CW00822325

DREAMING WITH OPEN EYES

Michael Tucker, born 1948, is a Principal Lecturer in the
Faculty of Art, Design and Humanities, Brighton
Polytechnic, and a reviewer for *Jazz Journal International*,
London. Co-author of the recent monograph *Alan Davie*, he
has published several innovative cross-disciplinary articles
and catalogue essays on twentieth-century Nordic art and
music.

His particular interests include the problems and
potentialities of primitivism in nineteenth- and twentieth-
century Western art and the relevance of shamanic ideas to
contemporary life. In 1992 he was invited by the University
of Sussex to become External Assessor for the course in
shamanic consciousness which is offered there, a post
previously held by the late R.D. Laing. *Dreaming With Open
Eyes* is the result of some ten years' research into the
relation between shamanism and twentieth-century art and
culture.

Dreaming with Open Eyes

*The Shamanic Spirit in Twentieth-Century
Art and Culture*

MICHAEL TUCKER

Aquarian/HarperSanFrancisco

Aquarian/Thorsons
An Imprint of HarperCollins*Publishers*
77–85 Fulham Palace Road,
Hammersmith, London W6 8JB

Published by Aquarian/HarperSanFrancisco 1992

10 9 8 7 6 5 4 3 2 1

©Michael Tucker 1992

Michael Tucker asserts the moral right to
be identified as the author of this work

A catalogue record for this book
is available from the British Library

ISBN 1 85538 184 2

Typeset by Harper Phototypesetters Limited,
Northampton, England

Printed in Great Britain by
Scottprint Ltd., Musselburgh

Contents

List of Illustrations

Measurements are given in centimetres, height before width (and, where applicable, width before depth).

For my parents, James and Margaret Tucker, with love and gratitude, and to the memory of my grandfather, William Swanson.

How vast life is when one meditates upon its beginnings!
Isn't meditation upon an origin dreaming? And isn't dreaming
upon an origin going beyond it? Beyond our history extends
our 'incommensurable memory' . . .

GASTON BACHELARD

Dream and art are a magic hoard; they link man
with the life of light and darkness, with true life,
with true spiritual collaboration.

JEAN ARP

Walk the wide and inner way
GUNNAR EKELÖF

Acknowledgements

Of the many people who have contributed to the realisation of this book, none merits gratitude more than Dr Brian Bates of the University of Sussex. It was Brian who first encouraged me to develop my thoughts about the relations between shamanism and modern art into publishable form and I am indeed grateful to him — not only for that encouragement, but for years of stimulating discussion, including more than a few moments of helpless, healing laughter.

Marion Russell, my first editor, was both warmly supportive and sensitively critical of various initial attempts to turn intuition into idea and idea into argument. Fiona Brown, who took over Marion's role, was patient, discerning and helpful in equal degree, and did a great deal to expedite picture research. I could not have wished for a more caring and committed editor to see the project to completion. My gratitude also to Philip Lewis for his thoughtful and sensitive design.

The ideas in this book have been developed from courses which I have taught and exhibitions which I have researched within the Faculty of Art, Design and Humanities at Brighton Polytechnic. I would like to thank both the Polytechnic for the various opportunities it has afforded me to pursue research abroad and the several generations of students who have done much to stimulate my ideas. I am also grateful to the Department of Adult Education at the University of Southampton, Susie Herschkorn and the Faculty of Art and Design, Polytechnic Southwest, Exeter, Paul Blythin and the IBM Jazz Club of Hursley, the Nordic House in Reykjavik, Grimsby City Council, the Anglo-Norse Society, Ian Sinclair, and Michael Goldmark of the Goldmark Gallery, Uppingham, for inviting me to lecture on several themes which subsequently found their place in the book.

Over the years, Richard Cupidi's extensive knowledge of shamanism has been a constant source of inspiration. I am indebted to Richard, not only for the degree to which he has always been willing to share that knowledge, but for the several hours he devoted to constructive criticism of my initial ideas. Early drafts of various parts of the text were read by Dr. Keith Clements, Julian Freeman, Ken Hyder, Andrej Jackowski, Iain Roy, Dr. Peter Shield, George Ware and John Warr, to all of whom I offer my sincere thanks. I am especially grateful to Dr. Richard Palmer, for both the scholarly care and patience with which he read several drafts of the full text, and the richly-humoured generosity of spirit with which he helped me to sharpen ideas, sharing his deep knowledge and love of Romanticism, modern literature and jazz with me.

Other people have been no less generous in particular ways. Monica Sjöö recommended some excellent sources within the burgeoning literature of the Great Goddess; Graham Ackroyd introduced me to the poetry of Kenneth White and Frank Gray did much to stimulate my interest in the films of Andrei Tarkovsky. Ken Hyder shared the fruits of his and Tim Hodgkinson's research into contemporary Euro-Asian shamanism, volunteering several fresh insights into the relation between shamanism and jazz. Steve Follen was equally kind, allowing me to make as much use as I wished of the extensive material which he had gathered from his first-hand research into Australian Aboriginal art.

For various other assistance, information and inspiration I am most grateful to: Stefan and Bente Bakke; Marie Baekkerud and the late Kåre Baekkerud; Tom Baekkerud and Hilde Hjulstad; Thurman Barker; Paul Benjamin; Brighton Polytechnic Learning Resources staff; Jayne Byrne and Carol Miller of the British Film Institute; Roger Cardinal; Ian Carr; Brian Catling; David Chapman and Pat Gilham; Jon Christensen; + Contempo + Modern Art Gallery, Eindhoven; John Cumming and John Ellson of Serious Productions Ltd; Andrew Cyrille; the late Anita Dalén; Alan and Bili Davie; Richard Demarco; Steve Dilworth; Mary Beth Edelson; Mike Fearey; Jan and Vigdis Garbarek; Stephanie Garrett and Julius Tabaćek; Mark Gilbert; Gimpel Fils Ltd, London; Viviane Gray of the Department of Indian and Northern Affairs, Ottawa; Tor Hammerø; Steve Harris; Geoff Hearn; Anton Heyboer; Peter Higgins; Nicki Jackowska; Andrej Jackowski; Richard Johnson; Dorothy M. Kosinski; Elisabeth Hartmann Krafft; Tom Lowenstein; Barry McRae; John Marshall; Knut Moe; Helen Oppenheimer; Mari Boine Persen; Raab Gallery at Millbank, London; Iain and Fiona Roy; Galerie Michèle Sadoun, Paris; Steven Sanderson of New Note Distribution Limited; Caroline Saunders; Eric Shanes; Geoffrey Shaw; Dr Peter Shield; Hilbre Skinner; Gorm Sorensen and Mette Myhre; Jo Spence; Cecil Taylor; Betty Thoday; Margaret Thoday; Nigel Thomas; Caroline Tisdall; Margaret Tucker; Peter Urpeth; Nana Vasconcelos; Eberhard Weber; Kenneth White; Frans and Åsa Widerberg; Val Wilmer; Jill and Joe Lee Wilson; Jan and Peter Morgan-Winsdale; Heather Mousseau and Margot Rousset of the Winnipeg Art Gallery; Nadir Yakir; Robert Wood and Ellen Zaks.

Finally, and above all, I would like to thank my wife Louise, without whose loving support, advice and encouragement this book would simply not have been written.

The author and publishers wish to thank the following individuals and publishers who have kindly allowed the use of excerpts of copyright material, full details of the sources of which can be found in the Notes to the text:

Abbeville Press, for excerpts from E. Shanes *Constantin Brancusi* and M. Tuchman (ed.) *The Spiritual in Art: Abstract Painting 1890–1985*.

Rasheed Araeen and the Hayward Gallery, South Bank Centre, London for excerpts from R. Araeen *The Other Story: Afro-Asian artists in post-war Britain*; Basil Blackwell Ltd, for excerpts from J. Cazeneuve *Lucien Lévy-Bruhl* (translated by Peter Riviere), H.P. Duerr *Dreamtime: Concerning the Boundary between Wilderness and Civilization* (translated by Felicitas Goodman) and M. Heidegger *Being And Time* (translated by John Macquarrie and Edward Robinson); Beacon Press Ltd, for excerpts from G. Bachelard *The Psychoanalysis of Fire* (translated by Alan C. M. Ross), *The Poetics of Space* (translated by Maria Joles) and *The Poetics of Reverie: Childhood, Language and the Cosmos* (translated by Daniel Russell) and H. A. Murray (ed.) *Myth and Mythmaking*; Bear and Co Publishing, for excerpts from R. Erdoes *Crying For a Dream*; Bloodaxe Books Ltd, for excerpts from *Tomas Tranströmer Collected Poems* (translated and with an introduction by Robin Fulton) and *Edith Södergran Collected Poems* (translated and with an introduction by David McDuff); Bloomsbury Publishing, Ltd, for excerpts from F. Gilot *Matisse and Picasso: A Friendship in Art*; Robert Bly, Paul Lawson and The Charioteer Press, for excerpts from *I Do Best Alone At Night: Selected Poems of Gunnar Ekelöf* (translated by Robert Bly and Christina Paulston, and with an introduction by Robert Bly; also published in the currently out-of-print 1967 Rapp & Carroll London edition to which the Notes make reference); Robert Bly and Sierra Club Books, for an excerpt from *Truth Barriers: Poems By Tomas Tranströmer* (translated by Robert Bly); The Bodley Head, for excerpts from C. Castenada *A Separate Reality* and *Journey To Ixtlan: The Lessons of Don Juan* and A. Tarkovsky *Sculpting In Time: Reflections On The Cinema* (translated by Kitty Hunter-Blair); John Calder Ltd, for excerpts from T. Tzara *Seven Dada Manifestos and Lampisteries* (translated by Barbara Wright); Cambridge University Press, for excerpts from C. Innes *Holy Theatre: Ritual and the Avant-Garde* and J. Wilson *Octavio Paz: A study of his poetics*; Roger Cardinal, for excerpts from *Outsider Art*; Dover Publications Inc, for excerpts from E. Cassirer *Language And Myth* and W. Kandinsky *Concerning The Spiritual in Art* (trans. M.T.H. Sadler); ECM Records, Munich, for excerpts from various sleevenotes to recordings by Keith Jarrett; Mary Beth Edelson, for excerpts from *Seven Cycles: Public Rituals* and *Shape Shifter: Seven Mediums*; Educational Development Center, Newton Mass. and the heirs of Knut Rasmussen for excerpts from 'Magic Words' (after Nalungiaq); Element Books, for excerpts from N. Drury *The Elements of Shamanism* and K. Stockhausen *Towards a Cosmic Music* (selected and translated by Tim Nevill); City Lights Books, for excerpts from G. Snyder *The Old Ways: Six Essays*; Faber and Faber Limited, for excerpts from T.S. Eliot *Selected Poems*, T. Hughes *Wodwo, Crow*, and *River*; W. Kandinsky *Complete Writings On Art* Volumes One and Two, P. Larkin *The Whitsun Weddings* and *Required Writing: Miscellaneous Pieces* 1955–1982, C.S. Murray *Crosstown Traffic: Jimi Hendrix And Post-War Pop*, G. Steiner *Real Presences: Is There Anything* in *What We Say* and W. Mellers *A Darker Shade of Pale: A Backdrop To Bob Dylan*; The Fjord Press, for excerpts from Edith Södergran *Love and Solitude Selected Poems 1916–23* (bi-lingual edition; translated by Stina Katchadourian); Green Print/The Merlin Press, for excerpts from J. Plant (ed.) *Healing the Wounds: The Promise of Ecofeminism*; Harcourt, Brace & World, Inc., for excerpts from M. Eliade *The Sacred And The Profane: The Nature Of Religion* (translated by Willard R. Trask); HarperCollins Publishers, for excerpts from W. Benjamin *Illuminations* (translated by Harry Zohn), E. W. Gadon *The Once and Future Goddess*, M. Roskill (ed.) *The Letters of Vincent Van Gogh*,

C.G. Jung *Memories, Dreams, Reflections*, G. Roth (with J. Loudon) *Maps To Ecstasy: Teachings of an Urban Shaman* and J.R.R. Tolkien *The Lord of the Rings*; Harper and Row Publishers, for excerpts from P. Cousineau (ed.) *The Hero's Journey: Joseph Campbell on his Life and Work*, M. Heidegger *Poetry, Language, Thought* (translated by A. Hofstader), J. Hillman *Re-visioning Psychology*, R.A. Johnson *Ecstasy: Understanding The Psychology of Joy*, E. Neumann *Art and the Creative Unconscious*, R.M. Rilke *Selected Poems of Rainer Maria Rilke* (translated and with a commentary by Robert Bly), M. Sjöö and B. Mor *The Great Cosmic Mother: Rediscovering The Religion Of The Earth* and Starhawk *The Spiral Dance: A Rebirth of The Ancient Religion of The Earth*; Hodder and Stoughton Publishers, for excerpts from D. Sweetman *The Love of Many Things: a Life of Vincent Van Gogh*; Indiana University Press, for excerpts from Y. Biró *Profane Mythology: The Savage Mind of the Cinema*; Michele Jamal, for M. Jamal (ed.) *Shape Shifters: Shaman Women in Contemporary Society*; Lund Humphries Ltd, for excerpts from G. Atkins *Asger Jorn The Crucial Years: 1954–1964*, A. Bowness (ed.) *Alan Davie*, A. Bowness (ed.) *The Complete Sculpture of Barbara Hepworth*; MW Press, for excerpts from *Richard Long in Conversation* Part Two; The Macmillan Press Ltd, for excerpts from H. Marcuse *The Aesthetic Dimension*; Mainstream Publishing Limited, for excerpts from K. White *Handbook For The Diamond Country: Collected Shorter Poems 1960–1990*, *The Bird Path: Collected Longer Poems 1964–1988* and *The Blue Road*; Marion Boyars Ltd, for excerpts from T. Joans *A Black Manifesto In Jazz Poetry And Prose*; New Directions, for excerpts from D. M. Guss (ed.) *The Selected Poetry of Vicente Huidobro* and J. Rothenberg *Pre-faces and Other Writings*; W.W. Norton and Company, for excerpts from R.M. Rilke *Duino Elegies* (translated by David Young); Octagon Books (A Division of Farrar, Staus and Giroux), for excerpts from J. McFarlane *Ibsen And The Temper Of Norwegian Literature*; Oxford University Press, for excerpts from S. Giedion *The Eternal Present*, R. Hayman *Artaud And After*, J. Sturrock (ed.) *Structuralism and Since: From Lévi-Strauss to Derrida* and F. Kermode *The Sense Of An Ending: Studies In The Theory Of Fiction*; Pantheon Books Ltd, for excerpts from L. R. Lippard *Overlay: Contemporary Art and The Art of Prehistory* and E. Neumann *The Archetypal World of Henry Moore*; Parkett Publishers, for excerpts from B. Curiger *Meret Oppenheim: Defiance in the Face of Freedom*; Penguin Books Ltd, for excerpts from Apollinaire *Selected Poems* (translated by Oliver Bernard), P. and L. Berger and H. Kellner *The Homeless Mind*, A. Camus *Selected Essays and Notebooks* (translated by Philip Thody), J. Halifax *Shamanic Voices: The Shaman as Seer, Poet and Healer*, R.D. Laing *The Politics of Experience and The Bird of Paradise*, F.G. Lorca 'Theory And Function Of The Duende' in *Lorca* (translated by J. L. Gili), Mallarmé *Selected Poems* (edited and translated by Anthony Hartley), F. Nietzsche *Thus Spoke Zarathustra* (translated by R. J. Hollingdale) and *Twilight of The Idols* (translated by R. J. Hollingdale) and J. Richardson *Georges Braque*; Pergamon Press, for excerpts from G.F. Orenstein *The Reflowering of the Goddess*; Perigee Books, for excerpts from C. Bell *Art*; Peter Owen Publishers Ltd, for excerpts from T. Vesaas *The Seed* (translated by Kenneth G. Chapman), *The Birds* (translated by Torbjørn Støverud and Michael Barnes) and *The Boat In The Evening* (translated by Elizabeth Rokkan); Picador/Pan Books, for excerpts from B. Lopez *Arctic Dreams: Imagination and Desire in a Northern Landscape*; Laurence Pollinger Ltd, for excerpts from D.H. Lawrence *The Rainbow* and *Selected Essays*; Princeton University Press, for excerpts from G. Ekelöf *Songs Of Something Else* (translated by Leonard Nathan and James Larson), M. Eliade *The Myth of The Eternal Return, or, Cosmos and History* (translated by Willard R. Trask) and *Shamanism: Archaic Techniques of Ecstasy* (translated by

Willard R. Trask), R. Jacobsen *The Silence Afterwards: Selected Poems of Rolf Jacobsen* (translated and edited by Roger Greenwald) and S. Prince *The Warrior's Camera: The Cinema of Akira Kurosawa*; Quartet Books Limited, for excerpts from L. Feigin (ed.) *Russian Jazz: New Identity* and G. Lock *Forces In Motion: Anthony Braxton and the Meta-reality of Creative Music*; Routledge, for excerpts from A. Bancroft *Origins Of The Sacred: The Spiritual Tradition In Western Tradition*, S. Freud *Totem And Taboo*, C.G. Jung *The Spirit In Man, Art And Literature, Four Archetypes* and *Essays On Contemporary Events: Reflections On Nazi Germany*, S. Hiller (ed.) *The Myth of Primitivism: perspectives on art* and A. Stevens *Archetype: A Natural History Of The Self*; Claude Schumacher, for excerpts from *Artaud On Theatre* (edited by Claude Schumacher); William L. Rukeyser and Leif Sjöberg, for excerpts from *Selected Poems of Gunnar Ekelöf* (translated by Muriel Rukeyser and Leif Sjöberg. Copyright © 1967 by Gunnar Ekelöf, Muriel Rukeyser and Leif Sjöberg); Shambhala Publications, Inc, for excerpts from J.A. Argüelles *The Transformative Vision*, G. Doore (ed.) *Shaman's Path: Healing, Personal Growth and Empowerment*, H. Kalweit *Dreamtime and Inner Space: The World of The Shaman*, R. Lipsey *An Art Of Our Own: The Spiritual in Twentieth-Century Art*, D. Rudhyar *The Magic of Tone and The Art of Music* and G. Wehr *Jung: A Biography*; Souvenir Press Ltd, for excerpts from J. Campbell, *The Masks of God* volume 1 *Primitive Mythology* and *The Masks of God* volume 4 *Creative Mythology* and K. Hamsun *Mysteries* (translated by Gerry Bothmer); Jo Spence and Camden Press, for excerpts from *Putting Myself In The Picture: A Political, Personal And Photographic Autobiography*; Spring Publications Inc, for excerpts from J. Campbell (ed.) *Myths Dreams And Religion*, C. Gaudin (ed.) *Gaston Bachelard: On Poetic Imagination And Reverie*, J. Hillman *Anima: an Anatomy of a Personified Notion* and *The Thought of the Heart*; Station Hill Press, for excerpts from S. Larsen *The Shaman's Doorway: Opening Imagination to Power and Myth*; Tate Gallery Publications, for excerpts from J. Collins *Cecil Collins: A Retrospective Exhibition*; Thames and Hudson Ltd, for excerpts from S. Gablik *Has Modernism Failed?*, M. Gimbutas *The Language of The Goddess*, J. Halifax *Shaman: The Wounded Healer*, R. Long *Walking In Circles*, H. Read *Arp*, M. Rowell (ed.) *Joan Miró Selected Writings and Interviews* and D. Sylvester *The Brutality of Fact: Interviews with Francis Bacon* (third edition); Caroline Tisdall, for excerpts from *Joseph Beuys*; University of Nebraska Press, for excerpts from J.G. Neihardt *Black Elk Speaks*; The Usher Gallery and Redcliffe Press Ltd, for excerpts from *The Journey: A Search For The Role of Contemporary Art in Religious and Spiritual Life*; Universe Books, for excerpts from *The Voice And The Myth: American Masters*; University of California Press, for excerpts from J. Rothenberg (ed.) *Technicians Of The Sacred: A Range of Poetries from Africa, America, Asia, Europe and Oceania*, J. and D. Rothenberg (eds.) *Symposium of The Whole: A Range of Discourse Towards an Ethnopoetics* and R. Shideler *Voices Under The Ground: Themes and Images in the Early Poetry of Gunnar Ekelöf*; University of Chicago Press, for excerpts from M. Eliade *The Quest: History and Meaning in Religion* and *Ordeal by Labyrinth: Conversations with Claude-Henri Rocquet* (translated by Derek Coltman); Verso, for excerpts from J. Baudrillard *America* (translated by Chris Turner) and R. Williams *The Politics Of Modernism* (edited and introduced by T. Pinkney); Warner Chappell Music International Ltd for excerpts from J. Hendrix 'Voodoo Chile'; Vision Press Ltd. for excerpts from K. Hamsun *Pan* (translated by James W. McFarlane); Kenneth White and PAP, for excerpts from *Le Chemin Du Chaman* (translated by Kenneth White); Wildwood House, for excerpts from H. Richter *The Struggle for the Film* (translated by Ben Brewster); Wilhelm Fink Verlag, for excerpts from Velemir Khlebnikov *Collected Works* volume 1 book 2

Creations 1906–1916 (translated by Barbara Einzig); Val Wilmer, for excerpts from *The Face Of Black Music* and *Mama Said There'd Be Days Like This*; Yale University Press, for excerpts from W. Kandinsky *Sounds* (translated and with an Introduction by Elizabeth R. Napier).

All quotations have been selected and used within the spirit of the 'fair use' norm of a maximum of *c.* 250–400 words and every effort has been made to trace and clear copyright. The author and the publishers will be happy to rectify any omission in subsequent editions of the present book, if notified in writing by the respective copyright holders.

Several passages in Chapters 8 and 11 have appeared in a slightly different form in the monograph *Alan Davie: with essays by Douglas Hall and Michael Tucker* Lund Humphries, London 1992. The author and the publishers acknowledge their gratitude to both Alan Davie and Lund Humphries Ltd. for kindly granting permission for these passages to be reprinted here.

Preface

Between fifteen and twenty thousand years ago, the cave painters of the Upper Paleolithic period created some of the greatest art the world has ever seen. The representational skills with which these artists depicted the power of the animal realm have never been surpassed: neither has the mystery of the more free-ranging marks which flank the naturalistic images of bison and bull, reindeer and rhinoceros, horse and cow. While such marks may represent the hunting traps or magic formulae of prehistoric cultures, to a twentieth-century mind they can seem like the origins of abstract art.

The art of the prehistoric caves was first brought to the world's attention towards the end of the nineteenth century; the paintings in the Altamira caves of Spain, for example, were discovered in 1879. Such discoveries continued well into our century. In 1940, four boys from Montignac in southern France followed a dog down a large hole which had perhaps been left by an uprooted tree: the artistic treasures of the cave of Lascaux lay in wait for them. The richness of this completely unexpected find was such that Lascaux has come to be known as the Sistine Chapel of pre-historic art.

Deep in a well, somewhat aside from the main galleries of Lascaux, there is one of the most extraordinary images in all art. A stick-like figure, with a bird-like face, outstretched arms and what appears to be an erect penis, is shown either falling or leaping in front of a large wounded bison. To the side of the figure, near its right hand, stands a rod, or staff, with a schematic bird's head affixed to its top.

The meaning of this image has been debated for many years. Scholars now agree that it can be seen as a stylistically distinct cousin, so to speak, of an equally compelling image in the Trois Frères cave which lies some miles directly south of Lascaux, and which was discovered on the eve of the First World War. Here one can see the now-famous image of a half-human, half-animal hybrid, with ears like those of a stag and a sturdy pair of antlers on its head. Depicted some twelve feet up the cave wall, the hybrid's body has animal haunches and paws: its face is distinguished by the two large, round and seemingly astonished eyes which stare out into space with hypnotic force.

The stick-like figure at Lascaux and the hybrid of Les Trois Frères are two of the earliest images known to us of the *shaman*, or seer, of ancient cultures. Charged with the responsibility of maintaining the health of the tribe, the prehistoric shaman remains the archetype of all artists. Image maker, dancer and drummer; actor and singer, healer and holy one, the shaman epitomises the human need to bridge worlds — to fly beyond the everyday realm of the visual in order to conjure worlds of visionary presence and power.

Is it only a matter of coincidence that the period in which the art of the prehistoric caves was being unearthed witnessed an unprecedented, cataclysmic change in the imagery and intent of Western art? Painters and poets, sculptors and composers, dancers and dramatists alike felt the need to abandon many previous conceptions of form, and to create work in the light of highly-charged visionary imperatives. The results often had more in common with the values of non-European tribal cultures, or with survivals of paganism in Europe, than they did with either the Greco-Roman or Christian traditions which had previously underlain so much of the history of Western art. Again, is it only coincidence that the discovery of some of the prehistoric caves and the shift in Western art towards increasingly primal levels of inspiration occurred at a time when the psychologists Sigmund Freud and Carl Jung were exploring previously unsuspected depths of the psyche?

It is my belief that these contiguous developments suggest something more than mere coincidence. If they are considered in the light of what Jung called synchronicity — the acausal, yet meaningful cross-connection of events which fascinated the psychologist, and to which he devoted at least one book — they begin to suggest a potent idea. At the heart of all three events — the discovery of the caves, the shift in both the aims and appearance of Western art, and the discoveries of depth psychology — one can detect the stirrings of a fundamental shift in attitudes towards matters of consciousness and creativity: a shift towards shamanic ideas of the relation between life and art.

The return of the Western mind to the ancient shamanic idea of the artist as visionary healer is the chief subject of *Dreaming with Open Eyes*. The book also includes current examples of the shamanic consciousness which can be detected in the art of what one might be tempted to call non-industrial, traditional cultures. Unfortunately, such terminology can often imply reductive ideas and images of the deathless purity of the ethnographic museum. As such, its use should be vigorously resisted — or at the very least, tempered by an awareness of the extent to which traditional cultures have long been involved in a challenging process of self-definition with regard to both the (largely destructive) pressures and (sometimes welcome) potentialities of Western industrial life.

Take the Saami culture of the Nordic countries, for example. In the eighteenth century the Swedish botanist Linnaeus celebrated what he saw as the relatively unspoiled, 'Noble Savage' aspects of what was then known as Lapp culture. Today, thousands of miles of motor roads cross the country of the Saami, whose reindeer herds sometimes have to be driven from airfields in order that planes may land. But this does not mean that the traditional values of the Saami people are now to be found only in the ethnographic museum. The Saami shamans of today write books, produce films and plays and record their native music — enhanced by synthesiser sounds and compact disc technology — in order that the whole world may hear of their fight to defend and develop their culture.

Something of that fight, as it has been developed in a variety of cultures, is touched on in this book. However, to explore the shamanic spirit in twentieth-century art from all such potential perspectives would have meant researching and writing not one book, but two. As a Westerner who lives in an industrial culture, I have felt it both necessary and worthwhile to concentrate upon the extent to which twentieth-century artists of the industrialised West have helped to prepare the way for the shift in consciousness which is so sorely needed today: the shift from mechanistic, rationalist modes of thought to what has been called a sense of *participation mystique* in life.

It is the argument of this book that such artists have done far more than create the various (and often competitive) sub-categories of the art historical movement known as modernism. Rather, their innovations have done much to develop the enduring legacy of the shamans of old — those archetypal artists whose images, deep in the caves of Lascaux and Les Trois Frères, address us with such particular intensity today.

N ORVAL M ORRISSEAU *The Storyteller. The Artist and His Grandfather* 1978
acrylic on canvas   two panels, each 174 x 94cm
Department of Indian and Northern Affairs, Ottawa
© The Artist and Department of Indian and Northern Affairs

PAUL KLEE *The Wild Man* 1922
oil and mixed technique on canvas   58.6 x 38.8cm
Städtische Galerie im Lenbachhaus, Munich

JEAN ARP *Forest* c.1917
painted wood   34.2 x 20 x 6cm
National Gallery of Art, Washington D.C.
Andrew W. Mellon Fund   © DACS 1992

CONSTANTIN BRANCUSI
The Sorceress   1916–24
maplewood   100cm (height)
Solomon R. Guggenheim Museum, New York
© DACS 1992

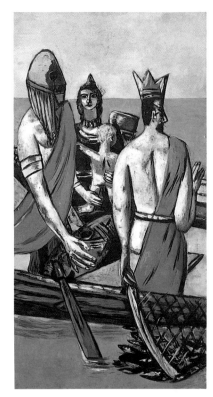

MAX BECKMANN *Departure* 1932–3
oil on canvas   triptych   centre panel 215.3 x 115.2cm   side panels each 215.3 x 99.7cm
The Museum of Modern Art, New York
Given anonymously (by exchange)   © DACS 1992

JACKSON POLLOCK *Guardians of the Secret* 1943
oil on canvas   123 x 191cm   The San Francisco Museum of Modern Art
Albert M. Bender Collection   Albert M. Bender Bequest Fund Purchase
Photograph: Don Myer   © ARS 1992

JOAN MIRÓ *Egg* 1963
ceramic   180 x 135cm   Miró Labyrinth, Fondation Maeght, Saint-Paul
Photograph: M. Tucker   © DACS 1992

ASGER JORN *In the Wingbeat of the Swans* 1963
oil on canvas   199.7 x 301cm   Stedelijk Museum, Amsterdam

FRANS WIDERBERG *Nordlys* [Aurora] 1980
lithograph   60 x 81cm   Collection of the Artist   © courtesy, the Artist
Photograph: Jan Ung, Oslo

NIKI DE SAINT PHALLE AND ALAN DAVIE *The High Priestess and the Magician* 1979–87
sculpture and fresco   cement, mirror glass and acrylic
Giardano dei Tarocchi (Tarot Garden) Southern Tuscany   © courtesy, the Artists   Photographs: Alan Davie

CONSTANTIN BRANCUSI *Endless Column* 1937–8
Cast iron 2935 x 122 x 152.5cm Public Park, Tîrgu-Jiu
Photograph: Eric Shanes © DACS 1992

1 Dreaming with Open Eyes

At first glance, the worlds of modern art and shamanism might seem as different as the proverbial chalk and cheese. What could all those zealously guarded paintings and sculptures in antiseptic galleries and museums — DO NOT TOUCH — possibly have in common with the shape-shifting, participatory world of the shaman of prehistoric and tribal cultures? Is it not the case that the more one considers these two worlds, the more one realises how far removed from life modern art has become, compared to the integration of artistic and vocational skills which one finds in shamanism? The shaman served the community: whether intentionally so or not, the modern artist often serves the interests of corporate finance. Remember the £25,000,000 or so which *Sunflowers*, a small-to-medium-sized Van Gogh painting, fetched at Christie's in London in 1987.

Such a statistic may seem unanswerable. However, it documents what is at best a half-truth. The price of much modern art *is* absurd, obscene even. But the amount which some individual or corporation is prepared to pay, in order to have a part of Van Gogh's soul locked away in a bank vault, cannot obscure the central implication of this artist's work. Van Gogh is the key, initiatory figure in the modern version of the Romantic perception of the artist as suffering visionary. At the heart of that occasionally risible myth, there lies the archetypal, essential idea of the artist as seer and healer — as shaman.

Van Gogh's life was one long struggle to develop and express an impulse to exalt life. Moving beyond what he came to regard as the restrictive horizons of his father's Protestant faith, the painter's personal sense of religious awe involved his conviction that one needed 'a certain dash of inspiration, a ray from on high' in order to create art that might inspire people. Beauty was to serve the soul: hoping that his art might offer spiritual comfort 'as music is comforting', Van Gogh revealed to his brother Theo how he wanted to paint men and women with 'something of the eternal which the halo used to symbolise'.[1]

Van Gogh felt that this might be achieved by the radiant vibrations of high-keyed colour. In the extraordinary last few years of his life, years when he finally realised the vocation which had eluded him for so long, canvas after canvas was to blaze forth with a numinous intensity which sang of the richness, the wholeness of life. A century later, all the absurdity and obscenity of high finance cannot dim this central aspect of his achievement — an achievement which is as manifest in all the books and

1

cheap postcard reproductions of today's Van Gogh industry as it is in the many works which now grace galleries and museums around the world.[2]

It is the idea of the struggle to exalt existence, to invoke the mysterious totality of life, which links the seemingly disparate worlds of modern art and shamanism. The shamans of pre-industrial cultures often had to suffer personal illness and psychic breakdown, as part of their preparation for an eventual breakthrough to transpersonal levels of visionary wisdom and healing activity. Equally, many modern artists have experienced the crisis of 'meaning' in industrial society with the sort of painful intensity which has prepared them for the struggle to respond (whether consciously or not) to the ringing, late-nineteenth-century call of Nietzsche's Zarathustra: 'Truly, the earth shall yet become a house of healing!'[3]

At one moment in the Saami writer and director Nils Gaup's 1987 film *Pathfinder*, a dramatic story of Saami (Lapp) tribal warfare from a thousand years ago, Raste, the old *noaidi*, or shaman, asks the young character Aigin what he can detect between himself and the walls of the tent in which he is hiding from the marauding Tschude tribe. Bemused, Aigin — who is eventually to inherit Raste's powers of spiritual leadership — can only reply that there is nothing. It takes a minute or more of near-suffocation by Raste to shock Aigin into awareness of the invisible, but nonetheless indisputable — and indispensable — existence of air. For Raste, air is the supreme symbol of the inter-relation of all things — of the chain of being which the Tschudes have violated.[4]

An ancient idea, the chain of being has been subjected to both philosophical scrutiny and environmental rape this century.[5] As a good deal of creative feminist scholarship has recently emphasised, to repair the chain of being, to reforge its links, is first and foremost a matter of reforging consciousness. In such books as Monica Sjöö's and Barbara Mor's *The Great Cosmic Mother: Rediscovering The Religion Of The Earth* (1975, 1987 and 1991), Elinor W. Gadon's *The Once and Future Goddess* (1989) and Gloria Feman Orenstein's *The Reflowering of the Goddess* (1990), the crisis of industrial culture has been addressed through both a critique of the patriarchal origins of its mechanistic world view and a celebration of the healing potentialities of the Goddess religion. This is the ancient, Earth-loving religion which once nurtured and revered all life as holy, rather than projecting spirituality into an exclusive and utterly trans-cendent 'beyond'. All three books underline the need to 'respell' today's ecologically-abused world through the rebirth and development of Goddess sensibilities. And all three underline the extent to which such a development involves a radical reappraisal of the role of art, of its shamanic capacity to shape — to heal — consciousness.[6]

It is the belief of Sjöö and Mor that the first shamans were women, wholly in touch with the rhythms of the earth. In keeping with such a belief, Monica Sjöö has done much in her painting to proclaim the holistic culture of the Earth Goddess. One of the prime intents of Sjöö's art is to

1 Monica Sjöö *Cromlech
Goddess/The Spirit of the Stone*
1982 oil on board 122 x 152.5
Collection of the Artist
© courtesy, the Artist
Photograph: Monica Sjöö.

stimulate the sort of life-participatory dreams that may awaken us to the creative evolution of consciousness which she believes is so sorely needed today. Such dreams stand in sharp contrast to the escapism of what she and Barbara Mor call the 'mass-produced dreams and commercial hallucinations' of industrial society.[7] Art must have a healing impact on the whole self, rather than feeding the split-off, shallow fantasies which are typical of that part of our culture which is so misleadingly called 'light entertainment.' (Misleadingly because, if it is not experienced with at least a measure of discrimination, such entertainment may eventually drown us in a sea of trivia.) Such holistic art can only be generated through an awareness of the roots of an integrated approach to life: and so Sjöö and Mor conclude their book with the simple, eloquent plea that 'The only way for human beings to survive the end is to return to the beginning.'[8]

The response of Sjöö and Mor to the crisis of industrial culture is a prime example of what historians of ideas, art historians and literary critics alike call 'primitivism'. This is a word, or term, which embraces an enormous range of issues. Put simply, it implies the desire to return to the origin of things, in order to gain maximum creative perspective on the present. Often inspired by a sense of dissatisfaction with that present, primitivism comes in a variety of emotional tonalities, as it were. The polar extremes of this variety are the sense of a Spartan call to order, and the idea of a luxuriant Arcadian dream. Between these extremes, various 'hard' and 'soft' varieties of the concept can combine to one degree or another.[9]

Western art has seen at least two great examples of a primitivism of a classicising kind: the Italian Renaissance, with its complex mixture of classical-pagan and Christian iconography and ideas, and the neo-classicism of the mid- to late-eighteenth century. The potential moral force of primitivism can be seen especially in the latter, with such stark 'Doricist' compositions of the French revolutionary painter Jacques-Louis David as *Oath of the Horatii* (1784—5) offering an implicit critique of the indulgent fantasies of Rococo art.[10] That moral force is also present in nineteenth- and twentieth-century primitivism, but often in a far less austere and civically-oriented manner than is to be witnessed in David.

The primitivism of much nineteenth- and twentieth-century art in the West is the (soft) primitivism of dream; a primitivism which encourages an enlargement of the psyche beyond the confines of both Judaeo-Christian thought and Descartian rationalism. Seeking to broaden and deepen their sense of both the world and themselves, primitivistic artists of such a persuasion have often abandoned the earlier classicising model for more 'primal' sources of inspiration. In this they have followed the precedent set by Paul Gauguin, the great romantic primitivist who left Europe at the end of the nineteenth century in search of inspiration in Tahiti.

Abandoning the idealised beauty of Athens and Rome for what he called 'the nourishing milk in the primitive arts', Gauguin believed that 'The great error is the Greek, no matter how beautiful it may be.'[11] Fifty years later, the American abstract expressionist painter Barnett Newman echoed Gauguin, preferring 'the barbarian's totemic fanaticism' to the idealised (and for Newman, irrelevant) beauty of Greek classicism.[12] And throughout the twentieth century, a host of artists have preferred the conceptual freshness and vivacity of child art, or even the painful authenticity of the mark-making of the mentally ill, to what they have considered to be the overly-polished perfection of the antique.[13]

Primitivism is thus an umbrella concept, which may well be as old as human consciousness itself: for the desire to recapture and make new the power of origins can be discerned in the mythic imagination and ritual practice of all traditional cultures. It has sometimes been suggested that the so-called 'primitive' of tribal culture cannot be primitivistic, since the latter term implies a sophisticated nostalgia arising from the awareness (of an essentially historical consciousness) that life has entered a period of change and decline. However, this is not the case. Tribal myths do not merely tell of genesis and decline; they *re-enact* these states, conjuring the awesome experience of aboriginal creation and destruction at appropriate moments within the yearly cycle of birth and death. As we shall see later, the shamans of traditional cultures might be called the first great primitivists, insofar as they periodically sought to return to the Paradisal time of origins.

Primitivism played an equally potent, albeit differently articulated role in the cultures of antiquity, helping to shape some of the most enduring classical approaches to the human experience of temporality and truth. (For example, Mircea Eliade, the late philosopher of religions, suggested that the conceptual rigour of Platonic thought can be seen as closely connected to archaic ideas of the paradigmatic celestial model of creation which preceded the human 'Fall' into temporality — a connection to which we shall return in Chapter 10.) The last 250 years of Western culture might be said to have witnessed the apotheosis of the primitivistic impulse, involving in equal degree the development of a many-sided nostalgia for the past and pointed criticism of the present.[14]

During the past decade or so, several aspects of such primitivistic nostalgia and criticism have come under sharp attack. Concerned to demystify what they see as an ultimately regressive 'myth' of primitivism, whereby Western artists and thinkers have projected a series of reductive stereotypes about a mythical 'Other' upon non-Western cultures, authors (and artists) such as Hal Foster, Rasheed Araeen, Jimmie Durham, Sally Price and Marianna Torgovnick have raised questions which are fundamental to any study of the shamanic spirit in post-Romantic art. Just as one might ask how closely the eighteenth- and nineteenth-century Romantics ever considered any of the shifting historical realities of the tribal cultures which they tended to see through the rosy glow, so to speak, of the myth of 'the Noble Savage', so one might ask whether the many late-nineteenth- and twentieth-century artists who have praised 'the primitive' have praised anything more than their own fantasies of an ahistorical 'Other', replete with all the nature-loving sensuality and spirituality which Western culture has been deemed to lack.[15]

The chief focus of such recent critiques of primitivism has been the exhibition which the New York Museum of Modern Art mounted in 1984 entitled ' "Primitivism" In 20th Century Art: Affinity of the Tribal and the Modern'. Co-directed by William Rubin and Kirk Varnedoe, both of whom contributed substantial essays to the exhibition catalogue, ' "Primitivism" In 20th Century Art' included pieces by such exceptional figures of modern art as Paul Gauguin, Pablo Picasso, Max Ernst, Paul Klee, Henri Matisse, Constantin Brancusi and Henry Moore. 'Tribal' works came from as far afield as the Zunis of New Mexico and the Inuit (Eskimos) of the Northwest; from Indonesia and New Guinea, and from such African peoples as the Dogon, Dan, Yoruba and Fang. Relating Western 'masterpieces' to their possible genesis in examples of tribal art, the exhibition purported to reveal an ennobling affinity between cultures. However, the fact that the individually-signed Western exhibits were scrupulously dated (sometimes to the month or even week of composition), whereas the supposedly anonymous 'tribal' objects were labelled by centuries, led many to suspect that the real message of the exhibition was — as Torgovnick puts it — 'Here is the primitive instance; here is the masterwork, with the primitive absorbed and transcended'.[16]

In other words, was not this exhibition simply another version of colonialism: a patronising acknowledgement of a mythical 'Other' as an essential, but nonetheless anonymous ingredient of the yeast of modernism — and thus a gross dimunition of what Sally Price rightly calls 'the complex humanity' of the creators of the many diverse 'tribal' pieces which featured in the exhibition?[17]

Similarly, further points which critics of the MOMA exhibition have made seem to me to be equally justified. However, in focussing attention on the inadequacies of the 'formalist' emphasis of ' "Primitivism" In 20th Century Art', and in (quite rightly) emphasising the rights of 'tribal' peoples to articulate and develop *their own* historical identities today, these critics seem to have themselves overlooked a key aspect of the whole question of post-Romantic primitivism: namely, the extent to which such primitivism should be seen in terms of a crucial development in *the history of religious ideas* — a development in which artists of the West have done their best to resurrect and develop ancient, fundamental conceptions of the sacred dimensions of existence.

I am completely sympathetic to Torgovnick's wish that Western primitivism might have encompassed what she calls 'a history in which primitive societies were allowed to exist in all their multiplicity, not reduced to a seamless Western fantasy; a history in which primitive societies were acknowledged as full and valid alternatives to Western cultures.'[18] But I am no less surprised by the extent to which Torgovnick ignores the possibility that post-Romantic Western primitivism might be interpreted *precisely in the light of her last remark*.

In common with such other critics of Western primitivism as Araeen, Price and Foster, Torgovnick eschews any mention whatsoever of the lifelong attempt of Mircea Eliade (1907—86) to encourage what he called 'a genuine encounter' between Western and non-Western cultures; an encounter which — as far as Eliade was concerned — the primitivistic concerns of modern art had done much to make possible. Thirty years before the current critiques of the alleged formalism and neo-colonialist paternalism of MOMA, Eliade argued in *Myths, Dreams And Mysteries: The Encounter Between Contemporary Faiths And Archaic Reality* that 'Western man is no longer the master of the world; he is no longer managing "natives" but talking with other men. It is as well that he should learn how to open the conversation.'[19] For Eliade, as for Joseph Campbell (another major interpreter of primitivistic ideas whose work has been curiously — not to say scandalously — neglected by recent critics of primitivism), the key to that conversation lay in a sensitivity to the layers of meaning that lie within myth.

Clearly, when critics of primitivism speak of the myth of 'the tribal Other' in twentieth-century art, they intend the term 'myth' to imply falsehood. Many a rational-minded critic of Western primitivism has followed Roland Barthes in interpreting myth as the attempt of 'false-consciousness' to turn what is historical (and thus subject to change) into what is 'natural' (and thus somehow beyond the play of socio-historical forces).[20] From this perspective, Frank Kermode's well-known distinction between fiction and myth might seem indisputable: 'Myth operates within the diagrams of ritual, which presupposes total and adequate explanations of things as they are and were; it is a sequence of radically unchangeable gestures. Fictions are for finding things out, and they change as the needs of sense-making change. Myths are the agents of stability, fictions the agents of change.'[21]

What, however, are we to make of what might be called the modern, secular fiction of life-as-history, a fiction which has gripped the imagination with such force that it must surely be accorded the status of myth? Spelled with a capital H, and fuelled by the utterly profane logic of capitalism, the 'march of History' today renders the idea of change permanent. This is the paradoxical myth — a simultaneous justification and destruction of the focus upon daily life — which suggests that there is no other terrain of human experience save that of the here-and-now: a here-and-now which until a moment ago was the future, and which, once having been lived, is immediately part of the past. And since time — History, Progress, Society — flows ever on, that moment can never be recaptured, save on the shifting, unreliable tides of memory. Hence the enormous anxiety of so much of our culture, the rush somehow to 'beat' or 'save' time, to re-experience it through the cycles of fashion, or to prolong or intensify the experience of it either at weekends or while on holiday.

According to Mircea Eliade, it is at such latter moments that modern, secular and thoroughly 'historical' humanity dimly intuits something of the aboriginal feeling which prehistoric humanity evinced for the sacred dimension in life — for the experience of time not as a simple succession of linear moments, as it were, but rather as a replenishing epiphany of the archetypal time of beginnings, of the 'Great Time' of sacred origins. The semantic roots of 'holiday' (holy day) should suggest to us something of this 'Great Time': the time which 'makes us whole' as it soothes and heals our fractured consciousness — heals it, that is, until the alarm clock summons us back to something we choose to call the reality of a working week.

Holidays thus reveal our nostalgia for the sacred, as we somehow deepen and transmute our experience of so-called 'everyday life'. And according to Eliade, much modern, primitivising art does no less. Following — but also deviating from — Kermode, one might say that the various challenging 'fictions' of modern art which we shall investigate have intimated a rebirth of myth: the rebirth of forms and images, sounds and movements which embody a replenishing sense of 'holy' time, of archetypal *presence*, of metamorphosing power. Contrary to both Barthes and Kermode, we may find that the essentially metaphoric nature of the myth-inflected thought and imagery of primitivistic art this century neither 'naturalises' nor 'stabilises' things, but rather precipitates psychological change and growth. Enhanced sensitivity to the mythic dimensions of life need not signify 'false-consciousness': on the contrary, it can open up far deeper and richer layers of consciousness than the purely historical mode of existence which has come to dominate so much of life today. Such was the belief, at least, of both Eliade and Campbell, two of the finest minds of twentieth-century hermeneutics, whose ideas about the relations between archaic thought and modern art will inform much of our subsequent discussion.

One of the most interesting and problematic aspects of primitivism is thus the attitude to time, to history and change, that it can involve. If one draws inspiration from the (sacred) past, and is critical of the (profane) present, what does that imply for one's sense of the future? Monica Sjöö and Barbara Mor offer a simple, but potent image, or metaphor, of what one might call a primitivistic approach to time. They suggest that the idea of returning to the culture of the Goddess today 'is not a backward trip through space or time . . .We *return* to the Goddess by *remembering, redefining, respelling* . . . Thus we complete a circle; but on a spiral, we revolve to a larger circle.'[22] Whatever its various faults may have been, or continue to be, the worthwhile nature of post-Romantic Western primitivism has been largely to do with the sort of ideas of regeneration and development which are embodied in such a figure of speech. Although it may be deeply involved with the sort of problems of a mythical tribal 'Other' which were adumbrated above, as the example of Sjöö and Mor makes evident, post-Romantic Western primitivism is also intimately related to its *own* cultural heritage.[23]

Given the particular nature of their anti-patriarchal argument, with its detailed emphasis on the historical realities of matriarchy, it is understandable that Sjöö and Mor did not wish to concern themselves with the extent to which their primitivistic concept of time has informed much post-Gauguin creativity in the West, insofar as that creativity has largely been the product of male artists. The completely female emphasis of Gadon and Orenstein is also understandable. It is an emphasis which has resulted in an impressive and inspiring documentation and explication of recent Goddess-oriented creativity, which I am grateful to have been able to draw upon in parts of the present text. However, I cannot help thinking that the struggle to repair the chain of being is a struggle which needs as many hands as can be found, no matter what their gender.

Orenstein (who claims that the Goddess tradition does not exclude men, but whose text excludes all but the briefest mention of any male artist) suggests that 'In the denigration of the powers of both women and nature, the patriarchy has never noticed that, as Leonora Carrington once said to me: "the Earth is a heavenly body." '[24] One wonders if such a critique of 'the patriarchy' enables Orenstein to excuse several generations of male Romantic philosophers, poets and painters from its all-embracing sweep — for the Romantics were obsessed with the spiral approach to time of which Sjöö and Mor speak, wishing to bring back the ancient, animistic idea of a living and fully integrated universe into Western consciousness. And what of Van Gogh, Rilke, Brancusi, Lawrence, Matisse, Klee, Miró, Moore, Beuys and Tarkovsky — to name only a few of those more recent male artists whose devotion to the earth is surely incontestable?

Meret Oppenheim (1913—85) welcomed the role that art might play in the social revolution of women today. At the same time, she believed firmly that in the context of creativity, 'There is no difference between man and woman; there is only artist or poet.'[25] Oppenheim is famous in the history of twentieth-century art for both the erotically-charged photographs which Man Ray took of her in the mid-1930s, and her own fur-covered cup, saucer and spoon piece of 1936, which André Breton, the so-called High Priest of Surrealism, entitled *Luncheon in Fur.* However, Oppenheim's contribution to twentieth-century creativity involves far more than might be inferred from either Man Ray's photographs or what Robert Hughes has called 'perhaps the most durable of Surrealist objects'.[26] In Oppenheim, we encounter a splendid example of the shamanic spirit in twentieth-century culture: the spirit, that is, which reaches back into prehistory, at the same time that it pushes the materials and the imagery of art towards a future untramelled by any previous notions of what art should look like.

In 1966 Oppenheim created a remarkable *Self-portrait since 60,000 B.C. to X.,* a portrait which epitomises the shape-shifting concerns of her art. Next to a dream-charged Indian ink drawing of what one might call psychic geology, where a primitive, cairn-like structure ascends through mountain and seascape, with flowers rather than lava bursting out of the mountain's peak, the following words are set: 'My feet stand in a cavern, on stones smoothed by many steps. The bear meat tastes good. Flowing around my stomach is a warm ocean current. I stand in the lagoons. I notice the reddish walls of a city. Torso and arms are decked in an armour of tightly overlapping scales. In my hands I hold a white marble. Thoughts are locked in my head as in a beehive. Later I write them down. Writing burned up when the library of Alexandria went up in flames. The black snake with its white head is in the museum in Paris. Then it burns down too. All the thoughts there have ever been roll around the earth in the huge mindsphere. The earth splits, the mindsphere bursts, its thoughts are scattered in the universe where they continue to live on other stars.'[27]

The mythic, metamorphosing tone of this portrait is evident throughout

Oppenheim's work. Her shaman-like search for psychic depth and balance — for what Jungians would call the health of individuation — resulted in an unclichéd range of both (painted and drawn) magical landscapes and masks. She made the latter in a rich variety of materials, the results often redolent of both ethnographic museums and the carnivals which she liked to attend in Basle. Landscapes and masks alike proclaimed a world of animistic myth, the world that writer Bice Curiger has emphasised in the following assessment of Oppenheim: '. . . speaking through her images, the artist becomes, on occasion, a shaman. Her images then release primal forces effecting magical transformation and unions: patterns of colour turn to stone, stone turns to sky and city, line turns to wood, wood to crocodile and snake . . .'[28]

From the point of view of myth, one might say that Oppenheim was led to release such primal forces by the energies of the cosmos — the cosmos which has been so threatened this century, and which spoke to her in the many dreams which she recorded from the age of 14 onwards. Gruesome nightmares of human abattoirs, social disintegration and sexual chaos came to her in the mid-1930s, to be balanced in later years by healing dreams of mountain ascents and vegetation myths. (It is perhaps appropriate to note that Oppenheim's doctor father had attended Jung's seminars in Zurich.) The psychic tension which stimulated Oppenheim's shaman-like capacity to bring such dream imagery into consciousness was particularly evident in the extraordinary sequence of self-portraits which opened the retrospective show of her work which London's Institute of Contemporary Arts housed in 1989.

In the earliest portrait, which was from 1943, pencil and watercolour registered Oppenheim's pale beauty in an image of intense, almost sacrificial frontality: this was the introspective, self-doubting person who had produced so much death-obsessed work in the 1930s, such as the drawing *One Person Watching Another Dying* (1933) or the oil *Anatomy of a Dead Woman* (1934). The next portrait, from 1964, was a profile photograph, an X-ray of Oppenheim's skull taken while she was wearing earrings, chain and rings. The bones of a hand could also be seen, again in profile. The final portrait, from 1980, was another photograph, entitled *Portrait with Tattoo*. A stencil and spray effect gave Oppenheim the appearance of a Native American. Strong and composed, but also revealing humour in the eyes and mouth, the image struck a dignified and affirmative tribal note — a note which could not have contrasted more sharply with the alienated and wan aura of the 1943 portrait.

Portrait with Tattoo may have been partly intended as a protest against purist tendencies in twentieth-century modernist art and design (as in the architect Adolph Loos's attack on tattooing in his critique of ornament early in the century). However, it was surely also Oppenheim's way of celebrating the fruits of the long, shaman-like journey she had taken into herself, once she had — in what we shall later come to see as the classic shamanic manner — 'died' to her old, doubting self and been reborn 'from the bone'.[29] *Portrait with Tattoo* is not an image of someone who has merely 'indulged' primitivistic ideas and aspirations, stereotyping a mythical 'Other'. On the contrary, it is the portrait of someone who was wholly sensitive to the transformation of consciousness which must take place if the healing possibilities of Eliade's 'genuine encounter' between cultures are ever to be realised.

In 1983 Oppenheim was invited to give a lecture at the Federal Institute of Technology in Zurich, where guest professor Paul Feyerband had convened a series of lectures on the subject 'Science and Art — Contrasts and Identities'. Oppenheim concluded her lecture with the following ringing words: 'When nature has stopped being treated as the enemy of man, when the battle of the sexes has become an unknown, when the so-called feminine traits that men share in full measure — feelings, moods, intuition — have been fully exploited, when the significance of woman's contribution to the preservation and development of human society has been recognised, when comfort is no longer mistaken for culture, when beauty has become a need again — then, at last, poetry and art will

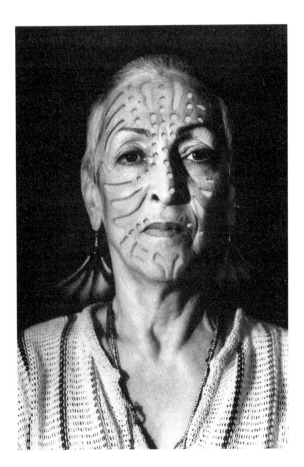

2 Meret Oppenheim *Portrait (Photo) with Tattoo* 1980 stencil and spray on photograph (photograph: Heinz Gunter Mebusch, Dusseldorf 1978) 29.5 x 21 Museum of Fine Arts, Bern © DACS 1992.

automatically come into their own again, even if the veil of longing always lies upon them like an eternal promise.'[30]

Oppenheim's life-long emphasis that 'The mind is androgynous!' was echoed by the inspiring Saami singer Mari Boine Persen, when I spoke to her in the spring of 1991 during her tour of Norway with the Jan Garbarek quartet and the Telemark folk singer Agnes Buen Garnås: 'I can understand why some people should wish to focus so strongly on women's creativity today, for it has been kept down for so long by male-dominated society. But I think it is dangerous to elevate only women in this way; it neglects much of the energy that is needed to change things. We all have male and female aspects within us; we should try to share our experiences, our feelings, not cut ourselves off from each other.'[31]

It is in such a spirit that I have tried to investigate some of the major links between modern art and shamanism this century. And such links can be seen to stretch back beyond the relatively recent (and thoroughly necessary and welcome) revival and development of Goddess-oriented creativity, to those roots of twentieth-century primitivism which can be discerned in late-eighteenth- and nineteenth-century European Romanticism.

Novalis's belief that 'Human beings, animals, plants, rocks and stars, flames, notes, colours must congregate in the end and "act" like a family or society, act and speak like a tribe'; Hölderlin's hymns in praise of 'lovely blue', his hope that humanity might someday 'dwell poetically on earth'; Wordsworth's conviction that 'Nature never did betray/The heart that loved her' . . .what were these if not heartfelt, primitivistic hopes that life might once again be experienced through the reverential, animistic terms of myth?[32] In his study *Romantic Roots In Modern Art,* August Wiedmann underlines the shamanic nature of such hopes in his description of Romantic creativity as an attempt to resurrect 'a *magical* universe in which man no longer felt separated from all that lived.'[33]

While a Romantic painter, like Turner, could be stimulated by the world of steam and speed which industrialism had brought into being, industrialism hardly repaid the compliment.[34] Romanticism's hopes for a 'magical universe' were to be swept aside in the name of progress and efficiency. The consequences of Benjamin Franklin's infamous idea that 'time is money' flowed out of the nineteenth century's 'dark, Satanic mills'; and the various ghosts of the 'lost magic kingdoms' of the tribal cultures which had so inspired Romanticism were assigned their carefully numbered glass tombs in ethnographic museums.[35]

The psychologist Erich Fromm has recently suggested that industrial culture makes it increasingly hard for people to *be* rather than to have. A century previously, Nietzsche had spoken in *The Birth Of Tragedy* about what he called 'the mythless man' of the industrial West, who was fired by the energies of material progress but at the same time troubled by an immense nostalgia: 'And now the mythless man stands eternally hungry, surrounded by past ages, and digs and grubs for roots, even if he has to dig for them among the remotest antiquities.' Reflecting on both the growth of ethnographic museums and the nineteenth century's obsession with historical styles (for example, the building of museums on neo-classical lines or churches in neo-Gothic proportions) Nietzsche continued: 'The tremendous historical need of our unsatisfied modern culture, the assembling around one of countless other cultures, the consuming demand for knowledge — what does all this point to, if not the loss of the mythical home, the mythical maternal womb?'[36]

A direct parallel can be traced between the extent to which industrialisation has intensified our sense of metaphysical homelessness and the extent to which post-Romantic artistic primitivism has intensified its search for a language of primal, healing power. We can see this relationship particularly clearly in the work of the Dada artists of the second two decades of this century. Protesting with great vigour against the mechanistic world view which had led to the obscenity of the First World War, these artists sought an elemental art which might put people back in touch with the poetic depths of both themselves and the world.

The origins of the word 'Dada' are still debated. Gauguin had spoken of going far back in his art, 'farther than the horses of the Parthenon . . . as far back as the Dada of my babyhood, the good rocking-horse.'[37] Something of this longing for the participatory directness of childhood experience certainly informed the early days of Dada, in the middle of the First World War, in Zurich. (Later, in Berlin and Cologne, Dada activity would acquire a tougher, more overtly political dimension.) The use of the word was also intended to convey a spirit of irreverent — and hence critical — nonsense. Centuries of so-called rationalism had ended with millions going to an absurd death in the trenches of the First World War. Jean Arp, one of the key Dada artists, described the Dada reaction: '. . . disgusted by the butchery of World War 1, we sang, painted, pasted and wrote poetry with all our might and main. We were seeking an elementary art to cure man of the frenzy of the times and a new order to restore the balance of heaven and hell.'[38]

Few artists of our century have felt the metaphysical sense of loss of which Nietzsche had written as keenly as did Arp. All his life, Arp (1886—1966) sought to inspire us to return to the womb of Nature. People had completely lost any sense of reality: by which Arp did not mean the ability to read a newspaper or understand a train timetable, but rather the capacity to sense what he called 'the mystical, the determinate indeterminable, the greatest determinate of all' in life. Aiming to free people from 'the rationalist swindle' and 'absurd over-evaluation of reason' whereby man had sought to place himself beyond nature, Arp sought an art which might be not so much a 'picture' of nature, in the sense of landscape art, but rather a 'parallel' to nature, in the organic quality of its forms and processes.[39]

Chance and improvisation thus featured strongly in Dada, as the creative process helped Arp and his fellow Dadaists to sense that existence was not a matter of oneself *and* the world, but rather oneself *in* the world. If the surface of life had become so terribly disfigured, then one must turn to the depths for replenishment: and so Dada brought the unconscious into full play. Despite all the horrors of the First World War, the painter and filmmaker Hans Richter, a close colleague of Arp, could speak of Dada's belief in 'the purity of man' — a purity which could only be realised by a journey down to the uncorrupted essence of his being, to that primal source of art 'welling up from the depths of the subconscious.'[40] Early in his life, Richter (1888–1976) came to believe that to be an artist was to search for a magical formula, 'to become a sorcerer with spiritual power who could instil divine POWER into or from the canvas.'[41] While he would eventually regard these words as somewhat hyperbolic, Richter retained a life-long belief in what he called the 'primeval magic power' of art.[42]

Dada is sometimes seen solely in terms of its virulent critique and negation of bourgeois hypocrisy — as the prototype of all the many subsequent varieties of youthful anarchist protest which our century has spawned. This is to overlook the deeply (albeit unorthodox) religious quality in artists like Arp and Richter. The latter, for example, spoke of how, in an age of 'general unbelief', Dada sought to restore to the work of art 'something of the numinous quality of which art has been the vehicle since time immemorial'.[43] Created in the spirit of nature, which — as Richter and other Dadaists emphasised — produces flowing forms rather than static 'works', art might once again come to be the way to 'what all the outdated religions call God — Unity with one's SELF.'[44]

In a memorable phrase, Arp once said that he hoped his work might help people to dream with their eyes open.[45] The aesthetician Henri Focillon has made the astute point that 'What distinguishes dream from reality is the fact that the dreamer cannot create a work of art; his hands are asleep. Art is made with the hands. They are the instrument of creation and the organ of understanding.'[46] Moving within the shape-shifting space which is neither dream nor wakefulness, as those two states are ordinarily understood, but rather reverie, Arp created such dream-charged pieces as *Forest* of *circa* 1917.

This humble, yet magical wooden relief makes a potent contrast with Paul Nash's bitterly titled *We Are Making a New World* of 1918. Rather than record the horror of history, as Nash did through the blasted trees which litter the foreground of his painting, Arp chose to mine the veins of mythology, taking us back to the origins of our imaginal life. In the child-

3 Paul Nash *We Are Making A New World* 1918 oil on canvas 77.1 x 91.4
The Trustees of the Imperial War Museum, London.

like forest which he fashioned, one senses a rebirth of both the poetic heart of the imagination and the ancient idea of the Tree of Life. The central image has a delightful fairy tale quality to it, uniting tree and human gesture as it does. And the luminous, moon-like shape in the upper right hand corner of the piece speaks not only of its evident physicality, its natural 'thingness', but also of the light of consciousness (the sun) and the energising, implicit darkness of the unconscious (the moon).

Arp's desire to help us to dream with our eyes open anticipated the beautiful insight of Gaston Bachelard, the French philosopher of the imagination, that one has never seen the world well, if one has not dreamed what one was seeing.[47] A friend of such major, mid-century artists of shamanic consequence as Asger Jorn, Bachelard (1884–1962) believed that 'Psychically speaking, we are created by our reverie — created and limited by our reverie — for it is the reverie which delineates the furthest limits of the mind.'[48] Bachelard, Richter and Arp would surely all have agreed with the advice which the Yaqui sorcerer Don Juan would later give to

Carlos Castaneda, which was that '*Dreaming* is as serious as *seeing* or dying or any other thing in this awesome, mysterious world.'[49]

Just as Arp and Richter looked back on a century or more of largely unsuccessful Romantic attempts to remind industrial culture of the awe and the mystery of the world, so do we have to acknowledge that the hopes of Arp and Richter have hardly been realised this century. The brutalities of war continue to supply sickening evidence of that insidious process of 'normalisation' which Dada deplored, and which the late psychiatrist R.D. Laing lamented with equal force. Writing in the 1960s, Laing described the condition of alienation, of being asleep to one's own potentialities, as 'the condition of normal man. Society highly values its normal man. It educates children to lose themselves and become absurd, and thus to become normal. Normal men have killed perhaps 100,000,000 of their fellow normal men in the last fifty years.'[50]

Given the numbing weight of this statistic, the world of art may seem of little consequence. However, we should not forget that Laing himself set great store by the potential of art to expand and alter consciousness. In *Apollo Versus The Echomaker*, a recent study of Laing, Anthony Lunt has drawn attention to the strong overtones of shamanism in his approach to questions of mental health and creativity. So it should come as no surprise that Laing valued art as much as he did: 'Creation *ex nihilo* has been pronounced impossible even for God. But we are concerned with miracles. We must hear the music of those Braque guitars (Lorca).' [51]

The potential miracle of modern art, such as that which Arp created in the middle of the hell of the First World War, is that it offers us ways back to beginnings which are simultaneously ways forward to a re-enchantment of both ourselves and the world. And if the miracle has not yet come to pass, that is scarcely surprising. For in its struggle to replenish the poetic heart of existence, modern art has had to engage in a constant struggle against an enormous backlog of aesthetic, religious and social conditioning — to say nothing of reactionary politics and critical myopia. [52]

The Russian painter Wassily Kandinsky signalled the plight of the poetic imagination with particular acuity in his *Concerning The Spiritual In Art*, which was first published in 1912. The greatest innovator in abstract art this century, Kandinsky was also a fine writer. He battled with both pen and brush against what he called 'the nightmare of materialism' which he felt had turned the life of the universe into 'an evil, useless game'.[53] Kandinsky spoke of how people's minds were 'only just awakening' after years of materialism, and how they were 'infected with the despair of unbelief, of lack of purpose and ideal'.[54]

In such contemporary works by the painter as *All Saints' Day* (1911), it is as though Kandinsky were forcefully seeking to hasten that awakening by reminding people of the spiritual truths of Christianity — truths which Marxism and Darwinism had done so much to challenge over the previous half-century. However, the painter would soon move away from such overtly Christian imagery, to conjure instead pre-Christian, shamanic layers of symbolism in imagery speaking of the nuances of unconscious (and what, spiritually speaking, one may call ecumenical) longing.

One wonders to what extent this immensely intelligent artist came to reflect upon how much Christian spirituality itself might have contributed to the diminution of the poetic imagination. While Saint Francis of Assisi might well be considered as the patron saint of ecology, as Lynn White suggested in a famous article of 1967,[55] scholars as diverse as the sociologist Max Weber (a contemporary of Kandinsky) and Mircea Eliade, doyen of shamanic studies this century, have suggested that there is something at the core of the Judaeo-Christian view of the world which is very much implicated in the neglect, or abuse, of the chain of being which has been such a disfiguring feature of recent Western culture. In a crucial sense, the shamanic spirit in twentieth-century art has had to do battle not just with the recent manifestations of a mechanistic and materialistic view of life, but with the much older spiritual framework within which that view of life first came to paradoxical birth.

The relations between the growth of both the capitalist work ethic and modern bureaucracy to Christian — and in particular, Protestant — beliefs about the utterly transcendent nature of divinity were investigated early this century by Max Weber. For Weber, modern man had become trapped in an iron cage of secular and rationalist activity. The cage had been long in the making: ironically enough, it had been forged out of principles once associated with transcendence and divinity.

The growth of the modern, unmagical world which so distressed artists such as Arp, Richter and Kandinsky was traced by Weber back to the disenchantment with the flesh and the world which Christian asceticism had proclaimed. Weber also pointed to the proto-bureaucratic behaviour associated with the growth of rational patterns of living and time-keeping in the medieval monasteries. Having gradually stripped the earth of the many protective layers of sacred significance which it had once revealed to the pagan mind (worshipful of rock and stream, tree and mountain), Christianity's eventual Protestant projection of spirituality into an increasingly distant, transcendent male realm was scarcely able to offer much resistance to the desacralising ideology of industrialisation. And the Christian development of the Judaic concept of time, whereby it is conceived as linear and historical, rather than cyclical, had long ago prepared people to neglect the present tense — what the East calls the ETERNAL NOW — of life. Paganism sees life in terms of the recurrent richness of cycles of activity: we are taught to relish — or fear — a future that by the very nature of our approach to time lies forever beyond our grasp.[56]

The spark of spirituality is a wondrous thing, but terrifying when it sets off self-igniting chains of abstraction. Mircea Eliade believed that the paramount problem of the present day is what he called 'the total desacralisation of both the cosmos and of human history' — something previously unthinkable.[57] Unlike Weber, however, Eliade did not see this process as irreversible. He was heartened by various indications of a return to the values of what he called 'cosmic religion'. In such a system of belief (of which the Goddess religion furnishes a strong, but not exclusive example) soul and spirit are to be found and celebrated throughout the world, rather than being regarded as the means by which we transcend the ground on which we stand, the water we drink or the air we breathe. In such an animistic conception, the sacred is revealed 'through phenomena that bind us to the cosmos, and not solely through man, as in Judaism and Christianity, with a dominating God who is lord of history.'[58]

As we shall see in subsequent chapters, it was developments in modern art which did most to encourage Eliade in his belief that, after centuries of transcendent and rationalising abstraction from the world, such a cosmic concept of religion was returning to human consciousness. The poet Apollinaire once spoke of the 'mystical, pagan imagination' of Marc Chagall; Chagall himself spoke of his search for a psychic fourth dimension, for 'a logic of forms that are *other*', a logic which might effect a revolution in the very depths of painting.[59] Despite the unmistakable Judaeo-Christian tenor of his work, Chagall is as good an example as any of the attempt by many modern artists to return to that state of consciousness which the Jungian psychologist Erich Neumann called *participation mystique* — a term which may be taken to summarise much of what the French philosopher and social scientist Lucien Lévy-Bruhl believed about the 'capacity for participation' which he felt distinguished tribal thought.

Lévy-Bruhl (1857—1939) wrote about what he called the 'pre-logical' mentality of tribal life and thought. The anthropological accuracy of this characterisation has since been challenged several times.[60] Nevertheless, Lévy-Bruhl's idea that the (so-called) primitive mind possesses the ability to be a real 'centre of participation' — to be both one and many in the world — does much to illumine the primitivism of much post-Romantic art, a primitivism which speaks simultaneously of the very old and the brand new with regard to matters of both artistic form and consciousness. Neumann — who is far and away the most perceptive of Jungian commentators on art — has spoken of the 'breakdown of consciousness' in modern art, a breakdown which carries the artist 'backwards to an all-embracing *participation* with the world'; but at the same time, he has stressed that such a return to archaic qualities of *participation mystique* contains 'the constructive, creative elements of a new world vision.'[61]

Obsessed with the notion of historical progress in both the realm of ideas and the material improvement of life, the conventional wisdom of our culture has tended to regard anything archaic as something which is irretrievably outdated. However, in *The Transformative Vision*, a pioneering study of visionary art in the West from the late Renaissance to the twentieth century, José A. Argüelles has pointed out that the root of the word 'archaic' is 'a verb meaning to *begin*. In a sense what is archaic may not be backward at all, but a beginning.'[62] Modern art is often spoken of as having effected a 'revolution' in both form and content: the root of the word 'revolution' implies a return to the beginning, to the alpha point. It is the basic argument of this book that the search for a primal language in

4 Marc Chagall *Time Is A River Without Banks* 1938 oil on canvas 100 x 81.3 The Museum of Modern Art, New York © DACS 1992.

modern art, for new beginnings, has been an 'archaic' search for *participation mystique.* In undertaking that search, the modern artist has inherited and developed (whether consciously so or not) the ancient role of the shaman.

In 1955, Georges Bataille published his *Lascaux Or The Birth Of Art.* This was a poetic study of the various depictions, both naturalistic and fabulous, of the power of the animal realm which can be seen — together with a range of mysterious shapes and signs — at the most famous of all sites of prehistoric art. The rolling, limestone hills and gorges of the Dordogne region in southwest France shelter what most scholars now agree to be one of the earliest depictions of a shaman. The ecstatic, ithyphallic figure is depicted deep in a well, separate from the main galleries of Lascaux and difficult to reach. Like the bird which perches on a rod or staff next to him, this haunting figure from some 15,000 to 20,000 years ago has been drawn with child-like schematic stiffness, in stark contrast to the marvellous representational skills evident elsewhere. [63]

The cave paintings were discovered fifteen years before the publication of Bataille's book, by some young boys who were playing at the site. *Can it be nothing more than coincidence that the century which has seen the development of Jung's idea of the collective unconscious should have stumbled upon these marvels of artistic and spiritual aspiration from so long ago?* Our current ecological crisis adds an extra, pointed dimension to both the fortuitousness of their discovery and Bataille's words: 'Little

5 *Shaman and wounded bison,* the Crypt, or Well, Lascaux Cave. Upper Palaeolithic Photograph source: The Ancient Art and Architecture Collection, Harrow-on-the-Hill.

6 Frans Widerberg *The Cave*
1987 oil on canvas 210 x 248
Private Collection
© courtesy, the Artist
Photograph: Tomas
Widerberg, Oslo.

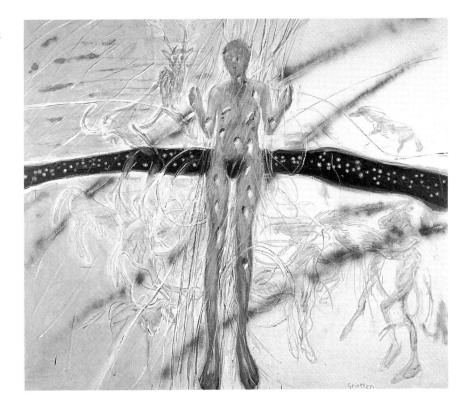

would it matter what those dead ancestors bequeathed to posterity were it not that we hoped to make them, if only for one fleeting instant, live again in ourselves.'[64]

In the 1988 preface to the second edition of his *The Shaman's Doorway,* an excellent, innovative study first published in the mid-1970s, Stephen Larsen underlined the relevance of shamanic ideas of holistic spirituality to late-twentieth-century life. In an unconscious echo of Arp and Richter, he suggested that wonder must eventually overcome terror in the balance of things: 'And the task of the shaman is to embody and transmit this message; to bring healing and meaning into life; and to create a glowing sense of accord with the informing root of all being. The modern shamanic path consists in a creative and affirmative relationship to life.'[65] Larsen went on to make the provocative point that it would be fruitless today to look for what he called 'true believers or card-carrying shamans'. This is not because the ancient figure of visionary and healing powers is no more to be seen. On the contrary, it is because shamans, according to Larsen, are currently to be found among all arts and professions: they are now therapists, artists, clergy, writers, poets, musicians and filmmakers.[66]

This insight should not be restricted to recent developments in the arts. At the end of his 1984 *Dreamtime and Inner Space: The World Of The Shaman,* Holger Kalweit suggested that over the past few years, the Western world has been witnessing the birth of a new mythos of the shaman. In fact, this mythos has been a long while in the making. As we have seen, its primitivistic roots lie deep in Romanticism. Argüelles speaks, quite rightly, of the 'absolutely shamanistic power' in the paintings and etchings of Goya;[67] and one can hardly read Wordsworth's *The Prelude, Or Growth Of A Poet's Mind*, with its famous line 'If prophecy be madness . . .', without remarking the author's shaman-like love of solitude and nature. However, as has already been suggested, it is from the late-nineteenth century onwards that the shamanic spirit in Western art really begins to develop the many formal and spiritual implications of Romanticism's dream of a magical world: develops them, that is, to increasingly primal (and at the same time subtle) levels of language and longing.

What one might call 'self-consciously advanced art' of the twentieth century is usually talked about in terms of its 'modernism' — at least up to the mid-1970s, when the often specious pluralism of the scrambled artistic codes of 'post-modernism' began to attract attention. Like primitivism, modernism is the sort of simple sounding word which becomes more complex the longer one studies it. Its artistic genesis is usually located in the increasingly self-conscious, mid- to late-nineteenth-century work of such painters as Manet and Cézanne. In its twentieth-century usage, the term continues to imply a high degree of formal self-consciousness on the part of the artist (with much parallel discussion by critics, concerning the moral implications of the allegedly requisite, non-illusionistic 'flatness of the picture plane' in painting or 'truth to materials' in sculpture). Social historians have related the origins of such self-consciousness to the general theme of bourgeois society's increasingly problematic sense of its own identity; and throughout the twentieth century, modernist artists have often sought to develop such self-consciousness into a would-be transformative engagement with the socio-historical dimensions of work and leisure.[68]

Whatever one may think of the fastidiousness of the Bauhaus or the megalomania of Le Corbusier, the example of Fernand Léger in painting is enough to show that the social side of modernism, so to speak, has produced some magnificent art. However, in the mid-1980s Suzi Gablik wrote a short, vigorous book called *Has Modernism Failed?*, in which she argued that a near-century of formal self-consciousness and Utopian ideology had largely failed to deliver the promised goods. Modernism had become formalistic, divorced from the social reality and spiritual aspirations of most people's lives. Gablik was equally critical of the mix'n'match games of post-modernism, which she saw as being all-too-knowing and empty at heart.[69]

If modernism had led to what another spiritually-oriented critic, the late Peter Fuller, called *kenosis* — a draining away of spiritual concerns, and a dispiriting emphasis on art-for-art's (or money's, or critical fame's) sake[70] — then art could only again become meaningful by a return to values of the distant past. Essentially, Gablik's book was a plea that art be 'remythologised'; that artists return to a 'devotional' state of mind; that the world be 're-enchanted'. Citing the work of such artists as Joseph Beuys and Anselm Kiefer in support of her argument, Gablik underlined the need to see the artist less as a celebrity *à la* Andy Warhol and more as a potential shamanic figure, or bridge-builder between worlds. And she insisted that the many tangled political problems of the late-twentieth century would only stand a chance of being solved if 'the visionary powers' were once again made central to life.[71]

I agree completely with the last part of Gablik's argument, just as I sympathise with her exposure of the artistic and moral vacuity of much of the art from New York which has flooded the international art market and magazines in recent years. However, *Has Modernism Failed?* considerably exaggerates the extent to which a quest for 'the visionary powers' has been absent from (modernist-inflected) twentieth-century art. Gablik's belief that 'Science, in the twentieth century, has had little to say about spiritual values; nor, it would seem, has art ... In modernist culture, nothing is sacred ...'[72] simply misses the point about an enormous amount of artistic endeavour this century. (As it also does about science, when one considers, for example, the parallels which Fritjof Capra's *The Tao Of Physics* drew between quantum physics and Taoism, the ancient Chinese philosophy of the earth which encourages us to still the ego and its desires, in order to attend to the great rhythmic oneness, or Way, which lies at the heart of 'the ten thousand things' of the world.[73])

One example may suffice to suggest not only the extent to which Eliade's idea of a return to cosmic religion can be detected in modern art, but also the degree to which that art may have been inspired by the discoveries of twentieth-century science. The Spanish artist Antoni Tàpies (*b.*1923) has become famous for the degree of his involvement with the material of existence. Mixing glue, plaster of Paris and sand, he has created mysterious relief-like images in dark, stained colours redolent of both the earth and the unconscious. Strange signs and forms emerge from the ground of the image, some scratched into the work's rich surface, others painted on. Tàpies has spoken of wanting to make his inert materials speak; of wanting to wake people up so that they 'are no longer lost in an artificial reality, distracted by advertising or by those advocating an ideology, for example.'[74]

Breathing life back into the humble but essential things of the world — resurrecting the presence of spirit in matter — Tàpies functions like a shaman, re-directing attention to the elemental dimensions of existence, to the animistic integration of self and world: 'I've always compared the attitude of the artist to that of the mystic. They both follow a path which slowly leads to an ultimate vision of reality. When you arrive at that point it's difficult to talk about it: what is ultimate reality, or the face of God, as the mystics would say? It's not so much knowledge as inner experience.'[75]

Like that of many Western artists this century, Tàpies's path to such experience has passed through the East. However, Tàpies tells us that he came to Oriental art through an early interest in science, when he was very concerned about the nature of reality, the structure of matter and problems of space, time and causality. Reading scientists like Albert Einstein, Niels Bohr, Erwin Schrodinger, Werner Heisenberg and Jacob Oppenheimer, Tàpies noticed that all these people, at one time or another, wrote of the Vedanta or Taoism or Buddhism, which encouraged him to read these Eastern philosophies.[76]

The example of Tàpies suggests that, rather than wondering if something called modernism has failed, one might seek to establish the extent to which modernist artists have prepared the way for a second Renaissance: the Renaissance of the 'mystical, pagan imagination' which Apollinaire sensed in Chagall; of that 'cosmic religiosity' which so concerned Mircea Eliade.[77] This is the other side of the social-historical modernist coin: the side which concerns the implications of pianist Keith Jarrett's remark that art exists 'as a reminder.'[78]

For this exceptional musician, who has been strongly affected by Sufi ideas of creativity and ecstasy, the purpose of art is to take us closer to the core of existence, to a sense of our place within the cosmos. Worthwhile art, art which 'wounds' the soul, the better to heal it, is a reminder of the larger dimensions of our existence — in contrast to the spiritual forgetfulness and imprisonment within the historical moment induced in us by a variety of political pressures and commercial blandishment today. In the sleevenotes to his 1989 release *Changeless,* Jarrett suggested that 'Our society has chosen its priorities quite clearly: surfaces . . . But only the knowledge of centers (or Center) will fix the core of our World (or worlds).'[79]

Arp and Richter would have agreed with Jarrett. So would Kandinsky; so would Meret Oppenheim. And so would Joan Miró, the Catalan painter and sculptor who was both one of this century's greatest shamanic spirits and a key figure in modernism: not the modernism of the socio-historical moment, but the modernism of post-Romantic primitivism, of the search for a healing language on the plane of cosmic religion.

In 1939 Miró declared: 'If we do not attempt to discover the religious essence, the magic sense of things, we will do no more than add new sources of degradation to those already offered to the people of today, which are beyond number.'[80] He felt that painting had been in decadence since the time of the Paleolithic cave artists: the cave-like 'graphism' of his work is a prime example of the primitivistic search for artistic and spiritual replenishment within twentieth-century modernism.[81] In 1964, the French poet Yves Bonnefoy underlined the importance of Miró's work for what he called the 'reinvention of faith' needed this century, a faith to be based upon a regenerative love of nature. For Bonnefoy, Miró had clearly inherited 'the ancient role of shaman.'[82]

Miró — whose work we shall consider further in Chapter 11 — visited America several times after the Second World War, and loved swing, or jazz music (as the Dadaists had done many years before). In the same year that Bonnefoy's book on Miró appeared, the saxophonist John Coltrane recorded the four-part composition *A Love Supreme*. This was a disturbing, yet ultimately affirmative work of great ritual power: drenched in the spirit of Afro-American gospel and blues, the turbulent, questing lines of the saxophonist were stoked to shamanic heights by the fattening, poly-rhythmic thunder of Elvin Jones's drumming. Religion as well as music was embraced in Coltrane's belief that 'you've got to look back at the old things and see them in a new light.'[83] In a far-ranging study of this master musician, Bill Cole rightly set what he called the 'visionary magic' of Coltrane's music in the context of the spiritual values of traditional, pre-industrial society — for the shamanic import of Coltrane's music, which we shall investigate in Chapter 8, is unmistakable.[84]

7 John Coltrane, London 1961
Photograph: © Val ⁇ ⁇ner.

Coltrane drew inspiration from a range of constantly expanding sources: from the whole Afro-American tradition, from Western concert music and folk music, from twentieth-century art and science, and from classic texts of both the Western and Eastern spiritual traditions. One of the many books he read was a life of Van Gogh, which affected him profoundly. In 1962 he wrote to the critic Don DeMichael: 'You know, Don, I was reading a book on the life of Van Gogh today, and I had to pause and think of that wonderful and persistent force — the creative urge. The creative urge was in this man who found himself so much at odds with the world he lived in, and in spite of all the adversity, frustrations, rejections and so forth — beautiful and living art came forth abundantly . . . If only he could be here today. Truth is indestructible.'[85]

In *A Separate Reality,* Don Juan tells Carlos Castaneda that the great thing in life is to learn how to *see*; which, he adds, is never a matter for the eyes alone.[86] He also remarks that, in order to see life well, in order to discover the joyful journey of a path with heart, you must first stop the world and dream real dreams.[87] Dreaming with open eyes, we may begin to sense that what links Van Gogh with Coltrane also links Paul Gauguin with Wassily Kandinsky, Jean Arp with Meret Oppenheim and Monica Sjöö, Hans Richter with Keith Jarrett, and Joan Miró with Antoni Tàpies: the ancient, indestructible truth of shamanism.

2 The Promise and the Search

It is one thing to dream with open eyes; it is another thing to reflect upon or to write about that experience. Equally, it is one thing to feel that there may be potent connections between twentieth-century art and the creativity of the prehistoric shamans, and another thing to attempt to substantiate such connections.

A key feature of the history that separates us from the prehistorical world is the growth of language. We often take it for granted that language is the medium whereby we communicate and develop ideas to the maximum. Yet rather than help to clarify our thoughts and feelings, language can often confuse and obfuscate matters. One might ask: how can our language, riddled with dualistic assumptions of the relations between active subject (or agent) and passive object (or world) as it is, hope to understand the nature of artistic activity in a world where such assumptions (and perhaps the very idea of 'artistic activity' as we comprehend it) may not have been linguistically present?

Leaving aside any consideration of such specialised 'languages' as are to be found in mathematics or the physical sciences, one might say that the growth of human consciousness has resulted in two great synthesising efforts of the human imagination: the language of the various systems of thought of the world religions, such as Hinduism, Judaism, Christianity or Islam, and the language of the historical and political self-consciousness which has (relatively recently) come to dominate Western thought. From the eighteenth-century European Enlightenment onwards, the language of history, politics and sociology has mounted a series of attacks upon the language of religion, claiming that the 'terrain' of history — of society and politics — is the sole terrain of human experience.

We can see this particularly clearly with regard to the change in meaning which the word 'alienation' has acquired over the past 150 years. Once, to be alienated meant to be cut off from God, to be outside the divine totality of life. But since Karl Marx's radical critique of religion in the 1844 *Economic and Philosophical Manuscripts,* the concept of alienation has come to have a quite different resonance.

From the perspective of Marxism, to be alienated is to have less than full control over one's powers and rights as an historical being, living in (or to be more accurate to Marxism, constituting) society. For Marx, religion was the heart of a heartless world, the opiate, or supreme 'false-consciousness' that prevented people from thinking about their position in capitalist-industrial society to the clearest possible extent. Only by a radical critique of religion might people be persuaded that they should thoroughly politicise themselves, and band together with others to effect the historical changes needed to create the unexploitative, classless world of first socialism and then communism.[1]

Religion thus came to be perceived as the prime vehicle of alienation, since it had encouraged people for so long to project their own ability to affect life into the absolute, transcendent powers of a distant and increasingly silent God. The language of religion — all religion — was the language of alienation; the language of human history — for what other kind might there be? — became the language of redemption, transferred from the sacred plane of religious transcendence to the dynamic, profane plane of society, of politics — of history with a capital 'H'.

The appalling consequences of the central irony of Marxism — of its dependence upon the eschatological framework of the very system of thought which it sought to destroy — have long been apparent.[2] The transference of a Judaeo-Christian understanding of 'the four last things: death, judgement, heaven and hell' to the realm of politics led to the murder of millions, as the Marxist ideology of historical progress came to rationalise the use of any means for the achievement of its supposedly glorious end. Having become a weapon of intellectual terrorism, language was itself murdered, as Orwell underlined in *1984*. And with the murder of language came the grimmest irony of all: the alienation of historically-defined humanity from itself.

It was suggested earlier that the growth of human self-consciousness has resulted in two great synthesising efforts of the imagination: the so-called higher religions and socio-political, historical consciousness. If the growth of the latter has meant an attack upon religious consciousness, what has it meant for art, the language that might be said to predate both religion and history?[3]

Just as Marxism, the philosophy which has taken an exclusively socio-historical perception of life as far as it will go, criticises religion in the name of the political realities and potentialities of life, so does it address art in the name of society. The central category of Marxist aesthetics is what the Marxist philosopher and literary critic Georg Lukács (1885—1971) called *realism*: a term which for the Marxist implies an awareness and understanding of the movement of history, and which is thus to be distinguished from mere reflective naturalism, with its tendency to be trapped within the historical moment, so to speak.

Most Marxist theoreticians harbour an intense nostalgia for what they call the 'totality' of social life. In his early work *The Theory Of The Novel* (written in 1914—15, before he became a convert to Marxism), Lukács contrasted the 'transcendental homelessness' of the individualistic modern world with what he saw as the 'integrated totality' of classical Greek culture, as expressed in the epic. In the various essays of the early 1920s which were gathered together in *History And Class Consciousness,* the full force of Lukács's conversion to Marxism became apparent: 'transcendental homelessness' could only be overcome and the 'integrated totality' of life and meaning achieved once more through the eventual world-wide historical triumph of the working class.[4]

Demanding an art which would reveal what he considered to be both the totalising, evolving potentialities and the realities of historical change, Lukács opposed both the stereotypical lies of 'progressive' Soviet Socialist Realism and what he felt to be the hopeless fragmentation and subjectivity of much modern art. He analysed the latter in terms of what he saw as its symbiotic relation to the decline in the bourgeois class's confidence in its historical power, a decline which Lukács thought had gradually accelerated from the mid-to-late-nineteenth century onwards. Too much modern art, felt Lukács, was nothing but navel-gazing.

Lukács believed strongly in the aesthetic category of the *type.* In selecting from the details of life, and thus raising those details to the status of the typical, an artist revealed his or her degree of historical consciousness. And the attainment of such consciousness in late-bourgeois society was a more subtle matter than simply depicting either the despair of the bourgeois class or the imminent triumph of socialism and communism.

The bourgeois realist artist, for example, could attain a position of what Lukács called critical realism, portraying both something of the death throes of capitalist society and the potentiality of human historical growth. Here, Lukács's exemplar was Thomas Mann, whose work Lukács contrasted with what he felt to be the ahistorical, falsely 'universalising' despair of artists like Franz Kafka and Samuel Beckett. In contrast to defeatist fragmentation and subjectivity, argued Lukács, 'True great realism . . . depicts man and society as complete entities, instead of showing merely one or other of their aspects . . . The central aesthetic problem of realism is the adequate presentation of the complete human personality . . . [which] . . . leads beyond pure aesthetics: for art, precisely if it is taken in its most perfect purity, is saturated with social and moral humanistic problems.'[5]

Key questions are begged here. For what does it mean, to speak of 'the adequate presentation of the complete human personality'? As an expression of that personality, how great a range of ideas, emotions and longings should art be expected — and allowed — to address? Is there anything more to the human being than 'class-consciousness'? How do individuals, for example, integrate awareness of mortality into their growth as persons? If the point of life is to develop towards 'integrative totality', what concepts can a Marxist use to at least indicate the enormous range of psychological issues involved in that process? In Brandon Taylor's recent *Modernism, Post-Modernism, Realism* the Marxist answer to such questions is clear. Taylor believes that 'In the art of the future, there must be no subjective representation which does not at the same time terminate in a problem of social relations, of class, of lived values in the exterior world.'[6]

But suppose all those problems were themselves part of a much larger problem — namely, the nature of the language within which we assume we are able to make such authoritative statements about 'art', 'social relations' and 'the exterior world' (not to mention 'integrative totality')? Taylor's language is the language of an exclusively socio-political, historical consciousness — the same kind of language that led the sociologist Janet Wolff to the central belief of her 1981 text *The Social Production of Art*, which was that 'the romantic and mystical notion of art as the creation of "genius"' must be abandoned, for 'the arts can adequately be understood only in a sociological perspective.'[7] Curiously, at the same time that she made the latter assertion, Wolff acknowledged that her text did not attempt to deal with the question of aesthetic value.[8]

What kind of would-be definitive discussion of art is it that does not attempt to deal with concepts of genius and aesthetic value? Exactly the kind of discussion one might expect from a language that has been drained of all reference to anything beyond itself; a language that has succumbed to the totalising *hubris* of socio-political, historical self-consciousness. In the late 1950s Raymond Aron called Marxism the opium of the intellectuals. One might say the same about sociological, or socio-political theorising today. No amount of luncheon vouchers will enable anyone to purchase a railway ticket; and yet the language of socio-political, historical self-consciousness persists in its logocentric delusion that the currency of historical, political and sociological thought will grant access to every experience under the sun. (Except the nature of aesthetic value, as Wolff so curiously reminds us. What, then, of the nature of religious experience, of morality, of imagination: the nature of everything, in fact, which may ultimately escape the relatively crude grasp of the *historically defined* categories of historical consciousness?[9])

Today, the concept of genius is often dismissed in left-wing circles as an embarrassing, politically regressive idea, redolent of an outdated romantic notion of art as the product of exceptionally gifted individuals. It is worth remembering what the Romantics themselves meant by the term. Here is Coleridge, in his *Philosophical Lectures,* defining joy as the state of abounding vitality essential to the creative power of genius — a power which takes one *beyond* individuality: 'To have a genius is to live in the universal, to know no self but that which is reflected not only from the faces of all around us, our fellow creatures, but reflected from the flowers, the trees, the beasts, yea from the very surface of the [waters and the] sands of the desert. A man of genius finds a reflex to himself, were it only in the mystery of being.'[10] As its semantic roots make evident, genius implies *spirit* — and Coleridge's words form a splendid bridge between ancient, animistic ideas of the creativity of the shamanic spirit and the key Jungian idea of the development of the human spirit, or soul, towards the state of individuation. We shall investigate the relation between shamanism and individuation in the following two chapters: for the moment, let us at least consider the possibility that in becoming sensitive to the genius of artists, we are doing more than paying lip-service to so-called bourgeois, 'elitist' notions of taste — as a sociologist like Pierre Bourdieu, for example, would have us believe.

Working in the field of inquiry known as the sociology of taste, Bourdieu's fundamental thesis is that 'The eye is a product of history, reproduced by education . . . there is no "love at first sight" in the encounter with a work of art.'[11] For Bourdieu, the ideology of 'natural taste' is a product of class distinctions: art museums are thus the 'sacred places' of the bourgeoisie, their 'true function' being to reinforce the barrier between 'those who have received Grace and those to whom it has been denied.' Everything about the gallery or museum, argues Bourdieu, serves to show that 'the world of art stands in opposition to the world of daily life, like the sacred to the profane: the untouchability of the objects, the religious silence imposed on visitors, the puritanical asceticism of the furnishings . . . the vast galleries, the painted ceilings, and the monumental staircases all seeming as if they were designed to reflect . . . a passage from the profane world to the sacred world.'[12]

It is a major part of my argument that the terms which Bourdieu uses with such sociological irony here — the sacred and the profane — hold the key to the 'esoteric' meaning of a good deal of twentieth-century art: the art of shamanic spirit, art which encourages us to rethink what we mean by speaking of 'the sacred' and its place in life. While this book is largely devoted to tracing the evidence of that spirit within a range of examples, rather than investigating the sociological conditions of its production and reception, it is worth pointing out that a broader, much less restrictive sociology of art than Bourdieu would seem to advocate is entirely possible to contemplate.

The French novelist and one-time Minister of Culture André Malraux (1901–76) believed that our century had made it possible for people to experience the transformative impact of an unprecedented amount of art, in what he called 'the museum without walls' which both high quality photographic reproduction and an enlarged, post-Romantic aesthetic sense had given us. (Before Romanticism's empathy — however stereotyped we now deem it to be — with the so-called 'Noble Savage', much of the world's non-classical, non-Christian art was dismissed by the West with a shudder: it was simply barbaric.) In a variety of books of the 1950s and 1960s, Malraux celebrated the endless process of mute, yet transformative dialogue in which he believed works of art of all ages — both secular and sacred — could now participate. For Malraux, the leitmotif of that dialogue — or 'song of metamorphosis' as he called it — was the affirmation of an archetypal 'antidestiny': the proclamation and celebration of the sacred *spirit* of humanity, in the eternal face of death.[13]

No matter how many sociologists and art historians have quarrelled with the Olympian (not to say neo-colonial) tenor of Malraux's ideas, it remains a fact that the twentieth century *has* developed a great number of 'museums without walls'. And these are now far more extensive than those of even Malraux's wildest dreams. For they have come to exist in the psyches of all those who are interested in moving beyond the 'local' sociology of art, so to speak, in pursuit of a broader vision. This is a vision in which — to employ a transmutation of Lukács's terminology — one's sense of both 'integrative totality' and exemplary 'type' embraces not the reductive fiction of class consciousness, but rather the sort of expansive, emergent mythical sensibility signalled in Erich Neumann's belief that 'The religions of the world, the saviors of the world, the revolutionaries, the prophets, and not least the artists — all these great figures and what they have created form for us a single whole. We all — and not just individuals among us — are beginning not to free ourselves from our personal determinants, for that is impossible, but to see them in perspective. The African medicine man and the Siberian shaman assume for us the same human dignity as Moses and Buddha; an Aztec fresco takes its place beside a Chinese landscape and an Egyptian sculpture, the Upanishads beside the Book of Changes and the Bible.'[14]

Neumann wrote the above words in the 1950s. To today's critics of Western primitivism, they may signify only the patronising naïvity of much Western thought about 'the Other': a neo-colonialist need to negate the realities of socio-historical and cultural *differences* in pursuit of some mythical (i.e. false) universalism. For example, Signe Howell, professor of Social Anthropology at the University of Oslo, has recently argued against the idea that inner states of consciousness, or emotional reactions to works of art, can be 'universalised'. As a disciple of Emile Durkheim, who was above all concerned to establish sociology as a discipline both independent of and superior to psychology, Howell believes firmly in social as opposed to psychological facts. Thus, for her, any claims for a transcultural, transhistorical understanding of 'art' (the quotation marks are Howell's) must be challenged by the proposition that 'symbolic artefacts made by members of any society . . . are only explicable within the cultural context in which they are produced . . . it is not acceptable to make encompassing generalisations concerning the meaning of any of these elaborations . . .

Each must be understood in terms of the overall cultural context in which they are elaborated. As such, they can be studied as social facts.'[15]

Leaving aside the rather large methodological problem that any Durkheimian has of explaining how a 'social fact' comes to be 'inflected' or even 'changed' by either individuals or groups of people, Howell's use of the phrase 'overall cultural context' surely begs the question with regard to much of the world's experience of life today. For the cultural contexts of 'social facts' are now, as never before, in a state of flux. As Howell's own examples make clear, just as images of so-called primitive, non-European art have appeared throughout the Western world this century, so do images of Western art now appear throughout the non-Western world — a prime example being Leonardo's *Mona Lisa*.

In a photograph which she took of a mountain lodge in Nepal, Howell reveals a reproduction of the *Mona Lisa* sitting next to images of Michael Jackson, Abba and the reigning monarch of Nepal — proof positive, Howell feels, of the difficulty of arguing that 'great art' (again, the quotation marks are hers) transcends cultural boundaries.[16] But whatever 'social fact' one might care to construct from such a photograph (and Howell herself offers us none), from a psychological point of view it seems to me entirely possible to argue that, in this particular ensemble of images, 'great art' has indeed transcended cultural boundaries. Leonardo's image of what Jungians would call the *anima* joins other (admittedly, elementary) examples of what psychologists or students of mythology would call 'heroic models': the models which help the soul to build itself, and which give it the strength to realise that life may in fact be more than the local, culture-bound experience of 'social facts' which Durkheimian sociology would have us believe.[17] To speak of life only in terms of 'social facts' is to deny the fundamental, shape-shifting mystery of the human spirit — to deny, that is, the distinctions between shamans and priests, or artists and anthropologists.

A painter paints a picture; a poet writes a poem; a musician composes, or improvises, a piece of music. And along comes an army of critics or historians, concepts of history and politics, sociology and anthropology in hand, ready to turn image, metaphor and overtone back into the 'chain of historical signifiers' (or some such) from which they emerged and to which they 'really' belong. Imagine a world where those critics or historians had to paint a picture, write a poem, compose or improvise a piece of music in order to reveal their reaction to art. Many critics and historians would soon be out of a job: those who remained should have acquired some sense at least of the 'otherness' of much art, and of the struggle which artists may have to undergo precisely in order to develop a language which *speaks of more than can be said*.

Wittgenstein suggested that, that of which we cannot speak, we must pass over in silence. I do not wish to argue for such an extreme view — although given the exponential growth of 'deconstructive' texts today, of language which would seem to have lost all desire (or ability) to speak of anything more than its own disillusioned odyssey through the 'de-centred' labyrinth of 'post-modernist' historical selfconsciousness, I would certainly wish to defend the right to be silent in the face of the (potentially transfigurative) experience of art.[18] However, I would not be writing this book if I did not believe in the power of language and ideas to alter — to deepen or extend — perception and imagination. One can hardly investigate the nature of twentieth-century art without remarking the extent to which artists, committed to the idea of art as a *mysterious* stimulus to personal and social change, have been prepared to discuss their ideas in written form: think only of Kandinsky's *Concerning The Spiritual in Art* or Malevich's *The Non-Objective World.* As both those artists knew, however, it is essential to regard language and ideas as aids towards the experience of art, rather than as substitutes for it — or, as in so much recent 'deconstructive' sociology, attacks upon it.[19]

Two authors have recently produced impassioned (and carefully reasoned) defences of the mystery dimension in art — of the possibility that if there *is* something in what we 'say' through art, then that something may well be of a metaphysical nature. In his *Real Presences* George Steiner urges us to reflect upon what he calls 'the openness to unknowing distinctive of myth', so that we might be prepared to suspend our notorious desire to 'know' what a work of art 'really means', and let the *presence* of art address us.[20] Joan Miró once spoke of how he worked like a gardener: if an artist's forms can take months and years to come to fruition, why should we presume that the resultant work will yield up its secrets to us in the minute or so of our time which we may be prepared to give to it in a gallery, or the quarter of an hour which we perhaps decide to devote to reading about it later? In *The Arts Without Mystery,* Denis Donoghue asks that no matter how much of our time we are prepared to give to art, we try to suspend what he calls 'the managerial function' of language. Why? So that the metaphors at the poetic heart of art, which fuel the imagination's flight, are not prematurely grounded by order of the rational mind — so that we may be able to feel something of the power of art to move us *beyond ourselves.*[21] This is the desire of Antoni Tàpies and Keith Jarrett, just as it was that of Jean Arp and Hans Richter.

Gaston Bachelard once observed that one does not 'explain' a flower by its fertilizer. What then might the relation between the language of historical consciousness and that of art be? Acknowledging that the 'languages' of social history and the sociology of art can tell us much of the circumstances surrounding the production and reception of art, and as such can go some way (but not, *pace* Wolff and Howell, all the way) towards helping us appreciate the complex range of meanings which art can embody, what effect might the language of art have upon the language of historical consciousness? Is it conceivable that the language of art might be able to help heal the wounds which we may inflict upon ourselves by using a language of exclusively socio-historical dimensions?

The Norwegian artist Frans Widerberg, whose startling images strike an unmistakably shamanic note, has suggested that the language of speech and writing can be seen as a two-way door. Used only one way, that door

8 Frans Widerberg *Near The Fire* 1976 black and white lithograph 80 x 60
© courtesy the Artist and Galleri K, Oslo
Photograph: Jan Ung, Oslo.

may lock the self inside itself and confirm the prison house of self-consciousness — of personality, society and history. Used another way, the door can open onto the essential, transmutative terrain of art — of mystery and metamorphosis. If language cannot traverse this terrain, it can at least point the way towards it. For Widerberg, who uses language with both discrimination and relish, the chief point of speech and writing is to enable the self to stand at the open threshold of both worlds — of history and politics, of cosmos and mystery — so that the healing energy of the latter may perhaps flow into the former.

Language — human self-consciousness — is thus both its own jailer and potential liberator. And if art is a language, then we should perhaps learn how to listen to it, rather than rushing to translate its various 'texts' into the words and ideas which can so insidiously confirm the prison house of everyday consciousness. Wittgenstein once suggested that the limits of our language are the limits of our world. Is this necessarily the case? When one raises one's arm and points to the moon, the gesture is usually not intended to draw attention to the condition of one's fingernails.

The language of speech, of writing, of prose and poetry is words; but it is also the silence between those words. The cliché of 'a pregnant silence' bears some thought: what is it that language may bring to birth? From the point of view of historical consciousness, language must give birth to yet more history — to more change and development within a horizontal plane of existence that opens out endlessly onto the future. But from the point of view of religion, poetry and mythology, language can give birth to a vertical dimension: the dimension that cuts through the profane flow of historical time to summon the sacred. And according to Mircea Eliade — in contradistinction to Marx — 'the "sacred" is an element in the structure of consciousness, not a stage in the history of consciousness.'[22]

The painter Wols once warned:

> '. . . Do not explain music
> do not explain dreams
> the elusive penetrates everything
> you must know that everything rhymes.'[23]

If everything rhymes, it must exist on a plane which is able to embrace and transfigure the 'social facts' of history (like the idea of the spiral which we encountered in the last chapter). For the energy of history — which as Claude Lévi-Strauss has argued, is always a matter of history *for* someone, as opposed to someone else — involves the dissonance and the detritus of change.[24] This is, of course, not to argue against the idea that everyone has an absolute right to proclaim their own history, their own sense of identity gathered from their understanding of the past, the present and the future — a point which concerned the seven black, British-born or domiciled painters who were featured in the *History And Identity* show which was curated by Eddie Chambers in 1991, for example, as much as it did the many Native American authors whose poetry was gathered together in Duane Niatum's 1988 *Anthology Of 20th Century Native American Poetry*.[25] It is to argue that, as much of that Native American poetry revealed, life can be understood as unfolding upon another plane than that of history *as understood in the fundamentally rationalist Western tradition* within which Janet Wolff and Brandon Taylor, for example, develop their understanding of art.

The transfiguring plane where 'everything rhymes' is the plane to which the ancient shamans flew, in search of the language that might cure the sickness of either individual or tribe. It is the plane of what Steiner calls 'the unknowing distinctive of myth', the (rational) unknowing which is in fact the deep 'knowing' of the poetic imagination, of mythological and mythopoeic consciousness. Here, language does not address the world in terms of (active) subject and (passive) object, but rather in terms of what the philosopher Martin Buber has called an I-Thou relation: a relation of numinous complementarity, where the world may *speak us*, as it were.[26]

In his study *Shelley's Mythmaking*, the literary critic Harold Bloom drew upon Buber's terminology to indicate a key distinction between mythological (and mythographic) consciousness and the realm of the mythopoeic. The first two terms refer to the use of already known mythic material by the imagination: whereas mythopoeisis connotes much more of the original, generative moment of mythic consciousness. This is the moment of an I-Thou relation between self and world, a moment when the details of existence are experienced freshly, in terms of Wols's epiphanic perception that 'everything rhymes'.[27] It is precisely the search for this plane of existence, or aspiration, which links the world of twentieth-century art with that of shamanism. And the fact that many twentieth-century artists have become deeply involved with the search for mythopoeisis goes quite some way to explaining the distrust of (historically conditioned) language which has been revealed by such a considerable number of them.

Jan Garbarek, the outstanding Norwegian composer and saxophonist whose often stark, yet always subtle work has done much to help resurrect and develop the 'mystical, pagan imagination' of which Apollinaire spoke, has said that 'The essential is that which cannot be put into words.'[28] Kandinsky felt that the whole point of art was to speak of mystery in terms of mystery; Georges Braque, the great Cubist painter whose work was often inspired — as was that of Kandinsky — by music, believed that the only thing that really mattered in art was the part of it that could not be verbalised. For 'to define something is to substitute the definition of the thing for the thing itself.'[29]

Towards the end of his life, Braque (1882—1963) developed this thought with regard to the metamorphosis of space and objects which had played such a central role in his art: 'No object can be tied down to any one sort of reality; a stone may be part of a wall, a piece of sculpture, a lethal weapon, a pebble on a beach, or anything else you like, just as this file in my hand can be metamorphosed into a shoe-horn or a spoon, according to the way I use it . . . Everything is subject to metamorphosis; everything changes according to circumstance . . . this "metamorphic" confusion is fundamental to what I am out to express. It is all the same to me whether a form represents a different thing to different people or many things at the same time. And then I occasionally introduce forms which have no literal meaning whatsoever. Sometimes these are accidents which happen to suit my purpose, sometimes "rhymes" which echo other forms, and sometimes rhythmical motifs which help to integrate a composition and give it meaning.'[30]

9 Georges Braque *The Studio VIII (Atelier VIII)* 1952—5 oil on canvas 132 x 197 Private Collection Photograph: John Webb © DACS 1992.

Cubism is sometimes regarded as a rather dry and dusty art, with little if any sense of metaphysical 'excitement' about it. Nothing could be further from the truth. The excitement of Cubism may not be that of Expressionism, with its clashes of colour and cries of longing for a world of renewed spiritual dimensions. But Cubism's poetic reshaping of

perception can be seen as very much part of the primitivistic thrust of twentieth-century art, of its longing to recapture something of the so-called primitive's experience of *participation mystique*. Building upon the achievements of Paul Cézanne (which we shall consider in the next chapter) Cubism broke with centuries of 'masterful' one-point Western perspective. Instead, it conjured a world of shallow pictorial space where the relation of objects to both each other and the viewer acquires something of a magical aura. Floating free of the laziness of everyday habits of perception, the objects of Cubism suggest a world where one can be a true 'centre of participation' – be 'one and many' at the same time.

The ultimate import of Braque's sensitivity to metamorphosis was expressed by the painter himself, again towards the end of his life. 'You see,' said Braque, 'I have made a great discovery: I no longer believe in anything. Objects don't exist for me except in so far as a state of rapport exists between them or between them and myself. When one attains this harmony one reaches a sort of intellectual non-existence – what I can only describe as a state of peace – which make everything possible and right. Life then becomes a perpetual revelation. That is true poetry.'[31]

Braque's carefully weighted words underline the metaphysical dimension in Cubism. It is a dimension that is particularly evident in the visionary space of Braque's *The Studio VIII* of 1952–5, or *Composition with Stars* from *circa* 1954–58. In the latter, a surreal image of a majestic, golden bird emerges from the rich spatial complexities of a studio, to send the eye soaring upwards to a Matisse-like galaxy of stars.[32] It is important to remember this metaphysical aspect of Cubism, rather than dwell exclusively on the purely formal or social characteristics which often dominate our understanding of this art. For the poetic world of (freshly analysed, and then synthesised) objects in shallow space of which Braque was such a master has provided the foundation for an enormous amount of *spiritually questing* art this century. Superficially, much of this art may seem to have little to do with the refinements of Cubism, but the relation (both formal and metaphysical) can be clearly established. The dramatic achievements of Miró and Jackson Pollock, for example, are scarcely imaginable without the inspiration which each artist drew from Cubism.

The primitivistic element of *participation mystique* which can be discerned within Cubism assumes a very different complexion in the contemporary work of the Italian 'metaphysical' painter Giorgio de Chirico (1888–1978), for whom *participation mystique* involved feelings of nameless dread as much as (if not more than) joy. De Chirico felt that 'the most amazing sensation' passed onto us by prehistoric man was that of presentiment. It is a feeling which haunts many of the elongated perspectives and ominous shadows in de Chirico's work. And it is a feeling which de Chirico believed would always continue: 'We might consider it as eternal proof of the irrationality of the universe. Original man must have wandered through a universe of uncanny signs. He must have trembled at each step.'[33]

Something of this feeling informs de Chirico's *Seer* of 1915. At the same time, the painting deepens its sense of mystery by managing to combine a distant echo of Blake's earlier, Romantic critique of Newtonian science (in the famous 1795 image of Newton on the sea floor, compasses in hand, as he 'murders to dissect') with a suggestion of the transfigurative knowledge which may be contained within the esoteric harmonies of geometry.[34]

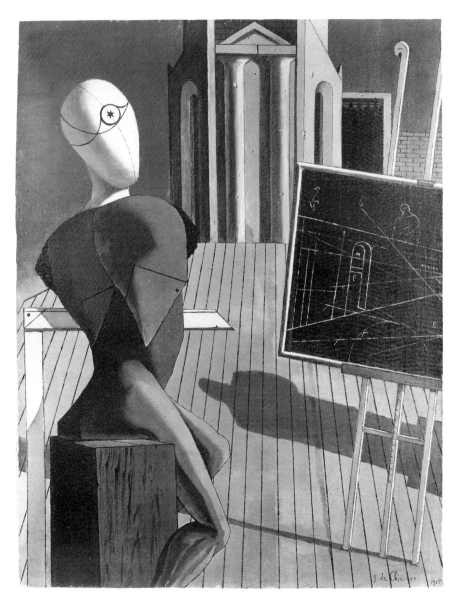

10 Giorgio de Chirico
The Seer 1915 oil on canvas
89.6 x 70.1
The Museum of Modern Art,
New York

Whatever levels of meaning we might care to read into *Seer*, we should remember that de Chirico shared Braque's belief that the power of a successful image transcends whatever words one might apply to it. De Chirico thought that 'To become truly immortal a work of art must escape all human limits: logic and common sense will only interfere. But once those barriers are broken it will enter the regions of childhood vision and dream.'[35] It is worth noting that at practically the same moment that de Chirico painted *Seer*, the Dada poet and activist Hugo Ball spoke of painters as 'advocates of the *vita contemplativa*: as advocates of the supranatural sign language . . .'. Ball asked: 'Is the language of signs the actual *paradise language*?'[36]

Years later, the American sculptor David Smith (1906–65), in whose work the importance of Cubism is again readily apparent, suggested that 'The promise, the hint of new vista, the unresolved, the misty dream, the artist should love even more than the resolved, for here is the fluid force, the promise and the search.'[37] A major artist in the mid-century development of what came to be known as Abstract Expressionism, Smith's painted and welded iron and steel sculptures bring to life a primitivistic, totemic world. It is a world where one can feel the full force of the sculptor's belief that 'Art is made from dreams and visions and things not known and least of all from things that can be said. It comes from the inside of who you are, when you face yourself. It is an inner declaration of purpose.'[38]

Smith — whose art has been described as 'totems for an ideal society'[39] — believed that 'In childhood we have been raped by word pictures. We must revolt against all word authority. Our only language is vision.'[40] His feelings were shared by the painter Clyfford Still (1904–80), another key artist of Abstract Expressionism. Still's large fields of bright, earthily impastoed colour carry strong, yet deliberately unspecific associations of immense landscapes: it was the landscape of the inner self that the painter sought. And this was a landscape which he felt to be charged with enormous, redeeming potentiality.

Still believed that 'a single stroke of paint, backed by . . . a mind that understood its potency and implications, could restore to man the freedom lost in twenty centuries of apology and devices for subjugation.'[41] Words, felt Still, had become a major part of such devices. Writing in his diary in 1945, he revealed how above all else he deplored 'the overemphasis on words. Not the poet's words, but words that explain, reason, debate, deduce, make "fact". Words have become omnipotent because so facile a tool have they become for the utilitarian and the practical . . . Verbiage becomes a substitute for comprehension. And everything leads to words and words become a substitute for everything . . . And the world is engulfed in the reasonable and the logical, and the sane and the pseudo-scientific.'[42]

11 David Smith *Zig II* 1961
Steel, painted black, red and
orange 255.5 x 137.2 x 85.1
Des Moines Art Center,
Permanent Collection, Iowa
Gift of the Gardner Cowles
Foundation in memory of
Mrs. Florence Call Cowles.

How might the translogical aspects of the twentieth-century pursuit of
artistic vision, the 'fluid force' of what David Smith called 'the promise
and the search', be related to shamanism? Mircea Eliade has described the
shaman as 'the archetype of *homo religiosus*'.[43] These five words are surely
worthy of a lifetime's reflection. For does religion imply to us the ritualistic
binding together of individual and group, the priestly conservatism
implicit in Durkheim's idea that in coming together to worship its gods,
a society is in reality reinforcing its own sense of communality? Or does
religion imply to us, rather, the movement away from the communal

and the familiar in the transcendent inspiration of the solitary visionary?

The history of religions shows that, sooner or later, these two dimensions tend to meet in the realm of 'social facts'. The seer generates a cult, and the cult eventually becomes an institution: what was once psychologically dynamic and socially explosive becomes analgesic and conservative. (Fundamentalist revivals may of course reverse something of this process.) But if the shaman is the archetype of *homo religiosus*, we must presume that shamanic — as opposed to priestly — consciousness forever has the potentiality to shock us out of the complacency of mistaking 'social facts' for total reality. The shaman is the person for whom religion means openness to other dimensions of existence than the everyday: for whom, as we shall later see, the very language of everyday consciousness and 'social facts' is abandoned in favour of a 'secret' language, shared with the spirits of animals and trees, sea, mountain and wind.

In her *Origins Of The Sacred: The Spiritual Journey In Western Tradition*, Anne Bancroft suggests that the great service of the shaman has always been to help shake people out of the rut of experience — out of the sheer forgetfulness of mystery which infects everyday life. We wake up; the world beckons. One day we wake no more. What traces of our soul, our spirit, did we leave as testimony to our brief sojourn on earth? According to Bancroft, the essence of mystical experience has always been to free the self from the premature death of routine, of habit, of boredom, as one comes to know the world *anew*. It was for this purpose that shamans entered a trance; that they were drummed into ecstasy; that their followers performed a dance. All partook of the shock of awakening to other realities — 'not because they went into a materially different world, but because they were able to see their own world with new eyes.'[44]

Bancroft's understanding of this aspect of shamanism accords with the views of the late Joseph Campbell, particularly as expressed in the first volume of his monumental study of the religious and mythological imagination, *The Masks Of God*. Here, Campbell (1904—87) drew a distinction between what he called the local and universal function of mythic images. A compelling myth may serve to contain the self within what Campbell called 'local', or historically conditioned feelings and aspirations. Until the last four or five centuries of Western expansion and exploitation, tribal life all over the globe revealed the healthy consequences of such a function of myth; while in our own century, fascism provides a chilling example of that function turned thoroughly sour and sick. But Campbell argues that compelling mythic imagery can also function to precipitate the growth of the sort of psychic energy that might eventually free the self from the framework of localised belief — and, indeed, from the overly familiar framework of the everyday personality. In this latter sense, the deeper rhythms and structure of myth, rather than its surface detail, work on an esoteric or hermetic level: one might say that at this level, mythology becomes mythopoeisis once more.

For Campbell, a certain 'tender-mindedness' was a prerequisite of the mythopoeic experience. The 'intuition of depth' in such experience was, he believed, 'absolutely inaccessible' to what he called 'the "tough minded" honest hunters [of life]' — whether they are seeking 'dollars, guanaco pelts, or working hypotheses'.[45] Open to mystery, the 'tender-minded' sense the non-historical dimensions of existence, whereas for the 'tough-minded', the historical factor is all: 'The whole reach of their experience is in the local, public domain and can be historically studied. In the spiritual crises and realizations of the "tender minded" personalities with mystical proclivities, however, it is the non-historical factor that preponderates, and for them the imagery of the local tradition — no matter how highly developed it may be — is merely a vehicle, more or less adequate, to render an experience sprung from beyond its reach, as an immediate impact. For, in the final analysis, the religious experience is psychological and in the deepest sense spontaneous . . .'[46]

Campbell saw the shaman as the original exemplar of such religious tender-mindedness — the prototype of the mystic, the poet, and the artist of later civilisations.[47] The various elements of shamanic experience, such as the initiatory patterns of privation and suffering which eventually lead to visionary wisdom, were thus seen in terms of what Campbell called the universal rather than the local function of myth. For Campbell, 'The Way of Suffering of the shaman is the earliest example we know of a lifetime devoted to . . . the use of myth hermetically . . . as a way to psychological metamorphosis . . . The shaman is in a measure released from the local system of illusions and put in touch with the mysteries of the psyche itself, which lead to wisdom concerning both the soul and its world . . .'[48]

The 'in a measure' which Campbell notes is crucial — for the shaman is able to hold both levels of the function of myth in stimulating balance. Divinity is sparked within the soul and, as Campbell says, the shaman thereby performs the necessary function for society of 'moving it from stability and sterility in the old towards new reaches and new depths of realisation.'[49] But such reaches and depths are never — as in some of the later monotheistic religions — projected into an utterly transcendent, 'unpicturable' realm. The shaman's world *is* a transcendent world, peopled with what we may like to think of as fantasy projections of the psyche in the shape of spirit helpers and the like. But at the same time, it is *this* world, pictured and experienced through numinous images of tree and mountain, forest and sea, bird and bridge. Long before Jean Arp and the Dadaists, the shaman encouraged people to dream with their eyes open.[50]

Art, suggested Keith Jarrett, is a reminder of ancient values. But as so much of Jarrett's own work shows, it is also an invitation to see and hear the world anew. Between the ancient and the new lies history — or rather, our understanding of that deceptively simple term. To suggest that twentieth-century artists have been in search of shaman-like experiences of mythopoeisis is in no way to suggest that they have ignored the socio-historical dimensions of existence. On the contrary: the vast nightmare which has been so much of our century's politics has precipitated an enormous amount of 'tender-minded' artistic endeavour aimed at countering the evil we have done to ourselves and the world.

We have already seen how fervently Dada artists committed themselves to the cause of peace during the First World War. In 1937, David Smith kept faith with the Dada spirit as he embarked upon the series of fifteen bronze medallions which he called *Medallions for Dishonour*. A forthright expression of idealist pacifist views, the medallions drew upon images from art history (e.g. Bosch, Brueghel), newspaper cuttings and medical books — and Picasso's *Guernica*.

One of the greatest resurrectors of the pagan imagination this century, Picasso was once asked (in March 1945) if he thought communists could understand *Guernica*, his myth-inflected protest against the fascist bombing of the Basque town in April 1937. Replying that some communists grasped the point of the painting, while others did not, Picasso scribbled down the following, so as not to be misunderstood: 'What do you think an artist is? An imbecile who has only eyes, if he is a painter, or ears if he is a musician, or a lyre in every chamber of his heart if he is a poet, or even, if he is a boxer, just his muscles? Far, far from it: for at the same time, he is also a political being, constantly aware of the heartbreaking, passionate or delightful things that happen in the world, shaping himself completely in their image. How could it be possible to feel no interest in other people, and with a cool indifference to detach yourself from the very life which they bring you so abundantly? No, painting is not done to decorate apartments. It is an instrument of war for attack and defense against the enemy.'[51]

At the same time, painting was not the same thing as reportage or propaganda. The 'message' of *Guernica* is encoded in — amongst other things — a highly personal series of meditations upon the Mediterranean mythology from which Picasso drew so deeply throughout his life. It is this 'encoding' which has enabled the painting to survive its immediate historical occasion, and to speak to subsequent generations of not only the horrors of April 1937, but the choice of good or evil which faces us at all times.[52] We can see much the same relation between the immediate and often horrific stimulus of twentieth-century history and mythological coding in the art of the German painter Max Beckmann, an artist obsessed (like Picasso) with the promise of, and the search for healing mythopoeisis in art.

One of the chief seers or prophets of the century, Beckmann (1884—1950) suffered a nervous breakdown during the First World War — at the outbreak of which, he had said to his first wife Minna: 'I won't shoot at Frenchmen, I owe too much to Cézanne. And at Russians neither: Dostoevsky is my friend.'[53] Like many modern artists, Beckmann was to suffer the wrath of the Nazis, because of the alleged 'degeneracy' of his work. In 1937, he emigrated to Holland, where he stayed for a decade before spending the last three years of his life in America. His life and work thus exemplify a major theme in twentieth-century art: the theme of the 'tender-minded' soul's exile from an unfeeling, insane world, and its longing for a return to a life of holistic meaning, expressed in art of shamanic, mythopoeic power.

In his 1938 *Self Portrait with Horn* Beckmann portrayed himself in an orange- and black-striped costume, connoting both convict and harlequin. The look on his face is as resolute as it is melancholic, as he listens for a sound from the magical, mythical horn which he holds up to his left ear. The Romantic overtones — the echoes of the *Waldhorn* — in this image are inescapable. All his life, Beckmann searched for that redeeming contact with the world which the Romantics had pursued. An avid reader in such fields as Biblical, Chaldean and Hindu mythology, as well as theosophy, much of his work conjures a timeless realm of soul journeys and spiritual flight, as in the extraordinary *Journey on Fishes* of 1934.[54] But for all his spiritual longings, Beckmann never avoided confrontation with the lacerating horror of much twentieth-century history. From *The Night* of 1920 to *Birds' Hell* of 1938, he created protesting, tellingly organised images of claustrophobic, Gothic intensity.

It is in *Departure*, his great triptych of 1932—3, that Beckmann achieved his most resonant blend of historical consciousness and mythopoeisis. The painting is a magnificent example of both Beckmann's command of bold, figurative imagery and the transformative breadth and depth of imagination which the shamanic spirit in twentieth-century art can evince. 'Departure, yes departure, from the illusion of life to the essential realities that lie hidden beyond' was Beckman's own summary description of a work which contrasts the depths of human banality and evil with a longing for spiritual fulfilment.

Stephan Lackner, a long-time friend of the artist, has written of the painting's 'almost hallucinogenic artistry', an artistry that 'welds confusion and clarity, hideousness and radiant beauty, into a unified whole'.[55] Replete with echoes of the healing symbolism of ancient mythologies, the central panel of *Departure* was described thus by Beckmann: 'And in the center? The King and Queen, Man and Woman, are taken to another shore by a boatsman whom they do not know, he wears a mask, it is the mysterious figure taking us to a mysterious land . . . The King and the Queen have freed themselves from the tortures of life — they have overcome them. The Queen carries her greatest treasure — Freedom — as her child in her lap. Freedom is the one thing that matters — it is the departure, the new start.'[56]

The journey to another shore is the journey of the shamanic spirit in twentieth-century art. To speak of that journey, of the connections between the shamans of old and artists of today, is finally more a matter of faith than anything else: faith that the 'tough-minded' language of Western history, of proofs, 'social facts' and political ideology is not the only language we have; faith that to speak of artistic 'realism' without acknowledging the 'fluid force' of the mythopoeic dimension in life is to speak of an alienated and vitiated world; faith that to deny the genius of exceptional artists is to deny the 'tender-minded' best of the human spirit in us all.

To speak of such faith is not to deny the justified force of Richard Wollheim's conviction that it is 'beyond the bounds of sense, even to entertain the idea that a form of art could maintain life outside a society of language users.'[57] It is, rather, to assert that, within that society, insofar as they propose a reductive interpretation of human potentiality, the languages of history and politics, sociology and anthropology must be resisted, or at the very least strongly qualified, by a language which attempts to speak of what is *other*, keeping one — in the words of Joseph Campbell — 'transparent to the transcendent'.[58] And as we shall see later, when considering the multi-layered shamanic work of such politically-committed artists as Joseph Beuys or Mary Beth Edelson, to speak of becoming 'transparent to the transcendent' does not imply any escapist refusal to face the world of 'social facts'. On the contrary: it suggests the need to gain access to *other energies*, energies which may help us to turn the pain and confusion of so many of today's 'social facts' into healing human potentiality.

In her sensitive study *On Not Being Able to Paint*, first published in 1950, the psychoanalyst Marion Milner revealed how she had gradually come to understand the implications of her own attempts at drawing and painting. Stressing the healing nature of the essential reverie involved in the production and reception of psychologically-charged images, Milner spoke of the joys of the 'contemplative action' to be found within the free-ranging, 'sensory, organic language' of art.[59] As Herbert Marcuse insisted in his *The Aesthetic Dimension: Toward a Critique of Marxist Aesthetics*, such a language 'breaks open a dimension inaccessible to other experience, a dimension in which human beings, nature, and things no longer stand under the established law of the reality principle.'[60]

Long ago, the shamans of Lascaux and Les Trois Frères lived the truth of Milner's and Marcuse's words. So have many artists this century. Their uncharted journeys beyond the horizons of history have discovered much that may initially seem new and strange, but which actually speaks of what one might call a 'great return'. Ultimately, the shamanic spirit in twentieth-century art speaks in the language of metamorphosis: a metamorphosis from the self-destructive 'tough-mindedness' of an exclusively historical self-awareness to the healing potentialities of mythopoeisis — to the moment when the world might reflect back to humanity's gaze not the horror which has been visited upon it so often, but rather the unspeakable mystery of a moment in which 'everything rhymes'.

3   A Heap of Broken Images?

With the important exception of the Goddess-oriented writers mentioned in the first chapter, most recent commentators on shamanism have ignored the shamanic dimensions of twentieth-century art. One author, Nevill Drury, is slightly unusual in this respect. In his 1982 *The Shaman and the Magician: Journeys Between Worlds*, Drury pointed out the striking graphic qualities in the work of the English visionary artist Austin Osman Spare (1888–1956). At one time affiliated with Aleister Crowley's group, the Argenteum Astrum, Spare's imagery moved from an early preoccupation with classical values of anatomy and modelling to the sort of looser, more atmospheric textures and shading which were redolent of the shape-shifting worlds revealed to the artist through trance.

We learn more about Spare's shamanic mindscapes of ecstatic nudes, masks and animal/spirit helpers in Drury's 1989 *Vision Quest: A Personal Journey Through Magic and Shamanism*. However, no matter how fantasy-oriented its subject matter, the work of Spare that Drury chooses to discuss remains rooted in post-Renaissance, Western conventions of classical and naturalistic representation. Also, in much the same way as the recent, lustrously detailed images of Susan Seddon Boulet which were gathered together in the 1989 *Shaman: The Paintings of Susan Seddon Boulet* — or the comparable work of Deborah Koff-Chapin, which complemented the visionary dreams of Marcia S. Lauck in the 1989 volume *At the Pool of Wonder: Dreams & Visions of an Awakening Humanity* — Spare's imagery might be said to *illustrate* ideas, rather than providing a self-sufficient formal equivalent or development of them.[1]

Since the end of the nineteenth century, when Paul Gauguin and other Symbolist artists argued strongly for the importance of the latter qualities of self-sufficiency in art, modern painting and sculpture have been much concerned to develop the metamorphosing, transformative power of what Georges Braque called an art of 'presentation' rather than representation. From a shamanic point of view, one might say that it is not enough for modern art to speak of, or about shamanism — as the British painter Malcolm Morley did in his *Arizonac* of 1981 for example, with its two enormous masked tribal magicians who advance towards us, pictured against a mountainous backdrop.[2] Like some of Susan Seddon Boulet's work, such an image tends to confine ideas of shamanism to the realm of illustration — to the somewhat sentimental terrain of the 'exotic'. For if shamanism is such a dramatic, ostensibly 'tribal' affair, one might feel bound to ask what it could possibly have to do with the international production and consumption of art in the twentieth century.

It is the argument of this book that, while the ancient roots of shamanism certainly do lie in the sort of dramatic tribal existence pictured by Morley, the continuing mythopoeic significance of shamanic ideas of life can be detected within a great deal of the art of industrial culture. To speak of a shamanic spirit in such art is not to suggest that one searches through the modern art galleries and museums of the world for 'pictures of shamanism'. It is rather a matter of searching for 'shamanic pictures' — and sculptures, dances, poems, music and so forth. In other words, one must search for art which contains *within itself* the mythopoeic (and formal) power needed to stimulate transformative, shamanic qualities of consciousness in the onlooker. And in such art, there may well be not a single (exotic) shaman in sight.

To say that much modern art has been an art of 'presentation' — of itself, so to speak — is not to suggest that such art should be seen as a purely formal matter of art-for-art's sake. Undoubtedly, there is a good deal of formalism in modern art; but there is also a good deal of transformative, mythopoeic power. As we shall shortly see, modern art has been distinguished above all by the challenging quality of its thought, its *ideas* about the world. Such ideas have been 'embodied in' rather than 'illustrated by' the materials and forms of art, developing through the artist's complete involvement in the manipulation of his or her materials, and often remaining open-ended at the end of the process. It is this approach to meaning — the combination of thought and feeling, ideas, process and form — which gives modern art its potential to be a truly democratic (and transformative) activity. For more than most previous art, it invites — and needs — creative participation from its audience.

It would be wrong to take this as implying that modern art is all 'feeling-based' or 'expressionistic', and devoid of any clarity or logic. In the late art of Paul Cézanne (1839–1906), for example, one can relish a supremely balanced approach to aspects of thought and feeling, ideas, process and form. Henri Matisse and Pablo Picasso both regarded Cézanne as 'the father of us all', the painter who laid the foundations for twentieth-century art. Cézanne himself lamented that, when compared to the old masters of the European tradition, modern artists such as himself were 'makers of fragments', for they no longer knew 'how to compose'.[3] However, in retrospect Cézanne can be seen as precisely the great composer of modern art — the man who combined aspects of the subjectivity and the objectivity of sight in such a way that art became freshly conscious of itself, as a struggle to realise a harmony parallel to that of nature. Cézanne did not paint a single shaman; but there can be no doubt that he is an artist of immense, shaman-like power.

The shamanic qualities in Cézanne's work are not merely to do with the fact that he became obsessed with painting what can be seen as an archetypal shamanic idea or image, namely the magnificent Mont Sainte-Victoire in Provence (i.e. the mountain of spiritual aspiration, struggle and revelation in shamanism). Rather, such qualities are to do with the extent to which he mastered those violent fantasies of his youth which are displayed in such paintings as *The Murder* of 1867–8 and *The Feast (The Orgy)* of *circa* 1870, and managed to channel a potentially destructive abundance of sensual energy into a transformative celebration of the *wholeness* of the world — a wholeness which included his own transformed and transforming consciousness of that world.

In his *Ecstasy: Understanding The Psychology of Joy* the Jungian analyst Robert A. Johnson has suggested that 'Dionysian ecstasy is found in the *sensuous* world, the world of poets and artists and dreamers, who show us the life of the spirit as seen through the senses.'[4] Johnson advises that we do not confuse this world with what he calls the sensual world, the materialistic world of pleasure that is destitute of spirit: 'The sensual world is the one we see all around us: the pursuit of money for its own sake, the desperate chasing after empty pleasures. The sensuous world is filled with the profusion of nature's fruits; it is the divine realm, the garden of the gods. What a beautiful thing!'[5] For Johnson, the key to psychic growth is to 'make the translation from the sensual world, devoid of spirit, to the sensuous world of Dionysus', for then 'one can begin a new era in one's life'.[6] This is exactly what Cézanne achieved — not just for himself, but for all the many subsequent artists who have drawn inspiration from his struggle to 'realise' the intensity of his passion for the motifs of his work.

In such a work as the 1890–5 version of the *Mont Sainte-Victoire* in the National Gallery of Scotland, we can see how a classical impulse towards order provides the unobtrusive, yet essential scaffolding which is able to marshal and contain the intensity of Cézanne's feelings for mountain and sky, tree and plain. At the same time, this implicit scaffolding ensures that the intensity of Cézanne's feelings is not just undiminished, but rather increased in the patient, yet energetic distribution of tones across the surface of the canvas. Every single inch of Cézanne's later paintings and watercolours — including those he deliberately left blank — exalts the harmony that he came to sense at the heart of nature. *'It's as if every place were aware of all the other places'* said Rilke, writing to his wife in wonder about Cézanne in 1907.[7]

The sense of order and structure in Cézanne precipitated a fresh amount of classical endeavour this century, which can be traced through such major figures as Matisse and Picasso, Braque and Léger, Piet Mondrian and Ben Nicholson, to Balthus and beyond. But it is also possible to feel

12 Paul Cézanne *Mont Sainte-Victoire c.* 1890—5 oil on canvas 55 x 65 National Gallery of Scotland.

in Cézanne that tremendous desire to hear the world *speak*, to share the language of wind and rain, sun and sea, rock and ravine, that we traditionally refer to as Romantic. If Rilke was astonished by the overall sense of order in Cézanne, he was no less sensitive to the feelings of primal intensity, of awe in the presence of nature, which contributed so greatly to the alchemical resonance of the painter's reshaping and overlapping of the relations of colour and form.[8] The logic of the light that plays across the canvases of Cézanne is anything but that of a disembodied eye and mind. Cézanne walked through, *lived in* the landscapes of southern France that he loved so much.

Regarding art as a religion, its aim the elevation of thought, Cézanne himself wondered if he might not be the primitive of a new way forward for painters. By a lengthy, complex process Cézanne came to rediscover and transmute ancient feelings of *participation mystique*, turning the empiricism of sight into the kind of vision that encourages us to feel both one and many in the world. It is this return to primal simplicity, to a feeling for the supernatural presence in things, and for that intense empathy with the world whereby it may 'speak us', that so struck Rilke. The painter thus led the poet to feel that 'One has to be able at every moment to place one's hand on the earth like the first human being.'[9]

Writing in 1912–13, in his book *Art*, the English critic Clive Bell praised Cézanne as 'the Christopher Columbus of a new continent of form'.[10] For Bell, Cézanne was the major figure in recent Post-Impressionist developments in painting — developments which had abandoned Impressionism's love affair with the form-dissolving play of sunlight and shade, to cultivate once more a world of what Bell called 'significant form'. What was 'significant form'? It was, suggested Bell, what the aesthetically sensitive observer could detect in 'the windows at Chartres, Mexican sculpture, a Persian bowl, Chinese carpets, Giotto's frescoes at Padua, and the masterpieces of Poussin, Piero della Francesca, and Cézanne' — without necessarily knowing anything at all about the particular historical circumstances which had shaped and given initial meaning to such examples of the concept.[11]

Bell admitted how difficult it was to define exactly what he meant by the idea of significant form. He was only sure that the element of artistic intention within the concept distinguished it from what he called 'the material beauty' of a butterfly's wings. It is all too easy today to see Bell as a bloodless aesthete, whose ideas imply little more than the somewhat ridiculous satisfaction which some people might get from believing that their choice of curtains, for example, indicates a greater sensitivity to 'significant form' than that of their friends or neighbours.[12] But we should remember that Bell was arguing against the immensely powerful legacy of essentially illustrative, Victorian ideas of taste in Edwardian and Georgian Britain; arguing, that is, that 'the subject' of art mattered much less than the mystery of the aesthetic and spiritual effect of artistic achievement. In Bell's view, a still life of three apples might be as ennobling an experience as the sculpture on the West façade of Chartres cathedral — provided that the still life had enough 'significant form' to it.

Again, it is all too easy today to see Bell as a harbinger of purely decorative or 'art-for-art's sake' ideas of aesthetics. To do so is to forget how fervently — albeit naïvely — he sought to link the idea of significant form to religious experience: not the exoteric experience of the world religions, but the esoteric experience of the mystic. Bell spoke of the rapture and the ecstasy which the experience of art could bring. It is not too fanciful to suggest that in another life he might have been a Sufi poet, hymning the majesty of God and nature as it has 'disposed itself in rhythm'.[13] Attending to the artistic transfiguration of such a humble object as an apple, Bell suggested that we might become aware of 'its essential reality, of the God in everything, of the universal in the particular, of the all-pervading rhythm. Call it by what name you will, the thing that I am talking about is that which lies behind the appearance of all things — that which gives to all things their individual significance, the thing in itself, the ultimate reality.'[14]

The concept of 'significant form' was thus the means whereby Bell sought to convey the ecstasy of what Robert A. Johnson would later call 'the sensuous world . . . the life of the spirit as seen through the senses'. In the chapter of his book which he called 'The Metaphysical Hypothesis', Bell concluded: 'And of one thing I am sure. Be they artists or lovers of art, mystics or mathematicians, those who achieve ecstasy are those who have freed themselves from the arrogance of humanity. He who would feel the significance of art must make himself humble before it.'[15] This, then, was the greatness of Cézanne: having humbled himself before nature, and having experienced something of the spiritual essence of life which animates the endless play of existence, he was able to pass on the fruits of that synthesising experience of surface and depth to others. And he did so in art which demands the creative participation of the onlooker, no less than the rituals of tribal shamans demand the active participation of the tribe.

The essence of the idea of significant form, as it had become manifest to Bell in contemporary painting, was that those artists whose work epitomised the idea were artists who had broken through the surface delights of Impressionism, creating a world where art was seen as 'a spiritual necessity' — a world which Bell believed was 'not altogether unworthy to be compared with that which produced primitive art.'[16] Breaking through the surface of twentieth-century history, artists would subsequently do much to deepen and extend the point of Bell's comparison. In the introduction to *The Eternal Present*, his 1962 comparison of our century's art with that of prehistory, Seigfreid Giedion suggested that 'Contemporary art was born out of the urge for elemental expression. The artist plunged into the depths of human experience. A real inner affinity suddenly appeared between the longings of the man of today and the longings of primeval man, crystallised in signs and symbols on the cavern walls.'[17]

After documenting such a correspondence, through such evidence as the seemingly parallel impulse to abstraction, the overlapping of imagery in fluid space, and the cultivation of multivalent symbols, Giedion turned to consider the shamans of old, as depicted at the Lascaux or Trois Frères caves in France. His conclusion was that, 'Perhaps the eternal figure of the creative artist, with his ability to find an approach to spheres that are inaccessible to the average man, comes nearest to the meaning of the shaman . . . [this] figure, expressing a relentless search to establish some connection with intangible forces . . .'[18]

As has already been suggested, primitivistic attempts to establish this sort of connection led much modern art to a radical break with previous Western conventions of form. In 1861 the French realist painter Gustav Courbet had declared that the art of painting should consist solely of the representations of objects 'visible and tangible to the artist . . . painting is a completely *physical language* . . . An abstract object, one which is invisible, non-existent, is not of the domain of painting. *Imagination* in art consists in knowing how to find the most complete expression of an existing thing, but never to suppose or create that thing.'[19] A century later, this positivist world view had been shattered not once but several times over, as painters and sculptors alike fought to reassert the priority of metaphysics, of imagination and feeling, over the dictates of 'empirical reality'. Alberto Giacometti, whose work passed through various primitivistic Cubist and Surrealist stages before attaining the elongated, austere forms for which the sculptor and painter is most famous, believed that 'Realism is a lot of rubbish . . . What we call the great styles in art are those that approach most closely the vision one has of things . . . the works of the past that I find most resembling reality are generally judged to be the farthest from it . . . For me, Egyptian painting is realist painting, although they call it the most stylised.'[20]

Instead of depicting images of countryside or town, made familiar by nineteenth-century Romanticism or Realism, and set in a field of vision stretching away into the distance, much modern painting offers curious images which sit 'flatly' on the picture plane. Shorn of both literary support and the illusory depth given by the laws of post-Renaissance perspective, the depths that such images may contain are of a predominantly psychological nature. They concern the emotions which may be stimulated in the labyrinth of the viewer's psyche, as attention is transferred from an exterior, 'masterful' view of either nature or society, to an inner-directed quest for the mystery and meaning which may flow out of a fresh encounter between self and world. Initially, the roots of such modern painting can be traced to both the transfiguring effect of Cézanne's intense sense of fidelity to the world and the symbolist concerns of many late-nineteenth-century painters and poets, such as Paul Gauguin, Émile Bernard and Stéphane Mallarmé. But beyond those sources lies the immense range of primitivistic tribal affinities suggested first by Bell and then by Giedion.[21]

Similarly, many sculptors have eschewed both the 'fleshiness' and the civic dimensions of centuries of Western, classically-based sculpture, to cultivate instead a disturbing, totemic-like art of forms oriented towards the unconscious depths of spirituality. Often inspired by artefacts from European prehistory or the pre-industrial cultures of Africa, Mexico or Native North America, such sculpture's restructuring of previous Western ideas of form and space contains clear cosmological implications and shamanic echoes.

The same tendencies are evident in poetry. Regular rhythms and rhyming schemes have often given way to the use of collage techniques; long, tumbling phrases recall the speaking-in-tongues of transfixed seers, or remind us of our century's Jungian fascination with the collective unconscious. And just as painters have at times sought to offer inspiration through the most delicate of marks, set in a plain of unprimed canvas, so have poets attempted to conjure an ocean of reverie with a few distilled drops of imagery and ideas.

It would be both unnecessary and tedious to continue such examples. The point is that the single most striking quality of twentieth-century art is that it *challenges* us: in search of the spirit of *participation mystique*, it neither looks, reads nor sounds like art did in the Renaissance, nor indeed as it did a century ago.

Common sense tells us that this is only to be expected. More than most, the artist surely feels the force of Honoré Daumier's famous belief that one must be of one's time. However, it is precisely common sense which has so often been offended by the sort of developments which have just been adumbrated. Modern poetry is often criticised for being too difficult, or obscure; two of the most familiar jibes against modern painting and sculpture are that 'a child of six could do it', or that 'the work looks like the ravings of a madman'.[22] When some of what Kandinsky called his *Improvisations* were shown at the Salon des Independants in 1912, paintings now regarded by many lovers of abstraction as some of the most beautiful that Kandinsky ever did, a reviewer writing for *The Scotsman* described them as 'looking as if a dog had dipped its feet or its tail, or both, in the palette, and walked across the canvas'.[23] Years later, the (in)famous presidential speech which Sir Alfred Munnings delivered to the Royal Academy in London in 1949 revealed that the post-Cézanne innovations of the School of Paris (e.g. Picasso, Braque, Matisse, Derain) had failed to convey anything very positive to the man whose advice to art students was that 'If you paint a tree — for God's sake try and make it look like a tree, and if you paint a sky, try and make it look like a sky.'[24] For Munnings, the School of Paris had produced 'violent blows of nothing'.[25]

The feelings of bafflement or rage concealed in such remarks are not peculiar to that mythical character, the man or woman in the street. The psychologist Carl Jung once asked: 'What is wrong with our art, that most delicate of instruments for reflecting the . . . psyche? How are we to explain the blatantly pathological element in modern painting? Atonal music?'[26] Jung himself painted and drew, and encouraged his patients to do likewise. But when the art historian J.P. Hodin tried to persuade him to write something about the Austrian expressionist painter Oskar Kokoschka, in 1955, Jung refused, saying that he could not pretend to have much to say about modern art: 'Most of it is alien to me from the human point of view and too disagreeably reminiscent of what I have seen in my medical practice.'[27]

It is one of the most baffling mysteries of recent times that Jung, who did so much to open up exploration of the depths of the collective unconscious, should have had so little appreciation of modern art. For this art has often displayed characteristics of deep dream imagery, just as it has often been

13 Wassily Kandinsky
Improvisation 26 (Ruder) [Oars]
1912 oil on canvas 97 x 107.5
Städtische Galerie im
Lenbachhaus, Munich
© DACS 1992.

inspired by the type of non-Western imagery and symbolism in which Jung delighted during his travels through Africa or Native America.

In *Memories, Dreams, Reflections*, Jung recalled that the camp life which he enjoyed in his travels through Kenya and Uganda in the mid-1920s proved to be one of the loveliest interludes in his life. He enjoyed the 'divine peace' of 'a still primeval country. Never had I before seen so clearly "man and the other animals" (Herodotus). Thousands of miles lay between me and Europe, mother of all demons . . . my liberated psychic forces poured blissfully back to the primeval expanses.'[28] The parallels with the feelings of many modern artists are inescapable.

Over thirty years before, one of the great pioneers of modern art, Paul Gauguin, had written from Brittany to his wife, Mette, in Denmark: 'May the day come — and perhaps soon — when I can flee to the woods on a South Sea island, and live there in ecstasy, in peace, and for art . . . far from this European struggle for money.'[29] In 1902 Paul Klee, another key figure in the development of modern art, noted to himself how he wanted to be 'as though new-born, knowing absolutely nothing about Europe, ignoring poets and fashions, to be almost primitive.'[30] Several years later, in Paris, painters such as Matisse, Derain, Vlaminck, Braque and (most famously) Picasso shattered centuries of European conventions of colour and perspective in their art; an art greatly inspired by both Cézanne and the startling qualities — both formal and spiritual — which they detected in much tribal work, particularly African masks. And in March 1914, Emil Nolde, a painter of intensely-hued coastal landscapes and stark Biblical visions, and a figure of great importance in the development of Expressionism, declared his belief that 'We are living at a time when primitive man and the primitive way of life are becoming extinct. Everything has been discovered and made European . . . The primitive people live together with Nature, are at one with it and are part of all creation. I often have the feeling that they are the only real human beings alive, while we are like puppets, manufactured and full of conceit. I paint, draw and try to hold fast something of this essential being.'[31]

Time and again, Nolde's sentiments are unconsciously echoed by Jung in *Memories, Dreams, Reflections*, as in his respect for the dignity of the beliefs of the Pueblo Indians whom he visited, compared to the poverty of European rationalism. Jung's lack of appreciation of modern art is made even stranger when one considers how closely the famous dream he had in 1909, while travelling with Freud in the USA, parallels the creative trajectory of many twentieth-century artists. In his dream Jung was led down through layer after layer (and historical era after historical era) of a house. He eventually reached 'a low cave cut into the rock. Thick dust lay on the floor, and in the dust were scattered bones and broken pottery, like the remains of a primitive culture. I discovered two human skulls, obviously very old and half disintegrated. Then I awoke.'[32]

What the dream revealed to Jung was the layers of his psyche; the collective unconscious at work. It was thus of inestimable importance for the development of his ideas over the next half-century. Similarly, in twentieth-century art, painters, poets, dancers, film makers and sculptors alike have broken through the surface of consciousness (the conventional, 'mirroring' representation of the world as we know it), in order to draw inspiration from ancient layers of imagery and imagination. Whether he knew it or not, Jung shared the great challenge of our century — making the old new — with the art he so disliked.

Jung followed the ancients in holding to the deceptively simple command: know thyself. Just as modern art suggests that we need to penetrate the surface of things, and make far-ranging and imaginative spatial and symbolic connections in order to sense the deeper aspects of ourselves, so does Jungian thinking place the quest for self-knowledge within a framework of breadth and depth. This framework initially suggests that, behind the *persona* which each of us adopts to meet society's demands, our true self should seek to develop, through an acknowledgement of the 'shadow' or dark side in the psyche which we usually keep repressed. One thinks of aspects of the fool's or the comedian's role in society — or of the trickster figure of tribal culture, the joker and breaker of taboos who functions as a sort of creative safety valve for that culture.

In an interesting essay, Jung once drew parallels between the healing roles of the trickster and the shaman;[33] in his 1988 article 'The Shaman Is A Gifted Artist' Mark Levy focussed attention on the recent trickster-like work of American Karen Finlay. Finlay turned to performance as a result of the death of her father, who committed suicide in 1979. She does not rehearse, but performs in a state of trance: other personae emerge during the course of performance, personae who can break taboos to the (scatological) extent that Finlay's work might seem pornographic to some. Finlay herself says 'I don't feel that my work is pornographic at all. I'm just telling it like it is.'[34]

From a Jungian perspective, 'telling it like it is' can also be to tell 'how it might be'. Besides acknowledgement of the shadow-side of ourselves (the hatred and intolerance that may lie underneath all the religious protestations of love and understanding that we may wish to make, for example) the development of the self also involves a creative awareness of not only one's capacity for rational analysis or intuition, thinking or feeling, but also the relation of the complementary contrasts of male and female drives within us which Jung called the *animus* and *anima*. If persona and shadow, animus and anima begin to come into fruitful relation, then the self may sense itself growing towards the key condition of psychic health and maturity which Jungians call individuation. If such development towards individuation does not occur, a twisted personality can result — a personality which may project its own unresolved tensions and frustrations onto others, with potentially disastrous results at both an individual and societal level. The hyper-'masculine' and 'purist' traits of twentieth-century fascism demonstrate this point only too well.

In an incisive introduction to the process of individuation, Marie-Louise von Franz makes the essential point that true individuation excludes any parrot-like imitation of others.[35] What could be closer to the hearts of twentieth-century artists, who have undertaken many a difficult personal journey in search of the sort of imagery that might have some transpersonal resonance? Despite Jung's own opinions of it, much modern art has an undeniable healing potential, in its capacity to trigger the sort of psychic growth which Jungian thought believes to be crucial to both self and society.

Depth psychology insists that the development and transformation of the conscious self means very little, unless such changes are matched by changes at the unconscious level of the personality — and *vice versa*. Modern artists have long worked at these two contrasting yet complementary levels. Not only that: with a single image or phrase, they have often been able to intimate what it may take a psychologist half a book to explicate. For example, Jungians summarise the process of individuation in the idea of the 'Great' or 'Cosmic' self, which can — and, in a healthy life, should — develop beyond the confines of the ego. Gunnar Ekelöf, the outstanding Swedish poet whose strongly shamanic work will be investigated in Chapter 6, once cut right to the heart of the matter when he suggested that we should try to 'walk the wide and inner way'.[36]

Jungian thought also emphasises the central importance of developing an understanding of the world of archetypes, that immemorial fund of images which is to be found at the deepest levels of the collective unconscious. Modern art has long anticipated and paralleled Jungian thought here: we have already seen how fruitfully Jean Arp engaged archetypal levels of imagery in his 1917 low-relief sculpture, *Forest*. Arp and many other twentieth-century artists long ago anticipated that revivifying process which David Feinstein and Stanley Krippner describe in their recent *Personal Mythology: The Psychology Of Your Evolving Self*, where they note how 'Shamans — the spiritual leaders, healers, and "technicians of the sacred" of tribal cultures — have been receiving increasing attention in recent years. They provide a model . . . for guiding the Western mind back to its estranged primal roots.'[37]

The journey which modern art has taken back to those roots has often gone via the East; a mythical East. Van Gogh envied the Japanese their ability to sit quietly and meditate on life's meaning in front of a blade of grass; the potter Bernard Leach drew the West's attention to the virtues of the simple Korean ware that seemed to him to be born, rather than made. John Coltrane admired the spiritual integrity and improvisatory élan so evident in classical Asian music, and recorded such extensive, modal tributes to that spirit as the 1961 *India*. And in his three part *Blue* series of the same year, Joan Miró conjured the poetry of (psychologically) deep, meditative space by placing the simplest of lines, circles and glowing bars of colour in spacious, Eastern-inflected asymmetry. Reminiscent of both the scale of American Abstract Expressionism (itself very much influenced by the East, as in the work of Mark Tobey) and the aesthetics of the Zen rock garden, these paintings are a superb testimony to the bravery of all those twentieth-century artists who have taken uncharted journeys to the deeper aspects of their lives.

The Western journey to the East — a journey of shamanic courage — has been a journey away from the would-be masterful ego. The response which Kandinsky's *Improvisations* elicited from *The Scotsman* in 1912 may thus acquire a different resonance, if we recall the classic story of Hokusai (1760–1849), one of the absolute masters of Japanese art, when he was summoned by the Emperor to paint at court. Dipping the feet of a chicken in blue ink, Hokusai gently dragged them over a long scroll of rice paper. He then dipped another chicken's feet in vermilion ink and simply let the chicken walk freely upon the scroll. When this was done, he bowed deeply to his royal patron and showed him the painting *Autumn Leaves Falling on the Yangtze River.*[38]

Hindu philosophy tells us that 'he who understands has wings'. The flight of the shamanic spirit in twentieth-century art has been a flight which suggests that transcendence is to be found, paradoxically enough,

14 Alan Davie *It's Heavenly Inside* 1962 oil on canvas 213.5 x 244
Collection of the Artist
© courtesy, the Artist
Photograph: Todd White.

in the depths of intuition and the blending of consciousness with the unconscious. The more one comes to appreciate this, the more ironic it is that the seeds of such an understanding were available long ago, in the work of the man who was unable to see anything very positive in the development of modern art. For such essays of Jung's as 'On The Relation of Analytical Psychology to Poetry' and 'Psychology and Literature', which were collected in the volume *The Spirit In Man, Art And Literature*, suggest a relationship between the artist and society which is thoroughly shamanic in import. Such insights of Jung's will be outlined – and their potentially positive application to modern art developed – in the following chapter.

For the moment, however, one must reiterate that Jung himself seemed incapable of seeing modern art as anything other than disturbing evidence of the fragmentation of contemporary life; the psychic breakdown of modern man, lost in his search for a soul. Reading Jung on Picasso or James Joyce, for example, one is often reminded of T.S. Eliot's inquisition in *The Waste Land*:

> What are the roots that clutch, what branches grow
> Out of this stony rubbish? Son of man,
> You cannot say, or guess, for you know only
> A heap of broken images . . .[39]

Jung's feelings about modern art have been shared by a great number of people. And indeed, it is not difficult to instance work which certainly does reveal the fragmentation and spiritual emptiness of much modern life. Consider, for example, the technically superb paintings of Francis Bacon (*b*.1909). Convulsed figures, frozen mid-gesture in anonymous, terminal wards of egocentricity, convey the full force of Bacon's belief that 'man now realises that he is an accident, that he is a completely futile being, that he has to play out the game without reason . . . painting has become – all art has become – a game by which man distracts himself.'[40] That game was played in a very different, but no less dispiriting way by media superstar Andy Warhol (1930–87). Why did people always have to feel that being an artist was so special? For Warhol, it was 'just another job'. And to prove his point, the dollar millionaire who manufactured his art with a 'Factory' of assistants produced perhaps the emptiest art of this century. 'If you want to know about Andy Warhol,' said this po-faced producer of silkscreened Coca-cola bottles and Campbell's soup cans, movie stars and murderers, car crashes and electric chairs, 'just look at the surface of my paintings and me, and there I am. There's nothing behind it.'[41]

Jung's case might seem proven. However – and it is a big however! – Bacon and Warhol do not represent the whole of twentieth-century painting, any more than Samuel Beckett and Jeff Koons represent the whole of twentieth-century literature and sculpture. Of course some twentieth-century art can be fairly accused of fragmentation and meaninglessness, or of meretricious, narcissistic novelty of one sort or another. The British 'artists' Gilbert and George join Jeff Koons in coming immediately to mind here. But there is a good deal more modern art which must be admired for its heroic, shaman-like attempts to transcend the domination of the ego, and to develop a language which breaks through the tired, familiar surface of existence: a language which is thoroughly new, at the same time that it is reminiscent of ancient spiritual wisdom.

Such a language is hardly likely to be immediately comprehensible in a world such as ours, which has placed so much emphasis on the 'communication skills' of politics and commerce. In fact, amidst the ceaseless drone of political propaganda and commercial blandishment, the worth of such artistic language might well be measured in direct proportion to the amount of resistance it has provoked from those who would wish art to 'communicate' to the maximum number of people possible. Therefore, before we investigate the shamanic spirit in twentieth-century art in detail, it is worth pausing in order to emphasise the various extraordinary degrees of resistance which this art has provoked, from such unlikely bedfellows as Adolf Hitler, Claude Lévi-Strauss and Theodore Roszak, for example.

Perhaps the silliest thing Jung ever wrote about modern art was in his 1945 article 'After the Catastrophe'. Following his familiar complaint about the pathological element in modern painting and music, Jung claimed with fatuous assurance that, 'Here we already have the germ of what was to become a political reality in Germany.'[42] Suggesting a parallel between the descent of the German collective psyche into primitive barbarism, and the fascination with the idea of the primitive which we have noted in such artists as Gauguin, Klee and Nolde, could not have been wider of the mark. For a correlation between modern art and mental disease had been a major feature of the Nazi attempt to bolster their spurious claim to be the guardians of culture, a culture which they expressed in a thoroughly debased form of Greek and Roman classicism — much like the USSR at the same time, with its proscriptive doctrine of Soviet Socialist Realism.

By 1937 the Nazi campaign against what they called 'degenerate art' had led to the confiscating of work by some 1,400 artists. Among these were Vincent Van Gogh, Paul Gauguin, Edvard Munch, Henri Matisse, Marc Chagall, Wassily Kandinsky, Emil Nolde, Pablo Picasso and Paul Klee. That year the Nazis organised an exhibition of over 700 such exhibits in Munich, in order to demonstrate the dangers of such 'degeneracy'. Such art scandalised the Nazis, because it so obviously had nothing to do with their belief that art should glorify the racial history of a nation. Its rejection of so-called classical ideals of beauty exposed the shallowness of the Nazis' psychic development, their unwillingness or inability to face the complexities and contradictions of their authoritarian personalities.

Transfigured landscapes and expressionist portraits, painted with allegedly 'deranged' colours and scant concern for perspective, could only signify to the Nazis the sort of mental sickness which they were committed to extinguishing throughout the world. Even worse, many of the artists had openly acknowledged that their high-keyed, 'distorted' expressionist imagery had been inspired by the culturally inadmissible 'barbarism' of prehistoric or tribal art. In the 1937 speech which he made to open a 'Great Exhibition of German Art', Hitler spoke of his determination to wage 'an unrelenting war of purification against the last elements of putrefaction in our culture ... those prehistoric stone-age culture-vultures and art stammerers may just as well retreat to the caves of their ancestors to adorn them with their primitive international scribblings.'[43]

It is hardly surprising that totalitarian governments have never been able to stomach the spiritual and political implications of modern art. What *is* surprising is the apparent inability of such usually far-sighted thinkers as Claude Lévi-Strauss, Theodore Roszak and James Hillman to sense the potential meaning and psychic health in much of such art. For example, in a series of interviews with Georges Charbonnier in 1959, the anthropologist Lévi-Strauss spoke of 'a sort of gratuitous playing about with artistic languages' which he claimed to discern in the twentieth century. Lévi-Strauss went on to express his doubts about the capacity of abstract art to be a meaningful language. For this champion of the powers of 'the savage mind', the various 'foreign elements' to which modern art had opened itself had not been assimilated to any truly communicative effect.[44]

Theodore Roszak's *The Making of a Counter Culture: Reflections on the Technocratic Society and Its Youthful Opposition* (1969) and *Where The Wasteland Ends: Politics and Transcendence in Post Industrial Society* (1972) are two of the most important post-Castaneda books relating shamanism to a wide range of contemporary issues. In both volumes, Roszak spells out his belief that 'the great artists are magicians ... conjurors with the sacramental consciousness of the race, reality makers or unmakers.' However, Roszak has virtually nothing positive to say about the artists of his own century. It is, rather, the great Romantic figures of Goethe and Blake, Wordsworth and Shelley who sustain his dreams of a world illumined once again by the loving power of what he calls 'rhapsodic intellect'. For Roszak, the art and literature of our time simply reveal 'with ever more desperation' and 'a nihilistic imagery unparalleled in human history' that 'the disease from which our age is dying is alienation'.[45]

To a certain degree, Roszak's views are shared by José A. Argüelles. In *The Transformative Vision* the question of art is bound up with the question of consciousness, as it must be. The role of art is placed at the centre of

Argüelles' argument that the West will not cure itself of alienation until the 'civil war of the mind' has ended with the resurrection of *psyche*, dominated for far too long — and with disastrous consequences — by *techne*. Art must cease to be based on what Argüelles sees as the enervating and ultimately sterile principle of avant-gardism for its own sake, which in Argüelles' view has resulted in a plethora of art this century. The cult of avant-gardism betrays the West's ridiculous obsession with the ceaseless movement of history: to be forever ahead of the game on the plane of art history and journalism is to be forever removed from the sources of genuine, lasting creativity. There must be a return to the symbolism of cosmos; a revivification of archaic principles of creativity, drawn from the deepest layers of an integrated psyche.

I am very much drawn to this argument. However, as with Jung and Roszak, I cannot help feeling that when it comes to twentieth-century art, Argüelles has a large blind spot. This is ironic, given both the wisdom of his belief that it is a profound metaphysical insecurity which drives us to imprison experience in fixed, familiar forms, and his statement that 'We do not understand modern art because we do not wish to understand ourselves.'[46] Although he is certainly more sympathetic than Jung or Roszak, Argüelles tends to damn such art with faint praise — particularly when compared to the attention which he gives to the art of late-eighteenth- and nineteenth-century Romanticism, and Symbolism. Thus a good deal of the work of Paul Klee, Wassily Kandinsky and Joan Miró, which is of major importance in any consideration of the healing, shamanic spirit in twentieth-century art, is described by Argüelles as 'an unconscious stuttering and stammering towards that symbolic language Novalis [the Romantic poet/philosopher] had called the true language of paradise.' [47]

The unconscious echo of Hitler is unfortunate. All three artists were in fact highly conscious of what they were doing, and their art reveals qualities far beyond those suggested by Argüelles' language — qualities which have done much to keep the Romantic spirit very much alive this century. Furthermore, and most importantly, not all avant-garde art is to be explained, or understood, as a compulsion to exorcise the past purely in order to stay ahead of history, as Argüelles argues. As we shall shortly see, when considering Mircea Eliade's very different interpretation of the supposed nihilism of avant-garde practice, there may be a surprising amount of healing, cosmic feelings and shamanic aspirations in such work.

Finally, let us consider the opinions of two other post-Jungian writers, James Hillman and Anthony Stevens, both of whom clearly subscribe to the view that too much modern art is but a heap of broken images. In his 1975 *Re-Visioning Psychology*, a generally superb, stimulating contribution to post-Jungian thought, even James Hillman's customary open-mindedness was soured by the issue of modern art. Hillman spoke of the twentieth century's 'contempt for representational painting; no recognisable images, no persons — anything, everything for the eye, nothing for the soul.'[48] In his *Archetype: A Natural History of the Self* Anthony Stevens echoes Theodore Roszak in seeing modern art as 'diagnostic of an imminent descent into barbarism'. And parallel to Argüelles, he deplores the sort of avant-gardism which for him only serves to reveal the increasing dominance of a left-hemisphere, overly analytical approach to life; modern art is full of 'mathematical sequences in music, incomprehensible abstractions in painting, elaborate gimmickry in sculpture — all needing books or words to "explain" what they are about in *conceptual* terms instead of allowing them to speak directly in their own perceptual idiom to the right hemisphere [of the intuitive powers] where they belong.'[49]

At best, the generalisations of Hillman and Stevens suggest only a small percentage of the truth. At worst, they are absurdly misleading. There has been plenty of excellent, well-received representational painting this century — think of Bonnard, Matisse, Balthus, Léger or Giacometti, for example; or Oskar Kokoschka, Max Beckmann, Edward Hopper, Stanley Spencer, Gwen John, Frida Kahlo, Lucien Freud, R.B. Kitaj and Paula Rego. Is Hillman seriously suggesting that there is 'nothing for the soul' in the liquid arabesques of Kandinsky's early work, or in the meditative stillness which the vast colourfields of Mark Rothko summon into being? Rothko believed that 'A picture lives by companionship, expanding and quickening in the eyes of the sensitive observer. It dies by the same token.'[50] When Stevens insists that 'If a good wine needs no bush, neither does a good painting'[51], one has to ask how he thinks that the sensitivity underlined by Rothko develops. A good wine may need no bush, but to recognise it as such surely requires an experienced palate. And it does sometimes happen that we read about a wine previously unknown to us . . .

To attempt to somehow separate seeing and knowing, as Stevens does here, is to do violence to both language and experience. For as Hillman reminds us, 'Ideas give us eyes, let us see. The word idea itself [from the Greek *eidos,* meaning in early Greek thought both that which one sees and that by means of which one sees] points to its intimacy with the visual metaphor of knowing, for it is related to both the Latin *videre* (to see) and the German *wissen* (to know). Ideas . . . allow us to envision, and by means of vision we can know.'[52]

There are two key, related ideas which may enable us to grasp the very real psychological worth of much modern art. One is the archetypal idea of shamanism. The other is cosmic religion.

At the end of his classic study *Shamanism: Archaic Techniques of Ecstasy,* Mircea Eliade suggested that shamans have traditionally played an essential role in the psychic defence of the community. They have soared beyond the bounds of convention, in order to pursue visions of transcendent, healing import. The innovations of many twentieth-century artists have been of no less potential import. The cry of Nietzsche's Zarathustra — 'Truly, the earth shall yet become a house of healing!' — found a potent echo in the belief of Rilke, expressed at the time of the First World War, that 'Only through one of the greatest and innermost renovations it has ever gone through will the world be able to save and maintain itself.'[53] The shamanic spirit in twentieth-century art has offered just such a renovation.

The innovations of such art, which have been so difficult for many to accept, have overturned centuries of Christian and humanist convention concerning the depiction of life and the spirit. They have reinforced neither Christianity's sin-ridden dualism of body and soul, nor outdated rationalist ideas of what Jung called 'the human point of view' — where humanity is placed firmly at the centre of Euclidean space, at the head of history and far away from all 'barbarians'. Instead, the innovations which have informed the shamanic spirit in modern art have conjured a world of multivalent dimensions, where humanity and the world *participate* in each other once more, through shape-shifting manifestations of dream and longing. Needless to say, these are neither the dreams nor the longing of Madison Avenue.

This is an artistic world still in the making; and since its values are closer to the cave of Lascaux than they are to the so-called real world which daily clamours for our attention, it is small wonder that it has so often met with bafflement and resistance. In *The Elements of Shamanism* Neville Drury points out that, in order to transform their perception from ordinary to magical reality, novice shamans have to undergo an 'unlearning process'.[54] Just as the novice shaman has to 'die' to his old self in order to be initiated into the healing mysteries of life, so does the shamanic spirit in twentieth-century art ask that we acquire a measure of courage, and attempt to transcend the assurances of the 'correctness' of our familiar values which the ego is ever ready to give us. In *The Hidden Order of Art*, the late Anton Ehrenzweig suggested that much of the problem of the alleged 'fragmentation' of modern art would disappear, if we could only succeed in evoking in ourselves 'a purposeless daydream-like state', wherein the unsuspected and deeper levels of formal coherence and meaning in modern art might have a chance to affect the appropriate levels of our consciousness. (He also pointed out how much 'dissonance' and 'fragmentation' there once was in Mozart's late music, for example, which we now assume to be all angelic melody and harmony.)[55]

'What is pure art according to the modern concept?' asked Charles Baudelaire, the great nineteenth-century Romantic poet and critic, and fervent supporter of the painter Delacroix — for whom colours were 'the music of the eyes'.[56] 'It is the creation', Baudelaire continued, 'of a suggestive magic which simultaneously contains object and subject, the world outside the artist, and the artist himself.'[57] For this astute observer, the paramount danger of the growth of photography in the mid–nineteenth century was that it might diminish such 'suggestive magic' by ensnaring people in the superficiality of appearances. In 'The Salon of 1859: The Modern Public and Photography', Baudelaire warned against the dangers of the artist simply 'bowing down before external appearance', and reminded his readership that *'it is a happiness to dream'*.[58]

The subsequent dominance of what one might call a mirroring, photographic approach to reality, reinforced every time we watch television or scan the pages of a newspaper or magazine, has freed the artist from any obligation to produce a replica of the world 'as we know it'. On the other hand, in cementing stereotypes about what it means to see — and, courtesy of advertising and much of the film industry, to dream — such dominance has obscured the worth of much of the 'suggestive magic' of modern art. But it is exactly this magic which offers us the way out of Max Weber's 'iron cage' of secular, rationalist thought and activity.

Baudelaire's celebration of dreaming anticipated the views of Paul Gauguin, one of the founding magicians of modern art. For Gauguin (1848–1903), as for his contemporary, the Symbolist poet Stephane Mallarmé, the essential thing in art was to *suggest*, not describe. And so Gauguin sought unusual combinations of both colour and mythic subject matter, in order to bring the mystery of music — its harmonies, its rhythms,

15 Paul Gauguin *Where Do We Come From? What Are We? Where Are We Going?* 1897 oil on canvas 139.1 x 374.6 Tompkins Collection Courtesy, Museum of Fine Arts, Boston.

its infinite melodic potential — into painting. There is much in Gauguin that makes him an archetypal figure for later generations. The eclectic range of inspiration that he drew upon, from the Bible through the myths of Polynesia to Buddhism, anticipated a good deal of our century's own restless search for a healing synthesis of spiritual insights. And the combination of decorative and spiritual boldness in Gauguin's use of colour makes him a remarkable harbinger of an enormous amount of twentieth-century art. For Gauguin, colour was 'a deep and mysterious language, the language of dreams'.

In the mid-1880s, a Sufi-like need for the common, replenishing depths of dream and mystery which might be found underneath the divisive, exoteric differences of religion and culture tore Gauguin away from bourgeois European family life. With their various transmutative blends of Western and Eastern iconography, the images that Gauguin went on to produce in Brittany, Provence and Tahiti are a marvellous, moving record of a soul in search of its home. The intensity of Gauguin's search for what he felt were 'the mysterious centres of thought' in life has something undeniably shamanic about it. For his flight from what he called 'this rotten and corrupt Europe' was in essence a flight in pursuit of healing magic, of psychic transformation at the deepest levels of the self. [59]

Like Van Gogh, with whom he lived and worked for a while in the South

of France in 1888, Gauguin was to die a lonely outcast. Our cynical age might be quick to detect a whiff of bohemian cliché here. However, José A. Argüelles is entirely right to call such artists suffering 'love-visionaries', for they surely were 'wounded healers', as Joan Halifax has described the shamans of old.[60] The healing gift that Van Gogh gave us is the passion of sight, a transfiguring love of *this* world. Gauguin took that love and turned it into the sort of seeing that, many years later, Don Juan would encourage in Carlos Castaneda — the seeing that can *hear* the invisible cracks between worlds, that can float free of all the absurd categories by which we humans often murder the mystery that is life.

In a famous letter of August 1888, Gauguin advised his friend Schuffenecker not to copy nature too much, for 'Art is an abstraction; derive this abstraction from nature while dreaming before it, and think more of the creation that will result [than of the model].'[61] In the twentieth century, many artists have followed Gauguin in pushing their search for such creation far back into the 'lost magic kingdoms' of either tribal life or childhood. The prescience of Baudelaire is again remarkable. For the poet anticipated these two chief strands of Western, twentieth-century primitivism: the veneration of pre-Christian tribal life and the cult of the child. Baudelaire suggested that 'Nomad peoples, shepherds, hunters, farmers and even cannibals, all, by virtue of energy and personal dignity, may be the superiors of our races in the West.'[62] And he believed that 'Genius is nothing more nor less than childhood recaptured at will — a childhood now equipped for self-expression with manhood's capacities and a power of analysis which enables it to order the mass of raw material which it has involuntarily accumulated.'[63]

In their summary of an ancient, primitivising theme in Western thought, Baudelaire's words in praise of nomad peoples recall the respect which the Roman historian Tacitus had for the marauding Germanic tribes. In his essay *Germania* of AD 98 Tacitus noted how 'The Germans do not think it in keeping with the divine majesty to confine gods within walls or to portray them in the likeness of any human countenance. Their holy places are woods and groves, and they apply the names of deities to that hidden presence which is seen only by the eye of reverence.'[64] Developed much later in the essays of Erasmus and Montaigne, this sort of celebration of natural spirituality was brought to a peak in the mid-to-late-eighteenth century by Jean-Jacques Rousseau.[65] Despite Baudelaire's obsession with original sin, there is a good deal of Rousseau in the poet, not least in his remark about childhood and genius. These famous words prefigure the sort of twentieth-century primitivism which would be developed to such potent and different effect by the painters Paul Klee, Joan Miró, Alan Davie and Jean Dubuffet, for example.

The modern world has often been trapped in political nightmares of childish malevolence and regression. In contrast, the primitivising, 'suggestive magic' of much modern art has offered pathways to psychic growth, through the healing potentialities of animistic, tribal-like imagery and child-like wonder. As the poet and critic Octavio Paz has observed in an essay on Miró, the journey of modern art in search of the 'wonder-filled eyes of the very first day' has been 'an apprenticeship in reverse; an unlearning of recipes, tricks, and clever devices so as to regain the freshness of humanity's pristine gaze.'[66]

In his beautiful short study *The Thought of the Heart* James Hillman is concerned that we develop the psychic qualities necessary to both 'ensoul' and 'be ensouled by' the world. In an unconscious summary of the century of artistic endeavour which such artists as Van Gogh, Gauguin and Cézanne precipitated, Hillman makes a key point about the potentially transformative nature of aesthetic experience. He suggests that the link between our heart and our sense organs is not simply mechanical, as empiricist thought would have us believe. For Hillman, it is aesthetic, for 'the activity of perception or sensation in Greek is *aisthesis* which means at root "taking in" and "breathing in" — a "gasp", that primary aesthetic response.'[67] To take in the world thus, is to open oneself to its beauty, to the implicit relation of its parts to a cosmic whole. And so for Hillman 'The transfiguration of matter occurs through wonder.'[68]

Think of Cézanne in his old age, on his way to the Mont Sainte-Victoire, under the immense, blue dome of a Provencal sky; or of Van Gogh, his soul coursing through the brushwork of the 1889 *Starry Night*, perhaps 'wrung by enthusiasm or madness or prophecy.'[69] Remember Gauguin, in troubled pursuit of enigma and reverie, opening up vast, mysterious continents of colour for subsequent generations. Or imagine the painter Georgia O'Keeffe, much later, in Southwest America. Loving the clear, starlit nights — the silence, the alfalfa fields and sage brush, the distant mountains which made her feel 'like flying'[70] — O'Keeffe (1887—1986) hymned 'the faraway nearby' of life with an ecstatic, Gauguinesque feeling for the music of colour and line. The advice that she gave to a friend in the early 1930s brings Rilke's love of Cézanne to mind: 'Try to paint your world as tho you are the first man looking at it — the wind and the heat — and the cold — the dust — and the vast starlit night.'[71]

A decade earlier, O'Keeffe had suggested to another friend that 'Making your unknown known is the important thing — and keeping the unknown always beyond you — catching crystalizing [sic] your simpler clearer vision of life.'[72] It was what she called the 'memory or dream thing' in her painting that brought O'Keeffe close to that sort of mythopoeic vision; a 'memory or dream thing' which came from a centre which felt to her like 'a plot of warm moist well tilled earth with the sun shining on it.'[73] Writing to William Howard Schubart in July 1952, O'Keeffe mentioned how she had had a Catholic priest visiting her for a week. The effect of the visit was to bring home to the 65 year-old artist how little she felt the

16 Georgia O'Keeffe *From The Faraway Nearby* 1937
oil on canvas 91.4 x 101.5
The Metropolitan Museum of Art, Alfred Stieglitz Collection, 1949
© ARS 1992.

need for the comfort of the Church: 'When I stand alone with the earth and sky a feeling of something in me going off in every direction into the unknown of infinity means more to me than any organised religion can give me.'[74]

For creator and audience alike, the difficulties of modern art have often occurred at exactly this point. For fresh attempts to 'transfigure matter through wonder', to use Hillman's words once more, have indeed 'gone off in every direction'. Whether consciously so or not, such attempts to conjure a mythopoeic sense of wonder have involved the rebirth of what Eliade called 'cosmic religiosity', that animistic feeling for the world which senses the presence of soul and spirit in all things. Hillman can help us understand why such a rebirth of primal vision might have involved labour pains. He points out that in Greek, *kosmos* was originally an aesthetic idea, and 'a polytheistic one. It referred to the right placing of the multiple things of the world, their ordered arrangement. Kosmos did not mean a collective, general, abstract whole.'[75] To conjure the rebirth of such a sense of cosmos in a secular world such as ours, driven as it is by a remorseless addiction to quarry efficiency out of everything from soil to sun, is hardly likely to have been an easy task. Nor is it yet.

Here, we approach the second key idea which can help us to sense the meaning within the supposed meaninglessness of much modern art. This is contained in Mircea Eliade's extraordinary intuition that, after centuries of rationalism, and the 'death of God' proclaimed by Nietzsche last century, much twentieth-century art has been a preparation for the return of a multivalent, sacred dimension to life.

Eliade's idea suggests a further reason why so much of this art has disturbed people, why it has often seemed no more than a heap of broken images. Neither wholly sacred nor wholly profane in the sense in which a Christian, Muslim or humanist culture, for example, would understand those terms, modern art has made enormous demands on what Jungians would call the collective psyche. It has dug both deep and wide in its search for the sort of mythopoeic vision that might summon a sense of cosmos, requiring — like the shamans of old — corresponding levels of energy and imagination from anyone wishing to share the fruits of its search.

One has only to think of the work of such diverse painters as Georges Rouault, Alfred Manessier, Marc Chagall, Eric Gill, Stanley Spencer, Cecil Collins and Graham Sutherland to be reminded of the rich inspiration which twentieth-century art has continued to draw from the Old and New Testament. However, for many artists what the painter and writer John Lane has called 'the flash of vision'[76] has been sparked by not only Biblical ideas, but by contact with prehistoric European art, tribal art, Tantric imagery from India, or Zen-inspired, egoless mark making from the Far East. Such a mélange of influence and inspiration has done much to qualify the impact of Judaeo-Christian ideas of linear time and singular, transcendent spirituality. Thus when the American sculptor Isamu Noguchi (1904—88) asked 'What is the artist but the channel through which the spirits descend — ghosts, visions, portents, the tinkling of bells?',[77] he conjured a polytheistic world of archaic, pre-Christian dimensions.

Noguchi studied with the Rumanian sculptor Constantin Brancusi in Paris in 1927. The key figure in twentieth-century sculpture's movement away from fleshy surface towards a more conceptual approach to life's energies, Brancusi believed that 'We will never be grateful enough towards the Earth that has given us everything.'[78] Writing about Brancusi in a 1965 essay entitled 'The Sacred and the Modern Artist', Mircea Eliade suggested that '. . . the contemporary artist seems to be going beyond [an] objectivising scientific perspective. Nothing could convince Brancusi that a rock was only a fragment of matter; like his Carpathian ancestors, like all neolithic men, he sensed a presence in the rock, a power, an "intention" that one can only call "sacred".'[79]

Eliade went on to suggest that the most significant impulse within the avant-garde this century has been to create the world anew — not for any trite reason of newness for its own sake, but because of a desire to overcome centuries of what might be called falsely flattering, 'masterful' human perspective (in several senses of the term), in order that the wholeness, the inter-relatedness of life, be manifest once more: 'In effect we might say that for the past three generations we have been witnessing a series of "destructions" of the world (that is to say, of the traditional artistic universe) undertaken courageously and at times savagely for the purpose of recreating or recovering another, new, and "pure" universe, uncorrupted by time and history.'[80] As seen in the sculpture of Brancusi — or the landscapes of such ostensibly disparate painters as Gauguin and Cézanne, Van Gogh and O'Keeffe — this 'new' universe contains layers of pre-Christian soul and spirit, expressed with an animistic sensitivity to the life which flows through all things.

The difficulties of modern art, the destructions which Eliade speaks about, have usually been seen by Marxists as clear evidence of an historical failure of nerve on the part of bourgeois artists. And, as we have seen, the primitivism which has fired so much of modern art's pursuit of mystery has been similarly criticised, for an alleged turning away from the realities and potentialities of historical change.[81] Unable to face up to the collective, secular challenges of history — so the Marxist interpretation goes — modern art collapses into the heap of broken images which is the inevitable result of a lack of progressive class consciousness. Stressing historical and social realism as the one aesthetic value above all others, Marxism necessarily attempts to demystify and deconstruct any cosmic aspirations that it detects in modern art.

The perspective of this book is very different. With Mircea Eliade, it seeks 'a demystification in reverse; that is to say, we have to "demystify" the apparently profane worlds and languages of literature, plastic arts, and cinema in order to disclose their "sacred" elements, although it is, of course, an ignored, camouflaged, or degraded "sacred".'[82] We have to find in modern art what Don Juan called 'the path with heart', and sense how much of its transfiguring, mythopoeic vision has been a product of the sort of 'eye of reverence' which Tacitus noted nearly two thousand years ago.

For Eliade, modern art revealed a fundamental nostalgia for an initiation into the cosmic heart of life: it is in the courage of the artist that one best discerns our culture's need for 'a total and definite renewal, for a *renovatio* capable of radically changing [its] existence.'[83] Is this the full, shamanic implication of Cézanne's belief that he was a primitive who heralded a new period of development for art?[84] It was the work of Cézanne which prompted D.H. Lawrence to reflect that 'In the flow of true imagination we know in full, mentally and physically at once, in a greater enkindled awareness. At the maximum of our imagination we are religious.'[85] Is this what Arp had in mind when he hoped that his work might help us to dream with our eyes open? Surely so: for just as Jungians hold that the personal ego must be absorbed within the 'Great' or 'Cosmic' self, so must our obsession with the modern myth of history as infinite progress be absorbed within a sacred sense of cosmos — otherwise there may soon be no more ego, history, or progress to worry about.

The aforementioned key ideas about modern art thus become one. No less than the shamans of old, modern artists have developed a 'suggestive magic' of redeeming potential. Viewed in the light of shamanic wisdom, much of what too many have taken to be a 'heap of broken images' in twentieth-century art can reveal its true identity, as a rich and variegated mosaic, inspiring dreams as ancient as they are new.

4 Call of the Shaman

We have seen how much the French poet and critic Charles Baudelaire (1821–67) anticipated primitivistic developments in late-nineteenth- and twentieth-century art. In the last few years of his life, Baudelaire set down a remarkable series of private maxims and reflections. Published posthumously as *My Heart Laid Bare*, they contain the advice that 'One must desire to dream and know how to dream', as well as the cryptic comment that 'Nothing upon the earth is interesting except religions.' This latter assertion prompted the question 'What is the universal religion?' Not surprisingly, perhaps, Baudelaire neglected to answer his own question. However, he did go on to declare his belief that there existed 'a universal religion devised for the alchemists of thought, a religion which has nothing to do with Man, considered as a divine memento.'[1]

Baudelaire was nothing if not an alchemist of thought himself. In the famous poem 'Correspondences', from the 1857 collection *Les Fleurs du Mal* (The Flowers of Evil), he painted an intriguing picture of how

> The pillars of Nature's temple are alive
> and sometimes yield perplexing messages;
> forests of symbols between us and the shrine
> remark our passage with accustomed eyes.[2]

What a wealth of questions, what histories of philosophy and religion are compressed here! Baudelaire went on to intuit the 'deep and shadowy unison' in Nature, wherein various sounds, scents and colours blend, like 'long-held echoes'. Could not such echoes, such a deep and shadowy unison, also be detected within the realms of culture and history? For if the poet inspires us to dream an enigmatic, animistic unity of the particular and the universal at the heart of the natural world, why should we not also dream a similar bridge across time?

Such a dream lies at the heart of much twentieth-century art. The late writer and diplomat Dag Hammarskjöld felt that 'Modern art teaches us to see by forcing us to use our senses, our intellect, and our sensibility to follow it on its road of exploration. It makes us seers ... Seers — and explorers — these we must be if we are to prevail.'[3] Explorers are often lionised for their opening up of supposedly virgin territory; more important is their excavation of unexpected or long-forgotten treasure. In the case of modern art, this treasure is the wisdom of the original seer, the shaman. And such wisdom is a long way indeed from the faith in science and technology, in social science and rational planning, and 'the romantic faith in speed and the roar of machines' by which Nikolaus Pevsner once characterised what he called 'The Modern Movement'.[4] It is a wisdom of an utterly different, yet no less challenging 'romantic faith'.

The call of the shaman is a call which breaks free from what José A. Argüelles has called the dream of reason, epitomised by history's promise of endless material progress, to stir instead ancient echoes of the cosmic mystery which life may contain. It is a call to acknowledge the 'vertical' dimension in life, the dimension of soul, of spiritual longing. And it is a call which is very much to do with the alchemy of that 'universal religion' of which Baudelaire dreamed.

Anne Trueblood Brodzky has called shamanism 'that *ur*-religion, that vibrantly interconnected life-way'.[5] To sense a shamanic note in life is to begin to intuit the wholeness of existence, the interdependence of self and world, body, soul and spirit. In his *The Shaman: Patterns of Religious Healing Among the Ojibway Indians*, John A. Grim considers that it is shamanism which has preserved the human capacity for evocation and wonder, rather than domination, in life.[6] To open oneself to the spirit of shamanism is thus to sense the possibilities of 're-animating' a world which monotheistic religion and mechanistic science have done much to deaden.

Mircea Eliade reminds us that 'It was the [Judaeo-Christian] prophets, the apostles, and their successors the missionaries who convinced the Western world that a rock (which certain people had considered sacred) was only a rock, that the planets and the stars were only cosmic *objects* — that is to say, that they were not (and could not be) either gods or angels or demons. It is as a result of this long process of the desacralisation of Nature that the Westerner has managed to *see* a natural object where his ancestors saw hierophanies, sacred presences.'[7] What the prophets started, the Inquisition and Newtonian science continued. Monica Sjöö and Barbara Mor have spoken of the 'rabid terrorisms' of the Inquisition, deployed with psychotic compulsion against the shamanic dialectic of self and world which the witches of late-medieval and Renaissance Europe continued to embody.[8] And Newtonian science's leap of faith into the belief that the ordered mechanism of the Universe must have been the responsibility of an Ultimate Watchmaker, so to speak, hardly diminished the enervating psychological consequences of its mechanistic world view. The world we live in today might be described, à la William Blake and Laurie Anderson, as the ironically diminished product of the single vision of Big Religion, Big Science, and Big Business.[9]

One recalls the philosopher Francis Bacon's belief that, if one wishes to wring her secrets from her, Nature must be put on the rack; or Descartes' assurance that animals have no feelings. In the famous 'I think, therefore

I am' of the 1637 *Discourse on Method*, Descartes unwittingly summarised —
and anticipated — hundreds of years of ever-increasing alienation of
humanity from itself and Nature. Why not 'I feel, therefore I am', or 'I
dream, therefore I am' — or even 'I am dreamed, therefore I am'? Descartes
could not trust his sensations, and there was no certainty in his dreams.
However, in doubting every aspect of his experience, he at least had the
certainty (or so he thought) of being the irrefutable agent of that doubt.
The ego thus secured its own little fortress, while the world retreated,
thoroughly depersonalised. That world would subsequently repay its hurt,
by haunting humanity in the shape of one psychologically destructive,
power-mad machine fantasy after another.[10]

To be alienated is to be outside, to be *apart from* as opposed to *a part of*
something. This includes one's own life. In his *Anima: An Anatomy of a
Personified Notion*, a free-flowing meditation on Jung's idea of anima as
embodied soul, breath, or spirit, James Hillman considers the consequences of the loss of anima in much of today's world. This is a loss
implying both the loss of internal animation (the sense of really being alive)
and external animism (the sense that the world is alive). Put bluntly, it
means dead people in a dead world. Naturally, for Hillman such a
condition is intolerable. His thoughts are worth quoting at some length:
'This loss is not just a psychiatric condition; it is also a cosmology. We
all live to a larger extent than we realize in the state of depersonalisation
. . . A self-knowledge that rests within a cosmology which declares the
mineral, vegetable, and animal world beyond the human person to be
impersonal and inanimate is not only inadequate. It is also delusional. No
matter how well we may know ourselves, we remain walking, talking
ghosts, cosmologically set apart from the other beings of our milieu.'[11]
And so for Hillman, there could scarcely be any more important task than
the work which aims to open the senses and the heart to what he calls the
life and beauty of an animated world.

What is the call of the shaman, if not a call to work on oneself in such
a manner — to safeguard the beauty of an animated world? Nevill Drury
describes shamanism as 'applied animism, or animism in practice.'[12] And
Hillman makes the key point that depersonalisation today presents a
striking similarity to what anthropologists have called 'loss of soul' in
traditional communities. Recovering soul, curing sickness by finding and
returning lost souls to the ailing, was perhaps the most important task of
the shamans of old.[13] It is no less an important feature of much modern art.

In *Shamanism: The Beginnings of Art*, Andreas Lommel suggests that the first
shamans of small scale, hunting and gathering cultures came into being at
a time when man could not help feeling inferior to his environment: 'He
began to carry on the struggle for existence by spiritual means and came
to attach special importance to the state of his soul as a condition of

survival.'[14] Lommel stresses the related importance of artistic skills: 'Without artistic creation in some form or another there is no shaman . . . The shaman is not merely the "sorcerer" who influences fortune in the chase, but also the poet and artist of his group . . .'[15] Here Lommel follows Eliade's thoughts in *Shamanism: Archaic Techniques Of Ecstasy*. A similar emphasis on the breadth of the shaman's capabilities informs many writers' understanding of this *ur*-figure of the arts. It is the control of such a breadth of activity, and the shamans' seemingly contradictory capacity to be ecstatically moved beyond themselves, which combine to distinguish shamans from mediums or prophets, yogin, sages or priests.[16]

Such exceptional, shamanic individuals battled against soul loss (whether caused by harmful magic, for example, or by the careless transgressing of taboos) in a world where, as Lommel suggests, humanity could easily feel dwarfed by the power of the natural environment. Today, a human being cannot help but reflect upon the continuous dwarfing of self and world which is caused by the insensate developments of industrialisation, and its attendant political and commercial 'noise'.

Whether reflected in the high street or the home buyer's catalogue, newspapers or radio, television or film, there is much within the mass cultures of industrialisation which 'magically' helps us to *forget* life and the fact that we are living it. In particular, there is much to help us forget the perhaps initially unpalatable paradox that it is only by reflecting upon our death that we may come to make the most of our lives. (The infantile dissimulations of much television and film violence have nothing to do with death, understood in any meaningful sense. They are, rather, evidence of our materialistic culture's inability to come to terms with mortality, and its compensatory obsession with the sterile fantasy that life can be mechanically replaced and reproduced *ad infinitum*.[17])

In these testing circumstances, the call of the shaman is as essential today as it was 20,000 years ago. For the shaman is a person who deals in magic that helps one to develop one's sense of the miracle that is life, rather than — like so much mass culture — facilitating escape from reflection upon its ultimate dimensions. And such shamanic magic is the product of a profound experience of death.

Shamans do not only think about death: in a symbolic, yet somehow lived manner, they have *been through it* during their initiation into the process of becoming a shaman. We shall shortly outline aspects of that process, the result of which is often a depth of wisdom reminiscent of the beliefs of the twentieth-century philosopher Martin Heidegger.

For Heidegger, a worthwhile, authentic life is one which has struggled to free itself from the debilitating distractions of the inauthentic world of the endlessly busy 'everyday', where 'everyone is another and no-one is himself'. The result of such a struggle may be a life lived in 'an impassioned freedom towards death'.[18] Similarly, Don Juan tells Carlos Castaneda that 'An immense amount of pettiness is dropped if your death makes a gesture to you, or if you catch a glimpse of it, or if you just have the feeling that your companion [death] is there watching you . . . Death is the only wise adviser we have . . . Our death is waiting and this very act we're performing now may well be our last battle on earth . . . I call it a battle because it is a struggle. Most people move from act to act without any struggle or thought . . . the only thing that is real is the being in you that is going to die. To arrive at that being is the *not-doing* of the self.'[19]

To arrive at such a 'not-doing' of the self is a matter of neither emptiness nor despair. On the contrary, it is to find oneself charged with energies from a far deeper dimension of the self than that of the ego or even the personal unconscious: it is to sense the still, yet completely energised point at the crossroads of time and eternity, history and cosmos within one. Musicians speak of such a moment, when they talk of feeling the music playing them rather than *vice versa*; and painters of no particular religious persuasion, such as Braque, have intimated the mysterious depths of such creativity by talking of the Grace which has visited a particularly — and otherwise inexplicably — successful work.[20]

To attend to such moments of depth is to suspect, for example, that the painter Francis Bacon did not discover any irrefutable truth about what he called 'the futility' of playing the game of life. Perhaps Bacon simply got stuck in his psychological development, never really living his despair to the point where he might have broken through to another side of the experience of life — to a whole, and perhaps holy perception of existence (as Edvard Munch, for example, was able to do). A character of Sartre's once remarked that life begins on the other side of despair. Attending to the call of the shaman, we may come to sense how rich that life might be.

Traditionally, shamanism is closely involved with the idea of a calling, or vocation. Future shamans may be recognised at birth, from the way in which the umbilical cord is perhaps wrapped around a part of the baby; or shamanising can be a matter of hereditary powers, passed down from generation to generation. But there is also the crucial factor of the 'call' from the spirit world, which may be made to anyone who — consciously or not — shows the potential for shamanising. Such individuals often become very vague and abstracted from everyday life. They may complain of headaches or fainting spells; sexual identity can be confused or ambiguous. Elders in the tribe recognise the signs and alert the chosen ones to the fact that the spirit world is calling for them to abandon their current identity and become shamans.

Resistance to the call, the refusal to take on the challenge of the personal transformation required to assume the role of visionary and healer, can be deadly. Shamans sometimes talk of the months, if not years, of debilitating sickness which accompanied their initial and continued refusal of the call, the sickness only passing when they agreed to become a shaman.

Underlining the great personal commitment required of a shaman, the Caribou Inuit (Eskimo) shaman Igjugargjuk once declared: 'True wisdom is only to be found far away from people, out in the great solitude, and it is not found in play but only through suffering. Solitude and suffering open the human mind, and therefore a shaman must seek his wisdom there.'[21]

In the solitude of wilderness, and in the wilderness of solitude, shamans come to experience what Hans Peter Duerr has called their 'wild' or 'animal aspect'.[22] Estrangement from their previous human dimensions enables shamans to gain a perspective on life which opens up the mystery dimension for which there are no adequate words. Don Juan describes this dimension to Castaneda as 'The *nagual* . . . the part of us for which there is no description — no words, no names, no feelings, no knowledge', and contrasts it with the familiar world of the 'island of the *tonal*.'[23] As Duerr puts it, in stepping over the border that separates wilderness from civilisation, in going where 'they can hear the "whispering" of the *nagual*, a whispering that is not of this world and yet is not outside of this world either',[24] shamans become truly conscious of themselves.

It is a familiar temptation to see shamanism in terms of its fantastic or exotic aspects, to become obsessed with such questions as 'do shamans *really* fly?' Much of Castaneda's initial training with Don Juan concerned this very point, as Don Juan sought to tease Castaneda out of the literal-mindedness which led him to be disappointed if his 'flying' only took place in the imagination, 'in [the] mind alone.'[25] The famous photograph which the French artist Yves Klein had taken of himself, as he 'flew' through space in the 1960 *The Painter of Space Hurls Himself into the Void!*, might be criticised on just such grounds — for its 'literalisation' of the subtleties of shamanic symbolism, its reduction of profound metaphor to a circus trick.[26] The Siberian Ostyaks on the Yenisei river used to tell an instructive story to future shamans. It is recounted by Hans Peter Duerr: 'A shaman once bragged that he had acquired powers of great significance. One day an eagle asked him what these powers might be? The shaman answered, "Do you see that cliff over there? Yesterday, I flew up to it." "Is that all?" the eagle countered. "I always fly up to that rock to relieve myself." '[27]

As Duerr says, the point to absorb is not so much the outer show of shamanism, as the fact that shamans live depths of personality, or the self, that are rarely suspected — or admitted — in our everyday world. We have to keep our mental and physical boundaries 'tight' in order to function in daily reality. (Sociologists such as Erving Goffman have pointed out that there may be a great deal of creative variety in the orchestration of the social roles which we play every day. However, this does not affect the basic thrust of Duerr's argument.) If we can follow the shamans — as many modern artists have done — in beginning to 'surrender' our boundaries, our sense of belonging in the world may both deepen and broaden.

Duerr summarises his thoughts thus: 'It is not so much that we fly [in shamanic consciousness]. What happens instead is that our ordinary "ego boundaries" evaporate and so it is entirely possible that we suddenly encounter ourselves at places where our "everyday body", whose boundaries are no longer identical with our person, is not to be found.'[28] The philosopher Maurice Merlau-Ponty, who wrote a penetrating essay on Cézanne's struggle to turn sight into vision, encouraged a similar expansion of our sense of self by reminding us of the magic that can lie — paradoxically enough — in literalism. He suggested that 'We must take literally what vision teaches us: namely that through it we come into contact with the sun and the stars, that we are everywhere all at once.'[29] Think only of Van Gogh, O'Keeffe and Miró: three very different artists, their luminous, shamanically-potent work offers a series of inspiring examples of the visionary knowledge of which Merlau-Ponty wrote.

The call of the shaman is a call to such visionary knowledge; a call which involves a severe shock to the conditioning of so-called normal, everyday consciousness. Having accepted the call from afar, the initiate shamans have to 'die' to the limits of their old selves, mastering their initiatory sickness during the painful and testing process of rebirth into various degrees of shamanic awareness and power. The symbolism of bone is important here. The initiate may be stripped down to skeletal existence, with the discovery of an extra bone within the skeleton confirming potential shamanic status.

The process of initiation varies in detail from tribe to tribe and area to area, but certain patterns are of universal importance. At root, shamans develop their powers as they develop the techniques which enable them to sense worlds within — and beyond — worlds. Holger Kalweit suggests that 'Every sickness is an attempt at healing and every healing an attempt to escape from the everyday neurosis of ordinary consciousness so as to arrive at a more subtle and, in the last resort, superhuman form of perception. The sicknesses that arise as a result of a calling are surely the highest form of illness — a sacred illness which by its power makes it possible for mystical and metaphysical insights to arrive.'[30] The acquiring of an animal or spirit helper, or familiar; the mastering of a secret language, usually derived from the animal world; the parallel mastery of certain techniques, such as prolonged, rhythmical drumming and singing — all these are of central importance in developing the possibilities for such mystical and metaphysical insights to occur.

The mirrors and quartz crystals often used by shamans symbolise such a power of insight, while iconographic details of shamans' costumes — such as the depiction of animals and a stylised tree with birds — indicate the cosmology which such techniques and resultant insights reveal to the initiates. The various techniques enable shamans to enter that ecstatic state where they are able to fly to, and move up and down, the world tree, or *axis mundi*, contacting great souls and spirits in the cosmos. Such flight produces synoptic vision, enabling shamans to bridge the lower and upper

17 Frans Widerberg *Seer* 1978
colour lithograph 30 x 45
Collection of the Artist
© courtesy, the Artist
Photograph: Jan Ung, Oslo.

worlds which surround the everyday plane of life. They are thus able to discern breaks, or blockages, in the flow of energy between the three worlds, which may have caused everyday life to have lost its vitality, and so to have 'gone wrong'. Charged with transcendental energy by such flights to other worlds, the shamans then return to the everyday world in order to perform healing ceremonies for an ailing individual, or perhaps for the whole tribe.[31]

Having been called to such a vocation, new shamans will start to use and develop their recently acquired healing power, as they begin to send out their own call to members of the tribe. Essentially, this is a call to recognise, and tune into, mythopoeic levels of integrated energy and aspiration. This aspect of the shaman's vocation has never been more beautifully suggested than in the song of Uvavnuk, a female Iglulik shaman:

> The great sea has set me in motion
> Set me adrift,
> Moving me as the weed moves in a river.

The arch of the sky and mightiness of storms
Have moved the spirit within me,
Till I am carried away
Trembling with joy. [32]

It is unfortunate that the word shaman is so (misleadingly) close to the English 'sham', with all that the latter implies of fraudulent trickery. The shaman may employ various theatrical 'tricks', but these are set in the service of a genuine quest for metaphysical insight and knowledge. [33] The word 'shaman' was first included in the *Encyclopaedia Britannica* of 1875, in an article by A.H. Sayce. According to the edition of some 110 years later, the term shamanism comes from the Manchus-Tungus word *śaman*. The noun is formed from the verb *śa* (to know); thus, shaman literally means 'one who knows'.

Not only what, but *how* the shaman — who can be either male or female — knows is of great importance. Joan Halifax strengthens our grasp of the semantics of shamanism when she tells us that 'Shamans the world over have a special relation to fire, heat and light. The Vedic term *śram* means "to heat oneself", and the shaman is one who is not only the supreme master of fire but also the embodiment of a heat so fierce that its spiritual luminescence is associated with purity and knowledge.' [34] Kalweit adds an interesting, confirmatory dimension here, in pointing to the luminosity and high-keyed colours associated with the documentation of out-of-body experiences in the modern world. [35] (Is it only coincidence that modern art has pushed colour to the levels of purity and luminescence

18 Agnes Nanogak, Holman (*b.*1925) *Song* 1975 stonecut on paper 45.8 x 61.3
Collection of the Winnipeg Art Gallery G-84-73
© the Artist, Holman Eskimo Co-operative
Photograph: Ernest Mayer; Winnipeg Art Gallery.

that it has?) And John A. Grim suggests that the word shaman is 'a transliteration of the Tungusic word *saman* or *hamman*, which functions as both a noun and a verb. As a noun it means "one who is excited, moved, raised"; as a verb it means "to know in an ecstatic manner."'[36]

It is the ecstatic element which is crucial to Mircea Eliade's understanding of shamanism; he defines it thus: 'shamanism = *technique of ecstasy*'. Eliade can help us to summarise some of the most important aspects of what he rightly calls a complex phenomenon: 'Shamanism in the strictest sense is pre-eminently a religious phenomenon of Siberia and Central Asia. The word comes to us, through the Russian, from the Tungusic *saman* . . . [however] . . . shamanic ideologies and techniques are documented among the primitive peoples of Australia, the Malay Archipelago, South America, North America, and other regions . . . Recent researches have clearly brought out the "shamanic" element in the religion of the paleolithic hunters . . . The shamans have played an essential part in the psychic defence of the community. They are pre-eminently the antidemonic champions; they combat not only demons and disease, but also the black magicians . . . The shamanic "miracles" not only confirm and reinforce the patterns of the traditional religion, they also stimulate and feed the imagination, demolish the barriers between dream and present reality, open windows upon worlds inhabited by the gods, the dead, and the spirits . . . shamanic ecstasy can be regarded as a recovery of the human condition before the "fall" . . .'[37]

This last point of Eliade's is of particular importance. We might immediately associate such a 'fall' with the Judaeo-Christian tradition of the tasting of the fruit of the Tree of Knowledge of good and evil, which led to the expulsion of Adam and Eve from the Garden of Eden. However, as both Eliade and Joseph Campbell (and, more recently, Richard Heinberg) have shown, the myth of the fall from Paradise is practically as old and widely dispersed as human consciousness itself.[38] In his article 'The Yearning for Paradise in Primitive Tradition', Eliade develops the implications of the shaman's mastery of the techniques of ecstasy in terms of this myth of Paradise. He suggests that 'through the exercise of special techniques the shaman tries to overcome the actual conditions of human life — those affecting "fallen man" — and to reconstitute the state of primordial man as we know it by the "paradisial myths".'[39]

Such myths speak of a Holy time of original harmony and unity between humanity, the animal realm, and nature; a time when there was complete 'communion' between all elements of life. In her survey *Primal Myths: Creating the World*, Barbara C. Sproul considers that these myths proclaim, in essence, how 'the structure of the absolute pervades the relative: the Holy is the ground of being. And further they argue that the ways of the absolute are appropriate models for the relative: they are eternal, abundantly powerful and vital, endlessly productive of being, existence and life.'[40] However, from evidence around the world and throughout time, it seems that humanity periodically finds its place within such a holy ground of being threatened; or it *forgets* its true relation to this ground. Sproul suggests that African myths, in particular, speak of the fall from Paradise as a result of man's distinguishing himself from the rest of nature. Rising above the animals and falling into disharmony with the natural world, the *hubris* of man's actions symbolically drives the divine away from earth.

How do shamans attempt to recover Paradise? Eliade argues that the structure and details of a healing shamanic séance are focussed on exactly this task. In order to prepare for the trance that will take them beyond ordinary time to the mythic time of beginnings and plenty, *in illo tempore*, shamans make use of a secret language, or, 'as it is called in some regions, "the language of the animals".'[41] They will imitate the behaviour of animals, their posture, their cries — those of the birds, above all.

Drum playing, dancing and singing bring them closer and closer to the mystic journey, which is finally undertaken in a trance. In April 1990 the Scottish jazz drummer Ken Hyder had the opportunity to listen to recordings of shamans in performance, from archive material in Novosibirsk. Hyder has made some interesting observations to me: while the drumming is not polyrhythmic, neither is it metronomic. The shaman will gradually speed up the drumming pattern and then slow it down. (Something which Hyder has subsequently taught himself with great difficulty, for one of the cardinal virtues of a jazz drummer is to keep the basic pulse of timekeeping steady.) Hyder interprets this as part of the shaman's strategy to disorientate ordinary consciousness, in preparation for the flight into other realms — a strategy which also makes use of the dramatic, shifting dynamics of the various sounds caused by the shaman's magical-protective paraphernalia.[42]

Breaking through the protective barriers of ordinary consciousness, the shaman *lives* symbols with an ecstatic, completely 'irrational' yet supremely focussed power. The small tree or pole which the shaman will actually use symbolises the Cosmic Tree upon which the soul of the shaman ventures its descent to the underworld or its ascent to Paradise: 'Thus the Altaic shaman uses for the séance a young birch tree with its lower branches lopped and seven, nine or twelve steps cut into the trunk. The tree symbolises the Tree of the World, the seven, nine, or twelve steps represent the seven, nine, or twelve Heavens, in other words, the different celestial levels. After having sacrificed a horse, the shaman climbs the steps, one after the other, till he reaches the ninth Heaven where Bai Ulgan, the supreme God, resides. As he ascends he describes to his audience, in great detail, everything he sees in each one of the heavens. Finally, in the ninth Heaven he falls down before Bai Ulgan and offers him the soul of the sacrificial horse.'[43]

Eliade traces a similar cosmic symbolism in the details of the shaman's drum, which is assumed to have been fashioned from the very wood of

19 Luke Iksiktaaryuk, Baker Lake (1909—77) *Untitled (Shaman) c.* 1974 antler, stone, caribou, skin, metal
71 x 41 x 28.5
The Peter Millard Collection, The Winnipeg Art Gallery; Gift of Peter Millard
G-89-179 a-d.
© Sanavik Co-op Association Ltd
Photograph: Ernest Mayer, Winnipeg Art Gallery.

the Cosmic Tree: drumming thus takes the shaman to the centre of the world. The drum has to be 'animated', or brought to life, before it can take the shaman on such an important journey. And so the Altaic shaman sprinkles it with beer, upon which the shell of the drum 'comes to life' and relates its history through the shaman. The same is then done to the skin of the oval-shaped, one-sided artefact; thus the animal in the drum — the shaman's spirit helper, his animal ancestor — speaks as well. Alive, and committed to the shaman, wood and skin can now conjoin worlds of mythic past and present.

Shamanic drums are often decorated with drawings of a rainbow, symbolising a bridge to Heaven. Among the Yurak-Samoyed the shamanic drum is called 'bow'; as Eliade says, 'the shaman's magic projects him to the sky like an arrow'.[44] Riding the drum — the Yakut say 'The drum is our horse'[45] — shamans experience the ecstasy of the musical magic that projects them beyond the deleterious divisions of this world to the melodic, harmonic and rhythmic heart of the cosmos. Through the orchestration of bodily-lived time they go back to the mythic *beginning* of time; and so they are enabled to remake (rather than repair) the world, on the model of its original harmony.

In her *The Catalpa Bow: A Study Of Shamanistic Practices In Japan*, Carmen Blacker documents how the Cosmic or World Tree is replaced in the symbolism of Japanese shamanism by the no less potent images of bridge and holy mountain.[46] Other images and artefacts of equal importance are those of boat and river, mask and staff (or ladder), found in many far-flung shamanic cultures. The central point of all such symbols is to help the psyche move towards the ultimate, 'unsayable' and 'unpicturable' mystery dimension, by paradoxically gathering both self and world into a 'picturable' and harmonic whole: a cosmology of potent thresholds and sacred places of power. If, as Blacker says, shamans are able to offer the community 'an invaluable lifeline' to the ultimate forces of the universe, they do so by their acute powers of balance. Moving between the *nagual* and the *tonal*, they are masters of what Joan Halifax calls 'sacred geography'.[47]

Some shamans acquire a greater mastery of that geography than others. The power of shamans is often related to how many times they were 'dismembered' during their initiation, or how high they are able to ascend the World Tree. The higher the ascent, the greater the power. In their *Studies In Lapp Shamanism*, Louise Bäckman and Åke Hultkrantz refer to research material which indicates 'at least three classes of *noaidit* [shamans] with their attributive designations as found among the Finnish Lapps. The most distinguished of the *noadit* were the *"kir'di noa'di"*, flying shamans, who could fly like arrows also named *"Hexenschuss"* or birds. They were also capable of appearing in the shape of other animals. Another type were the *"ecstatics"*, whose souls, while they were in a state of ecstasy (*Verzuckungszustande*), could manifest themselves in different animal forms. Finally there was the lowest of all, the *"conjuror"*, whose powers were limited to the word.'[48]

In his *Shamanism And Epic Poetry In Northern Asia*, A.T. Hatto suggests that 'Shamanism is but an extreme expression of a universal human capacity.'[49] His views would seem to be shared by such authors as Michael J. Harner and Nevill Drury, both of whom have recently encouraged (in a thoroughly responsible and intriguing way) a sort of participatory, 'do-it-yourself' approach to shamanism.[50] There is nothing at all wrong with such an approach. However, it should not be allowed to obscure the fact that tribal peoples have always acknowledged different degrees of shamanic power.

In a far-ranging, cross-cultural article entitled 'The roots and continuities of Shamanism', Peter T. Furst makes an essential point when he reminds us that shamans are not to be equated with neurotics, or even psychotics, as Georges Devereux, for example, has tried to argue.[51] Shamans are people who have *mastered* their initiatory illness, and who proclaim a world of healthy aspirations and ultimate psychic integration. However, this in turn does not mean that there is nothing out of the ordinary about them.

As Furst puts it, 'shamans as a rule are strong and healthy in body and mind, highly intelligent individuals, possessed of admirable self-control, strength of will and character, and in general capable of intellectual effort far beyond that of the collectivity . . . as inheritors, guardians, and transmitters of the sacred knowledge and heroic traditions of their people, the shamans of the non-literate and pre-industrial world . . . typically are masters of poetic vocabularies that far exceed those of their fellow tribesmen, and that equal, or exceed, those of the average educated individual in literate societies. An outstanding example here is the Yakut shaman in Siberia, whose poetic language has been calculated at no less than 12,000 words, as compared to 4,000 in the ordinary language of his community as a whole.'[52]

It is also worth reminding ourselves of something else which the recent, participatory school of literature on shamanism tends to overlook: such powers have to be paid for. Shamans are usually excused the ordinary, everyday obligations of work in the community — a fact which only very rarely precipitates a measure of cynicism about the shaman's motives among some members of the tribe.[53] When the great Scottish naturalist John Muir travelled around southeast Alaska in 1879 and 1880, he discovered that, despite public protestations of conversion to Christianity, shamanism was alive and well. Muir observed one case of a shaman who had been called in by a worried father to heal his son; the son's soul had been stolen by a crawfish who had been infuriated by some insulting remarks which the boy had made. The Tlingit shaman agreed to undertake this most difficult task, but pointed out that it would be expensive, to the tune of perhaps fifteen blankets.[54]

Overall, whatever the degree of power of individual shamans, and however great or small their remuneration, the call of shamanism is a call to guard the chain of being, and to acknowledge and develop what Drury describes as 'a dream of knowledge'. Derived from seeing with the heart, this is a dream of great intellectual and creative penetration; again, Drury talks of 'a lucid dream', which has the capacity to unite the left and right hemispheres of analytical and intuitive brain activity.[55] It is a healing dream, which brings body and mind, sensuality and soul, sexuality and spirituality together. For although shamans' souls leave their body on the descent to the Underworld or the ascent to Paradise, such soul-journeys would not be possible without the rhythmic drumming and singing and chanting which 'tune up' the body.

Sexual energy can play an important role here. We might say that it is this 'tuned up' body which is the bow of spiritual flight; if the bow is not correctly strung, the soul's arrow will not fly. And this is not to suggest anything of a fascist-like celebration of the body in shamanism, at the expense of the mind. What the body has led the mind to discover, the mind can then store and reflect upon to potent consequences of its own. (Once again we must reflect upon the dualist assumptions built into our language, and how inappropriate they may be *vis à vis* the totalising nature of shamanic consciousness.) Elderly shamans are amongst the most respected of all in tribal cultures, as they meditate upon and help preserve the shamanic 'dream of knowledge'.

What might this dream have to do with developments in art of the past hundred or so years? If Lommel is right to suggest that the first artists of prehistory were shamans, how applicable is such an insight to artists of the twentieth century? If the call of the traditional shaman was, according to Eliade, an antidemonic call, stimulating an exploration of healing, mythopoeic depths of imagination and creativity, how far can a parallel role be ascribed to the innovations of modern art? And where is the 'tribe' which attends to these innovations today, as the tribes of old attended to the shaman?

Nevill Drury has pointed out the amount of fruitless fantasy involved in trying to transpose the world of the traditional shaman to our own society in any literal, anthropological or sociological way. For Drury, the creative importance of reflecting upon the application of shamanism to today's world is twofold: shamanism reminds us of core feelings of 'the sheer "aliveness" of the universe', and it opens up the possibility 'for each of us to discover our own inner mythology, to explore our own transpersonal archetypes, to find our own Dreamtime.'[56] The very same words could be written about much twentieth-century art — art which, like shamanism, can help us to fly beyond the boundaries of a world which often appears to threaten the imagination from every side. And the 'tribe' which can attend to the innovations of such art is present within anyone and everyone who opens themselves up to the energies which precipitate such flight.

In a series of programmes called *The Power Of Myth*, broadcast on British television in 1990, Joseph Campbell outlined some of the most important aspects of the connection which I am proposing between the world of the prehistoric shamans and artists of our century. Using the terms which were first elaborated in Martin Buber's classic *I and Thou* essay from the 1930s (and echoing Harold Bloom) Campbell suggested that aboriginal cultures addressed the world as a *Thou*, as opposed to an *It*. Reminding his audience of Buber's fundamental point, that an ego which sees a holy Thou is not the same as an ego that sees an instrumental It (whether in the world, or in a person), Campbell suggested that the shamans of old were the great guardians and transmitters of such essential psychic and social knowledge. And this key role was the product, Campbell went on to assert, of what he called 'an elite experience'.

What was this experience? It was an experience, suggested Campbell,

20 Frans Widerberg *Magician*
1983 oil on canvas 165 x 107
Collection of the Artist
© courtesy, the Artist
Photograph: Jim Cooke.

which was common to prehistoric shamans and twentieth-century artists. Underlining the great versatility in the 'revelations' of the writer James Joyce and the painters Paul Klee and Pablo Picasso, Campbell drew an exact parallel between the experience of such modern artists and the ancient shamans. He declared that for them all 'the whole unconscious has opened up and they fall into it.'[57]

Campbell's words have an inescapably Jungian ring to them. In their study *The Grail Legend*, which was first published in 1960, Emma Jung and Marie-Louise von Franz suggest that 'The shaman and the medicine man and the analogous figure, the Celtic Druid, embody, as it were, the type of religious man [or woman] who, in complete independence and solitude, opens up a direct and personal approach to the collective unconscious for himself and tries to live the predictions of his guardian spirit, i.e. of his unconscious. The result is that he becomes a source of spiritual life for his surroundings.'[58] Campbell's references to Buber's I-Thou relation, and his parallel between the shaman and the modern artist, are deepened in equal measure when one reflects upon the further point of Jung and von Franz that 'the aspects and stages of his [the shaman's] personality correspond . . . to the process of individuation.'[59]

The shaman, that is to say, is not completely overwhelmed, his (or her) self is not obliterated by the experience of what Campbell calls 'falling into the unconscious'. (Such obliteration sometimes threatened the regenerating psychic impulses of late-eighteenth- and nineteenth-century Romant-icism, as we might infer from Novalis's beautiful line: 'I turn away to the holy, inexpressible, mysterious Night.'[60]) Rather, the shaman's personality is set on an alchemical path where, following the 'death' of the social persona or ego, conscious and unconscious aspects of the self are forged into a new, open and resolute unity. It is this process which illuminates Campbell's parallel between the ancient shaman and the modern artist: as with the shamans of old, the modern artist's courageous, innovative encounter with the world of image and symbol can help prepare the way for the development of what Jungians call the 'Great' or 'Cosmic' self. And it is this self which is able to sustain something of an I-Thou relation with life, a relation based on exactly the kind of 'dual animation' of self and world which, as we have seen, so concerns a contemporary psychologist such as James Hillman.

There should be no inference here of any strict and delimiting homology between the call of the tribal shaman and certain developments of shamanic import in twentieth-century art. For example, not every artist whose work exhibits shamanic qualities will necessarily have gone through a shaman-like initiatory crisis of illness and psychic disintegration — although there are more than a few cases of such a parallel. Nor will all the details and structure of shamanic cosmology necessarily be present in work which nevertheless exhibits strong shamanic qualities — although, again, there are more than a few examples where this is the case. And while some artists are fully aware of the shamanic dimension in their work and actively seek to develop it, there are others who may be quite unaware of shamanism, but whose work is nevertheless redolent of shamanic images and ideas.

What *is* essential to the relation between the call of the shaman and twentieth-century art is the dimension of mythopoeisis, the intimation of individuating myth or archetype, as understood in the sense in which Joseph Campbell addressed the tension or play between their 'local' and 'universal' dimensions in *The Masks Of God*. Discussing the Amazonian Yebamasa's classification of spiritual men — of which the Paye, or shaman, is the fifth and highest type — Holger Kalweit suggests that 'purely aesthetic experiences are not enough to make someone into a shaman. It is necessary for visions of the mythical past to occur, particularly visions of Jehino, the supreme being, or Romikumu' — the goddess and first shaman who created the world — 'or Vaihino, the mythical anaconda.'[61] There are few such purely 'local' mythical visions in the world of modern art. There may be, rather, a fruitful play between 'local' and 'trans-local' dimensions of imagery, myth and meaning, or intimations of the sort of deep, hermetic mythic structure which can encourage the psyche to grow towards various states of mythopoeic and individuated consciousness.

The idea of a journey — to one's own self, to the depths of one's longing and experience in the world — is crucial here. It is a journey which may initially seem both strange and disturbing, but which can ultimately come to be seen as partaking of healing, archetypal qualities. It is this sort of journey which distinguishes shamanic art from both purely decorative creativity and what might be called formalistic and priestly (or government-approved) art. The twentieth century has seen plenty of both these latter types, with their attendant trains of aestheticians and art critics, polemicists and politicians, rule books in hand.[62]

There was no rule book for the first shaman. And there can be none for the contemporary artist: the resonance of the shamanic spirit in modern painting, for example, is not to be found in anything which has been painted by numbers. And just as shamans exhibit different levels of power in their ability to wrestle with sacred energy, a difference symbolised by the height to which they are able to ascend the World Tree, so do twentieth-century artists of shamanic degree inhabit different positions on the Tree of Life.

To suggest that much twentieth-century art reveals its deepest dimensions — its most compelling 'call' — when approached through the spirit of shamanism, is to suggest that such art can play a major role in the development of the psyche, and hence of society. How crucial that role may be will become apparent if we now compare the approaches of Freud and Jung, the most important depth psychologists of our century, to the relation of art to aspects of both the self and — that endless enigma — 'reality'.

In the 1900 *The Interpretation of Dreams*, Freud frequently compared the construction of a dream to a poem, in terms of the simultaneous condensation and multiplicity of meanings which each embodies, and also in terms of their overall, associative unity of meaning. For Freud — in the famous phrase — dreams were the royal road to the unconscious. And to unearth the unconscious, one needed to tease out the 'latent' meanings (concerning aggression, or sexual complexes and neuroses dating back to childhood, for example) which were hidden within the 'manifest' dream content. Believing the unconscious, or *id*, to be a powerhouse of sexual energy, set in the service of what he called 'the pleasure principle', Freud held that dream images were subject to the censoring control of the half-slumbering ego. Turned into acceptable images, the raw, ravenous power of the id would not disturb the psyche. Thus, for Freud, the great function of dreams was to help us to sleep. This theory of sublimation, the idea that both the disturbing power of the id and the complexes of early childhood development could be turned into imagery which is acceptable at both a personal and cultural level, also informed Freud's understanding of art.

Only very occasionally was Freud able to admit the ineffable dimension in art. He spoke of Leonardo da Vinci's *John the Baptist* and *Bacchus* as pictures breathing 'a mystical air into whose secret one dares not penetrate';[63] but elsewhere, we find his lack of what he called 'the oceanic feeling' allowing ample room for his rationalising, analytical drive to come into play.

In *Totem And Taboo*, from 1913, Freud briefly essayed some broad ideas concerning the 'magic' of art. People, said Freud, spoke with justice of the magic of art, and rightly compared artists with magicians. For there could be no doubt that art had not begun as art for art's sake; it began in the service of magical impulses. It was in the arts that Freud detected the last residues of what he called the initial, animistic (or narcissistic) stage of human development: 'In only a single field of our civilization has the [animistic/narcissistic] omnipotence of thoughts been retained, and that is in the field of art. Only in art does it still happen that a man who is consumed by desires performs something resembling the accomplishment of those desires and that what he does in play produces emotional effects — thanks to artistic illusion — just as though it were something real.'[64]

In revealing how much Freud's mind had been shaped by centuries of mechanistic scientific presumption that something called 'reality' is ontologically superior to something called 'imagination', this remark is a classic indication of the limitations of Freud's understanding of both the psyche and art. In a strange way, Freud's ideas are grist to both the mind-numbing mills of everyday laziness and the logocentric aggression towards any notion of the sacred which can be seen in today's (generally) neo-Marxist ideologies of the 'deconstruction' of notions of author, text and 'meaning'. Encouraging a cynicism about the power of the imagination in the former, they help confirm the latter in their increasingly convoluted search for the *praxis* which might finally strip the world of all notions of (transhistorical) substance and transcendence.[65]

As a committed rationalist, Freud viewed both the individual and humanity in naïvely evolutionary fashion. Both had to develop from the diffuse magic of animistic, or 'wishful' thinking, initially to the wider, synthesising projections and perceptions which Freud associated with the emergence of monotheism. Such a development involved a gradual abandoning of the pleasure principle. In time, the psyche would come to acknowledge the role of both the ego and super-ego (the voice of conscience, of parental command, of inherited cultural mores) in helping it to adjust to the demands of social life and culture. The Freudian *credo* — 'Where Id was, there shall Ego be' — reveals how much Freud *distrusted* the unconscious. His Victorian fantasies of its ravenous sexual energy were a long way indeed from the wisdom of Pascal's mid-seventeenth-century belief, as expressed in the *Pensées*, that 'The heart has its reasons, which reason knows not', or Goethe's later trusting insight that 'Man cannot persist long in a conscious state, he must throw himself back into the Unconscious, for his root lives there.'[66]

The Freudian schema of development suggests that, having shed the last of their religious neuroses, individual and humanity can finally advance to the acknowledgement of something which Freud called 'the reality principle'. This was the lynchpin of his scientific world view: 'There is no court of appeal beyond that of reason' stated Freud in his 1927 study of religion, *The Future Of An Illusion*. In the 1930 *Civilisation And Its Discontents*, his evolutionary schema implied that in future, no-one need feel anything of the transformative power of art from any era, be it prehistoric or High Renaissance, twelfth- or twentieth-century. A completely rational mind could only grant art the role of 'a mild narcosis': for the beauty of art (and it is the beauty of art which Freud stresses) serves as but a temporary means of fending off the suffering which the ego must inevitably experience in life.[67]

Freud could not have been further from what Lommel and many others have described: the shamanic attitude to art and life. Here, suffering is not to be fended off by art. Rather, the fruits of suffering and art combine, and help to build up the power of the psyche. Nor is shamanic imagination simply wishful thinking, keeping reality at arm's length: it gives birth to, shapes and nurtures 'reality'. Art in shamanism is thus far more than the evidence of a personal or collective neurosis. It is one of the chief means by which the shamans master their personal initiatory illnesses, in order to fashion a life and work of inspiring, transpersonal import.

In *Memories, Dreams, Reflections* Jung revealed how Freud asked him in 1910 'never to abandon the sexual theory', which Freud said he wished to make into 'a dogma . . . an unshakable bulwark' against 'the black tide of mud — of occultism'.[68] The remark might be funny, were it not that it reveals how desperately narrow-minded and reductive so-called rationalist thought can be. As is well known, Jung could not share such dogma, and broke with Freud because of what Jung called the former's highly questionable attitude to the spirit.

Jung's attitude to the unconscious was far more trusting than that of Freud. The fundamental Jungian idea that the conscious and the unconscious must find a creative balance, or synthesis, recalls the *credo* of Eduard von Hartmann's 1868 *Philosophy of the Unconscious*: 'The principle of practical philosophy is to MAKE THE ENDS OF THE UNCONSCIOUS ENDS OF OUR OWN CONSCIOUSNESS.'[69] And so in Jung's various reflections on art, we find a very different interpretation from that of Freud, an interpretation which acknowledges both the mystery and the essential shaping power of art.

In the 1930 essay 'Psychology And Literature', Jung was quick to distinguish his approach from that of Freud, suggesting, for example, that when the Freudian school advances the opinion that all artists are undeveloped personalities with marked infantile autoerotic traits, 'this judgement may be true of the artist as a man, but it is not applicable to the man as an artist'.[70] *As artists*, human beings are not people endowed with free will, simply seeking personal ends; but nor are they the sublimated end-product of a determining childhood neurosis. They are the instruments of something much larger than themselves, and Jung insists that a person must pay dearly for 'the divine gift of creative fire'.[71]

Time and again, Jung speaks of the artist as someone immersed in the collective unconscious, who reaches back to the 'primordial images' which are best fitted 'to compensate the inadequacy and one-sidedness of the present'.[72] The great artist orchestrates the rhythms of our collective re-immersion in 'the state of *participation mystique*', offering images which are objective and impersonal, 'and yet profoundly moving'.[73]

Although Jung's idea that the artist somehow offers 'compensation' is a limiting one — why should the artist not offer something radically new and inspiring, perhaps taking us beyond a present in which we were perfectly content? — his understanding of creativity contains clear — if unconscious — echoes of the shaman's relation to the transformative power of art. For example, Jung believed that 'The normal man can follow the general trend without injury to himself; but the man who takes to the back streets and alleys because he cannot endure the broad highway will be the first to discover the psychic elements that are waiting to play their part in the life of the collective. Here the artist's relative lack of adaptation turns out to his advantage; it enables him to follow his own yearnings far from the beaten path, and to discover what it is that would meet the unconscious needs of the age.'[74] It is surely the shaman who comes to mind in Jung's description of the artist as someone who has 'plunged into the healing and redeeming depths of the collective psyche', where in the experience that will furnish his artistic material he meets 'something strange that derives its existence from the hinterland of man's mind, as if it had emerged from the abyss of prehuman ages, or from a superhuman world of contrasting light and darkness.'[75]

Like Freud, Jung compared the worlds of art and dream. Unlike Freud, Jung based his comparison on transpersonal factors, and relished the ambiguity which both art and dream contain: 'A great work of art is like a dream; for all its apparent obviousness it does not explain itself and is always ambiguous. A dream never says "you ought" or "this is the truth". It presents an image in much the same way as nature allows a plant to grow, and it is up to us to draw conclusions.'[76]

Given such views, the negative conclusions which Jung himself drew from modern art, as expressed in his essays on Picasso or James Joyce, for example, are somewhat irrational. In the latter essay, Jung thought it indicative of what he saw as the problem of modern art that Van Gogh had been schizophrenic. Perhaps Jung was too much drawn to the classical values implicit in his description of the 'objective and impersonal' nature of the great artist's 'profoundly moving' imagery; perhaps his aesthetic sense had been too deeply conditioned by the early twentieth-century bourgeois standards which Clive Bell had attacked through the concept of 'significant form'. And perhaps Jung was finally lacking in the sort of imagination that makes a person a creative artist, concerned with seeing the world afresh.[77] If it is true, as Nietzsche suggested, that we only catch the fish which our nets are capable of handling, then perhaps both Freudian and Jungian psychology, with their respective emphasis on the 'mild narcosis' and 'compensation' offered by art, are constitutionally unable to comprehend the total, transformative potential which lies in the magic of art.

Whatever the reasons, Jung could only see the art of Picasso in terms of what he called its 'psychic problems', which he compared to those of his patients. While Jung could talk with great insight in his Picasso essay of a 'descent into the cave of initiation and secret knowledge', it was impossible for him to sense anything positive in the artistic results of such a shaman-like descent into the depths of the unconscious. Nor was it possible for Jung to summon the enthusiasm to look very widely at modern art; he tended to generalise about its alleged, symptomatic significance on the basis of his reaction to only a very few artists.

Of all subsequent depth psychologists, it is Erich Neumann who has made the most noteworthy use of Jung's positive feelings about the role of art in general, extending them to an understanding and appreciation of the new and positive vision of *participation mystique* which, unlike Jung, Neumann was able to see emerging from the ostensible chaos of modern art. And in Neumann's thoughts on the nature of psychic and artistic transformation, we find an even stronger suggestion of the correspondence between the role of the shaman and the artist than in Jung.

In his 1954 essay 'Creative Man And Transformation', Neumann followed Jung in deploring the general reductiveness of Freudian approaches to art. Echoing shamanic ideas, he reminds us of the ancient myth that suggests that only a wounded person can be a healer, a physician. It is the creative person, suggests Neumann, who is forever 'wounded', because 'he does not, like other men, tend to heal the personal wounds involved in all development by an increased adaptation to the collectivity. His wounds remain open, but his suffering from them is situated in depths from which another curative power arises, and this curative power is the creative process.'[78] For that process to be really effective, Neumann felt that it was essential for the shadow side of the personality to be recognised, and brought into the play of creative vitality. There can be no light without darkness, and no order without chaos: the esoteric heart of the transformative process lies in the perpetual inter-relation and transmutation of these two sets of complementary contrasts in the psyche.[79]

It is thus, suggests Neumann, a 'total misunderstanding' to regard the apparent chaos of our century's art in a purely negative light. The modern artist helps to break up encrusted and restrictive ideas of both self and reality, preparing the way for a healing rebirth of the feeling of being one and many in the world, able to participate in life with enlarged psychic resources. Such a rebirth of (mythopoeic) potentiality can only be prepared in the depths of the psyche: and there are bound to have been labour pains throughout the time of transition which is our century. Like the call of the shaman, then, the dreams of the modern artist have nothing to do with helping us to sleep. Instead of offering us sublimated images of personal compromise and social adjustment, the modern artist attempts to *wake us up* to our place in the chain of being. And this may well be a place which we can only approach through experiencing the terror as well as the beauty of the depths that lie within us.

Late in life, Jung received an extraordinary letter from Herbert Read. From the 1930s onwards, the distinguished English art critic had done much to advance an understanding of modern art, writing such educative books as *Art and Society* and *The Philosophy of Modern Art*. Echoing many of Neumann's ideas, Read's letter of October 1960 anticipates the insights which Mircea Eliade would develop some five years later in his key article 'The Sacred and the Modern Artist'. At the same time, Read's thoughts may take our minds back to Baudelaire and his mid-nineteenth-century dream of the alchemy of a universal religion.

'The motive [of the artist]', Read wrote to Jung, 'has always been [since the beginning of the century] to destroy the conscious image of perfection (the classical ideal of objectivity) in order to release new forces from the unconscious. This "turning inwards" . . . is precisely a longing to be put in touch with the Dream, that is to say (as you say) the future. But in the attempt the artist has his "dark and unrecognisable urges", and they have overwhelmed him. He struggles like a man overwhelmed by a flood. He clutches at fragments, at driftwood and floating rubbish of all kinds. But he has to release this flood in order to get nearer to the Dream. My defence of modern art has always been based on this realization: that art must die in order to live, that new sources of life must be tapped under the crust of tradition.'[80]

Art must die in order to live. Does not this recall the classic pattern of shamanic initiation? Shamans do not develop their healing, mythopoeic powers without a considerable amount of time, pain, and effort. Why then should we expect the shamanic spirit in twentieth-century art to come clad in familiar guise, to little if any disruptive effect? The call of the shaman which can be discerned in modern art is a call to take wing beyond the familiar look and sound of things. At the same time, it is a call to dig deep into the ground of being. Such a call requires us to summon a participatory courage and open-mindedness. Initially, the alchemical journey inward towards that 'universal religion' of which Baudelaire dreamed may appear strange and disturbing, especially to eyes accustomed to centuries of ever-increasing domination of outer space and time. Ultimately, however, it is a journey, or path, of enormous heart, shot through with the healing spirit of shamanic evocation and wonder.

5   Journeys Home, Destination Unknown

The traditional world of the shamans has long been under threat. Seventeenth-century European illustrations of Saami shamans show the shaman conjuring not healing spirits, but the Devil: the all-important shamanic drum of the Saami, companion guide to the cosmos, was called 'this instrument of the devil' by Christian missionaries and priests.[1] As we have noted, a similar process of psychological reduction and crudely dualistic projections fuelled the Inquisition's war against witchcraft in Europe. And in America, the Puritans' discovery of the New World heralded the death of much of the Old. In the classic text *Black Elk Speaks*, first published in 1932, this *wichasha wakon* (holy man) of the Oglala Sioux summed up centuries of WASP genocide against Native Americans with the poignant words: 'There is no center any longer, and the sacred tree is dead.'[2]

When aged only nine, Black Elk had received a vision of great beauty and shamanic power. As transcribed much later by John G. Neihardt, it is an essential document of the role of *the marvellous* in shamanic imagination. Listening to Black Elk speak, one senses how much shamans — those 'technicians of the sacred' as Jerome Rothenberg (following Eliade) calls them[3] — inhabit a psyche that broadens and deepens itself through self-triggering layers of metaphor and metamorphosis.

Black Elk received his call to shamanic consciousness after a brief initiatory illness, when his legs and arms became badly swollen and his face puffed up. Two men from the spirit world invited him to visit his Grandfathers beyond the clouds; the invitation was strengthened by a sky full of dancing horses, turning into birds and animals of all kinds. A heaped-up cloud became a tepee with a rainbow as its open door. Meeting the Grandfathers there, Black Elk realised that they were 'the Powers of the World'. Of all the symbolic artefacts which they gave him, the most important was a bright red stick which was alive: as he looked at it, it sprouted branches full of singing birds.

Later in his vision, having returned to earth riding on storm clouds full of fructifying rain, Black Elk entered a dying Sioux village and with the help of his red stick, his *axis mundi*, brought back the plentiful time of origins. Thrust into the earth 'at the center of the nation's hoop', his stick turned into 'a waga chun, the rustling [cottonwood] tree, very tall and full of leafy branches and of all birds singing. And beneath it the animals were mingling with the people like relatives and making happy cries.'

This vision of Paradise was then threatened by the winds of war; after various tribulations and three attempts to ascend a symbolic, healing landscape, the young boy's vision came to its apotheosis as he finally stood on the highest mountain of all. Round about beneath him was 'the whole hoop of the world. And while I stood there I saw more than I can tell and I understood more than I saw; for I was seeing in a sacred manner the shapes of all things in the spirit, and the shape of all shapes as they must live together like one being.' In this supreme vision, so reminiscent of the last lines of Dante's *Divine Comedy*, Black Elk realised that the sacred hoop of his people was one of many hoops that made one circle, 'wide as daylight and as starlight, and in the center grew one mighty flowering tree to shelter all the children of one mother and father. And I saw that it was holy.'[4]

The aged Black Elk explained to Neihardt that the mountain upon which he had stood in his vision was Harney Peak in the Black Hills. But, Black Elk added, 'anywhere is the center of the world'.[5] The tragedy of this potentially great shaman's life was that the 'beautiful dream' of the vision which he had been given in his youth was never realised. Despite many efforts, Black Elk failed to become a technician of the lasting sacred. Instead, he lived to see his nation's hoop broken and scattered, the centre gone and the sacred tree dead. He lamented to Neihardt that, while nothing can live well except in a manner that is suited to the way the sacred Power of the World lives and moves, it is hard to follow one great vision 'in this world of darkness and of many changing shadows. Among those shadows men get lost.'[6]

People get lost; that is, they become homeless. The fate of Black Elk's people has been the fate of many over the past centuries, in both pre-industrial and industrial society. The Tree of Life has been uprooted; the 'immaterial', vertical foundations of life and longing sundered. They have been replaced by the concrete, yet curiously abstract, ever-shifting promises of politics and industrial technology: no more rainbows, but rather a neon sign across the industrial sky, proclaiming PROGRESS for all. Sociologists have spoken of the resultant 'deepening condition' of homelessness in the twentieth century, describing modern man as 'Don Quixote on his deathbed, denuded of the multi-coloured banners that previously enveloped the self and revealed to be *nothing but a man*.'[7]

Such a condition — *ecce homo* indeed — has been expressed in one or another variety of existentialist art and literature, with its emphasis on humanity's time-bound search for meaning in a profane world. The paintings of Francis Bacon might be taken to epitomise what Michel Leiris has called 'the inanity of our situation in the world as ephemeral beings . . . dispossessed of any durable paradise . . .'[8] However, illustration of the 'inanity' of our situation is hardly the theme of all existentialism. In the writings of Albert Camus, for example, one senses the Paradise-bereft soul in search of the healing rhythms of cosmos; rhythms that might deepen the self's sense of its journey to itself.

Camus (1913–60) did not believe in an afterlife. Instead, he felt that reflecting upon — and so creating — 'a conscious death' would add greatly to the lucidity of his life, to 'a certain weight of life' for which he asked. Reflection upon death was not a nihilistic exercise for Camus, anymore than it had been for Martin Heidegger: Camus considered that the amount of such reflection was the only true measure of a civilisation's progress. For Camus, creating conscious deaths meant lessening the distance which separates us from the world. However, although such consciousness could conjure a seemingly lyrical harmony of 'Sea, landscape, silence, scents of the earth', Camus still could write that, facing death without any transcendent hopes, he entered 'joylessly into fulfilment' with the world.[9]

This is terribly sad — and very indicative of the disenchantment of much twentieth-century life. Compare Camus' untransfigured fulfilment with that of the Iglulik shaman Uvavnuk, for example, who was set adrift by the great sea, shaken by storms and carried away 'trembling with joy'. (Alan Watts once wrote about the curious plight of modern man, sitting high in the branches of a tree and complaining bitterly about his fate, as he saws away the branches from underneath himself.[10]) The greatness of Camus's work is that, in a secular age, it reminds us of the language which self and nature might share. As Camus himself wrote, when thinking of how many modern scientific insights end up being expressed in poetic metaphor: 'What need had I of so many efforts? The soft lines of these hills and the hand of evening on this troubled heart teach me much more.'[11] The sadness of Camus's work is that this 'troubled heart', so representative of the more noble aspects of our century's time-bound consciousness, was unable to transfigure its own deepest levels of aspiration, its ultimate capacity to journey.

There is an important sense in which the 'deepening condition' of homelessness of which sociologists have spoken can transmute itself from the lucidity of existential dread into a shamanic quality of wonder at — and affirmation of — the inter-connectedness of all things. In much the same way that the shaman passes through the terror of psychic dismemberment to the state of *participation mystique*, homelessness can become a 'deepening condition', in a positive rather than negative sense: it can imply a healthy impulse to 'walk the wide and inner way', growing in wonder towards the unknown. Since so much of our crass culture professes to 'know' us — in both a political and commercial sense — may this not be a doubly good thing?

In Herman Hesse's novel *Steppenwolf*, a work of enduring shamanic power which was first published in 1927, Harry Haller, the chief character (and raging Steppenwolf of the title) reflects that 'Our whole century was a cemetery where Jesus Christ and Socrates, Mozart and Haydn, Dante and Goethe were but the indecipherable names on mouldering stones; and the mourners who stood round affecting a pretence of sorrow would give much to believe in these inscriptions which were once holy . . .'[12] Haller's own journey to holiness is a journey beyond both the futility of Bacon's painterly games and the existential lucidity of Camus's self-consciousness, towards the 'Magic Theatre' of his greater self. It is a search for a transcendent, yet embodied unity of soul and spirit, consciousness and the unconscious, persona and shadow, animus and anima. At one point in the novel, the clairvoyant-like character Hermine (friend of Pablo, the saxophonist whose jazz music does so much to set Haller on his healing journey to himself) says to him: 'Ah, Harry, we have to stumble through so much dirt and humbug before we reach home. And we have no one to guide us. Our only guide is our own home-sickness.'[13]

Homesickness can be a debilitating condition. It may lead to the sort of nostalgia that turns the psyche in upon itself, in a crippling refusal to face the challenge of living in the present: the cliché of 'the good old days' has been invoked by many an anti-modernist politician and artist this century. After the horrors of the First World War, it was understandable that much of Europe should have experienced a revival of classicism in the arts, as in the paintings of André Derain or the music of Igor Stravinsky, for example. But as we have already seen, turning to the authority and beauty of the classical past would soon assume a particularly unhealthy aspect, in fascism's regressive appeal to an hierarchical spirit of socio-political and artistic order.

However, not all twentieth-century homesickness leads to the reactionary nostalgia of fascism. On the contrary: the remarkable thing about the shamanic spirit in much modern art is the extent to which the old has been made new, with potentially expansive rather than constricting psychological consequences. Images of home and belonging need not imply the picturesque familiarity of being 'where the heart is', as the cliché has it. They can connote, rather, the unknown terrain to which the heart may be drawn, as it opens itself to mythopoeic moments of expanding intensity, quickening its appetite for life.

These are the moments which Joseph Campbell addressed with particular perception at the end of his synoptic study of world mythology, the four volume *The Masks Of God*. Here, Campbell suggests that there are now no more guaranteed paths to holiness, no more fixed horizons of meaning: 'Whereas formerly, for generations, life so held to established norms that the lifetime of a deity could be reckoned in millenniums, [sic] today all norms are in flux, so that the individual is thrown, willy-nilly, back upon himself, into the inward sphere of his own becoming . . .'[14] The heart is now what Campbell called its own mythogenetic centre. If it is not to fall victim to one or another repressive variety of literalising fundamentalism — whether political, religious or artistic — it must have the courage to 'let go the past'.

But if the particular, or 'local' details of mythologies had now lost their authority for Campbell, this hardly meant that archetypal structures of soul, of spiritual aspiration — and of myth — were suddenly of no relevance. Students of myth and religion often distinguish their exoteric and esoteric aspects (terms with which the late-nineteenth-century Symbolist poets and painters were thoroughly familiar). The former term refers to the particular, historically-conditioned details of ritual and belief, while the latter indicates the innermost essence of the mythical or religious experience, an essence which may resonate far beyond the boundaries of the exoteric.

In Harold Bloom's terminology, the esoteric could be described as mythopoeic rather than mythographic or mythological. In the series of television programmes entitled *The Power Of Myth*, Campbell singled out the vision of Black Elk as an exemplary 'translocal' mythic vision, with its successive circles of spiritual aspiration and its recipient's wisdom that 'anywhere' can be the mythical centre of the world. Black Elk may have failed to be a technician of the lasting local sacred, but he succeeded magnificently in transmitting a vision of metamorphosing, archetypal grandeur. And the central, esoteric process and structure of this vision are of continuing and essential mythopoeic relevance.

Black Elk's vision was a vision of Don Juan's path with heart, a vision of the development of the 'Great' or 'Cosmic' self which is as relevant to a schoolteacher in suburban Britain today as it was — and continues to be — to many Native Americans.[15] It comes as no surprise that the last words of *The Masks Of God* revivify the ancient archetype of shamanic transformation: for Campbell, the criterion of the heart's achievement must now lie in the courage it has 'to die to the world and to come to birth from within'.[16]

Writing about the problem of spiritual values in the art of our disenchanted, post-Darwinian world, the English critic Peter Fuller (1947—90) singled out Cecil Collins (1908—89) as an artist of especial importance. Fuller's criticism had moved from what one might call a position of discriminating Marxism to an agnostic engagement with what he saw as the fundamental problem of our culture: the lack of any compelling spiritual dimension to life, and the resultant world-weariness or cynical commercialism of a good deal of our art. For Fuller, the pilgrim fools and wounded angels, the dream landscapes and mountains of Collins had been of signal importance in helping to keep alive a sense of the marvellous in life, at a time when much painting was dominated by either reductive formal concerns or the banalities of mass culture.

Describing the painter's work as 'a search for a secular spiritualism', Fuller spoke of 'illusions' in Collins's work, illusions which demand of us 'the suspension, however momentary, of mundane disbelief'. He continued: 'The point is . . . that in order to live at peace with ourselves, each other and the world, in order to translate sensations into values, we need consoling illusions. The consoling illusion of God has been pricked forever. Perhaps we have to learn to gaze like grown-up children, or Collins' fools, who can still sustain "moments of illusion" in which they can see, and know not to challenge, their wounded angels.'[17]

To suggest that the 'consoling illusion' of God has been 'pricked forever' is problematic: it implies that the possibilities of spiritual experience develop and expire solely on the plane of history. From a sociological perspective, they undoubtedly do — and there are perhaps unintended echoes of Fuller's earliest, Marxist-oriented beliefs in this remark of his. But what we might call the existential possibilities of spiritual experience unfold within a dimension utterly distinct from that of linear, historical time: they are shot through with that mythopoeic quality which proclaims both the suspension of mundane time and the potentiality of transfiguring experience. Collins himself spoke of his desire to converse with 'that abundant life whose energy glows through the sad terrestrial curtain of time.'[18] If his work is worth anything — and it certainly is — that worth has little to do with 'consoling illusions'. It is rather a consequence of the fact that Collins's images engage esoteric archetypes of shamanic depth, archetypes which have everything to do with psychic *reality*.

Collins was very aware of both the homelessness of much twentieth-century life and the consequent temptation for the arts to turn into mere distraction and amusement. If artists were to produce something more than what Collins called 'visual confectionery', then they had to remember that 'There was a time when Artists were employed to create and set up altars to the gods of life in civilizations that were temples, and deep within us we Artists must endeavour to remember the services we were once able to give to humanity and to man's deepest experience of reality.' For Collins, to remember this was 'to understand why we feel like exiles'.[19]

Exiled, and in search of home, Collins produced imagery highly reminiscent of the world of the shaman. Chrysalis forms await meta-morphosis in landscapes which seem to hold a promise of a return to Paradise; a strange square-headed creature, part bird but also multi-winged seraphim, appears before a woman in a landscape lit by a fiery sun; pilgrims wander across terrain strewn with bones, which sometimes give off rays of light; a sybil dances, wearing horns on her head. Birds haunt a red-hued, spiky landscape, while angels and fools struggle across mountainous landscapes, finally to contemplate healing waters and the Tree of Life.

Collins never mentioned the shaman by name when discussing his work. However, it is clearly that world-bridging original seer, artist and healer who stands behind Collins's belief that, 'Beneath our technological civilization, there still flows the living river of human consciousness within which is concentrated in continuity the life of the kingdom of animals, plants, stars, the earth and the sea, and the life of our ancestors, the flowing

21 Cecil Collins *The Sleeping Fool* 1943 oil on canvas
29.8 x 40
Tate Gallery, London.

generations of men and women: the sensitive and the solitary ones, the secret inarticulate longing before the mystery of life. The artist is the vehicle of the continuity of that life and his instrument is the myth and the archetypal image ... Art is concerned with the transformation of consciousness.'[20]

Continuity of the mystery of life and the transformation of consciousness: do not these two phrases sum up the shamanic spirit in twentieth-century art — the spirit which offers us journeys home, but to destinations unknown? I should now like to look in some detail at the two great founders of such twentieth-century consciousness, Friedrich Nietzsche and Vincent Van Gogh, and then consider the related, shamanically-oriented work of four of this century's most important artists: Pablo Picasso, Henri Matisse, Wassily Kandinsky and Paul Klee.

Without Nietzsche (1844—90) and Van Gogh (1853—90), the mythopoeic dimension — the shamanic spirit — of much twentieth-century art is unimaginable. Both men produced their most important work in the 1880s, work which blew away the secular, positivist spirit of nineteenth-century rationalism. Both felt *inspired*, in a manner which goes back to the roots of shamanism — but which was expressed most famously in the classical era so dear to Nietzsche, in Plato's description of the poet as 'a light and winged thing, and holy, and never able to compose until he has become inspired, and is beside himself, and reason is no longer in him.'[21]

Nietzsche — who saw man as a sick animal who had to cure himself — spoke of being 'seized by an ecstasy', and thought it 'hardly . . . possible to set aside the idea that one is the incarnation, mouthpiece, and medium of higher powers.'[22] Similarly, Van Gogh wrote of experiencing 'moments when the *enthusiasm soars to the point of insanity or prophetic vision*, when I feel like the Greek oracle on her tripod.'[23]

Both men paid dearly for the revelations which they were granted. Van Gogh suffered severe bouts of mental illness, before shooting himself in the summer of 1890. A decade later, Nietzsche was to die insane. They both created out of a deep sense of suffering, in a manner very reminiscent of shamanic ideas: Nietzsche, for example, described suffering as 'the metamorphosis of the self', believing that 'Spirit is the life that itself cuts into life: with its own agony it increases its own knowledge.'[24]

Given the final tragedy of both men's lives, it may be objected that they can hardly be seen as shamanic figures: unlike the shamans of old, they were destroyed by the forces let loose within them. The Jungian psychologist Liliane Frey-Rohn has written a penetrating study of Nietzsche, where she argues that Nietzsche's crippling problem was that, while he came to experience a remarkable range of feelings concerning human longing for the divine, he could never really let go of his ego boundaries: 'What he "knew" as a result of his mystical experiences — the presence of a divine being — could not be accepted by his conscious ego. He remained ultimately unaware of the depth and extent of his religious problem.'[25]

Frey-Rohn thus sees Nietzsche's ego as being eventually inflated to megalomaniac, self-destructive proportions, rather than being absorbed within any greater or 'cosmic' Self. Similarly, in a sympathetic study of Van Gogh, while the existentialist psychologist Karl Jaspers acknowledges that 'From the beginning his [Van Gogh's] mind is directed towards the core, the essential, the meaning of existence . . .',[26] the evidence of developing, destructive schizophrenia is deemed to be overwhelming: 'The sick genius . . . creates for himself a new world, but he destroys himself in it.'[27]

However, if neither Nietzsche nor Van Gogh became a balanced, 'wounded healer' in the complete shamanic sense, this should not prevent our appreciating how much of the shamanic spirit they *were* able to revivify for subsequent generations. The intellectual and creative courage of both men was extraordinary. Given the tensions between the irrational, poetic depths of what they sought to recover and make new, and the mechanistic, utterly prosaic nature of much late-nineteenth-century life, it is small wonder that their lives were ultimately sacrificed in the quest to make the sacred a living part of consciousness again. And does not such a sacrifice place them very much within the tradition of shamanism?

Initially, it may seem strange to talk of the sacred in connection with Nietzsche. For was it not Nietzsche who in *The Gay Science* gave us the famous parable of the madman in the midday market place, come with burning lantern to look for God, but announcing 'God is dead . . . And we have killed him . . .'? And did not Nietzsche write in *Thus Spoke Zarathustra*: 'Once you said "God" when you gazed upon distant seas; but now I have taught you to say "Superman" '? The fact that Richard Oehler, one of the eulogists of Nazism, regarded Hitler as Nietzsche's thought in action, or that Nietzsche's own aged sister, Frau Elisabeth Forster Nietzsche, hailed Hitler as the incarnation of the Nietzschian Superman, has made it difficult for many to see anything but a proto-fascist justification of brute power in Nietzsche's ideas, which therefore come to seem a long way indeed from the sacred.

The rebuttal of any such connection between Nietzsche and Nazism can help us begin to understand Nietzsche's revivifying, shamanic approach to the sacred. As Janko Lavrin has argued, in his *Nietzsche: a Biographical Introduction*, it is a gross misunderstanding to see Nietzsche as a proto-fascist harbinger of aggressively nationalistic ideas, for Nietzsche himself was the last man to have a flattering opinion of the Germans whom the Nazis wanted to install in his name on the pinnacle of world history: 'Among Nietzsche's posthumous fragments one can find his statement that "The Teutonic Deutschland über alles [Germany above all] is the stupidest slogan ever devised in this world" . . . in one of his letters to Hippolyte Taine (1888) he bluntly states that all his instincts are "at war with Germany." '[28] The Nazis were to worship the machinery of State; for Nietzsche — as expressed by Zarathustra — only where the state ceased could greatness of spirit flourish.

Man, said Nietzsche, is a sick animal who must cure himself. In *Twilight Of The Idols*, Nietzsche described the great polymath Goethe as 'not a German event but a European one . . . what he aspired to was *totality*; he strove against the separation of reason, sensuality, feeling, will . . . he disciplined himself to a whole, he *created* himself . . .'[29] Clearly, it is Goethe, not Hitler, who best illustrates the sort of development of personality which Nietzsche intended by his use of the word 'Superman'.

In a letter of May 1888 to the Danish critic Georges Brandes, Nietzsche spoke of his own work in terms of alchemy. It was the alchemy of human totality that concerned Nietzsche; and it is within his constant search for such totality that his shaman-like approach to the sacred becomes evident. Nietzsche's loathing of Christian dogma, of what he saw as its turning away from the world — 'the one immortal blemish of mankind' — is (in)famous. Less well known is his appreciation of Christ's personality, his acknowledgement of Christ as a 'great symbolist . . . [who] . . . only saw and acknowledged *inner realities* . . .'[30] It was the mythopoeic world of inner realities that fascinated Nietzsche — a world opened up by an intense love of *this* world, the world of nature. We can read of Nietzsche's early childhood memories of the beauty of 'yellow, tall cornfields' and 'thickly leaved nut trees', or remark the tenderness with which he later described his walks on the hillsides of Genoa, and through the Mediterranean pinewoods along the Bay of Santa Margherita. And it was out of such a sensitivity to the *genius loci* — the spirit of place — that Nietzsche began to hear the voices within him that would eventually result in such extraordinary, shamanic flights of the imagination as *Thus Spoke Zarathustra*.

Long before Freud and Jung, Nietzsche suggested that 'all our so-called consciousness is a more or less fantastic commentary on an unknown, perhaps unknowable, but felt text . . .'[31] It is part of Nietzsche's greatness to have resurrected essential aspects of that text from distorting histories of the past. In the 1872 *The Birth Of Tragedy*, he corrected a century of cloyingly sweet interpretations of Greek culture, by pointing to the inter-relation of eruptive, Dionysian elements of ecstatic *participation mystique* with Apollonian values of lucidity and order in antiquity. Light *and* darkness, moderation *and* ecstasy contributed to the balanced genius of classical (i.e. pagan) Greece. Nietzsche saw a similar balance in the process of creativity; out of deep suffering can come joy, in art that is 'essentially the affirmation, blessing, adoration of existence.'[32]

It is *Thus Spoke Zarathustra*, of 1883, that exemplifies Nietzsche's own attempt to affirm and adore existence. Nietzsche himself felt that this book was his most profound work: Jacob Burckhardt, the venerated historian of the Italian Renaissance, wrote to him in September 1883 that '. . . even those who feel angry with the book cannot help being attracted by it. As for myself, I find a peculiar pleasure in listening to someone calling to me from a watchtower high up above my head and telling me of the horizons and depths he can descry. It is then that I realise how superficial I have been all my life . . .'[33]

The influence which *Thus Spoke Zarathustra* has had upon subsequent generations is immense. Echoes of its central ideas can be discerned in the work of Edvard Munch, Knut Hamsun, August Strindberg, Pablo Picasso, Wassily Kandinsky, Giorgio de Chirico, Paula Modersohn-Becker, Edith Södergran, Max Beckmann, Herman Hesse, Thomas Mann, Paul Klee, André Masson and Frans Widerberg. It is very likely that *Die Brucke* (The Bridge), the Dresden group of Expressionist artists which included Ernst Ludwig Kirchner, Max Pechstein and Karl Schmidt-Rottluff, and to which Emil Nolde belonged for a short while, took its name from a famous passage in the book: 'What is great in man is that he is a bridge and not a goal; what can be loved in man is that he is a *going-across* and a *down-going*.'[34]

Zarathustra is full of such spatial metaphors. It is as if Nietzsche were determined to resurrect a 'sacred geography', following the hammer blows which Marxism and Darwinism had dealt to the nineteenth-century world of Christianity (hammer blows to which Nietzsche himself would

22 Edvard Munch *Portrait of Friedrich Nietzsche* 1906–7 oil on canvas 200 x 130 © Oslo Community Art Collection Munch Museum Oslo.

contribute, in his intense effort to rescue soul and spirit from dogma, to return them to the fructifying womb of inner life). In a far-ranging and discriminating study, Eric Heller has described the post-Christian world of historical materialism and progress which was addressed by artists and thinkers like Nietzsche and Rilke, Kafka and Karl Kraus as a world of 'the disinherited mind'.[35] In much of Nietzsche, that mind is offered both ancient, pre-Christian solace and timeless, mythopoeic inspiration.

Returning to the world of social life after ten years of solitude in the mountains, and with a love of forests to balance his dislike of cities, Zarathustra notes the 'great sadness' which has come over humanity: 'A teaching went forth, a belief ran beside it: Everything is empty, everything is one, everything is past! . . . Truly, we have grown too weak even to die; now we are still awake and we live on — in sepulchres!'[36] Determined to fight such despair, Zarathustra receives inspiration from worlds of solitude and dream. He is befriended by serpent, eagle and lion; his animals implore him to 'go out especially to the song-birds, so that you may learn *singing* from them . . . Prepare yourself a lyre . . . New lyres are needed for your new songs.'[37]

The essence of Zarathustra's songs is in fact as old as the hills across which he flashes as lightning spirit; as old as the headland upon which he stands in a dream, reflecting that 'He who will one day teach men to fly will have moved all boundary-stones; all boundary-stones will themselves fly into the air to him, he will baptize the earth anew – as "the weightless."' Zarathustra dreams of flying; but he also advises that we 'Stay loyal to the earth . . . Truly, the earth shall yet become a house of healing!' Images of solitude and suffering, ecstasy and flight, mountain tree and 'highest, hardest, primordial hill', of 'the rainbow and stairways to the Superman' – all conjoin to revivify the numinous dimensions of the archaic world of shamanism, as surely as do Zarathustra's conversations with his animals, or the 'dance songs' which remind him that 'the dancer wears his ears – in his toes!'[38]

Just as some may find it hard to regard Nietzsche as a complete 'wounded healer', in harmony with the forces that precipitated his shaman-like flights of imagery, so may others wish to raise some queries about the overall development of *Zarathustra*. The book fascinated Jung, who conducted a yearly series of seminars on it: Nietzsche had clearly evoked for Jung the primordial image of 'a healer or teacher of mankind, or of a wizard'. However, the attempt to substitute a sort of Dionysian ecstasy for the orthodoxy of Christian resurrection only revealed to the psychologist how Nietzsche's religious self had been 'burst asunder', because 'he tried to imprison the divine paradox [of death and rebirth] within the narrow framework of mortal man.'[39] (This seems a strange observation from one committed to the notion of the unfathomable depths of the collective unconscious, and perhaps reveals more of Jung's ambivalence about Christianity than it does about Nietzsche.)

Gaston Bachelard once pointed out how much Zarathustra's reveries are dominated by cold, airy images of ascension. He also reminds us that it was while Nietzsche was staying at Sils Maria, '6,000 feet above sea level and even higher above all human things', as Nietzsche himself put it, that the idea of Zarathustra came to him.[40] Liliane Frey-Rohn sees the dominance of this ascensional element as revealing Nietzsche's final inability to integrate the different levels of his psyche. Zarathustra leaves his serpent behind as he journeys on with eagle and lion at the end of the book: to Frey-Rohn this reveals a dangerous separation of the conscious personality from its shadow side.[41] To put the point another way, we might say that there is finally too much air (and not enough earth) in Zarathustra's soul.

While Frey-Rohn's point is a good one, Jung's interpretation chiefly serves to underline the paradox of how near the psychologist came to understanding the shamanic spirit of much modern culture, while being finally blocked from grasping its true dimensions. In the last lines of *Zarathustra*, Nietzsche's prophet leaves his cave 'glowing and strong, like a morning sun emerging from behind dark mountains'.[42] Joan Halifax has pointed out the importance of solar symbolism in shamanism, suggesting that the end of the shaman's healing, transfiguring journey to the heart of the cosmos comes when the shaman flies through the Sun Door 'to the realm of eternally awakened consciousness'.[43]

Following Jung and Jaspers, psychologists and Christians alike may continue to experience difficulty with Zarathustra's songs, and wish to see Van Gogh's work purely in terms of schizophrenia. However, they would be hard put to deny a curious, healing synchronicity at work in the fact that, while Nietzsche was singing his great *amor fati* in *Zarathustra*, primarily in melodies of air rather than earth, Van Gogh was beginning to tap the energy that would soon explode into an equally vibrant celebration of existence — a celebration of water, earth and sun, in (unconsciously) complementary contrast to the aerial apotheosis of Nietzsche's adoration.

Van Gogh's road to his shamanic calling was long and hard. After several frustrating jobs, including a spell as an unpaid missionary assistant in the mines of the Borinage in southwest Belgium, he began to commit himself more and more to the laborious task of mastering silhouette and volume, line and wash, as his passion for drawing grew. He had to sink deep into the melancholy of such drawings as the 1882 *Country Road in Loosduinen*, the autumn 1883 watercolour *Landscape at Nightfall*, and the various water-bogged reveries of ditch and fen from early 1884, before he was finally granted access to the kingdom of colour that he explored in the last few years of his life. Then, what Van Gogh called his desire to know life and God 'deeper, better and more' poured itself into a fiery, yet earthy world of sun and stars, of human labour and mythopoeic longing. Orchards and olive groves, wheatfields and cypresses (trees of life, according to Jung in *Psychology and Alchemy*), sunflowers and peach blossom — all crackle and blaze with an intensity of what psychologists call 'affect' that has not dimmed an iota in a hundred years. Proclaiming the Paradise that is Earth, the luminosity of Van Gogh's colours and stabbing vitality of his draughtsmanship opened up both painting and the cosmos for subsequent generations. Late in life, Picasso would call Van Gogh 'the greatest of them all'.[44]

In *The Love of Many Things*, his 1990 biography of Van Gogh, David Sweetman offers the timely warning that it is 'all too easy to slip into the notion that Vincent was a poor innocent, a Holy Fool, utterly at odds with an artistic world that rejected him.'[45] Sweetman is rightly concerned to document the range of Van Gogh's reading and appreciation of art; his knowledge of the dealings of the late-nineteenth-century art world, in which he worked for quite some time, and his attempts, however unsuccessful, to participate in the normalities of everyday life.

For Sweetman, an article on Van Gogh entitled 'The Isolated Ones', which the young writer Albert Aurier published in 1890 in the Brussels journal *L'art Moderne*, set an unfortunate trend which remains to this day. Aurier neglected Van Gogh's devotion to such relatively traditional artists of the past as Meissonier, and saw the then-ignored Dutchman's work purely in terms of a visionary break from the past. With the substantial roots of his art in nineteenth-century culture all but forgotten, Van Gogh has thus passed into popular consciousness only as the mad harbinger of the violent distortions of twentieth-century Expressionism. His hacking away of part of his left ear on Christmas Eve 1888 has come to dominate the myth that has made Van Gogh 'the archetypal artist of the modern age: ignored and rejected while sacrificing himself physically and mentally in the service of his art.'[46]

One can imagine therefore that Sweetman might be wary of any attempt to see Van Gogh in shamanic terms: as a 'wounded healer' who helped to lay the foundations for a return of cosmic religiosity in twentieth-century art. However, the art historical and the shamanic perspectives on Van Gogh are not mutually exclusive. Much in both the immediate and more distant background of European art and culture does indeed help us to gain a deeper appreciation of Van Gogh's art. Where would Van Gogh have been without Millet and Delacroix, or the intense spirituality of Rembrandt — the luminosity of his *The Jewish Bride*, for example, which Van Gogh spent hours contemplating — as inspiration and example? Nevertheless, we should also remember that Van Gogh, who acknowledged his 'moments of melancholy, of distress, of anguish', declared himself 'sick of the *boredom of civilisation*'; just as we should remember how he felt that '*Colour expresses something by itself...*', believing that 'the painter of the future will be *a colourist such as has never yet been seen...*'[47]

Much inclined to religious and metaphysical speculation, as in the haunting thought that 'If we take the train to get to Tarascon or Rouen, we take death to reach a star',[48] Van Gogh was as 'tender-minded' as the shamans of old.[49] The discriminating range of his learning which is so evident in his letters only served to increase his passion for wholeness. And as the art historian Mark Roskill rightly suggests, this was a passion which Van Gogh set against the fragmentation of artistic sensibility that had increasingly characterised the nineteenth century.[50]

Like Nietzsche, Van Gogh sought to recreate and develop a 'sacred geography' in his work. Speaking of the *I-Thou* relationship (that relationship of mutuality with the world which Joseph Campbell saw as characteristic of shamanism), Martin Buber suggested that when we sense the Thou at the heart of life, then 'something lights up and approaches us from the course of being.'[51] Is it not just such an epiphany that we experience in such canvases of Van Gogh's as the April 1888 *Peach Trees in Blossom* and *Orchard Surrounded by Cypresses*?

In his *Vincent Van Gogh: Christianity versus Nature*, Tsukasa Kodera has recently traced the gradual displacement of overtly Christian subject matter and symbolism in Van Gogh's oeuvre by an intensely pantheistic love of nature, a love stimulated in great part by the painter's empathy with what he felt were the simple spiritual truths of Japanese life.[52] In part of Akira Kurosawa's 1990 film *Dreams*, a young man in an art museum — a memory of the director himself, who initially trained to be a painter — returns the compliment, so to speak, as he contemplates such irradiated Van Gogh paintings as *Sunflowers*, *The Bridge at Langlois* and *Wheatfield with Crows*. He 'walks' into one of the paintings, and in his reverie discovers Van Gogh under the broiling heat of a Provencal sun, working 'with the energy of a locomotive'. What was this, if not transfiguring, shamanic energy, attempting to bridge cultures and hymn the mythopoeic heart of life?

For all the visionary power of his work, Van Gogh saw himself as a realist painter. He was suspicious of purely imaginary painting, and once warned the painter Émile Bernard of the 'stone wall' waiting at the far end of the enchanted grounds of any Gauguin-like abstraction from nature. But the intensity with which he approached the actuality of nature has an undeniably hallucinatory quality to it. In his greatest work, such as the September 1889 *Wheatfield with Cypress*, he sees with the rhythmic integrity, the transfiguring magic, of a dancing seer. As Karl Jaspers says: 'He simple wants to paint present actuality; in return he conceives this presence as a mythos; by emphasising the reality he sees it transcendentally.'[53]

Extending and intensifying a century of previous Romantic effort to 're-animate' the world, Nietzsche and Van Gogh offered an extraordinarily important legacy to subsequent generations, a legacy comparable to the esoteric import of the vision of Black Elk. After centuries of mechanistic, post-Cartesian life, a sense of cosmos was reborn. A further part of the shamanic legacy of these two self-sacrificing men was to have brought the disturbing, yet potentially fructifying depths of life into full consciousness, reminding us of the intimate and paradoxical relations that can exist between suffering and creativity, pain and joy. We can see both aspects of this legacy being developed in Picasso and Matisse, Kandinsky and Klee, major shamanic artists of the twentieth century, to whose work we now turn.

The life and work of Pablo Picasso (1881—1973) have an outsize, Faustian dimension to them, inspiring interpretations ranging from hyperbolic adulation to feminist wrath, and from purely aesthetic delight to Marxist disparagement.[54] The comment in Patrick O'Brian's 1976 biography that 'Picasso, more than any painter in Europe since neolithic times, was susceptible to magic in every form'[55] contains more than a touch of hyperbole. However, it confirms the need to look closely at the cliché of

23 Vincent Van Gogh
Wheatfield With Cypress 1889
oil on canvas 72.5 x 91.5
The Trustees of the National
Gallery, London.

Picasso as a magician of the arts, capable of transforming the familiar world of appearances with the merest flick of pencil or brush.

Although Picasso himself said 'I don't seek, I find', he *was* the great seeker of twentieth-century art, exploring fresh means of expression in painting and drawing, sculpture and graphics, stage design and ceramics. What did he seek? Like Van Gogh and Cézanne, the two artists who (apart from Matisse) meant most to him, Picasso struggled to find an artistic language worthy of the metamorphosing energy — rather than the surface delights — of nature. And like the Iglulik Eskimos, who spoke to Knud Rasmussen of the fear which drove their lives — fear of weather spirits and sickness, of evil and death, of the demanding souls of dead human beings and animals[56] — Picasso had an acute sensitivity to the dangers as well as the joys implicit in nature's energies. Speaking of the impact which African masks made on him when he saw them for the first time at the old Trocadero Museum of Ethnological Art in Paris, early in the century, Picasso emphasised their role as '*intercesseurs*, mediators'. Their importance to Picasso was that they confirmed his growing belief that the function of art was to 'give spirits a form', in order to build up the psychic strength needed to survive and develop in life.[57]

When people described Picasso's art to him as sorcery, he took them at their word. He once said to Francoise Gilot that there should be darkness everywhere in the painter's studio — except on the canvas! — so that the painter might become hypnotised by his own work, painting as though in a trance. For Picasso, it was essential that the painter stay as close as possible to his own inner world, if he were to escape the limitations that reason would always try to impose on him.[58] Escaping those limitations led Picasso to some of the most resonant paintings of this century. Think only of the 1905 *Family of Saltimbanques*, a mysterious Tarot- and anima-oriented image of the near-shamanic world of circus entertainers which haunted Picasso all his life; the 1906–7 *Les Demoiselles d'Avignon*, a proto-Cubist exorcism of demonic virulence, ravaging both sexuality and the picture plane; the 1921 *Three Musicians* which, as Patrick O'Brian points out, has an uncannily magical quality, recalling the primal power of music, and the 1937 *Guernica* — that unrestrained, yet superbly organised *cri de coeur* against fascist brutality.

Nietzsche — whose importance for Picasso's development cannot be overemphasised — believed that 'Whatever is profound loves masks . . . around every profound spirit a mask is growing continually . . .'[59] Masks and metamorphosis are the joint keys to the searching quality in Picasso's art, an art which constantly switches back and forth between Apollonian and Dionysian elements. It is quite wrong to suggest — as did André Malraux — that Picasso had no capacity for praise, no feeling for the cosmos. For the art of Picasso is shot through with the spirit of what the Spanish poet Frederico Garcia Lorca called the *duende*.[60]

By the *duende*, Lorca (1896–1936) meant 'the spirit of the earth', something 'roused in the very cells of the blood'. The *duende* conjures the intensity of 'dark sounds', emissaries of both death and an expansive sense of wonder: 'in tender intimacy' our *duende*-inspired souls discover 'volcanoes, ants, gentle breezes, and the Milky Way clasping the great night to her waist'. The *duende* draws one to 'the edge of things, the wound' — to the place where forms fuse themselves 'in a longing greater than their visible expression'.[61] It is impossible not to feel this longing in the art of Picasso — who once said that he learned everything he knew from his stay in the isolated rural Spanish village of Horta in the late 1890s, when, recuperating from a violent attack of scarlet fever, he was to live in a cave with his friend Manuel Pallares for several weeks.

A bare hour spent at the Picasso Museum in Antibes should convince anyone of Picasso's richly affirmative feeling for the polytheistic *kosmos* of the ancient Mediterranean world. But the spirit of the *duende* in Picasso's art is finally most memorable for the eruptive, Dionysian power with which it addresses the problem of our homelessness, our need to journey into the unknown — a power which was never deployed with more shamanic intensity than in *The Three Dancers* of 1925.

The Three Dancers was one of Picasso's own favourite pictures. He kept it for forty years, before selling it to the Tate Gallery in London (when, predictably enough, protests were raised in the House of Lords about the misuse of public funds). Ronald Alley has written a scrupulously researched monograph which unlocks secrets of the various personal aspects of the painting's iconography. Alley sees the painting as a reflection by Picasso on the theme of the Dance of Life that is also a Dance of Death, a reflection occasioned by the death of an old friend, Ramon Pichot, whose profile can be seen on the right hand side of the canvas. Pichot's death apparently triggered memories of the death of another friend, Carles Casagemas, at the turn of the century — a death by suicide, which had been caused principally by Casagemas' unreciprocated love for one Germaine Florentin, later to be Ramon Pichot's wife. It is Casagemas, suggests Alley, whom we see crucified between Germaine on the left and Pichot on the right hand side of the picture.[62]

These personal memories are undoubtedly present in the painting.

24 Pablo Picasso *Family of Saltimbanques* 1905 oil on canvas 212.8 x 229.6 National Gallery of Art, Washington. Chester Dale Collection
© DACS 1992

25 Pablo Picasso *The Three Dancers* 1925 oil on canvas 215.3 x 142.2 Tate Gallery, London © DACS 1992

However, the strange, hieratic power of the work also encourages a broader interpretation of why Picasso should have kept the canvas for so long. Although O'Brian is doubtless right to suggest that parts of Picasso's life reveal the tragedy of being a 'successful phallocrat',[63] one should not forget how fascinating both metamorphosis and androgyny were to the painter. A good deal of his work, which feminist scholarship is often keen to see in the reductive terms of his sexism, can perhaps be seen in a more positive light than O'Brian's characterisation would suggest.

I have no wish to use shamanism (or anything else) to legitimise sexism. However, *sexuality* plays a key role in the development of at least some shamans' consciousness: one reads of helping spirits demanding sexual intercourse with the shaman — and threatening the shaman with dire consequences if such wishes are not met.[64] Picasso's frank engagement with sexuality is on one level exactly that: a frank engagement with aspects of experience which our culture often seems incapable of addressing without a good deal of cant and hypocrisy. On another level, that frankness can be seen as evidence of the struggle between the technical virtuosity of Picasso's artistic persona and the atavistic depths of his shadow side, and between his animus and anima. If Picasso did not 'win' this struggle — and it is difficult to think of the self's gradual realisation of its potentialities as ever coming to the state of resolution implied by that verb — he certainly left us some immensely potent images of the struggle we may all have to undergo in order to become more fully realised human beings.

At its best, as in *The Three Dancers*, Picasso's art reveals an astonishing, synthesised breadth and depth of sources, ambition and imagination. Who else, one wonders, could have combined in one transformative image the impact of Inuit (Eskimo) masks and Donatello's *Weeping Maenad at the Cross* from the San Lorenzo pulpits in Florence, as Picasso has done here in the double-faced, ecstatic dancer at the left of the picture?[65] Such a transmutative reworking of visual sources is matched by the shamanic depth of the picture's transpersonal, potentially healing theme.

The Three Dancers is a picture which tells of the struggle for psychic integration, of the 'crucifixion' of the self between the Dionysian and Apollonian forces of life. The picture reveals the sacrifice and the pain which may accompany the growth of the self towards individuation: lunar wisdom lies behind the Dionysian mask of sexuality, and Apollo has his shadow side. 'Painting', said Picasso, 'is stronger than I am. It makes me do what it wants.'[66] Here, painting led Picasso into the depths of both the personal and the collective unconscious. *The Three Dancers* partakes of that holy quality about which Picasso once spoke to Hélène Parmelin, when they were discussing what it was that distinguished the power of certain paintings from others: 'Something holy,' said Picasso, 'that's what it is. That's the kind of word you ought to be able to use, only people would get it wrong, give it a meaning it doesn't possess.'[67] Painting the holiness of *The Three Dancers* ensured Picasso's right to inhabit an elevated position in the Tree of Life of twentieth-century shamanism.

It seems inevitable to pair the shamanic power of Picasso's art with that of Henri Matisse (1869–1954), for the two were natural complementary contrasts. Whereas Picasso felt that the surface of a picture should 'bristle with razor blades', Matisse — the man who dreamed constantly, according to Louis Aragon — longed for an art 'of balance, of purity and serenity, devoid of troubling or depressing subject matter, an art which might be for every mental worker, be he businessman or writer, like an appeasing influence, like a mental soother, something like a good armchair in which to rest from physical fatigue.'[68]

By this, Matisse certainly did not mean the aesthetic equivalent of dozing off in front of the television. In 1953, the year of such majestic, sum-marising achievements as *Memory of Oceania* and *The Snail*, achievements realised in the cut-out, coloured paper technique which Matisse had mastered after a very serious illness the previous decade, the painter emphasised how 'Seeing is of itself a creative operation, one that demands effort. Everything we see in our ordinary life undergoes to a greater or lesser degree the deformation given by acquired habits, and this is perhaps especially so in an age like ours, when cinema, advertising and magazines push at us a daily flood of images which, all ready made, are to our vision what prejudice is to our intelligence. The necessary effort of detaching oneself from all that calls for a kind of courage . . .'[69]

If Picasso was the greatest draughtsman of our century, stimulating our courage with an unprecedented variety of linear invention, Matisse was his equivalent in colour. 'It is through colour that I am' said the man for whom green did not mean grass any more than blue meant sky. What then did colour mean to Matisse? Colour was Matisse's way of bridging soul and world, of realising his feelings, his sensations, in front of the external majesty of nature (to adopt a phrase from Cézanne, a painter who, together with Van Gogh and Gauguin, meant as much to Matisse as he did to Picasso). Matisse did not hold any orthodox religious beliefs, but he certainly felt religious awe in the face of life. In 1930 he spoke of how an artist or poet might possess 'an interior light which transforms objects to make a new world of them — sensitive, organised, a living world which is in itself an infallible sign of the Divinity, a reflection of Divinity.'[70]

26 Henri Matisse *Music* 1910
oil on canvas 258 x 399.5
The Hermitage, Leningrad
© Succession H Matisse/
DACS 1992

27 Henri Matisse *Interior with a
Violin* 1917—8
oil on canvas 116 x 89
Statens Museum for Kunst, J.
Rump Collection, Copenhagen
© Succession H Matisse/
DACS 1992

The organisation of Matisse's world is a thing of Paradisal wonder. His work offers us echo upon echo of the classical Arcadian dream of a harmony between people and nature: with the supplest economy, images synthesise figure and space, line and colour, object and feeling. Matisse spoke of using line to lead colour through the paths of the spirit, believing that at certain moments he was blessed with almost mediumistic abilities. The shamanic implications of such moments are clear. Matisse — who praised the power of cave drawings and amassed a superb collection of tribal art — offers us a replenishing journey to a non-denominational dream of Paradise, where space is not so much conquered as drunk deeply into the self.

If the range of Matisse's essentially contemplative, synthesising art was ultimately not as great as that which resulted from Picasso's relentless interrogation of life, then certainly, the healing, shamanic import of Matisse's Apollonian lucidity is just as remarkable as that of Picasso's Dionysian power. The monumental paintings *Music* and *Dance*, from 1910, take us all the way back to that first day of wonder of which Rilke spoke in connection with the art of Cézanne. In classic modernist manner, these magnificent paintings synthesise both the shifting, temporal evidence of their coming into existence (in *Music*, for example, close scrutiny of parts of the paint surface reveals how Matisse moved motifs around before reaching a satisfactory compositional balance) and simplifying mythopoeic power. And Matisse's art did not have to embrace such manifestly striking primitivistic subjects in order to deepen our sense of life's mystery.

Throughout his work, Matisse was able to turn the potentially mundane into the mythopoeic, as in the transmutation of such ostensibly naturalistic motifs as the interior of a room and the window which are featured in the *Interior with a Violin* of 1917–18. Although the 'spiritual' presence of the violin in its blue-lined case contrasts with the 'materiality' of the red table cloth in the right hand side of the picture, the balance of the whole composition underlines the extent to which Matisse's art pursued a non-dualistic, reverie-soaked synthesis of culture and nature, consciousness and the unconscious, intimacy and the infinite. And while the silhouetted arabesques of bird, star and fish in such late, cut-out masterpieces as *Polynesia, the Sky* and *Polynesia, the Sea* (both from 1946) cannot help but recall the distant exoticism of Gauguin's dreams, the 1947 collection of cut-outs and writings which Matisse called *Jazz* reminds us that we do not have to travel the world in primitivistic search of Paradise. Celebrating the energies of circus and dance, music and love, the synaesthetic grace of *Jazz* suggests that, ultimately, the search for Paradise is the self-transformative development of the wonder-struck heart, in endless, creative search of the transmutative harmony which lies at the core of life. As Matisse himself once said: 'Find joy in the sky, in the trees, in the flowers. There are flowers everywhere for those who want to see them.'[71]

It is the idea of synaesthesia — that blending of the senses whereby the visual may be 'heard' or even 'tasted' and sounds somehow 'seen' — which links the artistic worlds of Wassily Kandinsky (1866–1944) and Paul Klee (1879–1940). Synaesthetic experience in the arts may remind us of the original interplay of the elements of creative expression in shamanism, and the paintings of Kandinsky and Klee — who were life-long friends, with a mutual interest in the relations between painting and music — are full of shamanic resonance. Kandinsky takes us into the realms of pure, soaring spirit, while Klee passes to and fro between aerial and chthonic levels of mythopoeisis with a demeanour at once grave and humorous. 'Art', said Klee, 'does not reproduce what is visible; it makes visible'.[72] What he and Kandinsky made visible were the finest threads of desire hidden within the prophecies of Zarathustra or the swirling, impastoed rhythms of Van Gogh: a desire for a *renovatio* of soul and spirit, for a journey far from what Kandinsky called 'the nightmare of materialism'.

In his manifesto *Concerning The Spiritual In Art*, Kandinsky spoke of his faith in abstract art as a path to that regeneration of inner life which he believed was so sorely needed. In his *Reminiscences* he mentions once 'seeing' an abstract painting when he was ill with typhus: in terms of art history, the beginnings of his development towards abstraction, the most

28 Henri Matisse *Icarus* (image
number V111 from *Jazz*) 1947
© Succession H Matisse/
DACS 1992

provocative development in painting this century, can be traced to 1895, when the blurred luminosity of one of Monet's late *Haystack* paintings alerted Kandinsky to the power of enchantment which painting might have.

Monet's painting affected Kandinsky deeply, even though he had been unable to recognise the subject of the work without the help of the catalogue which had eventually revealed its title. In 1908, one of Kandinsky's own landscape paintings performed the same function for him. Returning home to his studio in Munich at twilight, he was astonished by an extraordinary, mysterious picture — 'beautiful, radiant, lit up' — on his studio wall. On closer inspection it turned out to be one of his own canvases, hanging upside down. When Kandinsky then deliberately tried to achieve the same effect, he was disappointed, for he could now recognise the objects in the painting at first glance. However, the experience confirmed him in his search for an art which might fly free of the familiar look of things, the better to stir soul and spirit by what he was later to call 'the romanticism ... of ... a flame burning in a block of ice'.[73]

Kandinsky's romanticism had been fuelled by both his Russian background — his father's family had lived in Western Siberia — and the theosophical reflections of such authors as Helena P. Blavatsky, Annie Besant and Charles W. Leadbeater, with their esoteric synthesis of elements from the great Eastern and Western mystical traditions.[74] In 1889 Kandinsky undertook a study trip in the province of Vologda, in the north of Russia, for the Society of Natural Sciences, Ethnography and Anthropology, and was particularly struck by the local peasant art.

It is interesting to speculate whether or not Kandinsky came across any evidence of shamanic practices on this trip. In her Jungian study of *Sounds*, Kandinsky's 1912 collection of synaesthetic poetry and woodcuts, Bettina L. Knapp asserts that 'Kandinsky was familiar with shamanism, having studied Russian folk customs in areas where such worship is still practiced.'[75] Speaking of Kandinsky's mid-1920s work, with its cosmic circles and triangles floating in space, Roger Lipsey has suggested that this imagery may have been inspired not only by such occult sources as Robert Fludd's Cosmic Monochord and the Kabbalistic Tree of Life, but also by shamanistic images which had been recently published by anthropologists.[76] The influence of such images might also be suggested in such metamorphosing, tribal-tinged works of Kandinsky's last years as *Accompanied Milieu* (1937) and *Sky Blue* (1940).

Whatever the evidence of direct shamanic inspiration in his work, there can be no doubt that Kandinsky produced some of the most ascensional, shamanic-spirited work of our century. In 1910 he met the painter Franz Marc, founding the short-lived *Der Blaue Reiter* (Blue Rider) group with him the following year. The group included Paul Klee and drew inspiration from the work of painters as different as Henri (le Douanier) Rousseau and Picasso, as well as from a world-wide range of spiritually-oriented art — ancient and modern, primitive and sophisticated. Marc felt a strong empathy with the world of animals, and his shaman-like views can only have confirmed Kandinsky's desire to produce art in a cosmic spirit, the spirit of *participation mystique*. Marc asked: 'For the artist can there be a more secretive idea than how nature is reflected in an animal's eye? How does a horse see the world or an eagle, a deer or a dog? How wretched and soulless is our convention, putting animals into a landscape which is viewed from our viewpoint, instead of submerging ourselves into the soul of the animal itself.'[77]

In the 1912 volume *Sounds*, Kandinsky tried to submerge himself in the souls of many things. The book was a deliberate attempt to subvert normal denotational aspects of both language and imagery, in order to 're-animate' existence. A shaman-like repetition of words complements Kandinsky's woodcuts, which range from *Jugendstil*-inspired representational imagery to fully abstract visions, soaked in the free-floating rhythms of reverie. One of the story-poems, 'In The Woods', takes us into an archetypal Romantic wood, with the urgency of the repeated imagery soon propelling our imagination into a world of vision-quests and mystical incantations: 'The woods grew deeper and deeper. The red trunks grew bigger and bigger. The green crowns heavier and heavier. The air darker and darker. The bushes lusher and lusher. The mushrooms thicker and thicker. Until there was nothing but mushrooms to walk on. It was harder for the man to walk, to force his way through without slipping. But he went on anyway, repeating faster and faster and over and over the same sentence:

> The scars that mend.
> Colours that blend.'[78]

29 Wassily Kandinsky *Rain Landscape* 1911 watercolour on paper 25.4 x 31.7
The Jacques and Natasha Gelman Collection
© DACS 1992

These last seven, simple words summarise Kandinsky's view that the mission of the artist was to attempt to heal the scars of centuries of materialism by the participative magic of colour. There are clear echoes of the shaman's triple role as seer, artist and healer in Kandinsky's belief

that the artist stands at the head of the triangle of spiritual development in society, where he is 'not the king of the castle but rather a servant of some nobler purpose'.[79] Speaking of his early experience of the process of painting, Kandinsky revealed that he sometimes heard a hissing of the colours while they were blending between brush and canvas, and likened the experience to being in 'the mysterious kitchens of the arcane alchemists'.[80]

His great aim was to speak of mystery in terms of mystery, cultivating the 'inner necessity' (or 'inner sound') of which theosophical writers had spoken, and which was Kandinsky's sole measure of whether or not an artist had produced spiritually significant rather than simply decorative work. And unlike the contemporary Russian artist Kasemir Malevich, whose liberation from representation in painting led him to such extreme depictions of the non-objective world as the 1913 *The Black Square*, a square metre of uniform, uncompromising black, Kandinsky's sense of mystery always embraced a creative tension of line and colour — a tension that meant genesis. (It is typical of the differences between these two artists that when Kandinsky produced his 1923 study for *In The Black Square*, his square contained a world in miniature.[81])

Experiments in chromotherapy early in the century, which according to Kandinsky had shown how coloured light could exercise 'very definite influences on the whole body', confirmed the painter in his belief that the artist's task was to orchestrate the play of his or her imagination in colour and line, so that it might somehow strike a healing chord in the onlooker: 'Colour is the keyboard, the eyes are the hammers, the soul is the piano with many strings. The artist is the hand which plays, touching one key or another, to cause vibrations in the soul.'[82] There is much of what Taoist aesthetics calls the flowing beauty of *li* (or organic principle) in Kandinsky. Psychologically, what is so satisfying about most of his work is that it avoids both rigidity and chaos — which Erich Neumann calls the two forms of the negative. Instead, it encompasses the richness of metamorphosis, balanced on 'the transformative axis of life and death'.[83]

Kandinsky was very much aware of the Nietzschian theme of the interrelation of suffering and joy in art. He once wrote on a ticket that if he were asked to define his artistic goal in a few words, he would choose the following: 'to elevate oneself through tragedy'.[84] This goal was no less crucial to Paul Klee, whose spiritual beliefs were forged in the tragedy of the First World War, when he lost two of his closest comrades, Franz Marc and August Macke. Klee spoke of abandoning the regions 'here below' in order to build a life and art 'on the other side'. There he could stand 'at a remote, original point of creation and from it presuppose the formulae proper to man, beast, vegetable, mineral, elements — to the cyclic forces as a whole . . .'[85]

'All art is a memory of our dark origins', wrote Klee, 'whose fragments live in the artist forever.'[86] As with Kandinsky, aesthetics here gives way to myth. Klee and Kandinsky taught together at the Bauhaus during the 1920s; and for both of them, reflecting on the way in which a point might become first a line and then a plane, or how one might, in Klee's famous words, 'take a line for a walk', was to search for underlying principles of cosmic genesis and development.

Metamorphosis was at the heart of Klee's artistic vision, a vision which he expressed most fully in his 1924 lecture *On Modern Art*. Placing more value on 'the powers which do the forming [in life and art] than on the final forms themselves', Klee asked his audience — to whom he wished to explain the freedom from naturalistic or photographic representation in modern art — to consider the simile of a tree. The sap of a tree flows from its roots to its crown — but between above and below 'there can be no mirrored reflection'. The artist stands at the trunk of the tree, 'battered and stirred by the strength of the flow', a humble transmitter of nature's energies, awed by genesis. The artist's responsibility cannot be to produce an inevitably inadequate copy of any one particular manifestation of those energies. Rather, the artist should seek to create art in the metamorphosing spirit of nature, making the invisible visible.[87]

The visions which Klee cultivated took him to the depths of the ocean and through Paradisal gardens to the heights of fairy tale mountain and World Tree. His 'miniaturist' style drew upon an enormous range of ideas and stimulation, from Goethe's concept of an *ur*-form in plant life to the work of Cézanne (whom Klee called his 'teacher *par excellence*'), and from the art of children and the mentally ill to eighteenth-century European musical polyphony.

We can see evidence of this last affinity in one of his most important paintings, the 1932 *Ad Parnassum*. However, if the linear boldness and tessellated richness of this composition grew out of Klee's reflections on the relation of melody to eighteenth-century voicings, the central elements of his homage to the home of the muses — the arc of a threshold, pathway, mountain and sun — strike a more mythologically resonant note than any to be found in eighteenth-century Europe. As in so much of Klee's work, it is a note of shamanic resonance, containing overtones of the ancient symbolism of the seer's ascensional journey through the 'doorway' which leads from the profane world to the luminous realm of enlightened consciousness.[88]

In the last five years of his life, Klee suffered from incurable scleroderma, a disease which causes the gradual drying up of the body's fluids. The knowledge of the nature of his illness precipitated both an astonishing amount of work and a deepening of his feelings about those fragments of the 'dark origins' which he believed artists carried within themselves. In the 1937 *Picture Album* Klee produced a virtual compendium of primitivistic imagery, with African and Egyptian elements fused with

30 Paul Klee *One Who Understands* 1934 oil and gypsum on unprimed canvas 54 x 40.8
The Jacques and Natasha Gelman Collection

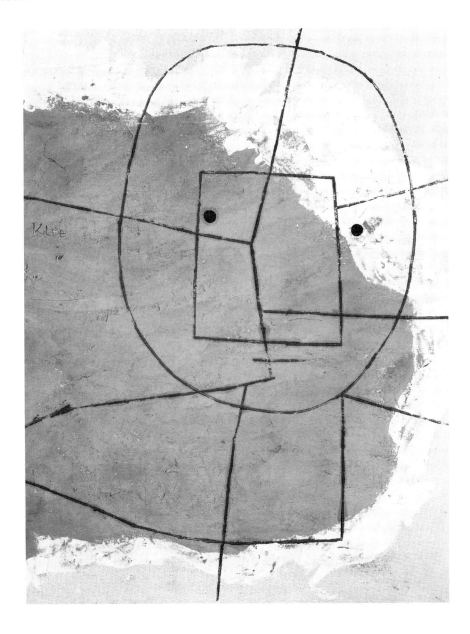

Aboriginal-style 'X-ray' drawing and a range of hieroglyphics. Much of Klee's later work, such as the 1938 *They Dance Through Fear* or the 1940 *Death and the Fire* is reminiscent of nothing so much as the yarn pictures of shamans and sorcerers made by the Huichol Indians and collected by Peter T. Furst in his *Myth in Art: A Huichol Depicts His Reality*.[89]

The shamanic depth of Klee's work, the sense of a journey simultaneously forwards and back to the origins of mythopoeisis, was already evident in such earlier images as *Mural From The Temple Of Longing* and *The Wild Man*. Painted in 1922, both works feature the arrow form that to Klee signified man's ability to 'measure the spiritual and cosmic despite his physical helplessness'.[90] In *The Catalpa Bow* Carmen Blacker underlines the importance of arrow symbolism and metaphors in shamanism, pointing to the fact that in shamanic rituals in Asia the arrow is 'less a weapon than an instrument which magically joins two worlds. Shot in the air, it will apprise a deity that a rite is about to take place.'[91]

What rite, what shamanic transformation is about to occur in *The Wild Man*? Like much of Klee's work, *The Wild Man* is an image at once humorous and a touch threatening, uplifting and a little sad, as the faintly ridiculous, top-hatted and very nineteenth-century-looking European feels the energies of ancient horned gods stirring in him. Was this not Klee's atonement (conscious or not) for centuries of Christian and rationalist attempts to obliterate all memory of the 'dark origins' of spirituality in shamanism? And what lies behind the flimsy veil of culture through which *The Wild Man*'s newly awakened eyes burn?

Klee had the soul of a true seer. Cutting away all the superfluities of everyday existence, the 1934 *One Who Understands* finds him using the simplest of lines to place a reflective, child-like schema of a face in the middle of a perspectiveless, desert-like terrain, of timeless mythopoeic import. *One Who Understands* is a humble, yet great image, with several of its ideographic lines continuing beyond the picture's border to the limits of our imagination. The 'wild man', the shaman in Klee, had the courage and the imagination to contemplate a journey home to the destination which on this side of the grave must remain forever unknown. On Klee's tomb are his own words: 'In this world I am not understood. So I am better with the dead or with those unborn. Closer than usual to the centre of creation. But not yet close enough.'

6 Northern Lights

Shamans believe that certain parts of the land are charged with power. If one goes to those parts of the land in the right state of mind, then that power may flow into the psyche, opening up previously untapped levels of feeling, perception and creativity. A crucial aspect of this process is the idea of (and capacity for) solitude. One thinks of the shaman Igjugarjuk's belief that true wisdom is only to be found 'far away from people, out in the great solitude'. Or one recalls Don Juan, leading Carlos Castaneda across the desert chaparral and into the mountains of Mexico, in search of those places of power that would enable Castaneda to really 'tackle' his dreams, seeing them not as 'just dreams' but rather as part of the deeper reality of life.[1]

Over the past 250 years, the Nordic countries — Iceland, Denmark, Sweden, Norway and Finland — have played a vital role in helping to preserve and develop such fundamental shamanic ideas. Throughout the nineteenth century, for example, the majestic fjords and mountain passes of Norway and the vast, uninhabited interior of Iceland increasingly attracted the attention of British and European artists, thinkers and travellers. Disturbed by the alienating pace and scale of industrialisation in their own countries, such lovers of the North sought a sublime, healing experience of landscape in countries where the great god Pan still seemed to hold sway over the imagination. By the beginning of the twentieth century, the idea of the North as a key to the renewal of inner life had acquired a magnetic aura — partly through the landscape itself, and partly through the (Nordic) art, music and literature which it had helped to inspire.[2]

To travel North today can be to feel a sea wind freshening in one's face, as the landscape changes from the agricultural plains of southern Sweden to first the heathlands of Denmark and then the rolling hills of the Oslo fjord. Beyond those hills, hundreds of miles of forest, mountain and lake stretch westwards to the icy fjords of Norway, or continue north to the mountains and plateaux of the Saami people, ancient guardians of the shamanic drum. To travel North is thus to travel towards the *idea* of something very powerful, something utterly primal. The Danish artist Asger Jorn once called the North 'the dream centre' of Europe — the place where one might defeat the thousand and one distractions of everyday existence and feel life stirring once more in the depths of both oneself and the world.[3]

To sense such a magnetism of the North is to hear the call of mountain and fjord, forest and lake, beyond the roar of traffic or the hum of telephone wires. It is to listen to what the Norwegian poet Rolf Jacobsen (b.1907) has called

> The silence that lives in the grass
> on the underside of each blade
> and in the blue space between stones. [4]

Jacobsen began life as an urbane modernist, much drawn to the idea of the city. 'Travel', from his first collection *Earth And Iron*, hymns 'the magic song of the rails. — Paris, Marseilles', as the poet relishes the thought of the smell of 'chestnut buds and exhaust' down by the harbour of a city — any city — of his imagination. But over the years, Jacobsen's imagination was drawn more and more to earth (nature) rather than iron (as turned into the steel of culture and history). Much of his 1979 collection *Think Of Something Else*, for example, focusses on the landscape beyond the city and its suburbs. The poet celebrates the enduring physical grandeur and symbolic richness of mountains, and the magical simplicity of

> Northern lights and a new moon
> instead of street lights. [5]

A similar feeling for landscape informs the work of the Swedish poet Tomas Tranströmer (b.1931), who is one of this century's greatest explorers of Europe's 'dream centre'. A psychologist as well as a poet, Tranströmer writes with a shaman-like sensitivity to the half-veiled moments of epiphany that life can offer, beyond the sweep of the headlights of what he calls 'the deaf cars [which] race towards the neon-line' today. [6] Thoroughly aware of the pressures of contemporary politics and technology, Tranströmer often builds aspects of the latter into his imagery. There is nothing remotely escapist or sentimental about his sensitivity to landscape: landscape offers him the essential 'breathing space' where he can feel life grow stronger at what he calls 'the open frontiers' of experience. These are the frontiers of reverie; the frontiers which can open up in the middle of work, for example, where there may be a sudden longing for wild greenery, for

> . . . the Wilderness itself, penetrated only
> by the thin civilisation of the telephone wires . . . [7]

Tranströmer is a poet of time, in several senses of that immense word. One of his finest poems is 'About History' from the 1966 collection *Bells And Tracks*. The poem is a meditation upon many things: the pressure of immediate political events; the transmission of ethical values; the problem of breaking free from the 'unhappy marriage' of 'Radical and Reactionary' today and searching for the sort of language which would enable one to 'Go like a bloodhound where truth has trampled'. The poem ends with an image of an abandoned newspaper slowly metamorphosing into a plant, into a cabbage-head — on its way to becoming

> united with the earth
> Just as a memory is slowly transmuted into your own self. [8]

'About History' epitomises the primitivistic trajectory of Tranströmer's work — the longing to heal the daily wounds of politics and history through the absorption of the self within the deeper rhythms of nature. History thus gives way to myth, transforming one's sense of time. And in Tranströmer, myth means mythopoeisis. In 'Further In', from the 1973 collection *Paths*, the poet senses a call to 'walk in the footsteps of the badger', deep in the forest where stones lie in the moss. One of these stones is precious. It can make everything change, make the darkness shine:

> It is a switch for the whole country
> Everything depends upon it.
> Look at it, touch it . . . [9]

The shamanic nature of such a calling is made specific in several of Tranströmer's poems, such as 'The Outpost', again from *Paths*. It is a calling rooted in the *genius loci*, or spirit of place, of the North — a spirit of place which embraces both the Romantic power of rocky outcrop and the humble beauty of lichen; the warmth of what Tranströmer calls 'a night of radiant sun', [10] and the purifying shroud of winter's snow. 'From March 1979', from the 1983 collection *The Wild Market Square*, exemplifies Tranströmer's Jacobsen-like turning to the earth:

> Weary of all who come with words, words but no language
> I make my way to the snow-covered island.
> The untamed has no words.
> The unwritten pages spread out on every side!
> I come upon the tracks of deers' hooves in the snow.
> Language but no words. [11]

The untamed has no words . . . does not this remind one of Don Juan's description of 'the *nagual*' to Carlos Castaneda — 'the part of us for which there are no words, no names, no feelings, no knowledge'? And do not Tranströmer's words also recall Hans Peter Duerr's description of the shamans discovering their 'wild' or 'animal' aspect in the solitude of wilderness, and the wilderness of solitude?

Tranströmer's empathy for the wilderness marks him as a poet of deep tradition — the tradition which informs the Icelandic artist Jon Reykdal's *In the Wilderness* (1987), for example. The Northern environment has long been of especial importance for the development of shamanic consciousness — just as the seemingly paradoxical idea of a nourishing wilderness has long been a quintessential aspect of Northern myth and legend. It is worth remembering that Christianity did not conquer the pagan world of Odin and Thor, Freya and Balder until around AD 1000. And as we have seen in the previous chapter, aspects of Saami shamanism were sufficiently alive to disturb Christian missionaries a good seven or eight centuries later than that.

Archetypal shamanism is usually seen as coming to birth in the North. The initiatory sufferings and subsequent visions of the Siberian or Inuit (Eskimo) shaman have been regarded as consequences of the extremes of Northern weather, sometimes being described as the product of 'Arctic hysteria'. In his recent, stimulating book *Arctic Dreams: Imagination And Desire In A Northern Landscape*, Barry Lopez pondered the mysterious artefacts of the Arctic Dorset culture which flourished between about 500 BC and AD 1000, such as the shamanic ivory carving known as the 'floating' or 'flying' bear.[12] Sensitive to the power in the landscape which the ancient *angakoq* (shaman) would have felt, Lopez writes with animistic, shamanic wisdom about the North, describing the 'vigorous and alive' Arctic landscape as 'an animal that contains all other animals.'[13]

31 Jon Reykdal (*b.*1945) *In The Wilderness* 1987 black and white linocut 14 x 18 Collection M Tucker © courtesy, the Artist Photograph: Mike Fearey

For Lopez, such a landscape has much more to offer today than the raw materials which industrial culture cannot wait to exploit. He speaks of the need to develop an 'elevated conversation' with the land, developing a psychologically enriching sense of reciprocity with it. The land thus becomes a dream-maker *par excellence*. Like Rolf Jacobsen and Tomas Tranströmer, Lopez opens himself up to a language beyond that of history, a language of mythopoeic weight. At the end of his book — a book that is distinguished by the sort of sensitivity that can turn precise scientific observation into poetry — Lopez stands at the tip of Saint Lawrence Island and looks out over the Bering Sea. He offers a humble, long-held bow to both the spirit of the North and the mystery of the totality which life weaves out of its myriad variety: 'When I stood I thought I glimpsed my own desire. The landscape and the animals were like something found at the edge of a dream. The edges of the real landscape became one with something I had dreamed.'[14] Like an *angakoq* of old, Lopez had dreamed of that uplifting and rare state that, like light, is 'unbounded, nurturing, suffused with wisdom and creation . . .'[15]

While Lopez is fully aware of the evolving historical dimensions of habitat and human presence in the Arctic, he believes that what the Arctic ultimately signifies is the transhistorical 'richness and sanctity of a wild landscape' — a landscape which Lopez believes can mean much today for what he calls 'the unfolding of a human life, the staying of a troubled human spirit . . .'[16] Exactly the same point obtains with regard to the healing potentiality of landscape in the Nordic countries. For these are countries where Lopez's dream of a state 'suffused with wisdom and creation' has been pursued with unmistakably shamanic intensity, in both the distant and recent past.

The work of the Norwegian author Tarjei Vesaas (1897–1970), for example — particularly his novels *The Birds* (1957) and *The Ice Palace* (1963), and the autobiographical collection *The Boat In The Evening* (1968) — develops exactly that 'elevated conversation' with the Northern *genius loci* which Lopez rightly deems essential to the healing of today's fractured, short-sighted consciousness.

Vesaas was born and raised in the remote interior of the rural Telemark district of Norway, but he also travelled widely, absorbing much of both world literature and the problems of twentieth-century politics. He spoke of how a change came over his writing at the time of the 1940 *The Seed*, which was the first book to feature the taut, lapidary language for which he became famous. Dealing with murder, mindless revenge and the subsequent search for atonement, *The Seed* reflects much of the shock and the horror of the Nazi occupation of Norway (a theme which Vesaas developed in *The House In The Dark* of 1945). Landscape reveals its hidden layers, speaking of the unacknowledged and potentially destructive shadow side in us all; but it also speaks of the potential good in the world, of our capacity to sense 'the seed in the dust'.[17] As such a phrase reveals, there is much of the New Testament in *The Seed*; but there is also a strong pagan quality of identification with the world of nature and animals. It is this latter quality which so distinguishes *The Birds*.

Perhaps Vesaas's finest achievement, *The Birds* evinces layer upon layer of ancient qualities of mythopoeisis and *participation mystique*. The novel presents a haunting picture of shamanic consciousness struggling to find its place in the modern world: the title may be taken as a dedication to all artists and dreamers. The book's chief character is Mattis, whom Vesaas saw as something of a self-portrait. Unable to function normally in the routines of rural working life, the 'half-witted' Mattis is blessed with a tender-minded, shamanic sensitivity to the animal and bird life of the magnificent Norwegian landscape.

One evening, a woodcock flies 'like an arrow' over the dwelling which Mattis shares with his long-suffering sister Hege, and changes his life forever. Something about the sound of the bird's wings in the night air touches his heart; later, following the flight of the bird down to some marshland, Mattis finds confirmation of his own path in life, 'a path full of joy.'[18] Finding a twig, he pricks a secret answer to the message which he feels the woodcock's graceful, dancing footprints have left in the mud for him. Thereafter, human speech becomes 'coarse and commonplace. He would have liked to have started using bird language for good — to have gone back home to Hege and never spoken in any other way. Then she might have begun to understand some of the things that were at present hidden from her.'[19]

Mattis's confidence begins to grow: he becomes a ferryman of sorts, rowing 'straight as an arrow' across the local lake. Eventually, however, this child-like visionary — who has inadvertently caused the death of the woodcock, by telling a young hunter of its evening visits — feels that he must sacrifice himself for the sake of Hege's happiness. With an allusive economy characteristic of Vesaas, the novel's last pages build to a conclusion of great pathos and power, including an extraordinary sequence when Mattis runs right up to the light grey stem of an alder, and bites his teeth into the bark 'so that the bitter juice smarted. This was something nobody must see, and it lasted only a moment.'[20]

In *The Ice Palace*, Vesaas created one of the most remarkable images of twentieth-century literature. Wary of the consequences of the friendship which she has just started with her classmate Siss, the eleven-year old Unn wanders further and further into the extensive, fabulous labyrinth of a frozen waterfall, eventually lying down to die in the extreme cold. The rest of the novel concerns Siss's struggle to break her own increasing sense of psychological isolation, as she strives to keep Unn's memory sacrosanct. On one level, the novel is a sensitive exploration of adolescent shyness and psychological and sexual growth. On another, it addresses archetypal patterns within the development of shamanic consciousness. The 'ice palace' of the frozen waterfall is the great, initiatory terrain of shamanic consciousness, the arena wherein the animistic message of the indivisible totality of life is forged out of fructifying suffering.

The collection of autobiographical fiction in *The Boat In The Evening* exemplifies Vesaas's conviction that 'Man belongs to the choir, but enters through his own perplexity.'[21] A key chapter is 'In the Marshes and on the Earth', which describes an early-morning encounter with a flock of wild cranes. Lying stiff and numb in the lonely cold, the narrator sights the birds approaching, and longs to experience 'An open channel, where we can search for the mystery we share while we walk in the marshes and on the earth.'[22] Begging the birds to dance, he muses to himself that if they do so, they will liberate himself as much as themselves. But a moment's reflection tells him that 'Liberation is a big word. It doesn't suit me; what am I to be liberated from? On the contrary, I must be able to receive. To fill a void.'[23] In the beautiful 'Beyond One's Grasp', such an ensouling sense of openness is conveyed through images as simple as they are mysterious — scent of the first rain on light clothes, over warm flesh, and the welcoming shift of a stone underfoot, on a country path: 'The stone will greet each new wanderer on the ascent in its reticent language. Throughout all ages and all ages. The restless wanderer will find peace and yet more peace. And you? Shyly you came to the path and asked. Shyly you came to know and understand.'[24]

Like Tarjei Vesaas, the Swedish poet Gunnar Ekelöf (1907—68), one of the greatest shamanic spirits of modern lyric poetry, 'shyly came to know and understand' the animistic essence of life through a deep feeling for nature — advising, for example, that if one wanted to hear music, one should

> Turn to the wilderness
> and you will perhaps even hear the forest's gongs
> if there is anything to you![25]

For Ekelöf, the staying of a troubled human spirit, as Lopez puts it, could only be achieved when one had learned to travel and be homeless, so to speak, expanding one's sense of self beyond the ego's cluttered and often self-destructive desires in order to live with 'the great, simple things: the sea, the forest, music — the music which . . . is built upon silence.'[26] In a transformation of both the classical ideal of a pastoral Arcadia and the Edenic tradition in Judaeo-Christian thought, such a Northern, shamanic road to Paradise — which we have already met in the work of Tomas Tranströmer — lies as much within the 'wilderness' of the self as without. Advising us to 'walk the wide and inner way', Ekelöf refused to offer any familiar signposts for the journey. 'If you ask me where I am' he wrote,

> Well I live here beyond the mountains
> It is far but I am near
> I live in another world
> but you live in it too
> It is everywhere, as rare as helium . . .[27]

The emotional overtones of such lines — and indeed, of all of Ekelöf's poetry — are inescapably Romantic; and it is a shamanic longing for wisdom which forms the backbone of this Romanticism. A key essay of Ekelöf's, in which he discusses the impact which evening sunsets and music had on him as a youth — when he used to clamber up to the ridges of the roofs near St John's Church in central Stockholm, and dream of flying off into the sunset — is called 'The Sunset: From A Romantic's Notes'. Regretting the loss of 'The whole longed for land of childhood . . . Sunrise over the troll lake, the hot fragrant hill of wild strawberries in the midday sun, the bells in the forest and the clear, echoing voices around the lake in the evening . . . And the simplicity and happiness of being — here and nowhere else . . .' the poet suggests that life's 'deepest streams' always evade the 'conscious-now-I, the near-sighted near'. He longs to learn 'only one hundred words of the supraearthly language', believing that then 'everything we had to say would soon be said'.[28]

Ekelöf spent a lifetime searching for such a Paradisal language. Believing strongly in the wholeness and indivisibility of art, he spoke of the lasting quality in modern art as representing 'an evolution in reverse, an evolution to something lost along the way.'[29] What Ekelöf's own art strove to recover was *participation mystique*; the urge towards shamanic totality which is particularly evident in a draft of an essay called 'Zoological Gardens': 'The awfulness of the fact that the concept "thing" ever arose! See life in everything, venerate everything! The animistic conception superior to the rationalistic. Poetry's to pragmatism's.'[30] For Ekelöf, poetry was mysticism and music; and by mysticism he meant what he called 'the deep experience of life itself, the apprehension of the eternally elusive, shifting, returning in everything which is related to picture, tone, thought, feeling and life.'[31]

Offering us a participatory mysticism of the self, Ekelöf's poetry cuts through layers of cultural conditioning and existential doubt in pursuit of the affirmative, esoteric core of life. Like a shaman, Ekelöf experienced initiatory suffering and crisis: in his 1932 debut collection *Late On Earth*, he tells us that he has sunk from the status of humanity to that of a floor rug. In 'Sonata Form Denatured Prose', from the same collection, language and the self are pulverised:

> crush the alphabet between your teeth yawn vowels, the fire
> is burning in hell vomit and spit now or never I and dizziness you
> or never dizziness now or never.[32]

Ekelöf experienced such a sense of meaninglessness for much of his life; what prevented him from becoming a Nordic Samuel Beckett was his intuitive understanding of the need to search and battle for meaning at the deepest — and 'wildest', most courageous — levels of the self. *Dedication*, his second collection of poetry, was prefaced by the famous words of Rimbaud: 'I say that one must be a seer, that one must *make oneself* a seer.' The influence of Rimbaud's *A Season In Hell* can be detected in much of Ekelöf's work: like the great French visionary, he was to cultivate an 'alchemy of the word', pursuing the mysteries that he felt lay in the tension-filled relation '*between* the words, *between* the lines, *between* the meanings.'[33]

With the faith of a seer in his own unconscious, Ekelöf developed dream associations of archetypal import in his work. Prime examples are the images of bird and stone which dominate 'Voices Under the Ground' from the 1951 collection *In Autumn* — a poem in which Ekelöf identified with *Archaeopteryx*, the forerunner of all birds. Nature was a constant, healing presence within his quest to wrestle a meaning from life while face to face with what he called 'sacred death'; and nowhere more so than in 'Euphoria', from his key collection *Ferry Song* of 1941. The poet feels the whole of nature 'strong in love and death' around him, as he sits in a garden one still, magical summer night, and senses with Bachelard-like reverie how 'all things are in all things, at once end and beginning.'[34]

In 'Open It, Write', from the same collection, Ekelöf sings like a Sufi mystic of

> . . . the only thing that can redeem,
> the only practical, the same for all:
> How seldom man holds the power
> to renounce power!
> To renounce the I and its voice, renounce —
> this alone gives power.[35]

Describing himself as 'a shipwrecked man who drifts in the shape-shifting dark', he proclaims his belief that

> There is no strength other than inner strength
> that from the outer comes
> from that mysterious thing that moves up there
> shines through those vaguely self-lit clouds
> streams over you in its galvanic force
> so that you feel yourself wrestling!
> Then it is the power wrestling, not you![36]

The concept of power here is as Taoist as it is shamanic; a combination developed in the short poem 'Solitude'. The worldly poverty of solitude opens the way to that 'song of something else' which haunted Ekelöf all his life:

> But isn't it necessary to be poor in spirit?
> To contract into something great!
> Poverty stands for something else
> Only he who is rich can afford poverty
> and he, who hears the voice, silence.[37]

The nature of the voice that Ekelöf longed to hear (and which so much of his poetry passes onto us) has been beautifully caught by one of his translators, the poet Robert Bly. As Bly says, Ekelöf's poems 'float along like souls above the border between religion and witchcraft . . . His poetry is constantly trying to hint to the reader the location of the road towards that transparent state of being the Easterners talk of. At the same time, curious images slip into Ekelöf's poems from somewhere else . . . from the heathen Swedish ground, from old Finnish swamps and that part of the Northern unconscious still obsessed by shaman hallucinations, changing of bodies, journeys of souls during trance. Ekelöf's poems are like a spider web strung between these two enormous trunks.'[38]

Attacking 'the near-sighted near', and listening to 'the silence of the deep night', Ekelöf's work — particularly 'Each Person Is A World', again from *Ferry Song* — stimulates us to listen to the voices of the Great, or Cosmic Self within us, voices often censored by an uneasy ego drawn to the false securities of one fundamentalism or another. Encouraging us to

> Be still, be silent and wait,
> Wait for the animal, wait for the sign that is coming,
> Wait for the miracle, wait for the defeat that is coming,
> When time has lost its saltiness.[39]

Ekelöf takes us to the border regions of our selves. His own search for the alchemy of individuation took him deep into such far-flung worlds as the poetry of Rimbaud, Edith Södergran and the twelfth- and thirteenth-century Sufi mystic Ibn Al 'Arabi; the art of the Paleolithic cave dwellers and so-called 'concrete' (or abstract) art of the early twentieth century. But the root of Ekelöf's conviction that

> . . . all the trees of the magic wood are one tree,
> the same tree forever[40]

is to be found within the sort of psychic terrain which the Norwegian philosopher and architectural historian Christian Norberg-Schulz once illuminated, in his characterisation of the Nordic world as 'a romantic world, in the sense that it brings man back to a distant "past" which is experienced emotionally rather than understood as allegory or history.'[41] At the heart of that past — a past which the Norse myths tell us began in 'burning ice, biting flame' — lies the ensouling power of a shamanic dream of life.

In *The Magic Of The Runes*, Michael Howard has recently spelled out the shamanic aspects of such central elements of Norse mythology as the mighty ash Yggdrasill. It was upon this Nordic World Tree that Odin — god of war, but also master of poetry — hung impaled on his own spear for nine days and nights, so that his suffering might gain him access to the psychic wisdom contained in the runes. Odin acquired the power to change into bird or animal at will; his eight-legged steed Sleipnir carried him through the air, while his ravens, Thought and Memory, helped him bridge worlds of past and future. According to one of the myths, Odin lost one of his eyes in payment for a drink from the fabulous spring of Mimir, which flowed beneath the World Tree — a drink which gave inspiration and knowledge of things to come. Odin has also been depicted as acquiring the gift of poetry in dangerous, shape-shifting fashion. Crawling in serpent form and flying as an eagle, he won the mead of poetic inspiration from the dwarves who had killed the wise giant Kvasir, and then mixed his blood with honey, in order to create the marvellous drink. [42]

Shamanic qualities can also be clearly seen in Freya, the 'gentle goddess' of the North, who was known as a *volva*, or seer. She would sit on a platform and sing her spells, often accompanied by music and singing from her audience. Attaining a state of ecstatic trance, Freya would then offer prophecies and answer questions concerning the spirit world. Anne Bancroft has drawn attention to Freya's costume of animal skins and the fact that she was said to travel in a carriage drawn by cats, her chosen animal spirits and helpers; [43] Monica Sjöö and Barbara Mor draw further attention to the 'priestesses of Freya ... [who] ... wore magic bird-costumes belonging to her; with these, they "flew" into other realities.' [44]

Today, those realities are very much part of the world of Sjöö (*b*.1938). While her imagery has long drawn inspiration from world-wide evidence of the roots of earth-affirming creativity in ancient cults of the Goddess, the North has played an essential role in helping Sjöö to develop her polemical sense of the healing values which art should proclaim. Today, the British-domiciled Sjöö still considers herself to be very much an artist of the Scandinavian North. [45]

Born in Härnosand on the Swedish Baltic coast, some seven hours north of Stockholm by train, Sjöö lived in Sweden until she was seventeen. She recalls with great affection the silent mystery of Northern moonlight on snow, or the late-summer, troll-like play of shadow and light over grassy-green boulders in deep, dim forests. In the 1984 painting *Nerthus/Freya* — an image of typically syncretic ambition, combining a central, lotus-like mandala with a paganistic, Nordic reclaiming of Christian iconography — Sjöö has depicted Freya guarding the caves and streams of ancient Earth mysteries. Freya is seen here with (as Sjöö believes) her mother Nerthus, the goddess who bore the title of Mother Earth (*Terra Mater*) in the ritual cults of 'the Germans' in Denmark, as described by Tacitus in the first century AD.

Further echoes of the rich shamanic past of the North can be sensed in the work of other twentieth-century Nordic artists, such as film directors Nils Gaup and Ingmar Bergman (the latter of whose work is considered in Chapter 9) and the painter, Bengt Lindström. Born in 1925 in Storsjökapell (The Chapel On The Great Lake), a small Swedish village in the midst of the mountains, forests and lakes of Saamiland (Lapland), Lindström is known today as one of Sweden's most striking colourists and celebrators of the pagan past. His father had a strong interest in Saami culture, and in fact asked a Saami godfather to baptise his son. Lindström was eventually to study painting in Stockholm, Copenhagen and Chicago, and today he lives in Paris. But like Monica Sjöö, he has always retained

32 Bengt Lindström *Sorcerer*
1989 oil on canvas 41 x 33
© courtesy, the Artist and
Galerie Michèle Sadoun, Paris

his early love of the landscape, myths and legends of the Far North, returning to Sweden each summer for inspiration.

The title of an important exhibition which Lindström had in London and Paris in 1990 — 'The Earth of the Ancestors' — encapsulates the atavistic, animistic qualities of his work. Swirling rapids of pure red, yellow and green oil paint, criss-crossed by rivulets of ice-cold blue and white, conjure a legendary world of lake spirits, hunters and mountain trolls. The contours of a forcefully handled landscape can simultaneously be the features of *Odin*, outstaring fate, or an enigmatic *King of the Lakes*. Informed by a thorough study of developments in painting since Van Gogh, Lindström's images — which are as beautifully crafted as they are bold — balance the shamanic power of the Nordic past with a thoroughly modern aesthetic, where colours are charged with the painterly responsibility of dramatising the force of their own (unillustrative) presence.[46]

It is impossible to think of much of what has come to be known as a modern aesthetic in twentieth-century culture, without acknowledging the essential role which such Nordic artists as Henrik Ibsen, Edvard Munch, Knut Hamsun and August Strindberg played in breaking through the smug and often hypocritical surface of late-nineteenth-century bourgeois life. (Just as it is impossible to think of the various developments of existentialist philosophy in our century, without the example and inspiration of the early- to mid-nineteenth century Dane Søren Kierkegaard.) In such disturbing images of Munch's as the 1885—6 *The Sick Child* and the 1893 *The Scream*, we witness the birth of modern Expressionism in painting; while Hamsun's subjectivity, fragmentariness and intense lyricism once prompted the Nobel Prize-winning author Isaac Bashevis Singer to remark that 'The whole modern school of fiction in the twentieth century stems from Hamsun.'[47] Ibsen and Strindberg, each in their very different way, remain the foundations of twentieth-century drama's obsession with the social, psychological and spiritual dimensions of the individual's search for meaning in an often indifferent or hostile world.

This much has come to be familiar in art history. What has not been sufficiently remarked is the extent to which the creativity of such artists — particularly Munch, Hamsun and Strindberg — revivified and developed archetypal patterns of shamanic consciousness and longing. These soul-searching artists of the North played an indispensable role in the rebirth of that sense of cosmic religion which Mircea Eliade discerned within the primitivism of much twentieth-century art, and which was such a particular feature of late-nineteenth-century Nordic art and literature.

This was a time when the William Morris-inspired Swedish writer and reformer Ellen Key emphasised that what she called 'spiritual culture' was in need of 'the vast open spaces and the loneliness [of Sweden's Norrland], where a man can grow strong by confronting himself with his insignificance . . .'[48] The Norwegian explorer Fridtjof Nansen spoke similarly of the transformative potential contained within impressions of 'the infinite spaciousness of the mountains', and of the 'supernatural . . . matchless power' of the Northern Lights – a power which Nansen conveyed with telling simplicity in several woodcuts of the mid-1890s. [49] Contemporary painters of all the Nordic countries shared something of this pantheistic sense of nature mysticism, a mysticism which put them back in touch with age-old metaphysical feelings. [50]

In *Night Glow* (1893) and *Summer Night* (1899) by the Norwegian painter Harald Sohlberg (1869–1935), for example, the fjordal location and interplay of foreground detail with the luminous Northern night proclaim a clear neo-Romantic worship of Nature. On initial acquaintance, such work may seem reminiscent of some of the imagery of the German Romantic Caspar David Friedrich (1774–1840), an artist whose work was particularly admired in avant-garde circles in Norway at the end of the nineteenth century. Anticipating late-nineteenth-century Symbolist ideas of an art sensitive to the nuances of the psyche, Friedrich had advised that a painter should depict 'not only what he sees before him, but also what he sees inside himself'. He suggested that an artist close his physical eyes 'so that you see your picture first with your spiritual eye. Then bring forth what you saw inside you so that it works on others from the exterior to their spirit.'[51]

Friedrich spoke as an artist of Christian convictions; and so, despite the parallels which might seem to exist between his work and that of a later painter like Sohlberg, it is important to remember that the earlier artist's Gothic ruins and forests, and couples contemplating moonlight and ships at sea, grew out of an intellectual and emotional climate very different from that of the late-nineteenth century. For example, Friedrich's 1820–6 *Moonrise over the Sea* and Munch's 1899 *Two People: The Lonely Ones* ostensibly share an archetypal Romantic location of shoreline and sea. But between Friedrich and Munch stand Marx and Darwin. Unlike Friedrich's figures, who sense the presence of Christ in symbolic details of ship and moon, Munch's couple see in the surrounding water only the depths of their own enigmatic longing. [52] Munch's 1898–1901 watercolour *The Empty Cross* furnishes further evidence of the extent of late-nineteenth-century doubt about Christian ideas of transcendence. An empty cross stands on a headland, as a pale sun is poised to sink into a grey-blue sea. The sea contains strange, floating faces and figures; on land, lovers and prostitutes cavort behind the stunned, questioning face of a monk-like figure – a self-portrait of Munch himself. [53]

Thirty years before this image asked 'Why?' of life with such post-Darwininian bleakness, the philosopher Eduard von Hartmann had expressed his belief that 'We stand directly before the time when the Jewish-Christian cosmic theory has only the chance of *dying out entirely or becoming pantheistic.'* [54] As we have already seen in Chapter 4, von

Hartmann's *Philosophy of the Unconscious* anticipated Jung's concern to bring the unconscious into fructifying relation with consciousness (and *vice-versa*). It is equally possible to see artists like Munch, Hamsun and Strindberg as anticipating Jung's ideas concerning the power of archetypes and the essential human need to achieve both individuality and (of ultimately greater, all-embracing importance) individuation. Sensitive to the ancient *genius loci* of the North, they offered a variety of animistic encouragement to the soul to hear the earth *speak* once again, and to search for life's meaning through archetypal shamanic paths of suffering and exaltation.

It is the shaman-like quest to conjure cosmos out of chaos — a quest which embraces both 'local' and 'universal' aspects of mythic sensibility, to use Campbell's terms once again — which gives their work deeper resonance than that of a neo-Romantic like Sohlberg. Excellent painter though Sohlberg was, his empathy with the Nordic landscape remained some way short of the transformative depths explored by Munch, Hamsun and Strindberg (and, as we have seen, Gunnar Ekelöf, who wrote penetrating essays about each of these artists). In his 1933 study *Dionysus: Myth and Cult* Walter F. Otto would suggest that true poets are 'divers' who constantly re-enter 'the eternal depths.'[55] In a lecture tour of 1891, Hamsun (1859–1952) had already digested this idea, maintaining that the true role of literature was 'to pursue thought in its innermost concealed corners, on its darkest and most remote paths, in its most fantastic flights into mystery and madness, even to the distant spheres, to the gates of Heaven and Hell.'[56] The shamanic implications of Hamsun's words are developed in his three great novels of the 1890s, *Hunger*, *Mysteries* and *Pan*.

From a shamanic point of view, it is intriguing to consider Hamsun's state of health while writing *Hunger*, the novel that established his reputation upon its publication in 1890. Choosing to isolate himself in the south of Norway's Valdres valley in order to write, Hamsun spoke of working in the grip of an hallucinated synaesthesia, in which he saw 'tones, notes, rhythms floating in the air not far away from me, like lines of light which I can hear.' Before the novel was finished, he had to write with a cloth bound around his left hand, because he was unable to bear the touch of his own breath on his skin.[57] A similarly exacerbated sensitivity marks the chief character of *Hunger*, a would-be writer who tramps the streets of Christiania (as Oslo, the capital of Norway, was then known) at the mercy of both an empty stomach and the quicksilver shifts of his own moods and aspirations. The result was a ground-breaking novel of refined psychological penetration and no little humour. Eschewing conventional ideas of morality and plot, *Hunger*'s prose — which seems as fresh now as the day it was conceived — reveals what Hamsun elsewhere called 'untrodden, trackless journeyings by brain and heart, strange workings of the nerves, the whisper of the blood, the entreaty of the bone, all the unconscious life of the mind.'[58]

There was a good deal of Hamsun's own life in the book, for he had experienced years of hard labouring and general scuffling for a living in the 1880s. However, the hunger of the novel is essentially psychological and metaphysical in nature. The influence of von Hartmann's *Philosophy of the Unconscious*, a book which Hamsun had praised while discussing it with friends in Copenhagen in 1888, is clear: at one point, the narrator of *Hunger* describes himself as 'nothing but a battleground for invisible forces.'[59] From a Jungian point of view, *Hunger* is a revelatory study of the creative tensions of the self's conscious and unconscious drives — of the shifting relations of persona and shadow.

Displaying a mediumistic trust in the promptings of his unconscious, the protagonist of *Hunger* is a striking combination of trickster figure and potential shaman. What others may see as a series of humiliating reversals of fortune, he experiences as initiation into deeper levels of being. Breaking social conventions practically every time he speaks, often to extremely humorous effect, he is clearly a man in search of metamorphosis. Physical, erotic and social privation all underline the paradoxical fact that he only really comes alive through the abstinence which an overwhelming, yet unspecified sense of longing breeds in him. In the following *Mysteries* (1892) and *Pan* (1894), Hamsun set that longing firmly within a pantheistic context.

Writing to his German publisher Albert Langen in 1894, Hamsun explained his intentions in *Pan*: 'I think of the Northern parts of Norway, the regions of the Lapps, the secrets and wide-spread superstition, the midnight sun; I think of J.J. Rousseau in these parts making the acquaintance of a Nordland girl — that is my book. I am trying to present something of the nature worship, the sensibility, the super-sensitiveness of a Rousseau-like soul.'[60] If the spirit of Rousseau's late-eighteenth-century *Reveries Of The Solitary Walker* — particularly the 'Fifth Walk', with its ecstatic identification with both the immediate natural world and the realm of celestial spirits — informs many of Lieutenant Glahn's meditations in *Pan*, it is Nietzsche's Zarathustra who comes most to mind in the nature reveries and psychological intrigue of *Mysteries*, which Hamsun set in a small Norwegian coastal town.

Both books celebrate the mysteries of a soul developing an animistic capacity for communion with nature; *Mysteries* partly through a refinement of *Hunger*'s innovative, stream-of-consciousness technique of free association, and *Pan* by the sort of measured, lyrical prose which at times turns itself into poetry of the deepest reverie: 'Summer nights and still water and endlessly still forests. Not a cry, not a footfall on the path, my heart was full as of dark wine.'[61] *Pan*'s title is indication enough of the extent of Hamsun's response to von Hartmann's call for a revivified pantheism, rooted in the nourishing soil of the unconscious. An ecstatic character, Glahn teeters on the edge of shamanic consciousness: '. . . all creatures came and regarded me, insects sat on the trees, and beetles crawled on the path. Well met! I thought. The mood of the forest suffused my senses through and through; I wept for the love of all things, and was utterly happy, I yielded myself up in thanksgiving. You good forest, my home, God's peace, shall I tell you from my heart . . . I look up to the hills and think: "Yes, now I am coming!" as if in response to a call . . .'[62]

The forest that Glahn loves so much signifies both a real Nordic forest of spruce and pine, aspen and birch, and the labyrinth of his own unconscious. The Finnish composer Jean Sibelius would later create a similar mythic unity of self and world in his 1926 tone poem *Tapiola*, dedicated to 'the Northland's dusky forests/Ancient, mysterious, brooding savage dreams . . .'[63]; and more recently, the spacious meditations of Jan Garbarek have been informed by a Hamsun-like sense of what Garbarek calls 'the forest we have within us, wherever we go.'[64] The continued potency of Hamsun's pantheistic reverie of the unconscious is also evident in the recent work of Finnish sculptor Olavi Lanu (*b*.1925). Sculpted from ice and wood, boulders, leaves and bark, and even from living plants, Lanu's figures inhabit otherwise unpeopled forest and lakeside with a rapt, Hamsun-like solitude that carries clear mythopoeic and shamanic overtones.[65]

In *Mysteries* and *Pan*, *Hunger*'s play with the unconscious is extended, as Hamsun weaves a polyphonic treatment of problematic animus/anima relations into the continuing dialectic of persona and shadow. Ultimately, all three books reveal a personality in search of — but finally unable to either achieve or sustain — the Great or Cosmic Self of both Jungian individuation and shamanism. One commentator on Jung has described individuation as consisting of 'the awareness on the one hand of our unique natures, and on the other of our intimate relation with all life, not only human, but animal and plant, and even of inorganic matter and the cosmos itself. It brings a feeling of "oneness", and of reconciliation with life . . .'[66] Both Lieutenant Glahn, the lonely hunter of *Pan* whose 'only friend was the forest and the great solitude', and the enigmatic, violin-playing Johan Nilsen Nagel of *Mysteries* are far more at ease with animal and plant, inorganic matter, and finally, the cosmos itself, than they are with society.

Like Glahn, Nagel is an ecstatic, near-shamanic figure, whose reveries take him 'rocking on the sea of the heavens, singing as he fished with a silver hook. His boat was made of scented wood, and the oars gleamed like white wings; the sail was of light blue silk and shaped like a half moon . . . A tremor of ecstasy ran through him. He felt himself carried away and engulfed by the magic rays of the sun . . .'[67] But the intricacies and demands of social life (which naturally include the projections and problems of the unconscious) confound and finally defeat Nagel, just as they do Glahn.

They are both classic outsider figures, restless and uneasy in society, but blessed with an extraordinary mythopoeic — and shamanic — sensitivity to the healing intimacy and grandeur of nature.[68]

In a famous passage in *Mysteries*, Nagel defends what he calls the religious *spirit* in man — by which he does not mean any religion in particular — from the attacks of one Dr. Stenersen, a rationalist who is strongly in favour of so-called progressive liberal thought. Suggesting that we really live only through our experience of symbols, Nagel asks the doctor 'what are we gaining by a pragmatism that robs our life of poetry, dreams, mysticism — are these all lies? What is truth? Can you tell me that?'[69] In the work of Munch and Strindberg, both of whom knew Hamsun and his work well in the 1890s, the pursuit of such questions led to a series of revelatory images and words. Completely unacceptable to bourgeois society at the time, these are images and words which anticipated by some six or seven decades the shamanic insight of R.D. Laing that 'True sanity entails in one way or another the dissolution of the normal ego, that false self competently adjusted to our alienated social reality: the emergence of the "inner" archetypal mediators of divine power, and through this death a rebirth, and the eventual re-establishment of a new kind of ego-functioning, the ego now being the servant of the divine, no longer its betrayer.'[70]

Munch and Strindberg are the two great wounded healers of Nordic art. If Hamsun's characters hover on the edge of shamanic insight and psychic transformation, Munch and Strindberg plunge over the edge of so-called normality to plumb archetypal depths of initiatory shamanic suffering and eventual wisdom. There is much which links their art thematically, particularly in the 1890s, when their paths joined — and crossed — several times, sometimes to explosive effect. Both men saw themselves as seers — and only attained that status through months and years of painful attention to what they each called 'the Powers' of life.[71]

The Strindberg family came from Norrland: the Swedish Strindberg (1849–1912) grew attached to the idea that he had Lapp (Saami) blood — and hence magical powers — in his veins. He loved the island of Kymmendö, in the Stockholm archipelago, with the sort of passion which could spark the following, shaman-like declaration: 'The great Pan is indeed not dead, though he has been ill. And now an Orpheus must go down into the underworld to sing life into the stones, which are not dead, only sleeping.' Seeing himself as 'the rival' of Orpheus, the great shaman-poet of Greek culture, Strindberg did not shrink from seeing it as his role 'to bring back to life an inanimate nature', a nature which had died 'in the hands of the scientists.'[72] Much of his poetry, which unfortunately remains relatively little known in the English-speaking world, takes up this task, as sensitive to the healing powers of wilderness as it is to the dispiriting capacity of humanity to sully such powers by thoughtless, short-sighted exploitation of natural resources. [73]

In a similar vein to Strindberg, Munch (1863–1944) spoke of the 'primordial power' with which a poet, or artist, could affect people, and of the fact that no matter how many mysteries scientists might come to explain, there would always be more to nourish the searching soul. Like Strindberg — and Hamsun — Munch had a strongly animistic feeling for life. He loved the winding streets and shoreline of Åsgårdstrand, the little town in the Oslo fjord which stimulated some of his most dream-charged work, such as *Starry Night* (1893) and *Girls on the Jetty* (1901), with the same sort of religious intensity with which Hamsun experienced northern Norway, or Strindberg the Stockholm archipelago. 'During the pale summer nights', wrote Munch, 'forms take on fantastic tones; at the seashore, stones appear like trolls and they move in the moon's rocking reflection. Then one has to move in silent adoration.' [74]

In 1897 Munch portrayed himself as Orpheus in *Self-portrait with Lyre*. Plucking the magical instrument, the painter's fingers stream blood. The idea of art being produced from one's life-blood was crucial to Munch, who insisted several times that he did not believe in art which had not forced its way into being from the need to open one's heart. *The Flower of Pain*, a cover design for a magazine on which he and Strindberg collaborated in 1897, epitomises this conviction, in an image of unmistakable shamanic import. Throwing his head back in agony, the naked figure of Munch clutches his wounded heart, as blood flows down from it to nourish the sort of slender, rising stem and flower which can also be seen as a nascent Tree of Life. Shamanic overtones are also manifest in the slightly earlier *Self-portrait with Cigarette*. Like a seer, Munch emerges from a hazy, dream-like background, his penetrating gaze cutting through blue-tinged, drifting cigarette smoke with hallucinatory intensity. As in so much of Munch's work, the mask-like face floats into focus from a psychologically enigmatic background shadow.

Art historians have speculated on the extent to which this 1895 image was influenced by the dramatically lit photographic self-portraits which Strindberg had taken by remote control a decade earlier. [75] Both artists were fascinated by photography and the role it played in Spiritualist circles towards the end of the nineteenth century. Strindberg once tried to cure his children of their illnesses by taking 'curative' photographs of them, and Munch used slow and double exposure techniques for many years, producing photographs of buildings, models and himself which have an unsettling, aura-like quality to them. [76] Whatever the medium they used, both men saw art as a means of getting in touch with elemental, metaphysical forces, forces that might give back to art something of its ancient transformative power.

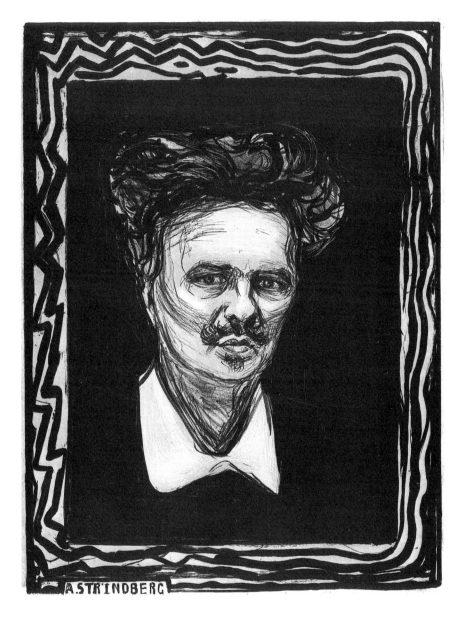

33 Edvard Munch *Portrait of August Strindberg* 1896 black and white lithograph 61 x 46 © Oslo Community Art Collection Munch Museum Oslo

In July 1896, Strindberg was living in Paris, at the height of what has come to be known as his Inferno crisis, after the title he himself gave to his half-fictionalised memories of the time. Over the previous few years, his Orphic ambitions had gone beyond novels, drama and poetry to embrace painting; he had also resurrected the age-old alchemical dream of creating gold, calling himself a 'poet chemist' and his chemical formulae 'chemical sonnets'.[77] In a neat reversal of Friedrich's advice to painters, Strindberg described himself as 'a naturalist occultist', who wanted to see 'first with my outer eyes and then with my inner eye.'[78] However, there is no doubt that it was Strindberg's inner eye which brought forth the most memorable of his paintings at this time: turbulent grey-green seascapes, with the paint applied thickly with the palette knife; or strangely symbolic landscapes, such as the *Lonely Poisonous Mushroom* of 1893.

It is possible that the red mushroom in the bottom right-hand corner of this painting, which adds a solitary note of naturalism to an otherwise practically abstract (and possibly Friedrich-influenced) composition in pale blue and yellow, is the fly agaric, *Amanita muscaria*, long used in Northern Asia as an intoxicant during shamanic practices.[79] Whether or not Strindberg followed suit has not been established. What *is* certain, however, is that the absinthe which he and his contemporaries consumed in impressive quantities at this time contained the potent oil of thuja, which has strong neuro-toxic and hallucinative properties. Its symptoms are exactly those which Strindberg described in *Inferno*, including feelings of anxiety and physical paralysis, loss of appetite and muscle power, and aural and visual hallucinations.[80]

From a shamanic perspective, it is obvious that Strindberg was courting something more than drugged or drunken distraction during these years. 'In the great crises', he wrote, '. . . when one's very existence is threatened, the soul acquires transcendental qualities.'[81] He spoke indirectly of his longing for rebirth, and in one of the letters which he wrote in July 1896 to Torsten Hedlund, a friend in Sweden, he pondered the fruits of his recent, often terrifying experiences: 'Hallucinations, fantasies, dreams, seem to me to possess a high degree of reality. If I see my pillow assume human shapes and those shapes are there, and if anyone says that they are only (!) created by my imagination, I answer — you say only? What my inner eye sees means more to me! . . . And I hear a sound in my pillow, sometimes like a cricket. The noise that grasshoppers make in the grass has always seemed like magic to me . . .'[82]

The transcendental qualities which Strindberg acquired through the suffering of his Inferno crisis were forged in the meeting of conscious research (into such different areas as the flight of birds, mediumship and world religions, for example) with fructifying, albeit disturbing unconscious energy. The magic of his post-Inferno dramatic work, particularly as revealed in the three-part *To Damascus* (1898–1901), is that it breaks through crusts of character and plot to reveal the alchemy — and the frustrations — of individualism developing into individuation.[83]

Strindberg described *A Dream Play* of 1901 as an effort to reproduce 'the disconnected but apparently logical form of a dream . . . Time and space do not exist; on a slight groundwork of reality, imagination spins and weaves new patterns made up of memories, experiences, unfettered fancies, absurdities and improvisations . . . The characters are split, double and multiply; they evaporate, crystallise, scatter and converge. But a single consciousness holds sway over them all — that of the dreamer.'[84] He had long been aware of Theosophy's pursuit of an esoteric synthesis of Eastern and Western mystical traditions; in both *A Dream Play* and *The Ghost Sonata*

(1907), something of the uplifting spirit of the Upanishads and Buddhism wrestles with the feeling that life here on earth is (literally) Hell, a feeling which Strindberg had developed from his reading of the eighteenth-century Swedish scientist and dream mystic Emanuel Swedenborg.[85] In both plays, there is an unnerving feeling of exploring force-fields of ultimate energies, or 'Powers', as Strindberg and Munch called them; a feeling suggested through both quicksilver, archetypally-inflected dialogue and an extraordinary, metamorphosing pictorial sense: one thinks of the burning Castle at the end of *A Dream Play*, with the flower bud on its roof bursting into a giant chrysanthemum.[86]

With its exposure of human self-deceit and cruelty, and free-flowing treatment of the soul's search for healing metamorphosis, such Strindbergian 'psychotheatre', as the French critic Guy Vogelweith has called it, has an undeniable shamanic quality.[87] Like a great shaman, Strindberg offers us a variety of testing ways to the metamorphosing mysteries of ourselves, countering what traditional shamans would surely have had very little hesitation in diagnosing as the 'soul-loss' of so much of the modern world.

Few painters can have contributed as much to the struggle against such 'soul-loss' as the Norwegian, Edvard Munch. His work is one of the most moving testaments in modern art to the suffering that a great individual may have to go through, in order that humanity be shown the way to a deeper sense of itself. In Jungian terms, Munch's life was one long struggle to achieve individuation.[88] According to the Jungian analyst and writer Aniela Jaffé, such a struggle centres on the fact that 'one must, in the course of life, accept death constantly as a pre-condition of inner transformation . . . Inner death . . . means the sacrifice of the ego and its will, the ceding of this position to a greater personality supraordinate to the human being.'[89] This is the transformative heart of shamanism; and it is the transformative heart of the life and work of Munch.

Born into a family prone to tuberculosis, Munch suffered from the disease himself as a child. When he was five, the disease claimed the life of his mother; when he was fourteen, that of his favourite sister — an event commemorated in *The Sick Child* (1885–6), an image which Munch was to repeat and vary in lithography and oils for much of the rest of his life. Munch's father was a doctor and strict Christian, who died when Munch was in his late twenties. To the young painter who reflects upon mortality in the blue-shrouded *Night (Night in Saint-Cloud)* of 1890, it must have seemed as if the only answer to Christian prayers was the vast, indifferent silence of eternity. In the 1895 *Self-portrait with Skeleton Arm*, Munch contemplates death head-on. His wan face stares directly out at us from the richly inked surface of a black lithograph: a disembodied, skeletal forearm in the bottom foreground of the image emphasises the

34 Edvard Munch *Self-Portrait*
1911 black and white woodcut
53.5 x 35
© Oslo Community Art
Collection Munch Museum
Oslo

extraordinary extent of the thirty-two year old's preoccupation with mortality.

From the point of view of both Jungian ideas of individuation and shamanic symbolism, such an image passes from the realm of the purely personal (an understandable obsession with his own sickly inheritance) to the transpersonal world of archetypes. Like a shaman, Munch here strips self-consciousness to the bone, 'dying' to his old self in order to open the way to replenishing levels of orientation and meaning. He reacted strongly to any suggestion that the preoccupation with death which marks so much of his work was morbid, claiming instead that it represented a sound release, a healthy reaction which one might learn from and live by.[90]

More than once, Munch observed that without sickness and death, his life would have been like a ship without a rudder. This hyper-sensitive individual once scrawled 'Could only have been painted by a madman!' in one of the blood-red arabesques which frame the swaying cataleptic of *The Scream*. But like a great shaman, Munch was to rise above such despair, confident that his imagery might enable people to live their lives with greater clarity and purpose.

In the sequence of paintings and graphics from the 1880s and 1890s which he called *Motifs from the Life of a Modern Soul* (generally known as *The Frieze of Life*, and divided into four sections: 'Seeds of Love', 'Flowering and Passing of Love', 'Life Anxiety', and 'Death'), Munch passed far beyond the surface delights of late-nineteenth-century Impressionism. Ripping away polite masks of social intercourse, he replaced them with primitivistic masks of suffering and desire. Wishing to paint 'living people who breathe and feel, suffer and love', as he summarised his artistic aims in the 'St Cloud manifesto' of New Year's Eve 1889, Munch hoped that people might feel something of the intensity which he wished to bring to such an ostensibly commonplace subject as a couple kissing: 'These two in that moment when they are no longer themselves but only one of thousands of links tying one generation to another generation. People should understand the sanctity of this moment and take their hats off as if in church.'[91]

No matter how blatant its sexual content, it is misleading to interpret Munch's work as simply a release of repressed Victorian sexuality, as José A. Argüelles does in *The Transformative Vision*. Rather than being regarded as 'the perfect accompaniment to the theories of Sigmund Freud, which began to appear in the 1890s', as Argüelles asserts,[92] Munch's work is better seen as an anticipation of Robert A. Johnson's much later, Jungian-inflected belief that the Dionysian ecstasy of art — the experience which enables one to 'stand outside oneself', as one is filled with emotion of divine, transformative power — is to be found 'in the sensuous [rather than the sensual] world, the world of poets and artists and dreamers, who show us the life of the spirit as seen through the senses.'[93]

The sexual energy which courses through such images of Munch's as the 1895 oil *Jealousy* or the 1897 woodcut *In Man's Brain* certainly reveals

35 Edvard Munch *To The Forest* 1897 coloured woodcut 52.7 x 64.7
© Oslo Community Art Collection Munch Museum Oslo

humanity to be human in Freud's understanding of the term: all-too-human, as it were. Elsewhere, however, the sexuality in Munch's work often flows out of, and into, a sense that, through sexual desire, humanity may begin to experience the full dimensions of its existence, with regard not only to its own history, but to that of the living cosmos: to the ancient presence of those troll-like stones before which Munch felt one should move 'as in silent adoration'; or to the presence of sun and moon, which cast their primordial light on so many of Munch's oneiric images of couples standing by the shoreline, or walking towards the pagan depths of forest and lake.

Such couples stand or walk in what often seems to be an attitude of reverential anticipation; *pace* Argüelles, the consummation they ponder is as much metaphysical as physical. In 1909, Jens Thiis, a distinguished administrator in the Norwegian art world and a friend of Munch, expressed his conviction that 'Munch's artistic temperament has a profound leaning towards the metaphysical, something which gives to his art an air of almost religious celebration of the wonders of life.'[94] Faced only with Munch's most famous work, the 1893 oil *The Scream* — where Munch, painting his neurasthenic experience of hearing 'the scream of Nature', produced an image which has become central to our century's *angst*-ridden sense of itself — many might experience understandable difficulties in concurring with Thiis. But the more one sees work like

The Scream and *Self-portrait with Skeleton Arm* in the totalising, shamanic light of such affirmative, anima-soaked images of Munch's as *Starry Night* (1893), *White Night* (1900), *Forest* (1903) and *The Sun* (1911—16), the more apparent it becomes how right Thiis was. Munch himself spoke of his art as being landscapes from the soul. It is part of the metamorphosing magic of Munch's ensouling vision that he often let the simplest of materials and designs speak of the most profound wonders, as in the way the grain of cheap packing case wood becomes the spacious ground of reverie in such emblematic woodcuts as *Melancholy* and *Moonlight*, both from 1896, *The Kiss* (1897/8) and *Towards the Forest* (1897/1915).

Insofar as Munch's celebratory, pantheistic feeling for life has been acknowledged by critics, it is usually seen as belonging to his later years. Certainly, it is unsurpassably present in the mandala-like synthesis of semi-abstract design and rugged coastline which distinguishes his enormous mural *The Sun*. However, as early as 1895, Munch's diary reveals the following animistic combination of religious ideas: 'A drop of blood is a whole world, with a sun at its centre and planets — and stars — and the sea is a drop of blood, a tiny part of a body — God is within us and we are within God — primitive and original light is everywhere, shining out wherever life is found — and everything is movement and light — Crystals are born and grow like a child in the mother's womb — and the flame of life burns even in the hardest stone . . .'[95]

36 Edvard Munch *The Sun*
1911—6 oil on canvas
455 x 780
Oslo University Aula
(end wall)
© Oslo Community Art
Collection Munch Museum
Oslo
Photograph: O. Vaering, Oslo

Like that of a shaman, Munch's mythopoeic sensitivity was forged through initiatory trials of suffering and solitude. His sense of what Eliade called cosmic religion grew in direct proportion to the painful honesty with which he faced the complexities and contradictions of his psyche: image after image in Munch's work reveals the urge to integrate persona and shadow, animus and anima, individual and Cosmic Self. In *Red Virginia Creeper*, a major Expressionist painting from 1900, nature seems to haemorrhage in sympathy with the painter's plight — with his desperate need to transform his consciousness. Munch received treatment for alcoholism and mental exhaustion several times in his life, undergoing electro-shock treatment in a Copenhagen clinic in 1908—9. But like a shaman, again, Munch's tremendous inner strength and openness to both the vicissitudes of experience and archetypal dream dimensions gave him access to worlds of transpersonal, healing imagery.

The extent to which such imagery partook of an archetypal dimension far beyond the imaginative scope of contemporary medical practice is nowhere more evident than in *Starry Night* (1893), the most resonant of all late-nineteenth-century treatments of the suggestive magic of the famous 'blue hour' of Nordic summer twilight.[96] In a thorough discussion of the painting, Louise Lippincott has recently revealed the esoteric fusion of Paradisal mythologies — Biblical, Norse and Hellenic, among others — which underlies this great work. Lovers' shadows touch a garden fence, which runs towards the sinuous Åsgårdstrand shoreline, under the massive, merged crowns of linden trees. The star-strewn infinity of a summer night enfolds all: there is an overwhelming feeling of well-being, of what Gaston Bachelard called 'cosmic reverie', in an image which — as enigmatic and multi-toned as it is simple — epitomises Bachelard's conviction that 'Space, vast space, is the friend of being.'[97]

As Lippincott points out, the equation of urbanism and modernity which was prevalent in Central Europe at the time that this work was executed was not felt as anything like binding by Munch. On the contrary: Munch happily combined sophisticated avant-garde ideas of colour, line and an increasingly flattened picture plane — ideas which he absorbed and developed during his many visits abroad — with a primitivistic approach to the resonance of both the *genius loci* and archetypal theme. Munch's great *Dance of Life* of 1899/1900, for example, takes place not under the lights of any urban dance hall, but in the hallucinatory light of a midsummer night, at the edge of the Oslo fjord. And of all the painters of the early modern period, it is Munch who offers the greatest range of 'site-specific' variations upon the *ur*-theme of the Tree of Life, or *axis mundi*.

The apotheosis of Munch's revivification of this theme is *Metabolism* (1898—1918), which places human self-consciousness firmly within an ancient, tripartite shamanic framework. It is an image which Munch regarded as central to his life's work, and where the totalising, sacred nature of his understanding of sexuality is fully apparent. In the middle of a

37 Edvard Munch *Metabolism or The Transformation of Matter (Man and Woman in a Wood)* *c.*1898 but overpainted later *c.*1918 oil on canvas 175 x 143 (excluding painted frame) © Oslo Community Art Collection Munch Museum Oslo

Hamsun-like forest, a naked man and woman stand on either side of an imposing tree trunk; the blue in the background distance could equally well be sky or water. Munch made a wooden frame for the painting, with details in low-relief: at the bottom, we see the roots of the central tree mingling with a human and an animal skull, suggesting the Underworld, while at the top, the tree's branches become masked by the walls of an imaginary, ancient Paradisal settlement. With its glowing streaks of primary red, yellow and blue, the bark of *Metabolism*'s central, world-bridging tree exalts the mystery of nature's shape-shifting divinity.[98]

During Munch's lifetime, the shamanic intensity of his feeling for landscape was echoed by another outstanding Nordic artist, the Icelandic painter Jóhannes S. Kjarval (1885–1972). In an age when many Central European (and not a few Nordic) artists came to feel that to work within what they regarded as an outdated Romantic landscape tradition was irrelevant to the urban imperatives of modernity, Kjarval continued to insist that 'the landscape has a thing or two to tell.'[99] What the vast and primal Icelandic landscape told this sophisticated student of world art was revealed in work noteworthy for both closely focussed, living detail and bold, sweeping design. In the 1931 *Summer Night at Thingvellir*, for example, the irradiated celebration of the lava-ridden hills and plains of the historic site of the first of all parliaments conjures a landscape of both pulsating animal presence and spiritual grandeur.

Attending to the language of the Icelandic wilderness — the profundity of its silences, the startling play of its unpolluted light over mountain and lake — Kjarval produced such other potent animistic images of the mid-1930s as *On the Shore of Dreams* and *Yearning for Flight*, which respectively revivify archetypal shamanic symbols of soul boat and animal spirit or familiar. The animistic quality of so much of Kjarval's work from this time — such as the ink and watercolour *Flowering Head* of 1940, with its metamorphosing combination of profile head and profusion of wild flowers — remains undiminished in such later images as *First Snow* (1953), *Mountain Milk* (1955) and *Esja in February* (1959). Here, as in so much of Kjarval, the spirits of Pan and the Earth Mother are very much alive. It is hard to imagine imagery more distant from the meretricious novelty of a good deal of the British and American Pop Art which was soon to dominate the international art world.

Since Munch's death, two Nordic artists have been of particular

38 Jóhannes S. Kjarval *Summer Night at Thingvellir* 1931 oil on canvas 100 x 150
© Listasafn Islands (National Gallery of Iceland) and heirs
Photograph: Kristjan Petur Gudnason

importance in extending the shamanic import of his work. They are the Dane Asger Jorn (1914–73) and the Norwegian Frans Widerberg (*b.*1934). As already mentioned, Jorn considered Scandinavia to be the 'dream centre' of Europe, believing that Nordic art epitomised what he called the joy of dreaming in 'a naked imaginative field . . . on the edge . . . of being, truth and life itself'.[100] Widerberg has spoken similarly of his own art: 'Deep inside me I find a vision, I try to bring it out, make it shine and be recognised by others . . . The inner landscape — that is what I am looking for.'[101] Jorn's dreams contained a strongly chthonic element, while Widerberg's inner journeys are often distinguished by their aerial, transcendent quality. Taken together, their art presents a rejuvenation of the range of shamanic 'miracles' of which Mircea Eliade spoke — miracles which 'stimulate and feed the imagination, demolish the barriers between dream and present reality, open windows upon worlds inhabited by the gods, the dead, and the spirits.'[102]

Like Munch, Jorn suffered from tuberculosis, and in the early 1950s, wrote about the importance that illness might have in helping to shape a person's creative destiny. A manuscript from this time which he called *The Human Animal* ends with the Taoist-like thought that 'nothing is eternal that is not earthly and nothing is earthly without being a part of eternity.'[103] The shamanic overtones of such reflections are also present in a subsequent description of the creative act: 'During every really creative act', wrote Jorn in 1958, 'the artist finds himself homeless. To overcome this state he has to call up his last reserves of strength. This mobilization of all his creative and formal resources, this passionate struggle with the medium, cannot be imitated. It is every man for himself. This explains the magic power of art. In every real experiment there is a zero point, where absolutely nothing can be predicted. A creative train of thought is set off: the unknown, the unexpected, the accidental, the disorderly, the absurd, the impossible . . . Art cannot be argued.'[104]

The late Guy Atkins summarised the result of such ideas as being Jorn's creation of a ' "chaosmos" . . . a world caught in the act of becoming . . . which represents what Klee calls a "primal state of myth" . . . a world of images that extends from the imaginary through the marvellous to the magic, and encompasses the whole range of spontaneous imaginative experience.'[105] In a painting like the 1958 *Re-encounter on The Shores of Death*, Jorn's debt to Munch is apparent in the central image of a couple by the edge of a mythical shoreline. However, here as elsewhere, Jorn's fluid and diverse approach to the overlapping relations of colour and form places his strongly primitivistic work intriguingly between figuration and abstraction, inviting a post-Munch range of 'form-giving' participation from the viewer.

Werner Haftmann, who like Guy Atkins knew Jorn well, once called him 'a king of the elves, an itinerant Odin'.[106] Jorn's life was full of travel, research and projects — both individual and collaborative — dedicated to re-awakening us to our participatory, creative place in what he felt was the paradise on earth which we had neglected for far too long. He had a strong interest in both Nordic prehistory and the general history of religions; his notebooks, for example, contain distilled reflections on Mircea Eliade's *The Sacred And The Profane*, and he collaborated with the Danish archaeologist P.V. Glob in gathering material for a book on Danish prehistoric art, as yet unpublished. An unusually intelligent man, blessed with a strong sense of dialectics, Jorn's concept of the North as Europe's 'dream centre' could not have been further from the reductive perversion of Nordic mythology propagated by the Nazis in mid-century. Jorn always argued, for example, that one of the strengths of Viking culture had been its openness to artistic currents from abroad.

There is in Jorn a unique blend of Nordic atavism with twentieth-century internationalism, of poetry with politics. Like Gaston Bachelard, whose portrait he painted in 1960, Jorn was convinced that the reverie and enchantment which art might bring into our lives (as both makers and creative spectators) were anything but escapist: on the contrary, they furnish the true means of awakening the self to the full extent of its transformative potentialities, thus enhancing our capacity for meaningful action. It is hardly surprising that Jorn played the key role that he did in the COBRA and Situationist International groups of the late 1940s and 1950s, for these were the two most important groups of post-World War Two European artists and writers dedicated to the idea that, without a revolution of the imagination, any ideology of 'a better life' (whether peddled by capitalists or communists) is worthless.[107]

The COBRA group of 1948–51 – the name signified the first letters of Copenhagen, Brussels and Amsterdam, where most of its members lived, but also struck a deliberate note of empathy with the animal world – stressed spontaneity and improvisation in the creation of both imagery and social life. Besides Jorn, COBRA contained such distinctive artists as Egill Jacobsen and Carl-Henning Pedersen, both from Denmark, and Holland's Karel Appel and Constant. The revolution of the imagination which such artists pursued took them back to the power of prehistoric art and the creativity of children. With its gestural exuberance and high-keyed colour, much of their work – Constant's *The Animal Sorcerer* (1949) or Appel's *Great Bird On The Roof* (1950), for example – contains clear shamanic overtones.[108] A good deal of COBRA activity was collaborative, such as Jorn's work with the poet Christian Dotremont in *I Rise, You Rise, We Dream* (1948) and the intriguingly titled *There Are More Things On The Earth Of A Picture Than In The Heaven Of Aesthetic Theory* (1949), both of which combine shape-shifting imagery (of bird and mask-like figures, respectively) with text. In 1957, while part of the anarchistic Situationist International, Jorn combined with the critical theorist Guy Debord to produce *Fin De Copenhague* – a mordant, collaged parody of post-Bauhaus, functionalist town planning and mass culture.[109]

Throughout his life, Jorn's sense of the healing, transformative power of art was developed and expressed in a totalising echo of the original shamanic unity of creative thought and action. Besides his involvement with painting and graphics, he wrote constantly, publishing several provocative books and numerous articles; distinguished himself in the fields of ceramics, sculpture and tapestry, and in the early 1960s, produced two records of spontaneously improvised *ur*-sounds and melodies with Jean Dubuffet, the French 'anti-cultural' painter and collector and advocate of *Art Brut*.[110]

From the strange, hybrid creatures who populate such paintings as *Birds of Paradise* (1948), *On The Silent Myth* (1950–1) and *Midsummer Night's Dream* (1953), through to the brooding, one-eyed *Outsider* (1964) and shape-shifting landscape, figures and masks of *In The Beginning Was The Image* (1965), Jorn's painting bears the unmistakable imprint of shamanic consciousness. Despite his belief in the possibilities of an earthly paradise, his primitivism was rarely idyllic. The pressures of the Cold War manifested themselves in such violent images as *The Eagle's Share*

(1949–50); elsewhere, he often chose to expose creative tensions and contradictions in himself, as in *The Timid Proud One* (1957) or *Loss of Centre* (1958). *Stalingrad, No Man's Land or The Mad Laughter Of Courage*, which Jorn worked on intermittently from 1956 to 1972, is an enormous, chilling image, its snow-white wastes and ghostly shards of human presence a painfully considered, inner response to the human tragedy and obscene scale of modern war.[111]

When Jorn *did* strike a lyrical note, as in *Letter To My Son* (1956–7) and *In The Wingbeat Of The Swans* (1963), it carried with lasting resonance. The former is a magical, free-floating orchestration of troll-like figures and nature spirits, emerging from the depths of Nordic folk memory; while the latter is one of the finest examples of his healing powers of spontaneous, metamorphosing dream imagery. There are no swans to be seen in the 2×3 metre painting which now hangs in the Stedelijk Museum in Amsterdam (and which is so reminiscent of Gunnar Ekelöf's poem 'Swan', where the poet hears wild geese one morning, trumpeting

> To the north? The south?
> Northward! Northward! —

reminding Ekelöf of a freshness deep within himself which no-one could deny, not even the poet himself.[112]) Eschewing naturalistic representation, Jorn's spacious passages of liquid, cool-toned loops and swirls of paint offer a sweeping subliminal impression of the flight of the Nordic imagination, conjuring primal realms of mythopoeisis and metamorphosis.

In the same year that he created this magnificent evocation of the spirit of *participation mystique*, Jorn was interviewed by the Copenhagen newspaper *BT*. Given the range of his interests and achievements — and his recent refusal to accept a prestigious award from Denmark's Establishment — it is natural that the interview should have ended with the question 'Who are you really, Asger Jorn?' Jorn replied: 'Do you know the village shaman, the wizard who has a sense of the supernatural and a little bit of magic? Johannes V. Jensen has written about this recluse who sits around in the villages and scratches about in the ashes and discovers the oddest things. They are called madmen . . . but people have always respected them because they represent magic and everything that's strange and inexplicable in life.' The reporter then pressed Jorn as to whether or not he was a shaman. 'Well,' said Jorn, 'how is one to answer that? . . . don't you know about the shamans?'[113]

Jorn's world of magic and 'everything that's strange and inexplicable in life' could not have been further from the trends which dominated the international art world in the early to mid-1960s. Obsessed with the idea

40 Asger Jorn *Letter To My Son* 1956–7 oil on canvas 130 x 195.5
Tate Gallery, London
© Arthur Tooth and Sons, London

that art's role be defined in relation to the material and social progress of city life, art critics and enthusiasts alike celebrated Pop, Op and all things dedicated to the omnivorous gods of industrial technology and so-called International Modernism. And these were gods, or idols, which had recently begun to hypnotise certain sections of the Nordic art world.

Thus, when Frans Widerberg exhibited his highly Romantic painting *Landscape, Torvo* for the first time in Oslo in 1963, modernist critics were quick to dismiss what they regarded as its 'antiquated formal language . . . beating on reaction's little drum'. To such observers, Widerberg's flagrant disregard of the Norwegian avant-garde's obsession with one or another variety of either abstraction or Pop Art could only signal what they called a position of 'spiritual isolation' in the modern world.[114]

One of the costliest mistakes of the International Modernism of the 1950s and 1960s (particularly evident in architecture, but no less damaging to the rest of the arts) was its insensitivity to the *genius loci* – to both the general ethos of a spirit of place and the specific details of places, as it were. It was Widerberg's so-called spiritual isolation that, in fact, first made him sensitive to the Nordic feeling for landscape which is manifest to such potent effect in the work of Hamsun, Strindberg and Munch.

Lying on the western edge of the Oslo fjord, the small island of Torvo

41 Frans Widerberg *Landscape, Torvo* 1963 oil on canvas
112 x 161
Collection of the Artist
© courtesy, the Artist
Photograph: O. Vaering, Oslo

42 Frans Widerberg *Landscape, Torvo* 1986 oil on canvas
115 x 145
Collection of the Artist
© courtesy, the Artist
Photograph: Jan Ung, Oslo

has meant as much to Widerberg over the past thirty years as Kymmendö did to Strindberg or Åsgårdstrand to Munch. In the 1986 version of *Landscape, Torvo*, the naturalistic colours of the 1963 painting have been transformed into a vision in primary colours, ablaze with numinous power. Such intense, transmutative empathy with the details of place has enabled Widerberg to dig deep into ancient layers of shamanic consciousness. Bringing such consciousness into new light, his art supplies a splendid demonstration of the import of Gaston Bachelard's belief that 'Imagination is not, as its etymology would suggest, the faculty of forming images of reality; it is rather the faculty of forming images which go beyond reality, which *sing* reality.'[115]

Widerberg's interest in shamanic ideas is made explicit in *The Cave*, a large painting from 1987 which sings several ideas – or layers – of place and time into being. In a glowing red and yellow space, which is cut across horizontally by a narrow, deep blue-black river of space and time, an upright, elongated female figure seems to dream images of Paleolithic cave art (such as the famous horned sorcerer of the Trois Frères site) into existence. Shamanic lines of communication flow around her, charging her body with startling pockets of light and energy. The image is the clearest indication to date of Widerberg's time-travelling, shamanic concerns. However, those concerns have been no less evident in work which has often drawn its initial inspiration from the more immediately-rooted achievements of Edvard Munch.

The affinity which Widerberg has always felt for Munch's work is particularly evident in an image like the lithograph *Couple* (1979), where a naked pair of lovers embrace at the end of a jetty, against a background of deep blue space. However, as is the case with Jorn, thematic echoes of the great Norwegian have been absorbed and transmuted within a language of inspiring freshness. Through a broad swathe of luminous yellow, for example, the jetty in *Couple* has been transformed into a near-abstract plane of pure energy.

To see, says Widerberg, is to listen to the language of light. What the painter hears is turned into visual poetry through the use of a concentrated palette of vibrant reds, yellows and blues, with the occasional touches of green and orange, ochre and black. Such a palette takes us into a world outside history: a metaphysical world of mythopoeic longing for both human contact and the infinite. Peopled by horses and riders, naked, contemplative couples and hovering, ecstatic figures, Widerberg's imagination conjures the farthest edge of experience, as in *Hoverer Over A Deep Valley* (1974), an image of glorious, shamanic exultation, or the haunting *Celestial Rider* (1979). Transcendent as they are, such images of primal reverie remain faithful to the earth, recalling a time when a similar sense of *participation mystique* flowed out of bodily experience, in cultures of this-worldly metamorphosis and natural piety.

One has to go back to the horse and chariot solar myths and rock engravings of the Scandinavian Bronze Age to encounter the sort of animistic vitality and shamanic intimacy between the human and animal worlds that Widerberg conveys in such paintings as *Swan/Rider* (1974), the lithograph *Landscape with Figures and Horse* (1977), and the woodcuts *Bird, Horse* and *Winged Dog* (1986).[116] Such atavistic power is embodied in a language of several layers of signification, as Widerberg himself explains: 'I'm not unfamiliar with the abstract [in painting]; nor with the naturalistic, the symbolic or the romantic. But I try to put these together in a new way, as a tool to help penetrate . . . the heart of substance. The colours I use are the colours of the elements to me, so perhaps in my spectrum I'm painting naturalistically; but the colours have their symbolic side too. The red suggests matter, blue the opposite; yellow is energy and green transformation. The point is to put them together in a way that provokes energy . . . for that is what most concerns me — the flow of energy, inside and outside.'[117]

The energy in Widerberg's painterly universe flows from the roots of various cultures and places. As a young artist, the early Italian Renaissance — particularly Masaccio — meant as much to him as Munch or such later twentieth-century masters of an existentially probing art as Marino Marini (1901–80) and Alberto Giacometti (1901–66). From a technical point of view, Bacon has been almost as interesting to Widerberg as Bonnard, a painter who has meant a great deal to the Norwegian from an emotional and spiritual point of view. Plato, Dante and Goethe have stimulated his metaphysical leanings as much as Kierkegaard and

43 Frans Widerberg *Bird* 1986
coloured woodcut 37 x 50
Collection of the Artist
© courtesy, the Artist
Photograph: Jan Ung, Oslo

44 Frans Widerberg *Tarot*
1984–5 etching and aquatint;
details from 2 sets of 10
images, each of total
dimensions 25 x 34
Private collection
© courtesy, the Artist
Photograph: Jim Cooke

Nietzsche; Eliphas Lévi has been as inspiring as Mircea Eliade. In Widerberg's superb *Tarot* etchings and aquatints of *1985*, occult wisdom reminiscent of Ouspensky flows through imagery redolent of both Nordic mythology and Tantric ideas, the whole series sparked by a fresh shamanic fusion of sexual androgyny and spirituality.[118]

Notwithstanding such internationalism, the core of Widerberg's vision is unmistakably Nordic. This is as evident in the contemplative depths of his ultramarine, cobalt and cerulean blues as it is in the fjordal location of so many of his images. Widerberg shares with Jorn the great spiritual legacy of Munch this century, singing worlds of soul and spirit into being through senses attuned to the transcendent implications of the distant soughing of pine forests or the surreal radiance of the midnight sun. And like Munch and Jorn, Widerberg does not shrink from acknowledging the violence which disfigures so much of our existence.

In the lithograph *Avengers* (1973), a helpless, outstretched figure is

clubbed to death by a faceless and grimly intent trio. Reminiscent of Tarjei Vesaas's *The Seed*, the image is as disturbing a protest against the inhumanity of humanity as Munch's *The Murderer* (1910) or Jorn's *Stalingrad* (op. cit.). Declaring himself wary of what he calls the power bargainers in life, Widerberg describes the political implications of his work thus: 'I do try to participate in the world, but from far away ... I'm not representing a "position", but I am appealing, in my way.'[119]

The unprecedented luminosity of Widerberg's images is a shamanic appeal to ensoul the world and ourselves once more. Like Gunnar Ekelöf, the painter encourages us to encounter each other on a trans-ideological basis, in the knowledge that we are all human beings, flawed and frail, but also potentially whole and holy, searching for meaning on a planet spinning in infinity. Schelling believed that every art must always return afresh to the world's 'primordial energy'; his fellow Romantic Philipp Otto Runge was convinced that the painter's function is to create 'symbols of our conceptions of the great forces of the world', realised through colour, 'the greatest art.'[120] It is hard to think of another figurative painter of the past quarter of a century who has developed these quintessential Romantic ideas to the extent that Widerberg — the finest poet of the Northern Lights in painting — has done.

In the lithograph *Nordlys* (Aurora) from 1980, a solitary figure contemplates the incandescent play of the Northern Lights in the depths of both the night sky and the Oslo fjord. We are taken back past Nansen's late-nineteenth-century nature mysticism, to that mysterious presence of 'deep water . . . and lovely fire' which Emanuel Swedenborg recorded in his dream journals of 1743—44, and which signified to him 'Love for what is high. Perhaps.'[121] In Widerberg, that 'perhaps' is given encouragement through some of the most inspiring, shamanically-oriented art of our century.

The sense of cosmic reverie which lies at the heart of Widerberg's images, and the musicality of so much of his work, serve as appropriate introductions to the writer and the musician who furnish two final — and vital — examples of the strength of the shamanic tradition in twentieth-century Nordic culture. Several generations separate the work of the Finnish poet Edith Södergran (1892—1923) and the Norwegian saxophonist and composer Jan Garbarek (b.1947). However, the bridging medium of the art of Widerberg enables one to suggest close connections between the creativity of these two great, essentially lyrical artists.

Garbarek has long drawn inspiration from the painter's ecstatic figures and transfigured landscapes. In pieces like 'Svevende' (Hovering) from the 1975 album *Dansere* (Dancers), or 'Blue Sky' from the 1978 *Photo With Blue Sky, White Cloud, Wires, Windows And A Red Roof*, the saxophonist floats spacious, reflective melodies across uncluttered arrangements, in a manner

46 Frans Widerberg *Hoverer Over a Deep Valley*
1974 oil on canvas 105 x 140
Collection of the Artist
© courtesy, the Artist
Photograph: O. Vaering, Oslo

reminiscent of Widerberg's control of both figure and ground and complementary contrasts of hot and cool colour. In turn, images such as Widerberg's *Celestial Bridge* (1982) — where figures stand, float and tumble in cosmic space, above a magnificent, curving river of primary-coloured energy — bring to mind such poems of Södergran's as 'On Foot I Had To Make My Way Through The Solar System', from the 1919 collection *The Rose Altar*:

> On foot
> I had to make my way through the solar system,
> before I found the first thread of my red dress.
> I already sense myself.
> Somewhere in space my heart hangs,
> sparks streaming from it, shaking the air,
> to other boundless hearts. [122]

Initially dismissed as a megalomaniac who wrote formless nonsense, Edith Södergran is now recognised as an artist of universal stature, largely responsible for the introduction of poetic modernism to the North. [123] Tarjei Vesaas and Gunnar Ekelöf shared a life-long passion for her work: Ekelöf made a pilgrimage to her home in Raivola on the Finnish-Russian border in the late 1930s and quoted from her poem 'Nothing' in *A Mölna Elegy* (1960), his book-length meditation upon a moment in time. His description of her as 'a Persian Princess living in Lapland' captures something of her magic; [124] more recently, the Danish author Thorkild Bjørnvig has called Södergran a 'shaman, gypsy woman, prophetic child'. [125] These are all appropriate words for this tragically short-lived woman, who produced a unique body of 'heart work', as Rilke once described the poet's task. Through her rhythmically free language — a language of both refreshing immediacy and fairytale beauty — Södergran brought ancient flights of the imagination to new life.

She developed this language through years of the most testing personal hardship and suffering. Like Munch before her and Jorn afterwards, Södergran suffered from tuberculosis: she died from the disease fifteen years after she had first contracted it from her father. And her struggle to affirm and exalt existence was not only physical. Coming from a Swedish-speaking minority in Finland, and attending a German-speaking school in St Petersburg, it is little wonder that an early poem of September 1908 confesses the following confusion:

> I do not know to whom to bring my songs,
> I do not know in whose language to write,
> I do not know whose heart to move
> Before whose eyes to stand. [126]

The poem — in which Södergran's characteristic directness is already evident — goes on to curse loneliness, announcing her longing for 'a *heart*' and a human soul that might understand her. Out of the lonely tensions of her erotic and spiritual desires, Södergran created a language of the Great or Cosmic Self. It was a language imbued with both a magical, child-like feeling for Nordic landscape, folktale and legend and a profound depth of existential reflection.

Describing herself as 'a bonfire of joy on mirroring ice', Södergran felt that beauty in life was 'to serve higher powers'. Offering her heart in sacrifice to 'an unknown god', she sang what she called 'pain's great hymn'.[127] An observation in her *Motley Observations* (1919) brings Georgia O'Keeffe to mind: 'It is not necessary to pray, one looks at the stars and has the feeling of wanting to sink down to the ground in wordless adoration.'[128]

Identifying with Orpheus, and believing that 'The inner fire is the most important thing that mankind possesses',[129] Södergran developed a taut, prophetic voice with a strong quality of Zarathustrian 'yea-saying' to it. In 'The Lightning's Yearning', for example, from the 1920 collection *The Shadow of the Future*, the poet pictures herself as an eagle, wheeling above the possibilities of a new world being born from the midst of a lightning storm. Elsewhere in the same collection, her close identification with Nietzsche is apparent in the pantheistic solar worship of several poems, particularly 'Animalistic Hymn'. Here death is faced, and accepted, with typical equanimity:

> There will come a day when our ashes will crumble,
> it does not matter when it is.
> Right now the sun shines deep into our hearts
> releasing us from every thought
> strong as the forest, the winter and the sea.[130]

Technical considerations aside, Södergran's greatness as a poet lay in her shaman-like ability to move convincingly between reverie of this-worldly forest, winter and sea and the ascensional heights of such poems as 'On Foot I Had To Make My Way Through The Solar System' and 'The Lightning's Yearning'. And when such heights finally acquired overtones of Christian transcendence, as in the famous title poem from *The Land that is Not* (1922), the poet could still remain faithful to the mystery and the beauty of the earth. In *The Land That Is Not*, the poem 'My Childhood's Trees' finds Södergran being reproached by the companions of her youth. Growing up to be 'a human being, foreign and hateful', she has forgotten the magic of childhood, of *participation mystique*:

> Now we want to tell you your life's secret:
> The key to all secrets lies in the grass in the raspberry patch.

> We would knock against your forehead, you sleeping one,
> we would wake you, dead one, from your sleep.[131]

In 'Homecoming' these same trees rejoice that the poet has returned 'from foreign lands' to rest her head in the grass, in the company of forest, shore and lake. Drinking power from 'the smallest and tenderest grasses', Södergran's shamanic sensibilities finally embraced both such pantheism and the monotheistic might of the protector who mercifully reaches out his hand to her.[132]

Just as Södergran's imagination can transport us from the intimacy of a woodland walk to the transparent majesty of the spaces which exist as much within us as without, so does the music of Jan Garbarek bridge worlds. Originating in impulses drawn from jazz, in particular the music of John Coltrane, Miles Davis, Albert Ayler and Johnny Hodges, Garbarek's mature voice is at times as close to twentieth-century classical music as it is to the folk music of his own country. He has spoken of his desire to be part of his own tradition, which he most certainly is. But as is the case with Munch, Jorn and Widerberg, a broad, yet discriminating internationalism nourishes the Nordic depth of his vision. Musicians as diverse as the Swedish pianist Bobo Stenson, American guitarist David Torn, German bassist Eberhard Weber, Norwegian drummer Jon Christensen and Brazilian percussionist Nana Vasconcelos have played a vital role in the development of Garbarek's music, which has always evinced a concern for subtly attuned group interaction.[133]

A poet of the saxophone, Garbarek sings worlds of soul and spirit into being with a uniquely resonant sound. On both tenor and soprano, as well as wood flute, it is a sound shot through with the Nordic *genius loci*: now redolent of the still, twilight gloom of Northern forests, or the keening of winter storms across mountain plateaux; now bringing to mind Ekelöf's 'sunrise over the troll lake, the hot fragrant hill of wild strawberries in the midday sun, the bells in the forest and the clear, echoing voices around the lake in the evening.' Like his sound, Garbarek's haunting compositions are full of the melancholy 'cry' of the North. But if Garbarek's music often conveys a sense of intense, yearning reflection, it also embodies irresistible feelings of healing, participatory joy, as in much of the noble, rhythmically diversified, five-part 'Molde Canticle' from 1990.

The brooding, tensile power of an earlier composition — the minor-keyed 'Vandrere' (Wanderers), from the 1976 recording *Dis* (Haze/Mist) — furnishes a particularly striking example of the Nordic spirit in Garbarek's art. As the shape-shifting, primal melodies of a wind harp give way to an extensive improvised duet by Garbarek and American guitarist Ralph Towner, the plangent accents in the music bring to mind Hamsun's 'untrodden, trackless journeyings by brain or heart', no less than Munch's

47 Jan Garbarek and Eberhard
Weber, The Royal Northern
College of Music Concert
Hall, Manchester, Winter 1990
Photograph: © Sefton
Samuels

love of the Åsgårdstrand shoreline or Ekelöf's fondness for 'the speech
of the men who wander forever' — as expressed in his poem 'I Do Best
Alone At Night', from the collection *Strountes* (Rubbish) (1955).

Much of the 1977 album *Ingentings Bjeller* (Nothing's Bells) which
Garbarek recorded with the Zen-inspired Norwegian poet Jan Erik Vold
(*b*.1939) sounds like the music that Ekelöf had in mind when he advised
us to turn to the wilderness: the music of the forest's gongs.[134] And on
the recent *Legend Of The Seven Dreams* recording, Garbarek's identification

with the Nordic spirit of place recalls both Ekelöf's ecstatic empathy with nature, as expressed in the poem 'Euphoria', for example, and the stimulation which the poet drew in particular from several trips to Lapland. This is particularly the case throughout 'He Comes From The North', the opening, major-keyed piece of the album, where Garbarek develops the melodic and rhythmic potentialities of a bright, wind-fresh Saami *joik* to epic degree.

On the solo soprano and synthesiser 'Mirror Stone', the last track of the album, another (ostensibly) simple melody of folk-like proportions takes us deep into the mystery of reverie. It is as though Garbarek had followed the advice of Tomas Tranströmer to walk 'in the footsteps of the badger', far into the forest — where a single stone beckons us with luminous, occult power. As rooted in the earth as it is open to the sky, such music sings 'pain's great hymn' with a lyrical intensity reminiscent of Södergran, giving our imagination essential, healing room to breathe.

Over the years, Garbarek's wide-ranging, yet fundamentally sculptural approach to improvisation has revealed more and more of a healing, Taoist quality of tenderness. The plaintive, yet affirmative melodies which so distinguish 'Footprints' and 'Still' from the *Paths, Prints* recording of 1981, 'Gentle' and 'Spor' ('Tracks') from the 1983 *Wayfarer*, 'Send Word' from *Legend of the Seven Dreams* (1988) and 'Star', from the 1991 album of the same title, are all particularly moving examples of this. Such tender-mindedness is reminiscent of the veneration with which shamans approach life — a connection reinforced by some of the interviews which Garbarek has given, where he has spoken of the transformative energy which can lie within a capacity for solitude.[135] As with the shamans of old, the courage with which Garbarek has explored worlds of solitude and suffering has led him towards a language of the Great or Cosmic Self.

For example, on the 1979 *Aftenland* (Evening Land), an album of duets with Swedish classical organist Kjell Johnsen, we are taken into an aural landscape of soul-wounding melancholy. It is a landscape reminiscent of the 'birdless, deserted regions' which the Swedish poet Pär Lagerkvist (1891–1974) explored in his collection *Evening Land* (1953). A poignant valediction to the 'absent God' of twentieth-century Christianity, and a lucent expression of natural piety in the face of nature, Lagerkvist's book inspired several of the titles of the compositions on Garbarek's recording.[136] Much of this highly abstract, chromatic music echoes the desolation of such images of Munch's as *The Empty Cross*. Such desolation can be seen to have functioned as a testing, transformative wilderness for Garbarek: for the Middle-Eastern-inflected supplication of 'Tegn' ('Sign'), the concluding piece on the album, is an hypnotic pledge to the mythopoeic heart of existence.

Following *Aftenland*, Garbarek's music has continued to explore tonally abstract regions of sound and space, most notably on the 1984 album *It's OK to listen to the gray voice* — a recording which drew all of its titles from the work of Tomas Transtömer. But the space which Garbarek sings into being here, through the limpid soprano melody which hovers above the distant (A minor and E flat minor) keys of 'It's OK to phone the island that is a mirage', for example, is very different from the space of much of the *Aftenland* album. It is the space of *participation mystique* rather than estrangement; a space that bids us dream and dance ourselves into the sense of wholeness created by both the sonorous, gospel-like meditation and (E major) affirmation of 'Mission: to be where I am' and the vibrant, ecstatic polyrhythms in the latter stages of 'The Crossing Place'.

Apart from a memorial dedication to Andrei Tarkovsky on one piece, no descriptive titles were given to any of the individual compositions on the extraordinary solo album which Garbarek recorded in 1986. But the overall title which he gave the album — *All Those Born With Wings* — was indication enough of the spiritual import of the music. The shamanic qualities which had long been implicit in Garbarek's work were finally made fully explicit in both the aforementioned *Legend Of The Seven Dreams* album and the 1990 *I Took Up The Runes* recording (which featured 'Molde Canticle').

On the *Dreams* album, 'Aichuri, The Song Man' set Garbarek's declamatory tenor and swirling (synthesised) harmonium riffs within staggered, *ostinato* drum patterns, recalling the insistent invocations of shamanic drumming. The very title of the 1990 recording induces images of Odin's initiatory suffering while hanging from Yggdrasill — images confirmed by the savage, spiralling power of the music in parts of the title composition. And on the lovely 'His Eyes Were Suns', from the same album, the Saami *joiker* Ingor Ántte Áilu Gaup joins Garbarek in evoking the presence of a traditional healer of the North, with a spirit as robust and infectious as it is liquid and mellow.

Rilke once called music the 'heart space' which grows out of us.[137] In the heart space that is Garbarek's music, it is possible to sense the resonance of the whole modern shamanic tradition in Nordic culture. Remaining in creative touch with the *genius loci*, this is a tradition which offers us the sort of journey to ourselves which is so sorely needed today. In the words of Tomas Transtömer, from the collection which inspired most of the titles on Garbarek's *It's OK to listen to the gray voice* album, it is the challenging — but potentially fructifying — journey

upward into
the depths.[138]

7 Bewitched by the Word

The *genius loci* of the North, the spirit of its myths and legends, informs one of the most popular works of the twentieth century, J.R.R. Tolkien's trilogy *The Lord of the Rings*. First published in the mid-1950's, the book's revivification of the genre of heroic romance successfully combined elements of Norse, Teutonic and Celtic mythology with key aspects of the symbolism of shamanism.

One thinks of the shaman-like death and rebirth of the wizard Gandalf in *The Two Towers*, book two in the trilogy, and of Gandalf's horse Shadowfax, flying far above the earth 'like the north wind'. As 'Gandalf the White, who has returned from death', the wizard battles with the treacherous Saruman in a contest of dramatic, anti-demonic shamanic import.[1] The spirit of shamanism is no less present in the climactic passage in *The Return of the King*, the concluding part of the trilogy. The initiate Frodo struggles to the death against Gollum for possession of the evil-working Ring of the Dark Lord; as Gollum bites the ring away from Frodo, thus inadvertently releasing him from its power, the shamanic theme of the wounded healer is made explicit, with Frodo's (self) conquering hand being left 'maimed and bleeding'.[2] (The motif of the maimed hand appears in a significant number of the prehistoric cave paintings. The stick-like shamanic figure of Lascaux, for example, has only four digits on each of his hands.)

Written at a time when much avant-garde literary ideology assumed that such a work — as rich in character detail as it is in mythological tropes — must be either impossible or inauthentic, *The Lord of the Rings* is an unashamedly Romantic document of the longing for magic, for psychological enchantment, which many have felt this century. A central passage in *The Return of the King*, where Frodo approaches the heartland of the Dark Power, reveals how much Tolkien's reworking of myth belonged within the European Romantic tradition of a critique of the post-Cartesian mechanisation of life. Frodo sees the 'ashen ruin' of Mount Doom in the deadly wastes of Mordor, and 'the great slave-worked fields away south in this wide realm, beyond the fumes of the Mountain by the dark sad waters of Lake Nurnen . . .'[3] Page upon page of Romantic cultural criticism lies behind Tolkien's further description of the 'great roads that ran away east and south to tributary lands, from which the soldiers of the Tower brought long wagon-trains of goods and booty and fresh slaves. Here in the northward regions were the mines and forges, and the musterings of long-planned war; and here the Dark Power, moving its armies like pieces on the board, was gathering them together . . .'[4]

The cult status of Tolkien's book has done much to divide critical opinion. Whereas C.S. Lewis praised what he saw as Tolkien's fine control of 'the almost endless diversity of scenes and characters — comic, homely, epic, monstrous or diabolic', Edmund Wilson once suggested that the basic appeal of the work is to readers with a 'lifelong appetite for juvenile trash'.[5] But whatever one thinks of *The Lord of the Rings* as literature — and personally, I incline more to Lewis's estimate than Wilson's — there can be no doubt that the fight of Gandalf, Frodo and Sam against the emissaries of Mordor has helped to alert many people to a major theme in post-Enlightenment literature. This is the theme of the search of the exiled, post-Cartesian soul for a language of replenishing mythic power, for a landscape of convincing poetic space.

As we have seen in the work of the Norwegians Knut Hamsun and Tarjei Vesaas, that landscape has been created to potent effect in the medium of post-Romantic prose. The novels of James Joyce, D.H. Lawrence, Herman Hesse and Gabriel Garcia Marquez furnish further rewarding examples of the richness of this theme. Joyce's non-Christian sense of epiphany, Lawrence's visceral intuition, Hesse's Jungian hermeticism and Marquez's magical realism have each manifested one degree or another of shamanic consciousness with regard to the healing potentialities of the creative word. However, no matter how vivid such post-Hamsun prose has been, it is within developments in twentieth-century poetry and theatre that one is best able to identify and examine key aspects of the post-Romantic pursuit of the shamanic power which may still be available within language.

Lorca, whose theory of the *duende* we have already encountered, believed that 'Only mystery makes us live. Only mystery.'[6] His intense empathy with the gypsy and the soil, the 'deep song' and the primordial pantheism of Andalusia mark Lorca as one of the most remarkable pagan outsiders of our century. Think of both the shaman-like lament of 'Sleepless City' in *Poet in New York* (1929), and the poet's contemporary drawing of himself in that city. Depicted as a primitivistic 'cosmic mask', with legs and arms transmuted into twirls of root-seeking energy, Lorca looks away from the *huecos*, the meaningless spaces of modernity. Animals — which are both comforting and menacing in *Poet in New York* — gather around him; while in the far distance, a sycamore-seeded shape (embodiment of the poet's soul, or anima) hovers above the desolate roof-tops.[7]

In his 'Ode to Walt Whitman' (1930) Lorca's critique of an America 'inundated with machines and tears' was fused with what Carlos Bauer has called 'a firm call for — or a return to — an all-encompassing pansexualism'.[8] Like Whitman, whose greatest poems — such as 'Crossing Brooklyn Ferry' — develop a shaman-like philosophy of death and

trans-historical *participation mystique*, Lorca was obsessed with essentially
Romantic ideas of the mysterious totality of life.[9] He once spoke of those
modern poets (including himself) who were concerned with 'pruning and
caring for the overluxuriant lyric tree left to us by the Romantics'.[10] This
is a particularly apt image. For at the same time that it underlines the
different power-to-weight ratio in the language of Romanticism and
modernism, it reminds us that for all their formal and philosophical
differences, modernists such as Lorca, Octavio Paz, Ted Hughes or
Kenneth White are linked to such Romantics as Whitman, Wordsworth or
Shelley through the immense, multiple root system of shamanism.

    In his 1964 review of the first English edition of Mircea Eliade's
Shamanism: Archaic Techniques of Ecstasy, Ted Hughes drew a direct parallel
between the phenomenology of shamanism and 'the basic experience of

the poetic temperament we call "romantic" '.[11] We can begin to appreciate the acuity of Hughes's comment by investigating the way in which modernists have inherited and developed the Romantics' fascination with Orpheus — the mythical musician of pagan antiquity, whose lyre could compel animals and trees, birds and fish to reverent attention (but who paid for such powers with the loss of his wife Eurydice); the psychopomp who journeyed to the land of the dead (but who was finally unable to bring Eurydice back to life); the wounded healer whose sacrificed head carried on singing as it floated down the river Hebrus, and which many poets believe continues to sing today, whenever — in the words of the Dadaist Tristan Tzara — 'The summit sings what is being spoken in the depths'.[12]

Orpheus is a paradigmatic shamanic figure: possessed of god-like powers, he is nonetheless a believable and sympathetic figure in both his ambitions and failures. He exemplifies the human striving to integrate conscious and unconscious forces, Apollo and Dionysus, animus and anima, the ego and the Great, or Cosmic Self. As such, he was bound to have a strong appeal for those Romantics who pursued Hölderlin's dream that humanity might yet learn how to 'dwell poetically' on earth.[13] Novalis, for example, felt that the Orphic myth symbolised the only path to true knowledge, believing that 'The perfected form of every branch of knowledge must be poetic.'[14] One senses Orpheus speaking in Wordsworth's dictum that 'poetry is the breath and finer spirit of all knowledge'; in the fourth act of *Prometheus Unbound*, Shelley spoke of language as 'the perpetual Orphic song' which brought harmony to the otherwise 'senseless and shapeless' flux of thoughts and forms in life. And it is surely Orpheus who lies behind Shelley's challenging declaration in *A Defence of Poetry* that 'the most glorious poetry that has ever been communicated to the world is probably a feeble shadow of the original conception of the poet.'[15]

Orpheus continued to weave his spell upon subsequent generations. We can detect his spirit in Baudelaire's theory of correspondences, which spun a synaesthetic thread between worlds of colour and sound, taste and sight. And he is no less present in Rimbaud, the eruptive visionary who spent 'a season in hell' in pursuit of the alchemy of the word that would enable him 'to give colours to the vowels', and who felt that the poet must be responsible 'for humanity, for *animals* even'.[16] For Rimbaud (1854–1891), to become a poet was to *make oneself* a visionary, a seer, through a shaman-like, systematic derangement of the senses. Thus one might take 'ecstatic flight' into 'the great dream' open to the '*I* [who] is an *other*'.[17] (Much later, another great eruptive visionary, Henri Michaux, would write: 'No need for opium. Everything is a drug for the man who chooses to live on the other side.'[18])

Rimbaud's Orphic dream was both intensified and refined through the symbolist ideas of Mallarmé (1842—1898). Like Rimbaud, Mallarmé acknowledged a fundamental debt to Baudelaire; and in his *Autobiography*, he spoke of 'the Orphic explanation of the earth' as being 'the sole duty of the poet'.[19] For Mallarmé, the flux of the world existed in order to be transmuted into the magical order of literature; the throw of dice in the famous 'Un Coup de Dés' thus symbolises the creation of a poem that challenges 'hazard'. As Raymond Williams has said, in Symbolism, 'the "poetic" word becomes a verbal symbol, at once material in embodiment and metaphysical in its revelation of a spiritual but still sensual reality.'[20] Mallarmé saw his task as being to help elevate consciousness, 'giving a purer sense to the language of the tribe'. For poetry was 'the expression, by means of human language brought back to its essential rhythm, of the mysterious sense of existence: thus it endows our stay on earth with authenticity and constitutes the only spiritual task.'[21]

Orpheus is no less present in the early decades of the twentieth century. The thirty short poems of Apollinaire's 1906—11 *The Bestiary, or Procession of Orpheus* (with woodcuts by Raoul Dufy) are both a modern version of the medieval bestiary and a hymn to:

> the voice which the first light made heard
> And for which Trismegistus found the word.[22]

And in 1922, during some two weeks of extraordinary inspiration, Rainer Maria Rilke wrote his fifty-five *Sonnets To Orpheus*, assuring the twentieth century that:

> . . . Once and for all
> if there is song, Orpheus is there.[23]

Throughout these sonnets, Rilke (1875—1926) revealed his faith in psychic transformation and *participation mystique* as the keys to life. It was a faith which he had declared some two decades earlier, in the beautiful 'Moving Forward' from *The Book of Pictures*. Written at a time when he was beginning to appreciate the integral structure — rather than the literary content — of paintings, the poem forms a magnificent Orphic bridge between Romanticism and modernism, East and West. It is a bridge of pure shamanic consciousness:

> The deep parts of my life pour onward,
> as if the river shores were opening out.
> It seems that things are more like me now,
> that I can see farther into paintings.
> I feel closer to what language can't reach.
> With my senses, as with birds, I climb
> into the windy heaven, out of the oak,
> and in the ponds broken off from the sky
> my feeling sinks, as if standing on fishes.[24]

How can a poet use language, precisely in order to take us beyond that medium? Part of the beauty of Rilke's poem is the way in which his images — such as river shores, birds, sky and fishes — are both utterly concrete, *things in themselves* as it were, and yet also — should we wish to read them as such — symbols susceptible to the transformations of hermeneutics. The poet is able to exploit the spaces between thing and symbol, denotation and connotation, music and 'meaning'. He thus takes us to the border regions of speech. And it is in those regions that language approaches the threshold of the mystery through which Lorca felt we truly live. Submitting to the alchemy of the poetic process, words can be seen to sacrifice the largely utilitarian role which they play in the everyday world. In exchange for such sacrifice — the Latin root of which is *sacra facere* i.e. 'to make sacred' — words assume their mysterious place within the totality of the poem, where they operate on a variety of complex and interlocked levels.

Gunnar Ekelöf suggested that the power of a good poem comes less through its content than through the state of tension *between* the words which form its content — from 'the poet's ability to place word and meaning in such refractive and subtle relationship that the emptiness quivers, lives, registers, transmits, and is a magnetic web of sorts, composed of invisible thread and power lines which attract or repel each other.'[25] Ekelöf's image encourages us to think of the transformative, shamanic power that lies stored in books — the power which Ezra Pound spoke of when he said that 'Properly, we shd. read for power. Man reading shd. be man intensely alive. The book shd. be a ball of light in one's hand.'[26] In the best lyric poetry, the 'materiality' of language — the way a poem focusses attention on the look and the sound, the rhythms and the rhyme of words — fuses with the yeast of simile and metaphor to produce something which is perhaps more astonishing than anything else within the rich legacy of shamanic consciousness. For the more 'substantial' or 'material' a (lyric) poem is — i.e. the more precise, potent and unalterable its language seems to be — the more it is able to precipitate the flight of consciousness, or language, beyond itself.[27]

To read such a poem is to fly beyond the boundaries of the separate ego into the participative depths of existence. The philosopher Francis Bacon once spoke disparagingly of poetry as 'a dream of learning'; but for the French phenomenologist Gaston Bachelard there was no better way to deepen one's knowledge of both self and world than by attending to the call of the sort of primal poetic images which are to be found in 'Moving Forward'. Challenging the frantic pace of so much of our lives today, such images recall us into the *being* of both ourselves and the world. The reverie induced by a great poetic image reminds us, said Bachelard, that 'we were meant to breathe freely'.[28] And in breathing freely, one remembers to breathe in before breathing out. One begins, that is, to absorb more and more of a sense of the true pulse of life, of the cosmicity of existence. The lyric poet — the poet of reverie — is thus a great healer. For reverie has the potential to make both words and life 'immense': it 'sacralizes its object'.[29] As shaman, as conjurer of reverie, the poet no longer describes, 'he exalts'.[30]

There is a marvellous sense of shamanic balance in Rilke's poem, a feeling that the poet is a vibrant channel for the creation of what Joan Halifax calls 'sacred geography' — for the holy intermingling of culture and nature, consciousness and the unconscious. Rilke's images anticipate Bachelard's conviction that reverie teaches us that 'the essence of being is well-being, a well-being rooted in the archaic being.'[31] They also exemplify the development of the Jungian spirit of individuation — the 'wide and inner way' which 'sings from the summit of what is spoken in the depths'.

Like a great shaman, Rilke achieved such psychic balance through a profound engagement with the idea of death, which, he believed, 'is the *side of life* that is turned away from us: we must try to achieve the fullest consciousness of our existence, which is at home in the *two unseparated realms, inexhaustibly nourished by both* . . . The true figure of life extends through *both* domains, the blood of the mightiest circulation drives

49 Marc Chagall *The Poet Reclining* 1915 oil on board 77.2 x 77.5 Tate Gallery, London

through *both*; *there is neither a here nor a beyond, but the great unity* . . . Transience everywhere plunges into a deep being.'[32]

Rilke's last seven words can be seen as a potential *haiku* of unsurpassable profundity. They speak of the sort of truth that only the greatest shamans of twentieth-century lyric poetry, such as Gunnar Ekelöf, Kenneth White and Rilke himself have been able to articulate with the sort of uplifting breadth and lucidity of vision which is to be found, for example, in Rilke's *Duino Elegies* (1912–22), Ekelöf's *Ferry Song* (1941) and White's *Walking The Coast* (1977/80).

For a variety of reasons, the sense of 'sacred geography' that these poets achieve in such works is largely absent from twentieth-century poetry. Instead of Rilke's transformational engagement with death, we are offered Philip Larkin's conviction that:

> Truly, though our element is time,
> We are not suited to the long perspectives
> Open at each instant of our lives.[33]

And instead of Ekelöf's death-fuelled euphoria or White's wonder-filled sense that 'the centre starts from everywhere' – his celebration of 'Ideas like fish and gulls. Swimming thinking, winged thinking'[34] – we encounter poetry which, from a shamanic point of view, is chiefly remarkable for the extent to which it reveals how the crisis of meaning, the split between humanity and nature which Romanticism had addressed, has assumed ever-larger proportions.

Orpheus has thus had to wander through T.S. Eliot's *The Waste Land* (1922), searching for those 'fragments' of spirituality from the past that might shore up the ruins of contemporary existence.[35] He has had to contemplate retreat into the austere Christian mysticism of Eliot's *Four Quartets* (1935–42), or brave the self-triggering detonations of automatic writing, trying desperately to unite self and other, life and death, psyche and politics in the ideological labyrinths of Surrealism.

'A day will come', said André Breton, 'when man will leave the labyrinth having gropingly found at night the lost thread. This thread is that of poetry.'[36] For a twentieth-century shaman-poet such as Allen Ginsberg (*b*.1926), the heart of the labyrinth is the terrain of politics: Orpheus must fight the demonic magic of the power structures which project their own 'Poem' of anti-life. At the height of the Vietnam War, Ginsberg spoke of creating a 'force field' of language with which to counteract and ultimately overwhelm 'the force field of language pronounced out of the State Department and out of Johnson's mouth . . . the War is a Poetry, in the sense that the War is the *Happening*, the *Poem* invented by Johnson and Rusk and Dulles . . . and all those people; so the end of the War is the *Happening*, the *Poem* invented by Spock, or myself, or Phil Ochs, or Dylan.'[37]

Politically-committed Orpheus has also spoken in the subtler, but no less powerful tones of the compassionate pacifism of Robert Bly (*b.*1926), as in *The Light Around The Body* (1968), or tried to unite politics and psyche with the nobility shown by the outstanding Chilean poet Pablo Neruda (1904–73). At other moments Orpheus has turned far inwards, suffering the disintegrative consequences of the hell-on-earth which much of our century has been. Refusing to project the shadow-side of existence onto others (be they nations or the Devil), poets as diverse as Ginsberg and Ted Hughes (*b.*1930) have grappled with the demons inside themselves, experiencing something of the full power (and terror) of shamanic initiation as they expose the psychic wounds of our culture.[38] And through all this, twentieth-century Orpheus has somehow managed to retain faith in the possibility that the healing shamanic power of the word can be preserved and developed; that the breath of poetry — the spirit of soul, of anima — can cure the sickness of an increasingly violent and violated world.[39]

In search of such a cure, the poet of Orphic ambition has looked to the ecstatic tradition of the Sufi mystics for inspiration;[40] reflected long and hard on the importance of both mantra-like repetition and diverse phrase lengths, for the effect they might have on the poet's and reader's understanding of questions of breath (and hence soul);[41] and generally searched far and wide in world poetry for the elements of a language that might ensoul consciousness once more.[42]

One such Orphic traveller through world poetry is the American Gary Snyder (*b.*1930), whose work has always exhibited elective affinities with both shamanism and the Taoist values which underpin much of the lyric tradition in Eastern poetry. Snyder's poetic voice is entirely his own: unfussy, direct and rhythmically free, it is distinguished in equal measure by a warm, yet unsentimental sense of compassionate animism and a welcome, leavening grain of humour — the last quality being particularly evident in his own readings of his work.[43]

As original as Snyder's voice is, it speaks from out of a deep sense of tradition. For Snyder, poetry today should be 'the eagle of experience', the far-ranging, far-sighted distillation of thousands upon thousands of years of spiritual wisdom: 'As a poet, I hold the most archaic values on earth. They go back to the late Paleolithic; the fertility of the soil, the magic of animals, the power-vision in solitude, the terrifying initiation and rebirth, the love and ecstasy of the dance, the common work of the tribe.'[44]

Believing that 'Whatever is or ever was in any other culture can be reconstructed from the unconscious through meditation', Snyder insists that 'primitive' is not a word that means past but *primary and future.*'[45] At the same time, Snyder hopes that what he calls 'the coming revolution' will 'close the circle' and 'link us in many ways with the most creative aspects of our archaic past'.[46] History is thus transmuted to myth. And at the centre of Snyder's circle of mythopoeic intuition, which gathers, synthesises and transforms energy from Taoism and Zen Buddhism, Trickster lore and Jungian psychology, anthropology and ecology, meditation and mythology, stands the primal figure of the shaman — initiate of a world where, as Snyder puts it, 'wilderness and the unconscious become analogous: he who knows and is at ease in one, will be at home in the other.'[47]

'In literature', suggested Thoreau, 'it is only the wild that attracts us. Dullness is but another name for tameness.'[48] Clearly, Snyder's poetics can be seen in terms of a direct line of descent from the mid-nineteenth-century views of the wilderness-loving wanderer who in *Walden, or, Life in the Woods* considered that a lake is 'the most beautiful and expressive feature in a landscape' — for 'It is earth's eye; looking into which the beholder measures the depth of his own nature.'[49] But Snyder's poetics can also be seen in terms of their relation to that faith in the regenerative powers of the unconscious which the Dada artists clung to so fervently during the early decades of this century. And it is in Dada that one finds some of the earliest evidence of the often desperate intensity with which twentieth-century poets have sought the healing magic of the word.

For the Dadaist Jean Arp, poetry was as important a weapon as painting or sculpture in his (essentially Romantic) fight to restore humanity to what he saw as its rightful place within — as opposed to above — nature. In 'Signpost', a short essay which he used as a preface to the retrospective selection of his poems which was published in 1953, Arp spoke revealingly of his life-long fascination with the transformative potentialities of (Orphic) language.

Recalling his adolescence, Arp remarked, 'Even then I was bewitched by the word. I filled page after page with unusual word-combinations and invented unusable verbs from nouns, altered well-known verses and declaimed them constantly with abandon and elation, on and on as if it would never end: stars stars many a star, on purpose to star stars, wood wood many a wood for the purpose of wooding woods, snag snag many a snag for the purpose of snagging snags.'[50] (One is reminded of Kandinsky's similar pursuit of an elemental word magic in *Sounds*.) 'Only much later', continued Arp, 'did I recognise the profound reality of such "senseless jokes" and then I consciously made such events happen. I wandered through many things, creatures, worlds, and the world of appearances began to slide, to grow and be transformed as in fairy tales. Rooms, woods, clouds, stars, hats, were alternatively made of ice, ore, mist, flesh, blood. Objects began to speak to me with the soundless voice of height and depth.'[51]

We can begin to grasp what Arp meant by speaking of the 'profound reality' of his play with language by considering a typically suggestive passage in Mircea Eliade's *Shamanism: Archaic Techniques of Ecstasy*. In the epilogue to this indispensable work, Eliade observes that 'Poetic creation still remains an act of perfect spiritual freedom. Poetry remakes and prolongs language; every poetic language begins by being a secret language, that is, the creation of a personal universe, of a completely closed world.'[52] But the ramifications of such a language spread into the wider world, for 'The purest poetic act seems to re-create language from an inner experience that, like the ecstasy of "primitives", reveals the essence of things.'[53] And in shamanism, the 'essence of things' is their animistic inter-relatedness — as is underlined by the following Inuit (Eskimo) recollection:

> In the very earliest time,
> when both people and animals lived on earth,
> a person could become an animal if he wanted to
> and an animal could become a human being.
> [. . .]
> All spoke the same language.
> That was the time when words were like magic.
> The human mind had mysterious powers.
> A word spoken by chance
> might have strange consequences.
> It would suddenly come alive
> and what people wanted to happen could
> happen —
> all you had to do was to say it.
> Nobody could explain this:
> That's the way it was.[54]

As Eliade emphasises, the shamanic path to such a sense of the totality of life is one of ecstasy. And for Eliade, the pre-ecstatic euphoria of the shaman may well be one of the universal sources of lyric poetry: 'In preparing his trance, the shaman drums, summons his spirit helpers, speaks a "secret language" or the "animal language", imitating the cries of beasts and especially the songs of birds. He ends by obtaining a "second state" that provides the impetus for linguistic creation and the rhythms of lyric poetry.'[55]

Shamans are distinguished from mediums by their overview, as it were, of the *consequences* of the ecstatic experience: they are what Eliade calls 'technicians' of ecstasy. Following Eliade, the poet and essayist Jerome Rothenberg has called the poets of tribal or so-called 'primitive' culture 'technicians of the sacred'.[56] By this, Rothenberg does not mean that such poets are the priestly guardians of the sort of sacred truth which is carved in stone. Rather, they are the shamans of the word, sensitive to the vibrant, shape-shifting wonder of the world, and constantly seeking to bring something of the animistic essence of that wonder into human consciousness. Their language is as alive, concrete and variable as the phenomenon of existence: and it is Rothenberg's belief that the poets of the so-called advanced societies of the West can learn an enormous amount from an engagement with (and contribution to) what he calls 'ethnopoetics'. Together with Eliade's *Shamanism, Symposium Of The Whole: A Range of Discourse Toward an Ethnopoetics* — the anthology which Rothenberg researched in the late 1970s and 1980s with Diane Rothenberg — is one of the essential documents of the revival of shamanic consciousness from Romanticism to today.[57]

In 1975, in a discussion with Rothenberg about oral poetry, William Spanos outlined those aspects of Martin Heidegger's thought which seemed to him to parallel some of Rothenberg's concerns: '. . . Heidegger keeps insisting that the fatal mistake of Western civilisation was when the post-Socratic philosophers translated the word Logos in the sentence "Man is the animal who has Logos" to mean "reason" or "judgement". This metamorphosis, he says, concealed the word's primordial meaning as "talk" or, rather, "oral speech" (Rede). And as a result the West gradually built up a civilization on the foundations of a coercive propositional language, a language of assertion, that in seeking to "take hold of", to master, the world, has ended up alienating "civilized" man from Being, the sacredness of existence, that it is only in the power of human speech to disclose.'[58] Heidegger himself said that 'To reflect on language means — to reach the speaking of language in such a way that this speaking takes place as that which grants an abode for the being of mortals.'[59]

As Mircea Eliade argued time and again, the modern mechanistic myth of History as infinite progress can offer no sense of any such abode. And this is surely a large part of the reason why the Orphic voice has had to struggle so hard both to find a healing language and to be heard this century. It is also why the attempts of poets to heal the split between culture and nature have at times assumed extraordinarily close parallels with ancient shamanic practice. Ernst Fischer's remark that 'In every poet, there is a longing for an original, "magic" language'[60] applies with especial force to all those poets who, like Rothenberg, have reacted against the thinning out of both language and life this century.

Octavio Paz, one of the most distinguished (and independent) of Surrealist poets, has written of the twentieth-century poet's attempt to transcend the ideological falsehoods of history; to resist the sorcery of 'force and numbers' which lies behind today's degradation of life into 'a mere sequence of events'; to conjure the magic of the regenerative word, so that every poem may be 'a Fiesta, a precipitate of pure time'.[61] Recollecting the years which he spent in the company of Surrealist painters and writers in Paris after the Second World War, Paz (b.1914) has said that he and his companions 'did not believe in art. But we believed in the efficacy of the word, in the power of the sign. The poem or painting were exorcisms, spells against the desert . . .'[62] Such spells were intended to induce dreams of resurrection: the resurrection of *participation mystique* – of ecstatic belonging – which is proclaimed in these lines from Paz's 'The Broken Jug'(1955):

We must sleep with our eyes open, we must sleep with our hands,
let us dream active dreams of a river seeking its bed, dreams of a sun
seeking its worlds,
we must dream aloud . . .
sing until the dream engenders and *spouts* from the side of the sleeper
the red wheat ear of resurrection . . .[63]

Such an open-eyed dream (a dream of the inner eye of soul and spirit) cannot help but recall Arp's desire to help people to dream themselves free of the alienating consequences of post-Cartesian rationalism. Equally, Paz's belief that poetry is 'the secret religion of the modern world'[64] cannot help but recall the intensity with which Dada artists addressed the question of the healing potentialities of the twentieth-century Orphic voice; the way in which the river of language might once again flow along the bed of shamanic consciousness.

In 'Note on Poetry', first published in *Dada 4 and 5* in May 1919, Arp's colleague Tristan Tzara spoke of the twentieth-century poet's task of rekindling that most essential of human attributes: hope. The poet must know 'how to recognise and pick up the signs of power we are awaiting, which are everywhere; in the fundamental language of cryptograms, on shells, on rails, in clouds, or in glass; inside snow, or light, or coal; on the hand, in the beams grouped around the magnetic poles, on wings . . . Logic no longer guides us . . . Other creative powers, flamboyant, indefinable, gigantic, are shouting their liberty on the mountains of crystal and prayer.'[65] In a 'Note on Negro Art', published a year earlier in *Sic* (Paris), Tzara had struck a similar shamanic note with his conclusion that 'Art, in the infancy of time, was prayer. Wood and stone were truth. In man I see the moon, plants, blackness, metal, stars, fish. Let the cosmic elements glide symmetrically . . . Mouths contain the power of darkness, invisible substance, goodness, fear, wisdom, creation, fire.'[66]

The shamanic nature of the translogical powers which Tzara and his fellow Dadaists sought was unmistakably manifest in the 'sound poem invocation' which Hugo Ball performed in Zurich on June 23, 1916. The date marks what is perhaps the most famous of all occasions in the history of twentieth-century performance art. Before his recitation, Ball read a few introductory words: 'In these phonetic poems we totally renounce the language that journalism has abused and corrupted. We return to the innermost alchemy of the word, we must even give up the word too, to keep for poetry its last and holiest refuge. We must give up writing secondhand: that is, accepting words (to say nothing of sentences) that are not newly invented for our own use.'[67]

Of the performance itself, Ball later recalled: 'I had made myself a special costume . . . My legs were in a cylinder of shiny blue cardboard, which came up to my hips so that I looked like an obelisk. Over it I wore a huge coat collar cut out of cardboard, scarlet inside and gold outside. It was fastened at the neck in such a way that I could give the impression of winglike movement by raising and lowering my elbows. I also wore a high, blue-and-white striped witchdoctor's hat.'[68] As Ball could not walk inside his cylinder, he had to be carried on stage. With three music stands of material spaced around him, he began to recite to an audience which, after an initial period of confusion, burst into laughter, screams and applause:

> gadji beri bimba
> glandridi lauli lonni cadori . . .
> hollaka hollala
> anlogo bung . . .
> bosso fataka
> ü üü ü . . .[69]

Ball's explanation of these sound poems could not have been more shamanic in import: 'We have charged the word with forces and energies which made it possible for us to rediscover the evangelical concept of the "word" (logos) as a magical complex of images.'[70] And Ball and the Dadaists were not alone in such a rediscovery: several years before Ball's performance, the Russian Futurist poet and dramatist Velemir Khlebnikov (1885—1922) had become fascinated by the possibilities of a new 'transrational' language. In the language of *zaum* new meanings would be created simply out of the sound of each element of the word. Thus in Khlebnikov's famous 'Invocation to Laughter' the whole composition is a series of variations on the Russian word *smekh* (laughter).[71] In contrast to the sheer 'materiality' of this poem's pursuit of magic, Khlebnikov's 'Numbers' reveals a curious — and moving — blend of Platonism and shamanic consciousness, as in the following extract:

> I look into you, o numbers,
> See you dressed in animals, in their skins,
> Leaning against uprooted oaks.

You — oneness between the snakelike
movement
Of the universe's spine and the
folkdance
of the
Great Bear. [72]

The 'transrational' resurrection of the word was to attain its (poetic) apotheosis in the work of the Chilean Vicente Huidobro (1893–1948). Octavio Paz has described Huidobro as 'the invisible oxygen of our poetry', while Huidobro once referred to himself as 'the mad cosmic' — 'Altazor, the double of myself/The one who sees himself working and laughs at the other face to face/The one who fell from the heights of his star.' [73] Huidobro/Altazor (the latter a compound formed from *alto*: high and *azor*: hawk) pursued what he called a Creationist vision, claiming that the cornerstone of his aesthetic — 'Make a POEM like nature makes a tree' — was derived from the following statement of an Aymara shaman: 'The poet is God. Don't sing about rain, poet. Make it rain!' [74] 'The Parachute Jump', the subtitle of the epic poem *Altazor* (1931), is a clear enough indication of the Orphic nature of Huidobro's journey through the seven cantos (heavens) of the poem, in search of a completely new and visionary language.

The shamanic ambition implicit in Huidobro's metamorphosis into Altazor was made explicit in the poet's belief that 'everything that passes through the body of the poet must be subjected to the greatest amount of his heat', for the poet is the person who 'puts himself into contact with the Universe, discovers its sense of unity, turns himself into a small God, and makes his cosmos.' [75] In Canto V the poet speaks in the relatively accessible metaphors of 'rosebush language', but by Canto VII the phonetic/would-be shamanic metamorphosis is complete:

Ai aia aia
ia ia aia ui
[. . .]
Isonauta
Olandera uruaro
Ia ia campanuso compasedo
[. . .]
Lalali
   Io ia
iiio
Ai a i ai a i i i i o ia [76]

Whether we consider Arp or Ball, Khlebnikov or Huidobro, the search to find the transformative magic of the word within 'transrational' language clearly raises a number of questions. Three of the most basic of these questions are as follows: Does anything of this 'secret language' carry over to the audience in anything like the way in which a shamanic 'performance' does to the listening tribe (or individual)? Can such work survive on the printed page, or does it demand performance? And in performance, how much of the impact of the work is carried by the 'words' themselves, and how much by the 'body language' of the poet? These were all questions which particularly concerned the actor, poet and dramatist Antonin Artaud (1896–1948). A key figure in the development of twentieth-century theatre, Artaud was the sort of person who in other epochs, as his biographer Martin Esslin has suggested, might have been 'a shaman, a prophet, an alchemist, an oracle, a saint, a gnostic teacher or indeed the founder of a new religion.'[77]

From the point of view of theatrical practice, it might be said that Artaud did indeed found a new religion. In his 1918 essay 'Modern Theatre: Points of View and Attack' the Swedish author Pär Lagerkvist had championed Strindberg at the expense of Ibsen, criticising 'the typical Ibsen drama' with its 'silent tramping on carpets throughout five long acts of words, words, words'.[78] For Lagerkvist, Strindberg's break from Naturalism in such proto-Expressionist works as *A Dream Play* and *The Ghost Sonata* pointed the way forward to a theatre which might offer the imagination of dramatist, actor and audience a simpler, more immediate and more expressive form. This is exactly what Artaud was to aim for in his revolutionary, so-called 'Theatre of Cruelty', through the basic idea of 'a new physical language based on signs' — such as 'angular postures', 'brutal jerks', 'syncopated modulations at the back of the throat', 'insect flights', 'the musical angle formed by arm and forearm' and 'animated puppet dances'.[79]

Artaud developed the central idea of such a 'metaphysics of signs' from seeing a troupe of Balinese dancers at the Colonial Exhibition in the Bois de Vincennes in Paris in July 1931. 'In the Balinese theatre', he commented, 'one senses a state prior to language, able to select its own language; music, gestures, moves and words.'[80] What did this imply for those 'words, words, words' for which Lagerkvist had earlier criticised Ibsen? In a 1932 article 'Mise en scène and Metaphysics' Artaud wrote of how language had to be replenished if 'ancient ceremonial magic' were to find 'fresh reality' on the stage: 'To make metaphysics out of spoken language is to make language convey what it does not normally convey. That is to use it in a new, exceptional and unusual way, to give it its full, physical shock potential, to split it up and distribute it actively in space, to treat inflections in a completely tangible manner and restore their shattering power and really to manifest something; to turn against language and its basely utilitarian, one might almost say its alimentary sources, against its origins as a hunted beast, and finally to consider language in the form of *Incantation*.'[81]

In a letter to Jean Paulhan of the same year, Artaud summarised his aims thus: 'To spoken language I am adding another language and trying to restore its old magical efficacy, its power of enchantment, which is integral to words, whose mysterious potential has been forgotten.'[82] 'What paganism divinized,' he believed, 'Europe has mechanised.' In January 1936 he sailed to Mexico; in August, after a 750-mile train journey, he travelled on horseback across the Sierra Madre to the territory of the Tarahumaras, a tribe that still celebrated their traditional rituals with peyote (mescalin). Thirty years before Carlos Castaneda first sat down by the side of Don Juan, Artaud explored those 'other worlds' of *participation mystique* which led him to conclude that the humanism of the Renaissance had resulted in 'a dimunition of man'.[83]

Towards the end of his life — a life often wracked by intense physical and mental pain — Artaud became particularly interested in what one might call a sort of refined glossolalia. His poetry of the late-1940s can seem like an elegant cross between Arp's 'nonesense' and Ball's phonetics:

o dedi
a dada orzoura
o dou zoura
a dada skizi

o kaya
o kaya pontoura
o ponoura
a pena
poni[84]

Artaud became convinced that he had found the way to a universal language, the potentially explosive, occult implications of which he recognised in the paintings of Van Gogh when he saw them at an exhibition at the Musée de l'Orangerie in Paris early in 1947. Within four weeks of seeing the exhibition, Artaud had written *Van Gogh le suicidé de la société* (a text which was to have a decisive impact on the young R.D. Laing). Van Gogh had been endowed with a 'superior lucidity' that enabled him 'to see further, infinitely and dangerously further than the immediate and apparent facts'. His paintings were 'atomic bombs'. 'What', asked Artaud, 'is a real madman? It is a man who has preferred to go mad in the socially accepted sense, rather than give up a certain higher idea of human honour. That is how society has organised the strangulation in lunatic asylums of all those it wants to be rid of or to protect itself from, because they refuse to be accomplices in certain supremely dirty acts. Because a madman is also a man to whom society does not want to listen. So it wants to prevent him from telling intolerable truths.'[85]

Discussing Van Gogh's last painting, the July 1890 *Wheatfield With*

Crows, Artaud suggested that the painter had succeeded in opening 'the occult entrance to a possible beyond, a possible permanent reality'.[86] This had been Artaud's entire ambition: 'Far from believing man invented the supernatural and the divine', he wrote in the preface to his 1936/37 collection of essays *The Theatre And Its Double*, 'I think it was man's eternal meddling that ended up corrupting the divine.'[87] Convinced that 'In our present degenerative state, metaphysics must be made to enter the mind through the body', Artaud's furious pursuit of 'fiery, magnetic imagery' and 'unforgettable soul therapy'[88] has had an enormous influence on many subsequent playwrights and directors, poets and performers with shamanic ambitions.[89]

One of the most important of these poets is Ted Hughes. Although he wrote eighteen plays between 1960 and 1971, Hughes does not consider himself a playwright. Nevertheless, before considering the shamanic qualities which so distinguish his poetry, it is worth paying some attention to Hughes's collaboration with Peter Brook and his Artaud-inspired 'theatre of ritual' in the 1971 *Orghast* production at Persepolis. Reminiscent not just of Artaud but the whole 'transrational' twentieth-century tradition, Hughes's invention of a primitive, guttural language (of some 2,000-odd words) for *Orghast* sought to cut through what he called the 'gabbled gibberish of static interference' in ordinary speech.[90]

The basic 'plot' of *Orghast* involved an Orphic descent into the underworld in order to retrieve evil, the buried husband of life, so that his true nature, that of light, might be released.[91] Jungian ideas of psychic integration were thus clearly operative within the complexity of the collage-like creation myth which Hughes wove out of aspects of chiefly Near Eastern mythology and legend. 'Orghast' was both the specific name which Hughes invented for 'the fire of being' (from ORG for 'life, being' and GHAST for 'spirit, flame') and the 'transrational' speech which Hughes created, with sounds being given particular emotional values. In Hughes's own words, 'if you imagine music buried in the earth for a few thousand years, decayed back to its sources, not the perfectly structured thing we know as music, then that is what we tried to unearth. A language belonging below the levels where differences appear, close to the inner life of what we've chosen as our material, but expressive to all people, powerfully, truly, precisely.'[92]

In the present context, the problematic aspects of the ambitions of Hughes and Brook in *Orghast* — the problems of negation and regeneration, context and connotation which are shared by all such 'transrationalists' — are less important than the fact that *Orghast* is such a striking example of Hughes's determination to dig down to something essential in language, to create on a level of mythic, Orphic significance. Few artists of our time have faced the need for regenerative myth as resolutely as Hughes has done in the head-on (and eventually trans-formative) confrontation with nihilism which can be traced in the poetry of *Wodwo* (1967), *Crow* (1972), *Gaudette* (Praise) (1977) and *Cave Birds: An Alchemical Cave Drama* (1978). As Ekbert Faas comments, 'With the possible exception of Jerome Rothenberg, none of his contemporaries seem to come closer than Hughes to rejoining the primitive shamanistic belief that it is possible to acquire the "technique for moving in a state of ecstasy among the various spirit realms, and for generally dealing with souls and spirits, in a practical way, in some practical crisis." '[93]

In a 1970 essay, Hughes echoed the whole Dada-to-Artaud tradition as he wrote that 'The story of the mind exiled from Nature is the story of Western Man. It is the story of his progressively more desperate search for mechanical and rational and symbolic securities, which will substitute for the spirit-confidence of the Nature he has lost.'[94] For Hughes, as for the Dadaists, all such substitutions had added up to very little — if anything at all — of real substance. So it was essential, as he put it in an interview with Faas in 1970, that people began to get back in touch with 'the bigger energy, the elemental power circuit of the Universe . . . it's obviously a pervasive and deep feeling that civilisation has now disappeared comp-letely. If it's still here it's by grace of pure inertia and chance and if the whole thing has essentially vanished one had better have one's spirit invested in something that will not vanish. And this is a shifting of your foundation to completely new Holy Ground, a new divinity, one that won't be under the rubble when the churches collapse.'[95]

In Hughes's view, poetry plays an essential role in the shifting of that foundation: he is convinced that poetry 'is nothing if not . . . the record of just how the forces of the Universe try to redress some balance disturbed by human error.'[96] With deliberate echoes of Blake, Keith Sagar has written of Hughes's shaman-like progression from single to fourfold vision over the years.[97] It is a progression from the existentialist bleakness of 'Pibroch' (from *Wodwo*), where 'The sea cries with its meaningless voice/ . . . Without purpose, without self-deception./Stone likewise . . ./Minute after minute, aeon after aeon,/Nothing lets up or develops . . .', through the Trickster-like trials and gruesome shamanic-alchemical initiations of *Crow* and *Cave Birds*, to the burgeoning acknowledgement of the Goddess spirit in nature in *Gaudette* and its full, loving celebration in the 1983 collection *River*.[98]

In a manner somewhat reminiscent of Lawrence — for whom creatures were 'little living myths', and whose animal poems anticipate a good deal of the resurgent animism of Jerome Rothenberg's 'ethnopoetics' — Hughes contemplates in *River* what he has called 'the elemental final beauty of the created world'.[99] The central organising idea of the life-cycle of salmon enabled Hughes to integrate individual and cosmos in the sort of lyrical, animistic mode which could not be further from the desolation of 'Pibroch':

The valley dark rapt
Hunched over its river, the night attentive
Bowed over its valley, the river

Crying a violin in a grave
All the dead singing in the river

The river throbbing, the river the aorta

And the hills unconscious with listening.[100]

Nor could we be further from Crow, 'spraddled head-down in the beach-garbage, guzzling a/dropped ice-cream',[101] as Hughes turns a memory of an Alaskan fishing trip with his son Nicholas into a moment of pure individuation and mythopoeisis:

Then for a sign that we were where we were
Two gold bears came down and swam like men

Beside us. And dived like children.
And stood in deep water as on a throne
Eating pierced salmon off their talons.

So we found the end of our journey.

So we stood, alive in the river of light
Among the creatures of light, creatures of light.[102]

The simplicity and concreteness of Hughes' language here, the deliberate, ritualistic repetitions, owe much to his long-term appreciation of the unsentimental strengths — the concrete vivacity — of tribal poetry. Like that of a shaman, the language of *River* speaks of the unity of light and dark, life and death — of the surpassing cyclical wonder of the world. As such, it assumes a central place within the quest of twentieth-century poetry to ensoul the world once more — to move beyond world-weariness and pessimism toward that 'completely new Holy Ground' which is in reality as old as the 'listening hills' of *River*.

Peter Redgrove has recalled how in the 1950s Hughes described Jung as 'the philosopher of the next hundred years'.[103] A similar estimate of Jung's importance marks much of Redgrove's own poetry, in which the fundamental themes of the rebirth of the nurturing Goddess and the growth of the individuated self are pursued with what would seem to be a good deal more serenity than is the case with the bulk of Hughes' work. [104] The animism of the 'awakened stones' and 'black-honeyed night' in 'Minerals of Cornwall, Stones of Cornwall', from Redgrove's 1972 *Dr Faust's Sea-Spiral Spirit*, speaks of a shaman-like search for individuation as potently as the 'shrugged-up riches of deep darkness' which sing in the same collection's 'The Idea Of Entropy At Maenporth Beach'. [105] In 'Silence Fiction', from *The Apple-Broadcast* (1981), the imagery of 'late houses built over early caves' combines with the alchemical play of the elements between 'chimney-vaults and cellar-roots' to bring Jung's famous dream of 1909 directly to mind. [106] Not for nothing did Redgrove preface his 1990 collection *Dressed As For A Tarot Pack* with the Jungian *credo* that 'One does not become enlightened by imagining figures of light, but by making the darkness conscious.' [107]

Redgrove has written of the healing, deepening effect of shamanic ideas and has spoken of his poetic 'mission' as 'attempting to arouse the feminine energies in men, and the feminine modes of perception . . . and to go some way to confirming them in some public sense so that both men and women may trust them in themselves to a greater extent.' [108] Hughes has praised *The Wise Wound*, the book about menstruation which Redgrove wrote with Penelope Shuttle, as being 'Far and away the most radical and inarguable case for the real dignity and sacredness of woman . . . therefore of the real feminine in spirit and in nature that I've read . . . the most important book about the Goddess since Graves' *White Goddess*.' [109]

What Redgrove and Hughes say naturally leads one to ask about women's own involvement with these issues. Writing about Sylvia Plath (1932–1963), Hughes once commented that the poet's psychic gifts had gained her access to depths 'formerly reserved to the primitive ecstatic priests, shamans and Holy men'. But she had 'none of the usual guards and remote controls to protect herself from her own reality.' [110] In the quarter of a century and more which has passed since Plath's tragic death, the many-sided development of feminism has done much to alter the way in which one might think about such 'guards and controls', emphasising as it has done the collective, supportive sharing and understanding of experience. And the comparatively recent feminist development of Goddess beliefs must surely lead one to reconsider the implications of Arp's recollection of being 'bewitched by the word.'

In 1960, Hughes's collection *Lupercal* was published. It contained a somewhat prescient meditation on the power of witches, in which Hughes criticised the 'small psychology' of our time — the reductive male rationalism which would 'unseam' the ancient shamanic powers of women through the insistence that such powers were but the stuff of dreams. [111] In the mid-1970s, Monica Sjöö and Barbara Mor were to develop their celebration of the holistic witch/wiccan power of women's shamanic creativity, as documented in *The Great Cosmic Mother* (1975, rev. eds. 1987 and 1991); while in *The Wise Wound: Menstruation And Everywoman* (1978), Penelope Shuttle and Peter Redgrove devoted a chapter to witchcraft, thereby underlining their belief that 'Shamanism was originally a female practice, linked to Moon, and therefore menstrual, cults'.[112] And in 1979 Miriam Simos (aka Starhawk) published what was to become one of the most successful guides of the 1980s to the 'be-witching' of the word through the dreams and practice of both historical and contemporary witchcraft: *The Spiral Dance: A Rebirth of the Ancient Religion of the Great Goddess.*

Starhawk took her name from a combination of the Star card in the Tarot pack and a power vision of a hawk (turning into an old woman) which she had in the mid-1970s. In the revised and updated, tenth anniversary edition of her book, she describes it as a work of 'poetic thealogy . . . a tool chest for visionaries, containing many processes for engaging our collective imagination, developing rituals, communities of support, spaces in which to create and enact something new.'[113] In the present context, what is particularly interesting is Starhawk's original insistence that 'Witchcraft offers the model of a religion of poetry, not theology. It presents metaphors, not doctrines, and leaves open the possibility of reconciliation of science and religion, of many ways of knowing. It functions in those deeper ways of knowing which our culture has denied and for which we hunger. The world view of Witchcraft is cyclical, spiral. It dissolves dualities and sees opposites as complements.'[114]

In *The Spiral Dance* the contemplative sensitivity to nature and the sacred which one associates with such poets as Kathleen Raine (*b.*1912) and Frances Horovitz (1938–1983) largely gives way to primitivistic chants and rhythms of collective, ritualistic affirmation. Is this the ultimate manifestation of Orpheus's post-Romantic search for the magic words that might heal the split between culture and nature? Whether one thinks so or not, one of the most pleasing aspects of *The Spiral Dance* is the way in which its ideas and energies move between poetics and politics, never sacrificing the one to the other.

Echoing Dion Fortune's belief that magic is 'the art of changing consciousness at will', Starhawk asserts that 'Poetry, itself a form of magic, is imagic speech. Spells and charms worked by witches are truly concrete poetry.'[115] The book gives various examples of the power chants, word association trances, invocations and spells which may help devotees of the Goddess to develop their psyches — in accordance with 'the three core principles of Goddess religion' which are 'immanence, interconnection, and community'.[116] The way in which the breath of such Goddess poetry becomes song is deemed to follow the spiral wisdom that 'activity is balanced by passivity. Exertion must be followed by rest; creativity by quiescence.'[117] Thus, within the framework of its own ambitions and beliefs, the poetry of *The Spiral Dance* might be described as combining aspects of the poetics of Ginsberg and Bachelard. Communal, earth-rooted praise to the Goddess who does not rule over us, but rather lives within us, it offers complementary contrast to the more diversely manifested 'transrational' bewitchment sought by such wordsmiths as Arp and Artaud, Khlebnikov and Tzara.

In *Healing the Wounds: The Promise of Ecofeminism*, an important collection of various feminist authors' essays, stories and poems which appeared in 1989, Starhawk spoke of the need for healing stories of power today, and of how

> the cries we hear may be those of labor
> the pain we feel may yet be that of birth[118]

In her article 'Awakening to the ecological self', from the same collection, Joanna Macy argued that 'we are summoned now to awaken from a spell. The spell we must shake off is a case of mistaken identity, a millennia-long amnesia as to who we really are.'[119] For Macy, to discover who — or what — we really are is to transcend the idea of a limited, suffering (and not infrequently insufferable) ego, in order to feel a responsive and responsible part of the animistic, ecological totality of life.

A key part of the argument of the present book is that such essentially shamanic perceptions of Starhawk and Macy are not gender-based — as, indeed, Macy's examples make clear and Starhawk insists in *The Spiral Dance*. In her excellent anthology *Tongues In Trees: Studies in Literature and Ecology*, which was published in the same year as *Healing the Wounds*, Kim Taplin drew upon a range of mainly male Romantic and post-Romantic authors to drive home her point that 'part of poetry's function is the reminding us, magically, what is our relationship to the earth.'[120] And it is to a male author that I turn for a final, particularly inspiring example of the presence of shamanic power in twentieth-century poetry — Kenneth White.

A double first class honours graduate of Glasgow University, White (*b.*1936) currently holds the Chair of Twentieth-Century Poetics at the Sorbonne. He is one of that increasingly rare breed of creative thinkers whose command of scholarly detail is matched — and enriched — by the depth of his intuition (and *vice versa*). When White first read Eliade's *Shamanism: Archaic Techniques of Ecstasy* in Paris at the end of the 1950s, the book had an enormous impact on him, largely because it suggested so many correspondences with the experiences of his early adolescence. Hour upon solitary hour had been spent exploring the hills and moors of Ayrshire, listening to birdsong — and 'talking' with owls at night — as White sought and relished what he later came to realise were the equivalents of the shaman's places of ecstasy and power-vision.[121]

In the lecture 'A Shaman Dancing on the Glacier' which he gave in Glasgow in November 1990, White suggested that it must never be forgotten that if the shaman is a 'medicine-man', concerned with individual sicknesses and collective problems in the tribe, 'he also practises simply "for joy". What the shaman, or the "dawn-man", as the Ojibway call him, is out for is an ecstasy (getting outside one's-self as well as outside history) and a de-conditioning . . . the shaman comes to know an identity larger than the one coded in the community, by giving it breathing space . . . A whole mystic geography, cosmic topography is involved.'[122]

With elective affinities which range from Eliade and Lao-Tsu to the ninth-century Celtic intellectual John Scot Erigena (*sunt lumina*: there are lights), and from Thoreau, Whitman and Lawrence to Hölderlin, Nietzsche and Artaud, Rimbaud and Bashō, Snyder and Uvavnuk, White is essentially a Romantic. But he is the sort of a Romantic (and he himself has worked out a whole series of fresh terms) whose soul-wandering tolerates absolutely no excess baggage, as it were. Few other poets have done as much to prune and care for that 'overluxuriant lyric tree' which Lorca saw as modernism's inheritance from Romanticism.

Like Gary Snyder, about whom he has written an illuminating short book,[123] White's sense of form and place has been strongly influenced by the 'less is more' approach of much Eastern thought and poetry:

> Write poetry?
>
> rather follow the coast
> fragment after fragment
>
> going forward
>
> breathing
>
> spacing it out[124]

Mindscape and landscape thus meet in a Romanticism which has been stripped to the shamanic — and cosmological — bone:

> I take quick notes
> like this:
> winter morning light
> and a black-winged gull
> keening over the hut —
> no more than that
> no metaphor-mongering
> no myth-malarkey

> I think of lines
> like lightning flashes
> lines that in their flying energy
> would make things
> touch and radiate in the mind[125]

As things 'touch and radiate' in the mind, consciousness deepens, clarifies itself. White has written about the figure of the *vajrasattva*, the 'diamond-being' of the yoga-tantra texts, who has reached 'if not a total clarification of himself as body-speech-mind, at least a little light'.[126] This is the light of 'the whiteness' to which the poet is so drawn: the whiteness of wilderness, of the far places of the earth, of the deconditioned, totalising mind. In *The Blue Road* (1983/90), the account of a physical and mental journeying (what White calls a 'way-book') to Labrador, White reflects on the power of the Northern landscape and the beauty of such a poem as Uvavnuk's 'The great sea': 'Spaced out poems, way beyond the person. To stand up to a landscape such as this, it takes a poetry close to the bone and open to the winds.'[127]

Several of White's poems have dealt directly with shamanism. In the eleven-part 'The Master Of The Labyrinth', from *The Bird Path*, White ponders the mystery of the stick-figure of Lascaux with a characteristic, refreshing absence of ponderous solemnity: the several little 'shaman's songs' which can be found in his work are distinguished by a similarly lucent blend of animistic mystery and leavenous humour.[128]

In the beautifully illustrated *Le Chemin Du Chaman* (The Shaman's Path), from 1990, White takes us on the shaman's sexually-charged journey of death and resurrection in language of both concrete vitality and unforced metaphysical import. Against his will, the poet-shaman is called away from the everyday world. But he soon comes to relish the metamorphoses of the soul journeys and spirit flights which take him through a multi-layered cosmos of wind and water, mountain and desert, cave and light — of primal *participation mystique*. At the climax of his transformation, he beats the shamanic drum: gull and crow, heron and great white goose join him in an ecstatic dance through space. The birds speak joyously to (and through) him, conjuring the ultimate, pure vista of mythopoeisis:

> higher and higher I go
> with the great sea-eagle
> come from the west
> so high now
> I'm only moving silence[129]

It would be entirely wrong to interpret such words as somehow 'escapist'. In 1968 White had launched the slogan 'Pas Mao, le Tao!': it is the expansive transfigurations of shamanic cosmology, not the 'local' politics

50 Kenneth White *Le Chemin du Chaman* PAP, Lausanne 1990. Composite image, with the permission of the author, of front cover and (mirror image) frontispiece, incorporating engraving of shaman from George Wilhelm Steller *Voyage to Kamchatka* (1774) and drawing of 'The journey of the shaman', Altai region
Photograph: Mike Fearey

of divisive ideology, which he has always seen as essential to life's well-being. And this does not mean that White is insensitive to the fact that post-Romantic poetics involves the politics of communication and inspiration. In *Letters From Gourgounel*, his diary of the time he spent living in an abandoned farmhouse in south-east France at the beginning of the 1960s, White spoke (via Nietzsche) of the crying need of our civilisation to get away from 'politics, nationality, education, newspapers', in order that the soul or spirit might accumulate in strength, to the point of spontaneous activity.[130] This is the ancient anarchism of the Tao; the politics which embraces all those free spirits who would sing of the wonder of the world.

In *The Blue Road*, White imagined 'a company of "wild geese" gathered from all over the world, forming an archipelago of live minds. Not so much artists as explorers of being and nothingness. Erratics and extravagants, looking for new configurations, outwith the field of ordinary culture. New mental energies. Fresh air blowing over the world!'[131] In the inaugural text which he wrote for the International Institute of Geopoetics that he founded in 1989, such poetic hopes and images were grounded in an ecological awareness very similar to that within the aforementioned *Healing the Wounds* collection of essays: 'One question is paramount: how is it with life on earth, how is it with the world?'[132] A decade earlier, White had already spoken of his conviction that 'the richest poetics come from contact with the earth, from a plunge into biospheric space, from an attempt to read the lines of the world.'[133]

It is the firm hope and belief of White that through geopoetics, poets and thinkers of all times and places can meet in the late-twentieth-century mind — poets and thinkers who have contributed to what one might call the sacred, Orphic understanding of existence (though again it must be stressed that White has his own terminology): 'A whole network can come into being, a network of energy, desire, competence and intelligence.'[134] What else would this network be but the dawning of a shamanic force-field of healing energy and desire — radiating outwards from the bewitchment of the reverie-inducing word, and bound together by all those 'lines like lightning flashes' which might yet make things 'touch and radiate' in the mind?[135]

8 The Body Electric

Shamans journey between Heaven, Earth and the Underworld — and the individual and collective psyche — in search of the wisdom and the power that can help to make existence meaningful, help make life whole. Crucial to this journey is the triple magic of sound, rhythm and song. In his far-ranging study *The Magic of Tone and the Art of Music* Dane Rudhyar reminds us that 'The music of primitive societies is not music in our sense of the term; it is *tone-magic* . . . Sound is the basic means for the transmission of the magical will. Magical tones can be particularly powerful when associated with physical body movements, that is, with specific rites and magical dancing . . . The shaman chanted as birds sing or cats in sexual circumstances moan and yell in intense melodic development.'[1]

Rudhyar suggests that the shaman was not preoccupied with the possibility of uttering 'wrong' notes, since 'Magical results are very different from intellectual and *esthetic* responses'.[2] While this is so, it remains the case that the shaman's sense of being charged with the ultimate powers of life is connected to a respect for — and lived encounter with — archetypal patterns of consciousness. For as the shaman's hypnotic drumming, chanting and singing combine to propel consciousness beyond the limits of ordinary feeling and perception, music becomes myth. A state of ecstasy is achieved, as a drum becomes a horse, taking the psyche into the transformative depths of itself; or as the shaking of the shaman's rattle synthesises the sexual dualities of both self and the world and song lends the soul wings. As Orpingalik, a Netsilik Inuit (Eskimo), once said to the explorer Knud Rasmussen: 'Songs are thoughts which are sung with the breath when people let themselves be moved by a great force, and ordinary speech no longer suffices.'[3]

That force is the transmutative power which stirred the Iglulik Inuit Uvavnuk so profoundly that when she sang with joy of the great sea and the sky which had set her adrift, she would always fall into a trance. It is the force that brings into being the ecstatic moment when, as Rudhyar puts it, 'Music is a myth in which the actors are tones uttered by the creative-destructive, transformative-regenerative power of the One Life — the sacred Tone of cosmic being, which operates both macrocosmically and microcosmically.'[4]

In her *Maps To Ecstasy: Teachings of an Urban Shaman*, Gabrielle Roth suggests that music is every bit as essential to the modern shamanic journey as it has been in the past. And for Roth, it is rock'n'roll which is 'today's shamanic call' — a call 'back to the beat, the heartbeat, back to the body, back to basics'.[5] Seeing rock concerts as the modern tribal rituals 'where communal ecstasy is a real possibility', Roth chooses to underline the healing, shamanic import of 'Rock for the rain forests, for starving children and burned out farmers — rock for the homeless, rock for political prisoners.'[6] As she puts it, 'Rock it, roll it, change it'. With her group Mirrors, Roth performs music to put us back in touch with essential dimensions of rhythm — what she calls 'flowing, staccato, chaos, lyric, stillness — the fluid structure, the DNA, of our physical lives'.[7]

Apart from its intrinsic interest, *Maps To Ecstasy* serves as a potent reminder of the extent to which twentieth-century music and dance might be considered in terms of shamanic ideas. In European dance, one has only to think of the myth of divinity which has long been associated with the performances which Vaslav Nijinsky gave while part of Serge Diaghilev's Ballets Russes early in the century. One might also consider the differently inflected primitivism of such innovative figures as Isadore Duncan and Martha Graham, or the work of Emil Jacques Dalcroze and Rudolf von Laban, and in particular, the way in which the latter's principles of 'pure shapes' were developed by Mary Wigman and her Dresden school of dance around the turn of the second and third decades of the century. Laban's theory of dance distilled opposed pairs of stylised movement (such as 'scooping' and 'scattering') to their essence: the resultant archetypal nature of the dancers' performances was deemed able to express such elemental feelings as anger and fear, love and joy. (Roth works on the similarly archetypal level of 'five basic emotions: fear, anger, sadness, joy and compassion'.[8]) The resultant rhythms were intended to produce an hypnotic, therapeutic effect, inducing the 'universal celebratory state' of the dancers' self-transformative participation in group movement.[9]

Moving away from classical ballet's emphasis on aesthetic harmony and balance, Mary Wigman's dance-drama sequences were developed as group improvisations, based, for example, on Laban-like tensions between the extension and contraction of movement. For Wigman, each improvisatory impulse, to be valid, had to come 'from the heart, [from] the depths of a nature shaken by the sacred fury'.[10] Her dancers often created their own musical accompaniment, by the sound of their feet or drum beats — for the repertoire of the group was intended to reveal authentic inner states rather than preconceived characterisations of personality. Among the mythopoeic pieces which the Wigman ensemble performed were *Ecstatic Dance* (consisting of four parts: 'Prayer', 'Sacrifice', 'Religious Rite', 'Temple Dance') and *Rites* (including 'The Call', 'Migration', 'Chaos', 'The Turning Point', 'Vision' and 'Greeting').

The potential shamanic overtones of such work are evident in contemporary descriptions of the performances, which drew attention to a nervous energy 'verging on hallucination . . . Most of the dance-dramas . . . demand a painful tension of the whole being. The dancer's eyes exclaim; her fingers flare; her body writhes with terror; she squirms on the ground, stamps furiously, collapses exhausted.'[11] As Colin Innes concludes, in his study *Holy Theatre: Ritual and the Avant-Garde*, Wigman's approach to dance revealed 'the atavistic, one might almost say Jungian aspect of expressionism, with its search for ritualistic or mythical archetypes to incarnate emotions so deeply felt that they become universal and transfigure the individual by a return to the roots of human nature . . .'[12]

Critics who approved the approach of the Wigman school described it as 'liturgical', while those who disapproved condemned it as 'barbarism'. At the same time that Wigman's visionary work was dividing taste, opinion in Europe and America was becoming similarly split over the question of the growing popularity of jazz music. For example, the Swiss conductor Ernest Ansermet was astonished by the power of the music which he heard from Sidney Bechet when the great jazz clarinettist and saxophonist played at London's Royal Philharmonic Hall in the summer of 1919. For Ansermet, the blues-playing Bechet was clearly an artist 'of genius'.[13] A couple of years later, however, America's *Ladies Home Journal* felt it had to defend the morality of millions by asking 'Does Jazz Put The Sin In Syncopation?', demanding 'Unspeakable Jazz Must Go!'.[14] In England, Clive Bell wrote an equally silly, contemporary article entitled 'Plus de Jazz', where he argued that 'Jazz art is soon created, soon liked, and soon forgotten'.[15]

Such a diversity of opinion and response has always attended jazz. The music's vigorous and varied history has embraced both the spontaneous joy of house parties and the calculated hysteria of the Swing Era; the bordellos of New Orleans and the concert halls of the world; the snappy syncopation of traditional forms and the fiery experimentation of the avant-garde. So vigorous has the growth of jazz been, in fact, that its avant-garde developments have often alienated enthusiasts of its earlier days, who claim to miss the uplifting melodies and rhythms of the music's older forms.

The late English poet and critic Philip Larkin, for example, very much regretted the development of jazz into a self-conscious art form, loathing the music of avant-garde saxophonist John Coltrane as much as he loved that of Sidney Bechet. After Coltrane, opined Larkin, 'all was chaos, hatred, absurdity'. Coltrane was a modern jazz musician — and modernism signified nothing but 'mystification and outrage' to Larkin. Reading about the innovations of Charlie Parker (the greatest saxophonist of the 1940s and early 1950s bebop era in New York, and a musician who had a profound effect on Coltrane), Larkin vehemently rejected the way in which various writers had tried to praise Parker by relating the challenge of his work to the development of twentieth-century modernism in the arts: '*Of course*! This was the language of criticism of modern painting, modern poetry, modern music. Of course! How glibly I had talked of *modern* jazz, without realising the force of the adjective: this was modern jazz, and Parker was a modern jazz player just as Picasso was a modern painter and Pound a modern poet. I hadn't realised that jazz had gone from Lascaux to Jackson Pollock in fifty years . . .'[16]

One wonders if Larkin ever came near to realising how unintentionally close to the truth his grossly inaccurate diatribe had been. For there certainly is a profound connection between modern jazz and modernism in all the arts, a connection which does indeed link Jackson Pollock with Lascaux. And it is exactly this connection which can help us to make sense of much of what Larkin could only see as 'mystification and outrage': the connection supplied by the archetypal spirit of shamanism.

In his *Shamanism: The Foundations of Magic*, Ward Rutherford suggests that we can begin to grasp something of the magic of the drumming, dancing and singing which are such key elements within the performance of shamanism by thinking of the improvisatory powers of a jazz soloist.[17] Rutherford's point is a good one. When the English singer and guitarist David Sylvian (*b*.1958) began to look for something more substantial than the commercial success which he had enjoyed with the techno-pop group Japan, his imagination was especially stimulated by listening to such jazz masters as Coltrane and Miles Davis. One of the first fruits of Sylvian's change of heart was his three-part *Words With The Shaman* recording from 1984, a meditative, yet intriguingly rhythmic piece which found Sylvian's hypnotic tape loops and sound effects enhanced by the jazz-inflected trumpet of Jon Hassell.[18]

Jazz musicians have long been — and continue to be — some of the greatest shamans of the twentieth century. More than any other music of this century, jazz challenges us at the core of our being, questioning and stimulating our ability to synthesise body and soul, dance and dream at the mythopoeic heart of life. Speaking at the Berlin Jazz Festival in 1964, Dr Martin Luther King underlined the importance of jazz in the fight against the sense of meaninglessness which has afflicted so many this century: 'Jazz speaks of life . . . When life itself offers no order and meaning, the musician creates an order and meaning from the sounds of earth which flow through his instrument.'[19] It is in jazz that one finds the most inspiring musical response to the problem which haunted such key nineteenth-century thinkers and poets as Thoreau and Walt Whitman, and which continues to haunt us today: the problem of the alienation of consciousness from its own roots, of the dualisms of body and soul, heart and mind in the Platonic and Judaeo-Christian traditions — dualisms which have done so much to shape Western attitudes to the world.[20]

'Why,' asked Thoreau (1817—62) in his study of the pleasures and responsibilities of life in the woods in *Walden*, 'has man rooted himself thus firmly in the earth, but that he may rise in the same proportion into the heavens above?' For this Taoist-like sage, who felt that in an era of increasing mass culture and cheap distraction, more and more people were coming to live lives 'of quiet desperation', it was essential to realise that 'Every man is the builder of a temple, called his body, to the god he worships . . . We are all sculptors and painters, and our material is our own flesh and blood and bones.'[21] In similar vein, Walt Whitman (1819—92) saw his soul reflected in nature. Hymning the sacredness of the bodies of men and women, Whitman's great poem 'I Sing The Body Electric' asks, 'And if the body were not the soul, what is the soul?'[22]

A century later, the innovative jazz group Weather Report offered a richly orchestrated response to Whitman's rhetorical question in their 1971/72 album *I Sing The Body Electric*. In this recording, where the spirit of the blues meets that of jazz, rock and twentieth-century 'classical' composition, the music of keyboardist Josef Zawinul, saxophonist Wayne Shorter, bassist Miroslav Vitous, drummer Eric Gravatt and percussionist Dom Um Romao ranged from spacious tone pictures — reflecting both the self-inflicted human misery ('Unknown Soldier') and healing mystery of existence ('The Moors', 'Crystal') — to hypnotic dances of improvisatory celebration and exultation ('Second Sunday In August' and much of the second, 'live' side of the album).[23]

At their best, Weather Report epitomised jazz's ability to synthesise composition and improvisation, individual and group, as tellingly as body and soul, heart and mind. Like jazz itself, born of a hybrid synthesis of African, European and American elements, the group drew inspiration from a wide range of cultures: elements of African, Hispano-Arabic, South American, Central European, Indian and Far Eastern scales and rhythms added nuances of colour, dynamics and rhythm to an already potent blend of Afro-American blues and swing. The driving, compulsive power of such pieces as 'Nubian Sundance' (1974), 'Between The Thighs' (1975) and 'Gibraltar' (1976) lay in the group's command of subtly layered rhythmic repetition; while the reflective qualities of such pieces as 'Morning Lake' (1971), 'Will' (1973), 'The Elders' (1978) and 'The Peasant' (1984) bore witness to the animistic fruits of Shorter's belief that 'Some people can only relate their soul to God. They think that the soul in relation to the universe has to do with [institutionalised] religion all the time. They can't see any practical use in relating their soul to a table, to a bug on the window sill, to musicians on a bandstand, or a picture hanging on a wall . . .'[24]

Shorter's words are quintessentially Romantic. In both their Eastern-inflected reverence for all life and their emphasis on the healing potentiality of music and art, they recall the Romantic belief that at the core of existence, nature resolves all ostensible dissonance into harmony — a belief epitomised by the conviction of Novalis that 'every illness is a musical problem.' Sickness is thus a matter of being 'out of tune' with both oneself and the world, and healing a question of 'making whole'.[25] Hence the prevalent sense of shamanic nostalgia in much Romanticism: the longing for nature's sympathy in Wordsworth, for example, or the pursuit of ecstasy in both the myth-cycles of Wagner and the harmonic clusters of the tone poems of the Russian composer Scriabin.

Before investigating the shamanic qualities of jazz in more depth, it is worth pausing to consider the extent to which such qualities might also be discerned within the worlds of (for want of a better phrase) notated compositions within the concert hall tradition of this century. Such a consideration may enable us to appreciate not only the degree to which shamanic ideas can be discerned within a wide range of twentieth-century creativity, but also the extent to which jazz music is this century's most potent inheritor and developer of shamanic approaches to the transformative power of music.

Through his highly Romantic music, Alexander Scriabin (1872–1915) was able to experience what he described as 'light . . . rapture . . . soaring flight . . . suffocation from Joy!'[26] Aspects of a shamanic sense of music as transformative myth are clearly present in the programmatic ascension of the 1908 *Poem of Ecstasy* and the 1910 *Prometheus – The Poem of Fire*: in the last years of his life, Scriabin drew very close to theosophy and occultism, his musical aim being to produce 'a glimpse of higher spiritual planes'. He grew obsessed with the idea of the 'mystical chord' — composed of the notes A, D #, G, C #, F # and B — which can be heard in *Prometheus*, and intended that this piece be performed in synaesthetic conjunction with a 'light keyboard' or 'colour organ'. Scriabin planned a final meta-composition, *Mysterium*, which would embrace all the arts. At the projected climax of what was to be a seven-day festival in the Himalayas, music would dissolve the world in an abyss of flame, returning all being to its spiritual essence within 'the plane of unity'.[27]

No less reminiscent of the dramatic totality of the shaman's approach to music are the violent, visceral rhythms of the early work of Scriabin's fellow countryman Igor Stravinsky (1882–1971). As Christopher Small has suggested in *Music, Society, Education*, a bold comparison of the various 'world views' which can be detected in Western music from the late Renaissance until now, Stravinsky's *The Rite of Spring* of 1913 (which Mary Wigman's group performed) restored nature to the realm of the sacred: the realm from which 'it had been so rudely torn by the efforts of western man from the sixteenth century onwards.'[28]

The shamanic overtones of this ballet about the spring rituals of prehistoric Russia — rituals involving the voluntary sacrifice of a virgin as propitiation to what Small calls the 'mysterious, unknowable, even menacing' forces of nature — are reinforced when one listens to the description of the work's origins which Stravinsky himself gave much later. Explaining how little immediate sense of musical theory and tradition lay behind the music, Stravinsky tells us that he simply *heard* — and what he heard, he wrote down: 'I am the vessel through which *Le Sacre* passed'.[29] As Small comments, such language resembles that of the shaman or priest rather than that of the artist as commonly thought of in the Western tradition; and while Stravinsky was never to repeat the *success de scandale* of *The Rite of Spring*, the idea of replenishing ritual can be traced through much of his subsequent work.

Once one has appreciated the shamanic overtones of the respective concerns for tone colour and rhythm in Scriabin and Stravinsky, it is entirely possible to see such different composers as Jean Sibelius (1865–1957), Gustav Mahler (1860–1911), Carl Orff (1895–1982), Harry Partsch (1901–1974), Olivier Messiaen (*b.*1908), Karlheinz Stockhausen (*b.*1928), Toru Takemitsu (*b.*1930) and Steve Reich (*b.*1936) in the light of shamanic ideas about the magical capacity of music to awaken a mythopoeic sense of the cosmos within one.[30] In this respect, it is particularly interesting to compare Stravinsky's recollection of how he came to compose *The Rite of Spring* with Stockhausen's description of himself: 'For many years I have said it innumerable times and sometimes written it: that I do not make my music, but only relay the vibrations I receive; that I function like a translator, that I am a radio.'[31]

The development of Stockhausen's music from the collaged, electronically-treated speech fragments of the 1955–6 *Song of the Youths*, through the meditative vocal harmonics of the 1968 *Tuning* to the ongoing, music drama cycle *Light* — which is variously arranged for solo voices and instruments, solo dancers, choirs, orchestras, ballet and electronic music — reveals much of the urge towards shamanic totality which informs Stockhausen's many comments on what he describes as 'cosmic music'. In 1971, for example, Stockhausen proclaimed his belief that the composer should be seen as a sort of spiritual guide — 'Like musicians were in African tribes, in American Indian tribes, and still are in India and Bali. What he does is always part of a spiritual activity. He makes the sounds others can fly on — on which they can get together in this sacred act of making contact with the divine.'[32] The shamanic overtones of Stockhausen's concerns are even more noticeable in his suggestion in an interview of 1987–8 that 'Only music is capable of bringing about experiences of supernatural time processes and of flying through unlimited space . . .'[33]

Much of Stockhausen's music does intimate an uplifting, cosmic dimension to existence; and as *Dream Formula*, his 1983 piece for solo basset-horn reveals, the composer has not shunned the sensual side of life.[34] However, one of the unresolved tensions in Stockhausen's belief that 'We're all working in this world to implement spiritual dreams'[35] is the extent to which his ideas reinforce — rather than heal — the aforementioned dualisms of body and soul, heart and mind. Stockhausen speaks of music's power of 'making you really feel you're a spiritual being which is not primarily identified with its body',[36] and his own idealistic elevation of the role of the composer shows a very limited appreciation of both the 'corporeal' role of improvisation in jazz and the possibilities of what he calls 'pop music'. In an interview with Peter Heyworth in 1971, for example, Stockhausen revealed that he could see little in pop beyond what he considered to be the 'very banal, militaristic' elements of 'this periodic beat, which makes people march without knowing'.[37]

To a degree, Stockhausen has a point. Much modern pop music of both the Tin Pan Alley and sampled House variety is as insidiously dangerous in its negation of the imagination as it is lacking in any sophisticated command of melody, harmony or rhythm. However, one wonders what Stockhausen would make of the relatively simple, repetitive accents of shamanic drumming, which are anything but militaristic or reductive in their effects.[38] One also wonders what this composer might make of the combination of spiritual and socio-political aspirations within the 'periodic beats' of blues and reggae music, both of which share jazz's strong relation to shamanism. Shortly before he died in 1959, the great New Orleans drummer Warren 'Baby' Dodds suggested that *drumming is spirit. You got to have that in your body. In your soul . . .'*[39] The contrast of such an approach with the dualist tendencies in Stockhausen is instructive.

Stockhausen's dismissal of jazz and pop music becomes further questionable when one considers the extent to which the power music has to move listeners may have nothing at all to do with definitive-sounding, cross-stylistic judgements of aesthetic quality. Criticising the Western tendency to split aesthetics from life, the radical black critic and poet Amira Baraka (aka Leroi Jones) has spoken of the *verb process* of life and art. He suggests that 'The most valuable quality in life is the will to existence, the unconnected zoom, which finally becomes in anyone's hand whatever part of it he could collect . . . Art-ing is what makes art.'[40]

It seems reasonable to suggest that people of different ages and backgrounds will both produce and 'collect' different aspects of art's affirmative power. And what may strike a middle-aged European composer (or black radical) as hopelessly banal may contain exactly the right amount of power needed to spark the beginnings of other people's journey to the deeper aspects of themselves. As the *Tao Te Ching* says, 'A tree as great as a man's embrace springs from a small shoot . . . A journey of a thousand miles starts under one's feet.'[41]

Thus, while the music of such rock groups as The Beatles, The Doors and Led Zeppelin rarely approached the power of the Afro-American sources from which they drew so much inspiration, over the past quarter of a century these groups have nonetheless played an undeniable role in helping to bring body and soul, heart and mind together for a wide range of listeners. Celebrating what he saw as the virtues of 'the drop out' generation, Allen Ginsberg spoke in 1966 of 'teenagers dancing Nigerian Yoruba dances and entering trance states to the electric vibrations of the Beatles who have borrowed shamanism from Afric [sic] sources . . . All the available traditions of U.S. Indian vision-quest, peyotl ritual, mask dancing, Oriental pranayama, East Indian ear music are becoming available to the U.S. unconscious through the spiritual search of the young.'[42]

It would be easy to smile at Ginsberg's naïvete and simply take his words as evidence of how shallow the so-called Swinging Sixties really were. But if the Beatles hardly approached the intensity of the music of such contemporary Afro-American seers as John Coltrane, Cecil Taylor and Albert Ayler, the primitivistic, initiatory impact which their music had — and continues to have — on many cannot be denied.

Psychologist Evan Davies has written about what he calls the archaic aspect in the early Beatles albums: 'The melodic simplicity, limited range, simplicity of rhythmic content, modal tonality, elements of fourteenth-century style, clarity of diction, are all elements of bardic style.'[43] Speaking of Beatle Mania, Davies notes that the (live) combination of regular rhythm and high volume created a strong physiological sensory response; combined with the reiteration of sexually charged (and yet somehow curiously innocent) lyrics, this inevitably led to a hypnogogic state among the audience.[44] And on the later Beatles albums, tracks such as the 1966 'Tomorrow Never Knows' and 1967 'A Day In The Life' struck a broadening note of meditative absorption in life's mysteries — a note enhanced by George Harrison's involvement with various aspects of Indian music.

The initiatory, shamanic impact of The Doors is again difficult to gainsay. In the 1978 *An American Prayer* album, the band whose very first record had advised us (courtesy of Aldous Huxley and a strong rhythm and blues riff) to 'break on through to the other side' produced one of the most completely realised statements of primitivistic longing in rock music. Released some seven years after Jim Morrison's death (or, as some still believe, disappearance) in Paris, this multi-layered recording finds Morrison telling us, *sotto voce*, of a formative experience of his childhood, when he saw a group of 'dead Indians' by the roadside. They had only just been killed in a truck accident, and it was Morrison's belief that the souls of some of these Native Americans somehow 'just leaped' into his soul. They stayed there all his life. Sick of doubt, sick of being dominated by the dour faces of corporate America which stared at him 'from the TV Tower', Morrison implores us — to an hypnotic, modal accompaniment soaked in the spirit of the blues — to reinvent all the gods, all the myths of the ages, in order to celebrate symbols 'from deep elder forests.'[45]

An American Prayer is the Doors' most extensive investigation of those twentieth-century 'shaman's blues' which Morrison shouted out on the 1969 *The Soft Parade* release.[46] As keyboardist Ray Manzerak reveals, the group were well aware of the shamanic implications of their music: 'We knew the symptoms of the [shamanic] state, so that we could try to approximate it. It was like Jim was the electric shaman and we were the electric shaman's band, pounding away behind him . . . Sometimes he was just incredible. Just amazing. And the audience felt it too!'[47] The extent of Morrison's shamanic concerns is reinforced when one considers the singer's reflections on yoga powers and the healing of illness through séance in *The Lords: Notes on Vision*,[48] as well as the 'abiding interest in dreams and visions' revealed in *Wilderness*, his posthumously published collection of poetry.[49]

The year that Morrison died (or disappeared), Led Zeppelin released their fourth album. This contained what was to become one of their most popular numbers, the anthemic, eight minute 'Stairway To Heaven'. Now pensive, now screaming, Robert Plant's vocal revitalised the cliché of 'all that glitters is not gold' through imagery which inescapably recalls shamanic ideas: a spirit which is 'crying for leaving', 'rings of smoke through the trees', and a stairway which lies 'on the whispering wind'. The stairway suggests the alchemical path to the self's state of grace; and the mythic, metamorphosing qualities of the lyric are underpinned by a fine arrangement, which moves from passages of folk-like, acoustic reflection and repetition through more accented, floating sequences (based on jazz-derived triplet rhythms) to the ringing affirmation of Jimmy Page's blues-based electric guitar solo.[50]

Of all the singer/songwriters — or as Bob Sarlin calls them, songpoets[51] — of rock, two in particular deserve great credit for the shamanic implications of their work. Early in their lives, Bob Dylan (*b.*1941) and Van Morrison (*b.*1945) both drank deeply from the life-giving well of the blues. (Later, they would share a taste for Rimbaud.) That elemental, cyclical form was to precipitate some of the most provocative, seer-like writing and performances of our century.

In a thoughtful article entitled 'Bob Dylan and the Poetry of Salvation', Steven Goldberg has suggested that the significance of such legendary Dylan albums of the 1960s as *Bringing It All Back Home*, *Highway 61 Revisited*, *Blonde On Blonde* and *John Wesley Harding* lies in the fact that their journey to mysticism embodies a concept of transcendence that flows through, rather than 'beyond' humanity.[52] From a shamanic point of view, the existential honesty of the various personae revealed in the loneliness and the horror of such tracks as 'It's Alright Ma (I'm Only Bleeding)', 'Desolation Row' and 'All Along The Watchtower' drew Dylan far into a soul-wounding wilderness. In compositions such as 'Mr Tambourine Man', 'Sad Eyed Lady of the Lowlands' and 'I'll Be Your Baby Tonight' —

songs rich in reverie — the soul is offered various related stimuli to the process of healing and transformation.

Describing the hallucinatory images, tonal ambiguity and cyclical, would-be endless patterns of 'Mr Tambourine Man', Wilfred Mellers suggests that 'The heart of the matter is that his [Dylan's] Pied-Piper myth encourages us to follow the unconscious wherever it may spontaneously lead us — ecstatically into the sky where there are no "fences" to confine "the skippin' reels of rhyme", but also into vaguely minatory regions "down the foggy ruins of time, far past the frozen leaves,/The haunted, frightened trees, out to the windy beaches". Poetically, Dylan wings to lyrical heights . . . as the rings of the melody unfold, we are liberated . . . The song is unexpectedly disturbing because its mythology plumbs unexpectedly deep.'[53] As Mellers realised, it could not have plumbed much deeper: ' What Dylan is dealing in here, on behalf of the spiritually if not materially deprived young of the sixties, is musical therapy with its origins in real folk art. He is a shaman who effects psychological fulfilment.'[54]

This observation applies with equal if not greater force to the art of Van Morrison. From the *Astral Weeks* album of 1968 right through to the 1991 *Hymns To The Silence* recording, Morrison's images and rhythms have been in healing touch with the unconscious. Spinning free-floating, yet highly focussed reveries of the Great or Cosmic Self across arrangements distinguished by a loving feeling for elements of jazz, gospel and country and western music, or digging deep into the blues to take the power of repetition to incantatory heights, Morrison has created some of the most consistently heartening music this century. Appropriately enough, he once described the title track of *Astral Weeks* as being like a transformation song: 'It's like transforming energy, or going from one source to another with it being born again like a rebirth. I remember reading something somebody said about you having to die to be born. It's kind of one of those songs where you can see the light at the end of the tunnel . . .'[55]

From the perspective of shamanism, Morrison's final image here transcends the realm of cliché. Like a shaman, the singer is able to put us in touch with 'the music of the spirit' as he sings 'the song of ages'.[56] That song takes us beyond the threshold of everyday consciousness into a world of ineffable presence and Paradisal healing. And if this is a convincing world, which it largely is, that is partly because Morrison's art has always been in touch with the sorrow that wounds, the better to heal. Exploring ensouling depths of experience and longing, this 'dweller on the threshold' has never been afraid to reveal the psyche's struggle and longing for transformation and individuation ('You Don't Pull No Punches But You Don't Push The River' — a title perhaps owing something to the Gestalt ideas of Barry Stevens — from 1974, 'Spirit' and 'When Heart Is Open', both from 1980, and 'Enlightenment', from 1990). The *rubato* reflections of the 1991 'On Hyndford Street', where Morrison asks to be taken back to the hushed magic of the long summer nights of his adolescence, are both an elegy for 'the days before rock'n'roll' and a celebration of cosmic reverie, of the feeling that, at the sacred heart of existence, 'it's always now'.

In 1991 Morrison was the subject of a BBC television documentary, *One Irish Rover*. He was seen performing in the typically varied company of his own touring band and Georgie Fame, Bob Dylan, John Lee Hooker (who, together with Leadbelly and Ray Charles, was a major early influence on the singer), The Chieftains and The Danish Radio Big Band. Discussing the question of where the spirit of his songs came from, songs which he suggested were concerned with 'transcending mundane existence', Morrison spoke of the essential need of the imagination for space and solitude. In characteristic, incisive manner he also volunteered his sympathy with Jungian ideas: 'Carl Jung says it comes from our collective unconscious and I'll buy that.'[57]

One of Morrison's songs from the 1984 *A Sense of Wonder* release is called 'A New Kind of Man' — a song rich in archetypal shamanic imagery of wilderness, mountain top and light. In creative touch with the collective unconscious, Morrison has long been a harbinger of the newly emergent male consciousness which the American poet Robert Bly has recently discussed. This is a consciousness aware of the need to transcend the reductive opposition of what Bly calls 1950s 'macho man' and post-1960s 'soft male'. Such a consciousness may be able to develop the strength needed to move towards a healing balance of assertion and reflection, animus and anima. Developing a shaman-like courage to experience what Bly calls 'the wild man' within, those who come to possess such consciousness may be able to express a genuine affirmation and creative celebration of life — qualities growing out of the essential capacity to acknowledge painful feelings, to open oneself to tenderness and to grief.[58] One thinks of the extraordinary, growling vocalese which gradually transcends the initial introspection and pain of Morrison's 1972 'Listen To The Lion', as the singer comes to search his soul for 'the lion' deep inside himself.[59]

As the programme *One Irish Rover* revealed, of all the many musical influences which Morrison has absorbed and transmuted, the blues has been of special importance. At ten or eleven, Morrison already loved the music of Leadbelly and John Lee Hooker, music which he still feels is 'the most natural thing I ever heard'.[60] Here, we approach one of the great, transformative mysteries of twentieth-century art — the relation of suffering and exaltation within the Afro-American tradition, and the impact of that tradition upon the world.

In 1989 Hooker released an album called *The Healer*. The title track featured the singer's urgent, repetitive celebrations of the power of the blues to heal, 'all over the world', delivered in classic call and response style with Carlos Santana's searing electric guitar lines. With its Latin rhythms and occasional touch of reggae drum accents, the track exemplifies the theme of the shamanic role of 'wounded healer' which has been played by so many artists of the Afro-American tradition this century.[61]

It is no exaggeration to say that millions upon millions of people around the world have been uplifted by music that would not have come into existence had it not been for the obscenities of slavery. Without the transporting of African slaves to the New World, followed by a (variously pursued) history of attempted cultural suppression and extinction of the survivals of African culture in America, there would have been no blues. And without blues, there would have been no jazz — none of the healing potions, for example, which jazz singer Bobby McFerrin celebrated on his 1990 *Medicine Music* release.[62] Hence the initially unpalatable observation of the late Oliver Nelson, excellent Afro-American saxophonist, composer

51 Albert King plays the blues, Odeon Theatre, Hammersmith, London 1969 Photograph: © Val Wilmer

and arranger: 'Thank God for slavery, because otherwise, I guess, jazz wouldn't have happened at all.'[63]

As we have already seen, jazz is many things to many people. To the Nazis and the Communists of the 1930s and 40s it was anathema: the Nazis vilified 'Nigger' music and the USSR twice tried to ban jazz officially.[64] They might just as well have tried to drain the oceans. For jazz has spread around the world, speaking to people of all colours and creeds. Born from the unspeakable misery of a people who had been branded as unworthy, jazz was the means by which that people asserted its worthiness, its dignity. And in giving the world jazz, Afro-American culture did far more than encourage a foot to tap here or a finger to snap there, in careless abandon.

As the Afro-American poet and painter Ted Joans emphasises in such poems as 'Jazz Is My Religion' and 'The Sax Bit', there is magic of the first order in jazz. In 'The Sax Bit', from the 1971 collection *A Black Manifesto in Jazz Poetry and Prose*, Joans celebrates the 'golden mine of a million marvellous sounds' and in particular, the key role which Coleman Hawkins (1901–69) played in the evolution of the saxophone from a novelty of the dance band to an instrument of immense transformative power:

> This saxophone salvation/modern gri gri hanging from
> jazzmen's necks placed there by Coleman Hawkins
> a full body and soul sorcerer whose spirit dwells eternally
> in every saxophone NOW and all those sound-a-phones
> to be[65]

The first great tenor saxophonist in jazz, Hawkins's October 1939 recording of 'Body and Soul' remains one of the outstanding achievements of the music. The huge sound and sweeping harmonic imagination which the recording revealed was developed even further in Hawkins's 1948 composition 'Picasso' — a solo performance and dedication which continues to serve as a sinewy reminder of the many links between jazz and twentieth-century painting.

Jazz has been one of the main vehicles to that primitivistic, potentially healing state of consciousness which has haunted the post-Romantic Western mind. When Jean Cocteau first heard American jazz in 1918, he felt that it was 'as fertilising to the artist as life itself.'[66] The Dadaists, particularly Richard Huelsenbeck, were fascinated by what they called 'Negro rhythms'. Huelsenbeck's obsession with 'the big drum' complemented Tristan Tzara's gathering together of African and Oceanic poems drawn from existing ethnographies and chanted at Dada performances in Zurich's Cabaret Voltaire.[67] As we have seen, a decade later jazz was to play a key role in Hesse's *Steppenwolf*. And it was at this time that the poet and critic Michel Leiris, who spent many a late evening in the 1920s listening to jazz with André Masson, memorably compared the effect of jazz to a form of possession — to a religious experience involving music, dance and eroticism. For Leiris, jazz unfurled 'an orgiastic banner to the colours of the moment'.[68]

Such a perception contains a large measure of truth. However, it also risks being trapped within one or another variety of potentially regressive myths. Consider, for example, Max Beckmann's 1930 *Self-Portrait*, with its phallic fantasy of a saxophone wrapped around the painter's waist and hips. Jazz *is* a very sensual music: but it is also music of much intellectual consequence. A major part of jazz's multivalent significance, in fact, is that it so convincingly transcends such deep-rooted dualisms of language. For in jazz, body and soul, heart and mind combine to epitomise what Robert A. Johnson calls 'the sensuous joy' of art. In this music, 'the life of the spirit' is indeed 'seen through the senses', as Johnson puts it.[69]

The avant-garde saxophonist and composer Anthony Braxton (*b*.1945) has described 'the total body' of the history of jazz in America as 'the most important alternative aesthetic and vibrational reality for America that's happened since black people were brought here as slaves.'[70] As *Forces In Motion* (Graham Lock's excellent study of this Chicagoan multi-instrumentalist) reveals, Braxton appreciates a wide range of twentieth-century music, including the work of Partsch, Stockhausen, Arnold Schoenberg and John Cage. And he is also aware of how white musicians have made telling contributions to jazz, citing the late alto saxophonist Paul Desmond as both his first major influence and an enduring personal favourite — 'a lightning-fast improviser, who understood sound logic and how to prepare the event.'[71] However, it is the essential Afro-American contribution to the ideas of 'sound logic' and 'event' in twentieth-century music which Braxton wishes to stress — a contribution which he has developed and refined in a variety of racially-integrated groups. And whether intentionally so or not, Braxton's understanding of music's transformative power is strongly reminiscent of shamanism.

For example, taking issue with the Zen-pragmatist John Cage's idea that we should stop choking the natural flow of existence with the various human glues of melody, harmony and rhythm, and just 'let a sound be a sound', Braxton points out that 'to study the meta-reality dynamics of creativity as it's viewed in world culture terms is to understand that music is not just a sound, the experience of listening to music is not just listening to sound. For those who are able to enter into abstract music, that phenomenon involves unifying what is being transmitted; and to enter the upper partials of music is to gain insight into the wonder of music, the wonder of existence. Really to enter the world of sound is to understand what a given function affirms in terms of a primary force — I'll say it like that.'[72] Marilyn Crispell, the very fine (white) pianist in Braxton's mid-1980s quartet, has spoken similarly of music as being 'an energy field, with waves of feeling that rise and fall, a feeling of going higher, to a non-mundane state . . . when you're really hooked into the music, you reach another level of energy that goes beyond the mechanics of it. I think it comes through getting in touch with your energy or with the primal energy that exists in the universe. That's the level I'm interested in reaching.'[73]

The perceptions of Braxton and Crispell parallel those of one of the strongest spirits in twentieth-century art: the Afro-American pianist, composer, poet (and sometime dancer) Cecil Taylor (b.1933). Since his first release on the Transition label in the mid-1950s, the dense, stabbing power and lightning lyricism of Taylor's fiercely percussive music have proclaimed a world of inspiring intensity. In recent years, the shamanic overtones of that intensity have been reinforced and developed by Taylor's readings of his poetry and collaborations with such Afro-American modern dance ensembles as The Dianne McIntyre Dance Company, with whom he performed at London's Roundhouse in 1984.

In 1987, I was fortunate enough to spend several hours in the company of this exceptional, extremely cultured musician, when he came to Brighton Polytechnic to give a lecture and performance to students of the Jazz Studies class which I teach there. When I suggested to him that the 1984 performance with McIntyre's company had exhibited clear shamanic qualities, Taylor's silence was as equivocal as his smile. His answer came in the performance which he later gave for the students. Appearing unannounced from behind stage curtains, Taylor moved slowly across the stage, his body undulating with stylised, dramatic force. As his growling phonemes and barking speech fragments gradually turned into incantatory poetry, and he moved to the piano to begin a blistering half hour of improvisation, one began to grasp the full force of his belief that 'Part of what this music is about of course is not to be delineated exactly, it's about magic, and capturing spirits . . .'[74]

Long fascinated by all sorts of dance, from the tap of Bill Robinson to the flamenco of Carmen Amaya, as well as the whole modern tradition of Afro-American dance which one associates with such luminaries as Katherine Dunham and Alvin Ailey, Taylor has said that he tries to imitate on the piano the leaps that a dancer makes in space.[75] His formidable technique has sometimes led commentators to associate his work with the complexity of the latter-day European tradition, as evinced by a composer such as Bela Bartók. However, Taylor himself much prefers to underline the relation of his music not only to such central pianists of jazz as Duke Ellington, Thelonious Monk, Bud Powell and Horace Silver, but also to jazz's inheritance and development of ancient traditions of ecstasy and inspiration. The ultimate import of the ability to improvise, which is a crucial aspect of jazz, has been described by Taylor as 'the magical lifting of one's spirits to a state of trance. It means the most heightened perception of one's self, but one's self in relation to other forms of life . . . It has to do with religious forces.'[76]

52 Cecil Taylor,
New York 1982
Photograph: © Val Wilmer

The effect of Taylor's shaman-like approach to what he calls 'rhythm-sound energy' — of his belief that 'Rhythm is life the space of time danced thru'[77] — is particularly evident in such pieces as the 1968 'Communications', which saw trumpeter and composer Michael Mantler setting Taylor's ecstatic pianism in dialogue with the twenty-strong Jazz Composer's Orchestra; the 1974 *Silent Tongues* solo recording from the Montreux Jazz Festival; 'Cun-Un-Un-Ùn-An' and 'Winged Serpent' from the 1984 large group recording *Winged Serpent (Sliding Quadrant)*; 'Glossalalia' from the 1986 solo release *For Olim*, and much of the 1989 *In Florescence* album, with its cryptic, animistic poetry and multi-layered, condensed trio interaction.[78]

On the wild, primitivistic 'Cun-Un-Un-Ùn-An' nine musicians from a variety of continents — including Taylor's constant musical companion for twenty-six years, the selfless alto saxophonist Jimmy Lyons (1932—86) — begin the piece with freely-phrased vocal cries and moans over waves of rich 'rain forest' percussion. Throaty *glissandi* and fast moving drum figures then precipitate passages of massive orchestral resonance, delivered in an hypnotic combination of *staccato* accents and gradually swelling dynamics. The music would seem to epitomise what the Native American shaman Brook Medicine Eagle meant when she once spoke of the shamanic challenge of playing on the edge: for it is at 'the edge of the unformed' that the special nature of the shamanic approach to the sacred comes into its own.[79] Chaos must yield to a sense of cosmos; but that sense should never solidify into the sort of fixed form that is the delight of the death dealers of abstract aesthetics, political ideology and institutionalised religion. It is hard to think of another musician who has addressed this challenge with such uncompromising vitality as Taylor has done over the past thirty-five years.

Braxton's emphasis on the vibrational force of Afro-American music, Crispell's belief that music is 'a spiritual expression and has a healing and transcending power',[80] and Taylor's conviction that the deepest aspect of creativity is always 'an attempt to understand the nature of the most sacred areas of one's own body temple'[81] all point to how much the European Romantic goal of healing the fractured consciousness of post-Cartesian culture has been continued and deepened by Afro-American culture this century. (And on this note, it is appropriate to reflect how clearly the smoking of ganga, which is so much part of the Rastafarian involvement with reggae music, can be related to Thoreau's celebration of the temple which is the body. According to Howard Johnson and Jim Pines, in their study *Reggae: Deep Roots Music*, religious Rastafarians see smoking the 'holy herb' as a purification of the body, where 'the body represents the "church" in which the holy spirit indwells. This belief and practice contrasts sharply with the Catholic church, for example, where incense is used to purify the church building.'[82]) It should hardly be necessary to underline how much the celebration of the body in jazz contrasts with the repression of sensuality in much institutionalised religion, nor the extent to which the so-called blue notes of jazz scales handle emotional contradictions and complexities in ways which can help to release us from the false promises of absolutes, be they those of politics or religion, love or hate.[83]

'Why', asked Thoreau nearly a century and a half ago, 'should we be in such desperate haste to succeed and in such desperate enterprises?'[84] He advised that we respect the person who does not keep pace with his sadly driven companions; the person who perhaps steps to the pace of 'a different drummer'.[85] As Thoreau wrote, American slaves were singing themselves out of their misery through the spirituals and field hollers which have since become such an emotional touchstone for the Afro-American musical tradition. And it is precisely within that tradition that the most potent transmutations of Thoreau's metaphor into fact are to be found. For example, jazz's various approaches to time (such as early syncopation, the Swing Era's more legato 4/4, Afro-Cuban and Latin polyrhythms, bebop's clipped, speedy accents, the simultaneously rolling and floating polyrhythms of Elvin Jones, or post-1960s 'energy/pulse' playing) can serve to unite body and soul, heart and mind and release us from the

53 Rashied Ali,
New York 1972
Photograph: © Val Wilmer

straitjacket of Judaeo-Christian historical (i.e. linear) time. Jazz, blues and reggae may all intensify our sensitivity to sound and the interaction of melody, harmony and rhythm, to the extent that we begin to experience the replenishing, mythical and magical circles of time that exist deep inside us.[86]

Underneath the exultant, dancing swing, the technical innovations and the flair of such modern Afro-American jazz masters of the drum as Sonny Greer, Baby Dodds, Jo Jones, Big Sid Catlett, Kenny Clarke, Max Roach, Art Blakey, Philly Joe Jones, Dannie Richmond, Ed Blackwell, Billy Higgins, Elvin Jones, Tony Williams, Rashied Ali, Sunny Murray, Milford Graves, Andrew Cyrille, Famoudou Don Moye, Jack DeJohnette, Thurman Barker and Roland Shannon Jackson lies an ancient archetype: the archetype of the shaman and the drum and the magical flight to both the heights of the Tree of Life and the centre of the Great, or Cosmic Self.[87] (Such an archetype also informs both the rhythms of the legendary Jamaican master drummer Count Ossie, whose work with The Rasta Family — such as 'Mystic Memories', 'Drums for Wise Man' and 'Chanting Higher Heights' — supplies a primal counterpart to the later 'redemption songs' of Bob Marley and The Wailers,[88] and the work of such diverse, outstanding European drummers as John Marshall and Han Bennink, Jon Christensen and Paul Lovens.)

The Brazilian dancer Ismael Ivo, whose highly expressive choreography is often based on strong Afro-American and Latin rhythms, has spoken of his desire to explore the labyrinth of suffering and aspiration in his art, in order to 'set the primitive instinct free in modern civilisation'.[89] As anyone who has seen such solo pieces by Ivo as *Phoenix* (a seven-part reflection on the African diaspora and Afro-Brazilian ritual) can attest, such a goal is pursued with the most sophisticated command of both vision and technique — elements which are sometimes divorced in the Western avant-garde, but which are completely interdependent in Ivo's work. And this is exactly the case with regard to the shamanic heart of the Afro-American musical tradition. The magic-working musicians are those who have applied themselves ceaselessly to their craft: such effort has not been directed towards technical perfection for its own sake, but rather towards a deeper understanding of the transformative pulse which lies at the heart of the labyrinth of suffering and aspiration of which Ivo speaks.

In *The Bluesman: The Musical Heritage of Black Men and Women in the Americas* the modern blues singer Julio Finn has recently argued that the true significance of the blues tradition (which one can argue is the spiritual backbone of jazz, reggae and funk/rap) can only be grasped through an appreciation of the religious, social and anthropological themes which bind the blues to the ancient African world of animistic magic — to the voodoo and the hoodoo which helped to carry aspects of this world over to the (so-called) New World. The blues singer is the *griot* of the modern world; the free-thinking singer of power, of faith in the unconscious.[90] Think of Jimi Hendrix (not mentioned by Finn, curiously enough) digging into the history of the blues on the fourteen minute 'Voodoo Chile', from the 1968 album *Electric Ladyland*. As Charles Shaar Murray comments in *Crosstown Traffic*, his stimulating book on the guitarist, this track is the most remarkable example of 'the alchemical processes' whereby Hendrix (1942—70) extended the power and the mystery of the blues 'into his own personal dreamscape . . .'[91]

At its best, as on 'Voodoo Chile', 'Third Stone From The Sun' and '1983 (A Merman I Should Turn To Be)', this was a dreamscape which conjured the triple shamanic magic of sound, rhythm and song. Soprano saxophonist Steve Lacy, one of the most open-minded, questing jazz musicians of the past thirty-five years, has described Hendrix as 'one of the gods, and that's the only name that'll go because he played like nobody's business. Hendrix was beyond all the categories, and that's the kind of stuff I like, stuff that transcends those earthly categories. To hell with the rest of it, the most interesting thing in music is the magic. That's what we're after — pure magic!'[92] In 'Voodoo Chile', Hendrix created such magic through images which are as reminiscent of shamanism as is the brooding power of the opening, solo guitar riffs:

54 Jimi Hendrix, Royal Albert Hall, London 1967
Photograph: © Val Wilmer

Well, the night I was born
Lord I swear the moon turned a fire red . . .
Well, my poor mother cried out 'Lord, the gypsy was right!'
And I see her fall right down dead. Have mercy!

Well, mountain lions found me here
And set me on an eagle's wing
He took me past the outposts of infinity
And when he brought me back he gave me Venus witch's ring . . .

And he said fly on . . . fly on
Voodoo chile![93]

Hendrix's music raises the thorny question of the seemingly compulsive need to categorise experience which afflicts late-twentieth-century culture: if we don't know how to label music, how are we supposed to sell the stuff — let alone listen to it? There are blues purists who will swear that Hendrix did not play the blues, just as there are jazz enthusiasts who will insist that Hendrix did not play jazz. As Shaar points out, however, the whole point of Hendrix's music is that it grew out of a rich, transmutative feeling for the totality of the Afro-American tradition — a tradition that has been split time and again into divisive categories, for the sake of commercialism, lazy ears or a racist desire (sometimes conscious, sometimes not) to diminish the overall significance of black culture.[94] There are aspects of gospel, soul, blues and jazz music in Hendrix; but above all, there is the magic that Steve Lacy talks about. And the deepest roots of that magic lie in the original, shamanic manifestation of uncompartmentalised, yet highly developed creativity.

The same point can be made about the history of jazz. This has often divided enthusiasts of various periods in a manner reminiscent of holy wars. But if jazz is seen in the light of shamanism, rather than the contrasting history of specific styles — some of which some listeners and critics will insist until Doomsday are not 'the real jazz'[95] — one may begin to share something of the jazz-loving wisdom of an Afro-American sculptor like Ed Love or a bandleader such as Sun Ra (aka Herman 'Sonny' Blount).

From 1984 to 1988, Love (b.1936) worked on *The Arkestra*, a twenty-seven piece welded steel, paint and mixed media celebration of the Afro-American musical tradition. His vibrant kinetic pieces are dedicated to a wide range of artists, from Sweet Honey in The Rock and Duke Ellington to Bob Marley and The Wailers, Charlie Parker, John Coltrane and The World Saxophone Quartet.[96] The collective name of Love's various pieces was a tribute to the legendary orchestra which keyboardist Sun Ra has led for the past thirty-five years. One of the great jazz visionaries, Sun Ra (*b.*1914) pioneered the use of electric keyboards in the 1950s. More importantly, he has led one of the most stimulating ensembles of twentieth-century music, whose repertoire extends from shape-shifting performances of jazz classics by Jelly Roll Morton, Fletcher Henderson, Duke Ellington and Thelonious Monk, through energising blues and funk workouts, to the sort of mystical, volatile tone poems found on *The Heliocentric Worlds Of Sun Ra* recordings of the mid-1960s.

For Sun Ra, music is a vehicle that takes one to what he calls the Omniverse — a state of mind that acknowledges that 'space is the place', and which is as far beyond the twentieth-century rational norm as the glittering 'space coats' worn by The Arkestra in performance or Sun Ra's insistence that he is not part of mundane history, but belongs instead to 'the Kingdom of Mythology'.[97]

In 1967 Sun Ra gave a mixed media show in New York's Central Park, with some one hundred players, singers and dancers and a large crew of

55 Sun Ra Arkestra, Wigan 1989
Photograph: © Sefton Samuels

light and sound technicians. During a performance in Berlin in 1970, he gazed at stars through both a telescope and the solid roof of the Berlin Kongresshalle, while a fire eater and light show added further touches of surreality to the proceedings. As the astute German critic Ekkehard Jost has suggested, such performances should be seen in the context of 'the rites of the voodoo cult, a blend of magic, music and dance; and in [the context of] the vaudeville shows of itinerant troupes of actors and musicians, where there was room for gaudilly tinselled costumes and the stunts of supple acrobats, as well as for the emotional depths of blues sung by a Ma Rainey or a Bessie Smith.'[98] But the roots of Sun Ra's mythopoeic activities stretch back beyond voodoo, beyond even his obsession with all things Egyptian, to the shamanic core of musical-dramatic activity. The titles of such Sun Ra pieces as 'Medicine for a Nightmare', 'Cosmic Tones for Mental Therapy', 'The Sun Myth' and 'Other Worlds' all underline the shamanic import of his work — as did the art work which he created for the *Heliocentric Worlds* recordings. This featured a strong, frontal image of a metamorphosing, masklike face and abstract landscape, with currents of energy flowing in and out of various spirals and labyrinths.

Only slightly less surreal than Sun Ra, the late Rahsaan Roland Kirk — who is also honoured in Love's *Arkestra* — is another jazz musician whose work transcends narrow historical categories to send the imagination spinning off in the direction of shamanism. Before he died in 1977, at the age of 41, Kirk had recorded tributes to a whole range of jazz luminaries. In the seventeen minutes of the 1970 'The Seeker', this blind multi-instrumentalist takes us from New Orleans voodoo (via a chuckle box) and 1930s swing through the 1940s bebop of Charlie Parker to the spiritual intensity of so much 1960s jazz. 'Seek! Seek! Seek!' the saxophonist implores.[99]

What we should seek, according to Kirk, is an understanding of both the totality of jazz and the healing import of its greatest practitioners. One thinks immediately of the central achievement of Duke Ellington (1899—1974), with his various orchestral and pianistic syntheses of rhythmic élan, harmonic sophistication and blues power; and of the no less remarkable blends of propulsive affirmation and spacious lyrical introspection in the work of such constantly creative individuals as Charles Mingus (1922—79), Miles Davis (1926—91) and Stan Getz (1927—91). Or one remembers such very different, but complementary figures as saxophonists Lester Young (1909—59) and Eric Dolphy (1928—64).

Young is famous for his light tenor saxophone sound and a more floating, linear style of improvisation than Coleman Hawkins: a 'cooler' approach which still works its magic upon listeners and musicians alike. Young used to listen to song birds at night, calling out and playing back to them in the various keys in which they sang.[100] He thus anticipated something of the controversial fascination which multi-instrumentalist Dolphy felt for the quarter tones of bird melodies. At the end of the 1950s and beginning of the 1960s, Dolphy's highly vocalised sound and volatile improvisations disturbed several jazz critics, one of whom felt obliged to ask the saxophonist if bird imitation could be 'valid' in jazz.[101]

Today, Dolphy's playing is recognised as some of the most emotionally compelling of all jazz. From the perspective of shamanism, rather than stressing the considerable stylistic differences between their music, it may be more productive to recognise the communality of inspiration which Young and Dolphy drew from nature. Like the shamans of old, these two great musicians developed potentially healing dialects of 'the language of the birds'.[102]

Roland Kirk once said that the idea of playing several instruments together came to him in a dream — as did the name Rahsaan. Kirk seems to have had an unusually heightened feeling for the dream-like quality of jazz's

56 Rahsaan Roland Kirk,
New York 1967
Photograph: © Val Wilmer

revivification of ancient, timeless wisdom. On the 1975 'Theme For The Eulipions' his soulful tenor saxophone accompanies a lyric by Betty H. Neals, a lyric which celebrates the activities of a mysterious traveller, who

> Calls himself a 'Journey Agent', a Eulipion.
> Says his friends, the poets, the artists,
> the musicians are journey agents too.
> Listen!
> Listen to his tune.
> Calls it his 'Duty Free Gift', for the traveller. [103]

The critic Michael Ullman has commented that, at its best, Kirk's music is filled with 'the wild spirit' that informs the greatest jazz — the spirit that makes one feel that the music might 'heal the sick and raise the dead'. [104] Like Sun Ra and so many other artists of the Afro-American tradition, this 'Journey Agent' functioned as a creative explorer of the psyche, developing the role of the shaman in the world of the twentieth-century city. This is exactly what one thoughtful commentator on shamanism, Serge King, believes is the key, 'really tough' task for shamanism today. [105]

The idea that musicians within the Afro-American tradition have managed both to remain in touch with and develop deep-rooted feelings and spiritual aspirations is not intended to suggest any reductive, racist notion that such musicians have a 'natural' capacity for the sort of highly rhythmical music which may precipitate ecstatic experience, any more than it is intended to suggest that 'whites can't play the blues'. Nor is it intended to obscure the fact that spiritually significant music within the Afro-American tradition may be music which is more concerned with relatively arhythmic aspects of structure, instrumentation, timbre and voicings. One should also remember that within this broad tradition, a sophisticated sense of structure has often been combined with hypnotic, propulsive rhythm: the work of pianist and composer George Russell, whose 1959 *The Lydian Chromatic Concept of Tonal Organisation* remains one of this century's most profound works of musical theory, furnishes an outstanding example of this sort of synthesis of body and mind, heart and soul. [106] Today, many an Afro-American musician — such as pianist and composer Anthony Davis (*b.*1951) — not only produces work of refined structural interest and sophisticated rhythmic intensity, but will also emphasise verbally the extent to which such a breadth of achievement has long been a central aspect of the Afro-American tradition. (Think only of Ellington's 'Concerto for Cootie' and 'Ko-Ko' from 1940, for example.) [107]

From a shamanic point of view, the importance of the Afro-American musical tradition is that within its rich, multi-layered heritage one finds so many musicians who have combined an unprecedented level of technical ability and innovation with a visionary feeling for the beauty and the sacred significance of the world.[108] One of the most important of these musicians was the saxophonist and composer John Coltrane (1926–67).

Discussing what he called 'the life side' of music, Coltrane once said that 'All a musician can do is to get closer to the sources of nature, and so feel that he is in communion with the natural laws.'[109] As his music brought him closer and closer to such laws, Coltrane was taken beyond conventional notions of beauty: ' . . . it's more than beauty that I feel in music – that I think musicians feel in music . . . over-all, I think the main thing a musician would like to do is to give a picture to the listener of the many wonderful things he knows of and senses in the universe. That's what music is to me – it's another way of saying that this is a big, beautiful universe that we live in, that's been given to us, and here's an example of just how magnificent and encompassing it is. That's what I would like to do. I think that's one of the greatest things you can do in life, and we all try to do it in some way. The musician's way is through his music.'[110]

Before establishing his own quartet at the end of the 1950s, Coltrane worked with such jazz masters as Johnny Hodges, Dizzy Gillespie, Thelonious Monk and Miles Davis. As Bill Cole says in his ground-breaking study of the saxophonist, Coltrane 'first listened to his elders, gained proficiency on his instrument, and then brought that proficiency to his art.'[111] Anticipating Julio Finn's comparison of the blues singer with the African *griot*, the tribal emphasis of Cole's approach places the visionary power of the music of the last seven or eight years of Coltrane's life in the context of the traditional wisdom of the African musician who acknowledges the magic of sound: 'For him [Coltrane], the magic of his sound came through the process of making his own music. [He] sought out the influences of sound – the magic of sound – that aspect which takes people to another level.'[112]

If ever a musician of the twentieth century pursued what Rudhyar calls 'the sacred Tone of cosmic being' it was Coltrane. On the sleeve notes to his 1964 *A Love Supreme* recording, the saxophonist spoke of the 'spiritual awakening' which, 'by the grace of God', he had received in 1957. Helping him to break his previous dependence on alcohol and drugs, this experience of the numinous opened the gates of the collective unconscious for Coltrane. Thereafter, he would approach questions of religion and metaphysics with a Sufi-like humility and breadth of vision.[113]

Throughout much of the magnificent music which Coltrane created in the last decade of his life, there is a feeling of ever-deeper, primal currents of energy flowing into both the individual and collective psyches of the musicians. This energy broke up historical crusts of musical form and set sound, rhythm and song in original, incantatory relation once again.

57 John Coltrane,
London 1961
Photograph: © Val Wilmer

Recordings such as *A Love Supreme*, the June 1965 *Ascension*, October 1965 *Om* and *Kulu Se Mama*, November 1965 *Meditations*, February 1967 *Interstellar Space* and March 1967 *Expression* all embody what Rudhyar calls 'the creative-destructive, transformative-regenerative power of the One Life' with an overwhelming intensity of sound and plasticity of rhythm.

At the same time, there is an intensification of the lyricism which had always lain at the heart of Coltrane's sound. The beautiful 1959 ballad 'Naima' is given an extensive, transmutative reading on the 1966 *Live At The Village Vanguard Again!* album, while tracks like 'After The Rain' (1963), 'Wise One' (1964) and 'Dear Lord' (1965) develop the transcendent serenity of such earlier solos of Coltrane's as that on 'Blue In Green' from Miles Davis's epochal *Kind of Blue* recording of 1959. Such lyricism is as reminiscent of the wonder of Orpingalik or the exaltation of Uvavnuk as it is of the ballads of Johnny Hodges, one of Coltrane's favourite musicians.[114]

At the end of the 1950s, Coltrane was known above all for his unprecedented exploration of complex chord progressions: the critic Ira Gitler once caught something of the nature of Coltrane's development of

Charlie Parker's earlier, sophisticated harmonic sense in his description of his playing as 'sheets of sound'. Such technical command was never an end in itself for Coltrane, who was always interested in the struggle of other artists — such as Van Gogh, whom (as we have seen) he read about with particular interest in the early 1960s — to realise their vision. In the last decade of his life, Coltrane's hard-won mastery of the tenor and soprano saxophones was to merge with a multiphonic, primal approach to questions of both vision and music.

Stimulated by both the spirituality and polyrhythms of African and Asian music, and drawn increasingly away from sophisticated chord progressions to both the gospel and blues roots of the jazz tradition and the pentatonic scales of much folk music, Coltrane was able to turn a 12-bar blues such as 'Chasin' The Trane' or a popular tune like 'My Favorite Things' into an hypnotic half hour or more of mesmeric 'speaking in tongues'.[115] The doctor and author Cuthbert Ormond Simkins documents a moment late in Coltrane's career which illustrates how far the saxophonist's final approach to 'sheets of sound' had come from any purely technical approach: 'John was merging more and more with the music. The sounds were heavy, and had filled the club almost to the point that it would fly. John was wailing, screaming out feelings, weaving lines of notes. It got so mean that he walked up to the mike, expanded his chest and beat on it, screaming: "Aaaaoooaa!!!" Some in the audience walked out: "Oh no, oh no, Trane done went mad now!" '[116]

Several reasons have been advanced for the development which Coltrane's music underwent in the 1960s. Obviously, the man who recorded the stark, infinitely sad 'Alabama' in 1963 was acutely sensitive to the political and social divisions of America at the time, a sensitivity which emerges in Frank Kofsky's long interview with Coltrane in his *Black Nationalism And The Revolution In Music*.[117] Psychiatrists have described the saxophonist's music as sounding like that of a driven, compulsive personality, or as that of someone tied down and screaming to be let free.[118]

From the point of view of shamanism, the political and psychological aspects of Coltrane's music merge into the transmutative idea that, like a shaman of old (and like Sun Ra, whom he first met in 1959 and who was important for his development in a number of ways), Coltrane was inexorably drawn to the archetypal intuition that the world's ills cannot be healed exclusively in the profane realm, so to speak. For the world — the sacred *cosmos* which dominated Coltrane's imagination in the last years of his life — must be periodically recharged with primal energy from the *ur*-domain of mythopoeisis. A particularly intense, lengthy modal blues of the mid-1960s, which Coltrane recorded with his regular quartet partners McCoy Tyner (piano), Jimmy Garrison (bass) and Elvin Jones (drums), is called 'Transition'. There could not have been a more appropriate title for the music which Coltrane created in this period. For it is precisely the (embodied) search for the transition from the realm of the profane to that of the sacred which so distinguishes the last decade of this exemplary musician's life.[119]

In the sleeve notes to *Om*, a recording which found his regular quartet augmented by saxophonist Pharoah Sanders, flautist Joe Brazil and bassist and bass clarinettist Donald Garrett, Coltrane spoke of his understanding of the ultimate Asian mantra: 'Om means the first vibration — that sound, that spirit which sets everything else into being . . . it is the first syllable, the primal word, the word of Power.'[120] In searching so fervently for that word in music, Coltrane left 'true records of his spirit on earth'[121] — records of immense importance for any consideration of the shamanic spirit in twentieth-century art.

Equally important to any such consideration are the spiritual and socio-political concerns of such other key musicians of the 1960s as Ornette Coleman and Don Cherry, Pharoah Sanders and Leon Thomas, Albert Ayler and Archie Shepp, most of whom worked with Coltrane at some time or other and helped confirm him in his pursual of a primal concept of music. In the sleevenotes to his 1967 recording *Mama Too Tight*,

58 Elvin Jones,
New Jersey 1972
Photograph: © Val Wilmer

saxophonist Shepp (*b*.1937) might have been speaking for all these musicians (as well as many of the exceptional drummers mentioned earlier): 'I play music out of an overwhelming need to play; to make the rains come; to abolish wars . . . the question is not whether one chooses to be "far out". It is rather the sudden, wonderful, intuitive transmogrification of one's entire biological, sociological, political being into a living line — so that the moment of performance is less a technological feat than a prayer.'[122]

In 1969 tenor saxophonist Albert Ayler (1936 — 70), who cultivated a pleading, barn-wide vibrato in his huge, grainy sound, recorded a lengthy piece of cross-rhythmic intensity entitled 'Music Is The Healing Force Of The Universe'. Vocalist Mary Maria joined Ayler, imploring the listener to 'let it [the healing power of music] come in/oh let it come in/the music of the Universe/the music of love . . .'[123] For Ayler, whose 1964 *Spiritual Unity* recording with (white) bassist Gary Peacock and drummer Sunny Murray is a three-way classic of the vibrant, so-called 'New Thing' music which disturbed many traditional critics at the time, music was more about feelings than notes. Like Shepp, Coleman and Sanders, Ayler played out of a deep feeling for the folk roots of music. It was exactly this feeling which led so many jazz musicians in the 1960s back to the potential shamanic magic of music: the healing magic of incantatory sound, rhythm and song.[124]

On *Spirits Known and Unknown*, his debut recording of 1969, vocalist Leon Thomas took the jazz tradition of scat singing (a tradition originated many years earlier by Louis Armstrong) beyond jazz to its ultimate roots in world music: 'At the very beginning of all music was the voice. Now we're getting back to the importance of that primary human instrument' wrote Thomas in the sleevenotes to the album. 'The voice can be the most evocative of all instruments' he continued, 'but as I hear things, for that to happen requires going into the most ancient forms of musical expression — what the pygmies and others sing in Africa, Indian ragas, music of the Himalayas. If you listen, although some people regard these people as "primitive", what they're doing is really very complex and subtle but at the same time it's a free expression of the voice.'[125] Thomas described his spirited combination of the jazz, blues and gospel tradition with a fast-moving, yodel-like 'shake' of the voice as 'egoless' — 'because it goes into the unconscious. It can be a moan or a cry or a tear. It can be a great big sigh — but under control. The thing is, however, not to be limited to what you consciously think or feel — you have to let it all well up.'[126]

The singer's collaboration with saxophonist Pharoah Sanders on the latter's *Karma* album of 1969 resulted in one of the strongest expressions of the (old) New Thing. Moving from richly percussive, *rubato* moods to *ostinato* bass patterns and passages of glorious tenor affirmation and vocalese, the music hymned both 'The Creator' and 'Mother Nature' as it moved with regenerative, shaman-like balance between worlds of primal sound and serene order. A similar sense of balance can be discerned in the music of trumpeter Don Cherry and pianist Keith Jarrett, two musicians who over the past quarter of a century have taken the fervent spirit of so much jazz of the 1960s into more refined, but no less potent areas of expression.

Don Cherry (*b.*1936) describes what he plays today as 'Primal Music'. Like Leon Thomas on *Spirits Known and Unknown*, the half Native American, half Afro-American trumpeter and multi-instrumentalist is above all concerned to get to the egoless heart of life. From his first, late-1950s recordings with alto saxophonist Ornette Coleman — where the musicians were as one in emphasising melodic improvisation which was sensitive to the flowing spirit of their folk-like compositions — to the 1989/90 recording *Multikulti*, Cherry has sought the healing vibrations of music, in a manner which is reminiscent of nothing so much as the process of Jungian individuation. Travelling the world, Cherry has integrated aspects of Indian, African, Native American, Far Eastern and European instrumentation, scales and rhythms into a suite-like approach to sound, rhythm and song. He has learned to play the African doussn'gouni (a kind of hunter's harp) and studied Indian vocal technique with the great master of Indian singing, Pandit Pran Nath; brought the spirit of both Tantric Buddhism and rapping reggae into his music, and worked creatively with electronics — while also producing some of the purest acoustic music of recent years.

Two records in particular indicate the extent to which Cherry early on preserved and extended Coltrane's key role as a harbinger of music of the collective unconscious. *Eternal Rhythm*, from 1968, combined the meditative tranquillity of gamelan music with the urgent, protesting spirit of the blues, while *Humus – The Life Exploring Force*, from 1971, embraced ragas, South American bird flute melodies, 1930s big band vamps, 1960s 'free' outbursts of energy and Chinese pentatonicism: there was even a spot for Cherry's three-year-old son to contribute his drumming and guitar improvisations. Such a breadth of vision (which included a dedication to Herman Hesse) typifies the music of a man who has long abandoned the strictures of professionalism: 'I've been a professional musician long enough and have shown that I can do it. But professionalism became like a religion in certain quarters. To me, there's more to religion than that.'[127]

Cherry has said that what he admires in high quality improvisation (which is not necessarily achieved by highly professional musicians) is the combination of 'earthly and godly' elements that he has felt in listening to much world folk music.[128] It is a combination which was particularly evident in the music which Cherry created with multi-instrumentalist Collin Walcott (1945–84) and percussionist Nana Vasconcelos in the CODONA ensemble of the late 1970s and early 1980s. Tracks such as

59 Don Cherry and Dewey
Redman, New York 1982
Photograph: © Val Wilmer

'Like That of Sky' and 'New Light', from the trio's first, eponymous
release, struck a spacious, meditative note redolent of Tibetan temple
music; 'Que Faser', from their second album, remains one of the great
manifestations of world music Utopianism, with its bright, swinging
combination of soaring vocalese, jazz–inflected trumpet, Indian sitar and
Brazilian polyrhythms. The French critic Alain Gerber once described
Cherry's exoticism as 'not that of the Orient and not that of Africa: it is
the exoticism of Somewhere, the Here and Somewhere; and this means it
is the exoticism of dreams.'[129] How appropriate then that in 1989 Cherry
should record 'Love in Outer Space' and 'Of Invisible Them' with Sun
Ra and his Arkestra. The collaboration could not help but underline the
shamanic note of psychic exploration in each man's music — music which
gives us invaluable hints of the wholeness of life.[130]

It is the relation of music to the wholeness of life which fascinates Keith
Jarrett (*b.*1945), who is one of the major, shaman-like musicians of the past
few decades. Like Don Cherry, Jarrett is the sort of thorough professional
who knows how important it is not to be restricted by professionalism.

A child prodigy, of Central European background, Jarrett studied piano from the age of three and presented his first full-length solo recital (of classical pieces) when he was seven. Years later, having established himself as one of the greatest jazz pianists and composers of the 1970s and 80s, Jarrett returned to the world of classical recitals for a while, playing the music of, among others, Bach, Mozart, Bartók, Stravinsky, Samuel Barber and Lou Harrison.

From a shamanic perspective, it is interesting to learn of the chief reason for the particular affinity Jarrett feels for the work of Bach, Beethoven, Mozart and Handel, composers who were the leading keyboard improvisers of their day: 'I wouldn't say I like their music because they were all improvisers, but there was something in the music, and I would say that it is the ecstatic knowledge that comes through in Bach's music and in Beethoven's music. It's the knowledge of the ecstatic state — which means that's why their music conveys so much . . . I know that when you're an improviser, a true improviser, you have to be familiar with ecstasy, otherwise you can't connect with music.'[131]

The improvisations of Jarrett's solo (jazz) concerts of the 1970s and 1980s were full of rhythmic heat, with strong overtones of the gospel, blues and boogie-woogie traditions; but they were also distinguished by their sophisticated harmonic sense and hymnal, European Romantic quality. Like Don Cherry, Jarrett has extended and refined Coltrane's legacy, taking us deep into the labyrinths of longing that connect self and world. Convinced that music 'is about your blood flowing',[132] the pianist has been particularly struck by Sufi ideas of inspiration and ecstasy.[133] In a manner similar to Cecil Taylor (a musician with whom he is sometimes pointlessly contrasted, by critics who find his European Romanticism hard to stomach), Jarrett places improvisation firmly within the context of ecstatic spirituality.

For Jarrett, it is essential that improvisation comes from the deepest layers of the self, rather than 'off the top of the head'. True improvisation is thus 'more than the word expresses . . . It is a "blazing forth" of a "Divine Will" (Divine if only because of its greater force). This means you (the pianist) are not only the victim of a message (impulse) quite beyond your own human ideas and thoughts, but you must put out (into the world of sound) as large a portion of it as possible (having first put complete trust in the "impulse").'[134]

The shamanic implications of these thoughts are evident not only in Jarrett's many hours of solo improvisations at 'the edge of the unformed', to quote Brook Medicine Eagle, but also in much of the music which he recorded in the 1970s with either his American group (with Dewey Redman, Charlie Haden and Paul Motian) or his European 'Belonging' quartet (with Jan Garbarek, Palle Danielsson and Jon Christensen).[135] Three very different recordings from the 1980s furnish further compelling evidence of the shamanic import of Jarrett's wide-ranging work.

60 Keith Jarrett,
New York 1971
Photograph: © Val Wilmer

On the 1980 *Invocations*, recorded in Ottobeuren Abbey, Jarrett plays pipe organ and soprano saxophone, his approach on the latter lending a more spacious ambience to the Middle Eastern overtones which Coltrane brought to the instrument. The music — all of which was extemporised — is as earthy as it is ethereal. The organ growls and shudders, like some mythical creature of the steppes ('Power', 'Resolve'), setting up hypnotic drones and *ostinato* patterns ('Mirages', 'Realities'). Beseeching, single soprano notes ('First: Solo Voice') complement sustained passages of unaffected lyricism ('Recognition'), while the extraordinary contrasts of timbre on 'Shock, Scatter' are suggestive of nothing so much as what Rudhyar calls 'the creative-destructive, transformative-regenerative power of the One Life'. The music has an unmistakable mythopoeic quality, summoning 'the sacred Tone of cosmic being' with a variety of wild and brooding episodes redolent of East European folk music or ancient pagan ritual.[136]

Similar qualities can be discerned in much of the 1985 *Spirits*, which Jarrett recorded at his home studio in New Jersey. Coming from somewhere deep in the collective unconscious, this music helped to heal the pianist of the paralysing depression from which he was suffering at the time. After he had improvised a variety of folk-like melodies on a number of recorders, Pakistani flute and the piano, and had overdubbed tabla and shaker rhythms, Jarrett was led to reflect on the spirit of place that had perhaps flowed into both his blood and the music. There are shades of both Thoreau and Jim Morrison in Jarrett's appreciation of the strong spirit of Native America which he felt in the grounds around his house and studio.[137] And in the sleevenotes to the album, the primitivistic force of Jarrett's approach to music emerged in full flood.

His words constitute a striking plea for a mythopoeic, shamanic approach to art's role today. As such, they merit quoting at some length: 'Music is part of life . . .[it] should not remind us of the control we seem to have over our lives. It should remind us of the necessity of surrender, the capacity in man for understanding the reason for this surrender, the conditions that are necessary for it, the Being necessary for it . . . If there is such a thing as cosmic music, that music should certainly be in touch with the earth, which is the largest part of the cosmos to which we have access. What if so-called "ethnic" or "primitive" music really has been cosmic all along? . . . What if our separation, through science and specialization, from our living context, is a sin? (or a sign?) What if there is only one channel left for remembering this since [institutionalised] religion has condoned it in order to survive . . .? What if this channel were "art", because in its deepest sense, its moral sense, it is participation, not separation . . .'[138]

Jarrett expressed similar sentiments in his sleevenotes to the 1987 *Changeless*, a live album of four improvisations from the hands of Jarrett, bassist Gary Peacock and drummer Jack DeJohnette. The music is a superb example of jazz interaction at its best, moving with complete naturalness from passages of urgent, fiercely swinging celebration ('Dancing') and limpid reflection ('Endless') to moments of mesmeric repetition ('Lifeline') and rumbling, primal sound deep in the bass register ('Ecstasy'). In Jarrett's hands, the piano truly comes alive. As Ian Carr comments in his fine study of the pianist, Jarrett has always treated the instrument 'like a live creature, crouching before it, standing up before it, coaxing sounds from it, stroking the strings, kicking the pedals, attacking the keyboard.'[139] And this is not done out of any cheap sense of theatricality. Like the cries and groans with which he often accompanies himself, it is all part of Jarrett's shaman-like quest to see with the 'eyes of the heart'; to participate 'in the center'; to connect with 'a greater power'.[140]

With its increasing emphasis on both the power of improvisation and the scales and tones of folk music, the emotional directness of so much jazz of the 1960s and after had an enlivening effect on the nature of jazz's development outside America. There had long been excellent non-American players: Django Reinhardt, Stan Hasselgard, Lars Gullin, Hans

Koller, Phil Seaman and Joe Harriott are but a few of the most important names that come immediately to mind. And several of these musicians — such as Reinhardt, Gullin and Harriott — have an indisputable claim to originality. But with Coltrane's heart-on-sleeve emotionalism and the mixture of folkish composition and wide-open improvisation in the music of Coleman, Cherry and Ayler, non-Americans committed to jazz were really encouraged to dig into their own folk roots and develop a music of their own. Here too, strong shamanic echoes can be discerned.[141]

We have already seen how potently the music of Norwegian Jan Garbarek — who early in his career was indebted to Coltrane, Ayler, Shepp, Sanders and Don Cherry, working with the last-named in Oslo in the late 1960s — embodies the spirit of the modern Nordic shamanic tradition. Such fellow Nordic musicians as Finnish drummer Edvard Vesala (*b*.1945) and saxophonist and flautist Juhani Aaltonen (*b*.1935) have also produced much refreshing music redolent of the shape-shifting mysteries of the North.

On Vesala's 1974 *Nan Madol*, for example, spacious, reflective pieces such as 'Love For Living', 'Call From The Sea' and 'The Wind' broadened traditional jazz instrumentation, with harp and violin, percussion, flutes and bells striking a mystical note of nature reverie.[142] 'Star Flight', from the 1976 *Satu*, found Vesala's forceful drumming and arrangement combining rock and free accents to send Norwegian guitarist Terje Rypdal and Polish trumpeter Tomasz Stanko into the stratosphere.[143] On Aaltonen's 1978 *Springbird* the mood is again mystical, with Vesala contributing Japanese koto, Indian tambura, guitar, piano, accordion, bells and percussion to Aaltonen's arrangements: the percussionists of the National Ballet of Senegal increase the rhythmic power of the music on several tracks. As one might infer from titles like 'Winds of the Mystical Night', 'Hibernate', 'Ghostrider' and 'Dance of the Witches', the overall impression which the music gives is that of a primitivistic homage to the spirit of place of the North. A long way from the urban resonances of much of the American jazz tradition, it is music of the living sea and rock, of ancient earth and sky.[144]

If one stands by the water's edge in Helsinki, where *Springbird* was recorded, and looks southeastwards across the Gulf of Finland, St Petersburg is but a day's travel away. Far beyond that monument to Russia's one-time love affair with Western classicism lie the Volga and the Ural rivers. And to the East, beyond the forbidding Ural mountains, lies the vastness of Siberia — home of the Yakut, people of the shamanic drum whose heartbeat is that of a horse. And also home, in recent years, to some extraordinary jazz.

In 1983 the London-based company Leo Records released *Homo Liber* by the Siberian 4. Like such previous Leo releases of Russian jazz as *Live in West Germany* (1979) and *Con Fuoco* (1978/80) by the Vyacheslav Ganelin Trio, the music of Vladimir Tolkachev (saxophones and flute), Yuri Yukechev (piano, vibes, flute and percussion), Sergey Panasenko (bass) and Sergey Belichenko (drums) greatly impressed Western critics. While influences from Sun Ra and Keith Jarrett were inferred, the group's overall originality of vision could not be denied.[145]

What is remarkable about the music of the Siberian 4 is the refusal to settle comfortably into any one style. While there are echoes of the intensity of free jazz, there are also passages of unabashed lyricism and tonal beauty. The tradition of vocalising into a flute, which in jazz terms can be traced back to Roland Kirk and Eric Dolphy, acquires something of an original shamanic mystery, and together with the discreet use of bells, does much to establish *Homer Liber*'s unclichéd aura of spiritual quest and affirmation. Pianist Yukechev comments: 'You know, sometimes a musician gets into that special mood and he becomes practically a "priest" of art. There are rare moments when he enters into some unusual religion. Those are moments of enlightenment, refinement, catharsis. There are such moments with Ellington, the Ganelin Trio, Peterson, Basie; but it happens very seldom.'[146] Drummer Belichenko continues the theme, but with more recent exemplars: 'I feel very close to the ideas of Alice Coltrane, Sun Ra, Sanders, about music as an emanation of the universal spirit, as an expression of man's belonging to the cosmic world.'[147] Saxophonist Tolkachev eschews examples, but reinforces the overall theme in his belief that 'music is itself a religion, which I value above all, as an opportunity to go beyond the limits of everyday experience, to exist in another world.'[148]

With the music of the Siberian 4, the dance of the body electric comes full circle. When an interviewer asked Sergey Belichenko what was special about Siberian jazz, he suggested that 'Siberia has in concentrated form some essence of a pre-European past, thousands of years old, untouched by professionalism. A sort of musical matrix. All these musical influences [such as the improvised music of the Buddhist Touvinians, 'full of echoes of China and India'] could be very fruitful for the future of our jazz.'[149]

At the heart of the musical matrix which Belichenko describes stands the *ur*-figure of the shaman. And as Norman Weinstein — the distinguished Jungian commentator on jazz — recognises, in a world dominated by the sick imperatives of mass culture (be it the culture of communist bureaucracy or capitalist consumerism), the musician who wants to get in touch with the essence of creativity 'is set up as a shaman whether or not he wants the role or wears the outward trappings'.[150]

Weinstein's words are addressed to the present, intriguing situation of Russian jazz, but they apply with equal force to musicians worldwide: 'To follow the daimon living within keyboards horns drums is to define a life as a quest for new and possible form. Within the context of a society where

61 Henri Matisse *The Clown*
(image number 1 from *Jazz*)
1947
© Succession H Matisse/
DACS 1992

life-shapes are mass-produced the musician finds his spiritual callings in inventing that technology which permits the odd mutation, "odd man out". The odd-sounding music relieves the strain of being dully ordinary. Hear, in "idiosyncratic", "idiot" (thank you, Dostoevsky) and "sin" or "syn-". The sin of acting like a fool among those for whom the heart's music is chronic palpitation.'[151] All praise then to all the holy fools of the body electric, as they sing the song of ages: the song of infinite longing, the song of infinite love.

9 Magic Lanterns

In Inuit culture, the shamanic term *elik* signifies 'one who has eyes'. Shamans the world over are seers: visionaries whose capacity to see beyond the everyday realm gives them access to healing knowledge, wisdom and power. As 'technicians of the sacred', they draw upon both a technology — of drum and rattle, cap and coat, hallucinogens and amulets — and a range of what one might call performance skills. Discussing the feelings which he had before submitting to an all-night experience of the healing work of the Nepali shaman Sakrante, John T. Hitchcock, a professor of anthropology, recollected that 'Both my apprehension and confidence derived from the skill of an accomplished actor; and were released in me by the same suspension of disbelief that I experience during a good play or dramatic film. Sakrante's acting and his all-night "play" belong to an ancient Himalayan shamanistic tradition, handed down for countless generations . . . I do not think it does Sakrante or his shamanistic tradition a disservice to speak of it as remarkably good theater. I know Sakrante thought of himself as a performer, a better performer than other shamans.'[1]

We have already remarked the extent to which shamanic ideas can be traced in twentieth-century drama in the West, from their origins in the 'psychotheatre' of Strindberg through to the extremes of gestural and guttural primitivism found in the work of Artaud, Peter Brook and Ted Hughes, for example. It is through the reflections of another outstanding Nordic artist, film director Ingmar Bergman — whose devotion to Strindberg has been life-long — that we can begin to appreciate the many implications of Hitchcock's comparison of the effect of Sakrante's shamanising with the 'suspension of disbelief' experienced while watching a 'dramatic film'.

'Film', says Bergman, 'has a very hypnotic effect on the audience. You sit there in a completely dark room, very anonymously. You look at a spot in front of you, and you don't move. You sit and you don't move, while your eyes are concentrated on that white spot on the wall. This is exactly what some hypnotists do. They light a spot on the wall and ask you to follow it with your eyes, while they talk to you and then they hypnotize you. The film medium is some sort of magic. Also, it is magic that every frame comes and stands still for a fraction of a second and then it darkens. This means that while you are watching a film, you remain in complete darkness. Isn't that fascinating? That is magic. In this medium, as in music, we go straight to the feelings.'[2]

The shamanic overtones of Bergman's words become increasingly evident as one considers the comparison which the film theorist and professor of film studies Vlada Petrić has drawn between the technology of prehistoric and twentieth-century art. Petrić believes that, with its 'unique spatial dynamism' and capacity to alter 'the shape, time, and place of things and events', cinema can make the world of dreams more tangible than any other art: 'In the "dawn period" of mankind the cave-artist wanted to create a painted illusion of moving animals appearing as bizarre as the imagery in his dreams. Today, modern technology permits such a strong creation of oneiric visions that viewers feel they are experiencing their own dreams.'[3] And we do not have to travel back to the European cave artists to appreciate that, for all the sophistication of film technology, there may be something at the heart of the experience of film which links that experience with shamanism. Writing of the time he spent in Brazil making the film *The Emerald Forest* (1985), director John Boorman has suggested that 'The Indians, with their music, dance and ritual, are constantly striving to escape from their material lives into the spirit world. In making a movie we take the material elements of our society and transmute them into a stream of light flowing on to a wall, hoping that it will contain something of our spirit.'[4]

No matter how problematic we may find Boorman's idea of 'escape' from the material world to be with regard to the beliefs of South American tribes, his words are important, signalling as they do the issue which dominates so much of the film theory, discussion and debate of our century. Insofar as it involves the elemental question of whether art be regarded as a mere diversion from the pressing realities of life, or as the chief means of engaging with and transforming those realities, that issue — the nature of the experience which is offered to us through the film medium — is the same as it is in any of the arts. But there is something absolutely peculiar to the medium of film — its ability to capture photographically the most material of realities, while simultaneously transcending everyday materiality; to project both the presence and absence, as it were, of materiality — that lends an extra, essential dimension to such perennial questions of aesthetics and ethics.

This extra dimension, or ontological 'doubleness' of film, is intimately bound up with essential questions concerning the presence and development of the shamanic spirit in twentieth-century art. For example, one of the greatest exemplars of that spirit, the late Andrei Tarkovsky, often stressed that what he called 'the basic element' of film lay in the faculty of careful, patient observation. Undoubtedly, a large part of Tarkovsky's genius — and I use the word unashamedly, with an intent which will become evident later — lay in his ability to register the sheer material *presence* of the world. But at the same time that Tarkovsky's images are some of the most intensely physical ever made — or as the director himself might have said, 'sculpted in time' — they are some of the most *metaphysical* ever to have been 'captured' on film.[5]

Film is thus admirably suited to be the shamanic art *par excellence* — an art of simultaneous substance and illusion, materiality and transcendence; of memories and dreams, ghosts and spirits. Its roots in mesmerism and magic are apparent enough in the fact that Georges Méliès (1861–1938), the great French film pioneer and producer of the first 'trick films', took over Robert Houdin's theatre of magic and illusion in 1888, adding photographic slides, glass plates and projectors before turning it into an actual cinema in 1896. A year earlier, visitors to the film cellar of Louis (1894–1948) and Auguste (1862–1954) Lumière had been amazed not by any primitive cinematic tricks, but rather by the simple recording of visual 'facts' — people walking out of a factory, perhaps, or trains arriving at a station. In *The Struggle for the Film*, the history of early film which the Dadaist Hans Richter wrote in the late 1930s, but which was not published until 1976, we learn of Richter's admiration for what he calls the *primal cinema* of the Lumière brothers: the cinema of a moment when 'it was as if the movement of things — of the surrounding world — of oneself had been discovered for the first time. The sheet hanging at the other end of the room provided a plane on which one could examine things as if they were on another planet and oneself an alien being.'[6]

While Richter argued that 'Our age demands the documented fact',[7] he was also sensitive to the needs of the imagination. The words of this painter who was also the maker of some of the most uncompromising of purely 'abstract', rhythmic films this century are worth quoting at some length: 'It is no accident that Méliès' early films are so concerned with magic. And, in case we have forgotten (or no longer want to admit it), there remains the invisible world, the realm of the imagination, of ideas and thoughts, a world just as real for us as the visible one. It is to find this world expressed, to feel its reality, to experience it, that we are drawn into museums, concert halls and to the magical screen . . . it is the machinery of the cinema, apparently so earthly, so purely physical, that has given receptive humanity knowledge that will not be restricted to the domain of the immediate. Complex technological inventions and plans have made it possible for this machine, this refined version of the magic lantern, to make an incomparable contribution to the welfare, the recovery of humanity.'[8]

Richter here touches on several of the chief issues of not only film criticism, but also the general sociology of the arts in the twentieth century, the central issue being — exactly what is meant by 'the recovery of humanity'? Does this pregnant phrase imply simply the ability to master the linear flow of history in a manner which is as unexploitative of one's fellow human beings as possible? (Which is not to say that the development of such an ability is a simple matter: far from it.) Or does it involve the recovery of something ahistorical, as it were: namely, a sense of *participation mystique*, of circular, mythic time — of cosmos rather than history? Will humanity only really ever 'recover itself' if it abandons the logocentric values of post-Cartesian, 'progressive' humanism? It is through a consideration of aspects of the development of film, above all other media, that something of the complexity implicit in what one might call the sociology of such questions — of the shamanic spirit in twentieth-century art — can be addressed.

In Chapter 2, we encountered the sociologist Pierre Bourdieu's ironic use of the terms 'sacred' and 'profane'. For Bourdieu, such terms helped to illuminate the extent to which a middle-class experience of art in either a gallery or museum is not so much a pseudo-religious experience of the essence of life as a disguised exercise in the power play of social class and status. (Such sociologistic perceptions can be applied, of course, to any domain of the arts, such as concert halls and cinemas.) Suppose, however, that we approach those archetypal concepts, the 'sacred' and the 'profane', in the spirit not of sociology, but rather of phenomenology and hermeneutics, as Mircea Eliade did for most of his adult life. Suppose, that is, that we return to Eliade's fundamental idea that we have to effect not a sociological demystification of the experience of art this century, but rather 'a demystification in reverse; that is to say, we have to "demystify" the apparently profane worlds of literature, plastic arts, and cinema in order to disclose their "sacred" elements, although it is, of course, an ignored, camouflaged, or degraded "sacred." '[9] In so doing, we might discover not so much the latent sociology of class distinctions, as the esoteric history of religion: a history where ancient ideas of the relation of art to religious ritual have been revived, transmuted and developed — just as our whole sense of the sacred might be said to have been revived, transmuted and developed by the arts this century.

Whether it be an ignored, camouflaged, degraded — or triumphantly proclaimed — sacred, sooner or later, any discussion of the sacred dimension in twentieth-century art has to attempt to come to terms with the ideas of Walter Benjamin's famous essay of 1936, entitled 'The Work of Art in the Age of Mechanical Reproduction'. In recent decades, this has become a key text for anyone who wishes to reflect upon the sociology of art from what one might call a broadly left-wing perspective. The opening sections of John Berger's contentious television series and book *Ways of Seeing* (1972), for example, were followed by Berger's acknowledgement of the fundamental indebtedness of his ideas (concerning the commodification of art in late-capitalist society) to Benjamin's text.[10] However, the richness of Benjamin's essay is such that (critical) reflection upon some of its central ideas may enable us to sense the extent to which, underneath the vast and miserable desecration of life which has been the history of so much of the twentieth century, a sense of the sacred may be said to have survived and developed in the arts. [11]

The burgeoning development of photo-mechanical means of reproduction in the nineteenth and twentieth centuries was central to Benjamin's argument that art had lost both its 'aura' and its relation to 'tradition'. By aura Benjamin meant the essential 'otherness' and ultimate unapproachability of the unique work of art, characteristics which could be traced back through the various threads and interstices of tradition to art's origins in cult and magic. Benjamin also explained what he meant by the concept of aura through reference to such natural phenomena as the branch of a tree, defining its aura as 'the unique phenomenon of a distance, however close it may be'. [12] Photomechanical means of creativity and reproduction had combined to annul the 'otherness' or 'aura' of both the natural world and art, as they had been progressively 'invaded' by the replicative thrust of modern technology. Emancipated from what Benjamin saw as its 'parasitical dependence on ritual', the essence of art had been transformed from the appeal of a singular 'cult' object to something 'designed for reproducibility'. [13]

Much of Benjamin's essay was concerned with developments in film. Noting the diversity of reactions which the new medium had aroused earlier in the century, Benjamin underlined the extent to which those in favour of early film had spoken of its potential cult, or ritual values. The response of Severin-Mars is typical here: 'What art has been granted a dream more poetical and more real at the same time! Approached in this fashion the film might represent an incomparable means of expression. Only the most high-minded persons, in the most perfect and mysterious moments of their lives, should be allowed to enter its ambience.' [14] Or one might consider the words of Alexandre Arnoux: in 1929, praising the virtues of the (already outmoded) silent film, Arnoux had asked: 'Do not all the bold descriptions we have given amount to the definition of prayer?' [15]

Benjamin was less struck by such comments about the sacred potentialities of film than he was by the mounting evidence of film's contribution to what sociologists would later call the desacralisation of the world. Noting the plethora of relatively worthless 'entertainment' in recent film production, Benjamin paid less attention to analysing the emotional or narrative content of such works than he did to addressing the import of the *technology* of film, developing a provocative analogy between what he called the boldness of the cameraman and the skills of a surgeon.

What continues to make this comparison so suggestive is that Benjamin contrasted cameraman and surgeon with painter and magician. While magicians, said Benjamin, respect the bodies of their patients, restricting themselves in their search for a cure to a 'laying on of hands', surgeons cut into the bodies of their patients. And while the painter – again, according to Benjamin – 'maintains in his work a natural distance from reality', the cameraman 'penetrates deeply into its web'.[16] That is, the cameraman breaks up the surface of reality, as he assembles countless aspects of it – what Benjamin called 'multiple fragments' – through a variety of hitherto unsuspected techniques of visualisation and film recording. Adding the play of the dualism of the sacred and the profane to Benjamin's ideas, one might say that the ultimate contrast between painting and film is the contrast between (sacred) contemplation (time held, and condensed in order that the psyche might both gather itself and expand) and (profane) shock (time scattered, along with space, with the result that the psyche is scattered on the winds of history): 'Let us compare the screen on which a film unfolds with the canvas of a painting. The painting invites the spectator to contemplation; before it the spectator can abandon himself to his associations. Before the movie frame he cannot do so. No sooner has his eye grasped a scene than it is already changed. It cannot be arrested.'[17]

While Benjamin suggested that such filmic shocks should be cushioned by 'the heightened presence of mind', he went on to conclude that 'Reception in a state of distraction, which is increasing noticeably in all fields of art and is symptomatic of profound changes in apperception, finds in the film its true means of exercise. The film with its shock effect meets this mode of reception halfway. The film makes the cult value recede into the background not only by putting the public in the position of the critic but also by the fact that at the movies this position requires no attention. The public is an examiner, but an absent-minded one.'[18]

Several points suggest themselves in response to Benjamin's ideas. The first is the adequacy, or otherwise, of the language within which we may wish to make prescriptive statements about art through the discipline of sociology. Exactly who — or rather, what — is 'the absent-minded public' whose potential ability to view films with a 'heightened sense of mind' Benjamin was able to dismiss with such apparent certainty? Is this 'public' likely to remain the same from one year to the next? Does this essentially abstract idea of a film audience actually 'take on flesh' anywhere at all? And if it does, how does one set about quantifying it? (If I am from social class B, to offer a hypothetical example, and I like both watching James Bond movies and reading Raymond Chandler in paperback, does this make me part of the same 'public' constituted in part by my friend, also in social class B, who shares my taste for James Bond movies but who cannot stand Chandler, much preferring D.H. Lawrence? Does the fact that my friend joins me in watching James Bond movies imply that we have the same political views? Offer money to the same charities? Treat our friends and relatives the same way? Feel the same way about tourism? Or feminism?

A thousand other objections to such a conceptual abstraction as 'the public' might be offered — such as, what exactly is 'social class B'?[19])

Secondly, why did Benjamin assume that viewers of a film cannot 'abandon themselves' to their sensations, simply because the images of films pass by their eyes at relatively fast speed? How did Benjamin know that at the subconscious level, viewers' minds were not capable of sensing both the overtones of such images and the deeper, *subliminal* rhythms of the films into which such passing images may have flowed? Benjamin placed his reflections upon the changing impact of imagery within a broad historical context of technological change. It is thus strange that he did not develop his provocative insight that what people reject in avant-garde painting (the distortions of Picasso), they will accept in film (the body language of Charlie Chaplin), into the possibility that given enough (historical) time, people may be able to synthesise a quite unprecedented amount of stimulating material within their experience of film language.

Finally — and from the present point of view, most important of all — if it has now become obvious that cult values *do* survive in film, in however degraded a form, through the so-called 'star' syndrome, why should it not be possible to imagine film serving deeper, and more complex 'sacred' values? Why, that is, should the cinema screen not serve as the altar — or cave wall — of our imagination?

Rather than destroying our links with tradition, the development of film this century can be seen — *together with* such 'traditional' means of expression as literature and painting, music and dance — as having given us the possibility of reclaiming and developing the most ancient and essential aspect of the tradition of art: its shamanic spirit. We may be able to see how much this is the case if we now take Benjamin's metaphor of the cameraman as surgeon, and ask whether or not it is possible to make something rather different, and — as far as ideas of the sacred are concerned — more positive out of it than Benjamin himself did.

Whether the image of a surgeon cutting into a body strikes one as more or less appealing than that of a magician, or shaman, laying on hands, the fact remains that surgeons are concerned to heal their patients. A cameraman, says Benjamin, 'penetrates deeply' into the web of reality. If a film director such as Tarkovsky was able to orchestrate a complex variety of impressions of that reality, developing the possibilities of artistic expression which lie within such matters as variety of camera angle and length of shot; slow motion, dissolve and flashback; long tracking shot and static close-up; mixture of dialogue, music and silence, black and white and colour film, or sepia processing, for example, why should we suppose that he was unable to offer us a *healing* picture of the sacred totality of life? That is, if the camera penetrates everywhere, in a variety of registers, why should it not be the vehicle for a return to feelings of *participation mystique*, enabling us to be both 'one and many' in the world?

While Benjamin makes an astute point in saying that the mechanisation of vision in film (including such aspects of production as the cutting room) has reached such a point of saturation that, paradoxically enough, technology is able to play an extremely convincing disappearing trick upon the film audience, he draws too pessimistic a conclusion from his insight: 'The equipment-free aspect of reality here has become the height of artifice: the sight of immediate reality has become an orchid in the land of technology.'[20] Such a conclusion is surely as 'forced' and provisional, as it were, as Benjamin's final image. In an interview of the late 1970s, Tarkovsky revealed that during the editing stage, he had made *nineteen* different versions of his film *Mirror.*[21] Of all Tarkovsky's films, this is the one which precipitated the most letters to the director from viewers: viewers who were as astonished as they were grateful that Tarkovsky had managed to tell the story of their lives with such poetic power. (What does this tell us, incidentally, about the state of the so-called film 'public' today?) There is nothing 'orchid-like' about the poetic power of Tarkovsky — a power which emerged partly from an absolute technical mastery of the film medium and partly from an intense, shamanic sensitivity to life. More than that of any other director, Tarkovsky's work surely encourages us to ask why an encounter with technologically mediated 'immediate reality' should not lead to perceptions, or intuitions, of the deep structures of experience, structures which give that experience lasting, potentially sacred meaning: the structures of myth.

In her *Profane Mythology: The Savage Mind of the Cinema* (1982), the film theorist Yvette Biró suggests that what she calls 'film-thought' should be considered as 'a branch of the tree of mythical thinking'.[22] Arguing that 'cognition that precedes pure reason encompasses a far larger realm than does categorical thought', Biró defends the power of thinking in images. Aware of the many complexities of film language, she suggests nonetheless that in the very 'primitiveness' of film lies its superiority to so-called rational modes of communication: 'Just like child-thought, the film communicates in dramatized actions, and perhaps this is precisely what facilitates the presentation of the whole and makes what may not attain comprehensiveness in speech prevail on the screen.'[23]

Thus for Biró (in contrast to Benjamin), the camera's abilities 'cannot be relegated to the narrow category of technical miracles. Cinema's earliest pioneers understood well that film eye = film truth; in other words, the camera — with its boundless appetite, curiosity and mobility reaching heaven and earth, far and near, inside and outside of everything — not only gathers data of human activity but, out of the sum of reference points, fragments, and signs, creates a world-image, a coherent view. This view is at once a component of and the result of our collective consciousness; its wisdom urges us to think.'[24]

All technology contains the possibility of good or evil: it is the human mind that has decided whether the principle of locomotion should serve farmers or militarists, poetry or political propaganda. And so it is with film: if the wisdom of the best films urges one to think in healing images of *participation mystique*, the banality of the worst encourages us to sleep the sleep of gross unreason. In the late 1930s, Han Richter had already protested that 'To varnish our lives with entertaining stories is too petty a task for this mighty technology, too petty if it is grow to artistic maturity.'[25] Half a century later, Joseph Campbell was asked if he saw the filmmakers 'in what they've called "the dream factory" of Hollywood' as modern myth-makers. Campbell's answer was that such filmmakers 'could be . . . if they'd make myths. All they do is put people into bed and take them out again. This naturalism in our art world', Campbell continued, 'is . . . all flat-footed prose. And in all flat-footed prose there are only two things that are interesting: violence and sex. That's what it's come down to.'[26]

Campbell's sense of the mythic potentialities of cinema had been encouraged by his recent exposure to the work of George Lucas, who has himself acknowledged the debt which his *Star Wars* trilogy owes to such books of Campbell's as *The Hero With a Thousand Faces* and *The Masks of God*.[27] By his own admission, although he felt there was 'no better medium in the world than film', film played a relatively minor role in Campbell's life. The advent of what Campbell called 'the talkies' had killed his early interest in the medium, in that it had led to far too much naturalism — 'the death of the art' for Campbell.[28] One wonders what this immensely sophisticated, yet thoroughly primal person would have made of the theatrical play of (essentially shamanic) ideas about the calling of the artist in Cocteau's *The Blood of a Poet* (1930) and *Orpheus* (1950); of Fellini's related exploration, in *8½* (1963), of creative stasis and personal crisis; of Godard's primitivising nihilism in *Weekend* (1967); or of the liberating combination of shamanic and trickster qualities projected by Jack Nicholson in Milos Forman's immensely popular film of Ken Kesey's *One Flew Over the Cuckoo's Nest* (1975). Above all, one wonders what Campbell would have made of the subtlety of Bergman's investigation of the problematic legacy of Protestantism and the possibilities of a primitivistic rebirth of mythic imagination today; of Tarkovsky's intensely mythopoeic preoccupations; and of the tensions between the dynamics of history and cosmos which have driven so much of the work of Akira Kurosawa, a director of immense mythic power, whose influence upon Bergman has been as substantial as it was upon Tarkovsky.

In the course of a discussion of the work of Swedish director Bo Widerberg, in *Profane Mythology*, Yvette Biró suggests that beautiful as they are, the landscape elements in such films of Widerberg's as *Elvira Madigan* (1967), *Adalen 31* (1969) and *Joe Hill* (1971) reveal the dangers of projecting too much of the mythic imagination into nature today. For 'at the bottom of this view lie mythicizing simplicity and romantic archaization.'[29] Wary of the sentimentality which she suspects may lie within any contemporary use of the idea of nature as part of a critique of social life, Biró claims that 'The true territory of myth has remained the big city, the jungle of the metropolis.'[30]

I believe that this is a fundamental error of judgement. While the risk of sentimentality is always present in the use of landscape imagery, in the work of Kurosawa, Bergman and Tarkovsky the achievement of what Biró calls 'mythicizing simplicity and romantic archaization' embodies, at its best, a completely unsentimental call to rethink our priorities: to move, that is, from the increasingly destructive ideology of history as the only space of (profane) human action and fulfilment to an acknowledgement of our (sacred) responsibilities to cosmos. And this is a call shot through with the spirit of shamanism, expressed in the sort of demanding, yet fulfilling language that addresses what Hans Richter felt was perhaps the central problem of twentieth-century life: the antagonism between thought and feeling.[31]

In dreams, said W.B. Yeats, begin responsibilities. Kurosawa (*b.*1910) has always thought of himself as an artist working in a global art form, with commensurate responsibilities: in his fine study of the director, Stephen Prince has rightly spoken of Kurosawa's 'almost missionary use of the cinema'.[32] However, Kurosawa has always drawn a sharp distinction between political ideology and the capacity of art to move human beings to action. Kierkegaard believed that while knowledge might be communicated directly, 'All communication of capability is indirect communication.'[33] Rather than quantifiable knowledge or political propaganda, it is mythopoeic, shamanic capability that Kurosawa is interested in communicating in his art.

Over the past forty years, Kurosawa has been driven to a 'mythicizing simplicity and romantic archaization' not out of any sentimental impulse, but rather out of a slowly forming, and increasingly intense conviction that humanity *must* rediscover the sources of cosmicity within itself. In *Living* (1952), Kurosawa depicted the last few months of the life of Kanji Watanabe, a petty official who learns that he has incurable cancer. Avoiding the bathos that might have attended a straightforward narrative treatment of his theme, Kurosawa juxtaposes the dramatic irony of a voice-over technique with an extraordinary series of perspectival and narrative ellipses, until Watanabe finally becomes the complete 'absence' in the film which he was always destined to be — but an 'absence' that has provoked his relatives and colleagues into a deeper sense of their capabilities.

Having tasted dreams of the 'good life' — dreams of drunkenness and pinball machines — Watanabe finally finds meaning in the face of death by committing himself wholeheartedly to the building of a children's park on a patch of reclaimed city wasteland. Expressed as baldly as that, the film's conclusion may sound sentimental. However, this is anything but the case. Watanabe has struggled to find a space — psychic space — where, as Stephen Prince says, 'the individual could stand' without becoming blind to the social world or simply collapsing into self-pitying solipsism. [34] This is the space of individuation: and given the later developments of Kurosawa's films, the fact that in *Living* this space was symbolised by a park for children assumes a special significance.

In *Red Beard* (1965) Kurosawa developed the existentialist theme of *Living* — the basic, shocking sense of suddenly standing beyond the familiar, comforting reach of social mores, and having to search for the roots of oneself within something utterly distinct from the distractions of daily life — into a subtly conceived framework of cosmicity. The film traces the gradual development of the wisdom of humility in a brash young doctor, who finally comes to realise that true healing involves more than the application of textbook medical formulae to his patients. Kurosawa here intimates what one might call a transcendental, or meta-perspective upon suffering: in a world of (profane) strife and violence, the hospital clinic in the film offers the (sacred) space of solitude and calm within which true healing may occur. [35]

Over the past quarter of a century, Kurosawa's shaman-like quest for a sacred framework of healing has involved a reprise and development of the animism which so distinguished his treatment of landscape in *Throne of Blood* (1957). In this masterly interpretation of *Macbeth*, bleached sky, fog and desolate plains offer a mute, sacred contrast to the profane banality of human evil. As Prince, once again, comments: 'The film attempts to speak a discourse of enlightenment to the violence and power hunger of human behaviour . . . such wisdom is no longer of this world. It is incarnate in the spirits, the mists, and the cosmic emptiness from which they issue.' [36]

In *Dodeskaden* (1970) and *Dersu Uzala* (1975), Kurosawa's quest for animistic wisdom took him from the dreams and disappointments of the poverty- and disease-stricken inhabitants of a combined garbage dump and shanty town (*Dodeskaden*) to the vast, cleansing spaces of Siberia (*Dersu Uzala*). The adolescent Rokuchan, the central character of *Dodeskaden*, drives an imaginary trolley through the slum wastelands, his spirit buoyed by fantasies. Kurosawa has described Rokuchan as a symbol of the artist, 'the cineaste who creates entirely by the power of his imagination'. [37] One wonders how aware Kurosawa was of bringing that imagination back to its ultimate, replenishing shamanic home in *Dersu Uzala*.

Set in the early years of this century, the film is a study of the friendship

62 *Dersu Uzala* 1975 director Akira Kurosawa, photographers/cameramen Asakadzu Nakai, Uri Gantman and Fyodor Dobronravov © Moss Film/Toho Film/British Film Institute

which develops between Arseniev, a Russian explorer who is surveying and mapping the Ussuri region on the Pacific seaboard, and Dersu, the hunter and trapper whom he meets and who becomes his guide. In 1971, Kurosawa had tried to commit suicide. In *Dersu Uzala*, his camera pans across magnificent vistas of the Siberian wilderness with epic, healing dignity. The wilderness supplies Dersu with an animistic, essentially shamanic wisdom. He talks to fire and wind and water as if they were people: when a soldier laughs and asks him why, he replies it is because they are alive. Isolation produces not madness, but wisdom, enlightenment: the enlightenment of a mythopoeic consciousness, in tune with cosmic rather than historical forces.

If *Dersu Uzala* is a celebration of animism, it is also an elegy to cosmicity. Profane, banal history begins to spread its cankerous way through the sacred spaces of life: Dersu ends up alienated in a city, and is killed by someone for the sake of the modern rifle which he has been given by Arseniev. All that is left for Kurosawa thereafter is an increasingly desperate, albeit poetic statement of his central theme: without a sense of cosmicity, the world *cannot* survive.

At one moment in *Dersu Uzala*, the camera lingers over a rainbow which has appeared above the shack in which the explorers have sheltered from a storm. One could say that the rainbow is a sanctification of the magnanimity of Dersu, who has befriended and helped the explorers out of — as the cliché has it — the simple goodness of his heart. At the end of 'Sunshine Through Rain', the first section of Kurosawa's eight-part, and largely autobiographical *Dreams* (1990), a young boy walks into the resplendent majesty of a pastoral and mountain landscape, which is vaulted by an enormous rainbow. Simultaneously embodiment and sanctification of the glory of being, this rainbow landscape speaks of the cosmicity of sacred time, of the 'Great Time' of both origins and individuation: of mystery, magic and the mythopoeic core of life.[38]

Discussing the film at a press conference in France, Kurosawa commented: 'Dostoevsky once said that dreams express our deepest fears and greatest hopes more vividly than anything else. That's what I've tried to put on screen.'[39] It is the search for cosmicity within the attempt to express 'our deepest fears and greatest hopes' which links the work of Kurosawa with that of Ingmar Bergman (*b*.1918) and Andrei Tarkovsky (1932–1986), both of whose work clearly reflects their admiration for the Japanese director.[40] In Bergman and Tarkovsky, the tension between the forces of (profane) history and (healing) cosmos which has driven Kurosawa for so long acquires an even deeper resonance. It is no exaggeration to say that in the work of these two consummate masters of film, the shamanic spirit in twentieth-century art attains its apotheosis.

The mutual respect between Bergman and Tarkovsky was such that while Bergman is said to have seen Tarkovsky's *Andrei Roublov* (1966) at least ten times during Tarkovsky's lifetime, describing it as his favourite film of all, Tarkovsky repaid the compliment by the comparable amount of attention which he paid to such films of Bergman's as *The Seventh Seal* (1956), *Wild Strawberries* (1957), *The Silence* (1963), *Persona* (1966) and *The Shame* (1968). The two directors — who came within yards of each other one winter's day in Stockholm, in 1985, but who never actually met[41] — shared such elective affinities in film as Bresson and Kurosawa, Antonioni and Buñuel. Nonconformists both, they shared a compulsive desire to poeticise existence, to deepen our sense of the rhythms of cosmos: to precipitate the search for the presence of the sacred not in the 'outer casing' of religious dogma, but rather at the mythopoeic, creative heart of life.

'No form of art', Bergman has said, 'goes beyond ordinary consciousness as film does, straight to our emotions, deep into the twilight room of the soul. A little twitch in our optic nerve, a shock effect: twenty-four illuminated frames a second, darkness in between, the optic nerve incapable of registering darkness.'[42] Taking us back to the basic duality of film's potentiality already present within the work of the Lumière brothers and Méliès, Bergman has also said that when film is not a document, it is a dream. And this is why he believes that Tarkovsky is 'the greatest of them all' — because the Russian director moved 'with such naturalness' in the world of dreams. 'All my life', writes Bergman in *The Magic Lantern*, his autobiography, 'I have hammered on the doors of the rooms in which he [Tarkovsky] moves so naturally.'[43]

Although Tarkovsky's dream language, which is as assured in his first film, *Ivan's Childhood* (1962), as it was to be in his last, *The Sacrifice* (1986), is indeed unique, Bergman is being far too modest here. For if Tarkovsky moved ceaselessly through the rooms of his imagination, in restless, yet fluid search of the poetic core of life, the filmic and spiritual foundations of those rooms had to a great extent been laid by Bergman in his work of the 1950s and early 1960s. The fundamental Tarkovskian idea of the experience of film as a journey to the centre of the self; the metaphoric, animistic density of the landscape imagery which both stimulates and embodies that journey; the chamber music-like intensity of the interplay and development of motifs; the distilled, sparing use of what one might call 'sound montage' — all these Tarkovskian 'signatures' can be detected (albeit in a different personal register, of course) in the Bergman of *Summer Interlude* (1950) and *Sawdust and Tinsel* (1953); *The Seventh Seal* and *Wild Strawberries*; *The Face* (1958) and — above all — the trilogy of 'metaphysical reduction' of the early 1960s, which Bergman himself described in terms of chamber music: *Through A Glass Darkly* (1961), *Winter Light* (1962) and *The Silence*.[44]

Over the years, all these films have elicited an enormous amount of critical attention, from Christian theologians as well as film critics, and from feminists as well as Marxists.[45] Bergman has often been seen as a quintessentially Protestant artist, a sort of late-twentieth-century equivalent of Edvard Munch — the anguished Munch of *The Scream*, rather than the affirmative Munch of *Metamorphosis* and *The Sun*. The cliché about Bergman, as about Munch, is that his is a depressing art, locked within the destructive, dualistic legacy of Lutheranism: the world of the flesh is but a vale of tears. However, in these magnificent films of the 1950s and 1960s, Bergman not only registers and explores the destructive effects of this legacy, but also prepares the ground for a return of archaic qualities of *participation mystique*.

Implicit in all these films is an acute exploration of the potential of art to give our lives meaning in a post-Darwinian world. As thoroughly, yet economically based in history as it is subtly developed from the point of view of artistic form, this exploration enables Bergman to acknowledge the historical nature of contemporary nihilism and despair, at the same time that his formal mastery can speak of the healing possibilities still contained within archaic qualities of mythic, cosmicising thought. It is a very special mind indeed that can offer such a self-conscious study of film language as Bergman does in *Persona*, allied to an exploration of contemporary despair — and yet which encourages us, nevertheless, to leave the cinema aesthetically and spiritually refreshed, our sense of life's mysteries deepened rather than destroyed.[46] No matter how existentially bleak their ostensible 'narrative' content may be, practically all of Bergman's films are structured in the cyclic, regenerative form of myth, the final frames concluding on an open-ended note, even as they recall initiatory motifs and developmental passages in the films.

Few other artists of the past forty years have offered us so much to think about, in terms of that deceptively simple phrase 'significant form'. While what one might call mainstream or Hollywood cinema was stuffing its products full of as many ingredients as possible, from colour photography to the degraded pageantry of history, Bergman allied the multi-toned magic of black and white photography to an essentially modernist reduction of narrative concerns. The most pregnant moment in Bergman's medieval allegory *The Seventh Seal*, for example, is supplied by neither the famous chess game between the Knight and Death early in the film, nor the equally well-known (and very beautiful) sequence when the Knight sits down, early one evening, to share wild strawberries and a bowl of milk with the troupe of Jof, Mia and Skat. It occurs, rather, when a group of flagellants — who have listened, lying down and moaning, to a Christian soldier's verbal excoriations of the lust for life shown by various members of a local community — raise themselves up, and continue their pathetic pilgrimage. As the flagellants move out of shot, all sounds cease: the camera registers, momentarily, the luminous purity of the play of light across the field upon which the hapless sinners have just degraded themselves.

Tracing the withdrawal of the Protestant God — a silent, and in Bergman's films, hostile and authoritarian God — from the world, the historical *tabula rasa* which Bergman effects allows him to focus on the inner, archetypal dimensions of spirituality. In a stimulating article on the psychological implications of Bergman's trust in dream, in those 'inner voices' to which he has listened all his life, the psychotherapist Ira Progoff has drawn upon a revealing but relatively little-known American television interview with Bergman which took place sometime in the mid- to late-1960s. When he made *The Silence*, Bergman said, he was 'still bleeding' after the experience that God 'didn't exist anymore'. He continued: 'But I'm now still convinced that there is no God anymore in the world. That God is dead. But I am also convinced that in every man, you have — there is, there is a part of man who is — a human being in his mind — a room that is holy. That is, that is very special. Very high. Very secret room that is — that is a holy part of the human being.'[47]

After pointing out the subtlety with which Bergman intimates the nature of this (rationally inexpressible) intuition in his films, primarily through examples in the medium of music, Progoff suggests that the director's words are a clear enough indication of the extent to which his psychic development has followed the classic patterns of growth discussed within holistic psychology. For Progoff, Bergman is 'an excellent instance of how the dialectic of the psyche leads beyond itself in the life of a creative person to intimations of a spiritual dimension of reality. Inward for the imagery, outward for the artworks, unified in the waking dream that coheres each creative act, the continuity of experience brings forth a living myth.'[48]

The fundamentally shamanic nature of Bergman's creation of that 'living myth' — of his progressive 'internalisation' of questions of spirituality, and the consequent, gradual awakening and strengthening of the anima, or qualities of soul, in his work — becomes particularly apparent when one reflects upon such diverse films as *Sawdust and Tinsel*, *The Face*, *Through a Glass Darkly* and *Hour of the Wolf* (1968). For in every one of these films, Bergman explores what has been called the liminal realm of shamanic experience (from the Latin *limen*, meaning 'threshold').[49] He acknowledges the many dangers of the inner quest — the psychosexual dangers, for example, which lead Karin to mental illness in *Through a Glass Darkly*, or which in *Hour of the Wolf* bring the painter Johan Borg to a beak-slashed death in a dark forest. And he also explores various implications of humour, that fundamental 'threshold' mystery of the human psyche, a mystery which can help to take the self far beyond the confines of rationality.[50]

In *The Face* (or *The Magician*, as the 1958 *Ansiktet* is sometimes known), Bergman offers a rich examination of both the sociology and phenomenology of shamanism, as the members of Albert Emanuel Vogler's nineteenth-century travelling Magnetic Health Theatre encounter the rationalist cynicism of Dr. Vergerus, royal counsellor of medicine, Starbeck, chief of police, and Egerman, wealthy bourgeois. In an extensive, illuminating discussion of the film, Paisley Livingston underlines both the interplay of faith and doubt about the power of art which runs through the work and Bergman's constant desire not to send viewers to sleep, so to speak, by the dream-like power of his art. On the contrary: Bergman's chief desire has always been to *wake us up* to the complexities of experience (from the point of view of both the artist and the audience).

As Livingston suggests, it is entirely appropriate that *The Face* should end with an image of a lantern swinging in and out of the light: for the whole film is an exploration of the dialectics of ego and unconscious, animus and anima, vision and trickery, cynicism and belief, transcendence and immanence.[51] It has sometimes been claimed that Bergman's final view on such matters is that, divorced from its roots in religion, art today is a shallow business at best. One thinks of Bergman's own words upon receiving the Erasmus prize in 1965, when he compared modern art to the illusion of life which one might receive upon seeing a dead snake's skin

63 *The Face* 1958 director
Ingmar Bergman,
photographer/cameraman
Gunnar Fisher
© Glenbuck Films/British
Film Institute

move, as countless ants continue to eat away at what remains of its innards;
or one recalls the empty 'ritual' performed by the none-too-subtly named
troupe Les Riens in *The Rite* (1969).[52] Seen from the perspective of
shamanism, however, it is hard to doubt that the overall thrust of
Bergman's work has involved the healing attempt to put the 'living juice'
of the sacred back into art, through a revival and development of the
aboriginal, cosmic roots of artistic practice in shamanic states of
consciousness.

The nihilism of *Hour of the Wolf* and *The Rite* should thus be seen within the overall context of Bergman's shaman-like struggle to bring a 'living
myth' of the holy back into existence.[53] At the end of *The Silence*, perhaps
Bergman's finest film, a young boy strains to understand the few words
of the 'foreign language' which his dying aunt has scribbled on a piece of
paper for him. To use a beautiful expression from the Norwegian Tarjei
Vesaas, one might call these the words of an esoteric language, 'quietly
hidden on the tongue behind words of love':[54] the language of that brief
epiphany of stillness and wonder in *The Seventh Seal*, after the flagellants
have disappeared; the language which might eventually enable us to walk
'the wide and inner way' to which Gunnar Ekelöf was so drawn.[55]

This is the mythopoeic language of cosmicity and individuation – a
language which Bergman spent over forty years developing and refining
in film. Time and again, but particularly in the work of the 1950s and
1960s, Bergman's increasingly taut manipulation of the relations between
image and sound, narrative and myth brought fundamental questions of
persona and shadow, animus and anima into consciousness, seeking to

acknowledge and integrate, or fructify, the eternal presence of death in life. In the resonant affirmation of his film version of *The Magic Flute* (1975), and in the epic recapitulation of so many of his ideas and motifs in *Fanny and Alexander* (1982) — the central moments of which are the shape-shifting triumph of Isak Jacobi's magic-working powers over the insane Lutheran asceticism of Bishop Edvard Vergerus and Alexander's subsequent introduction to the androgynous 'wild man' and psychic, Ismael — Bergman proclaimed the full, sensuous beauty of individuated consciousness, with a richness that has been matched by only one other film maker this century: Andrei Tarkovsky.

If cinema is, as Susan Sontag has suggested, 'the natural home of those who suspect language', [56] the work of Tarkovsky compels an especial awareness of the potential banality which lies within all attempts at either written or spoken film exegesis. As Mark Le Fanu has observed, in the course of his sensitive study of the director, 'An idea, in the cinema, is a camera movement, not a speech.' [57] But the *idea* of speech — in both a literal and metaphorical sense — is absolutely central to Tarkovsky's oeuvre. At the beginning of *Mirror* (1974), Tarkovsky's most autobiographical film, an adolescent is cured of an atrocious stutter by a speech therapist, who uses hypnosis upon her patient. It would not be stretching a point to suggest that, by the mythopoeic power of his images, Tarkovsky sought to bring a long-buried, almost forgotten language back into historical consciousness: the language of reverie; of animism; of cosmic religion — the language whereby the earth may speak us.

'Why do people go to the cinema?' asked Tarkovsky in *Sculpting In Time*, his collection of meditations upon film theory and aesthetics. 'What takes them into a darkened room', he continued to muse, 'where, for two hours, they watch the play of shadows upon a sheet? The search for entertainment? The need for a kind of drug?' Distancing himself totally from what he called the world of 'entertainment firms and organisations which exploit cinema and television and spectacles of many other kinds', Tarkovsky suggested that the starting point for an answer to his question should lie not in such sociological details of corruption, but rather in 'the essential principles of cinema, which have to do with the human need to master and know the world.' [58]

Such language might lead us to suspect the *hubris* of rationalistic humanism, reminding us perhaps of the profane penetration of the world achieved by Benjamin's surgeon-like cameraman. But Tarkovsky was both surgeon *and* magician, and his concept of 'knowing and mastering' the world had very little indeed to do with rationalistic humanism. Tarkovsky's camera does not cut into, but rather caresses the world: the director was above all a poet of reverie, extraordinarily sensitive to the potential ensouling beauty of the elements. [59] But at the same time that his work mirrored the beauty of nature (and how absurd it is, incidentally, that in today's so-called sophisticated climate of post-modernist irony, one might be expected to worry about the potential sentimentality of such a phrase), Tarkovsky's concept of artistic form cut deeply into the structure of experience, giving his films an implacable formal and spiritual strength. As surface detail and psychological depth combine, we sense the rebirth of mythopoeic consciousness: time is no longer simply a matter of linear moments, differentiated only by the nature of our passing moods. Time could not exist, said Aristotle, without a soul to count it. In Tarkovsky's films, however, the soul is *shaped by time*, as the subjective time of memories and free-flowing poetic associations dissolves into the Paradisal time of myth and cosmos, of *participation mystique*.

The answer which Tarkovsky gave to his own question about cinema-going was that people visit the cinema in search of *time* — 'for time lost or spent or not yet had'.[60] He defined film as 'sculpting in time', and in language curiously reminiscent of Brancusi (whose work we shall investigate in the following chapter), spoke of how, just as a sculptor takes a lump of marble and, 'inwardly conscious of the features of his finished piece, removes everything that is not part of it', so does the film-maker, 'from a "lump of time" made up of an enormous, solid cluster of living facts', cut off and discard whatever he does not need, 'leaving only what is to be an element of the finished film, what will prove to be integral to the cinematic image.'[61]

A filmic image lives in time; but it was also essential, said Tarkovsky, that *time be allowed to live in the image*. Compare the length of so many of the magisterial tracking shots in *Mirror*, *Stalker* (1979) and *The Sacrifice*, for example, with the fact that, in *Rambo II*, the average shot lasts for just 2.9 seconds.[62] Is it any exaggeration to say that, in constructing such transparent fictions of mass culture today, we murder time? A large part of the healing power of Tarkovsky's films lies in the resurrection of time which they embody: for in resurrecting mythic time, they sharpen our sense of that 'very secret room that is — that is a holy part of the human being' of which Bergman spoke in the 1960s.

As we have learned, Bergman considers Tarkovsky to be 'the greatest of them all'. From a shamanic point of view, it would be difficult to disagree. It is, of course, impossible to watch any of Tarkovsky's films — *Ivan's Childhood* (1962), *Andrei Roublov* (1966), *Solaris* (1972), *Mirror* (1974), *Stalker* (1979), *Nostalgia* (1983) and *The Sacrifice* (1986) — without becoming aware of how different Tarkovsky's attitude to the legacy of Christianity was from that of Bergman. Whereas Bergman traced the disappearance of the Protestant God from his world, leaving the 'negative impression' of the 'absent father' in *The Silence*, for example, Tarkovsky's films are full of positive Christian images.[63] But as we shall shortly see, Tarkovsky's

Christianity has to be viewed within the wider shamanic framework of pan-religiosity — of archaic cosmicity — which is so evident in his oeuvre.

When Bergman used the music of Bach in *The Silence*, it seemed to signify both a lost world (especially when set against the dance-band, sub-Modern Jazz Quartet sounds which are also featured in the film) and the hope of a pure, humane contact between people, above and beyond that which is possible in language. In Tarkovsky, the use of Bach still carries a traditional transcendental import. Part of the extraordinary condensation achieved in the last frames of *The Sacrifice*, for example, where we hear Bach's *Saint Matthew Passion*, is the subliminal intimation of a crown of thorns, as the camera moves slowly up the bare branches of a pine tree, framed against an 'eternal' background of shimmering light-on-sea. As 'Little Man' lies under the (dead) tree which — following the parable which Alexander, his father, told him at the beginning of the film, he is to water 'religiously', until it comes back to life — he speaks for the first time in the film, as he asks his (now) absent father: 'In the beginning was the Word. Why, Papa?'[64]

As always with Tarkovsky, the stunning simplicity of such moments contains a more complex resonance than might appear from a purely Christian interpretation of the imagery. If one has seen *Ivan's Childhood*, for example, it is impossible not to note the mythic circularity of Tarkovsky's work which is manifest in these final frames from *The Sacrifice*. For the very first seconds of *Ivan's Childhood* featured a young boy's enchanted contemplation of a pine tree, set within a Paradisal, yet thoroughly real context. The first and the last shots of Tarkovsky thus feature the archetypal idea of the Tree of Life: and just as Tarkovsky's camera remained fixed on the earth in the opening moments of his film career, so does the horizontal, this-worldly dimension complement the ascensional impulse within the final moments of *The Sacrifice*. As Antoine de Baecque has suggested in a fine, Bachelardian study of the director, Tarkovsky is truly a poet of the earth: only very rarely does his camera embrace the sky, and never at the expense of the things of this world.[65]

At the end of *The Sacrifice* it is not the sky which frames the somewhat battered reprise of the archetype of the Tree of Life, but rather the shimmering expanse of the sea. Water is absolutely central to Tarkovsky's imagery: and although the director himself was antipathetic to any talk about symbolism in his films, preferring to stress the 'sculpting of an image of reality' which film at its best could achieve, it is impossible not to associate this element with the flow of the unconscious, both personal and collective. A large part of the genius of Tarkovsky surely lay within his capacity to open himself to the stirrings of his unconscious; to let his dreams tell him of both ancient and more recent 'signatures' of human longing. And the most ancient of all such signatures is shamanism.

The last thing I wish to suggest here is that Tarkovsky somehow 'illustrated' a series of shamanic ideas in his films. Whatever ideas there are in Tarkovsky (and there are many) emerge naturally from the flow of his images: nothing is imposed, or 'literary', in his conception of film. However, Tarkovsky was a person blessed with a good deal of intellectual curiosity. As the recently published extracts from his diaries make clear, he was a widely read man, to whom Rilke meant as much as Dostoevsky, and Lao Tsu as much as — if not more than — the prophets. In the latter years of his life, it would appear that he developed a fascination with one author in particular: namely, Carlos Castaneda.

In a diary entry of January 1979, Tarkovsky writes: 'Reread Castaneda's *The Lessons of Don Juan*. A marvellous book! And very true, because —

1. the world is not at all as it appears to us.

2. under certain conditions it could well become different.'[66] A month earlier, he had written of his wish to make a film 'based principally on Castaneda'. And in April 1979 he asked himself again, 'What about making a film of Castaneda's Don Juan?'[67]

Tarkovsky never made that film. But in a sense, he had no real need to. For from the very first Paradisal moments of *Ivan's Childhood*, Tarkovsky revealed himself as a person of extraordinary shamanic sensitivity. The more one sees his films, the more evident it is that the 'signature of things' which he read into the earth he loved so much was thoroughly shamanic in import. It would be both tedious and banal to offer a 'check-list' of all the many shamanic images and themes in Tarkovsky: but think only of the 'weightless' motif in *Mirror* and *Solaris*, for example; of Tarkovsky's empathy with the Russian tradition of the *iurodstvo*, or holy fool in *Andrei Roublov* and *Nostalgia*; of the way in which a simple ladder propped against a country building retains its natural being, even as it becomes part of an extraordinary ensemble of images of purifying 'immanent transcendence' in the scene where a barn burns down in lightly dripping rain in *Mirror*; of the trials of initiation and the themes of sacred space, animal spirit or helper, and cosmic reverie in both *Stalker* and *Nostalgia*; and of the centrality of the liminal motifs of ladder, fire and water in *The Sacrifice*.[68]

At one point, Tarkovsky planned to call his last film *The Witch*: the 'witch' Maria plays a relatively small, but absolutely pivotal role in what became *The Sacrifice*. In a recent article in *Soviet Film*, the Swedish film scholar, historian and author Layla Alexander has revealed how Tarkovsky spoke of the occult in the last few years of his life: 'Andrey introduced me to his Italian colleague as "la strega", the sorceress or witch. Surprised at the ensuing protests on my part, he asked me whether I had anything against witches. The Russian word for witch "ved'ma" has its origin in the verb "vedat" — to know, be aware of, to have knowledge about.'[69] Later, Layla recalls, she and Tarkovsky spent an evening listening to Saami *joiks*, which she describes as 'shepherd's cries, wailings reminiscent of a shaman's invocations. They occur in the film [*The Sacrifice*] just as something threatening or inexplicable is about to happen. This calling, this captivating woman's voice can be heard both when Otto, the postman and

64 *Stalker* 1979 director
Andrei Tarkovsky,
photographer/cameraman
Aleksandr Knyazhinsky
© Contemporary Films/
British Film Institute

Alexander fall into "psychic trances" and, similarly, when Alexander has his apocalyptic dream.'[70]

In his study *Transcendental Style in Film: Ozu, Bresson, Dreyer*, the director Paul Schrader makes the point that any film maker concerned with expressing the transcendent has to be wary of what he calls 'overabundant means': for the spectre of kitsch (Charlton Heston in *The Ten Commandments*, for example) threatens the sublime now as never before. Here, the quintessential modernist idea that 'less is more', which has usually been given a formal — or 'profane' — meaning, comes into its own. As Schrader says, it is in the sparseness of cinema that its true riches lie; just as it is in its 'unique ability to reproduce the immanent' that one may find 'its unique ability to evoke the Transcendent'.[71] It was Tarkovsky's extraordinary achievement to have evoked the transcendent, through a dialectical synthesis of the seemingly opposed traditions of the Lumière brothers and Méliès. For in the filmic shamanism of this Russian seer, every blade of grass, every drop of water, every flicker of that fundamental aspect of both life and film — light — is both itself, and an intimation of something *other*.

10 Sculpting the Cosmos

Some of the most striking examples of the humanist energy which drove the Renaissance are to be found in the massive statues of horse and rider (such as the one of Marcus Aurelius from which the blazing Domenico falls at the end of Tarkovsky's *Nostalgia*) which dominate many an Italian square. The contrast with our century could hardly be greater. Instead of the civic and martial dignity of Donatello's *Gattemelata Monument* in Padua (*c.*1443—53) or Verrocchio's *Colleoni Monument* in Venice (1479—96), for example, the work of Marino Marini — the most memorable equestrian sculptor of the past fifty years — features a series of variations upon the motif of a startled, rearing horse and naked rider. Marini chose to depict horse and rider in what would seem to be a moment of anguished disarray, presaging cultural and social disaster. Describing his work as 'the decomposition of a myth — that of the heroic and victorious man, of the *uomo di virtù* of the humanists', the sculptor believed that 'we are heading towards the end of a world'.[1]

If one believes that twentieth-century art is remarkable chiefly for what it reveals about the loss of spirituality and meaning in the modern world, Marini's words might seem to require little further comment. However, as we have seen, socio-historical despair hardly constitutes the sole theme of modern art. Far from it: as creative recollection, as primitivising anamnesis, such art has spoken of the regeneration and development of potentially healing qualities of *participation mystique*. In one guise or another, the shamanic spirit of modern art has revealed how much we still experience that 'thirst for *being*' which Eliade felt to be characteristic of all archaic, religiously-oriented life.[2] And in this regard, sculpture has played at least as great a primitivising role as any of the other arts this century.

Thus, beyond the pessimism of Marini's twilight terror, much twentieth-century sculpture speaks not of death but of birth — of the sculpting of those mythopoeic ideas, forms, textures and rhythms which might counter the increasingly voracious demands of history and politics, and conjure a healing sense of cosmos. Of all the arts this century, sculpture is the one which has expanded its 'field of operation' the most. To speak of the shamanic spirit in twentieth-century sculpture is to speak of both 'timeless' objects and video performance; of large scale monuments and magical boxes; of walks in the Scottish Highlands and vigils in Neolithic caves; of the worship of the Great Goddess — and the planting of seven thousand oak trees in the middle of a town.

We have already remarked the extent to which Jean Arp's low-relief sculpture *Forest* embodied the healing power of what Gaston Bachelard called 'cosmic reverie'. The contemporary, Dadaesque sculpture of Marcel Duchamp — another artist whose work, like that of Arp, contains far more 'cosmicity' than might be apparent at first sight — is a comparably stimulating, albeit ascetically realised example of the extent to which the ostensible 'meaninglessness' of much twentieth-century art contains an esoteric core of potentially healing power.

The tendency of post-Romantic art to stress the 'object-ness' of the art work, while at the same time emphasising the extent to which that 'object-ness' embodied rather than illustrated ideas about the world, meant that a post-Symbolist artist like Duchamp (1887–1968) could take the simplest of everyday objects, and by the power of the transformative idea with which he invested them, turn them into sculpture of provocative resonance. Sculpture thus became the perfect medium within which to realise an occult transmutation of idea into object, and object into talisman.

In recent years the writers Jack Burnham and John F. Moffitt have done much to illuminate the shamanic and alchemical import of such (in)famous Duchamp 'ready-mades' as *Bicycle Wheel* (1913) and *Bottle Rack* (1914). In the case of the former, the first of the 'ready-mades', Duchamp simply mounted an inverted bicycle wheel (minus tube and rubber tyre) on a painted wooden stool. In characteristically low-key manner, he once described the pleasure he took from this piece: 'To see that wheel turning was very soothing, very comforting, a sort of opening of the avenues onto other things than the material life of every day. I liked the idea of having a bicycle wheel in my studio. I enjoyed looking at it, just as I enjoy looking at the flames dancing in a fireplace.'[3]

For Moffitt, *Bicycle Wheel* brings to mind a metaphor employed by the Russian occultist P.D. Ouspensky in *Tertium Organum* (1911) to illustrate the transrational workings of the fourth dimension: once put into rapid spinning motion, the open spokes of a bicycle wheel paradoxically become a solid plane, through which an object such as a stick or ball cannot penetrate.[4] There is also the key fact that the reverie which the spinning wheel induced in Duchamp came from something *round*, elevated — literally and symbolically — into a principle of contemplation. (It is worth noting the conjunction of the Latin *tempus* i.e. time and *templum* i.e. space in the last word.) In *The Poetics of Space*, Gaston Bachelard speaks of the healing phenomenological significance of 'roundness'. This can be related to the emphasis he places elsewhere upon the idea or experience of being *centred*: 'Every universe is concentrated in a nucleus, a spore, a dynamised center.'[5] As we shall presently see, both concepts — roundness and centredness — are crucial to Mircea Eliade's understanding of the cosmic dimension of existence in archaic or traditional cultures.

Initially, the quietly-spoken Duchamp, a man much given to irony, might seem the very last person in whom to discern the post-Romantic shamanic spirit at work. But in his early 'ready-mades' Duchamp exploited the tension between object, context and idea in such a way as to poeticise the world, opening up its mythopoeic, cosmic dimensions. Just as the shaman is able to turn a notched stick into the World Tree upon which the healing journey to the spirit world is undertaken, so did Duchamp endow the everyday object with potentially healing, talismanic power. And in his emphasis upon the fact that, through the various levels of attention they bring to a piece, the audience of an art work brings that piece to varying degrees of life, Duchamp opened up questions of idea and image, and energy and transformation to an extraordinary degree.

Aspects of Duchamp's radical aesthetic can be discerned in much of the twentieth-century avant-garde: one senses his spirit in many of the Fluxus artists of the 1960s, for example, with their anti-formalist emphasis and their desire that art function not as a commodity but as (an ultimately disposable) stimulation to social change.[6] In the present context, however, one must remark the complementary echoes of Duchamp's intensification of symbolist concerns in such later 'box sculptors' as the American Joseph Cornell (1903–63) and the Canadian Tony Urquart (b.1934).

A great admirer of Duchamp, Cornell transformed a twilight world of romantic or Victorian *bric à brac* in such a way as to somehow combine formal austerity and surrealist fantasy. His boxes have been described as 'star maps of a private universe': the shamanic overtones of their post-Mallarmé cosmicity have been beautifully captured in Brian O'Doherty's suggestion that 'The past is full of voices seeking to ventriloquise themselves through what the present provides. In divining that past, Cornell engaged in voyages of retrieval through his "chains" of communication ... At the heart of Cornell's universe was this system of equations: celestial bodies = light = time = memory = decay = nostalgia = grand design = common objects = celestial bodies.'[7]

In Urquart's work, the nostalgia for cosmicity is conveyed by the ubiquitous motif of the hole or aperture. Joan M. Vastokas relates Urquart's use of this motif to Eliade's ideas concerning the holy space, or centre, of archaic or traditional cultures — a space which is never chosen by man, but rather revealed to him. Besides this fundamental motif of the hole, which enabled the shaman to break through the various planes of existence and thus open the tribe to the healing energies of divine cosmicity, Urquart's boxes also feature the motifs of the creation of the world and the enclosed, Paradisal garden. As Vastokas says, these highly finished works are essentially 'creations out of chaos that define a sacred space, a sanctuary.'[8]

The idea of sacred space, of art as a sanctuary, is central to the work of Constantin Brancusi (1876–1957). The key figure in early modernist sculpture's development of primitivistic 'significant form', and an artist of immense shamanic consequence, Brancusi believed that 'a well-made sculpture should have the power to heal the beholder.'[9] Describing sculptures as 'occasions for meditation', the son of a Romanian peasant and weaver who became one of the chief figures of the Parisian avant-garde summarised the affirmative, transformational essence of his art thus: 'I made stone sing — for humanity.'[10]

Technically, Brancusi's great contribution to twentieth-century sculpture lay in his early abandonment of modelling in favour of direct carving, a technique which was to lead such later sculptors as Henry Moore and Barbara Hepworth to emphasise the 'truth to material' which, like Brancusi, they felt should be manifest in their art. The cosmological implications of this shift in technique are evident in Brancusi's belief that 'The artist should know how to dig out the being that is within matter and be the tool that brings out its cosmic essence into an actual visible existence.'[11]

In an excellent study of the sculptor, the English painter and art historian Eric Shanes has suggested that such a remark clearly confirms the intellectual sophistication and Platonism of an artist-savant who has on occasion been mythologised as a sort of holy innocent. One should recall that this academically-trained artist — who was to overturn all academic conventions of sculptural form — could at various times count Picasso, Apollinaire, Léger and Marcel Duchamp among his friends and acquaintances. Brancusi owned a copy of Poincaré's 1914 edition *Oeuvres de Platon*, and in a famous remark, once suggested (with unmistakable Platonic force) that 'It is only fools who could say my works are abstract; what they are categorising as abstract is in fact the most realistic thing possible, for reality is not the outer form but the idea, the essence of things.'[12]

As Shanes points out, such Platonism can be traced back to Brancusi's youth. Before his legendary 1904 journey halfway across Europe to Paris, a large part of which was undertaken on foot, Brancusi had studied aesthetics while attending the School of Fine Art in Bucharest — and such studies would have included an analysis of Platonic and neo-Platonic thought. From a shamanic point of view, however, one is tempted to see Brancusi's Platonism — his abandonment of the fleshy surface of life, so to speak, in pursuit of the ideal forms which lay waiting in matter, forms which might 'materialize meaning' as they revealed 'the essence of things' — as part of an even older tradition of cosmological thought.

Mircea Eliade, compatriot of Brancusi, argued that Plato's emphasis on the timelessness of the ideas and concepts which lie behind the shifting veils of the phenomenal world can be related to the belief of archaic and traditional cultures in the regenerative power of myth. For the experience of myth returns the members of such cultures to the archetypal time of origins, thus taking them beyond everyday, profane time to the sacred time of cosmic creation. Eliade has suggested that, insofar as so-called primitive thought always returns to the idea of generative, mythic archetype, temporarily abolishing the exhausted 'everyday' experience of life in favour of the divine, replenishing model which first set that life in motion, Plato might be regarded as 'the outstanding philosopher of "primitive mentality", that is, as the thinker who succeeded in giving philosophical currency and validity to the modes of life and behavior of archaic humanity.'[13]

For Eliade, therefore, Brancusi's significance lay not so much in his Platonism as in the fact that 'he succeeded in rediscovering the "presence-in-the-world" specific to archaic man, whether Lower Paleolithic hunter or Mediterranean, Carpatho-Danubian, or African Neolithic hunter.'[14] What did Eliade mean by this? There has long been an art historical debate over the extent of Brancusi's debt to the examples of either African or Romanian tribal and folk motifs, and these cultures' technical excellence with regard to wood carving.[15] For Eliade, the point at issue was not so much whether Africa or his native Romania had had the biggest influence on Brancusi, but rather the primal nature of the mental and spiritual universe which such influences jointly helped to bring to life in the sculptor. Eliade speaks of the journey of 'interiorization' towards a distant past which was triggered off in Brancusi — who himself believed that 'The journey is really within oneself', and who once declared: 'I am not Surrealist, Baroque, Cubist, nothing of this kind. My new I comes from something very old.'[16] This 'something very old', Eliade believed, was the mental and spiritual universe of prehistoric humanity: an animistic universe, structured by the fundamental concepts of the sacred and the profane.

In such works as *The Myth of the Eternal Return or, Cosmos and History* (1954), *The Sacred And The Profane: The Nature Of Religion* (1957) and *The Quest: History and Meaning in Religion* (1969) Eliade elaborated upon his fundamental intuition that 'The chief difference between the man of the archaic and traditional societies and the man of the modern societies with their strong imprint of Judaeo-Christianity lies in the fact that the former feels himself indissolubly connected with the Cosmos and the cosmic rhythms, whereas the latter insists that he is connected only with History.'[17] Connected only with the broken, uncertain rhythms of history and politics, the secular ideologies of post-Enlightenment modernity posit something unthinkable in traditional society — the development of what Eliade called 'the *completely* profane world, the wholly desacralized cosmos'.[18] For Eliade, Brancusi's sculpture had done much to help counter such a development. Replenishing the 'vertical', cosmic dimension of the psyche, it had resurrected key aspects of that archetypal imagination which had once given meaning to archaic and traditional culture.

Archaic and traditional societies experience space and time in terms of the inter-relation of what are (for them) the ontologically essential categories of the sacred and the profane. For these cultures, the creation of all aspects of human society is dependent upon a paradigmatic model — the creation of the universe by the gods. And if life is to continue, and to continue well, it must be periodically recharged with such paradigmatic creativity. This is encountered within the magical realm of myth, the metamorphosing dimension of existence where humanity returns to the time of origins, and thus gains replenishing, participative access to aboriginal archetypes of energy and orientation.[19]

Experience of the mythic dimension of divine creativity involved archaic or traditional cultures in an enormous intensification and transmutation of their everyday, profane sense of both time and space. The myths of such cultures not only 'took' their tellers and listeners back to the time of origins (*in illo tempore*); they also 'placed' them at the aboriginal heart of the world, the initial and ultimate place of creation. The symbolism of the generative centre is all-important here — the centre from which members of archaic and traditional cultures were able to develop and sustain an organised and meaningful 'horizontal' (i.e. socio-geographical) orientation in their lives.

Of most importance for Eliade is the fact that such a mythic experience of the centre also involved a vertical dimension, through which life could be experienced as open to the transcendent plane of sacred, celestial archetype. Hence the crucial image of the *axis mundi*, an image — or rather, artefact — which features in both the most nomadic and settled of archaic and traditional cultures. The symbolism of the *axis mundi* can be both a matter of architectural support for the 'dome' of organised life, and a sign of potential transcendence. Until the recent proliferation of the skyscraper office block, the power of this elemental religious image was apparent enough in non-tribal life in the symbolic dominance of town or city proclaimed by church tower or cathedral spire.

'In short,' says Eliade, 'whatever the dimensions of the space with which he is familiar and in which he regards himself as situated — his country, his city, his village, his house — religious man feels the need always to exist in a total and organised world, in a cosmos.'[20] The strength of that need emerges with particular force in Eliade's précis of the famous anthropological report of the 1920s by Spencer and Gillen, concerning the consternation and desolation into which the nomadic Arunta tribe, the Achilpa, were plunged when their sacred pole, which they had always used to help discern the direction in which they should travel, broke.

The pole of the Achilpa had been shaped from a gum tree, the same tree from which their mythical ancestor Numbakula had fashioned the very first sacred pole — the *axis mundi* of the tribe. Having cosmicised their territory with the pole, anointed with his blood, Numbakula climbed up it and disappeared into the sky from whence he had come. Only around the sacred pole was territory subsequently habitable, as the pole's physical and symbolic power transformed the natural world into a cosmos of horizontal and vertical order 'guaranteed' by the paradigmatic creativity of the divine ancestor. For the pole to be broken denoted catastrophe, the rupturing of the spiritual backbone of life. Isolated in the profane world, bereft of any sense of divinely organised cosmos, the tribe wandered around aimlessly for a while. Finally, they simply lay down on the ground together and waited for death to come.[21]

The story of the Achilpa is a vivid example of the extent to which archaic or traditional cultures *lived* the symbolic dimensions of their lives: a pointed contrast to the experience of many today, where — thanks to dictionaries of symbolism and all manner of socio-historical and psychoanalytical exegesis — we often seem to 'know about' much more than we experience of this fundamental aspect of life. The fate of the Achilpa also clarifies what Eliade meant by speaking of archaic or traditional man's religious 'thirst for *being*' — for that thirst arose precisely from archaic man's terror of the nothingness, the chaos, that lies outside a sense of cosmos. Hence his overwhelming need 'to take his stand at the very heart of the real, at the Center of the World'.[22] Finally, what a rationalist mind may be quick to see as this nomadic tribe's neurotic need for a cosmology underlines Eliade's key point that the multiplicity, or even the infinity of centres of the world raises no difficulty for religious thought. For 'it is not a matter of geometrical space, but of an existential and sacred space that has an entirely different structure, that admits of an infinite number of breaks and hence is capable of an infinite number of communications with the transcendent.'[23]

As we have seen in chapter 4, the shamans of archaic or traditional cultures were the ultimate guardians of the pre-Judaeo-Christian sense of sacred being, of a multi-dimensional, animistic cosmos. With their highly developed, mythopoeic sensitivity, such individuals were able to experience what Eliade calls the mystery of the breakthrough in plane: the breakthrough from everyday time to the Paradisal Great Time, and from everyday space to the Great Space of Origin. The pre-eminent shamanic technique, says Eliade, is the passage from one cosmic region to another — from earth to the sky or from earth to the underworld.[24]

Given the appalling consequences of fascism's various attempts to 're-tribalise' life this century, it is natural that some may suspect the spectre of a regressive, de-humanising conservatism in Eliade's various anti-historical, cosmological concepts of 'centre', 'thirst for *being*' and 'break-through in plane'. However, this would be to misunderstand entirely the thrust of Eliade's thought. For all its critique of aspects of Judaeo-Christianity and modernity, Eliade's work was very much oriented towards both the thinking, feeling and 'suffering' individual and the problems and potentialities of cultural interchange today. At the end of *Myths, Dreams and Mysteries*, for example, Eliade spoke of the possibility of a 'genuine encounter' between peoples today, a mythically-informed encounter that might constitute the point of departure for a new humanism, upon a world-wide scale. Like Joseph Campbell, Eliade believed that '*Every* people is a chosen people'.[25]

To suspect the ghost of fascism in Eliade's respect for primitive ontology would be to forget the emphasis which he placed upon the multiplicity of cosmologies in archaic cultures. It would also be to overlook the emphasis which he placed upon shamanism as a testing experiential bridge from the profane to the sacred dimensions of life — or what Jungians would call the passage from individualism to individuation.[26] While the essential nature, or foundations of that bridge might be homologous from culture to culture, Eliade was the last person to suggest that there was only one way to either construct or cross it. Hence his passion for shamans rather than priests, and for modern art rather than political theory. Like the shaman, the sort of modern artist who attracted Eliade's attention — such as Brancusi — had broken away from the tired, sick or overly familiar world of appearances, in personal search of the replenishing cosmological core of (individuated) existence. And as the 1937 Degenerate Art exhibition organised by the Nazis made absolutely clear, the exploratory courage of such a search has had precious little in common with fascism.

Rather than reflecting the shifting details of historical consciousness in his work, Brancusi sculpted what one might call the mythopoeic core of the archetypal forms of the cosmological imagination. He can thus be seen as the great, initiatory shaman of twentieth-century sculpture, working with wood and stone, polished bronze and marble to offer us a world of profound simplicity and regal symmetry. Brancusi's sculptures constitute a world of 'sacred geography', in which idea and appearance, spirit and matter are in healing, mythopoeic equilibrium. From a Jungian point of view, the radical equality of the disposition of the male and female figures in the 1907–08 *The Kiss*, the faces and upper torsos of which press together with a desire which is as unexploitative as it is unsentimental, reveals the extraordinary degree to which Brancusi was able to synthesise animus and anima, the rational and the supra-rational in his work.[27]

The Brancusi scholar Sidney Geist has drawn attention to the way in which the greatest weight of the triple-forked piece of maple from which *The Sorceress* (1916) was carved is placed in the upper rather than the lower part of the sculpture. *The Sorceress* is thus an excellent example of both Brancusi's animistic sensitivity to the elemental forms lying in wait within material, and what was to be his life-long concern for the transmutation — rather than any simplistic, dualistic transcendence — of matter. 'Throughout my life', said the sculptor, 'I have searched for the meaning of flight. Flight, what happiness!'[28] From the folk-like robustness of the *Maiastra* (Magic Bird) of 1912, to the many elegant refinements and transmutations of this motif which are to be found in the later *Yellow Bird* and *Bird in Space* series, Brancusi sought to sculpt 'not a bird' but rather 'the meaning of flight', as he put it in old age.[29]

For Brancusi, the meaning of flight lay in the alchemy of the self's passage from the realm of the personal to the transpersonal: from the inevitable vicissitudes and exhaustion of historical existence to the exaltation of cosmological consciousness. A biography of the eleventh-century Tibetan monk Milarepa, published in French in 1925, was one of Brancusi's favourite books; he also read Lao-Tzu and Helena Blavatsky with much pleasure. Those are who are nearest to God, said the sculptor, had seen his work best: work intended to give the beholder the experience of 'pure joy'.[30]

The cosmicity of Brancusi's work is nowhere more evident than in *Endless Column*, which he first carved in wood in 1916 and developed in various scale and material throughout the years. With this piece, Brancusi created what is both one of the most striking examples of the modernist faith that 'less is more', and the greatest single example of the shamanic spirit in twentieth-century art. The column attains its most compelling realisation in the cast iron version at Tîrgu-Jiu in Romania, where it constitutes the climactic part of the war memorial ensemble which Brancusi created in 1937–8.[31] The formal aspects of the piece could hardly be simpler: a sequence of rhomboids which, as Eliade noted, make the column 'akin to a tree or to a notched pole'.[32] Brancusi himself described the piece as 'a stairway to heaven'.[33]

What did the idea of heaven mean to Brancusi? 'In the art of other times', he remarked, 'there is joy, but with it the nightmare that the religions drag with them. There is joy in Negro sculpture, among the archaic Greeks, in some things of the Chinese and the Gothic . . . oh, we find it everywhere. But even so, not so well as it might be with us in the future, if only we were to free ourselves of all this . . . It is time we had an art of our own.'[34] Freeing himself of the accumulated and often divisive and deadening historical weight of religious orthodoxies, Brancusi revivified the most ancient of divine archetypes, as he sought the 'break-through in plane' of the shaman: the creation of that 'existential and sacred space' which gives the imagination healing access to a world of cosmic reverie. In the mid-1920s, Brancusi spoke of his dream of building an *Endless Column* in New York's Central Park, taller than any building and with a 'great bird' poised on its tip. The revolution of twentieth-century art here came full circle, paying unconscious homage to that anonymous artist of fifteen to twenty thousand years ago who once drew a bird's head on top of the stick, or staff, which stands beside the shaman of the Lascaux Cave.

The rhomboid module of *Endless Column* not only reminds one of the notches whereby the archaic shaman climbed the Tree of Life: it is also

65 Constantin Brancusi
Maiastra 1912 polished bronze
55.2 x 17.1 x 17.8 on stone
base with stone reliefs
34.9 (height)
Tate Gallery, London
© DACS 1992

reminiscent of a sculptural base. (In his study of Brancusi, the museum director and author Pontus Hulten is certain that the module began life as a base.[35]) The question of the role of the base or pedestal in sculpture was fundamental to Brancusi, indicating the extent of his concern to create an integrated ensemble, where the base of a sculpture does not so much elevate the world of form above the earth, as help it to grow out of the latter. In turning what had traditionally functioned as mere support (and indication of sculpture's separation from the earth) into the ascensional heart of the piece, Brancusi said much about the human struggle to transmute the divisions of body and soul, sexuality and spirituality.

Endless Column exemplifies what one might call the sublimating and synthesising power of individuated, unitary consciousness: rooted in the earth, the column nevertheless conjures the space of pure ascension.[36] What Eliade has observed with respect to Brancusi's work in stone surely applies with equal if not more force here: 'One might almost say that he performed a transmutation of "matter" or, more precisely, that he brought about a *coincidentia oppositorum*, since he achieved in one and the same object a coincidence of matter and flight, of weight and its negation.'[37]

The column has stood seven degrees off true vertical since the early 1950s when, as Eric Shanes recounts, 'a Stalinist mayor of Tîrgu-Jiu decided the work was a piece of Western formalist junk and tried to pull it down for smelting into industrial machinery. He had guy ropes attached, and for three days horses tried to pull the column over. Fortunately Brancusi had fixed the base of the column in a pyramidal steel footing and embedded it in fifteen cubic feet of concrete, so it proved immovable, though it was left with a slight lean.'[38] Triumphing over the short-term 'logic' of such perverse historical consciousness, *Endless Column* stands as an unsurpassable monument to cosmological consciousness: a marvellous shamanic image of the sense of integral transcendence that may grow out of what Bachelard called 'centralized solitude'.[39]

A sacred feeling of cosmicity is no less part of the art of Henry Moore (1898–1986) and Barbara Hepworth (1903–75), artists who were both positively affected not only by Brancusi's primitivising idealism, but by the biomorphic forms which Jean Arp developed in the early- to mid-1930s. Arp wanted his free-standing 'sculpture in the round' (as opposed to his low-reliefs) to find what he called 'its humble place in the woods, the mountains, in nature'.[40] Similarly, Moore and Hepworth developed strongly organic forms which, inspired by nature, came to full life in a natural setting. Following the precedent set by Gauguin and Brancusi, Jacob Epstein (1880–1959) and Henri Gaudier-Brzeska (1891–1915), both were greatly inspired by sculpture from beyond the Greco-Roman tradition of idealised (human) beauty. For Hepworth, for example, to make sculpture was to create something talismanic — something 'primitive, religious, passionate, and magical — always, always affirmative'.[41]

While he had been deeply impressed by the work of Giotto, Masaccio and Donatello which he saw on a student study trip to Florence in 1925, it was not until the 1940s that Moore allowed an affinity with classicism to become as evident in his work as it is in the Masaccio-like dignity of the 1943—4 *Madonna and Child* which he carved for St Matthew's Church, Northampton. Throughout the formative 1920s and 1930s, decades when he was as influenced by Roger Fry's celebration of Negro sculpture in *Vision and Design* as he was by the power of sculpture from beyond the classical tradition which he saw and drew in the British Museum, Moore celebrated the vitality of so-called primitive art.[42] Declaring that 'All art has its roots in the primitive', he described primitive art as 'a channel for expressing powerful beliefs, hopes and fears' — 'something made by people with a direct and immediate response to life'.[43] In 1934, he contributed the following key reflection upon his work to *Unit One*, a book edited by Herbert Read: 'Beauty, in the later Greek or Renaissance sense, is not the aim in my sculpture. Between beauty of expression and power of expression there is a difference of function. The first aims at pleasing the senses, the second has a spiritual vitality which for me is more moving and goes deeper than the senses. Because a work does not aim at reproducing natural appearances it is not, therefore, an escape from life — but may be a penetration into reality ... an expression of the significance of life, a stimulation to greater effort in living.'[44]

After the Second World War, Moore would emphasise that the great challenge of his work was 'to combine sculptural form (POWER) with human sensitivity and meaning i.e. to try to keep Primitive Power with humanist content.'[45] But as his biographer Roger Berthoud has pointed out, ultimately, there is more pantheism than there is humanism in Moore's world — the pantheism which integrates body and landscape, 'inside' and 'outside', for example, in such a masterpiece of resurgent *participation mystique* as the elmwood *Reclining Figure* of 1936.[46]

Erich Neumann devotes several pages to this commanding work in his study *The Archetypal World of Henry Moore*. For this Jungian psychologist, *Reclining Figure* epitomises Moore's ability to take us beyond our ego-centred consciousness, which 'knows only a reality polarized into outside and inside, a world of objects that the ego, so far as it is conscious, confronts as a separate subject.'[47] Transcending the ego, we approach the *participation mystique* of the 'unitary reality' of archetypal and transpersonal experience: 'When the artist, when Moore, puts his figures into reality, it is never the reality of our consciousness and of everyday. Always these figures belong to another world than the "normal" one, and always they

66 Henry Moore *Reclining
Figure* 1936 elmwood
64 x 115 x 52.5
Wakefield City Art Gallery
© The Henry Moore
Foundation

have the effect, in our everyday world, of an invasion from another dimension of being.'[48] Sculpting an animistic cosmos, redolent of both the potentially healing majesty of the Great Mother, or Earth Goddess, and the mysteries of those cave-like paths of initiation which follow the 'night sea journey' of the sun (consciousness) into the labyrinth of the unconscious, Moore here attained the status of a great seer.[49]

As Neuman says, the wood of *Reclining Figure* is treated as living matter, the flow of its grain heightening — and to a certain extent determining — the plastic effect of the carving. But at the same time, nature's materiality has been transmuted into a highly organised sculptural field of devotional, rhythmic and tactile power. Contemplating the initiatory implications of *Reclining Figure*, the extent to which it intimates a world of cosmic, primordial integrity, one senses how much in tune Moore was with what Mircea Eliade called 'primitive ontology'.

The same point applies to Barbara Hepworth, albeit in a somewhat different register. An artist of consummate subtlety, whose work might be said to develop the Eastern overtones in Brancusi's oeuvre, Hepworth produced some of the most psychologically unified pieces of sculpture of the century. (In 1932 she visited Brancusi's studio in Paris, where — as she recalled later — she encountered 'the miraculous feeling of eternity mixed with beloved stone and stone dust'. Hepworth felt the power of Brancusi's 'integrated personality' and 'clear approach to his material' very strongly.[50])

Whether one considers the rhythmical counterpoint of wood and string in *Wave* (1944), the ascensional interaction of sheet metal planes and strings of *Orpheus* (1956), or the compelling invitation of the cool, circular hole which runs clean through the Irish green marble of *Ritual Stone* (1967), it is obvious that we are in the presence of an artist who was able to combine romantic and classical sensibilities to an unusually high degree. The completely unillustrative, formal self-sufficiency of Hepworth's work has sometimes tempted observers to see it in terms of pure geometry or abstraction. Even so sympathetic and intelligent a commentator as A.M. Hammacher has spoken of Hepworth's work as displaying 'rhythmic spatial feeling' as opposed to the 'mythological spatial feeling' of Moore.[51] But however rhythmically pure the spatial feeling in Hepworth's approach to 'significant form' may have been, there can be no doubt that it both emerged from and contributed to a mythopoeic sense of the cosmicity, the sacred significance of life.[52]

For Hepworth, the sacred forces of life were to be sought, above all, in landscape — whether it be the Yorkshire moors, the Cornish coast or the islands and inlets, the mountains and valleys of Greece. In 1934 she wrote: 'In the contemplation of Nature we are perpetually renewed, our sense of mystery and our imagination is kept alive, and rightly understood, it gives us the power to project into a plastic medium some universal or abstract vision of beauty.'[53] Later, while discussing the 'practical and passionate' business of responding to what she called 'the embrace of land and seascape' — an embrace which was of fundamental importance for her

67 Barbara Hepworth *Curved Form (Trevalgan)* 1956 bronze 90.2 x 67.3 x 59.7 Tate Gallery London © courtesy, Alan Bowness

drawings — she remarked: 'I rarely draw what I see — I draw what I feel in my body. Sculpture is a three-dimensional projection of primitive feeling: touch, texture, size and scale, hardness and warmth, evocation and compulsion to move, live, and love. Landscape is strong — it has bones and flesh and skin and hair.'[54]

Such animism emerged with even greater force in the last few years of her life. In 1970, the year she produced the mysterious, hieratic group of abstract bronzes which she called *The Family of Man*, she suggested to the art historian Alan Bowness that she thought of her sculpture as 'objects which rise out of the land or the sea, mysteriously. You can't make a sculpture without it being a thing — a creature, a figure, a fetish . . . It's something you experience through your senses, but it's also a life-giving, purposeful force.'[55] There could scarcely be a clearer statement of the shamanic role of the modern sculptor, concerned not with lamenting the end of a world, as in the case of Marini, but with recharging existence through the revivification of ancient ideas of animistic power and cosmic consequence — ideas 'reborn' and developed in the body as much as in the mind.[56]

Hepworth's faith in the affirmative magic of sculpture, her sense of herself as a shape-making medium for the larger forces of life, recalls the rhetorical question of Isamu Noguchi: 'What is the artist but the channel through which spirits descend — ghosts, visions, portents, the tinkling of bells?' Sharing the love of natural materials shown by Hepworth, Moore and Brancusi, Noguchi is perhaps the finest example of a twentieth-century sculptor bridging the cultures of East and West. In search of the shamanic 'break-through in plane' that might gain him access to healing currents of spiritual energy, Noguchi spoke thus of art: 'I don't think that art comes from art . . . I think it comes from the awakening person. Awakening is what you might call the spiritual. It is a linkage to something flowing very rapidly through the air . . .'[57]

Without any sense of self-grandeur, Noguchi described himself as both nomad and shaman in spirit, believing that 'If you allow yourself to be — or imagine yourself to be — part of all phenomena, then you are able to be anywhere, and the artist is merely the shaman who is able to contact all these other phenomena. Therefore, you are really free and you really don't belong anywhere.'[58] Such a blend of (sociological) homelessness and (animistic) belonging produced some of the most telling examples of the fusion of Far Eastern and Western sensibilities in the arts this century. One thinks especially of such works as the spacious, three-part *Garden Elements* of 1962, executed in bronze; the various skeletal, yet magical sets which Noguchi created for dancer Martha Graham from the mid-1930s onwards, and the beautiful UNESCO garden in Paris of 1956—8. (Although this garden drew upon the contemplative, asymmetrical aesthetic of the Zen rock garden, it was also — contrary to most Japanese gardens — designed to be walked in.)

Noguchi was born of Japanese-American parentage in Los Angeles in 1904; two years later, the family moved to Japan. Returning to America in 1918, Noguchi took premedical studies at Columbia University, before eventually gravitating to New York and deciding on a career in art. Travelling to Paris in the mid-1920s, he became Brancusi's studio assistant for a while. This was a key, formative episode in Noguchi's life, as he began to reflect upon the import of Brancusi's integration of the highest standards of craftsmanship with strong philosophico-religious ideas about the significance of direct carving, truth to material and pure form.

Returning to New York, Noguchi formed a friendship with a very different figure, the visionary architect, engineer and planetary planner Buckminster Fuller. In 1930 he made his first return to the Far East as an adult, studying painting in Beijing and pottery in Kyoto. Later, he remembered how important this period was for him: 'I have since thought of my lonely self-incarceration then, and my close embrace of the earth, as a seeking after identity with some primal matter beyond personalities and possessions. In my work I wanted something irreducible, an absence of the gimmickry and clever.'[59]

The search for something irreducible was to lead Noguchi to a revivification of the ancient Japanese veneration of the power of stone. He described stone as 'a direct link to the heart of matter', suggesting that when he tapped it, he received the echo of 'that which we are — in the solar plexus — in the center of gravity of matter. Then, the whole universe has a resonance!'[60] While in his early twenties, he had already spoken of a desire to view nature not through the eyes of (humanist) man, but rather through those of nature, his goal being to attain 'a fine balance of spirit with matter'.[61] *Great Rock of Inner Seeking*, a 10½ feet tall basalt piece from 1974, is a summarising example of the shamanic fruits of this ambition, testimony to the sculptor's belief that if religion had died as dogma this century, it had been reborn as direct personal expression in the arts.

The shadowed concavities and bold, ladder-like striations of this magnificent piece generate both subliminal and tactile intimations of the shamanic struggle for ascension which lies within potential reach of us all. The more overt cultural and spiritual resonances of the sculpture have been well captured by Roger Lipsey, who has described it as 'a truly commanding abstract sign, part stone calligraphy, part Easter Island head of massive size and presence . . . the front a forcefully carved but peaceful calligraphic sign, the back an intense pattern of drillmarks, pecking, and planes of relief that suggest the cloak — and character — of a Zen or Taoist patriarch.'[62]

Great Rock of Inner Seeking exemplifies what psychologists have called the 'haptic' (bodily, or touching) element in the primitivism of such modern sculptors as Gaudier-Brzeska, Brancusi, Arp, David Smith, Moore and

68 and 69 Isamu Noguchi
Great Rock of Inner Seeking
1974 (front and back view)
Basalt 324.5 (height)
National Gallery of Art,
Washington. Gift of Arthur
M. Sackler, M.D. and
Mortimer D. Sackler, M.D

Hepworth — and of course Noguchi himself. In recent years, the bodily import of primitivism in sculpture has both increased and diversified enormously, in parallel with an increased interest in both the cosmology of prehistoric sites and the possibilities of the body as a medium of expression. Instead of producing a durable piece of sculpture which symbolically synthesises aspects of the body and landscape, as in the case of Moore, Hepworth or Noguchi, land artists of the past two or three decades have chosen to work directly in nature, recording their activities by means of diary, still photograph or video film. The diversity of such activity has raised a number of key questions, prime among them being whether or not art has anything very meaningful to 'say' now, at a time when more and more evidence would suggest that the world is poised on the edge of ecological catastrophe. Are the arts to be anything more than 'the dance band on the Titanic'?[63]

In this respect, it is interesting to consider the pioneering land art of Richard Long in comparison with some later, strongly feminist and Goddess-oriented art. Born in Bristol in 1945, Long opened up a quietly fresh and radical direction for sculpture in the late 1960s, with a piece entitled *A Line Made by Walking*. The artist simply made a briefly visible line in a field, by walking to and fro for a while: he then documented the result with a photograph. Subsequently, Long exchanged the sleepy familiarity of a farmer's field for the sublimity of the wildernesses of the world: the line has been joined by a ubiquitous circle, constituted by rocks, stones and boulders, or by the imprint of Long's boots. The photographs have been complemented by road maps and minimal descriptive statements — which some critics are happy to call poems — and together with his hand-imprinted mud circles and spirals, Long's beautiful stone or slate circles may now be found in museums and galleries around the world. The essence of Long's work, however, remains the same as it was in that modest piece of 1967: a refined, yet direct interplay between the primal human impulse to make (delimiting) marks and the (comparative) immensity of nature.

Recently, Long has been described as 'capable of sustaining many roles as well as that of artist, including traveller, explorer, pilgrim, shaman, magician, peripatetic poet, hill-walker and ordinary twentieth-century person from Bristol.'[64] The artist himself remains wary of at least some of these — and several other — classifications. When comparisons with either the British Romantic landscape tradition or Zen Buddhism are suggested to him, Long prefers to stress the simple facts of what he does: walking in a landscape, making marks, recording the activity.[65] And when comparisons are drawn between his work and the henges and menhirs of prehistory, his response is immediate: 'I actually hate that approach to my work. It is very academic. I was interested in landscape art long before I saw Stonehenge. You have to consider that Stonehenge and all the circles in Britain, they came about from a completely different culture, for different reasons. They were social, religious art. They were made by society. I make my work as an individual. There are enormous differences, really.'[66]

While Long is undoubtedly correct to stress such differences, it can nevertheless be argued that, at a mythopoeic level of the psyche, his mark-making reveals exactly the same nostalgia for cosmicity which Eliade saw to be such an important feature of archaic and traditional cultures. Long has suggested that the questions which arise when deciding where to make and place his pieces are 'like in one of the Carlos Castaneda books where everyone has to find their special place in the room.'[67] And when pressed recently as to whether or not he would describe his sensitivity to certain landscapes as a feeling for sacred place, he replied: 'Well, sacred I suppose has particular religious meanings and my work is not about religion. Probably a special place would be a better word. I suppose, sacred really means a place of intense feelings. If you think of religion as being about intense feelings and emotions, art can be close to religion. I think when I do a good work, I don't really think about it but . . . it seems as if the world and myself are completely in harmony at that place . . . It does not happen always but I am talking about when everything comes right. It really does feel like the centre of the world at that moment.'[68]

Thus, if Long's work is not about religion in the social — or priestly — sense, it is certainly religious in its shaman-like sensitivity to cosmicity. Long has said that he believes in modernism, in 'the excitement of new ideas', because in his view 'really profound art has in some way to be original, a new view of the world.'[69] The fundamental argument of this book is that much of the formally 'new' in modernist art can be seen in terms of the profundity of the very 'old' in human culture: and that in the shamanic moment of creativity (and aesthetic perception), the new and the old dissolve into the cosmicity of mythopoeic consciousness, or what Eastern thought has called the Eternal Now. In this light, it is particularly interesting to read of Long's belief that his work is both exactly the same as the handprints which he once saw in the cave at Lascaux, and entirely different. His sense that what he does may be part of a mysterious circle of continuity, difference and regeneration becomes further evident as he

70 Richard Long *Six Stone Circles* 1981. *c.* 150 pieces of Delabole slate: diameter 731.5 © courtesy, Anthony d'Offay Gallery, London Photograph: Prudence Cuming Associates Limited, London

speaks of the mud with which he makes his gallery circles and spirals: 'But it is amazing to think that my common, local mud, from the Avon, is the product of millions of years of powerful tides which themselves are controlled by the moon. It is a mixture of time, water and stone. So it is possible that small human choices and cosmic forces come together.'[70]

It is the belief of many feminist artists of the past twenty-five years that the conjunction of such 'small human choices and cosmic forces' must be seen in the light of the cyclical wisdom of what Marija Gimbutas, Monica Sjöö and Barbara Mor respectively call the religion of 'the Great Goddess' or 'the Great Cosmic Mother'. In Gimbutas's words: 'The Goddess in all her manifestations was a symbol of the unity of all life in Nature. Her power was in water and stone, in tomb and cave, in animals and birds, snakes and fish, hills, trees, and flowers. Hence the holistic and mythopoeic perception of the sacredness and mystery of all there is on Earth . . . In Europe she ruled throughout the Paleolithic and Neolithic, and in Mediterranean Europe throughout most of the Bronze Age.'[71]

If primitivism implies a (creative) return to — and development of — the values of the distant past, what richer renaissance of ancient qualities of *participation mystique* could there be than in art which returns to the values of a religion which once worshipped the dialectical life-forces of the earth? Gimbutas suggests, for example, that the menhirs of prehistory — which in our post-Freudian culture we may be tempted to see in phallic terms — were actually epiphanies of the Goddess, associated with mysterious healing powers.[72] Underlining the connection between menhir and well, Goddess and water of life, she also suggests that the circular form featuring so strongly in archaic and traditional cultures — 'be it fairy dance or ring of standing stones' — transmits what she sees as the healing, transformational Goddess energy which is increased by 'the combination of the powers of stone, water, mound, and circling motion'.[73]

After century upon century of violent repression and exile from consciousness, is the Great Goddess trying to speak through the art of Richard Long? Should this seem a far-fetched suggestion, consider the extent to which many of the primal forms favoured by modern artists might be seen as having their roots in the old European culture of the Goddess. For example, in her *Overlay: Contemporary Art and the Art of Prehistory*, easily the richest survey of its subject, Lucy Lippard suggests that 'The spiral, water meander, lozenge, zigzag, and bird, snake, and egg of this goddess-centered Old European culture turn up in different guises until (and into) Christian times . . . The androgynous bird-snake goddesses of Old Europe, with their phallic heads and fertile bodies, were the predecessors of the Cycladic idols that inspired Constantin Brancusi (who was raised in Romania, in the heart of Old Europe) and Max Ernst, with his androgynous bird alter ego — "Loplop".'[74]

For many feminists, the question of whether or not the Goddess is speaking through their art today is a non-question: She *is*, and the real question to be addressed is how to make Her voice as powerful as possible. For such artists, the return to what Gimbutas calls 'holistic and mythopoeic perception' involves an integration of politics and poetics, an integration based upon a thoroughly 'immanent' understanding of such terms as 'awareness' and 'spirituality.' Elinor W. Gadon, for example, suggests that 'The term spiritual is controversial when applied to political movements like ecofeminism and Green Politics. The problem lies in the association of the spiritual with the supernatural, a worldview that is contrary to earth-based spirituality that sees the divine as the immanent life force grounded in the natural world.'[75] Thus, to sculpt the cosmos today is to address fundamental issues of ideology and social change, while drawing transformational energy from the most ancient of sources.

According to the sculptor Cristina Biaggi, 'Sculpture in the Western world has lost the mystical magical presence that it had during the Neolithic period when a temple or a sculpture was considered to be the body of the deity.'[76] For Biaggi, therefore, to sculpt is to resurrect ancient, *embodied* mysteries of the earth. Having researched megalithic sites in Malta and the British Isles, she has produced a series of drawings for a Goddess Mound oriented towards the movements of sun and moon. She speaks of wanting to create 'a space that inspires mystery; that evokes the dark caves of the Goddess — places of rebirth and revitalized consciousness'.[77]

Biaggi's Goddess-oriented ambition to 'revitalize consciousness' has been shared in recent years by such diverse sculptors and performers as Ana Mendieta (1950–86), Michelle Stuart, Vijali Hamilton and Mary Beth Edelson.[78] It is in the work of New York-based Edelson that one is best able to see the extent to which the Goddess-inspired feminist artist committed to social change has been willing to move from the realm of private, ritualistic encounter with the cosmic energies of the Earth to public, communal (and often confrontational) activity.

The 1979 ritual *Where Is Our Fire?* which Edelson performed with other women at a 'Feminist Visions of the Future' conference in the Chico Mountains, California furnishes a good introduction to her concerns. Dressed in amorphous, shape-shifting black robes, the performers drew in the air with torches, developing a visual and collective meditation upon the element most associated with sacrificial, regenerative themes of threshold and transformation. As can be seen in the films of Tarkovsky, the phenomenology of fire fuses sexuality and spirituality, dread and delight, immanence and transcendence to an extent unmatched by any of the other elements. In *Where Is Our Fire?* the women participants are in control of the element which was once used to murder so many women visionaries. The sculpted, aerial arabesques of the piece proclaim Edelson's

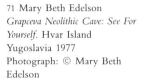

71 Mary Beth Edelson
Grapceva Neolithic Cave: See For Yourself. Hvar Island
Yugoslavia 1977
Photograph: © Mary Beth Edelson

desire to help women determine their own place in the world – to find their way through the labyrinth of history to the transformative, cosmic heart of existence.

Lucy Lippard describes Edelson as 'The American artist most deeply immersed in the study of the Great Goddess, resurrected from prehistory as a medium between nature and humanity . . . For over a decade she has combined a number of ingredients – Jungian psychology, feminism, dreams, fantasies, the collective unconscious, politics and collaborative artmaking – into a body of work that spans many mediums and millennia . . . Her utterly serious (and equally humorous) battle cry has been "Your 5,000 Years Are Up!" '[79] Two pieces of work from 1977 – *See For Yourself: Pilgrimage To A Neolithic Cave* and *Memorials to 9,000,000 Women Burned as Witches in the Christian Era* exemplify the dialectic of poetics and politics in Edelson's work.

In 1977 Edelson made a pilgrimage to the Neolithic Goddess site of Crapceva Cave on Hvar Island, off Yugoslavia. She had been performing private, Goddess-oriented rituals for some years, both in her studio and out of doors in nature, but had felt an increasing compulsion to visit an actual Goddess site. She describes her experience — which she documented by means of a time release camera — as follows: 'The cave was dazzling. It was magnificent. The main room, the great hall, sparkled and glistened with coral quartz. Stalagmites and stalactites, suggesting great temple pillars, divided the room into chambers. The atmosphere created a feeling of reverence and awe; . . . for me it was a holy place . . . I felt like the center of the universe . . . The cave contracted and expanded with my rhythms, and shimmered on its way back and forth. I made a pact with the cave; it would tell me some of its secrets in exchange for my rituals, rituals it had not seen for millennia. I in turn would learn some secrets now and some later — I had only to listen, to keep in touch.'[80]

Edelson regards her photographic images of such rituals (which she often adds to through drawing) as defining '*not who I am* but who *we are*', her intention being to restore what she calls 'a living mythology that cuts across many areas — political and spiritual'.[81] In the *Memorials* ritual of 1977, the animistic, shamanic nature of her experience of solitude and sacred space in Yugoslavia assumed strong historical and political overtones.

Edelson describes the complex, yet clearly articulated installation and ritual performance which took place at the A.I.R. Gallery in New York as follows: 'To enter the space [of the gallery] one went through the portals of a passage, *Gates of Horns/Fig of Triumph*, which set the exhibition apart as a sacred space. Both sides of the gate were lined with close-up photographs of hand gestures; on the front side *mano cornuta*: reclaimed as a sign of the horned bull and of female magic and power, and on the backside *mano in fica*, the fig, sacred fruit of the Goddess reclaimed as a symbol of Her Body/Our Body. Through the gate one faced a fire ladder surrounded by a circular table. The table contained books that further discussed witch hunts and sacred spaces. The ladder in the center of the table symbolized both positive and negative energy; during the Christian era when prosecutors were in a hurry to rid themselves of an accused witch they sometimes did not spend the time and money on a proper pyre, but grabbed a handy ladder and tied the poor woman to it, thrusting her into the bonfire. The positive energy refers to the ladder as a universal mystical sign of leaving behind, of being able to transcend.'[82] On Hallowe'en Eve, a public ritual took place in the gallery and then in the streets, with participants performing a litany of the names of persecuted witches, before walking by torchlight to a final, chanting and dancing celebration of the presence of the Goddess within themselves.

A more cryptic, yet equally expansive interplay of poetics and politics informs the work of the late German artist, Joseph Beuys, who developed a revolutionary approach to sculpture in the light of what he called 'this position where the umbilical cord is cut away from the cosmic powers'.[83]

For Beuys (1921—86) it was essential that humanity regenerate both itself and the earth through a return to an animistic, cosmic sense of existence. However, such a return was to be simultaneously a move forward towards a world in which what Beuys defined as 'social sculpture' — 'Sculpture as an evolutionary process; everyone an artist'[84] — could flourish. For Beuys, art and spirituality, mythopoeisis and politics were inextricably linked. During a public dialogue in New York in 1974, he spelled out his belief that 'The whole problematic of understanding the function of art in the society is to change our understanding of ourselves and humankind — the problem is only to understand that man is a being who needs nourishment for his spiritual needs, and that if he could cultivate and train this primary nature, this spiritual nature, he could develop whole other energies.'[85]

Beuys sharply distinguished his understanding of art from that of Marxism. Rather than being part of the 'ideological superstructure' built upon the realities of class struggle and economics, art was, for Beuys, the essence of humanity's capacities. Only from deep, sustained reflection upon the nature and purpose of creative activity could essential social change arise. When he was asked if his concept of 'social sculpture' implied the 'politicisation' of art, he replied that it meant exactly the opposite: the stale and increasingly meaningless ideologies of politics had to be broken up by the power of artistic activity, understood in its widest sense. For Beuys, being a teacher was his 'greatest' work of art.[86]

One of the most contentious figures of recent avant-garde art, Beuys spoke repeatedly of his belief in art as a therapeutic process, on both an individual and societal level. This was the therapy of the intelligence and feeling which might flow from a unitary consciousness, perpetually open to ideas of transformation and development. Using such unconventional sculptural materials as felt, fat and copper, blood and honey, a dead hare, bicycle pumps and a Volkswagen bus, Beuys shaped a multi-layered art of provocative bodily presence and animistic nuance. His drawings often reveal a mediumistic quality, their flowing, ethereal images of horse and stag, swan and hare indicating the essentially Celtic and Romantic cast of his mind; while the blackboards which he used to explicate his ideas during his performances, or actions, are full of diagrams and equations reminiscent of nothing so much as Novalis's conviction that 'the sciences must all be made poetic'.[87]

As redolent of the spirit of the laboratory as of a shamanic trance, Beuys's work constantly challenges us to think in terms of transformational dialectics. He once used the analogy of complementary colours (whereby, for example, if someone sees a red light and then closes their eyes they will see an after-image in green, and *vice-versa*) to explain how by using such an unprepossessing material as felt, he hoped to evoke in the engaged onlooker a sort of vibrant 'anti-image'. It was, he said, 'a matter of evoking a lucid world, a clear, a lucid, perhaps even a transcendental, a spiritual world through something which looks quite different, always in an anti-image process.'[88] Eschewing conventional notions of beauty, Beuys's sculpture moved between extremes of chaos and order, heat and cold, simplicity and complexity, in tandem with his belief that the psychological task for humanity is to unite the Apollonian and Dionysian principles in an animistic, metamorphosing development of life.

One might describe Beuys as the artist who has given the concept of 'significant form' the most radical of (non-formalist) reappraisals this century. Beuys did not become fully engaged with the practice of art until several years after the Second World War, following a period of study of the natural sciences, and he did not have a major exhibition of his work until the mid-1960s. But the drawings of the late 1940s and 1950s, with their essentially Nordic fascination with Romantic and shamanic themes, reveal what was coming to birth in him.[89] In a simultaneous negation and transcendence of the Nazi perversion of both Romanticism and primitivism, Beuys sought to reclaim and develop shamanic consciousness in the light of the homoeopathic principle 'Similia similibus curantor: heal like with like': hence the distinct sense of unease his imagery can sometimes arouse.[90]

The story of the transformation of Beuys's consciousness which began when the Ju-87 fighter plane which he was flying crashed in a snowstorm in the Crimea in 1943 has become as much a part of the legend of modern art as Gauguin's exile in Tahiti or Van Gogh's suicide in Auvers. Thrown from his plane, the unconscious Beuys was found by nomadic Tartars, who nursed him back to health, covering his body in fat and wrapping him in felt. (Part of the myth that grew up around Beuys was that the hat he so often wore hid the scars he bore from this experience. Whether this was true or not, the ritualistic use of this hat had clear shamanic implications, as Beuys knew: certain shamans consider their cap to be the most important part of their dress, the focal point of a good deal of their power.[91]) Much of Beuys's subsequent work would allude to both his traumatic experience in the Crimea and the general horrors of war: images of wounding and survival are ubiquitous in his art. In the 1964 action *The Chief*, for example, Beuys was wrapped in a shroud of heavy felt for nine hours, accompanied by two dead hares: from time to time, he cried out in a primal manner, reminiscent of the roar of a stag.

During the war, Beuys had read some of the Anthroposophical works of Rudolf Steiner (1861–1925), which made little if any positive impression on him at the time. However, shortly after the war Beuys attended some lectures and began to feel a considerable empathy for Steiner's ideas.[92] In his study *Occultism in Avant-Garde Art: The Case of Joseph Beuys*, John H. Moffitt has demonstrated the considerable extent to which the ideas which Beuys would finally develop about art can in fact be related to both Anthroposophy and Romanticism: for Steiner and Beuys were equally committed to the transformative union of art, religion and science. The greatest single influence in Steiner's intellectual life was Goethe, and for Steiner, it was essential that the twentieth century regain Goethe's perception that nature is 'God's living garment'.[93] Only then might humanity heal itself of the crippling dualisms that had come to dominate life: inner-outer, male-female, physical-spiritual, thinking-feeling, scientific-artistic.

Steiner placed consistent emphasis upon the arts as the means to such spiritual development. In 1923 he gave a series of eight lectures outlining the consequences of his belief that 'only a person who participates in spiritual life has an impulse for a creative activity transcending the merely natural [in appearance] . . .'[94] Looking back to what he regarded as the cosmic unity of spiritual and creative life in archaic culture, Steiner suggested that 'If we wish to reawaken in mankind the true artistic mood, we must, to a certain degree, transport ourselves back into those ancient times, when the celestial, the poetic mood, lived in the human soul.' 'Then', Steiner continued, 'we will receive an impression of how best to use other media to carry art to the world of the spirit; which is what must happen if art wants to be art.'[95]

Like Steiner, Beuys looked to the past for the inspiration needed to precipitate a fundamental change in our understanding of art's role. There was thus nothing at all sentimental in his approach to shamanism, which he described as 'the deepest root' of the idea of spiritual life: 'I take this form of ancient behaviour as the idea of transformation through concrete processes of life, nature and history. My intention is obviously not to return to such earlier cultures but to stress the idea of transformation and substance. That is precisely what the shaman does in order to bring about change and development: his nature is therapeutic . . . while shamanism marks a point in the past, it also indicates the possibility for historical development . . . So when I appear as a kind of shamanistic figure, or allude to it, I do it to stress my belief in other priorities [than those of late-industrial society] and the need to come up with a completely different plan for working with substances. For instance, in places like universities, where everyone speaks so rationally, it is necessary for a kind of enchanter to appear . . .'[96]

In 1909 Steiner had argued that 'The self is formed out of, born out of the whole universe, and our own [spiritual] ascent leads us finally to merge in the whole Cosmos. The aim of self-knowledge is to give man his place in the great world in order to reveal to him the true meaning of the word, self-knowledge.'[97] Two particular actions, or performances, by Beuys epitomise the extent to which his work explored the shamanic implications of Steiner's words: *How to explain pictures to a dead hare* (1965) and *Coyote: 'I Like America And America Likes Me'* (1974).

In the former piece, Beuys spent three hours in a gallery, his head covered with honey and gold leaf, 'explaining' pictures to a dead hare. An iron sole, complete with magnet, was tied to Beuy's right foot, companion to a felt sole on his left foot. While Beuys remained mute throughout the action, his right foot tapped on the hard stone floor as he limped slowly around the gallery, carrying the hare from picture to picture. For Beuys, this aspect of the performance was a means of attracting occult powers through getting in touch with the energy of the earth; a dialectical complement to the questions he wished to raise through the alchemical and apian overtones of the materials with which he had dressed his head.

He described the total action as 'a complex tableau about the problem of language, and about the problems of thought, of human consciousness and of the consciousness of animals, and of course the abilities of animals. This is placed in an extreme position because this is not just an animal but a dead animal. Even this dead animal has a special power to produce . . . The idea of explaining to an animal conveys a sense of the secrecy of the world and of existence that appeals to the imagination. Then, as I said, even a dead animal preserves more powers of intuition than some human beings with their stubborn rationality. The problem lies in the word ''understanding'' and its many levels which cannot be restricted to rational analysis.'[98]

Coyote intensified and developed such animistic concerns, as Beuys spent a week in the company of a coyote in New York. Wrapped in felt, and thus 'insulated' from the profane, everyday world of America, Beuys was driven from Kennedy Airport to the Rene Block gallery in an ambulance and taken by stretcher to a bare, caged space. Here he was 'introduced' to a coyote. For a week, Beuys and the coyote established a sort of a mute dialogue in mythic space. Every day, Beuys would ritually ring the triangle which hung from his neck, and watch the coyote as it either circled around him or tore bits of his felt robe away. The coyote was introduced to various aspects of the human world: walking stick (doubling as shepherd's crook), gloves (symbolising the creativity of hands), and the *Wall Street Journal*. He urinated on all of them, but especially the *Journal*. At the end of the action, Beuys was driven away from the gallery in an exact, cyclical echo of the opening of the piece, confirmation — were any needed — of the strongly mythic quality of the whole event.[99]

Beuys had chosen to explain pictures to a (dead) hare not only because of the animal's reputed magical qualities, but because he felt the hare had 'a strong affinity to women, to birth and to menstruation, and generally to chemical transformations of the blood.'[100] In choosing to spend a week in America in the sole company of a coyote, Beuys felt that he had made contact with what he called 'the psychological trauma point of the United States' energy constellation: the whole American trauma with the Indian, the Red Man.'[101] For Native Americans, Coyote had been one of the mightiest of deities, the epitome of shape-shifting transformation and power, of the sexually redoubtable, shaman-related energy of the rule-breaking Trickster. Coyote is thus both an unpredictable and extremely potent figure. As Gary Snyder suggests, 'For those who can handle such a Helper the power of being a Healer may be gained.'[102]

In a later interview, Beuys observed that: 'When I do an action like the one I did with the coyote, I wasn't interested in giving some kind of zoological lecture or anything, I was trying to show people that there is a realm that exists below the human realm and which is a precursor to human evolution, an autonomous animal realm. I took a creature out of this realm and brought it into contact with human beings, and people felt

72 Joseph Beuys: *Coyote: I like America and America likes me* Rene Block Gallery New York 1974 Photograph: © Caroline Tisdall

provoked — in the end it provoked them to asking themselves whether there might not be other realms that exist "above" the human realm. We really ought to reconsider our sense organs and what they're capable of, you know, because they can penetrate far into other realms, realms we have lost touch with . . .'[103]

For Beuys, the *Wall Street Journal* upon which the coyote had so persistently urinated epitomised the 'ultimate *rigor mortis*' afflicting thinking about life today: economic capital is the only 'substance' revered by a culture that is prepared to sacrifice everything else in its name.[104] What Beuys meant by the term 'substance' (or capital) was utterly different, growing out of a shamanistic perception of art (capital) as creative, animistic energy and imagination: the ultimate root of any possibility of growth towards a non-totalitarian world of social and cosmic totality. As he said at the time of *How to explain pictures to a dead hare*: 'It's a question again of Which Reality? Is it the limited materialist understanding of *materia*, or is it *substance*? Substance for me is the greater issue and includes evolutionary power which leads ultimately to the real meaning of Materia, with its roots in MATER (mother — as in "mother earth"), as one pole of spirituality, while the other encompasses the whole process of development.'[105]

In the last fifteen years of his life, Beuys devoted much of his energy to developing institutions wherein his ideas of radical democracy and 'social sculpture' could flourish, such as the Free International University which he founded in 1977.[106] One of the root meanings of education (from *educere*: to lead forth) is to 'bring out' what is already in present in potentiality: the essentially Romantic project of Beuys was to 'bring out' the cosmicity which he felt had lain slumbering in us for so long.

As his contribution to the art show DOCUMENTA 7 in 1982, Beuys proposed the planting of 7,000 oak trees in the town of Kassel, each to be set next to a basalt column of just over a metre in height. Speaking of the regenerative nature of such an extension of the possibilities of sculpture, Beuys explained that in his eyes the oak had 'always been a form of sculpture, a symbol for this planet ever since the Druids, who are called after the oak. Druid means oak. They used oaks to define their holy places.'[107]

In the idea of *7,000 Oaks*, evolution and revolution, history and cosmicity, mythopoeisis and politics combine in an inspiring, dialectical and ecological whole. As with the work of Mary Beth Edelson, we are led to reflect that it is only by 'breaking the plane' of (linear) history that we can gain access to the symbolic realm of cosmicity, of healing *participation mystique*. And if we are not prepared to follow the example of such artists as Edelson and Beuys today — if, that is, we ignore the need to sculpt the cosmos from out of the depths of our individual and collective psyches — we should hardly be surprised if we become the victims of that very chaos and nothingness which once fuelled archaic humanity's 'thirst for *being*'. For life — whether we call it 'mother earth', the Great Goddess, or as Beuys did, the Great Generator[108] — may soon have no other choice than to remind us forcefully that the symbolism of the Tree of Life is founded on the surest of facts: no trees, no life.

11 Bird Through the Wall

Shamans give life wings, singing it through the pain and confusion of existence into the glory of being. Mircea Eliade reminds us that 'the German word for magic formula is *galdr*, derived from the verb *galan*, "to sing"', a term applied especially to bird calls.'[1] Flying beyond everyday boundaries of space and time, shamans sing themselves to the heights of the World Tree, or *axis mundi*. At the same time, they relive the Paradisal condition which was shared by all before the Fall into the various divisions of species-consciousness, sexuality and language.[2] In the mid-1980s, in his poem 'Vermeer', Tomas Tranströmer conjured a distant but nonetheless resonant echo of the shamanic flight towards totality, when he reflected that

> It hurts to go through walls, it makes you ill
> but it is necessary.
> The world is one. But walls ...
> And the wall is part of yourself —
> we know or don't know, but it's true for us all
> except for small children. No walls for them.[3]

In his last essay, which he completed only some ten days before his death in 1961, Jung focussed attention on the recently-built Berlin Wall, seeing it as an all-too-graphic symbol of humanity's schizoid dissociation from itself.[4] Today the Berlin Wall lies in ruins. But does anyone doubt that Jung's general point still holds? On whatever scale one wishes to consider the question, how often do we really experience any transformative sense of breaking through the self-made walls of human isolation? In the following poem, published a year after Jung's death, Tranströmer gives us some Thoreau-like hints of what he calls 'the half-made heaven' that lies outside (or rather, deep within) the fortress of the ego (or class, aggrandising nationalism and general bigotry):

> Despondency breaks its course.
> Anguish breaks its course.
> The vulture breaks its flight.
>
> The eager light streams out,
> even the ghosts take a gulp.

73 Alan Davie *Bird Noises*
1963 gouache 50.5 x 76
Private Collection
© courtesy, the Artist
and Gimpel Fils, London

And our paintings see daylight,
our red beasts of the ice-age studios.

Everything begins to look around.
We walk in the sun in hundreds.

Each person is a half-open door
that leads to a room for all.

The endless ground beneath us.

The water shines between the trees.
The lake is a window into the earth.[5]

Of all the various movements in twentieth-century art, it is Surrealism which has pursued such a 'half-made heaven' with the most revolutionary fervour. In terms of art history, the creativity which one associates with such figures as André Breton, Max Ernst, Luis Buñuel, Salvador Dali, Joan Miró, Yves Tanguy, René Magritte, André Masson, Man Ray, Alberto Giacometti, Antonin Artaud, Louis Aragon, Robert Desnos, Leonora Carrington, Remedios Varo, Freda Kahlo and Meret Oppenheim resulted in the most consequential range of innovations in modern art next to those of Cubism. From a shamanic point of view, much within those innovations merits the closest attention.

Growing out of Dada's intransigently anarchic attack on bourgeois hypocrisy, and sharing the Dadaists' sympathy for the creativity of anyone uncontaminated by Western rationalism,[6] the more systematic critique of Surrealism transformed not only painting and sculpture, but the theatre, literature, photography and revolutionary politics. In the laudatory catalogue essay which he wrote for the Mexican artist Frida Kahlo's 1938 debut New York exhibition, André Breton — long the leading polemicist and self-styled leader of the Surrealists — asked the crucial Surrealist question: 'What meaning can be ascribed to the eye's capacity to pass from visual power to visionary power?'[7]

Influenced by the early metaphysical paintings of de Chirico and the theories of Freud, and inspired by the transformation masks of Native North American and Inuit (Eskimo) culture, the Surrealists sought the sort of internal vision that might liberate the psyche — and hence society — from centuries of self-imposed alienation.[8] To dream with open eyes was thus to first *close* one's eyes to the triple dictatorship of Christendom, capitalism and commonsense. Salvador Dali, who collaborated with Luis Buñuel on the two Surrealist film classics of the silent era, the 1928 *Un Chien Andalou* and the 1930 *L'Age d'Or*, believed that the best film was the one that could be seen with one's eyes closed: in 1929 the Surrealist journal *La Revolution Surréaliste* featured a Magritte collage of a reproduction of one of his word-pictures, *I do not see the* [nude woman] *hidden in the forest*, surrounded by a series of passport-like photographs of various Surrealists with their eyes firmly shut. Intensifying the idea of interiority which we have already encountered in Caspar David Friedrich and Knut Hamsun, the Surrealists sought a collective alchemy of psychic and political transformation, in pursuit of 'the marvellous' — or what Breton was later to apostrophise, *the absolute* — in life.[9]

The marvellous might be experienced and expressed through what Breton's first *Surrealist Manifesto* of 1924 called 'pure psychic automatism'. Or it might be sensed within the transfiguring nature of what Breton, again, called *l'amour fou*.[10] Juxtaposition of disparate elements in collage; the stream of images released by automatic writing or drawing; a random walk through the backstreets and parks of a city; photo-montage, solarisation techniques and the blurring of gender distinctions in nude photography — all were prime Surrealist vehicles to the moment when the imprisoning, dualistic distinctions of life might dissolve into an epiphany of this-worldly ecstasy, fuelled by the power of the unconscious.[11]

One commentator on Surrealism, Joseph Jablonski, has suggested that 'The capacity to bring the mind into focus on the marvellous requires a development as private and sensitive as a shamanic initiation.'[12] To experience the marvellous — or the *convulsive* beauty which fascinated

Breton — thus required a qualitative leap of the imagination. 'To be a Surrealist as I am', said Magritte, 'means barring from your mind all remembrance of what you have seen, and being always on the lookout for what has never been.'[13] For this painter of dream-like visual paradoxes and logical contradictions, the content of any particular dream was not as important as the general fluidity and freedom of the dream experience. Magritte's 'magic realist' imagery was very much his own, entirely different from the free-flowing metamorphoses of Miró, for example. Nonetheless, Magritte might have been speaking for all Surrealists when he declared that 'Surrealism requires a freedom in waking life that is similar to that we have when dreaming.'[14]

From the perspective afforded by later developments in the relation between Surrealism and society — such as the superficially 'Surrealist' nature of much advertising imagery today — it is understandable that many should have become somewhat doubtful (if not downright dismissive) about Surrealism's success in pursuing such freedom. Such doubters and dismissers of the Surrealist faith have included some of the Surrealists — or artists closely associated with the movement — themselves. And some of these artists voiced their doubts about Surrealism long before its imagery and ideas had been corrupted by the mass media. One such artist was the Mexican painter Frida Kahlo (1910–54).

As we have seen, André Breton (1896–1966) thought highly of the work of Kahlo, and indeed, there is much within the primitivistic, myth-oriented art of this exceptionally brave woman which exemplifies the shamanic idea of the 'wounded healer' — an idea which is central to the Surrealist craving for an animistic, integrated universe. An horrific bus accident in her youth had left Kahlo with her spinal column broken in three places and her body wracked by multiple fractures. Her 1944 self-portrait *The Broken Column* is a grim testimony to the strength with which she faced a lifetime of excruciating pain and some thirty-odd surgical operations: the 1946 *The Little Deer* depicts Kahlo as a mythical woman/horned deer, stepping lightly through a wooded landscape even as she is pierced by bloody arrows, bringing ancient images of the wounded shamanic healer clearly to mind. Like a series of magical invocations to health (in the widest sense of the word), Kahlo's art of the earth grew out of her pain, celebrating a vitalistic pantheism in such potent images as *My Nurse and I* (1937), *Roots* (1943), *Tree of Hope* (1946) and *The Love Embrace of the Universe* (1949).

In their animistic fusion of body and earth, night and day, such images might seem to be quintessentially Surrealist.[15] But once elected to the Surrealist pantheon by Breton, Kahlo soon became less than enthusiastic about what she saw as Surrealism's parasitical intellectual posturing, which she distinguished sharply from the psychological realism and Mexican rootedness of her own work. Under the influence of the Marxist ideas which in the last years of her life led her to place more and more faith in 'the Party', Kahlo finally came to see Surrealism as 'a decadent manifestation of bourgeois art. A deviation from the true art that the people hope for from the artist.'[16]

For Marxists and non-Marxists alike, no Surrealist can have revealed that decadence — the decline from potential shamanic power to parasitic posturing — more flamboyantly than Salvador Dali (1904—89). In the late 1920s and 1930s, the 'paranoiac-critical method' whereby Dali attempted to see like a medium, thereby conjuring a stream of freely associative imagery from his unconscious, resulted in such hallucinatory, disturbing paintings as *Self-Portrait Splitting Into Three* (1927), *The Great Masturbator* (1929) and *Soft Construction With Boiled Beans: Premonition of Civil War* (1936). But in the same year that Dali created the last-named, premonitory and gruesome image of humanity (literally) tearing itself apart, the Dalinian 'dream landscape' was being featured in *Vogue*.

A few years later, Breton conveyed his disgust at what he saw as Dali's commercial and ideological betrayal of the Surrealist movement, coining the pointed anagram Avida Dollars for the man whom he had once praised for having '[opened] the mental windows really wide, so that one can feel oneself gliding upwards towards the wild sky's trap'.[17] Unconcerned, Dali continued to amass a fortune, becoming in the process the media's favourite artist-buffoon. His famous quip — 'The only difference between a madman and Dali is that Dali is not mad' — had once contained overtones of shamanism: in 1970, the lucid madman accepted $10,000 for a fifteen second commercial on French television, during which he 'rolled his eyes roguishly and said "I am mad, I am completely mad . . . over Lanvin chocolates."'[18] As any number of advertisements featuring 'freely associative' imagery have since suggested, the Surrealist quest to liberate the imagination might be seen to have functioned as nothing more than an unintended, but nonetheless extraordinarily successful research and development department of capitalism.[19]

In *The Transformative Vision*, José A. Argüelles suggests that it is a testimony to what he calls 'the suicidal tendencies' of the European mind that in the decades following the Great War, the Surrealists looked 'not to Jung but to Freud, who was incapable of seeing beyond the limits of his own ego'.[20] Excepting Artaud and Ernst from his critique, Argüelles contrasts what he sees as the residual egocentricity and intellectualism of Surrealism with the far greater shamanic quality of imagination which he discerns in the work of a man who actually was 'mad', the incarcerated schizophrenic, Adolf Wölfli (1864—1930). One of the chief historical figures in the anti-cultural ideology of *Art Brut* (Raw or 'Outsider Art', as it has become known) which the French painter Jean Dubuffet developed after the Second World War, Wölfli is described by Argüelles as an exemplary 'love-visionary' — a hero of the inner voyage, in the tradition of Van Gogh and Gauguin.[21]

The combination of some particularly cruel childhood experiences and extreme loneliness in adolescence led Wölfli to sexual desperation and degradation: in 1890 he attempted to rape a fourteen-year-old girl and a year later he attacked a five-year-old. Following a further attack on a three-year-old, in 1895 Wölfli was pronounced insane and sentenced to an asylum for the rest of his life. Initially, he was extremely quarrelsome and violent, which led to his being put into solitary confinement in 1897. (He was to remain alone in his cell for the next twenty years.)

It is at this point, says Argüelles, that Wölfli's tremendous latent creativity began to be 'finally metamorphosized — shamanized — into the exuberantly creative, gentle, and monastic St. Adolf 11 . . .'[22] St. Adolf 11 was Wölfli's alter-ego, the enigmatic figure who eventually came to dominate the 'cosmic biography' which Wölfli began around 1900, some two or three years after he had heard voices forecasting his imminent death. Argüelles suggests that there are clear parallels to be drawn between Wölfli's experience of burgeoning creativity and the initiation of a neophyte shaman.[23]

There is no doubt that the unique combination of writing, drawing, poetry and musical composition which Wölfli developed over the last three decades of his life is an extraordinary testament to the power of the human spirit — to its ability to transcend circumstance and affirm life. The *Vögeli* (little birds) which appear in so many of the twisting, crowded labyrinths which dominate Wölfli's thousands upon thousands of pages of writings and drawings are poignant evidence of the shaman-like struggle for meaning in his work. Further aspects of shamanic symbolism suggest themselves in the description which Roger Cardinal, a noted authority on Outsider Art, gives of Wölfli's 'fantastic biography'. 'Wölfli', says Cardinal, 'casts himself in the role of "Saint Adolf 11", a child divinity in the care of an almighty God who acts as his guide in various adventures. Saint Adolf goes on endless journeys through the cosmos, plunging through infinite space, across mountains, oceans, jungles, and visiting gigantic cities . . . A repertoire of gods and goddesses often accompany him. Among the animals that appear is the serpent, both a destructive and lifegiving force . . . The basic form of the snake, the ring, symbolizes the unbroken supremacy of Saint Adolf, who rules over a limitless world — as indeed Wölfli the artist ruled over a limitless imaginary kingdom.'[24]

As Argüelles notes, there are some striking parallels between the overall configuration of many of Wölfli's works and the mandala forms of medieval European, Indian and Tibetan art. But at this point, some unavoidable — and difficult — questions arise, concerning the extent to which Wölfli's work really did break through the walls of circumstance and conditioning in a manner analogous to the shamanic transmutation of suffering and solitude. Are the mandala-like forms in Wölfli a means to

74 Adolf Wölfli *Saint Adolf Wearing Glasses, Between The Giant Cities of Niess and Mia* 1924 coloured crayons on paper 51 x 68
© courtesy of the Collection De L'Art Brut, Lausanne
Photograph: Germond

psychic development and cosmic transcendence? Or are they, on the contrary, a series of rigorous defences set up by the ego against the world? Is the compulsion to fill up pictorial space in Wölfli evidence of the rich, metamorphosing expansion of the psyche? Or is it, again, evidence of an understandably deep-rooted defensiveness, an inability to 'let go' of the controlling ego and 'float off' into transfiguring space? There is no doubt that, as Argüelles says, Wölfli's art can be seen as '*a tool for self-transformation*'.[25] But to what extent did that transformation yield images, rhythms and ideas which might take anyone else very far up the Tree of Life?

In his 1976 study *Art Brut*, Michel Thévoz suggests that Wölfli takes us back to 'a pre-objective stage in which things have not yet taken form. Or, if they have, they remain unstable, labile . . . So it would be pointless to assign a fixed meaning to this or that object, for every object here is always subject to an unforeseeable transformation . . . In his [Wölfli's] hands, all objects are treated metaphorically in a way that makes them endlessly convertible.'[26] Some might see this as the ultimate manifestation of 'the marvellous' which the Surrealists pursued with so much passion. From my own point of view, however, Wölfli's work is finally more moving than it is marvellous. Only rarely (for me) does it strike the sort of mythopoeic note which really compels the attention. More often than not, one's eyes (and psyche) tend to flicker over the surface of the work, unable to sense the sort of rhythmical power or energising interplay of colour and line, image and ground which might conjure a truly shamanic quality of *participation mystique*.[27]

I hope it will not sound like a dry-as-dust argument for formalist aesthetics if I say that, extraordinary and moving as it is, there may not be enough 'significant form' in Wölfli's work to make it shamanic art of any particularly high degree.[28] What I mean by this may become a little clearer if we now return our attention to Surrealism, and see if there may not be more to it than either Argüelles or Kahlo would have us believe.

While he is quite right to emphasise the unhealthy aspect of the Surrealists' dependence on Freud (just as he is right to underline the reductive effect of Surrealism's later, somewhat forced marriage with Marxism), Argüelles gives a less than complete picture of the range of Surrealist ambition and achievement. For in the work of Max Ernst (which Argüelles acknowledges, but does not treat in any detail), Leonora Carrington, Remedios Varo and — above all — Joan Miró and Meret Oppenheim (whose work was discussed in chapter 1), there is a rich shamanic dimension, which brings their imagery much closer to Jung than Freud.[29] And rather than Freud, it is Jung whom one senses, once again, in the Surrealist-inflected work of Jackson Pollock and Alan Davie, two of the greatest shamanic spirits in twentieth-century art. The extent to which their post-Surrealist, strongly mythopoeic imagery might inspire us to break through the walls of self-alienation will be considered in the conclusion to this chapter.

Transmutative, shaman-like bird imagery plays a key role in the art of Varo, Carrington and Ernst. In her 1958 painting *The Creation of Birds*, the Spanish-Mexican Varo (1913—63) depicts a hybrid owl-artist working at a desk in a convent-like room. In her *The Reflowering of the Goddess* Gloria Feman Orenstein describes the painting as depicting 'a Woman/Bird Being who is both an alchemist and an artist. Sitting in her laboratory, which is also her art studio, she uses the energies of the cosmos and the chemicals of the earth to sketch the image of a bird, which then flies off the paper and soars into the sky. Dressed as a bird herself, she [Varo] has created a being in her own image, and has given it both artistic and biological life simultaneously.'[30] The bird is a product of three types of transformational symbolism: the mysterious, organically-shaped alchemical equipment which feeds the energy of star dust from the outside darkness into the bird-artist's palette; the triangular-shaped magnifying glass which refracts light from a far-off star onto the artist's paper, and the violin-shaped instrument which hangs near the bird-artist's heart, sending its vibrations down into the life-giving hand of the surreal hybrid.

For Orenstein, Varo's image should be seen as a tale of power — the sort of power that links us with both nature and the 'invisible', showing spirit alive *in matter*. It thus enacts what Orenstein calls 'a sacred shamanic or magical Creation ceremony, breathing life into the animistic world view that preceded patriarchy and that was symbolised by the Great Goddess Creatress, Mother of all.'[31] This is Orenstein's far-reaching, metamorphosing reading of the (male) Surrealists' obsession with Woman as nurturing dream presence — a reading which stresses the extent to which female Surrealist artists broke through the wall of socio-sexual stereotyping which one might suspect in Magritte's aforementioned *I do not see the* [nude woman] *in the forest*, for example, in order to reclaim and develop their *own* Goddess heritage.[32]

Wary of the dangers of ahistorical stereotyping which she suspects within ideas of the collective unconscious, Orenstein stresses the extent to which women artists' *conscious* and often (deliberately) ambiguously-coded creation has informed such an artistic reclamation of the Goddess. However, Orenstein also acknowledges the indisputable importance which Jungian ideas had for many of the Goddess artists whom she interviewed in the mid-1970s.[33] One of the most intriguing of these artists was Leonora Carrington, a close friend of Remedios Varo.

As Whitney Chadwick has documented in her study *Women Artists and the Surrealist Movement*, Carrington and Varo shared 'dreams, stories, and magic potions' while living near each other in Mexico City in the 1940s. Different as their imagery was to become, the notion of creativity as both a recording of and stimulus to transformational spirit-journeys was common to both artists.[34] In her 1974 novel *The Hearing Trumpet*, Carrington (*b*.1917) told the story of a 92-year-old woman named Marion and her Grail-like quest for self-knowledge. Telepathy and mystical visions help to bring ancient layers of Marion's true identity to light; the last line of the novel reads: 'If the old woman can't go to Lapland, then Lapland must come to the Old Woman.' When Gloria Feman Orenstein asked Carrington why the Old Woman should want to go to Lapland, Carrington replied that it was simply because 'The shamans of Lapland are the most magical people on Earth.'[35]

With its various magical-realist transformations of rocking horse into fabulous animal, the interior stage-set of Carrington's 1938 *Self-Portrait* had long ago revealed the Celtic strain of Romanticism in her. Orenstein has suggested that the mental breakdown which Carrington suffered soon afterwards, following separation from her lover Max Ernst during the confusion and disorientation of the early days of the Second World War,

75 Leonora Carrington *The Pomps of the Subsoil* (detail) 1947 oil on canvas 58.3 x 93 Collection Robert and Lisa Sainsbury, University of East Anglia © Leonora Carrington/ARS, NY Photograph: James Austin

is better seen as a 'breakthrough' to deeper levels of psychic awareness.[36] In 1939, Carrington had painted Ernst as a shaman-like figure, striding across a glacial wasteland (within which a white horse stands, expectant but frozen) with a miniature horse (Carrington's symbol of magical transformation) instead of a flame within the lantern which he carries.[37] Following her breakdown, Carrington would transform *herself* from the *'femme enfant'* fantasy of the male Surrealist imagination into an artist of unmistakable shamanic consequence.

In paintings such as the 1975 *Grandmother Moorehead's Aromatic Kitchen*, for example, one can see how much Carrington's early Romanticism was deepened and developed by years of research into and reflection upon Goddess imagery. An outsize goose is about to step inside the magic circle which dominates the interior of a large 'dream-kitchen', which seems to float in space. At the centre of the circle, by the side of an imposing cauldron (or alchemical oven), three hooded figures prepare a meal, the shamanic implications of which are underlined by the broom-carrying, horn-headed figure who stands to one side of the outsize goose. The painting contains several layers of esoteric significance, signified by the mirror-writing in the magical circle. Part of this reads 'The Goddess Dana became and is the Sidhe . . . The Old Races died — Where did they go?'[38]

Orenstein makes an astute point about the link between the culinary arts and alchemy in Carrington's work, when she says that 'The chemistry involved in the act of painting is a mode of culinary alchemy in its spiritualization of matter, creating the painting as a kind of surrealist food for thought. Digestion is also a chemical process . . . art is a magical food that we ingest through the eyes, but which brings a subtle chemistry to our beings in a way that is similar to what we experience when we eat.'[39] The food for thought in Carrington's work concerns the ancient, animistic knowledge that both she and Orenstein see epitomised in the *historical reality* and ongoing symbolic strength of 'prehistoric' Goddess culture.

In the 1947 *Pomps of the Subsoil*, Carrington depicted humans and animals intermingling happily in the underworld where, as Orenstein describes the painting, 'the Goddess, from whose brain a Tree of Life evolves, presides over the birth of the Tree of Life from the Cosmic Egg or, on an analogical level, the birth of life from woman.'[40] The theme of women's creative reclamation of their original shamanic power is summarised in Carrington's 1969 *Bird Seizes Jewel*, where a Varo-like bird-woman or Bird-Goddess leads patriarchal Rabbis to the moment of ancient gnosis: an aureole above the bird-woman's head signifies her enlightenment as she seizes the original, esoteric jewel of knowledge from a guru who inhabits a tower of concrete.[41]

In the same year that Leonora Carrington painted *Pomps of the Subsoil*, her former lover Max Ernst (1891—1976) produced a small watercolour which he called, simply, *Bird*. This ostensibly minor image of Ernst's is important to consider, not just because of its subject, but because of the way that Ernst has brought the theme of the flight of the imagination to fresh life. One of the most important of Surrealist artists, Ernst did much to both expand and intensify the idea of 'significant form'. Often less illustrative (in both the obvious and esoteric sense of the word) in his work than Varo and Carrington, Ernst transformed the relation of images to materials in a way which encourages us to sense the potentiality of 'the marvellous' in a highly textured, dream-rich integration of form and content.[42]

Bird features a silhouette of a large-billed avian archetype, set within the richly glowing colours of an imaginary landscape. The landscape sits 'flatly' on the picture plane, shorn of all allegorical, esoteric or perspectival support. It could be the weathered surface of a wall, seen from close-up: the sort of surface into which one might 'daydream' the evanescent shapes of the foothills and clouds which Ernst has conjured into being in parts of the image. The bird's neck is tilted upwards, suggesting a longing for transcendental flight: its large oval-shaped body speaks simultaneously of gravity and the earth, of primal egg and metamorphosis. *Bird* is thus at once an idea and an image of exemplary Surrealist presence, dependent on little if any esoteric knowledge to achieve its enigmatic, energising effect. At the same time as we see the bird *in* the wall which is the ground of the image, we are also encouraged to feel that this giant (yet curiously vulnerable) creature is poised to fly off into the far distance of our imagination, fly off *through* the wall. Earth and sky, near and far, actuality and potentiality, the finite and the infinite here combine in an image of the utmost simplicity, celebrating the presence of *spirit in matter*.[43]

Ernst considered the bird motif crucial to the development of his creativity. He claimed that during what he called 'the Great Mess' of the First World War, he had died to his old self, to be reborn in life-long contact with his alter-ego Loplop, Superior of the Birds: 'Max Ernst died the 1st of August 1914. He resuscitated the 11th of November 1918 as a young man aspiring to become a magician and to find the myth of his time. Now and then he consulted the eagle who had hatched the egg of his pre-natal life. You may find the bird's advices in his work.'[44] There could hardly be a clearer indication of the shamanic nature of Ernst's approach to art than the 1920 collage and photo-montage *Switzerland, Birth-Place of Dada or Physiomythological Flood-Picture*, which he executed jointly with Jean Arp. Against a primeval background of sea and emergent dinosaur, a youthful, sleeping figure dreams the metamorphosis of an older, muscular person into a bird. Another bird perches on a nearby branch, calmly surveying the transformation of the man's calf and foot into a giant, scaly bird's foot and claws.

Like all the Dadaists and Surrealists, Ernst despised bourgeois ideas of 'the beautiful', and spoke of the need to find a 'painting beyond painting'. The point of destroying bourgeois notions of the beautiful was to help art recover and develop its archetypal dimensions of healing myth and metamorphosis. Confronted with such images (and titles) of Ernst's as the 1922 *Oedipus Rex* and 1941 *Totem and Taboo*, one naturally thinks of Freud's importance for the Surrealists — and Werner Spies, the distinguished Ernst scholar, reminds us that Ernst was 'demonstrably the first artist to read Freud'.[45] But as Spies also documents, there is much within Ernst's work that reveals a fundamentally Romantic desire to 'poeticise' the world. Rather than the Freudian shibboleth of sexual sublimation, it is the Jungian spirit of individuation that one senses at work within the cosmic sweep of such later paintings of Ernst's as the 1943 *Flute of Angels*, 1953 *The Cry of the Gull* and 1964 *The Sky Marries the Earth*.[46]

The emergence of Loplop was eventually to help Ernst to move beyond the debunking irony of much of his early Dada work — the dehumanised images of machine-part or behatted people which we find in the 1919/20 *Ambiguous Figure* or 1920 *The Hat Makes the Man*, for example — and acknowledge the deep strain of Romanticism within himself. When nine paintings by Caspar David Friedrich were destroyed during the fire which burned down the Crystal Palace in Berlin in June 1931, the loss affected Ernst almost to the point of physical illness. Like all Surrealists, Ernst longed for the power of the 'inner spiritual eye' of which Friedrich had spoken (albeit without the Christian overtones of Friedrich's work).

Rejecting the positivism of Western rationalism (but finding much inspiration in the illustrations of scientific journals), Ernst searched long and hard within himself for the sort of artistic language which might finally bring the great Romantic Novalis's hopes of an integrated universe into realisation. Novalis, the spirit of whose late-eighteenth-century *Hymns to the Night* can be detected in much of Ernst's work, believed that 'Human beings, animals, plants, rocks and stars, flames, notes, colours must congregate in the end and "act" like a family or society, act and speak like a tribe.'[47] For the Surrealists, the key question was: what sort of artistic means might help to take art beyond itself and bring such a vision to life?

In 1924, Max Morise had suggested a criticism of de Chirico, while discussing what he felt to be the poverty of any notion of realistic representation with regard to the development of Surrealist imagery. He declared that '... the images [of de Chirico] are surrealist but their expression is not'.[48] Whether or not one agrees with Morise, there is no doubt that he had put his finger on one of the great problems for those Surrealists whose primary passion was painting. If the point of art was to effect a radical transvaluation of life, how could that be done — how could the marvellous be brought into consciousness — unless form *and* content, medium *and* 'message' were equally radicalised?[49]

Collage was one of the first means by which the Surrealists pursued the marvellous. Theirs was not the relatively sober, aesthetically pleasing collage of the Cubists. Rather, they sought the sort of irrational, electric juxtaposition of elements which might provide a visual equivalent to that 'accidental meeting of a sewing machine and an umbrella on an operating table' which Isidore Ducasse (Comte de Lautreamont and one of the chief influences on the Surrealists) had once dreamed up, and which Ernst quoted as a classic example of Surrealist poetry in his 1934 essay 'What is Surrealism?'[50] Shortly after reading Morise's strictures — and having already distinguished himself in collage — Ernst was to happen upon one of the major Surrealist innovations of form and content.

One rainy day in 1925, while contemplating the bare floorboards of the boarding house room in which he was staying, Ernst drifted off into a state of reverie. Recalling an experience in childhood when the sight of an imitation mahogany panel opposite his bed had induced 'one of those dreams between sleeping and waking', he decided to encourage what he called his 'powers of meditation and hallucination' by generating imagery through rubbing a pencil over sheets of paper dropped at random on the floorboards.[51] The technique of *frottage* (rubbing) soon led to one of Ernst's most striking works, the series of rubbed images known as the *Histoire Naturelle*. First published in Paris in 1926 with a poetic preface by Jean Arp, the hypnagogic quality of these images of mysterious planets and forests, horses and birds, eyes and leaves was to inform the generation and resonance of much of Ernst's subsequent work. The sequence of petrified forests of the late 1920s, within which Loplop can be seen imprisoned, but ever hopeful of flight; the primeval, but post-historical landscapes of the late 1930s and early 1940s, such as the 1940–2 *Europe After the Rain*, and the aforementioned *Bird* of 1947 may all be cited as exemplary here.

Frottage took Ernst deep into the realms of both the unconscious and visual poetry. In his 1936 essay 'Beyond Painting' he described the results as based on 'nothing but the intensification of the irritability of one's nervous faculties by suitable technical means, ruling out any conscious mental guidance (of reason, taste, or moralizing) and reducing to the utmost the active share of the man who has hitherto been called the "maker" of the work . . .'[52] The artist thus becomes a channel between worlds, whose role is 'to gather together and then give out that which makes itself *visible* within him'.[53] But the sheer range of Ernst's work (in both subject matter and technique) gives the lie to any notion that he was nothing but a passive recording medium for the eruptive forces of his unconscious. Like a great shaman, Ernst gave archetypal shape to those forces: and in the frightening, ironically-titled *Fireside Angel* of 1937, he warned of the psychic imbalance which had already led to the atrocities of the Spanish Civil War, and which would soon plunge the world into even greater destruction. On a bare deserted plain, clearly redolent of Spain, a Loplop-like figure fails to restrain (and thereby perhaps ensoul, or spiritualise) the ravenous energy of an enormous, grotesquely dancing creature, which looks like nothing so much as a 'demonic' (i.e. evil-working) shaman gone berserk.[54]

In contrast to such horror, Ernst's 1942 *Surrealism and Painting* summarises the hopeful – and humorous – pantheism of the man who that year had himself photographed in New York surrounded by his large collection of Hopi Kachina dolls. A giant, Loplop-like hybrid caresses its avian family, while its enormous left arm and hand mix colours and lines of post-Kandinsky, abstract forms and non-Euclidean space on a canvas. The surreal avian family is perched on a table, underneath which can be seen the same sort of magic-working tools which fascinated Remedios Varo. The canvas-within-a-canvas is a prime example of what the Chilean painter Roberta Matta would later celebrate in Ernst, namely 'The power to create hallucinations [which] is the power to exalt existence'. Matta continued: 'It can be argued that this constitutes a form of madness, but I think that Max Ernst accepts this as part of the task of the artist. The artist is the man who has survived the labyrinth.'[55]

76 Max Ernst *Surrealism and Painting* 1942 oil on canvas 195.6 x 233.6
The Menil Collection, Houston
Photograph: Hickey-Robertson, Houston

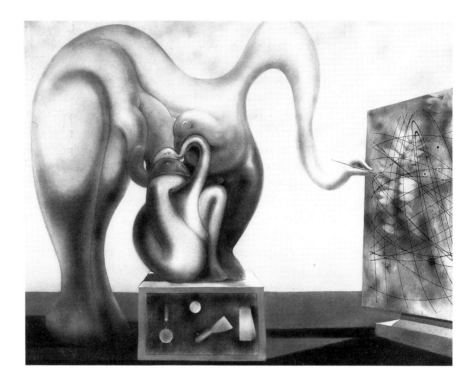

Surviving the labyrinth, Ernst shaped some of the most significant of all Surrealist images. Within the broad orbit of Surrealism *per se*, the shamanic importance of his work is only surpassed by the magic contained within the work of the man with whom he created the sets for a memorable 1926 Ballets Russes production of *Romeo and Juliet*: Joan Miró.[56]

The voluminous range of paintings, graphics, ceramics, sculpture and tapestries which Miró created constitutes one of the richest and most uplifting examples of the shamanic spirit at work in twentieth-century art. With his feet planted firmly on Earth, this Catalan liberator of the human spirit took the imagination into the farthest realms of cosmic reverie, helping us to dream ourselves into the space which was so crucial to Gaston Bachelard — the space that is the friend and not the enemy of being.[57]

At the beginning of his 1928 text 'Surrealism and Painting' Breton had declared: 'The eye exists in an untamed state. The only witness of the Wonders of the Earth at an altitude of thirty metres and the Wonders of the Sea at a depth of thirty metres is the wild eye that can see colours only in terms of the rainbow. It presides over the conventional exchange of signals that the mind's navigations would seem to require. But who will set up the ladder of vision?'[58] As Alain Jouffroy notes in his 1987 monograph on the artist, every single word here holds true for Miró, whom Breton went on to describe in 'Surrealism and Painting' as 'the most surrealist' of them all, and one of whose chief motifs is precisely the ladder of vision (or escape, as Miró sometimes called it) which links earth and sky, the here and the beyond.[59]

The motif that Miró (1893–1983) would later float across moon and stars, within the transparent infinity of the night which he loved so intensely, is first noticeable in the relatively prosaic form of the stepladder which leans against an outhouse in the 1921–2 *The Farm*. The painting is usually described as Miró's first masterpiece and Miró himself considered this crystal-clear, meticulously detailed homage to his parental home in Montroig to be the foundation and key to all his work.[60] A decade earlier, the adolescent, would-be artist had tried to meet his parents' wishes by pursuing a career in accountancy rather than art. After two frustrating years, he fell seriously ill, with a nervous breakdown being followed by typhoid fever. To help Miró recover, his father bought a farmhouse in Tarronga, between the Catalan village of Montroig and the Mediterranean.[61] There was no more talk of accountancy. Free to hone his burgeoning artistic talent on solitary, loving expeditions into the countryside, Miró experienced what was tantamount to a shamanic rebirth.

The Farm epitomises the early fruits of Miró's acute, complementary powers of observation and artistic organisation. Even-toned, high-keyed Southern light reveals woman, child and watering can, axe and cart, donkey and dog, goat and chickens, rabbit and pigeons, snail and lizard, stepladder and trellis in *Quattrocento*-like, minor counterpoint with the major pictorial elements of weathered farmhouse and fabulous blue sky, ploughed earth and eucalyptus tree — the last-named dominating the centre of the composition like some battered but triumphant Tree of Life. The startling clarity with which the elements of farm life have been rendered and laid out before us brings a surrealistic aura of the marvellous to the painting's scrupulous details. *The Farm* thus transcends realism to function as a talismanic invocation to health — to the ecstatic, animistic sense of identity with the earth which had healed the young Miró, and which the painter never tired of emphasising as being central to the broader issue of the healing of twentieth-century consciousness in the West.

Strength, believed Miró, flowed into the soul through the earth. Hence the enormous feet of *The Farmer's Wife* of 1922–3; and hence the painter's conviction that in order to leap high into the sky, one must have one's feet set firmly on the ground. The primitivism which Miró revealed in a 1937 interview with George Duthuit is typical: 'Each grain of dust contains something marvellous. But in order to understand it, we have to recover the religious and magical sense of things that belong to primitive people.'[62] Whereas Magritte's sense of the marvellous led him to attempt to bar from his mind all remembrance of what he had seen, and so be 'always on the lookout for what has never been', for Miró the road to the marvellous led through the visible, revered world of earth and sky, sun and moon, women, birds and stars, to the timeless moment of mythopoeic creation.

Several times, Miró declared forcefully that painting had been in decadence since the age of the cave-dwellers; and in the mid-1950s, when Miró and his old Catalan friend Joseph Llorens Artigas were commissioned to produce two large decorated wall ceramics for the UNESCO building in Paris, the first thing to which they turned for inspiration was the prehistoric art of the Altamira caves.[63] For Miró, art was above all 'a magic force-field' in which creator and viewer alike might get in touch with elemental energies.[64] He spoke of painting on canvas as being similar to walking the earth; walking that earth, he revivified ancient, essential constellations of longing.

Early in his career, Miró responded to Parisian avant-garde art, absorbing both Cubist ideas of shallow space and the Fauves' high-pitched approach to colour. Ultimately, however, neither of these influences seems to have been as important as the spiritual affinity for the East which lies behind the Japonisme of Miró's 1917 *Portrait of E.C. Ricart.* The East helped to confirm the painter's intuitive feeling for the divinity of all things — for the blade of grass which could be 'as enchanting as a tree or mountain'.[65] Devoid of hierarchy, Miró's world is one of endless metamorphosis, where 'the horizon has unbuckled its belt' and images that are simultaneously man and woman, embryo and spermatophore listen intently to the dialogue of insects, or trace the magical flight of birds between sun and moon.[66] And it is no sentimental idyll that Miró creates: we sense the pain as well as the pleasure of nature's eternal, regenerative dialectic of birth and death. In his study of Miró's poster art, José Corredor-Mattheos has recently suggested that 'Carlos Castaneda, lying on the floor face to face with a beetle — in an encounter which fuses and identifies it with him — discovers that same truth to which Miró gives prominences . . . Human beings or animals, plants or crystalline transfigurations of matter, all these forms from Miró's world defy any linear classification, because they are the fruit of an imagination that allows us to discover, better than with the naked eye or a scientific instrument (which we know finds only its own reflected image) what nature *may be . . .*'[67]

Raymond Queneau once described Miró as the poet of prehistory. All his life, the healing capacity of poetic metaphor was of the utmost important to Miró (as was the inspiration he drew from music, from Bach and Mozart through Webern, Stockhausen and Cage to jazz). Walt Whitman (whose *Leaves of Grass* he read in adolescence) joined such Dadaists and Surrealists as Tristan Tzara and Paul Eluard (both of whose work he illustrated in the 1930s, 40s and 50s) in furnishing Miró with examples of what he called 'the divine spark' necessary to create really worthwhile art. A volume of Rimbaud was always at his bedside; scarcely less important to him were Mallarmé and Rilke.

Just as Rimbaud attempted to make himself a seer, and Rilke sought the 'great song' within himself, so did Miró look all his life for the healing

77 Joan Miró *Une Etoile caresse le sien d'une negresse* (A Star Caresses The Breast of a Negress) 1938 oil on canvas 129.5 x 194.3
Tate Gallery, London
© DACS 1992

language that Jungians speak of in terms of individuation. At times that search led him to a spacious, painterly combination of image and *haiku*-like poem, as in the 1925 *Ceci est la couleur de mes rêves* (This is the colour of my dreams) or the 1938 *Une étoile caresse le sein d'une negresse* (A star caresses the breast of a negress). At other moments, Miró abandoned painting for the challenges of ceramics and sculpture, inspired by the many natural objects which he collected on various walks, and which he subsequently arranged in his studio like a surreal family of spirit familiars. He spoke of his friend and close collaborator Artigas as working 'like an alchemist of old' to find 'secrets as old as the world' in the process of ceramic firing, and relished what his biographer Jacques Dupin calls 'this perfect union of earth and fire, which is like the celebration of some primitive mystery'. [68]

The primitive, archetypal mystery that Miró's life reveals is the mystery of the alchemy of individuation: in two self-portraits of 1937–8 and 1938, for example, he inhabits the firmament and the ocean depths with an equal, burning intensity of vision. Admiring both the simple, direct power contained within the Romanesque frescoes of his native Catalonia and the diverse strengths of world folk art, Miró spoke of the need to fuse an absolute individuality and 'locality' of artistic gesture with a corresponding anonymity and universality. Several times in his career, he 'destroyed' the artistic language which he had mastered, in order to advance yet further towards the possibility of a language where matter and spirit might be in complete equilibrium. Despite the seriousness of that search, the primitivism of Miró's universe is often leavened by a refreshing touch of humour. Transcending bourgeois notions of individual virtuosity and the ponderous collectivism of Soviet socialist realism alike, Miró created some of the most compelling and diverse examples of the process of individuation — the emergence of the Great, or Cosmic Self — in twentieth-century art.[69]

Although Miró was to distance himself from what he regarded as the dogmatic, overly intellectual side of Surrealism (particularly as represented by Breton), he was at one with the Surrealists in their desire to restore to art something of its aboriginal, healing power.[70] The point of art was thus not to produce beautiful objects, but rather to stir increasingly powerful currents of transformative energy into motion. Equating new forms in art with the potentiality of social change, Miró spoke of the artist's task as being to liberate humanity — to *wake people up* to the spark of divinity that he felt lay within potential reach of everyone.[71]

As we have seen, Miró underwent something of a shamanic crisis and rebirth in his adolescence. Similar shamanic qualities can be discerned at certain key moments in Miró's subsequent development, such as the lonely suffering of the hunger-induced hallucinations in Paris which precipitated his breakthrough to visionary, Bosch-like imagery in the 1924–5 *Harlequin's Carnival*; the bold, metaphorical leap into space which marks what one might call a Taoist-like ensouling of the void in so many of the 'dream-paintings' of the next few years; and the desire to 'murder painting' which Miró expressed at the end of the 1920s, when he insisted that the only thing that interested him was the collective unconscious. His aim in murdering painting was to die to his old self (like a shaman), in order to move ever deeper into the psyche in search of the sort of imagery that might work like a magical potion, by-passing all need for intellectualisation and rationalisation in both the artist and viewer.[72]

In the 1960s, Miró — together with Artigas — created one of our century's richest ensembles of shamanically-oriented sculpture, in the *Miró Labyrinth* at the Fondation Maeght in Saint-Paul in France. At the heart of the labyrinth lies a large ceramic piece entitled, simply, *Egg*. The sculpture is a marvellous image of 'immanent transcendence'; a healing, non-dualistic reminder of both the potentiality for spiritual ascension which lies deep within humanity and the essential 'ground' of the Paradisal earth which makes the very thought of such ascension possible. The late English Surrealist artist and author Roland Penrose was entirely right to describe Miró as an Orpheus-figure: a shaman who journeyed far into the labyrinth of both the universe and his unconscious to emerge triumphantly with the mysterious, shape-shifting signs which we find in such paintings as *Woman and Bird in Front of the Sun* (1942); *Hope* (1946); *Woman, Snake Flying in front of the Horizon* (1949); *The Half-Open Sky Gives Us Hope* (1954; its several direct handprints a clear echo of the spirit of the prehistoric caves) and *The Glitter of the Moon Spurs the Dance of the Dragonfly* (1955). All this work is strongly redolent of the eternal shamanic search for the primal, Paradisal unity of things — as are so many of the richly textured graphic images which Miró developed in the 1960s and 1970s, such as *The Great Sorcerer* (1968), *The Spirit* (1969), *Migratory Bird* (1970) and *The Seers* (1970).[73]

Such works epitomise the lyrical, ascensional tendencies within Miró's art. But Miró — whose name carries Spanish connotations of 'he looked, or observed' (from the past tense of *mirar*) — also looked unflinchingly into the mire of much twentieth-century history. In the agonised heads and bizarrely elongated bodies which feature in his work of the 1930s — and especially in such lurid images as *Man and Woman in Front of a Pile of Excrement* (1935—6) and *Still Life With an Old Shoe* (1937) — the pursuit of the marvellous has been abandoned for a grotesque, protesting battle with the horror and the banality of fascism.[74]

With such paintings, Miró revealed how passionately he responded to the specific evils of our century. But in the *Constellations*, the series of twenty-three small, intensely poetic gouaches which he created during some of the most depressing of the early days of the Second World War, Miró was to strike a note of healing, cosmic reverie which broke clean through the walls of historical consciousness. Withdrawing deeply into himself, and sustained only by the night, the stars, and music, Miró created what are generally agreed to be some of his greatest works. Their shaman-like resurrection of a sense of (sacred) cosmos from (chaotic and profane) history merits some detailed consideration.

It is one of the shibboleths of our time that the only time that we can know is that of history. As we have noted, the sociologist Pierre Bourdieu has gone so far as to say that 'the eye is the product of history'.[75] However, as Mircea Eliade never tired of arguing, both the potentiality and the experience of the sacred dimension in life exist upon a plane fundamentally different from that of history. Experience of the sacred involves a break in the flow of profane historical time, a break which is symbolised in the arrangement or 'architecture' of all ritual observance. For Eliade, as for many if not all pre-industrial cultures, to recognise the sacred is to recognise that there is something 'irreducibly *real* in the world', something to counter 'the terror of history' — of the thought of time devouring even itself.[76] For Marxists, any such idea of the sacred must be considered part of the false consciousness that is to be abandoned if humanity is to move into a future of complete historical self-determination. But as we have seen, for Eliade 'the "sacred" is an element in the structure of consciousness, not a stage in the history of consciousness'.[77]

It was Miró's great achievement to have trusted what Breton called the 'wild eye' within himself so completely that he was able to break through the walls of mid-twentieth-century history, in triumphant pursuit of at least part of the means by which we might *re-cognise* the sacred within ourselves. At a time when history seemed bent on eradicating all traces of nobility and hope from the world, one of the first of the *Constellations* series which Miró created was called *The Escape Ladder*. The naturalistic stepladder of *The Farm* has here turned into a schematic, or ideogrammatic ladder, resurrecting the imaginal purity of our desire for a sense of orientation and ascension. There is nothing here which is 'escapist' in the derogatory sense of that word. Quite the contrary: the image sends us on a shaman-like journey through and beyond the horrors of history, into a healing world of mysterious, floating signs and symbols. Experiencing the magical, musical calligraphy of the *Constellations*, we begin to sense anew the transcendent depths of our soul's longing for a sense of ultimate purpose in life — for a sense of sacred cosmos.

In depicting the descent of so many into the historical hell of the 1930s, Miró had returned to the modelling and *chiaroscuro* which he had previously abandoned in the 1920s, in order to give his symbolic figures and objects a certain suffering presence and weight, thereby underlining their tragic immersion in contemporary history and politics. In the *Constellations* of 1940—1, however, Miró abandoned all traces of realism and perspectival depth in favour of a subtly variegated flat ground. This ground supports what Jacques Dupin has called 'a pure glissando of lines and figures, darting back and forth, twirling together on the absolutely flat surface'.[78]

Archetypal, primitivistic men and women, insects and birds, sun, moon and stars — and above all, the lineaments of worshipful desire which animate their graceful, twirling dance — are presented, rather than represented, through the simplest (and hence most demanding) of colours and lines. Under the spell of the reverie induced by *The Morning Star* (where the shamanic ladder of vision has become an arrow of ecstasy), we are encouraged to ascend *The Escape Ladder* and fly *Toward The Rainbow*. Later, we hear *The Nightingale's Song at Midnight with Morning Rain*, and explore a world where *Acrobatic Dancers* and *The Poetess* celebrate *The Beautiful Bird Revealing The Unknown to a Pair of Lovers*. As in so much of Miró's work, sexuality here resumes its aboriginal, sacred significance. Like a Sufi poet, Miró reaffirms the participatory pulse of life: across the centuries, the *Constellations* offer a confirmatory echo of the compassionate faith of Muhyi' ddin Ibn Al-'Arabi: 'O marvel! a garden amidst fires!/My heart has become capable of every form . . ./I follow the religion of Love; whatever way Love's camels take, that is my religion and faith.'[79]

In the text which he wrote to accompany a 1959 facsimile edition of the *Constellations*, Breton praised Miró for stepping 'outside the world, and outside time, too' as he encouraged us 'to penetrate into the cosmic order with all that is involved in going beyond our condition.'[80] The last of the series, which Miró completed at Montroig ('red mountain') in September 1941, celebrates the soul's recovery of a sense of cosmos from chaos with a title of unmistakable shamanic resonance. In retrospect, it can be seen

78 Joan Miró *Constellation: Toward the Rainbow* 1941 gouache and oil wash on paper 45.8 x 38 The Jacques and Natasha Gelman Collection © DACS 1992

to summarise the import of Miró's whole career. For this astonishingly productive man — who considered that all his dreaming was done while creating, and who once noted to himself that his work should be made 'in a highly poetic and musical spirit, done without any apparent effort, like birdsong, the uprise of a new world or the return to a purer world . . . full of love and magic'[81] — surely did map *The Passage of the Divine Bird* in twentieth-century consciousness.

Smuggled out of war-time Europe in a diplomatic bag, Miró's *Constellations* were the very first European work to be shown in America at the end of the war. When they were exhibited at the Pierre Matisse Gallery in New York in 1945, they confirmed the impact which the 1941 retrospective of Miró's work at New York's Museum of Modern Art had had upon many American artists. One of the artists to be particularly affected by Miró was Jackson Pollock, the most mythologised of all modern American painters and an artist much involved with both Jungian ideas of individuation and shamanism.

Pollock (1912–56) held his first individual show at Peggy Guggenheim's Art of This Century gallery in November 1943. A key work in the exhibition was a mysterious, hieratic painting called *Guardians of the Secret*. Veiled totemic figures, somewhat reminiscent of Northwest Coast Native American pole sculpture, stand guard at each side of the imposing, four foot by seven foot canvas. In the centre foreground of the image, a large dog or wolf joins these figures in protecting the threshold to an inner realm of scumbled dream landscape and pictographic mysteries. Its gestural power, ritualistic organisation of space and hallucinatory mixture of high-keyed and meditative colour combine to make *Guardians of the Secret* a powerful, strangely disturbing manifestation of shamanic energy in painting. In retrospect, it can be seen as a potent harbinger of the rhythmic alchemy of the self that Pollock would later cultivate in such famous 'drip' or 'poured' paintings as *Alchemy* (1947), *Number 1, 1948* (with its echoes of the handprints of cave painting underlying rich, lyrically disposed ribbons of freely orchestrated paint) and *Autumn Rhythm* (1950).

Miró spoke several times of the tragic side to his personality, a side which he generally tried hard not to force onto the attention of others. In Pollock, a similar ambivalent depth and range of feeling manifested itself in periodic outbreaks of alcoholism and aggressive, self-destructive behaviour. Beginning in 1937, Pollock underwent years of (initially Freudian, but for the most part Jungian) therapy. There is a remarkable parallel in the search for integration and individuation which his art reveals, particularly in the 1940s. Drawing inspiration from the Surrealism of both Miró and André Masson (the latter a pioneer of automatic drawing, who lived in Connecticut during the war years), Pollock was to completely redefine pictorial ideas of the ancient theme of a figure in a landscape. When the influential German-American painter and theoretician Hans Hofmann saw Pollock's work for the first time in 1941, he was impressed, remarking that Pollock clearly worked 'from the heart'. However, he also suggested that it might be a good idea for Pollock to enrol in his (Hofmann's) school and learn to work from nature. Pollock replied — 'I am nature'.[82]

Hofmann's advice must have seemed somewhat gratuitous to Pollock, who throughout the 1930s had struggled long and hard to work from nature. Having been introduced to the idea of the spiritual in art at a relatively early age, when an art teacher at school managed to communicate his love of both theosophy and modern art to the somewhat gauche youngster, Pollock first developed his feelings for landscape through the relatively prosaic regionalist ideas of Thomas Hart Benton. By the end of the 1930s — a decade which he survived partly thanks to being on the WPA Federal Art Project, set up in 1935, and through which he met and worked with the Mexican muralist David Alfaro Siqueiros — Pollock's feeling for landscape had begun to acquire a strongly primitivistic, metamorphosing quality.[83]

Two paintings in particular reveal the growing shamanic nature of Pollock's quest for a magical vocabulary of healing, transmutative forms at this time: the 1938—41 *Naked Man* and the 1941 *Bird*. In the former, a figure of heavy, Picasso-esque classicism wears a tribal-like mask that appears to send waves, or circles of energy down towards the wearer's torso. The torso, however, remains stiff and unresponsive. In *Bird* a central, Miró-esque eye (albeit executed with little if any of Miró's aerial grace) hovers above a stylised, primitivistic avian image, reminiscent of both Native American pictographs and the Phoenix myth. Taken together, these paintings are a moving documentation of Pollock's struggle for psychic integration. They also indicate the considerable extent of his interest in Native American imagery.[84]

Raised in the Western states, Pollock had long been fascinated by Native American culture. As an eleven-year old, he used to explore the Indian ruins of cliff dwellings and mounds north of his home near Phoenix; and some time between 1930 and 1935 he and his brother bought twelve volumes of the *Annual Report of the Bureau of American Ethnology*, volumes profusely illustrated with reproductions of Native American ritual paraphernalia and rare documentary photographs of late-nineteenth- and early-twentieth-century Indian rituals. In New York, Pollock's various visits to the Museum of the American Indian and the American Museum of Natural History further broadened his anthropological knowledge, preparing him in part for the inspiration offered by such major exhibitions from New York's Museum of Modern Art as the 1936 'Fantastic Art, Dada and Surrealism' and 1941 'Indian Art of the United States'.

At the time of the latter exhibition, Pollock was undergoing Jungian analysis with a Dr Violet Staub de Laszlo, with whom he discussed the sand paintings made at the Museum by visiting Navajo artists. The essence of Navajo sand painting is that it is a healing, participatory art, in which patients suffering soul loss are brought back to the sacred centre of their being by the mythic images, chanting and singing of the painter-shaman. Once the process has been completed, the sand images are swept away, to be recreated only when strictly necessary.[85]

In a recent detailed discussion of the development of Pollock's art in the 1940s, W. Jackson Rushing has established that Pollock was thoroughly aware of the shamanic nature of his dual exploration of his unconscious in therapy and paint.[86] And Pollock was hardly alone in the eclectic range of shamanistic inspiration which he drew at this time from Native American art, Jungian ideas, Surrealism, and the recent work of Picasso — particularly *Guernica*, which had been exhibited at New York's Valentine

Gallery in early 1939. To many American artists perplexed by the pressing question of the relation of art to both politics and the psyche, *Guernica*'s myth-inflected protest against fascism justified the search for a language which exploded the surface of history, allowing the individual to engage creatively with the (potentially healing) depths of the unconscious.[87]

Pollock's mythopoeic quest for imagery which might contain something of the power of tribal art, without necessarily embodying either the stylistic characteristics or particular mythic details of that art, was shared by such other major, New York-based painters as Richard Pousette-Dart, Adolph Gottlieb, Barnett Newman and Mark Rothko.[88] In his 1937 *System and Dialectics of Art*, the influential New York-based painter and theorist John D. Graham had argued that 'The purpose of art in *particular* is to reestablish a lost contact with the unconscious (actively by producing works of art), with the primordial racial past and to keep and develop this contact in order to bring to the conscious mind the throbbing events of the unconscious mind.'[89] Graham's primitivising emphasis on the 'primordial racial past' became a key element in the development of Abstract Expressionism, as can be seen in the letter which Gottlieb and Rothko wrote — with the then unacknowledged assistance of Barnett Newman — to *The New York Times* in June 1943.

Reacting to a negative review of their work, the painters stressed their belief that 'art is an adventure into an unknown world, which can be explored only by those willing to take the risks'. They also emphasised the importance of subject matter in art. Wishing to cultivate 'the simple expression of the complex thought' through such means as the avoidance of perspectival depth (because of their belief that flat forms 'destroy illusion and reveal truth'), they asserted that 'the subject is crucial and only that subject matter is valid which is tragic and timeless. That is why we profess spiritual kinship with primitive and archaic art.'[90]

The subject matter of Abstract Expressionism became nothing less than the self's struggle to realise the simultaneously awesome and healing depths of its own mythopoeic capacities; not out of any narcissistic impulse, but so that the ancient 'bird' of exalted (and individuated) consciousness might break free of the nightmare of history and ensoul the world once again. Eschewing any obvious recourse to previous conventions of religious or landscape painting, the Abstract Expressionists attempted to make cathedrals out of themselves.[91] And none of them tried to do this with more determination than Pollock.

The shamanic nature of Pollock's quest was beautifully captured in the series of photographs which Hans Namuth took of the artist in 1951. Namuth photographed Pollock while at work on the sort of 'drip' or 'poured' paintings which had recently brought him to the attention of *Life* and *Time* magazine reporters, who were anxious to establish if 'Jack the Dripper' really was 'America's greatest living artist'.[92] These jazz-tinged documents of Pollock stepping in and around his canvases, paint flowing freely from brush, stick or pot, have contributed a great deal to the image of Pollock as a 'caricatured cowboy existentialist', the 'action painter' who allegedly epitomised the utterly unfettered, individualistic spirit of the so-called American way.[93] On a deeper level, they reveal just how far the painter had advanced towards an archetypal, individuated state, particularly when compared to the somewhat desperate mythologising of a decade previously, as revealed in *Naked Man* and *Bird*.

Body and soul now have no need to be pictured separately, at the threshold of shamanic transformation. They are as one in the shape-shifting line which drips and dances its way across the canvas, endlessly alive, endlessly transformed — a calligraphy of consciousness in total, metamorphosing tune with itself. As W. Jackson Rushing says, 'The drip paintings speak of a oneness . . . the merger of opposites: the image and pictorial ground become one, the gesture and image become one, drawing and kinds of writing become painting, and, finally, the work of art is the ritual process.'[94] Like a great shaman, Pollock swept far down into himself in these paintings, gliding through the hieratic threshold of *Guardians of the Secret* into a healing, mythopoeic space: the space of cosmos, of ecstatic reverie, of *participation mystique*.

79 Jackson Pollock *Number 1, 1948* 1948 oil on canvas 172.7 x 264.2 The Museum of Modern Art, New York. Purchase © ARS 1992

The dreams of Miró, as earthy as they are aerial, and the dancing, visceral energy of Pollock can help to prepare us for the work of Alan Davie (*b*.1920), the outstanding Scottish artist whose 1971 series of paintings *Bird Through the Wall* supplies the title for this chapter. An accomplished musician, Davie had a successful career as a jazz saxophonist in the 1940s, before deciding to concentrate on painting. Like Miró, Davie — who is one of the most striking of all shamanic spirits in twentieth-century art — has been greatly inspired by the art of prehistory, as well as by tribal art from all over the world. And like Pollock, he has created a vibrant world which can send us dreaming and dancing deep into ourselves — into the *ur*-terrain of shamanic transformation.

Breton's hope that the eye might pass from visual to visionary power is completely met in such paintings of Davie's as the 1971 *Magic Serpent* and *Bird Through the Wall* series. The latter represents neither bird nor wall as we might ordinarily think of them, even after contemplating Ernst's *Bird* of 1947. In number twelve of the series, for example, a surreal, speckled snail-shaped hybrid with wings and tail hovers above an ochre ground in 'irrational', non-Euclidian space, where the various perspective lines offer no familiar footing for the imagination. A spacious combination of Egyptian Ankh and light blue crescent moon complements a variety of elemental, interlocking shapes at the bottom of the painting, offering a further stimulus to abandon conventional notions of perception and inhabit the dream world of the marvellous which the painter has conjured for us.

The music that Davie recorded in the same year, and to which he gave the same title as the *Bird Through the Wall* paintings, offers similar challenges and reward. Recorded with some of Britain's finest jazz musicians, including saxophonist Ray Warleigh, bassist Chris Lawrence and drummer Alan Jackson, the improvised forty minutes or so of *Bird Through the Wall* float free of clichés of bar divisions and harmony, to offer a world where fiercely phrased passages of ululation and delicate traceries of sound co-exist in shape-shifting surreality. It is the surreality of reverie, with silence and dramatic dynamic transitions flowing in and out of rich, chromatic voicings as naturally as the winds circle the seas.

Bird Through the Wall was one of the five very stimulating albums of jazz-related improvised music which Davie recorded between 1970 and 1975, with a variety of personnel including the distinguished drummers Frank Perry, Daniel Humair and Tony Oxley. Intuition and improvisation, which are crucial to jazz, have always been of central importance to Davie; and as such titles of his improvised pieces as *Offering To The Ram-Headed Serpent*, *Adventures with a Magic Ring* and *Fish Fascinator* indicate, he sees music — like painting — as a bridge to the sort of magical, animistic world which the Romantics hymned.[95] For Davie, the painter's and the musician's encounter with the vibrations of light and sound are entirely similar, in that they are both dealing with the *mysteries* of the energy which nourishes

80 Alan Davie *Bird Through the Wall No. 12* 1971 oil on canvas 122 x 152.5
Private Collection
© courtesy, the Artist and Gimpel and Weitzenhoffer Ltd, New York

existence — mysteries which finally elude all attempts at rational analysis. In either case, if the vibrations are right, they may help us to slough off the dead skin of habit, and perhaps waken to a sense of the numinous in life.

Few artists of the post-Surrealist era have pursued the marvellous with such sustained intensity and vigour as Davie. Early in his career, he was inspired equally by Van Gogh and Cézanne, Klee and Picasso, the poetry of both Walt Whitman and the Far East, and Romanesque and tribal art. From the late-1940s onwards, Surrealism's (undogmatic) pursuit of the marvellous in the depths of the unconscious seems to have been second nature to him.[96] Together with Miró, whom he acknowledges as a painter of major consequence, Davie stands as an outstanding exemplar of the Surrealist imagination — provided that imagination is seen in Jungian rather than Freudian terms, and that one focusses on its mythopoeic nostalgia for the sacred (as in the work of Miró, Carrington or Varo, for example) rather than its notorious cultivation of culturally-bound sacrilege (as in the work of Buñuel).

In 1949 Davie saw works by Pollock in the Peggy Guggenheim collection in Venice. He was to meet the artist later, shortly before Pollock's death and at a time when the American's inspiration seemed to have run dry. Pollock's 'drip' or 'poured' paintings are often compared with jazz music, and rightly so. However, it is Davie who has created this century's most striking painterly equivalents to the process of jazz improvisation and composition, in works which are completely eloquent of their own rhythmic, melodic and harmonic power. Such irradiated, gesturally potent paintings as *Blue Triangle Enters* (1953), *Crazy Ikon* (1959), *Cornucopia* (1960), *Music Man's Dream* (1963), *Cure For The Blues* (1964), and *Jazz By Moonlight* (1966) offer a shaman-like exaltation of existence. Their free-flowing drawing with paint thickens and twists, advances and recedes in a glorious, polyrhythmic dance of hypnotic intensity, singing of those ecstatic moments when we sense the transcendence of all imprisoning dualities.

Whether painting, writing poetry, making jewellery or playing classical and improvised music on a wide variety of instruments — including piano, xylophone, saxophone, bass clarinet, flute and cello — Davie has always revealed an alchemical, or shamanic attitude to creativity. In a lecture which he gave at Brighton Polytechnic in Autumn 1989, he summarised a lifetime's quest for a language that might realise the Romantics' desire to 'dwell poetically on earth', in his suggestion that 'Basically the creative state would appear to amount to a kind of religious communion with the *great eternal*. Here it is apparent to me that what I am doing is fundamentally the same as the artists of remote times — the same as artists in tribal society — engaged in a shamanistic conjuring up of visions which will link us metaphorically with mysterious and spiritual forces normally beyond our apprehension.'[97]

81 Alan Davie *Jazz By Moonlight No. 3* oil on canvas 1966 122 x 152.5
Collection of the Artist
© courtesy, the Artist

Long interested in Zen Buddhism (as were several of the Abstract Expressionists), Davie sees art as a crucial aspect of the struggle of humanity to free itself from the restrictions of the ego, or what Sufism calls the lower self, in order to reach and realise what he calls 'the eternal spirit' which dwells within us all. Writing in 1960 about his experiences of teaching, he expressed a desire to awaken a sense of 'total immersion in the eternity of now' in both himself and anyone who might wish to participate in the creative process through learning to trust the intuition which 'knows' without knowledge. His hope remains that 'In time perhaps an "inner knowing" can be cultivated to supplant the dead knowledge which is of the past, yet which continues to rule the lives of men in a lingering age of materialism; and perhaps through art man will rediscover the mystical key to the magic that is life.'[98]

The search for magic has led Davie far into the collective unconscious; and as the disturbing, brooding power of such paintings as the 1952 *Blood Creation* and 1956 *Sacrifice* suggests, that search has had to pass through shaman-like stages of initiatory pain and struggle. The result is a splendid example of what James Hillman has called 'the imaginatively thinking heart', concerned to both 'ensoul' and 'be ensouled by' the world.[99] Dogma of any kind is distasteful to Davie; the initial spark of religious feeling, wherever and however it may occur, warms his heart. His is a quest to *shake the bones of the past*, as it were, and bring them into fresh, inspiring configurations. Painting after painting (and recording after recording) manifests a desire to be at the mythopoeic heart of things, at the primal intersection of culture and nature.[100]

Dreaming one's way into Davie's open-ended imagery, one encounters transmutative echoes of ancient shamanic rites (Tree of Life symbolism, hypnotic rhythmic patterns, animal or bird familiars, bodily or psychic metamorphosis); Egyptian symbolism (especially the Ankh, symbol of life, the all-seeing, protective eyes of Horus, and snake souls); Tantric art (the power of Kundalini, both asleep and arising); the Western magical tradition (the seals and symbols of Medieval and Renaissance magicians, and the energising shapes of Tattwa cards), and a host of other cultures from Neolithic Britain to Aboriginal Australia, and from West Africa to Native America and the Indian sub-continent (cup markings, spirals and labyrinths, transformation masks and Hopi migration symbols, meditations on Jain cosmology). And throughout, there is the unmistakable mark of Davie's own Celtic heritage, in both the luminosity of his colours and the organic interplay of his linear invention.

Like Miró, Davie sees the creative process as being far more important than the inevitably retrospective (yet sometimes proscriptive) categories of critics or historians. In such myth-oriented, metamorphosing works of the 1970s and 1980s as the *Shaman's Drum*, *Dancer Myth*, *Homage To The Earth Spirits* and *Magic Fountains* series, he abandoned the relatively 'flat' or shallow space of much of his earlier work (which had endeared him to modernist critics and curators) to develop a more theatrical and playful sense of space and revelation (which was sometimes shamefully ignored by the so-called *cognoscenti* of the art world).[101] And like Miró again, a lasting 'surreal' or shamanic quality underlies and unifies all the various periods of Davie's work, no matter how different the treatment of space, scale, surface, motif or gesture may seem to be.

Just as Miró loved the earth, so has Davie at various times in his life devoted himself to gardening, gliding, sailing or underwater swimming with a passion redolent of the shaman's ecstatic empathy with nature. 'How much more important than Art, just to be a bird', he once wrote.[102] In the mid-1980s, the shamanic nature of Davie's art was firmly underlined in the commission which he received from the French sculptor Niki de Saint Phalle, when she invited him to the Tarot sculpture park which she had created some sixty miles north of Rome. Using acrylic paint for the first time in his life, Davie fashioned a magnificent, undulating fresco for the interior of the combined structures of de Saint Phalle's *High Priestess and Magician* sculpture. Reminiscent of the shamanic symbolism of magic crystals and mirrors, the shards of mirror glass which Davie worked into his highly luminous, primitivistic images create a multiplicity of refracted viewpoints. Wandering around within the sculpture, viewers are thus encouraged to dream themselves clean through the walls of everyday perception and relish a world where the shamanic ladder of vision, or

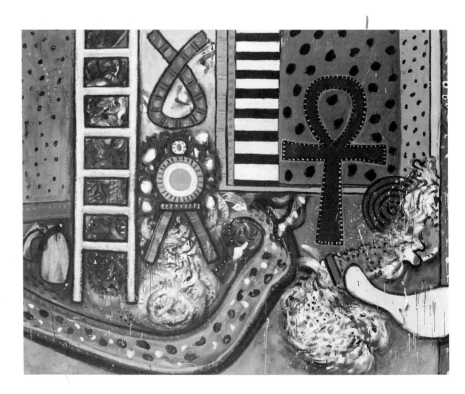

82 Alan Davie *Dragon Fetish*
1967 172.75 x 213.45
Private Collection
© courtesy, the Artist and
Gimpel Fils, London

83 Alan Davie *Shaman's Drum No. 4* 1973 oil on canvas 76.2 x 101.6 Private collection © courtesy, the Artist and Gimpel Fils, London

escape, passes through a vibrant, energising space of synthesised, yin/yang creativity. [103]

While developing the idea of her sculpture garden, de Saint Phalle (*b.*1930) had drawn inspiration from a wide range of sources: Italian gardens of the sixteenth and seventeenth centuries, Antoni Gaudi's Guell Park in Barcelona (created between 1900 and 1914), and the 'ideal palace' of the 'outsider' artist Ferdinand (Facteur) Cheval (1836–1924) — a particular favourite of the Surrealists. As with Davie's work, however, a single archetype of creative vision lay underneath all such influences — for de Saint Phalle worked on the heavily wooded and sloping site out of a strong sense of compassion for all the female seers of the Christian European past. She has described the Tarot garden as being for 'all the women who over so many centuries were not allowed to create and if they dared they were burned as witches or locked up in a madhouse. The garden is a homage to them and also to an ancient, lost wisdom . . .' [104]

The combination of de Saint Phalle's sculpture and Davie's fresco is one of the most potent examples of how modern art has sought to bring that ancient wisdom back to life. It is also a superb example of the potential (Jungian) fruits of Surrealism's pursuit of the marvellous. In the *High Priestess and Magician* of the Tarot Garden, the mutual resonance of twentieth-century art and prehistoric vision unites landscape and sculpture, sculpture and painting, female and male, in an ensemble of vital, shamanic power. If we wish to break through the walls of our conditioning, of our isolation; if we wish to break through the plane of history, and recover a mythopoeic sense of sacred cosmos; if we wish to fly towards the 'half-made heaven' that lies deep within us . . . then there could scarcely be any better place than this in which to open our eyes and dream.

12 Rainbow Bridge

'Imagine that you can fly through the rings of Saturn or travel inside a blood cell around the body; imagine being able to walk around a building that doesn't exist . . . Imagine a world where the laws of physics do not apply, where you can pass through walls or float inside a cloud.'[1] Imagine, that is, that the needs of your imagination have been met courtesy of recent developments in computer technology — developments which have led to the creation of what has been called Virtual Reality, or Cyberspace.

From 1985 to 1990 California-based Scott Fisher was founder and director of the Virtual Environment Work Station Project at NASA's Ames Research Center near San Francisco. With scientist Michael McGreevy, he developed the first VR headset — a 'helmet' with goggles made of screens adapted from two Japanese miniature televisions. Wearing the helmet inside a space station, an astronaut could be linked to a robot working outside on repairs: when the astronaut's head turned, the robot's camera eye would move in the same direction. The potential social applications of such a development range from advanced surgery to supermarket shopping; from games of 'virtual' tennis or golf to military training. It has been suggested that the nature of the Allied preparations for the air battle in the Gulf War of 1991 made it the first 'virtual war'.[2]

What has all this got to do with shamanism? Could there be any parallel between the shamans' use of their caps and drums to summon the spirit world and the fact that, to move into Cyberspace, one has to don a headset and DataGlove? Discussing the implications of Virtual Reality, Fisher comments: 'The caves of Lascaux were a primitive virtual environment. The idea's been around for a long time. It's a kind of dreamspace . . . where you're not bound by normal laws'.[3] According to writer Simon Worrall, 'It is no accident that the term VR is so close to the title of one of the cult books of the Sixties [sic], Carlos Castaneda's *Separate Reality*. Castaneda's accounts of his experiments with peyote feel very like a "trip" in Cyberspace. There is the same sense of immersion in other worlds, the same dizzying shifts of scale, even the same experience of "flying" '.[4]

In the mid-1960s, when computer power was in its infancy, Marshall McLuhan had already suggested that electronic technology would bring us rapidly to 'the final phase of the extensions of man — the technological simulation of consciousness'.[5] A choice example of the potential delights of this 'final phase' is given by Worrall, regarding the application of VR to design developments by the Japanese corporation Matsushita: 'At a booth in a Tokyo shopping-centre, housewives equipped with a headset and DataGlove were able to "shop" in Cyberspace, matching "virtual refrigerators" with their "virtual" kitchens. Only the bill they received at the end was real.'[6]

Whether one regards Cyberspace as a potential nightmare or a liberating breakthrough into interactive technology, it seems to me that the parallels Fisher and Worrall suggest between so-called Virtual Reality and shamanism are as dangerous as they are banal. Epitomising the 'touch of a button' syndrome of late-capitalist culture, they reduce the spiritual richness of shamanic experience to a (very expensive) question of technological wizardry. Such a paradoxically empiricist travesty of the idea of vision ignores both the *specific* qualities of the results which accrue from the shaman's understanding of the technology of vision, and the *totalising* nature of the shaman's vision quest.[7] The idea of shamanism surely implies far more than the ability to indulge in some kind of 'way out' optical and sensory experience, abstracted from the sensuous reality and diversity of the world.

There may be readers who have felt slightly different doubts about the parallels I have tried to draw in this book. That is to say, in detecting the archetypal spirit of shamanism in a variety of developments in twentieth-century art, does one not run the risk of stretching the connotations of the concept 'shamanism' to the point where it becomes meaningless?

As Starhawk has observed, shamanism has recently become a 'trendy' word — so 'overused and commercialized', she believes, that out of respect for its traditional meaning, she refuses to use it with regard to the present day practice of witchcraft.[8] Viewing shamanism from what one might call a fundamentalist perspective, she maintains that 'A shaman is a healer who is trained within a traditional society and uses her or his skills in the service of that community . . . The interest in spiritual traditions that offer direct encounters with dimensions beyond the everyday has grown enormously, spawning a minor industry in workshops and exotic tours. But real spiritual growth takes place in the context of a culture. People of European heritage, out of hunger for what that culture lacks, may unwittingly become spiritual strip miners, damaging other cultures in superficial attempts to uncover their mystical treasures.'[9] Rather than flock to 'the sad tribe of "Wannabees" — want to be Indians, want to be Africans, want to be anything but what we are — '[10] Starhawk suggests that people of industrial cultures should focus attention on aspects of their own long-suppressed spiritual background: hence her commitment to the Great Goddess and witchcraft.

There is, of course, a good deal of truth in what Starhawk says. However, one wonders to what extent her respect for tradition runs the risk of reinforcing the very things she wishes to criticise. Dividing the world into categories of 'us and them', distinctions between cultures — no matter how well-intended — can serve both to disguise the fact that we are *all* ethnic, as it were, and to imprison people within history through a puristic denial of the possibilities of cultural interchange and development.[11] In this respect, it is interesting to compare Starhawk's views on shamanism with the beliefs of Brook Medicine Eagle, the great-great-grandniece of Grandfather Joseph, the Nez Percé Native American leader and holy man.

Born on the Crow Reservation in Montana, where Native American traditions were fading, Brook Medicine Eagle was in her twenties when she undertook ritual training with the Northern Cheyenne medicine woman Stands Near the Fire (Josie Limpie), one of the highest traditional leaders among her people. Raised in economically straitened circumstances, Brook Medicine Eagle was awarded a full scholarship to the University of Denver, where she earned a bachelor's degree in psychology and mathematics and a master's degree in counselling psychology.[12] Her understanding of the shamanic spirit today is couched in language of transition and growth: 'Fortune has taken me back to native medicine people and to healers around the world, yet I still get the same basic message from them: "You will never be given a traditional form. The form that is yours is the formless form, which breaks through to Spirit." This is what has been given to me.'[13]

Initially, Brook Medicine Eagle suffered because of such advice. Missing the security of tradition, she longed to hear someone tell her '*This* is the way!' Gradually, however, she matured into the realisation that, 'whatever path is mine, however it's related to tradition, it is a *new way*. This is a new time on earth we're coming into; one of my challenges is to bring us gracefully over the rainbow bridge into a new age . . . to step into a pattern that we've never ever had before.'[14]

Reflecting upon Brook Medicine Eagle's words, one recalls the vision which came to Ursula in Lawrence's *The Rainbow*: the (much less charitably expressed) vision of a rainbow arching above the 'dry, brittle corruption spreading over the face of the land' — the rainbow that might yet bring the people who crept 'hard-scaled and separate on the face of the world's corruption' to a 'new germination, to a new growth, rising to the light and the wind and the clean rain of heaven.'[15] Or one thinks of the Austrian artist Friedrich Hundertwasser (*b*.1928), who has chosen to add both Friedensreich (Kingdom of Peace) and Regentag (Rainy Day) to his name. For this painter of raindrops and rainbow houses, of luminous, aerial views of dream landscapes, dominated by the visionary motif of the spiral, 'the sun is finest when it rains'.[16]

Hundertwasser calls himself a painter of vegetation. He is an artist for whom creativity is above all a recognition and development of organic relations, of *humus* (= humility). Loathing the straight lines of our

84 Iain Roy (*b.*1944) *Rainbow,
pylons and prehistoric site*, on the
edge of the Lammermuir,
Kingside, East Lothian. 1989
silver bromide print
27.7 x 36.5
Collection of the Artist
© courtesy, the Artist

century's so-called 'rationalist architecture', he has created both anti-Bauhaus architectural manifestos (such as the *Mould Manifesto* of the late-1950s) and a curving, variegated housing complex in Vienna, which was built in the mid-1980s.[17] Having long protested against the domination of both external and internal nature by rationalist ideas, his settling in the Bay of Islands, New Zealand in the mid-1970s could not help but recall Gauguin's flight to Tahiti, following his dismissal of 'this rotten and corrupt Europe'. Like Gauguin, Hundertwasser can be seen as a shamanic figure, actively seeking to remind us of the transformative dimensions of creativity which lie beyond (or rather, deep within) the everyday realm. And Hundertwasser has long been aware of the ecological implications of his faith in the regenerative powers of nature, travelling the world to speak on environmental issues and working on occasion with Greenpeace.[18]

In 1975, the year that he settled in New Zealand, Hundertwasser spoke of his belief that regenerative art comes from a transrational level of the psyche — that painting is a religious activity, that 'the actual impulse comes from without, from something else that we do not know, an indefinable power which comes or does not come and which guides your hand . . . the only thing one can do is to prepare the ground, so that this extraterrestrial impulse or however else one might describe it can reach you. That means keeping oneself ready. That means eliminating the will, eliminating the intelligence, eliminating "wanting to do better", eliminating ambition. I should perhaps like to be known as the magician of vegetation or something similar. We are in need of magic. I fill a picture until it is full with magic, as one fills up a glass with water. Everything is so infinitely simple, so infinitely beautiful.'[19]

Lawrence's 'clean rain of heaven' and Hundertwasser's magic-filled glass of water combine to bring to mind Brancusi's hope that we might develop an art from what he called 'the source of pure water' — so that everyone might be able to drink from it: 'Art begins to be born. Once rid of the religions and the philosophies, art is the thing that can save the world. Art is the plank after the shipwreck, that saves someone . . .'[20] As we have seen, while Brancusi could speak thus of the potentialities of an art free from the divisive details of religion and philosophy, his own art was nonetheless shot through with archetypal religious and philosophical meaning. The painter Henri (Le Douanier) Rousseau (1844–1910) once said to him: 'I see what you are trying to do; you want to transform the ancient into the modern.'[21] This is exactly the nature of the 'rainbow bridge' of which Brook Medicine Eagle speaks: the (shamanic) transformation of the essence of the archaic wisdom of the past into a new, world-wide pattern — 'a pattern that we've never ever had before'.

It is this pattern which so interested Mircea Eliade and Joseph Campbell: the possibility of what Eliade called an enlarged humanism, on a world scale, inspired by a participatory respect for the mythic dimension of existence. In *Myths, Dreams and Mysteries* Eliade suggested that, just as the discovery of the unconscious had compelled Western man to confront 'his own individual, secret and "larval" history', so would the encounter with non-Western cultures oblige him to 'delve very profoundly into the history of the human spirit and . . . perhaps persuade him to admit that history as an integral part of his own being.'[22] 'It is not enough', Eliade continued, 'as it was half a century ago, to discover and admire the art of Negroes or Pacific islanders: we now have to discover the spiritual sources of these arts in ourselves; we must become aware of what it is, in a modern existence, that is still "mythical", and survives as such simply because this, too, is part and parcel of the human condition, in that it expresses the anxiety of man living in Time.'[23]

Eliade suggested that the obsession with anxiety, chaos and death which marks so much of the culture of modernity might be radically transformed, were we to reflect upon the way in which animistic, archaic thought confers positive values on situations which we might at first glance find either terrifying or absurd. (For example, the fundamental mythic idea that in order to be reborn, the world must first die, which in turn feeds into archaic notions of socio-spiritual initiation and development. Of course, Eliade did not intend such thoughts to feed any insane rationalisations of either nuclear war or any other ecological catastrophe.) As we have seen, it was Eliade's sensitivity to such aspects of archaic thought which enabled him to discern the regenerative 'cosmic meaning' within what many have taken to be the sheer meaninglessness of modern art's abandonment of immediately familiar forms. As Eliade observed in his key article 'The Sacred and the Modern Artist', 'From a structural point of view, the attitude of the [modern] artist in regard to the cosmos and to life recalls to a certain extent the ideology implicit in cosmic religion.'[24]

I have tried to argue that that 'certain extent' is best understood in terms of the ideas of shamanism: just as the shaman had the courage to 'exit from time', as Eliade puts it, flying beyond the familiar in search of the cosmic core of existence, so has the modern artist broken through the socio-political plane of history, in search of the mythopoeic power which might regenerate our sense of the sacred in life.[25]

Describing the art of Aboriginal Australia, Peter Sutton and Christopher Anderson call the Dream Time or Dreaming from which such art derives 'the power-filled ground of existence'.[26] For well over a century, modern artists (a category that, as we shall shortly see, is here intended to include artists of Aboriginal background) have sought a new understanding of what that ground might be — how the power of archaic, 'local' truths might be transmuted into forms and images that speak of a pattern which is redolent of the ancient past, at the same time that it is 'one that we've never ever had before'. The English artist Andrzej Jackowski (b.1947), for example, who has often spoken very positively of the relation of shamanic ideas to painting, has referred to his work as 'archaic fiction': stepping stones to the inner ground, or 'where the stories come from', as Bruno Schultz, one of Jackowski's favourite authors, has put it.[27] This is the realm of reverie: the healing, cosmic realm which fascinated Rilke and Tarkovsky as much as it did Gaston Bachelard, all of whom stir elective affinities in Jackowski. Painted on a half-chalk ground, scraped and sanded, rubbed and glazed, Jackowski's images seem to light themselves from within, as they float into our consciousness to speak of the mythopoeic gathering and expansion of the self: the future of the child whom *Earth-Stalker* (1987) carries on his shoulders lies as deep in the past as that past's future lies within both ourselves and her.

It is the mythic interplay of past and future in the *expanded* and *intensified* present which so fascinated Joseph Campbell, for whom developments in modern art were of no less importance than they were to Eliade. Speaking

85 Andrej Jackowski *Earth-Stalker* 1987 oil on canvas
152.5 x 233.5
Private collection
© courtesy of the Artist and
Marlborough Fine Art
(London) Ltd

of the 'field of deep problems' addressed by artists such as Thomas Mann and James Joyce, Paul Klee and Pablo Picasso — problems of the relation of the 'here and now' to 'knowledge of the other foci . . . of the whole totality range' — Campbell asked 'Why should these men have given their whole lives to working on problems like this if they weren't of life-shattering depth? This is the problem of the relationship of art to life. Is it a killer or fosterer of life? It's a fosterer.'[28] One of this century's most profound and rounded of minds, Campbell's various studies of mythology did a great deal to explicate the idea that, as Eliade insisted, 'the sacred lies within the structure of consciousness'. And for Campbell, there was no contradiction involved in believing, as he did, that it was the sensuous, *embodied* nature of art which made it the greatest vehicle to the spiritual. For 'The artist with a craft remains in touch with the world; the mystic can spin off and lose touch and frequently does. And so it seems to me that art is the higher form.'[29]

Brancusi once remarked that while simplicity should not be a conscious aim or end in art, we arrive at simplicity in spite of ourselves, in approaching the real sense of things: 'Simplicity is at bottom complexity and one must be nourished on its essence to understand its significance.'[30] His insight would seem to parallel Campbell's intuition concerning the luminous, transcultural core which he sensed at the heart of all mythologies. Shortly before his death, Campbell spoke of the bliss of the *mythologically inspired life* — where mythology is 'lived' as layer upon layer of fluid metaphor, leading the self to the exalted state of being 'transparent to the transcendent'.[31] Campbell was fond of quoting Joyce's famous comment (via the character Stephen Dedalus) that 'History is a nightmare from which I am trying to awake'. He regarded Joyce's words as confirmation of his own cryptic insight that 'history is simply a function of misunderstood mythology'.[32]

Whether we be theists or atheists, so to speak, if we insist on taking mythology literally, we imprison ourselves in its exoteric or 'local' resonance. But if we allow the metaphoric dimensions of mythology to speak to us, and so begin to peel away the socio-historical layers within which its central 'message' is both encoded and buried, we can begin to grasp the healing import of the liberating, esoteric function of myth: 'When you have seen the radiance of eternity through all the forms of time, and it's a function of art to make that visible to you, then you have really ended life in the world as it is lived by those who think only in the historical terms. This is the function of mythology . . .'[33]

For Campbell, this was precisely what linked the world of the prehistoric shaman with that of the twentieth-century artist: the tender-minded sensitivity to mythopoeisis, the 'break-through in plane' of which Eliade spoke — the search for the luminous core of life. As I have already stressed in Chapter 2, such a mythopoeic perspective does *not* imply any Olympian disregard for the various problems and potentialities of historical existence which press upon consciousness today as never before. On the contrary: it suggests that without a respect for the mythopoeic dimensions of life, for *participation mystique*, for the recreative mythic power of humanity, historical existence is doomed to extinction — a central, particularly cheerless aspect of the legacy of Christianity. Paradoxically enough, it is becoming increasingly evident that only by abandoning the myth of (linear, unique) history is it likely that any history may be preserved: the history which from time to time has the grace to gather itself into those archetypal moments when its relations to the constitutive sacred — the cosmos — are acknowledged and celebrated.[34]

In preparing the way for a return to such a sense of cosmicity, the shamanic spirit in twentieth-century art has indeed suggested that, in the words of Brook Medicine Eagle, we need 'to step into a pattern that we've never ever had before'. For the 'rainbow bridge' of the new shamanic consciousness has had to fuse the exoteric and the esoteric, the archaic and the evolving manifestations of *participation mystique*, the poetic and the political. To step towards that bridge is not to rush to join any tribe of 'Wannabees': on the contrary, it implies the ability to move between cultures, with what one might call the mythopoeic heart as a guide, sensitive to both what distinguishes mythologies and what may ultimately link them. Just as the shaman broke through the plane of everyday consciousness, in search of an integrated cosmic vision, so do we have to break through the 'fundamentalist' crust of 'local' socio-political and religious consciousness, and 'fly' to those realms where we may at least catch a glimpse of the bridge of which Brook Medicine Eagle speaks. Or would we prefer the impact of oil spills and nuclear accidents, international terrorism and corporate capitalism to be our only stimuli for thinking of the world in holistic terms?

Arching over and away from 'local' terrain, the 'rainbow bridge' is nevertheless built from the very ground of our being. And while that ground may ultimately lie outside any purely 'local' history, we may not be able to discover it until — to employ the famous image of Seamus Heaney — we have dug down through layer after layer of history and myth.[35] In this regard, two contemporary German artists are of particular interest: Anselm Kiefer (*b.*1945) and Sigmar Polke (*b.*1941).

Both artists might be described as healers, insofar as they have brought aspects of the previously repressed 'unspeakable' in Germany's Nazi past into consciousness. Kiefer's *Your Golden Hair, Margarete* (1981), *Nuremberg* (1982) and *Sulamith* (1983) and Polke's *Camp* (1982) and *Watchtower* series (1984—5) have all touched a number of (understandably) raw nerves. In 1984 Kiefer became the first contemporary German painter to be given a one-person exhibition at the Israel Museum in Jerusalem, where his work was received with no little sensitivity and understanding. Meir Ronnen, of the *Jerusalem Morning Post*, wrote: 'In murdering the Jews, we Germans, thus Kiefer might be translated, have murdered a part of ourselves . . . But mourning might be the key to the psyche of Kiefer. It is not mourning comparable to the mourning of the Jews of our times. Kiefer seems to be mourning the indigestibility of his heritage by battling with it in an ongoing series of waking dreams.'[36]

The (latent) intention of those 'waking dreams' was nothing less than to rescue mythopoeisis from recent historical perversions of myth. Kiefer's paintings often depict fields of scorched stubble, an ambiguous image redolent of both the barbarity of an army in retreat and the farmer's expectation of cyclical renewal. Fire is here both destroyer and purifier, medium of the soul's Phoenix-like rebirth. Eagles often feature in Kiefer's work: it is worth noting the extent to which the legend of the eagle-sized Phoenix, graced with certain features of the pheasant, carries strong overtones of shamanism. When it saw death drawing near, the Phoenix would make a nest of sweet-smelling wood and resins, which it would expose to the full force of the sun's rays. Having burnt itself to ashes in the flames, another Phoenix would then arise from the marrow of its bones.[37]

In the early 1970s, Kiefer visited Joseph Beuys frequently: he has described the sculptor as his teacher 'in the largest sense of the word'.[38] There is the same feeling of rehabilitation in Kiefer as there is in Beuys: a rehabilitation not of Nazism, of course, but of Romantic primitivism, of nature as the site of (mainly Nordic) mythology, of art as a ritual act, bound up with psychic transformation and development. A 1970 watercolour by

Kiefer depicts a minuscule figure beneath a transparent blue dome, set within a sweeping panorama of field and sky. The figure's right arm is raised in fascist salute: seen against the enormity of the surrounding earth, his pose becomes both pathetic and ridiculous. Entitled *Every Human Being Stands beneath His Own Dome of Heaven*, the work may be taken as both a statement of sociological relativism and illustration of Campbell's fundamental point concerning the need to transcend the 'local' dimension of mythology, and become ever more 'transparent to the transcendent'.[39]

For Kiefer, the path to the transcendent has lain deep within materiality. With their predominantly sombre — often blackened — earth tones, his paintings have been distinguished by their evident physicality, not only with regard to their size but, more importantly, with respect to their various integrations of painted image, photograph and word, sand and straw, cardboard and lead, oil and acrylic, shellac and emulsion, zinc and steel, charcoal, wire and gold leaf. The last-named substance suggests the alchemical heart of Kiefer's work, which becomes particularly evident in such paintings as *Nigredo* (1984), *Astral Serpent* (1986), *Jerusalem* (1986) and *Saturn Time* (1986).[40] In working his way so thoroughly into and through his material (in several senses of the word) Kiefer has done as much as — if not more than — any other artist of the past three decades to suggest that, while history may be based in mythology — and may at times render that mythology thoroughly base — the mythopoeic core of mythology cannot be reduced to history.

Some of Sigmar Polke's paintings have made this point in a very different, but equally extraordinary way. One might call Polke the Quesalid of contemporary painting. Much of his early work seemed to question the possibility of saying anything at all meaningful in art: *Modern Art* (1968) is typical in its cynical (albeit clever) parody of a number of the high ambitions of modernism (Constructivism, Abstract Expressionism, Hard Edge Painting). But then Polke began to experiment more and more with both historical iconography and materials, eventually producing the distinctly unsettling *Camp* and *Watchtower* paintings of the early 1980s. In retrospect, it is as though his engagement with the utter horror of the Nazi past released something very deep — and transmutative — in his psyche. For whereas Polke had previously painted extremely self-conscious paintings about 'the problem of the subject in painting', in the late 1980s he created a series of what are perhaps the most potent alchemical-shamanic paintings of the century.

The five 'abstract' works which constitute the series *The Spirits that Lend Strength are Invisible* received their collective name from a Native American proverb. Created for the 1988 Carnegie International exhibition in Pittsburgh, the suite can be seen as an homage to the Americas, for all of the materials used were associated with the so-called New World as opposed to Europe. The suite cannot be said to be painting in any traditional sense of the term — or rather, its sense of tradition goes back to both the alchemists of the Renaissance and the days of the cave painters. Here is Polke's description of the media which he used in three of the works: *I*, tellurium (pure) blown onto artificial resin on canvas; *IV*, silver nitrate painted on invisible, hermetic structure and artificial resin on canvas; *V*, silver leaf, neolithic tools, and artificial resin on canvas.[41]

The result was a commanding, subtle reprise and development of the painterly scale and spiritual ambitions of Abstract Expressionism, reminiscent of both Jackson Pollock and Cy Twombly. Because of the chemistry of their materials, these immense, enigmatic 'soulscapes' develop and change through the joint effects of light and time. It is hard to think of a better example of Brook Medicine Eagle's 'formless form' which 'breaks through to the Spirit' than these liquid, aerial works, as they continuously alter, and thus preserve their ritualistic 'aura' from any desacralising, would-be definitive photographic reproduction.[42] In a generally enthusiastic essay, the poet and critic Peter Schjeldahl has written of Polke's 'sarcastic shamanism'.[43] However, it seems to me that, like Quesalid, Polke has finally begun to believe in his tricks: for these are surely paintings from the (mythopoeic) heart.

Several centuries ago, Pascal reminded us that the heart has its reasons, which reason knows not. Today, Brook Medicine Eagle has suggested that the essence of the Native American approach to life is 'To allow the heart to be the distributor of energy on this planet; to allow your heart, your feelings, your emotions to distribute your energy; to pull that energy from the earth, from the sky; to pull it down and distribute it from your heart, the very center of your being — that is our purpose.'[44] In the spirit of Brook Medicine Eagle's remarks, I would now like to consider some final examples of the shamanic spirit in twentieth-century art. Taken from a variety of cultures, these examples should suggest something of the complexity of the current relations of mythopoeisis and history, poetics and politics which inform the 'rainbow bridge' of the shamanic spirit in art today.

Some of the most centred and heartfelt music that I have heard over the past three decades has been that of the Norwegian saxophonist Jan Garbarek. As we have seen, Garbarek is an artist whose work has gradually reflected and 'made new' more and more of the shamanic tradition of the North. But at the same time that he has created music with an unmistakably Northern ring to it, Garbarek has developed as an artist of the world. The contributions which he has made to records by Keith Jarrett, Ralph Towner, Bill Connors, Egberto Gismonti and Charlie

Haden, Eberhard Weber, David Darling, L. Shankar, Eleni Karaindrou, Paul Giger and Trilok Gurtu, for example, have all helped to shape 'a pattern that we've never ever had before'.[45] Inspired as he is by a variety of art and music from Japan and Brazil, Native America and Russia, Poland and Greece, England and Germany, India and Italy — as well as the Nordic countries, of course — it is little wonder that Garbarek once told *Downbeat* writer Michael Bourne: 'You might say that I live in a spiritual neighbourhood which is scattered geographically all over the world.'[46]

In 1991 Garbarek played a series of concerts in his native Norway, with his regular quartet partners, pianist Rainer Brüninghaus, bassist Eberhard Weber and drummer and percussionist Marilyn Mazur, and two singers of very different but equally compelling qualities: Agnes Buen Garnås from Telemark and Mari Boine Persen from Saamiland. Drawing upon musical ideas from all around the world, the concerts were a superb example of the spiritual potentialities of so-called 'world music' — when that music is played by people who are genuinely concerned with getting to the cross-cultural heart of the mystery of music's existence as both acknowledgement and transcendence of (linear) time.

One arrangement in particular, featuring Mari Boine Persen on vocal, epitomised the new shamanic spirit of the 'rainbow bridge' of which Brook Medicine Eagle speaks. Beginning with the tender, *pianissimo* invocations of her *coloratura* vocal and Eberhard Weber's bass, Persen's composition 'Du Lahka' (Near You) gradually built to the ecstatic heights of a beautifully realised melodic and dynamic arch, before the musicians moved seamlessly into a collective improvisation upon the theme of 'Witchi Tai To', a composition by the Kaw-Creek Native American saxophonist Jim Pepper. The music had a quite extraordinary resonance to it: rarely, if ever, have I heard such a simultaneously piquant and exultant affirmation of existence.

When I asked Mari Boine Persen what had inspired her composition, she explained that it had begun life as a song celebrating the closeness of a lover. However, as she had performed it with increasing frequency, it had come to seem to her to be more a song in praise of the Spirit: the Spirit which lives 'far out there' — here she gestured away into the distance — at the same time that it exists in all things in nature and 'deep in here' — at which point she motioned towards her heart. In the strictly musical sense, Persen knew that the vocal of 'Du Lahka' could not be described as a *joik* — the lilting musical form peculiar to the Saami people, and through which they somehow bring into being the person, landscape or event which they are *joiking*. Nevertheless, she felt that the spirit of *joiking* was implicit not only in 'Du Lahka' but in a great deal of what she sang.

It was thus more than a matter of musical key or tempo which linked 'Du Lahka' with Jim Pepper's 'Witchi Tai To': for the latter song began life as a Comanche peyote vision chant which Pepper used to hear his grandfather sing. The song became a top 40 hit in 1968; the trumpeter Don

Cherry heard it and taught it to the Swedish pianist Bobo Stenson, who together with Garbarek gave it a superb instrumental reading in 1973.[47] A decade later, Pepper's equally fine tenor sax and vocal version revealed the visionary, shamanic core of the piece — 'all the strange feelings' in the singer's head, feelings that make him 'glad that I'm not dead'.[48]

Speaking to Mari Boine Persen, it soon became evident not only how strong her sense of tradition is, but also how determined she is that that tradition should be developed and made new. She spoke of her awareness of the ancient cultural tradition of the *noaidi* (shaman) — the person who, as she put it, had a particularly developed sensitivity to nature — and of how something of that tradition *had* to be preserved and developed in the world today.

Originally educated as a teacher, Persen did not remain long in the profession: the questions she had long asked herself about contemporary Saami identity were to be best articulated through performance. Featuring 'Du Lahka', her second album *Gula Gula* (Hear the Voices of the Foremothers) was recorded in 1989 in Oslo and released on Peter Gabriel's Real World label in 1990. Revealing a loving, unsentimental respect for folk wisdom, within arrangements which drew upon a novel, refreshing breadth of instrumentation (using, for example, hammered dulcimer and electric bass clarinet as well as claypot and drone drum), *Gula Gula* epitomises the growing strength of Saami self-determination today.[49]

Several of the Icelandic sagas mention Saami sorcerers, male and female. A famous chapter ('De Finnis') in the thirteenth-century work *Historia Norwegiae* offered further documentation, and Johannes Schefferus's *Lapponia*, issued in Latin in 1673 and shortly afterwards in English, German, French and Dutch, devoted an equally well-known chapter to magic and shamanism. Given the richness of shamanic consciousness within Saami culture and history, it is particularly heartening to note the strong shamanic overtones of Saami art today, after centuries of aggressive Christian missionary work, when many examples of 'the Devil's instrument' were burned.[50]

In Ailo Gaup's 1988 novel *Trommereisen* (The Drum Journey), for example, a man dreams that an archetypal Saami shaman's drum is in danger: he must find it, whatever the cost, and restore it to its rightful place in both the community and consciousness. The man journeys by car to the far north of Saamiland, where he has to battle with various negative, shape-shifting forces before gaining access to the artistic and spiritual powers of the drum. His journey to the heartland of Nordic shamanic consciousness is simultaneously a journey to the slumbering, animistic roots of his own self: a journey where landscape and mythology become increasingly alive, as room upon room of animistic feelings opens up within him.[51]

We have already remarked the excellence of Nils Gaup's 1987 film *Pathfinder*. To Persen and both Gaups must be added the name of Nils-Aslak Valkeapää, composer of the music for *Pathfinder* and the central figure in the recent renaissance of shamanic values in Saami culture. One of the great architects of the 'rainbow bridge' today, Valkeapää (*b*.1943) is both *joiker* and poet, artist and musician: inheritor and developer of the pride in Saami values which was earlier proclaimed by the poet Paulus Utsi (1918—75).

In Utsi's work, we learn of his sadness at the State policies of the Nordic countries during his lifetime, which were often aimed at destroying Saami language and culture in a policy of 'integration'. We also learn of his faith in ancient, animistic values. In one poem, for example, there are echoes of the pre-Christian worship of the *seite* — generally a rock unusually shaped by nature, or even a curiously formed tree stump — by the Saami. Utsi whispers into 'the rock', to someone who is hiding 'in a secret place', and who receives the word, 'carries it forward' and 'makes it come true'.[52] In another poem, we learn of Utsi's equal faith in the power of the *joik* (regarded by many as the oldest known music in Europe) — the *joik* which 'elevates the mind of man' as it flies with his thoughts 'above the clouds', and 'in the beauty of nature'.[53]

The modern powers of the *joik* are central to the shamanic spirit within the work of Nils-Aslak Valkeapää. His poetry-epos *Beavi, Ahcazan* — or as it has been called in Norwegian, *Solen, Min Far; Jorden, Livets Mor* (The Sun, My Father, The Earth, Life's Mother) — celebrates the mystery of the balance of nature's forces with a language which is as fresh and direct as it is rhythmically compelling. Able to combine the concrete and the metaphysical with compassionate, *haiku*-like precision, Valkeapää brings subtle twists of assonance and dissonance to his highly effective use of folk-derived techniques of repetition.[54] Both this book and the 1990 trilogy *Vindens veier* (The Ways of the Wind) were superbly illustrated by Valkeapää: his drawings range from unclichéd and atmospheric evocations of life among the reindeer herds on the *viddene* (mountain plateaux) to boldly dispersed, stark ideograms, redolent of the petroglyphs of the Nordic Bronze Age. There are also marvellous images of the shaman's drum, depicted in line with the ancient belief that this drum, with its three cosmic worlds, is a resonant symbol of the Universe.[55]

In 1988, Valkeapää — together with Esa Kotilainen — set parts of *Beavi, Áhčážan* to music. Using a wide range of warm synthesizer tones, the music's epic vocal sweep is sustained by a series of dramatically swelling, shaman-like drum patterns. Sequences of highly danceable, infectious rhythms contrast with rapt, withdrawn moments of reverie, as the hour-long recording revivifies and develops both shamanic ideas of music as an exalted state and the concept of the tone poem.[56] *Beavi, Áhčážan* has also inspired a drama production by the Saami Dálvadis Theatre, which is based in Karesuando, 250 miles north of the Arctic Circle, and which counts an Iroquoi Native American and a Greenlandic Inuit among its cast.

In the final part of his *Vindens veier* trilogy, Valkeapää tells of a trip to America, when he met members of the Blackfoot tribe and came to sense the strong links between their view of the world and Saami culture. In the 'mild, dark prairie night', the poet hears drum beats which seem to summon the spirit of the *joik*; drumbeats redolent of the *sjamantromme* (shaman's drum); drumbeats which send his blood racing; which fill his heart with joy . . . and which precipitate his mordant comments to the *store hvite herre* (big white lord) who has cheated so many native cultures out of their land and rights.[57] As the Navajo Ginger Hillis has said: 'They came with the Bible in one hand and the gun in the other. First they stole the gold. Then they stole the land. Then they stole souls.'[58]

In 1990, Richard Erdoes's beautifully illustrated book *Crying For a Dream* revealed the extent to which such 'soul loss' among Native Americans has been tackled in recent years by a combination of traditional means and political organisation. Erdoes's book is a valuable counter to the conventional wisdom of many enervated city dwellers that shamanism must surely be a thing of the long-distant past. It documents the survival of such time-honoured means of 'crying for a vision' as the Sun Dance and the Sweat Lodge, the 'vision pit' and the (Sioux) *yuwipi* ceremony. In the last-named, the medicine man, or 'stone dreamer' is wrapped in a star blanket, tied completely round with rawhide thong, and laid face down on the floor to await a vision. Lame Deer, a Minneconjou Sioux, explains: 'This is tying us together, ending the isolation between one human being and another; it is making a line from man to the Great Spirit. It means a harnessing of power. The man is tied up so that the spirits can come and use him. It pulls the people together and teaches them.'[59]

If the essence of shamanism is the combination of vision and healing, and the consequent strengthening of one's sense of soul, then it would not appear to be stretching a point to suggest that in the present context, the consequences of the actions of the American Indian Movement in the 1960s and early 1970s should be noted. Participant Dennis Banks underlines the positive results of the AIM's militant emphasis on Native American pride: 'Before the American Indian Movement, there were more suicides among Indians than any other racial group in the United States. Young people drank themselves to death and sniffed glue. They lived in despair . . . They were ashamed to be Indian . . . At Wounded Knee [the massacre site where hundreds of Sioux women and children had been killed by Custer's Seventh Cavalry, and which was occupied by Native Americans in 1973, precipitating a modern-day 'shootout' in which two Indians were killed] they became warriors again and began feeling good about themselves, feeling good about being Sioux, and Cheyennes, Ojibway, Navajos, Crees, Iroquois, Saultaeux, and Nisquallys . . . after almost one hundred years, they were ghost-dancing again. Even if AIM had not achieved anything else, it would have done its job.'[60]

It is a grim irony, indeed, that the cultures from which Romanticism once drew so much healing inspiration (albeit through the cliché of the 'Noble Savage') and to which Surrealism looked with equal enthusiasm should have suffered so much. Sadly, the same point applies to many other of the cultures from which twentieth-century Western artists have drawn primitivistic inspiration.[61] As I stated in the preface, it has been the purpose of this book to document the shamanic spirit in twentieth-century art from a largely Western-industrial perspective. However, whether from the point of view of either morality or historical accuracy, one would hardly wish to avoid at least some consideration here of recent evidence of the shamanic spirit in the art of what were once known as 'traditional' or 'tribal' cultures.

This is especially the case inasmuch as that art has come to be created in line with Western-style criteria of 'fine' and 'applied' art, and as so-called 'traditional' artists have exercised their right to be as innovative and eclectic in their work as artists of the West have been in theirs. If the Western avant-garde has felt free to be spiritually and technically inspired by the art of non-European cultures, why should those cultures not have the right to repay the compliment? And why should 'traditional' cultures not have the right to borrow freely from each other? (Especially as their understanding of tradition often embraces a far more flexible approach to innovation and cross-cultural exchange than any old-fashioned Western myth of the 'authentic Other' may be prepared to acknowledge. The range of material on Jim Pepper's aforementioned *Comin' and Goin'* recording is a prime example of this.[62])

In the Inuit artist Joseph Senunetuk's 1970 lithograph *Where Goes The Shaman's Spirit?*, which was entered in the Sixth Annual Festival of Native Arts in 1971, ancient ideas and contemporary imagery combine in a sophisticated composition, redolent in parts of early twentieth-century Expressionist prints.[63] The shaman is pictured between the shape-shifting worlds of native cosmology and the flight of a jet aircraft over a modern city: a summarising statement of the problem of what Theodore Roszak has called the secularization of symbols. Discussing the metamorphosis of the ancient dream of flight into the sort of routine that finds the businessman yawning as his flight circles around an airport, queuing for airspace, Roszak asks: 'how *could* so great and ancient a dream turn out to be so trivial? . . . somewhere along the line we have lost touch with the traditional aspiration. We have made it real — materially, historically real — but at the expense of some other, greater reality . . . something that eludes us for all our greater power and cunning.'[64]

The sense of 'some other, greater reality' was very much to the fore within the Inuit sculptures, drawings, stonecuts and stencils which were gathered together in the exhibition, 'The Coming and Going of The Shaman: Eskimo Shamanism and Art', mounted by the Winnipeg Art Gallery, Manitoba in 1978. Using a combination of whale-bone, antler, stone, fur, leather and wood, sculptors such as Elsie Emuk (*b*.1901), Luke Iksiktaaryuk (1909—77), Davidialu Alasua Amittu (1910—76), Karoo Ashevak (1940—74), Thomas Suvaaraq (*b*.1935) and George Arlook (*b*.1949) have created some of the most extraordinary free-standing images of shamanic metamorphosis this century.[65] Stonecuts, stencils and drawings by Agnes Nanogak (*b*.1925) and Simon Tookoome (*b*.1934) are scarcely less impressive. The simplicity of their full frontal and silhouette images strikes exactly the note of pure lyric affirmation which is implicit in such respective titles as *Song* (1975) and *The World of Man and the World of Animals came together in the Shaman* (1973).

For anthropologists and art critics alike, such an exhibition can raise some difficult questions. For example, if shamanism was originally a totalising unity of what much later were to become the separate activities of healing and prayer, music and dance, painting and performance, what exact 'status' or 'power' do such latter-day 'art' pieces have, produced as they were during a period when the traditional shaman's power was in decline?[66] Are they *about* shamanism, as opposed to *being* shamanic? Have these artists succumbed to the lure of Western commodification, negating the once fluid power of shamanism as they turn it into a collectable object?

Such questions lead one to reflect upon the complexity of what one might call the sociology of shamanism today. For these art works can be seen from at least two sociological perspectives. If they demand to be seen

87 Simon Tookoome, Baker
Lake (*b*.1934) *The World of
Man and the World of Animals
Came Together in the Shaman*
1973 coloured pencil on paper.
50.9 x 65.8
Collection of the Winnipeg
Art Gallery. Purchased
through a grant from Petro-
Canada. G-80-240
© the Artist, Sanavik Co-op
Association Ltd
Photograph: Ernest Mayer;
Winnipeg Art Gallery

in terms of the decline of a once-vigorous tradition, they can at the same
time be regarded as potent objects of shamanic transformation and growth.
For, insofar as they have distilled the essence of shamanic experience within
images which can carry far beyond their original context, they have carried
the tradition which informed them into the consciousness of a world sorely
in need of the healing insights of that tradition. The whole thrust of my
argument has been that there is a power in (twentieth-century) art which
can — and should — be seen in the light of shamanic ideas about life. If
creative people from a 'traditional' culture have chosen to express
themselves in the language of 'fine art', one might suggest that a potent
circle has been joined: a circle with a multitude of points of potential
contact and transformation.[67]

Recently, the exact nature of that circle has caused a good deal of debate
in Australia. The shaman-like power of some of the images of such
internationally-fêted Australian artists (of ultimately European background) as Sidney Nolan (*b*.1917) and Arthur Boyd (*b*.1920) has long been
apparent: one thinks of the visionary force of Nolan's *Rimbaud at Harrar*
(1963), or Boyd's *'Figure with rainbow and rain' with artist* (1973), for
example.[68] But it is only relatively recently that the healing, shamanic
import of twentieth-century Aboriginal art has begun to receive due
recognition: art in which questions of modernity and Aboriginality,

cosmos and history, and — not least — primitivism, poetics and politics come into sharp focus.

In 1990 two Aboriginal artists — Rover Thomas (*b*.1926) and Trevor Nickolls (*b*.1949) — were chosen to represent Australia at the Venice Biennale. It was only 23 years earlier that a referendum had been held in Australia, asking white people if constitutional change could be made to allow Aboriginal people to be acknowledged as Australian citizens and be included in the census. On one level, therefore, such a selection of two Aboriginal artists assumes an immense, general symbolic importance. Of equal importance, however, is the fact that the work of these two artists is utterly individual. The spacious qualities of the 'outback' paintings of Rover Thomas resist stereotypical notions of what Aboriginal art should be as surely as do the pointed, crowded and ironic contrasts between 'Dreamtime' and 'Machinetime' which inform so much of Nickolls's work.[69]

One of Thomas's most enigmatic paintings is called *Roads Meeting* (1986). Here, the modern world of motor roads and 'stop' signs seems to transmute itself into a pregnant echo of prehistory. In Nickoll's work, the 'roads which meet' underline the clash between cosmos and history — precisely the clash which so concerned Mircea Eliade. *From Dreamtime 2 Machinetime* (1979), for example, places an animistic, Paradisal sense of cosmos in opposition to the robotic alienation of money-driven history, in the sort of sophisticated, perspectiveless and 'all-over' composition in which one might imagine Joan Miró, Paul Klee, Eduardo Paolozzi or Alan Davie, for example, feeling perfectly at home.

88 Rover Thomas kukaja/Wangajunka (*b*.1926) *Roads Meeting* 1987 natural ochres on canvas 90 x 180 Australian National Gallery, Canberra
© the Artist

In Jennifer Isaacs' recent study *Aboriginality: Contemporary Aboriginal Paintings and Prints*, Nickolls speaks of the marriage of Western culture and Aboriginality in his work, work which he calls 'traditional contemporary'.[70] Isaacs' valuable study includes such diverse artists as Nickolls, Pooaraar, or Bevan Hayward (*b.*1939), Heather Walker (*b.*1942), Jenuarrie, or Judith Warrie (*b.*1944), Raymond Meeks (*b.*1957), Avril Quaill (*b.*1958) and Fiona Foley (*b.*1964). The last-named was one of the founding members of the Boomalli Aboriginal Artists Ko-operative in Sydney, which began in 1987, and of which Avril Quaill is a prominent member: the cooperative is dedicated to developing the cause of urban Aboriginal art, and to breaking down any and all received stereotypes of allegedly 'prehistoric' Aboriginal art. For both Quaill and Foley, the 'Dreamtime' of (so-called) prehistory has lost none of its relevance today: on the contrary, its animistic, holistic approach to life is needed more than ever before. However, they express such wisdom through contemporary, modernist means, where the many issues of the politics of contemporary Aboriginal identity may be addressed through highly lyrical, poetic sensibilities, as in Quaill's *Denis Nueue and Biami Figure at Kuringai Chase, NSW* (1985) or Foley's *Moon Fish* (1988).[71]

Sociological questions about the relation of shamanism and contemporary art from 'traditional' cultures came into similar focus when the C.E. Smith Museum in Hayward, California mounted an exhibition in 1990 entitled 'California Indian Shamanism'. Featuring such artists as Frank Day and Harry Fonseca, Jean LaMarr and Brian Tripp, Dalbert Castro, Frank LaPena and George Blake, the work embraced painting and installation pieces, lithography and watercolours. While the coyote-trickster theme was in plentiful evidence, so was the impact of modernist art ideas. Impressed by the power and emotional variety of the work, as well as by the blend of what the European tradition of art criticism would call 'craft' and 'fine art' pieces, writer Jeanette Ross asked the curator of the show, author and lecturer Carol Morrison, what the relation of artist and shaman meant to her. Morrison, a masters degree graduate in anthropology, replied: 'The shaman, like the artist, looks into the self, into the earth, into the stars and beyond, and brings back something of power.'[72]

Ross then asked whether or not displaying Native American work in a blend of the 'fine art' context of a gallery and traditional anthropological museum — as Morrison had done — was not somehow 'muddying the cultural waters'. Stressing her belief that 'There's no such thing as tribal or ethnic purity — at the boundaries, whether it's between tribes or nationalities in Europe, there are all sorts of mixes' — Morrison's reply emphasised her faith in the transformative powers of both shaman and artist, and the especial relevance of these powers to such an uncertain time as our own: 'The shaman and the artist have taken similar roles. The shaman was often an artist and philosopher, one who saw the big picture. It was the shaman who would recognise the need for something new, could see the need to act out a new idea . . . an artistic expression of an idea . . . The shaman and the artist help us to find strength in change.'[73]

Such a perception of the parallels that exist between the roles of shaman and ('fine art') artist today is given confirmation by the beliefs of Norval Morrisseau, an Ojibway Native American artist and one of the most rewarding painters of recent years, no matter what the context within which one might wish to discuss his work.

Born in 1931 in Thunder Bay, Ontario, Morrisseau was raised by his grandfather, from whom he gained ancestral knowledge of the shamanic traditions of the Ojibway. Such knowledge enabled Morriseau to withstand the effects of the mainstream cultural policies of the time, which forbade the speaking of his native language at school. However, combined with the objections which the elders of his tribe raised, when he announced his intention of making visual 'fine art' statements about the tribe's beliefs, such State cultural suppression led to a period of psychic confusion and traumatisation as Morrisseau moved into young adulthood.

In 1957 he contracted tuberculosis and was sent to a sanatorium at Fort William. While he was there, he had a number of visions, one of which finally gave him the courage of his convictions. An early pen and ink drawing on cheap brown wrapping paper summarises the emergence of his metamorphosing concerns, with lines of power and interspecies communication surrounding such traditional Ojibway animal-spirit helpers as Thunderbird, Sacred Turtle and Sacred Beaver. Technically, Morrisseau's work quickly distinguished itself by its practically total absence of shading, or modelling, his images sitting 'flatly' on the picture plane, handled with an unerring feeling for both primary colours and bold design.

Having had many successful shows of his work, and with his art represented in the national museums, Morrisseau has spoken of his mature identity thus: 'I am a shaman-artist. Traditionally, a shaman's role was to transmit power and the vibrating forces of the spirit through objects known as talismans. In this particular case, a talisman is something that apparently produces effects that are magical and miraculous. My paintings are also icons; that is to say, they are images which help focus on spiritual powers, generated by traditional belief and wisdom. I also regard myself as a kind of spiritual psychologist. I bring together and promote the ultimate harmony of the physical and the spiritual world.'[74]

While Morrisseau has always seen his art as rooted in tradition, he has always wanted to create it in the non-traditional form of paint on canvas, welcoming the opportunity to express himself within the 'fine art' networks of Western art: 'My art speaks and will continue to speak, transcending barriers of nationality, of language and other forces that may be divisive, fortifying the greatness of spirit which has always been the foundation of the Great Ojibway.'[75] In 1989 several of his paintings were shown at the enormous 'Magicians of the Earth' exhibition in Paris. Reminiscent of both the technique and spiritual power of the best stained glass windows, his striking combinations of flat black outlines and saturated colours could be appreciated in such diverse images as *Sacred Bear*, *Artist With Thunderbird Vision* and *The Gift* — the last-named a relatively rare overt political statement, depicting a Christian white man

89 Norval Morrisseau *Joseph With Christ Child and St. John the Baptist* 1973 acrylic on canvas 101.6 x 81.3 Department of Indian and Northern Affairs, Ottawa. © the Artist and Department of Indian and Northern Affairs

bestowing the 'sacred gift' of smallpox on a Native American and his child.[76]

Despite such a critique of Christian hypocrisy, and notwithstanding his determination to be an artist of the Ojibway traditions, Morrisseau has at times used Christian motifs with entirely positive intent in his work. As well as shamanism, his early upbringing exposed him to strong Catholic beliefs. While he has spoken of how Christianity weakened and confused his sense of identity at one stage in his life, and of his preference for the shamanic as opposed to the Christian understanding of personality, especially with regard to sexuality, he has also revealed that, for him, Christ is 'still the greatest shaman'.[77] (One recalls even Nietzsche's deep respect for Christ as a master of inner mysteries.)

In his growth as a shaman-artist, Morrisseau would seem to exemplify Joseph Campbell's ideas concerning the working through of layers of mythology towards the ultimate state of becoming 'transparent to the transcendent'. In *Levels of Consciousness* (1977), for example, circles of intense primary colours surround a profile of the artist's head, as he meditates upon the passage towards the uppermost circle of the soul's development, depicted in white. But at the same time that Morrisseau has painted such rarefied statements about the mysteries of spiritual development, he has also kept faith with more sensuous Ojibway ideas of transformation, sometimes depicting the process of animistic metamorphosis in series of five or six canvases or panels, as in *Man Changing Into Thunderbird* (1977) and *Ancestral Figure With Spiritual Helpers* (1978).

We Are All One (1978) may be taken as representative of the many luminous works where Morrisseau has depicted humanity in spiritual (and decorative) harmony with fish and falcon, bear and moose, raven and loon. In intuitive accord with the mythopoeic heart of such different spiritual traditions as Native American animism and Christianity, Morrisseau has contributed an enormous amount to the shamanic pattern that 'we've never ever had before'.

Where else might the 'rainbow bridge' of the new shamanism be detected? Before answering that question in some further contemporary detail, one should emphasise how long the bridge has been in the making. In a recent article, 'Art in the Age of Ecology', Suzi Gablik reiterated her discontent with what she sees as 'the old schismatic energy of modernism', suggesting that it is high time that that energy gave way to 'a unifying, more healing energy of reconciliation'.[78] Once again I find myself both agreeing and disagreeing with Gablik. For it was precisely the 'schismatic energy' of primitivistic modernism which brought the cosmic, animistic dimension of existence back into Western consciousness this century. If artists in industrial cultures today are to cultivate the kind of art which, as Gablik puts it, 'speaks to the power of connectedness and establishes bonds; art which calls us into relationship',[79] they will do so thanks to — rather than in spite of — the many achievements of the modernist artists whose work we have examined.

That said, there is a plurality of approaches to the making of art now which makes the 'rainbow bridge' of the contemporary shamanic spirit in art considerably more diffuse than was the case thirty or forty years ago. The English painter Jennifer Durrant (b.1942), whose work has a strongly meditative, Taoist quality to it, has said that 'The cry for wholeness in our lives is our attempt to find a way home.'[80] That cry can be heard in many different registers today: and perhaps the best way to begin to appreciate the range of the new shamanic spirit in art is to examine some of the major spiritual, technical and social implications of the different inflections which the idea of 'wholeness' — or 'healing' — has recently acquired in art practice.

In the work of the Dutch painter and graphic artist Anton Heyboer (b.1924) one finds what might be called classic evidence of the 'bohemian theme' of art as a means to shamanic self-healing. In 1943 Heyboer was arrested by the Nazis and made to work in a labour camp in Berlin, where he fell seriously ill. This proved to be a turning point in his life. After the war, partly blind, tubercular and subject to fits of unconsciousness, he broke with his parents, took up drawing landscapes and began a wandering, unemployed existence. For a number of years, he lived a life of near-total isolation, eventually suffering a severe mental crisis, which culminated in his request for admission to the local asylum in Santport. Months later, he gravitated to Amsterdam. After several years of bohemian existence in that city, he moved with his wife Maria to an old farmhouse in Den Ilp, cutting himself off from society once again.

During all this time, Heyboer had worked constantly at his art, primitivising his landscape and animal motifs and developing a curious graphic image or 'system' of crossed lines, numbers and written texts. The crossed lines are Heyboer's own representation of the force-fields of animus and anima, hatred and love, suffering and guilt, creativity and frustration which he has experienced. Interspersed with his stick-like representations of men, women and animals, they project a compulsive, primal power, partly through Heyboer's mastery of a tar and zinc etching technique which uses colours mixed from soil and raw oil.

In recent years, Heyboer has become recognised as one of the Netherlands' finest artists. In fact the painter Pierre Alechinsky, a disciple of the COBRA school, once described Heyboer as 'maybe the most important artist in Northern Europe, someone who succeeds best to visualize new truths. [sic]'[81] As many of Heyboer's gouaches from the mid-1980s make clear, with their variations upon the theme of 'the spirit of crystals taken out of mountains is eternity', those 'new truths' have in fact had much to do with ancient shamanic ideas. 'You can learn to draw

90 Anton Heyboer *The spirit out the mountain cristal gives the honour to the man back* [sic] 1984 gouache on paper 78 x 108 Private collection © courtesy, the Artist and + Contempo + Modern Art Gallery, Eindhoven

in half an hour,' Heyboer has said, 'but the subject that is identical with your feelings is a life's work.'[82] Heyboer's art — which he describes as 'pure expression' — is one of the most moving records in recent years of a soul's journey towards individuation, undertaken at the absolute margins of existence.[83]

A very different approach to the idea of healing through a sort of visual diary-writing informs the work of British photographer Jo Spence. Whereas Heyboer came to his shaman-like perception of the interplay of forces needed for psychic balance from the perspective of a complete 'outsider', Spence's key idea that photography can help people to break free from the stereotypical, alienating 'scripts' of so much family life and social role-playing emerged from what one might call her total immersion in the social realm. *In Putting Myself in The Picture: a Political, Personal and Photographic Autobiography* Spence recounts her development from successful mainstream photographer to critical theorist, revealing how she became 'a completely fanatical workaholic, dedicated only to the struggle to help make the world a "better place". In the process I just about burnt myself out, finally becoming totally confused about who I was actually doing anything for and breaking down, both mentally and physically. When, eventually, I ground to a total halt, I shut myself away for a month and cried incessantly. That same month I was admitted to hospital.'[84]

As Spence says, her body had been giving her warning signals for months, but she had not understood what was being 'said'. Cancer of the breast was diagnosed, and a mastectomy suggested as the only possible cure. Preferring to seek alternative means of healing in traditional Chinese medicine, Spence began to reflect upon the tensions which had built up in her over the years, tensions which she traced back to the seemingly innocuous world of the family photographic album. Here she found evidence of power struggles and thwarted desires, of gender stereotyping and 'false stories'. And so she hit upon the idea of replaying these 'stories', but with her own script — a script that allowed room for gender-breaking roles, for example, and which she could play out with the help of her partner.

Photography thus became one of the chief means of her self-healing, unlocking many of those deeper, unfulfilled aspects of her self which she had long kept from consciousness. And so she recommended that people begin a radical transformation of their approach to the ubiquitous 'snapshot': 'It is there in the high-technology-but-low-cost of amateurism that the future of photography lies for me . . . Initially we could use the camera for a dialogue with ourselves, as in photo-therapy, to de-censorize ourselves . . . Long live amateur photography! Long live the healing arts!' [85]

It may be objected that while such an approach to photography obviously has a good deal to do with healing, that does not necessarily mean that it has anything to do with shamanism. My reply would be that the relation of shamanism to contemporary life takes many forms today. Discussing the application of shamanic ideas in a hospital pain clinic, Frank Lawlis, a professor of psychology, has suggested that 'magic can happen even in modern science, even in the controlled sterility of a hospital. More importantly, however, spirituality can once again be considered as a crucial variable in the healing process.' [86] It seems to me that Spence's work suggests an accessible and valuable way for people to increase their powers of imaginative 'self-visualisation', powers which Lawlis suggests are crucial to the healing process.

We have already remarked the key role which such photographic 'self-visualisation' played in the art of Mary Beth Edelson in the 1970s, as she documented both private and communal Goddess rituals, rituals intended to make ancient shamanic powers new. While Edelson was creating such spectral, figurative photo-pieces as the 1979 *The Nature of Balancing* which, as Edelson puts it, 'evokes shamanic powers and the desire to fly, but settles for balancing on the edge', [87] Marilyn Bridges was flying in a light aircraft over the Nazca lines of southern Peru, photographing their mysterious mixture of spirals and zigzags, birdmen and killer whales. Later, Bridges photographed the Mayan sites at Yucatan and Chiapas, as well as Native American sites in Arizona — including rattlesnake patterns around 165 feet long, believed to have been made by Mojave shamans about two hundred years ago — and the megalithic henges and dolmens of Brittany and southwest England.

The photographs were published in 1986 as *Markings: Aerial Views of Sacred Landscapes*. In her introductory essay, Lucy Lippard contrasted Bridges's sensitivity to the way in which the cosmicity of the earth 'speaks' through these ancient sites with the profane surveillance of the satellite camera. She suggested that in offering us such an extraordinary record of the cosmic dimensions of archaic culture, Bridges had performed a shamanic service: 'Shamans are said to be able to fly. Marilyn Bridges can; she does so "from a witch's distance", as John Szarkowski once put it — as low as 200 feet. In a kind of spiritual surveillance, she "keeps an eye on" those values that our society is in danger of forgetting.'[88]

Bridges herself speaks of the creative process thus: 'There are moments when I seem to have reached beyond everyday experiences and found a balance of emotional, intellectual, spiritual, and physical energies. It is at these times that I feel most creative. Flying lifts me into this state almost immediately.'[89] Recently, the idea of 'spiritual surveillance' has acquired a directly critical edge, as Bridges' attention has shifted from a celebration of the pre-industrial symbiosis of culture and nature to a lamentation of the post-industrial disharmony symbolised by storage tanks and highway interchanges. 'The way man treats the earth is the way man treats himself' says Bridges.[90]

From Heyboer through Spence to Edelson and Bridges, one can thus trace the expansion of both the technology and the 'social field' addressed by artists concerned with seeing their work in holistic terms. The shamanic overtones of this process are particularly evident in recent developments in sculpture. From the Russian Ernst Neizvestny's dream of a massive Tree of Life that would combine the latest technology with ancient ideas of cosmology,[91] to Agnes Denes's planting and harvesting of two acres of wheat on the Battery Park landfill in downtown Manhattan, sculpture has addressed key, pressing questions regarding the need for a transformation of the relations between poetics and politics, transcendence and immanence. 'The new role of the artist is to create art that is more than decoration, commodity or political tool', wrote Denes in 1982, the year she brought two acres of swaying grain to life in the shadow of New York's World Trade Center.[92]

A large part of that role has involved what could be called the resurrection of the body. Multi-media artists like Kjartan Slettemark from Norway, and Helen Chadwick from England, for example, have explored some of the shamanic implications of Chadwick's remark that 'Progress has to be made through self-understanding, self-awareness, but one of the taboos has been an exploration of one's own body. To understand the

91 Helen Chadwick *Of Mutability: The Oval Court* (detail) 1986 mixed media Collection of the Victoria and Albert Museum © courtesy, the Artist Photograph: Edward Woodman

capacity for transcendence through the flesh, one has to move in the face of theory into areas that cannot be comprehended by theory. I want the body to be as much a site of victory as the brain.'[93] Chadwick's intellectually stimulating, 'enfleshing' photo-sculptures and installations draw upon a wide range of both art historical references and photographic techniques. Yet she has described art as 'like crying, an act of self-repair, to shed the natural tears that free us, that make us strong . . .'[94] Intellect and emotion, so often split apart in the West, here come together — as they do in a very different, more confrontational way in the work of Slettemark.

After a series of grotesque facial reliefs in the late-1960s, in which he let streams of chaotic plastic letters run out of open mouths, or glue themselves like ants on long tongues, Slettemark's primitivistic disgust at the hypocrisy of rational linguistic culture manifested itself in a variety of well-planned, yet seemingly spontaneous intrusions into the 'body politic'. In one carnivalesque guise after another, he attacked both the academic abstraction of art institutions and the dogmas of institutionalised religion. Arrested by the police, and risking enforced hospitalisation on more than one occasion, Slettemark's shamanistic provocations 'broke the codes' of both respectably modernist and Pop-oriented Scandinavian art.[95]

Today, Slettemark's actions seem curiously prescient. Paralleling the contemporary 'anti-psychiatry' work of R.D. Laing and David Cooper, they anticipated much of today's performance work, where the (personal) body has become the transformative terrain in which the social script of the 'body politic' is challenged and examined, torn up and 're-written'. The Japanese Butoh dancer and choreographer Isamu Ohsuka has spoken of the fluid mixture of structure and improvisation which helps Butoh dancers to get in touch with 'the internal tiger' that wanders through 'the forest with no name' which lies at the heart of the bodily self. Strongly redolent of shamanism, Ohsuka's image applies as much to post-Beuys performance art as it does to contemporary dance.[96]

In the work of the English sculptor, performer, film maker and writer Brian Catling, for example, what Catling calls 'the inedible thinness' of the 'soapy fictions' of much of today's media-mediated existence is challenged by an art in which the body projects both the palpable strength

92 Brian Catling *Luna Prayer*
Oxford Museum of
Modern Art 1989
© courtesy the Artist and
Oxford Museum of
Modern Art
Photograph: Paddy
Summerfield

93 Steve Dilworth (*b.*1949)
Rook (1982) bog oak, rook and
iron nails 45x18 and *Hooded
Crow* (1990) yew, bog oak,
steel, hooded crow 49x17
Private collection. Featured in
the exhibition 'The
Shamanism of Intent: Some
Flights of Redemption',
Goldmark Gallery,
Uppingham, July-August 1991
© courtesy, the Artist
Photograph: Beka Dilworth

and the ghostly evidence of its longing for transformation.[97] Desiring a
language of substance and metamorphosis, the self bleeds its frustration
into cryptic invocations — both written and performed — of allusive,
shape-shifting power. As the poet and novelist Ian Sinclair has said,
'Wounded in the tongue, Catling insists upon the shaman's right to
stumble, to draw stones from traumatised flesh.'[98]

In 1991 Sinclair helped Michael Goldmark to organise an exhibition
entitled 'The Shamanism of Intent: Some Flights of Redemption' at the
Goldmark Gallery, Uppingham. Bringing together a refreshing variety of
British painters and poets, sculptors and performance artists, novelists and
academics, the exhibition was a potent indication of the extent to which
inter-disciplinary ideas of creativity as a stimulus for psychic growth can
help us to transform our understanding of art.[99] And it is surely high time
that we did this, in the light of the sort of shamanic passion which fired
Sinclair's catalogue essay: 'We have been walking too long in someone
else's sleep. There is a nagging sense — we reward ourselves by insisting
upon it — of having travelled through a dark night of the soul, a sooty
tunnel of indolence and mechanistic frenzy: a tooth-chattering, skull-
rattling dance of the zombies . . .'[100]

Discussing such artists as sculptors Steve Dilworth and Gavin Jones, and
painter Laurence Bicknell, Sinclair spoke of today's 'deregulated
shamanism' — of the fact that the shaman-artist 'without a tribe' is still 'a

nib of energy'.[101] For Mary Beth Edelson, as for Ian Sinclair, it is essential that that energy helps us to rethink the implications of such words as 'spirituality', 'art' and 'politics'. In an interview at the end of the 1980s, Edelson reflected on what the term 'shamanism' had come to mean for her. Her thoughts shed further light on the question upon which we have already touched through consideration of the differing ideas of Starhawk and Brook Medicine Eagle regarding the 'authenticity' of contemporary cross-cultural approaches to shamanism. 'Ultimately,' said Edelson, 'I believe that everyone can have access to primal levels of consciousness and to shamanic experiences. However, how that comes about, as well as a resolution to this question of shamanic authenticity, is no longer self-evident. We need new terms to describe this kind of experience. "Shamanism" suggests indigenous cultures. Nonetheless, when used as a metaphor for healing, direct access to our essential self, and transformation, then I think that it is a well-chosen term.'[102]

As the title of her 1990 travelling retrospective exhibition — *Shape Shifter: Seven Mediums* — made apparent, Edelson developed, throughout the 1980s, the healing implications of her dance-inflected rituals of the 1970s in a rich variety of media. While the sculptural installation piece *Black Spring: Room for New Beginnings* (1989) reflected the trauma of the *Exxon Valdes* oil spill disaster in Alaska, the overall tone of Edelson's paintings and drawings, photo-rituals and texts remains resolutely optimistic. It is an optimism reminiscent of nothing so much as the integrated sensibilities of Meret Oppenheim, and which is rooted in the (ultimately shamanic) conviction which lies behind Edelson's simple, but potent question: 'how else can we proceed without first dreaming of what might be possible?'[103]

Edelson speaks of the 'paradigm shift' that is needed today as never before: a shift from cynicism and fear to commitment and hope; from short-term, exploitative business and politics to holistic thinking, feeling, and action; from the isolated ego to the engaged Self. Her art intimates a metamorphosing dream of wholeness: a dream where critical, analytical and discursive language and 'primal' levels of consciousness and inspiration inform each other; where the destructive legacy of such enduring dualisms as heart and mind, body and soul is finally overcome; where the transcendent flows through the immanent — and where the idea of 'spirituality' only comes to fruition insofar as it helps to connect us 'to one another, to our ecological environment, or to a broader story.'[104]

In this book, I have tried to show something of the 'broader story' of twentieth-century art — a story which has suggested, I hope, just how much the shamanic spirit within that art has to offer us, in terms of Edelson's understanding of the metaphoric import of the term 'shamanism' today. 'Our wounded crippled nature', says Niki de Saint Phalle, another contemporary artist of much shamanic consequence, 'is destroying the universe.'[105] It is my belief that that process will only be halted when we have finally broken free from what Max Weber called the 'iron cage' of secular and rationalist activity, and from one-dimensional fictions-cum-myths of history as the exclusive terrain of our being-in-the-world — the terrain which must be endlessly profaned, as it would appear today, in the name of material progress. It is also my belief that, far from producing 'a heap of broken images', redolent of socio-historical despair and psychic disintegration, twentieth-century artists have laid the essential, multi-dimensional foundations for the 'rainbow bridge' of the new, synthesising consciousness which is so sorely needed today.

Alan Davie has described the shamans of the Lascaux and Les Trois Frères caves as seeking 'the visible sign and sacrament of all that the artist and his people felt to be the inner meaning, the everlasting element in man and in nature, present, past and future.'[106] When the Scottish drummer, composer and improviser Ken Hyder toured the length and breadth of Russia in the spring of 1990, with saxophonist and multi-instrumentalist Tim Hodgkinson, he found that one question came up time and again among audiences who were transfixed by the power of the music which this shamanically-inspired duo played. Expressed in relation to the growing Westernisation of the Soviet Union, that question was: 'Is it possible to become "civilized" yet retain a cultural spirituality?'[107] My

94 Alan Davie at Gamels Studio, Rush Green, Winter 1989
Photograph: © Iain Roy

95 Ken Hyder with Saami shaman drum, at the author's home, Brighton, Spring 1991 Photograph: © M. Tucker

answer would be that, if we do not attend to the everlasting message, or spirit, of shamanism, no civilisation worth the name is possible.

Speaking about the renaissance of classical learning in the twelfth century, Bernard of Chartres is alleged to have remarked that 'We are like dwarves alighted on the shoulders of giants, who see more numerous and distant things not by virtue of their own keen vision or stature, but because they are raised aloft by the giants' enormous height.'[108] Transposing such wise words to our own century, I would speak rather of giants standing on the shoulders of giants: the 'tender-minded' giants of twentieth-century art, who have fought long and hard to build a replenishing vision of existence upon the most ancient and durable of foundations. One of Ken Hyder's most treasured possessions is a Saami shaman's drum, which he acquired one day in a second hand shop in Helsinki: the drum which is both animal and cosmos; earth, underworld and heaven; heart and mind, body and soul. Long may we listen to its rhythms, as we seek to build the rainbow bridge: the bridge of praise and compassion, of wonder, creativity and love.

Notes

CHAPTER ONE

1. *The Letters of Vincent Van Gogh* (ed. Mark Roskill) Fontana/Collins, London 1974 pp. 335 and 286.

2. The word *numinous* (from the latin *numen*, signifying 'divine will' or 'divinity') was used by Rudolf Otto to summarise the experiential qualities of the human perception of the holy. See Otto, R. *The Idea of the Holy* (trans. John Harvey) Oxford University Press, London 1923. Van Gogh (and his brother Theo) managed to sell but a single example of his work. At the time of the great Van Gogh retrospective in Amsterdam in summer 1990, various media sources suggested that Van Gogh reproductions are now the most popular in the world.

3. *Thus Spoke Zarathustra* (trans. R.J. Hollingdale) Penguin, Harmondsworth 1967 p. 46.

4. Shot in the most difficult (sub-zero) conditions, *Pathfinder* is an excellent example of the possibilities of combining 'exoteric' narrative with 'esoteric' mythical qualities in film today. On 'exoteric' and 'esoteric' qualities, see e.g. Chapter 5 below.

5. Lovejoy, A.O. *The Great Chain of Being* Harvard University Press, Cambridge, Massachusetts/ London 1964 (first ed. 1936) investigates the idea as it has developed in Western intellectual history, *vis à vis* e.g. the legacy of the tension between 'otherworldliness' and 'worldliness' which exists in the thought of Plato. On environmental rape, see e.g. Carson, R. *Silent Spring* Penguin, Harmondsworth 1971 (first pub. 1962) and Collard, A. with Contrucci, J. *Rape of the Wild* The Women's Press Ltd, London 1988.

6. *The Great Cosmic Mother: Rediscovering The Religion of The Earth* Harper and Row, San Francisco 1987 and 1991 (second edition); *The Once and Future Goddess* The Aquarian Press, Wellingborough 1990; *The Reflowering of the Goddess* Pergamon Press, New York 1990.

7. Sjöö and Mor 1987 op. cit. p. 362.

8. Ibid. p. 431.

9. See e.g. Goldwater, R. *Primitivism in Modern Art* The Belknap Press of Harvard University Press, Cambridge, Massachusetts/London 1986 (rev ed.) and Bell, M. *Primitivism* Methuen and Co Ltd, London 1972. Duncan Macmillan's 'Magic Pictures' in *Alan Davie: works on paper* Talbot Rice Gallery, The University of Edinburgh/British Council, London 1992, pp. 6—13 supplies an incisive introduction to key aspects of primitivism, from the early eighteenth-century thoughts of the Earl of Shaftesbury, and the impact of tribal designs in Owen Jones' influential *A Grammar of Ornament* of 1856, to the diffusion of ideas in J.G. Frazer's *The Golden Bough* among many twentieth-century thinkers and artists.

10. See Goldwater 1986 op. cit. and Honour, H. *Neo-Classicism* Penguin, Harmondsworth 1975.

11. Goldwater 1986 op. cit. p. 66.

12. Hess, T.B. *Barnett Newman* The Tate Gallery, London 1972 pp. 26-7.

13. See Goldwater 1986 op. cit. The antique has sometimes been misunderstood by those twentieth-century minds which (even after Nietzsche's emphasis on the balance of Apollo and Dionysus in Greek culture) tend to see it through the exclusively Apollonian 'image' created by eighteenth-century neo-classicism.

14. On primitivism in antiquity see Lovejoy, A.O. and Boas, G. *A Documentary History of Primitivism and Related Ideas in Antiquity* Baltimore 1934. Bell 1972 op. cit. contains a good selected bibliography on the idea of primitivism.

15. The relevant texts are Foster, H. 'The "Primitive" Unconscious of Modern Art, or White Skin Black Masks' in his *Recodings: Art, Spectacle, Cultural Politics* Bay Press, Seattle, Washington 1985; Araeen, R. 'From Primitivism to Ethnic Arts' *Third Text* No 1, London Autumn 1987; Price, S. *Primitive Art in Civilized Places* The University of Chicago Press, Chicago and London 1989; Torgovnick, M. *Gone Primitive: Savage Intellects, Modern Lives*

University of Chicago Press, Chicago and
London 1990; Durham, J. 'The Search For
Virginity' in Hiller, S. (ed.) *The Myth of
Primitivism: Perspectives on art* Routledge, London
1991 (which includes Araeen's 1987 article). On
Romanticism and the 'Noble Savage' see
Fairchild, H. N. *The Noble Savage: A Study in
Romantic Naturalism* Russell and Russell, New
York 1961.

16. Torgovnick 1990 op. cit. p. 121.
17. Price 1989 op. cit. p. 43. The responses of
Rubin and Varnedoe to similar criticisms from
Thomas McEvilley can be found in Ferguson,
R., Olander, W., Tucker, M. and Fiss, K. (eds.)
*Discourses: Conversations in Postmodern Art and
Culture* The New Museum of Contemporary
Art, New York/The MIT Press, Cambridge,
Massachusetts and London 1990. In the same
volume, Clifford, J. 'Histories of the Tribal and
the Modern' is also relevant to the present
theme.
18. Torgovnick 1990 op. cit. p. 247.
19. Eliade, M. *Myths, Dreams and Mysteries: The
Encounter Between Contemporary Faiths and Archaic
Reality* (trans. Philip Mairet) The Fontana
Library of Theology and Philosophy/Collins,
London and Glasgow 1972 p. 38. Neither
Eliade nor Campbell is mentioned at all in
Hiller (ed.) 1991 op. cit.
20. Barthes, R. *Mythologies* (trans. Annette Lavers)
Jonathan Cape, London 1972 e.g. 'We reach
here the very principle of myth: it transforms
history into nature.' (p. 129). Locked within
recent social history, Barthes's exclusively
sociological and 'deconstructive' approach to
myth offered little if any illumination of what
one might call the positive 'psychodynamics' of
mythic imagination, such as one finds in the
works of Eliade and Campbell.
21. Kermode, F. *The Sense of an Ending: Studies in
The Theory of Fiction* Oxford University Press,
London, Oxford, New York 1968 p. 39.
22. Sjöö and Mor 1987 op. cit. p. 430.
23. See the discussion of shamanism and modern
art in Chapter 2 below.
24. Orenstein 1990 op. cit. p. 71.
25. Belton, R.J. 'Androgyny: Interview with Meret
Oppenheim' in Caws, M. A., Kuenzli, R. and
Raaberg, G. (eds.) *Surrealism and Women* The
MIT Press, Cambridge, Massachusetts/London
1991 p. 66.
26. Hughes, R. *The Shock of The New* British
Broadcasting Corporation, London 1980 p. 243.

27. Curiger, B. *Meret Oppenheim: Defiance in the Face
of Freedom* Parkett Publishers, Zurich, Frankfurt,
New York/ICA, London 1989 pp. 6-7. The
information about Oppenheim's dreams which
follows below was taken from the ICA London
retrospective, Winter 1989, curated by Ewona
Blazwick and Stuart Morgan. At the time, *Meret
Oppenheim: Dream Diaries* (trans. Shaun
Whiteside) was said to be in preparation for
publication by Polygon, Autumn 1990.
28. Ibid. (Curiger) pp. 83–5.
29. See Chapter 4 below for the phenomenology
and symbolism of shamanism.
30. Curiger 1989 op. cit. p. 87.
31. Interview May 11, 1991, Frederikstad, Norway.
See Chapter 12 below.
32. On Romanticism and the recovery of the sacred
see especially Abrams, M.H. *Natural
Supernaturalism: Tradition and Revolution in
Romantic Literature* Oxford University Press,
London 1971 and Wiedmann, A. *Romantic Roots
in Modern Art* Gresham Books, Old Woking
1979.
33. Ibid. (Wiedmann) p. 9.
34. See Gage, J. *Turner: Rain, Steam and Speed* Allen
Lane The Penguin Press, London 1972 for the
impact of the 'Railway Revolution' on the
English and French Romantics and
Impressionists. In the year that Turner painted
Rain, Steam and Speed (1844) Ruskin asked 'Is
there no nook of English ground secure/From
rash assault?' (p. 28). In contrast, Gage
interprets *Rain, Steam and Speed* as a celebration
of the Railway Age 'with an allegory developed
from the Baroque, and in a style deriving from
a study of Rembrandt.' (p. 65).
35. 'Lost Magic Kingdoms' was the title of an
exhibition which the Scottish sculptor Eduardo
Paolozzi (*b.*1924) arranged at the Museum of
Mankind, London in 1985. The exhibition was
a significant contribution to the whole area of
'primitivism', focussing on the question of the
influence of ethnographic collections on a
Western artist such as Paolozzi. See Paolozzi, E.
Lost Magic Kingdoms British Museum
Publications, London 1985.
36. *The Birth of Tragedy* (trans. Walter Kaufmann)
Vintage Books, New York 1967 p. 136.
37. Goldwater 1986 op. cit. p. 68. As Goldwater
points out 'A whole aesthetic may indeed be
there, but it is not the aesthetic of Gauguin.'
38. *Arp 1889–1966* Cambridge University Press,
Cambridge 1987 p. 65.

39. Ibid. See also Arp *On My Way poetry and essays 1912–1947* Wittenborn, Schultz, Inc, New York 1948 passim.

40. *Hans Richter by Hans Richter* (ed. Cleve Gray) Holt, Rinehart and Winston, New York 1971 p. 101.

41. Ibid. p. 50. Richter would later look not for such dramatic magic, but rather 'the balance between an inner voice and an outer occasion'.

42. Richter, H. *Dada: Art and Anti-Art* Thames and Hudson, London 1966 p. 59.

43. Ibid.

44. Richter 1971 op. cit. p. 180. Richter often spoke of the need for a feeling of ONENESS. Jungian thought would interpret this in terms of the concept of individuation – the growth of the Great, or Cosmic Self. See Chapter 3 below.

45. Quoted in Elsen, A.E. *Origins of Modern Sculpture: Pioneers and Premises* Phaidon, London 1978 p. 152.

46. Quoted in Raillard, G. *Miró: The Masterworks* Bracken Books, London 1989 p. 25.

47. *The Poetics of Reverie: Childhood, Language and the Cosmos* (trans. Daniel Russell) Beacon Press, Boston, Massachusetts 1971 p. 173. While Nash's *We are Making a New World* registered the horror of history, much of the rest of his work has precisely the qualities of reverie which so interested Bachelard, with motifs of dream-charged landscape and flight suggesting a shaman-like quest for poetic transfiguration. See e.g. the discussion of Nash in Lane, J. *The Living Tree: Art and The Sacred* Green Books, Hartland, Bideford 1988 pp. 117-19, which draws specific attention to the shamanic quality of Nash's late work (where sun and moon exist in healing symbolic balance) and Cardinal, R. *The Landscape Vision of Paul Nash* Reaktion Books Ltd. London 1989 passim.

48. *The Psychoanalysis of Fire* (trans. Alan C.M. Ross) Beacon Press, Boston, Massachusetts 1968 p. 110.

49. Castaneda, C. *Journey To Ixtlan: The Lessons of Don Juan* Penguin, Harmondsworth 1987 p. 114.

50. *The Politics of Experience and the Bird of Paradise* Penguin, Harmondsworth 1967 p. 24. See Schell, J. *The Fate of the Earth* Picador/Pan Books Ltd, London 1982 for the transmutation of such a statistic into the potential nightmare of nuclear catastrophe. Unfortunately, Schell's impassioned argument for (non-nuclear) sanity includes several somewhat misleading paragraphs on artistic developments this century: he is much less hopeful than Laing about the potentially healing power of art. See pp. 162–5.

51. Ibid. (Laing) p. 38.

52. See Chapter 3 below.

53. *Concerning The Spiritual in Art* (trans. M.T.H. Sadler) Dover, New York 1977 p. 2.

54. Ibid. pp. 1–2.

55. 'The Historical Roots of Our Ecological Crisis', *Science* 1967 pp. 1203–7. For an introduction to Saint Francis and his place in the history of Western thought, see Stock, D. and Cunningham, L. *Saint Francis of Assisi* Scala/Harper and Row, San Francisco 1981.

56. See Freund, J. *The Sociology of Max Weber* Allen Lane The Penguin Press, London 1968 pp. 167–217. On different interpretations of time see e.g. Frazer, J. (ed.) *The Voices of Time* Allen Lane The Penguin Press, London 1968.

57. 'A conversation with Mircea Eliade' *Encounter*, London Vol LIV No 3 pp. 21–7.

58. Ibid. The English anthropologist Sir Edward Tyler (1832–1917) applied the term 'animism' (after the Latin *anima*: soul) to the earliest phases of magical and religious thought. In these phases, according to Tyler, soul and/or spirit inhere in all things, not just humanity. See Chapter 4 below.

59. Walther, I.F. and Metzger, R. *Marc Chagall* (trans. Michael Hulse) Taschen, Cologne 1987 pp. 22-4 and Roditi, E. *Dialogues on Art* Ross-Erikson, Santa Barbara 1980 p. 19.

60. See Neumann, E. *Art and The Creative Unconscious* (trans. Ralph Mannheim) Harper Torchbooks/The Bollingen Library, Harper and Row Publishers, New York 1966 passim (on *participation mystique*) and Cazeneuve, J. *Lucien Lévy-Bruhl* (trans. Peter Riviere), Basil Blackwell, Oxford 1972. Radin, P. *Primitive Man as Philosopher* Dover Publications, New York 1957 (first ed. 1927) offers a critique of Lévy-Bruhl's concept of the 'prelogical' mind, and documents the differences between the 'active' and 'thinking' (reflective-religious) mind in 'primitive' culture. The book is an extraordinary account of the richness and variety of so-called 'primitive' thought. Lévi-Strauss, C. *The Savage Mind*, Weidenfeld and Nicolson, London 1972 explores 'the science of the concrete' in tribal thought from a more theoretical (structuralist) perspective, thus increasing further our sense of the complexity of what Lévy-Bruhl had called 'pre-literate mentality'. Lévy-Bruhl's ideas of

primitive *participation mystique* can be traced in
his writings from *c.*1910 to the 1927 *L'Âme
primitive.* By the time of his (posthumously
published) *Carnets,* Lévy-Bruhl had abandoned
his earlier distinction between the (mystical)
primitive mind and others: '. . . let us expressly
rectify what I believed correct in 1910: there is
not a primitive mentality distinguishable from
the other by *two* characteristics which are
peculiar to it (mystical and prelogical). There is
a mystical mentality which is more marked and
more easily observable among "primitive
peoples" than in our societies, but it is present
in every human mind.' Cazeneuve 1972 op. cit.
p. 87. This is in close accord with the views of
Joseph Campbell concerning the 'tender-
minded', mystically-oriented personality which
is as evident in twentieth-century art as it is in
prehistoric shamanism: see Chapter 2 below.

61. Neumann 1966 op. cit. p. 125.
62. Argüelles, J.A. *The Transformative Vision*
    Shambhala, Berkeley 1975 p. 277.
63. See Davenport, D. and Jochim, M.A. 'The
    Scene in the shaft at Lascaux', *Antiquity* 62,
    1988 pp. 558—62 for detailed analysis and
    interpretation of the shaman/bird motif. Lewin,
    R. 'Stone Age psychedelia' *New Scientist* Vol.
    130 No. 1772 June 8 1991 pp. 30—4 documents
    recent research into the enigmatic (non-
    naturalistic) mark-making of the prehistoric
    caves which was mentioned in the Preface
    above. On the basis of comparisons with
    southern African prehistoric rock art, and
    developing a neuropsychological model of
    interpretation, researchers David Lewis-Williams
    and Thomas Dowson have suggested that the
    (non-naturalistic) marks at Lascaux were the
    result of shamanic hallucinations. See also
    Cardinal, R. 'The Primitive Scratch' in Gilroy,
    A. and Dalley, T. (eds.) *Pictures At An Exhibition:
    Selected Essays on Art and Art Therapy*
    Tavistock/Routledge, London 1989, pp. 113-26.
64. *Prehistoric Painting: Lascaux or The Birth of Art*
    Albert Skira, Geneva/Macmillan, London 1980
    p. 50. See Campbell, J. *The Way Of The Animal
    Powers. Historical Atlas Of World Mythology* Vol 1
    Times Books Ltd, London 1984 passim for the
    Paleolithic 'world-view'.
65. *The Shaman's Doorway* Station Hill Press,
    Barrytown, New York 1988 (second edition)
    p. ix.
66. Ibid.
67. Arguelles 1975 op. cit. p. 99.
68. See Frascina, F. and Harrison, C. (eds.) *Modern
    Art and Modernism: A Critical Anthology* Paul
    Chapman/The Open University, London 1988
    passim.
69. Gablik, S. *Has Modernism Failed?* Thames and
    Hudson, London 1985 passim.
70. See e.g. Fuller, P. *Beyond the Crisis in Art,*
    Writers and Readers, London 1980. Fuller's
    worthy emphasis on the values of the British
    Romantic landscape tradition sometimes
    threatened to become little more than the other
    side of the unnecessarily cheap — and often
    unreal — coin which he fashioned out of the
    internationalism of modern art for his own
    didactic purposes. For example, Joseph Beuys —
    an artist much concerned with bringing
    Romanticism's dreams of a magical universe
    alive in the late twentieth century — was crudely
    dismissed by Fuller as 'that low charlatan'
    (p. 17). A good deal of Fuller's criticism was on
    a higher plane than this. However, one must
    ask to what extent his approach to questions of
    the spiritual in art might have been broadened
    by an awareness of e.g. the works of Bachelard
    or Eliade, neither of whom seems to have
    featured in the development of his ideas. See the
    discussion of Fuller's approach to Cecil Collins
    in Chapter 5 below.
71. Gablik 1985 op. cit. pp. 92—3 and 124.
72. Ibid. p. 94.
73. Capra, F. *The Tao of Physics*, Flamingo/Fontana,
    London 1981. See also Willis, B. *The Tao of Art:
    The inner meaning of Chinese Art and Philosophy*
    Century/Hutchinson, London 1987.
74. Peppiatt, M. 'The Soul Revealed by the Hand:
    An Interview with Antoni Tàpies' *Art
    International* 13, Winter 1990 p. 34.
75. Ibid. p. 35.
76. Ibid. See also Waddington, C.H. *Behind
    Appearance: A study of the relations between painting
    and the natural sciences this century* Edinburgh
    University Press, Edinburgh 1968.
77. See Davenport, G. 'The Symbol of the Archaic'
    in (Davenport) *The Geography of The Imagination*
    Picador/Pan Books, London 1984 for an
    excellent discussion of the primitivistic
    Renaissance of the twentieth century. Davenport
    suggests that the 'discovery, or invention, of the
    archaic is as splendid a donation as that of
    Hellenism to the Renaissance' (p. 28). While he
    makes the astute point that 'The heart of the
    modern taste for the archaic is precisely the
    opposite of the Romantic feeling for ruins'

(p. 22), Davenport mentions neither Eliade's theme of the return of cosmic religion nor the idea of the modern artist as shaman.

78. Sleevenotes to his recording *Spirits*, recorded 1985 and released 1986 on ECM 1133/34. Jarrett's work is discussed in Chapter 8 below.

79. *Changeless* (ECM 1392), recorded in 1987 and released in 1989.

80. Rowell, M. (ed.) *Joan Miró: Selected Writings and Interviews* Thames and Hudson, London 1987 p. 166.

81. 'Graphism' is a term used by the French poet Jacques Dupin in his outstanding 1961 monograph on Miró. See Chapter 11 below and Cardinal 1989 op. cit. ('The Primitive Scratch').

82. Bonnefoy, Y. *Miró* Faber and Faber, London 1967 pp. 27–8 (first edition 1964).

83. *Down Beat*, September 29, 1960 p. 27.

84. See Cole, B. *John Coltrane* Schirmer Books/Macmillan, New York/Canada 1978 pp. 11 and 160 and Chapter 8 below.

85. Simpkins, C.O. *Coltrane A Biography* Herndon House, New York 1975 p. 160.

86. Castaneda, C. *A Separate Reality* Penguin, Harmondsworth 1986 pp. 174 and 258.

87. Castaneda, C. *The Teachings of Don Juan: a Yaqui way of knowledge* Ballantine Books, New York 1973 p. 106; Castaneda 1987 op. cit. pp. 13 and 108.

CHAPTER TWO

1. See McLellan, D. (ed.) *Karl Marx Early Texts* Basil Blackwell, Oxford 1971 pp. 130–83 and Masterson, P. *Atheism and Alienation: A Study of the Philosophical Sources of Contemporary Atheism* Gill and Macmillan, Dublin/Macmillan, London 1971 (for e.g. the key relations between the Marxist concept of alienation and the earlier ideas of Hegel and Feuerbach). On alienation and language, see e.g. Collard and Contrucci 1988 op. cit. pp. 5–7 and passim for the contrast between the holistic speech of Native American (cultural) existence and the exploitative abstractions of much of the language of (patriarchal) industrial culture.

2. See MacIntyre, A. *Marxism and Christianity* Gerald Duckworth, London 1972 and Bentley, J. *Between Marx and Christ: The Dialogue in German-Speaking Europe 1870–1970* Verso, London 1982. For a succinct philosophical critique of Marxism, see Turner, D. *On The Philosophy of Karl Marx* Scepter Books, Dublin 1968.

3. By 'predating history' I mean predating consciousness of (linear) history in the sense in which we ordinarily take the term in the West. The origins of art remain a moot point: did the impulse to sing or make a mark predate (or even cause) the impulse to worship or propitiate the powers of life? Was art a product of exclusively collective, social forces? If so, what was the genesis and role of the visionary shamanic experience? Fischer, E. *The Necessity of Art: A Marxist Approach* Penguin, Harmondsworth 1963 (Chapter 2 'The Origins Of Art') is a socially-oriented but broad-minded approach to such questions. It takes an exceptional Marxist to suggest, as Fischer does here, that 'In every poet there is a longing for an original, "magic" language.' (p. 27) See Chapter 7 below.

4. See Lukács, G. *The Theory of The Novel* (trans. Anna Bostock) Merlin Press, London 1971 and *History and Class Consciousness: Studies in Marxist Dialectics* (trans. Rodney Livingstone) Merlin Press, London 1971.

5. Lukács, G. *Studies in European Realism* Grosset and Dunlap, New York 1964 pp. 1–19. Quoted in Girvetz, H. and Ross, R. (eds.) *Literature and The Arts: The Moral Issues* Wadsworth Publishing Company, Belmont 1971 p. 108.

6. Taylor, B. *Modernism, Post-Modernism, Realism* Winchester School of Art Press, Winchester 1987 p. 154.

7. Wolff, J. *The Social Production of Art* MacMillan, London 1981 p. 1.

8. Ibid. p. 7. A more complex approach informs Wolff's earlier *Hermeneutic Philosophy and The Sociology of Art* Routledge and Kegan Paul, London 1975.

9. See Aron, R. *The Opium of the Intellectuals* Secker and Warburg, London 1957; Turner 1968 op. cit. and Leff, G. *The Tyranny of Concepts: a Critique of Marxism* The Merlin Press, London 1961.

10. Quoted in Abrams 1971 op. cit. p. 276. Compare the emphasis on the relation of creation and joy to the Infinite in the Chandogya Upanishad: *The Upanishads* (trans. Juan Mascaró) Penguin Books, Harmondsworth 1988 pp. 119–20. Weisberg, R.W. *Creativity: Genius and Other Myths* W.H. Freeman and Company, New York 1986 furnishes a sustained critique of the idea of genius, stressing an 'incremental' (rather than 'God-given' or 'mysterious') approach to questions of

'problem-solving' in creativity, as well as underlining the importance of society's reaction to the work of artists in determining whether that work be judged the product of 'genius' or not. While Weisberg draws attention to Freudian theories of the unconscious, he does not mention Jung at all. It is precisely within the Jungian concept of individuation that one is able to explore the links of 'genius' (i.e. spirit) which exist between archetypal shamanic approaches to the import of creativity and the aims of much Romantic and post-Romantic art. For a comparison of Freudian and Jungian approaches to creativity, see Chapter 4 below.

11. Quoted in Price 1989 op. cit. p. 19 from Bourdieu, P. *La Distinction: Critique sociale du jugement* Les Editions de Minuit, Paris 1979.

12. Ibid. (Price) pp. 18–19. Quoted from Bourdieu, P., Darbel, A. and Schnapper, D. *L'Amour de l'art: Les musées d'art européens et leur public* Editions de Minuit, Paris 1969. See Januszczak, W. 'Art in the godless world' *New Statesman* 14 August 1987, pp. 22–4 for an 'agnostic' reaction to the fact that 'The art gallery has replaced the church as the public building *par excellence* of our times'.

13. See Malraux, A. *Museum Without Walls* (trans. Stuart Gilbert and Francis Price), Secker and Warburg, London 1967 pp. 239–40 and *André Malraux* Fondation Maeght, Saint-Paul 1973 passim. On shamanic themes in Malraux's novels, see Mary Ann Frese Witt 'Malraux's Shamanism: Initiatory Death and Rebirth' in Thompson, B. and Viggiani, C.A. (eds.) *Witnessing André Malraux: Visions and Re-Visions* Wesleyan University Press, Middletown, Connecticut 1984 pp.169–78.

14. Neumann 1966 op. cit. pp. 128–9.

15. Howell, S. 'Art and Meaning' in Hiller (ed.) 1991 op. cit. p. 236.

16. Ibid. p. 228.

17. See the discussion of myth by Campbell below and Chapter 5 passim. Howell's article makes for some interesting, provocative reading, including e.g. a revealing consideration of the changing, Western-inflected 'social facts' of cultural production among the Jah Hut people of the Malay Peninsula. However, the conscious avoidance of a psychological dimension considerably weakens the possibility of Howell's approaching the (fresh and ancient) meanings which might be discerned in the world-wide cross-cultural flow of images and artefacts today. I am sympathetic to Howell's wish to qualify or contradict some of the biologically-based claims which have recently been advanced in support of a 'universalism' of aesthetic response. However, I am not convinced that citing a Chinese secretary's view of Henry Moore in 1986 — 'What are these strange bodies? I am frightened. I do not like these things. Why they have holes where their stomachs should be? Is not possible to tell what they are meant to be doing. Is most confusing. Bad statues. Mr. Moore bad man.' — tells us anything very significant (p. 227). Moore's work had long been subjected to similar criticism from within his own culture: it is possible to argue that the 'bodily knowledge' in Moore's work which psychoanalysts and critics like Eric Neumann and Peter Fuller have spoken of in 'universalist' terms is a potential, esoteric knowledge, hidden within layers of exoteric conditioning. But Howell displays a resolute antipathy to any such attempt to go beyond the realm of the local 'social fact'.

18. According to the late Michel Foucault, 'The researches of psychoanalysis, of linguistics, of anthropology, have "decentred" the subject in relation to the laws of its desire, the forms of its language, the rules of its actions, or the play of its mythical and imaginative discourse.' *The Archaeology of Knowledge* quoted in Sturrock, J. (ed.) *Structuralism and Since: From Lévi-Strauss to Derrida* Opus/Oxford University Press 1979 p. 174. If this were a 'shamanic decentring' (see Chapter 4 below) one might expect evidence of the self's eventual breakthrough to at least some sense of what Jungians call individuation i.e. a deep sense of 'centring'. Why should this not be possible in our so-called post-modern world? We might begin to learn from the enormous achievements of the world's cultures, expanding our 'decentred' sense of self in an entirely positive sense. However, the 'decentring' of much post-modernism is often more reminiscent of a regression to primary narcissism. For example, the 'desert' which so fascinated the French post-structuralist sociologist Jean Baudrillard in his 1986 study *America* is not the transformative desert of Georgia O'Keeffe or Don Juan and Carlos Castaneda. It is, rather, the deathly desert of Baudrillard's solipsism. Unwilling or unable to pursue any of the implications of the diverse

historical realities contained within the concept of 'America', Baudrillard collapses what one might call immense historical landscapes of desire into such stunningly banal comments as 'Why do people live in New York? There is no relation between them. Except for an inner electricity which results from the simple fact of their being crowded together.' Rather than learn about, or pass on anything of the rich heritage of African-American culture — which is one very good reason why people might choose to live in New York — Baudrillard prefers to tell us of 'The beauty of the Black and Puerto Rican women of New York . . . [for] . . . it must be said that black, the pigmentation of the dark races, is like a natural make up that is set off by the artificial kind to produce a beauty which is not sexual, but sublime and animal — a beauty which the pale faces so desperately lack.' *America* (trans. Chris Turner) Verso, London 1988 pp. 15—6. Clearly, the 'decentred' post-modern mind has come a long way since the days of de Tocqueville and dances at Congo Square. See 'Jean Baudrillard: America' in Hughes, R. *Nothing if Not Critical* Harvill/HarperCollins, London 1991.

19. For an introduction to questions of language and art this century, see Vaizey, M. 'Art Language' in Michaels, L. and Ricks, C. (eds.) *The State of the Language* University of California Press, Berkeley, Boston and London 1980 pp. 331—42. In querying the relation between discursive or analytical language and art, it is not my intention, of course, to suggest any grossly misleading stereotype of the mindless artist who is either unable or unwilling to think and/or write about art, anymore than it is my intention to deny that art takes on meaning(s) within a social context. I am suggesting, rather, that discursive and/or analytical language functions well when it becomes aware of its limitations; and that within a social context, it should be possible for people to acknowledge that the social construction of reality contains signifying systems (such as art) which may well speak of more than that reality — of dimensions of experience which cannot be completely 'translated' back into either discursive or analytical language.

20. *Real Presences. Is there anything in what we say?* Faber and Faber, London 1989 p. 222.

21. *The Arts Without Mystery* British Broadcasting Corporation, London 1983 p. 96.

22. *The Quest: History and Meaning in Religion* University of Chicago Press, Chicago and London 1975 Preface (unpaginated).

23. Quoted in Lambert, J-C. *Abstract Painting* (trans. Anne J. Cope) Heron Books, London 1970 p. 121.

24. Lévi-Strauss 1972 op. cit. p. 257. Chapter 9 'History And Dialectic' is an incisive examination of the key question of the 'coding' of historical dates i.e. the impact which an event has within a framework of days is obviously different than it would be were it to be placed within a framework of decades or centuries or (as is the case with prehistory) tens of thousands of years. Lévi-Strauss argues that the writing of history (particularly from the committed, left-wing humanist viewpoint of someone like Jean-Paul Sartre, with whose ideas Lévi-Strauss here took issue) is often irrational in the way it which it switches between these various frameworks. On the 'detritus' of history (compared to the 'steady-state' nature of tribal society) see Charbonnier, G. *Conversations with Claude Lévi-Strauss* Jonathan Cape, London 1970 Chapter 3 'Clocks and Steam Engines'.

25. Chambers, E. *History And Identity: Seven Painters* Norwich Gallery, Norfolk Institute of Art and Design 1991 and Niatum, D. (ed.) *Anthology of Twentieth Century Native American Poetry* Harper and Row, San Francisco 1988 (see e.g. 'Taku Skanskan' by Paula Gunn Allen (b.1939), with its Lakota meditation on God and history, on 'horsebreath, mybreath, earthbreath/skybreathing air. ing.' pp. 119—20). Aspects of the aesthetic and spiritual beliefs of editor Duane Niatum are discussed in Chapter 12 below.

26. Buber, M. *I and Thou* (trans. Ronald Gregor Smith) T. and T. Clark, Edinburgh 1970.

27. *Shelley's Mythmaking* Ithaca 1969. See also Bellquist, J.E. 'On Myth and Myth-making in Strindberg' *Scandinavica* Vol 23 No 1 May 1984.

28. 'Det essentielle er det du ikke kan si noe om': Jan Garbarek interviewed by Bjørn Stendahl, *Jazznytt* No 3 1984 (Norway) (this trans. M. Tucker).

29. Quoted in Golding, J. 'Braque And The Space Of Still Life' *Braque: Still Lifes and Interiors* The South Bank Centre, London 1990 p. 26 (source Richardson, J. *Georges Braque* Penguin, Harmondsworth 1959). See Chapter 7 below for a different perspective on the power of words.

30. Ibid. p. 18.

31. Ibid. p. 26.

32. This extraordinary painting was exhibited (and reproduced) for the first time as part of the 1990 South Bank Centre Touring Show *Braque: Still Lifes And Interiors* (see p. 55 of catalogue for colour reproduction).

33. 'Mystery and Creation' (1913) in Chipp, H. B. (ed.) *Theories of Modern Art* University of California Press, Berkeley, Los Angeles and London 1968 p. 402.

34. Waddington 1968 op. cit. p. 61 considers that de Chirico is here painting 'the poetry of romantic intuitive man constrained to live in a world of which he can understand only the mechanical aspects.' But theosophical (and other) ideas concerning the esoteric/spiritual nature of geometry (e.g. Plato: 'God geometrizes'; St Augustine's cardinal concept of God as 'a circle whose centre is everywhere, and circumference nowhere') were in circulation in avant-garde circles of European art at this time, and may have had an influence on this picture. See Tuchmann, M. (ed.) *The Spiritual in Art: Abstract Painting 1890–1985* Los Angeles County Museum of Art/Abbeville Press, New York 1986 pp. 17–87 and passim. Whatever its levels of meaning, *Seer* makes an interesting comparison with the later blackboard demonstrations of Joseph Beuys, an artist much influenced by occult ideas. See Chapter 10 below.

35. Chipp 1968 op. cit. p. 401.

36. Richter 1971 op. cit. p. 94.

37. Gray, C. (ed.) *David Smith by David Smith: Sculpture and Writings* Thames and Hudson, London 1988 p. 166.

38. Ibid. p. 137.

39. ' "The Secret Letter": Interview with Thomas B. Hess' in Merkert, J. (ed.) *David Smith Sculpture and Drawings* Prestel-Verlag Munich 1986 p. 164.

40. Gray 1988 op. cit. p. 137.

41. 'An Open Letter to an Art Critic' (1959) *Artforum* 11 (December 1963). Quoted in Cox, A. *Art-as-Politics: The Abstract Expressionist Avant-Garde and Society* UMI Research Press, Ann Arbor, Michigan 1982 p. 54.

42. *Clyfford Still* San Francisco Museum of Modern Art, San Francisco 1976 pp. 110–11.

43. Eliade, M. *Birth and Rebirth: The Religious Meanings of Initiation in Human Culture* Harper and Row Publishers, New York 1958 pp. 77-8.

On various intrepretations of religious experience from the point of view of individual psychology see James, W. *The Varieties of Religious Experience* The Fontana Library/Collins, London and Glasgow 1971. (First delivered as the Gifford Lectures in Edinburgh, 1901–2.) Discussing mysticism, James observes that 'Music gives us ontological messages which non-musical criticism is unable to contradict, though it may laugh at our foolishness in minding them. There is a verge of the mind which these things haunt; and whispers therefrom mingle with the operations of our understanding, even as the waters of the infinite ocean send their waves to break among the pebbles that lie upon our shores.' (p. 406). Joseph Campbell's term 'tender-minded' came from James, but Campbell gave it his own meaning.

44. Bancroft, A. *Origins of The Sacred: The Spiritual Journey in Western Tradition* Arkana/Routledge and Kegan Paul, London 1987 p. 30.

45. Campbell, J. *The Masks of God* Vol 1 *Primitive Mythology* Penguin, Harmondsworth 1982 p. 253.

46. Ibid. p. 263.

47. Ibid. p. 264.

48. Ibid. p. 471.

49. Ibid.

50. Of course, the shaman also encouraged people to dream with their eyes closed. Reflection on the various dimensions of shamanic vision may contribute much to the familiar debate about the 'meaning' (or otherwise) of abstract art. For example, one might imagine using the information about the Lascaux Cave in Chapter 1 note 63 to counter the criticisms which Claude Lévi-Strauss has made of the communicative capacities of abstract art (see Chapter 3 below).

51. Tery, S. 'Painting Is Not Done To Decorate Apartments' in Cooper, E.C. (ed.) *Picasso's Guernica* W.W. Norton and Company, New York and London 1988 pp. 152–3.

52. Ibid. passim. See Tankard, A.D. *Picasso's Guernica after Rubens's Horrors of War* Art Alliance Press, Philadelphia/Associated University Presses, London and Toronto 1984 for a thorough iconographic, stylistic and compositional comparison of these two paintings – plus a Freudian psychoanalytical interpretation which (in my view) does much to reveal the reductive nature of Freudian thought

e.g. p. 76 'I propose that the dove of peace which Picasso has made his symbol [after World War Two] and which has been said to fly over half the world is the phallic pigeon which he wrested from his father in the Oedipal conflict and that Picasso flaunts it as a symbol of his victory over the castration of his father . . .' (p. 99); 'Fish have the same time-honoured [sexual] symbolism as birds . . .' etc. See Chapter 4 below for a comparison of Freudian and Jungian approaches to art, in terms of shamanic ideas of creativity.

53. Lackner, S. *Max Beckmann* Harry N. Abrams, New York 1977 p. 15.

54. See Hart, C. *Images of Flight* University of California Press, Berkeley, Los Angeles, London 1988 pp. 241—43 for discussion of the winged siren/flying fish motif from the perspective of Christian iconography, where 'The promise of sensual flight is illusory and can lead only to unhappy communion with the earth.' There is a good deal of this feeling in Beckmann's image, which may well have been inspired by medieval representations of the Last Judgement (Lackner 1977 op. cit. p. 122.) However, more positive interpretations are also possible. Like Picasso's *The Three Dancers* of 1925 (discussed in Chapter 5 below) Beckmann's extraordinary image can be seen as a compellingly honest depiction of the struggle which the self may have to experience in its development towards what Jungian thought calls individuation (see Chapter 3 below).

55. Lackner 1977 op. cit. p. 116.

56. Ibid.

57. Quoted from 'Introduction' to *Art Language* May 1969 in Vaizey 1980 op. cit. p. 342.

58. Cousineau, P. (ed.) *The Hero's Journey: Joseph Campbell on his Life and Work* Harper and Row, San Francisco 1990 p. 40. Campbell took this expression from the twentieth-century German psychologist Karlfreid Graf Durkheim. According to Campbell, Durkheim thought that the whole problem of life is to become 'transparent to transcendence', to be able to live the divine life within oneself, 'not as the final term but as a vehicle of consciousness and life' (ibid.). Durkheim's phrase led Campbell to define myth as 'a metaphor transparent to transcendence' (ibid.). See Chapter Five below.

59. Milner, M. *On Not Being Able to Paint* Heinemann Educational Books, London 1987 pp. 95—105 and 164—5.

60. Marcuse, H. *The Aesthetic Dimension: Toward a Critique of Marxist Aesthetics* Papermac/Macmillan, London 1978 p. 72. Marcuse believed that 'The institutions of a socialist society, even in their most democratic form, could never resolve all the conflicts between the universal and the particular, between human beings and nature, between individual and individual' (pp. 71—2). This does not mean, of course, that Marcuse was not committed to the idea of a thorough (but non-totalitarian) critique of capitalist society. Similarly, the various critiques of the ideologies of 'H'istory and 'P'rogress in the present book should not be taken to imply any rationalisation of class structures and inequality.

CHAPTER THREE

1. *Shaman: The Paintings of Susan Seddon Boulet* Pomegranate Artbooks, San Francisco 1989; Lauck, M.S. and Koff-Chaplin, D. *At The Pool of Wonder: Dreams and Visions of an Awakening Humanity* Bear and Company, Santa Fe 1989.

2. I am grateful to Eric Shanes for drawing my attention to this picture, which is in the ownership of Doris and Charles Saatchi, London. See Pradel, J-L (ed.) *World Art Trends 1983/4* Harry N. Abrams, New York 1984 p. 125 for colour reproduction.

3. Kendall, R. (ed.) *Cézanne by himself* Macdonald Orbis, London 1988 p. 305 (original source Gasquet, J. *Cézanne*). The classical side of Cézanne is summarised in his famous remark about imagining 'Poussin redone entirely from nature' while his Romanticism is evident in his enthusiasm for both Delacroix and the Old Master colourists of the Venetian school. Ibid. pp. 308—9. As a 'composer' Cézanne was able to synthesise and transmute classical and Romantic qualities of structure and colour to animistic effect. His later paintings in particular are uncannily — one might say mesmerically — 'alive'. Cézanne himself believed that 'Colour is alive, it alone can convey living things' ibid. p. 305.

4. Johnson, R.A. *Ecstasy: Understanding The Psychology of Joy* Harper and Row, San Francisco 1989 p. 12. Johnson tells us how the Greek god Dionysus was thrice born from his mother's mortal womb, his immortal father's thigh and the wisdom of the earth, represented by his grandmother. He lived a life of shape-shifting,

poetic intoxication, accompanied by the wildly dancing female Maenads ('last devotees of the Great Goddess') and nature spirits. Dionysus's qualities of *participation mystique* distinguish him from the rest of the Olympian pantheon, whose forms are fixed in their idealised, deathless aloofness. For Johnson, 'To worship Dionysus is to worship the life force' (p. 34). See Chapter 4 note 36 and the discussion of the Great Goddess in Chapter 10 below.

5. Ibid p. 12.

6. Ibid.

7. Rilke, R.M. *Letters on Cézanne* (ed. Clara Rilke, trans. Joel Agee) Jonathan Cape, London 1988 p. 80. The remark was occasioned by Cézanne's *Madame Cézanne In a Red Armchair* of *c.*1877, but it applies with equal force to the landscapes and portraits of Cézanne's later years.

8. See e.g. Cézanne's description of the Mont Ste Victoire in Kendall 1988 op. cit. p. 303: 'What *élan*, what an imperious thirsting after the sun, and what melancholy, of an evening, when all this weightiness falls back to earth . . . These masses were made of fire. Fire is in them still.' In an essay on Cézanne which he wrote in 1929, D.H. Lawrence praised the painter for capturing 'the mysterious *shiftiness*' of landscape: 'it is *not* still. It has its own weird anima, and to our wide-eyed perception it changes like a living animal under our gaze. This is a quality that Cézanne got marvellously.' 'Introduction to His Paintings' in (Lawrence) *Selected Essays* Penguin, Harmondsworth 1968 p. 342.

9. Rilke 1988 op. cit. p. 74.

10. Bell, C. *Art* Perigee Books, New York 1981 p. 139. Compare Cézanne's own feeling that he was far more traditional than people thought — a remark that confirms Bell's understanding of 'significant form' as resurrecting ancient qualities of both spirituality and 'design': Kendall 1988 op. cit. p. 305.

11. Ibid. (Bell) p. 17.

12. A point which left-wing criticism is sometimes keen to make about the Bloomsbury/Charleston aesthetic of the decorative arts which grew out of the Cézanne-influenced ideas of Bell and the English critic and painter Roger Fry. The latter's *Vision And Design* Oxford University Press, London 1981 (first ed. 1920) both develops and qualifies Bell's idea of significant form. See Watney, S. 'The Connoisseur as Gourmet' in Formations Editorial Collective *Formations of Pleasure* Routledge and Kegan Paul, London 1983 and the defence of Fry in Spalding, F. 'Roger Fry and his Critics in a Post-modernist Age' *The Burlington Magazine* July 1986 No 1000.

13. Baktair, L. *Sufi: Expressions Of The Mystic Quest* Thames and Hudson, London 1979 p. 110 (quoting Ardalan, N. and Baktiar, L. *The Sense of Unity: The Sufi Tradition in Persian Architecture*).

14. Bell 1981 op. cit. p. 54.

15. Ibid. p. 55. Lawrence 1968 op. cit. passim attacks the idea of significant form as being too intellectual and abstract a concept to illuminate what he sees as Cézanne's struggle to break through the clichés of mental concepts to the intuitive depths of a bodily love of the world. He also suggests that Cézanne was not so much humble as honest with himself. While there is a good deal of penetrating thought in Lawrence's essay, I think he was less than fair to critics like Bell and Fry. The concept of significant form was an attempt (however naïve) to do justice to the synthesising totality of Cézanne's achievement: the dualism of body and mind which often appears in Lawrence's essay sunders that totality.

16. Bell 1981 op. cit. p. 159.

17. Giedion, S. *The Eternal Present: A Contribution on Constancy and Change* Oxford University Press, London 1962 p. xx. (Originally delivered as the A.W. Mellon Lectures in the Fine Arts, The National Gallery of Art, Washington 1957).

18. Ibid. p. 512.

19. Hodin, J.P. *Modern Art And The Modern Mind* The Press of Case Western Reserve University, Cleveland and London 1972 pp. 251–2.

20. Lamarche-Vadel, B. *Alberto Giacometti* (trans. Kit Currie) Tabard Press, New York 1989 p. 70. See also the belief of the Jamaican-born, British-domiciled sculptor Ronald Moody (1900—84) that 'Art is not primarily concerned with the mirror image, but with the inner significance of things . . .'. Quoted from article in *Flamingo*, November 1964, by Wilmer, V. in Araeen, R. (ed.) *The Other Story: Afro-Asian artists in post-war Britain* Hayward Gallery, London 1989, p. 19. The exhibition and book *The Other Story* addressed a complex range of issues with regard to Afro-Asian artistic achievement in post-World War II Britain. See p. 11 for Araeen's reflections on what he regards as the distorting myth of 'the magical power of the modern artist (white, male, individual, heroic)' and that artist's fascination for 'the Other'. While I am

sympathetic to many of the points Araeen makes, I believe that there is much more to this myth than its alleged function of masking 'the contradictions of the bourgeois/imperial society'. Ibid.

21. On the relations between primitivism and symbolism see Goldwater, R. *Symbolism* Allen Lane The Penguin Press, London 1979 and Goldwater 1986 op. cit.

22. See *A Child of Six Could Do It! Cartoons About Modern Art* The Tate Gallery, London 1987.

23. Vergo, P. *Kandinsky: Cossacks* Tate Gallery Publications, London 1986 p. 13.

24. *Munnings v. The Moderns* Manchester City Art Galleries 1986 p. 11.

25. Ibid. p. 12. In 1956 Munnings satirised modernism in his painting *Does the Subject Matter?*, which can be seen in the Sir Alfred Munnings Art Museum, Castle House, Dedham (see *Munnings v. The Moderns* for colour reproduction).

26. Jung, C.G. *Essays On Contemporary Events: Reflections on Nazi Germany* Ark Paperbacks/Routledge, London 1988 p. 66.

27. Hodin 1972 op. cit. pp. 95–6.

28. Jung, C.G. *Memories, Dreams, Reflections* Flamingo/Fontana Paperbacks, London 1989 p. 293.

29. Gauguin, P. *Noa Noa: A Journal of The South Seas* (trans. O. F. Theis), The Noonday Press, New York 1974 p. vi.

30. Goldwater 1986 op. cit. p. 199.

31. Quoted in Whitford, F. *Expressionism* Hamlyn, London 1970 p. 180.

32. Jung 1989 op. cit. p. 183.

33. Jung, C.G. *Four Archetypes: Mother; Rebirth; Spirit; Trickster* Ark Paperbacks/Routledge, London 1988 p. 136.

34. Levy, M. 'The Shaman is a Gifted Artist: Shamanism in the work of Yves Klein, Joseph Beuys, Mary Beth Edelson and Karen Finlay' *High Performance* Fall 1988 Vol 11, No 3 p. 61. This useful article contains a brief overview of (sometimes critical or cautious) reactions to the idea of seeing shamanic themes in twentieth-century art.

35. 'The process of individuation' in Jung, C.G. (ed.) *Man and his symbols* Aldus Books/Jupiter Books, London 1974 p. 217. In his introductory contribution to this collection of essays, Jung seemed to take a more positive view of modern art than he had done previously. Two chapters in this collection — Henderson, J.L. 'Ancient myths and modern man' and Jaffé, A.

'Symbolism in the visual arts' — outline the many positive correspondences which can be established between Jungian ideas and modern art. On the interplay of animus and anima and the relation of 'soul-making' to individuation, see Hillman, J. *Anima: An Anatomy of a Personified Notion* Spring Publications, Dallas, Texas 1985.

36. 'I Believe in Individual Man Himself', *Selected Poems of Gunnar Ekelöf* (trans. Muriel Rukeyser and Leif Sjöberg) Twayne Publishers Inc, New York 1967 p. 60.

37. *Personal Mythology: The Psychology of Your Evolving Self* Mandala, Unwin Paperbacks, London 1989 p. 39.

38. Watts, A. *Tao: The Watercourse Way* Penguin, Harmondsworth 1981 p. 30.

39. 'The Waste Land', Section 1: *The Burial of the Dead*, lines 19–22, *Selected Poems,* Faber and Faber, London 1965 p. 51.

40. Sylvester, D. *The Brutality of Fact. Interviews with Francis Bacon* Thames and Hudson, London 1987 (third edition) pp. 28–9 (from an interview of 1962). In an interview in the early 1970s, Bacon acknowledged Sylvester's point that he was not concerned 'to say something about the nature of man, in a way that an artist like, say, Munch was'. p. 82.

41. *Andy Warhol: A Retrospective, a Guide to the exhibition* The South Bank Centre, London 1989 (unpaginated).

42. Jung 1988 op. cit. p. 66.

43. Chipp 1968 op. cit. p. 482. For the Nazi attitude to art, see Hinz, B. *Art In The Third Reich* Basil Blackwell, Oxford 1980.

44. Charbonnier 1969 op. cit. p. 77.

45. *Where The Wasteland Ends: Politics and Transcendence in Post Industrial Society* Faber and Faber, London 1973, pp. 372 and 379; *The Making of a Counter Culture: Reflections on the Technocratic Society and Its Youthful Opposition* Faber and Faber, London 1970 pp. 232 and 252–3.

46. Argüelles 1975 op. cit. pp. 149 and 191.

47. Ibid. p. 220.

48. *Re-Visioning Psychology* Perennial Library/Harper and Row, New York 1977 p. 11.

49. *Archetype: A Natural History of the Self* Routledge, London 1990 pp. 279 and 283.

50. Waldman, D. *Mark Rothko, 1903–70: A Retrospective* Harry N. Abrams Ltd/The Solomon R. Guggenheim Foundation, New York 1978 p. 62.

51. Stevens 1990 op. cit. p. 283.

52. Hillman 1977 op. cit. pp. 179—80.

53. Argüelles 1975 op. cit. pp. 179—80.

54. *The Elements of Shamanism* Element Books Ltd, Shaftesbury 1989 p. 82.

55. *The Hidden Order of Art* Paladin/Granada Publishing Ltd, London 1970 pp. 89 and 90. Ehrenzweig believed that we are far too intolerant of 'superficial fragmentation'.

56. Benz, E. Portmann, A. Izutsu, T. et al *Color Symbolism (Six Excerpts from the Eranos Year book 1972)* Spring Publications, Dallas, Texas 1977 p. 158.

57. Quoted in Goldwater, R. *Gauguin* Harry N. Abrams, Inc, New York (undated) p. 44.

58. Quoted in Argüelles 1975 op. cit. p. 121. The subsequent role of photography in helping to preserve a consciousness of the wildernesses of the world merits a separate study. See e.g. Porter, E. *The Place No One Knew. Glen Canyon on the Colorado* (edited by David Brower), Ballantine Books, New York 1968 and the discussion of the work of Ansel Adams in Lipsey, R. *An Art Of Our Own: The Spiritual in Twentieth-Century Art* Shambhala, Boston and Shaftesbury, 1988 pp. 390—4 (and the discussion of Minor White, pp. 401—4).

59. See Ibid. (Argüelles) pp. 164—76 and Andersen, W. *Gauguin's Paradise Lost* The Viking Press, New York 1971.

60. Argüelles 1975 op. cit. pp. 194—5; Halifax, J. *Shaman: The Wounded Healer* Thames and Hudson, London 1982 p. 5.

61. Quoted in Goldwater (*Gauguin,* undated) op. cit. p. 28.

62. *Intimate Journals* (trans. Christopher Isherwood) Panther Books, London 1969 p. 68.

63. Baudelaire, C. *The Painter of Modern Life and Other Essays* (trans. and ed. Jonathan Mayne) Phaidon Press, London 1964 p. 8; quoted in Goldwater (1986) op. cit. p. 190.

64. Tacitus *The Agricola And The Germania* (trans. H. Mattingly; rev. by S.A. Handford) Penguin Books, Harmondsworth 1970 p. 109.

65. See Fairchild 1961 op. cit. pp. 1—139.

66. 'Constellations: Breton and Miró' in (Paz) *Correspondences: Essays On Art And Literature* (trans. Helen Lane) Bloomsbury, London 1987 p. 285.

67. *The Thought of the Heart* (Eranos Lectures 2) Spring Publications, Dallas, Texas 1987 p. 31.

68. Ibid. p. 32.

69. Van Gogh/Roskill 1974 op. cit. p. 310. The quote is from a letter from Vincent to Theo Van Gogh of February 3 1889.

70. Cowart, J. and Hamilton, J. *Georgia O'Keeffe: Art and Letters* (ed. Sarah Greenhough) National Gallery of Art, Washington/Bulfinch Press, Little, Brown and Company, Boston, Toronto, London 1987 p. 190.

71. Ibid. p. 214.

72. Ibid. p. 174.

73. Ibid. pp. 206 and 217. O'Keeffe did not feel that her centre came from her mind. See Chadwick, W. *Women, Art and Society* Thames and Hudson, London 1990 pp. 283—88 for O'Keeffe's rejection of male stereotyping of her art through the reductive use of the term 'femininity'. O'Keeffe was equally unsympathetic to 'attempts by feminist artists and critics during the 1970s to annex her formal language to the renewed search for a "female" imagery' (p. 288). The Jungian idea of the relation of animus and anima helps one to resolve such terminological-ideological issues.

74. Cowart, Hamilton and Greenhough 1987 op. cit. p. 263.

75. Hillman 1987 op. cit. p. 28.

76. Lane, J. 1988 op. cit. p. 101. 'The Flash of Vision' is the title of Chapter 6 of Lane's book, a chapter which looks at five twentieth-century painters: Chagall, Bonnard, Giorgio Morandi, Stanley Spencer and Paul Nash. Lane does not deal with specifically shamanic themes, although he does draw attention to the shamanic quality of such paintings of Nash's last years as *Eclipse of the Sunflower* (1945). See pp. 118—9. See *Resurgence* November/December 1990 issue 143 pp. 31—3 for Lane's interview with British painter Christopher Cook, where Lane's question — 'Do you think that the artist who relies on the subconscious is acting analogously to the shaman of primitive societies?' — receives a positive, sensitive reply from Cook. On Biblical themes in twentieth-century painting, see Usherwood, N. and Holberton, P. *The Bible In Twentieth-Century Art* Pagoda Books, London 1987.

77. Lipsey 1988 op. cit. p. 354. Like Lane, Lipsey pays little specific attention to shamanic themes. However, he provides an illuminating reappraisal of the motivations of many (predominantly abstract) artists.

78. Ibid. p. 246.

79. 'The Sacred and the Modern Artist', *Criterion* Divinity School, University of Chicago 1965

Vol 4 pt 2. Parts of this key article are anthologised in Beane, W.C. and Doty, W.G. (eds.) *Myths, Rites, Symbols: A Mircea Eliade Reader* (two vols) Harper and Row, New York 1975.

80. Ibid.

81. Further to Chapter 1, note 15, for a critique of primitivism see Harbison, R. *Deliberate Regression* Andre Deutsch, London 1980. Harbison explores what he sees as the grim trajectory of the Romantic impulse in the twentieth century: 'Nineteenth century subjectivism leads through personality to a depersonalised end' (p. xv). But however subtly argued or seemingly 'obvious' they are, the connections between Romantic and Expressionistic primitivism and fascism (e.g. Hitler as a pseudo-'shamanic' figure at the head of the German 'tribe') have to ignore the enormous differences between these phenomena which the 1937 Degenerate Art exhibition made fully apparent.

82. Eliade 1975 op. cit. p. 126.

83. Ibid.

84. As opposed, that is, to the predominantly formalist, proto-Cubist conclusions which many critics have drawn from both his work and his famous advice, as recorded by Émile Bernard, that one should learn to treat nature in terms of the simple forms of the sphere, the cone and the cylinder. Bernard himself acknowledged what he called Cézanne's 'mystical temperament'. See Brion, M. *Cézanne* Thames and Hudson, London 1974 p. 72 note 7.

85. Lawrence 1968 op. cit. p. 317.

CHAPTER FOUR

1. Baudelaire 1969 op. cit. p. 67.

2. *Les Fleurs du Mal* (trans. Richard Howard) The Harvester Press, Brighton 1982 p. 15.

3. Lipsey 1988 op. cit. p. 456.

4. Pevsner, N. *Pioneers of Modern Design* 2nd ed, New York 1949 p. 135.

5. Brodzky, A.T., Danesewich, R., Johnson, N. (eds.) *Stones, bones and skin: Ritual And Shamanic Art*, Artscanada/The Society for Art Publications, Toronto 1977 p. ix.

6. Grim, J.A. *The Shaman: Patterns of Religious Healing Among the Ojibway Indians* University Of Oklahoma Press, Norman and London 1987 pp. 207–8.

7. Eliade 1965 op. cit. See Bultmann, R. *Primitive Christianity in Its Historical Setting* Thames and Hudson, London 1983, for Christianity's relations to Judaic and Hellenic ideas, and its contrasts with Gnosticism. Macdermot, V. *The Cult of the Seer in the Ancient Near East* Wellcome Institute of the History of Medicine, London 1971 analyses the differences between earlier (world-affirming) pagan mysticism and Christian (world-denying) asceticism. On the latter, see also Waddell, H. *The Desert Fathers* Constable and Co Ltd, London 1987.

8. Sjöö and Mor 1987 op. cit. p. 307. On witchcraft, see also Duerr, H.P. *Dreamtime: Concerning the Boundary between Wilderness and Civilization* (trans. Felicitas Goodman) Basil Blackwell, Oxford 1987.

9. William Blake prayed to be kept from 'single vision and Newton's sleep!' Laurie Anderson's *Big Science* recording, with its critique of the 'Golden Cities, Golden Towns' of modernist ideology was released in 1982 on Warner Brothers WB K 57 002.

10. See Sjöö and Mor 1987 op. cit. p. 353 for a critique of the ideology of 'Bionic Man'.

11. Hillman 1985 op. cit. p. 109.

12. Drury 1989 op. cit. p. 5.

13. On the shamanic recovery of souls, see e.g. Blodgett, J./The Winnipeg Art Gallery *The Coming and Going of The Shaman: Eskimo Shamanism and Art* The Winnipeg Art Gallery 1979 pp. 119–26.

14. Lommel, A. *Shamanism: The beginnings of art* McGraw-Hill Book Company, New York and Toronto/Evelyn, Adams and Mackay Ltd 1967 p. 147.

15. Ibid. p. 140. This is the consistent theme of Lommel's book. For Lommel, the shaman is 'probably the first artistically active man known to us'. Ibid. p. 8.

16. Grim 1987 op. cit. pp. 180–208 contains a good discussion of these distinctions.

17. The subject of mass culture has spawned an enormous amount of literature, much of which attempts to demonstrate that there is no such thing (as mass culture), and that any use of the concept indicates a reactionary inability to appreciate the healthy diversity of cultural experience available this century. See e.g. Swingewood, A. *The Myth Of Mass Culture* The MacMillan Press Ltd, London 1977. This argument is not without its merits. However, what one might call the 'feeling-tone' of not just particular items of culture today, but much of its overall pattern and flow, is undeniably

reductive in a 'mass-cultural' way. See e.g. Pawley, M. *The Private Future* Thames and Hudson, London 1973. On developing meaningful attitudes to death, see e.g. Metzger, A. *Freedom and Death* Human Context Books/ Chaucer Publishing Co Ltd, London 1973 pp. 1–14 and Herzog, E. *Psyche and Death: Archaic Myths and Modern Dreams in Analytical Psychology* Hodder and Stoughton, London 1966.

18. Heidegger, M. *Being and Time* (trans. John Macquarrie and Edward Robinson) Basil Blackwell, Oxford 1967 p. 311.

19. Castaneda 1987 op. cit. pp. 51, 101 and 214. There are close links between such shamanic thought about death and Jungian ideas of individuation. See the discussion of Meret Oppenheim in Chapter 1 and of Edvard Munch in Chapter 6.

20. Malraux, A. *Picasso's Mask* (trans. J. and J. Guicharnaud) Macdonald And Jane's, London 1976 p. 235.

21. Halifax, J. *Shamanic Voices: The Shaman as Seer, Poet and Healer* Pelican/Penguin, Harmondsworth 1980 p. 69.

22. Duerr 1987 op. cit. p. 65. Duerr supplies a stimulating, richly documented study of the wilderness theme in shamanism.

23. Castaneda, C. *Tales of Power*, Simon and Schuster, New York 1974 p. 126.

24. Duerr 1987 op. cit. p. 69.

25. Castaneda 1973 op. cit. p. 131.

26. See Levy, M. 1988 op. cit.

27. Duerr 1987 op. cit. p. 105.

28. Ibid. p. 87.

29. 'Eye and Mind' in *The Primacy of Perception*, Northwestern University Press, Evanston 1964 p. 187. The essay 'Cézanne's Doubt' is in Merlau-Ponty, M. *Sense and Non-Sense* Northwestern University Press, Evanston 1971 pp. 9–25.

30. Kalweit, H. *Dreamtime and Inner Space: The World of The Shaman* Shambhala, Boston and London 1988 p. 89. For Kalweit, the greater the initiatory suffering, the greater the subsequent shamanic power. Ibid. p. 9.

31. See Eliade, M. *Shamanism: Archaic Techniques of Ecstasy* (Trans. Willard R. Trask) Bollingen Series 76/Princeton University Press, Princeton 1974, passim.

32. Kalweit 1988 op. cit. p. 73. This song always put Uvavnuk in a trance. See Lowenstein, T. *Eskimo Poems From Canada and Greenland* Allison and Busby, London 1973 for a slightly different

translation. The song was originally collected by Knud Rasmussen.

33. Lévi-Strauss, C. *Structural Anthropology* Allen Lane/The Penguin Press, London 1969 Chapter 9 'The Sorcerer and His Magic' contains a discussion of such 'tricks'. The cynicism of the Kwakiutl apprentice sorcerer Quesalid concerning shamanic 'tricks of the trade' diminished considerably during his four-year apprenticeship: Quesalid found that his tricks worked better than anyone else's. (Material originally collected by Franz Boas.)

34. Halifax 1980 op. cit. p. 14.

35. Kalweit 1988 op. cit. p. 52.

36. Grim 1987 op. cit. p. 15. Here Grim combines definitions from Eliade 1974 op. cit. and M. A. Czaplicka *Aboriginal Siberia*. Sjöö and Mor 1987 op. cit. suggest that shamanic ecstasy — 'the dance of the individual with the All' — was initially the experience of women shamans and seers: 'Among the Siberian tribes, male shamans have always worn ornamental and symbolic "breasts" on their robes. When "civilised" men become the moralistic priests of the new Father God, women (and pagans of both sexes) remain the shamans (the witches) of the ecstatic Mother.' Ibid. p. 52. On gender in early shamanism and the ideas of Earth Mother and Sky God see also Rutherford, W. *Shamanism: The Foundations of Magic* The Aquarian Press, Wellingborough 1986 pp. 21–30.

37. Eliade 1974 op. cit. pp. 4, 502–3, 508 and 511.

38. See Heinberg, R. *Memories and Visions of Paradise: Exploring the Universal Myth of a Lost Golden Age*, The Aquarian Press, Wellingborough 1990.

39. Eliade, M. 'The Yearning for Paradise in Primitive Tradition', in Murray, H.A. (ed.) *Myth And Mythmaking* Beacon Press, Boston 1968 p. 63. (First published in *Diogenes*, University of Chicago Press, Summer 1953.)

40. Sproul, B.C. *Primal Myths: Creating The World* Rider/Hutchinson, London 1980 p. 23.

41. Eliade/Murray 1968 op. cit. p. 63.

42. Personal communication April 1991. Hyder discusses his trip to Russia (which he undertook with multi-instrumentalist Tim Hodgkinson) in his article 'In Search of the Spirit' *Jazz Forum* Vol 127, No 6 1990 pp. 30–3. See Chapters 8 and 12 below.

43. Eliade/Murray 1968 op. cit. pp. 65–6. On the symbolism of the World Tree see Vastokas, J.M. 'The Shamanic Tree of Life' in Brodzky, Danesewich and Johnson (eds.) 1977 op. cit.,

pp. 93—117, and Cook, R. *The Tree of Life: Image For The Cosmos* Thames and Hudson, London 1988.

44. Eliade 1974 op. cit. p. 135.

45. Ibid. p. 233. See Halifax 1980 op. cit. p. 28 for the related, sexually unified symbolism of the shaman's rattle, which becomes a world axis, 'the instrument of balance, transformation and flight'.

46. Blacker, C. *The Catalpa Bow: A Study of Shamanistic Practices In Japan* Mandala, Unwin Paperbacks, London 1986, 2nd ed. pp. 19—33. See pp. 106—7 (for discussion of bow and arrow symbolism) and pp. 317—20 (for discussion of the ascent of the 'ladder of swords').

47. Halifax 1982 op. cit. p. 30. See also p. 94: ' . . . shamans are trained in the art of equilibrium, in moving with poise and surety on the threshold of opposites, in creating cosmos out of chaos.'

48. Bäckman, L. and Hultkrantz, Å. *Studies In Lapp Shamanism* Stockholm Studies In Comparative Religion 16/Almqvist and Wiksell International, Stockholm 1978 p. 70. See pp. 62—78 for a range of related distinctions.

49. Hatto, A.T. *Shamanism And Epic Poetry In Northern Asia* School of Oriental and African Studies, University of London, 1970 p. 19. Eliade sets a similar point within the context of Paradisial mythology: Eliade 1974 op. cit. p. 486.

50. See Harner, M.J. *The Way of The Shaman: A Guide to Power and Healing* Bantam Books, Toronto and New York, 1982 and Drury, N. *Vision Quest: A Personal Journey Through Magic and Shamanism* Prism Press, Bridport/Unity Press, Lindfield 1989.

51. See e.g. the discussion in Lewis, I.M. *Ecstatic Religion: An Anthropological Study of Spirit Possession and Shamanism* Pelican/Penguin, Harmondsworth 1975 pp. 180—1.

52. Furst, P.T. 'The roots and continuities of Shamanism' in Brodzky, Danesewich and Johnson (eds.) 1977 op. cit. pp. 25—6.

53. See e.g. the poem 'Contempt', concerning the 'prodigious humbug [of a shaman], who believes his lies', and the discussion of the rarity of such sentiments in Lowenstein 1973 op. cit. pp. 77—80 and 149.

54. Jonaitis, A. *From The Land of The Totem Poles: The Northwest Coast Indian Art Collection at the American Museum of Natural History* American Museum of Natural History, New York/British Museum Publications, London 1988 pp. 94—5.

55. Drury, N. *The Shaman and The Magician: Journeys Between the Worlds* Routledge and Kegan Paul, London 1982 pp. 20 and 93.

56. Drury 1989 (*Elements . . .*) op. cit. pp. 101—2.

57. *Joseph Campbell and The Power of Myth*, with Bill Moyers. The conversations took place in 1985—6; this particular one was broadcast on BBC2, August 12 1990. See Campbell, J, with Moyers, B. *The Power Of Myth* Doubleday, New York and London 1988 p. 85.

58. Jung, E. and von Franz, M-L. *The Grail Legend* Sigo Press, Boston/Coventure Ltd, London 1986 p. 360.

59. Ibid. p. 360 footnote 5.

60. Novalis *Hymns To The Night* (trans. by Jeremy Reed) Enitharmon Press, Petersfield 1989 p. 19. Jaffé, Λ. *Was Jung a Mystic? and Other Essays* Daimon Verlag, Einsiedeln 1989 sets such problematic aspects of Romanticism's immersion in the depths of the psyche within the perspective afforded by Jungian ideas of individuation: see the chapter 'The Romantic Period in Germany'.

61. Kalweit 1988 op. cit. p. 163.

62. Girvetz, H. and Ross, R. (eds.) 1971 op. cit. is a representative compilation of the many prescriptive pressures which have been applied to the arts this century.

63. Neumann 1966 op. cit. pp. 68—9. For an introduction to Freud's views on art see Miller, J. (ed.) *Freud: the man, his world, his influence* Weidenfeld and Nicolson, London 1972 (esp. Podro, M. 'Art and Freud's Displacement of Aesthetics' and Ades, D. 'Freud and Surrealist Painting'). See also Gombrich, E.H. 'Psycho-Analysis and the History of Art' in his *Meditations On a Hobby Horse* Phaidon Press, London 1963.

64. Freud, S. *Totem and Taboo* (trans. James Strachey) Routledge and Kegan Paul, London 1975 p. 90.

65. See the discussion in Donoghue 1983 op. cit. and Steiner 1989 op. cit. passim.

66. Whyte, L.L. *The Unconscious before Freud* Social Science Paperbacks/Tavistock Publications 1967 pp. 91 and 128. Whyte provides documentation of the European interest in the unconscious which can be detected long before Freud, as a sort of natural counterbalance to Descartes' emphasis on the *cogito*. In the present context, remarks such as that of the Romantic J.G.V. Herder (1774—1803) — 'The world of dreams

gives us the most serious hints about our-selves' — are of particular interest. For Whyte, Freud was 'the last pre-Freudian rationalist, passionately upholding a rationalism of the conscious intellect which his theories would soon do much to undermine.' Ibid. p. 179.

67. Freud, S. *Civilisation and Its Discontents* (trans. Joan Riviere; rev. James Strachey) The Hogarth Press, London 1969 p. 18.

68. Jung 1989 op. cit. p. 173.

69. Whyte 1967 op. cit. p. 165 (Hartmann's capitals).

70. Jung, C.G. *The Spirit in Man, Art and Literature* (trans. R. F. C.Hull) Ark Paperbacks/Routledge, London 1989 p. 101.

71. Ibid. p. 102.

72. Ibid. pp. 82–3.

73. Ibid. p. 105.

74. Ibid. p. 83.

75. Ibid. p. 90.

76. Ibid. p. 104.

77. I say this in the knowledge that Jung painted and drew himself, and encouraged his patients to do likewise. It is indeed strange that Jung, who recalled in *Memories, Dreams, Reflections* how he was only able to draw with pleasure at school when he was allowed to draw 'what stirred my imagination' (rather than copies from the antique or naturalistic studies), should have shown such a lack of understanding of modern art for so much of his life. Jung 1989 (*MDR*) op. cit. p. 45.

78. Neumann 1966 op. cit. p. 186.

79. Ibid. pp. 160–5. See also Feinstein and Krippner 1989 op. cit. p. 224.

80. Wehr, G. *Jung: A Biography* (trans. David M. Weeks) Shambhala, Boston, Halifax, Shaftesbury 1988, pp. 484–5. Read's words bring to mind the collages of Kurt Schwitters. See Pickstone, C. 'Kurt Schwitters — An Excremental Mystic' in *Modern Painters* Vol. 4 no. 4 Winter 1991.

CHAPTER FIVE

1. Bäckman and Hultkrantz 1978 op. cit. pp. 38 and 72.

2. Neihardt, J.G. *Black Elk Speaks* University of Nebraska Press, Lincoln and London 1989 p. 270.

3. Rothenberg, J. *Technicians of The Sacred: A Range of Poetries from Africa, America, Asia, Europe and Oceania* University of California Press, Berkeley, Los Angeles and London 2nd ed. 1985, p. xxv.

4. Neihardt/Black Elk 1989 op. cit. pp. 21–43.

5. Ibid. p. 43 footnote 8.

6. Ibid. p. 250.

7. Berger, P. L., Berger, B. and Kellner, H. *The Homeless Mind* Pelican/Penguin, Harmondsworth 1974 p. 82.

8. Leiris, M. *Francis Bacon* Rizzoli, New York 1983 pp. 45–6.

9. Camus, A. *Selected Essays and Notebooks* (trans. Philip Thody) Peregrine/Penguin, Harmondsworth 1970 pp. 74–9.

10. See e.g. Watts, A. *The Book on The Taboo Against Knowing Who You Are* Abacus/Sphere, London 1973.

11. Camus, A. *The Myth of Sisyphus* (trans. Justin O'Brien) Hamish Hamilton London, 1971 p. 23.

12. Hesse, H. *Steppenwolf* (trans. Basil Creighton; rev. Walter Sorell) Penguin, Harmondsworth 1972 p. 92.

13. Ibid. p. 180. For Hesse's relation to Jung, see Serrano, M. *C.G. Jung and Herman Hesse: A Record of Two Friendships* Routledge and Kegan Paul, London 1977.

14. Campbell, J. *The Masks of God: Vol 4 Creative Mythology* Penguin, Harmondsworth 1976 p. 677.

15. According to Vine Deloria Jr, *Black Elk Speaks* has become 'a North American Bible for all tribes'. Neihardt/Black Elk 1989 op. cit., back cover.

16. Campbell 1976 op. cit. p. 678.

17. Fuller, P. *Images of God: The Consolations of Lost Illusions* Chatto and Windus/The Hogarth Press, London 1985 pp. 125–29.

18. Collins, J. *Cecil Collins: A Retrospective Exhibition* Tate Gallery Publications, London 1989 p. 37.

19. Ibid. p. 36.

20. Ibid. pp. 36–7.

21. Plato *The Ion*, quoted in Rothenberg, A. and Hausman, C.R. (eds.) *The Creativity Question* Duke University Press, Durham N.C. 1976 p. 32.

22. Quoted in Nietzsche 1967 op cit. Translator's Introduction, pp. 19–20.

23. Van Gogh/Roskill 1974 op. cit. p. 310.

24. Quoted in Frey-Rohn, L. *Nietzsche: A Psychological Approach To His Work* Daimon Verlag, Einsiedeln 1988 p. 116.

25. Ibid. p. 292.

26. Jaspers, K. *Strindberg and Van Gogh* The University of Arizona Press, Tuscon 1977 p. 155.

27. Ibid. p. 190.
28. Lavrin, J. *Nietzsche: A Biographical Introduction* Studio Vista, London 1971, pp. 117–18.
29. Nietzsche, F. *Twilight of The Idols* (trans. R.J. Hollingdale) Penguin, Harmondsworth 1968 p. 102.
30. Frey-Rohn 1988 op. cit. pp. 247–8.
31. Ibid. p. 55.
32. Ibid. p. 219 footnote 126.
33. Nietzsche, F. *Selected Letters* (ed. O. Levy; trans. A.N. Ludovici) The Soho Book Company, London 1985 p. 286.
34. Nietzsche 1967 op. cit. p. 44. On Nietzsche's varied influence on German culture, see Frenzel, I. 'Prophet, Pioneer, Seducer: Friedrich Nietzsche's Influence on Art, Literature and Philosophy in Germany' in Joachimedes, C.M., Rosenthal, N. and Schmied, W. (eds.) *German Art in the Twentieth Century: Painting and Sculpture 1905–1985* Royal Academy of Arts, London/Prestel-Verlag, Munich 1985 pp. 75–81.
35. Heller, E. *The Disinherited Mind* Penguin, Harmondsworth 1961.
36. Nietzsche 1967 op. cit. pp. 155–6. Zarathustra is listening to another prophet here.
37. Ibid. pp. 236–37.
38. Ibid. pp. 102–3, 52 and 241.
39. Jung 1989 (*The Spirit . . .*) op. cit. p. 103 and 1988 op. cit. p. 38.
40. Bachelard, G. *On Poetic Imagination and Reverie* (ed. and trans. Colette Gaudin) Spring Publications Inc., Dallas 1987 pp. 42–53.
41. Frey-Rohn 1988 op. cit. p. 167.
42. Nietzsche 1967 op. cit. p. 336.
43. Halifax 1982 op. cit. p. 24.
44. *Late Picasso: Paintings, sculpture, drawings, prints 1953–1972* Tate Gallery Publications, London 1988 p. 32. For an overview of the impact of Van Gogh on early modern art, see the exhibition catalogue *Van Gogh and the Modern Movement 1890–1914* Museum Folkwang Essen – Van Gogh Museum Amsterdam/Luca Verlag Freren 1990.
45. Sweetman, D. *The Love of Many Things: A Life of Vincent Van Gogh* John Curtis/Hodder and Stoughton, London 1990 p. 311.
46. Ibid. pp. 1–2.
47. Van Gogh/Roskill 1974 op. cit. pp. 189, 229, 242.
48. Ibid. p. 273.
49. Campbell 1982 op. cit. pp. 253 and 263.
50. Van Gogh/Roskill 1974 op. cit. Editor's Introduction p. 30.
51. Buber, M. *I and Thou* (trans. Ronald Gregor Smith) T. and T. Clark, Edinburgh, 2nd ed. 1970 p. 126.
52. Kodera, T. *Vincent Van Gogh: Christianity versus Nature* John Benjamins Publishing Company, Amsterdam/Philadelphia 1990 e.g. Chapter 4 'Japan as primitivistic utopia'. See Yamada, C.F. (ed.) *Dialogue in Art: Japan and the West* Zwemmer, London 1976 pp. 208–9 for a discussion of the difficulties involved in any equation of Van Gogh's proto-Expressionist intensity and Eastern ideas of 'mu', or 'emptiness'.
53. Jaspers 1977 op. cit. p. 176.
54. See Berger, J. *Success and Failure of Picasso* Penguin, Harmondsworth 1966 for a sampling of the many different opinions which Picasso's achievement and myth have provoked. For a feminist critique, see Broude, N.F. 'Picasso: Artist of the Century (Late Nineteenth)' in *Arts Magazine*, Vol. 55 (1) October 1980 pp. 84–86.
55. O'Brian, P. *Pablo Ruiz Picasso: a Biography* Collins, London 1989 p. 337.
56. Lowenstein 1973 op. cit. pp. 134–37.
57. Malraux, A. 1976 op. cit. pp.10–11.
58. Gilot, F. and Lake, C. *Life With Picasso* Penguin, Harmondsworth 1965 p. 113. See Richardson, J. (with the collaboration of McCully, M.) *A Life of Picasso Volume 1: 1881–1906* Jonathan Cape, London 1991, p.207 for the early interest in the occult which Max Jacob inspired in Picasso. See also pp.273–4 for the possible influence of both Hermes Trismegistus ('as above, so below') and the Magician card of the Tarot pack *vis à vis* the iconography of Picasso's *La Vie* of 1903.
59. Frey-Rohn 1988 op. cit. p. 198. For the relation of Nietzsche's ideas to Picasso see Rosenthal, M. 'The Nietzschian Character of Picasso's Early Development' and Johnson, R. 'The "Demoiselles D'Avignon" And Dionysian Destruction' in *Arts Magazine*, Vol 55 (1) October 1980 pp. 87–91 and 94–101.
60. Malraux 1976 op. cit. p. 258 speaks of Picasso's 'basic hostility to any cosmos'. The relation of Picasso's art to the spirit of *duende* was posited by John Berger, who sees Picasso as a 'vertical invader' from the land of the *duende*. Berger 1966 op. cit. pp. 38–40. For Berger, writing from a Marxist viewpoint, this central, primitivising aspect of Picasso's 'Noble Savage' creativity prevented him – except in his early Cubist period – from coming to terms with the evolving historical potentialities of the twentieth century.

61. 'Theory And Function Of The Duende' in *Lorca* (trans. J.L. Gili) Penguin Books, Harmondsworth 1967 pp. 127–39.
62. Alley, R. *The Three Dancers* Tate Gallery Publications, London 1986.
63. O'Brian 1989 op. cit. pp. 315–6.
64. See Eliade 1974 op. cit. pp. 71–5 and 79–81.
65. A point made by John Golding in his 'Picasso and Surrealism', in Penrose, R. and Golding, J. (eds.) *Picasso in Retrospect* Granada Publishing, London 1981 p. 54.
66. O'Brian 1989 op. cit. p. 458.
67. Ibid. p. 455.
68. Chipp 1968 op. cit. p. 135. For an extensive discussion of the relations between Matisse and Picasso, see Gilot, F. *Matisse and Picasso: A Friendship in Art* Bloomsbury, London 1990. Highlights of this lucid study include the discussion of Matisse's mastery of colour relations — his discovery that 'colour was structure' (pp. 59–62) — and the treatment of the different development of the animus and anima in each artist's work (pp.288–98). Gilot reminds us (p. 232) that Matisse's engagement with art began when his mother bought him a box of watercolours as a distraction when, at the age of twenty — and having been employed as a clerk in a solicitor's office — he was suffering from not only chronic appendicitis but also hypochondria and depression. Matisse was invalid for a year. From a shamanic point of view, interesting parallels might be drawn between Matisse's illness and that which affected Joan Miró in his youth, before he too was able to cultivate his creative daemon with full, healing attention. See Chapter 11 below.
69. Quoted in Lynton, N. *The Story of Modern Art* Phaidon, Oxford 2nd ed. 1989 p. 209.
70. Elderfield, J. *The Drawings of Henri Matisse* Arts Council of Great Britain/Thames and Hudson, London 1984 p. 102. For a discussion of Matisse from a sympathetic Christian viewpoint, see Heyer, G.S. *Signs of Our Times: Theological Essays on Art in the Twentieth Century* The Handsel Press, Edinburgh 1980. Much in Matisse's art recalls the discussion of the synthetic, 'feeling-toned experience of the symbol' in Neumann 1966 op. cit. pp. 173–75. Speaking of his pursuit of 'the hypnotic power of the image', Matisse once declared: 'Integrating meaningful elements into a coherent whole is my unique goal.' Gilot 1990 op. cit. p.77.
71. Ibid. (Gilot) p.301. (For an extensive analysis of Matisse's cut-outs, see Elderfield, J. *The Cut-Outs of Henri Matisse*, Thames and Hudson, London 1978.) Gilot often describes Matisse in near-shamanic phrases: while discussing his liberation of colour in terms of the freeing of 'the instinctive impulses of the unconscious', for example, she suggests that 'Like Orpheus, he had to enchant the wild beasts of his unconscious, to rein them in without inhibiting their intensity' (p.59). She also suggests that 'the artist, like the sorcerer of old, ought to be a builder of myths but should dispel evil dreams among his countrymen and within humankind. The artist ought to break the chains that prevent humanity from surging forward toward better tomorrows' (p.241).
72. From his *Journal*. Quoted in Lambert, J.-C. 1970 op. cit. p. 172.
73. Quoted in *Homage to Wassily Kandinsky* Leon Amiel, New York 1976 p. 19. Here, Kandinsky was speaking specifically of his work from the 1920s. However, the description is valid for all his work.
74. See Tuchman, M. (ed.) 1986 op. cit. for a range of articles detailing the impact of such thought on the development of both Kandinsky and twentieth-century abstract painting in general.
75. Knapp, B.L. *Music, Archetype, and the Writer: A Jungian View* The Pennsylvania State University Press, University Park and London 1988 p. 92. The trip to the Vologda region is described with enthusiasm by Kandinsky in his *Reminiscences*. The impression of walking through the great wooden peasant houses, with all their carvings, was of 'magical' importance: it taught the painter-to-be to 'move within the picture'. But there is no mention of shamanism *per se* by Kandinsky here.
76. Lipsey 1988 op. cit. p. 208.
77. Tobien, F. *Franz Marc* Artline Editions, Bristol 1987 p. 8.
78. Kandinsky, W. *Sounds* (trans. Elizabeth R. Napier) Yale University Press, New Haven 1981 p. 79.
79. Kandinsky 1977 op. cit. p. 54.
80. From his *Reminiscences* in Lindsay, K.C. and Vergo, P. (eds.) *Kandinsky: Complete Writings on Art* Volume One *(1901–1921)* Faber and Faber, London 1982. Quoted in a slightly different version in Knapp 1988 op. cit. p. 90.
81. See Lacoste, M.C. *Kandinsky* Bonfini Press, Naefels 1979 pp. 57–62 for the differences

between these two artists. Clearly, there are shamanic elements in what Malevich called his Suprematist art, an icon-related art of cosmic space and subtly deployed, archetypal forms such as the cross. However, I have chosen to concentrate on Kandinsky: the combination of his theoretical and practical concerns, and the relation between his painting and his poetry, exemplify the shamanic dimension in early abstract painting, and shamanic elements continued to be manifest in his work all through his life. See also note 83 below.

82. Kandinsky 1977 op. cit. p. 25.
83. Neumann 1959 op. cit. p. 163. On *li*, see Watts 1981 op. cit. p. 15.
84. *Homage* 1976 op. cit. p. 28.
85. Lambert 1970 op. cit. p. 47.
86. Jaffe, H.L. *Klee* Hamlyn, London 1972 p. 46.
87. Klee, P. *On Modern Art* (trans. Paul Findlay) Faber and Faber, London 1969 pp. 45, 13 and 51.
88. See Halifax 1980 op. cit. p. 1 for the Huichol concept of the *neirika*, the cosmic portway or interface between realities of everyday and extraordinary consciousness. For the musical aspects of *Ad Parnassum*, see Kagan, A. *Paul Klee: Art and Music* Cornell University Press, Ithaca and London 1983.
89. Published in 1968; two illustrations are reproduced in Duerr 1987 op. cit.
90. From a lecture of April 3 1922. Quoted in Rewald, S. *Paul Klee: The Berggruen Collection*, Tate Gallery Publications, London 1989 p. 154.
91. Blacker 1986 op. cit. p. 107.

CHAPTER SIX

1. Castaneda 1987 op. cit. pp. 108–10. In terms of twentieth-century art, the idea of place in shamanism may initially seem to suggest a consideration of Mexico (and an artist such as Rufino Tamayo (1899–1991), for example). One thinks of D.H. Lawrence's *The Plumed Serpent*, or his 1928 essay 'New Mexico' — where Lawrence spoke of what he called 'the old, old roots of human consciousness still reaching down to depths we [Europeans moderns] know nothing of'. Lawrence 1968 op. cit. p. 183. Mexico was of great importance to the Surrealists. Breton's admiration for the country is legendary; Artaud journeyed across the Sierra Madre to the peyote-using Tarahumaras tribe in 1936. (See Hayman, R. *Artaud And After*,

Oxford University Press, Oxford 1977 pp. 102–14 and Chapter 7 below.) However, given the emphasis on the Northern origins of shamanism in most of the literature, it seems only natural to investigate the idea of place in shamanism with regard to the North; and particularly so since the modern, shamanically-oriented artistic achievements of the Nordic countries are as yet nowhere near as well known in the wider world as they deserve to be. See note 138 below.

2. See Mjöberg, J. 'Romanticism and Revival' in Wilson, D.M. (ed.) *The Northern World: The History and Heritage of Northern Europe AD 400–1100* Thames and Hudson, London 1980 and Tucker, M. 'Not the Land, but an Idea of a Land' in Freeman, J. (ed.) *Landscapes from a High Latitude: Icelandic Art 1909–1989* Lund Humphries, London 1989 for the historical-cultural background to the emergence of such an idea of the North. The idea can be approached from both the 'internal' perspective of nineteenth-century National Romanticism (and the subsequent nineteenth- and twentieth-century achievement of political independence in Norway, Finland and Iceland) and the 'external' perception of travellers such as William Morris, who travelled with much enthusiasm in Iceland in 1871 and 1873.

3. Quoted from 'Risk and chance. Dagger and guitar' (1963: from material as early as 1946) in Shield, P. 'On Reading Jorn', in Hansen, P. F. (ed.) *A bibliography of Asger Jorn's writings* Silkeborg Kunstmuseum, Silkeborg 1988 p. 36. My interpretation of the idea of the North is somewhat different from the famous thesis advanced by William Worringer in his *Abstraction And Empathy: A Contribution to the Psychology of Style* Munich 1908. Worringer drew a sharp distinction between what he called Northern (psychological and stylistic) 'abstraction' in the face of the hostile powers of nature and Southern 'empathy' with the more benign qualities of Southern climes. While Worringer's emphasis on the extreme emotional intensity — 'das unheimliche Pathos' — of the North certainly applies to a work like *The Scream* by Edvard Munch, I wish to argue that much shamanically-oriented art of the North (including that of Munch) reveals an intense, animistic *empathy* with nature. See Norberg-Schulz, C. *Genius Loci: Towards a Phenomenology of Architecture* Academy Editions, London 1980

for a valuable qualification of Worringer's characterisation.

4. 'The Silence Afterwards' (1965) in *The Silence Afterwards: Selected Poems of Rolf Jacobsen* (trans. and ed. Roger Greenwald) Princeton University Press, Princeton 1985 p. 155.

5. 'Beyond Grorud' ibid. p. 243. In 1978 Jacobsen made a beautiful recording of his work with, among others, fellow Norwegians Egil Kapstad (piano) and Karin Krog (vocal): *Til Jorden* (To The Earth) (Norwegian Zarepta ZA 34016).

6. 'The Nightingale in Badelunda' in Tranströmer, T. *Collected Poems* (trans. Robin Fulton) Bloodaxe Books, Newcastle upon Tyne 1987 p. 149.

7. 'On the Outskirts of Work' ibid. p. 78.

8. 'About History' ibid. pp. 75–6.

9. 'Further In' ibid. p. 99.

10. 'The Blue House' ibid. p. 138.

11. 'From March 1979' ibid. p. 134. In Winter 1990 Tranströmer was interviewed by Jeremy Hooker for 'Third Ear', BBC Radio 3. When asked about the religious quality in his work, the strong sense of 'the other' in his language, he replied 'Yes, I think I am one of the many in our time who have a strong religious feeling, without belonging to a special church dogma. I feel that I communicate very much with readers in these poems. But they are not orthodox at all. You could almost say that they are agnostic poems. But at the same time much more positive to religion than usually I connect with the word agnosticism.' In the interview, Tranströmer stressed how important dreams are to him, how close to his conscious life they are.

12. For the sculpture of Dorset culture, see Canadian Eskimo Arts Council *Sculpture of the Inuit: Masterworks of the Canadian Arctic* University of Toronto Press, Toronto 1971.

13. Lopez, B. *Arctic Dreams* Picador/Pan Books, London 1987 p. 411.

14. Ibid. p. 414.

15. Ibid. p. 414. Lopez speaks of this state as having absorbed 'that very darkness which before was the perpetual sign of defeat'; there are clear connections with his earlier discussion of the *angakoq's* role as 'an intermediary with darkness', who has *qaumaneq* – 'the shaman light, the luminous fire, the inexplicable searchlight that enables him to see in the dark.' Ibid. p. 243. It is worth noting that one of Tranströmer's collections was called *Seeing In The Dark* (1970): see Tranströmer 1987 op. cit. pp. 88–96.

16. Lopez 1987 op. cit. pp. 228 and 406.

17. Vesaas, T. *The Seed* (trans. Kenneth G. Chapman) Peter Owen, London 1966 p. 147. The book was written in the summer of 1940.

18. Vesaas, T. *The Birds* (trans. Torbjørn Støverud and Michael Barnes) Peter Owen, London 1968 p. 75.

19. Ibid. p. 77.

20. Ibid. p. 221.

21. Vesaas, T. *The Boat In The Evening* (trans. Elizabeth Rokkan) Peter Owen, London 1971 p. 130.

22. Ibid. p. 45.

23. Ibid. p. 41.

24. Ibid. p. 155. It is appropriate that the *festschrift Tarjei Vesaas,* Gyldendal Norsk Forlag, Oslo 1967 contains Tomas Tranströmer's poem 'A Few Minutes', from his *Seeing In The Dark* collection. Like Vesaas, Tranströmer uses a simple, direct image – the 'dark rag' of a squat pine's crown – to suggest the secret, animistic roots that take us 'Outside what one wills./Outside the Metropolis'. See Tranströmer/Fulton 1987 op. cit. p. 88.

25. 'Prescription' in Ekelöf 1967 op. cit. p. 75.

26. Ekelöf, G. *Promenader och Utflykter* (Walks and Excursions) Bonniers, Stockholm 1985 p. 40 (this trans. M. Tucker).

27. 'If You Ask Me' in Ekelöf 1967 op. cit. p. 40.

28. Quoted in Shideler, R. *Voices Under the Ground: Themes and Images In The Early Poetry of Gunnar Ekelöf* University of California Press, Berkeley 1973 pp. 137, 134 and 133.

29. Ekelöf, G. *Songs of Something Else: Selected Poems* (trans. Leonard Nathan and James Larson) Princeton University Press, Princeton 1982 p. 5.

30. Quoted in Thygesen, E.G. *Gunnar Ekelöf's Open-Form Poem: A Mölna Elegy* Almqvist and Wiksell International, Stockholm 1985 p. 137.

31. Quoted from *Poeter om poesi* (Stockholm 1947) in Shideler 1973 op. cit. p. 15.

32. Ekelöf, G. *Late Arrival on Earth: Selected Poems* (trans. Robert Bly and Christina Paulston) Rapp and Carroll, London 1967 p. 13.

33. Ekelöf 1967 op. cit. p. 28.

34. Ibid. p. 33.

35. Ibid. p. 104. In Ekelöf's posthumously published autobiography we can read of his youthful enthusiasm for the Sufi poet and mystic Ibn Al-'Arabi, whose *Tarjumán Al-Ashwáq* Ekelöf bought in London when he was living there for a short while in the 1920s. See Ekelöf, G. *En Självbiografi* (ed. Ingrid Ekelöf) Albert

Bonniers, Stockholm 1971 p. 52. Such enthusiasm stayed with Ekelöf all his life: there are distinct echoes of the *Tarjumán* in Ekelöf's late *Diwan over the Prince of Emgion*, for example. The following famous lines of the *Tarjumán* would seem to epitomise Ekelöf's pursuit of a creedless creed: 'I follow the religion of Love: whatever way Love's camels take, that is my religion and my faith.' *Tarjumán Al-Ashwáq* (trans. Reynold A. Nicholson) Theosophical Publishing House, London 1978 p. 67.

36. Ekelöf 1967 op. cit. p. 105.
37. Ekelöf 1982 op. cit. p. 115.
38. Ekelöf/Bly 1967 op. cit. pp. 7—8.
39. 'Trolldom In Fall' Ibid. p. 15.
40. 'In the Forests of Convention' Ibid. p. 21.
41. Norberg-Schulz 1980 op. cit. p. 42. This book is an excellent introduction to the idea of *genius loci* as both general ethos of place and particular place. For Norberg-Schulz, Nordic landscape (as compared to what he calls 'desert' and 'classical' landscapes) is characterised by *'an indefinite multitude of different places'*. While it is the kind of landscape where 'the original forces are still most strongly felt', it is also a landscape where 'Behind every hillock and rock there is a new place, and only exceptionally the landscape is unified to form a simple, univocal space. In the Nordic landscape, therefore, men encounter a host of natural "forces", whereas a general unifying order is lacking. This becomes clearly manifest in the literature, art and music of the Nordic countries, where natural impressions and moods play a primary role. In legends and fairy-tales we encounter the mythical inhabitants of this world: gnomes, dwarfs and trolls. Still today Nordic man carries these beings within his psyche, and when he wants to "live", he leaves the city to experience the mysteries of the Nordic landscape. In doing this he looks for the *genius loci*, which he has to understand to gain an existential foothold.' Ibid. p. 42. Such a characterisation spills over the boundaries of modern-day nation-states: its importance for an understanding of the survival and development of shamanic ideas in modern Nordic art hardly needs stressing.
42. See Davidson, H.R.E. *Scandinavian Mythology* Paul Hamlyn, London 1975 and (Davidson) *Myths And Symbols in Pagan Europe: Early Scandinavian And Celtic Religions* Manchester University Press, Manchester 1988.
43. Bancroft 1987 op. cit. p. 162.

44. Sjöö and Mor 1987 op. cit. p. 225. See also Achterberg, J. *Woman as Healer* Rider, London 1991 Chapter 3, 'Denmark: Woman as Shaman'.
45. Personal communication January 1991.
46. See Galerie Michèle Sadoun *Lindström: La Terre des Ancêtres* Paris 1990 and Boudaille, G. *Lindström* L'Autre Musée, Paris 1984.
47. Preface to Hamsun, K. *Hunger* (trans. Robert Bly) Duckworth, London 1974 p. ix.
48. *Tankebilder* (Stockholm 1898) quoted in *The Swedish Vision: Landscape And Figurative Painting 1885–1920,* Moser and Klang, Stockholm/ Shepherd Gallery, Associates, New York 1985 p. 15. This exhibition catalogue documents the Nietzschian nature-worship evident in various artist colonies in Sweden at this time. The animistic work of painter Johan Axel Gustav Acke (1859—1924) is particularly striking: in *The Sound of The Sea*, a naked man lies pressed flat against a rock, listening for what Tomas Tranströmer would later call 'language, but no words'.
49. Nansen, F. *Sporting Days In Wild Norway* Thornton Butterworth, London 1925 p. 77. See also pp. 116—20, where Nansen contributes to the twentieth-century mass culture debate with his observation that 'Deprived of the leisure to digest his new impressions, to deepen the current of his inner self, no human being can hope to develop.' Falk-Ytter, H. *Aurora: The Northern Lights in Mythology, History and Science* Floris Books, Anthroposophic Press, Edinburgh 1983 — a thought-provoking, wide-ranging study of the Northern Lights — contains several colour reproductions of Nansen's woodcuts.
50. See e.g. Varnedoe, K. *Northern Light: Nordic Art at The Turn of The Century* Yale University Press, New Haven and London 1988.
51. Quoted in Heller, R. *Munch: The Scream* Allen Lane/The Penguin Press, London 1973 p. 24.
52. A comparison drawn by William Vaughan in *Caspar David Friedrich 1774–1840* Tate Gallery Publications, London 1972 p. 44.
53. The theme of the artist and the cross would also occur in *Golgotha*, a James Ensor-like oil of 1900, where Munch suffers on the cross, surrounded by all-too-human evidence of life's idiocy and greed. On the relation between Munch and Ensor, see the Norman Mackenzie Art Gallery *James Ensor Edvard Munch Emil Nolde* Regina, Saskatchewan 1980. Munch's pantheism was paralleled by a deep respect for the teachings of Christ.

54. McFarlane, J.W. *Ibsen And The Temper of Norwegian Literature* Octagon Books, New York 1979 p. 143.

55. Otto, W.F. *Dionysus: Myth and Cult* Spring Publications, Dallas 1986 p. 161.

56. McFarlane 1979 op. cit. p. 119.

57. Ferguson, R. *Enigma: The Life of Knut Hamsun* Hutchinson, London 1987 pp. 67 and 102.

58. McFarlane 1979 op. cit. p. 122.

59. Hamsun 1974 op. cit. p. 15.

60. McFarlane 1979 op. cit. p. 142.

61. Hamsun K. *Pan* (trans. James W. McFarlane) Condor/Souvenir Press, London 1980 p. 51.

62. Ibid. pp. 90–1.

63. Layton, R. *Sibelius* J.M. Dent and Sons, London 1971 p. 78. Layton writes about a 'feeling for nature' in *Tapiola*, which is 'so intense as to amount to complete identification'. In the context of this chapter, it is interesting to note that Layton prefaced his study of this great explorer of Nature's depths with Hofsmannsthal's observation: 'The deeper a man's solitude the more powerful his language . . .' (*Book of Friends*).

64. Personal communication November 1984. In 1988 Garbarek recorded his *rubato* tone poem 'Pan' (composed for a Norwegian radio version of the novel) with Norwegian classical violinist Arve Tellefsen and keyboardist Kjetil Bjerkestrand. Issued in Norway: Arve Tellefsen *Pan* (Norsk Plateproduksjon IDCD 3).

65. Lanu's work is discussed by Jan Olof Mallander in Bløndal, T. (ed.) *Northern Poles: Breakaways and Breakthroughs in Nordic Painting and Sculpture of the 1970s and 1980s* Bløndal, Denmark 1986 pp. 255–8. Despite Mallander's comment that 'modern Finland is the society of engineers, not shamans' (p. 226), a significant proportion of the painting, sculpture and performance art which he discusses indicates that Lanu is not alone in exploring shamanic-oriented themes in Finland today. I have chosen Lanu as the most immediately striking example of such work in the context of the *genius loci*.

66. Fordham, F. *An Introduction to Jung's Psychology* Penguin, Harmondsworth, 1953 pp. 61–3.

67. Hamsun, K. *Mysteries* (trans. Gerry Bothmer) Condor/Souvenir Press, London 1973 p. 64.

68. Given the degree of sensitivity (including the ability to be ironic about themselves) in the early characters of Hamsun, and his (in)famous 1891 criticism of Ibsen's drama for its presentation of 'types' who can only think 'in whole numbers', Hamsun's eventual support of Hitler remains one of the strangest, most disturbing events in both recent Nordic literary history and the whole field of twentieth-century primitivism. See the discussion in Ferguson 1987 op. cit. pp. 324–410.

69. Hamsun 1973 op. cit. p. 194.

70. Laing 1967 op. cit. p. 119.

71. See Dittman, R. *Eros and Psyche: Strindberg and Munch in the 1890s* UMI Research Press, Ann Arbor 1982.

72. Sprinchorn, E. *Strindberg as Dramatist* Yale University Press, New Haven and London 1982 pp. 63 and Bellquist, J.E. *Strindberg as a Modern Poet: A Critical and Comparitive Study* University of California Press, Berkeley 1986 p. 160.

73. Ibid. (Bellquist) pp. 53 and passim. This text is a most useful combination of many of the poems themselves (in Swedish and English) and a thorough critical commentary, which places Strindberg's longing for 'the golden age of dreamers' in the context of both Romanticism and modernity.

74. Heller, R. *Munch: His Life And Work* John Murray, London 1984 p. 90.

75. See Eggum, A. 'Munch and Photography' in Martin Friedman/Walker Arts Center *The Frozen Image: Scandinavian Photography* Abbeville Press, New York 1982 pp. 108–15.

76. See Eggum, A. *Munch And Photography* Yale University Press, New Haven and London 1989 and *Munch And Photography* Newcastle Polytechnic Gallery, Newcastle upon Tyne 1989 for a thorough discussion of such techniques and effects.

77. Lagercrantz, O. *August Strindberg* (trans. Anselm Hollo) Faber and Faber, London 1984 p. 271. Meyer, M. *Strindberg* Oxford University Press, Oxford 1987 suggests that Strindberg's materialist researches into alchemy should be seen as a contrast to the ancient alchemists' esoteric understanding that they were searching for what Jungians call 'philosophical gold'. Meyer sees Strindberg's alchemical research as 'a symbol of his defiant unwillingness to accept the existence of a God, and of his search for an alternative explanation of the human condition.' Ibid. p. 335. Another perspective might be that Strindberg's experiences at the time of his Inferno crisis took him back to precisely the sort of ancient, animistic experience of the world which transcends the dualism implicit in Meyer's assessment.

78. Sprinchorn 1982 op. cit. pp. 58–9.

79. See Fraser, C.C. 'August Strindberg and "The Lonely Poisonous Mushroom"' *Scandinavica* November 1987 pp. 151–6.

80. See the discussion by Mary Sandbach in her Introduction to *Strindberg: Inferno and From An Occult Diary* (trans. Mary Sandbach) Penguin, Harmondsworth 1979 pp. 48–9.

81. Sprinchorn 1982 op. cit. p. 277.

82. Strindberg/Sandbach 1979 op. cit. p. 56.

83. Sprinchorn 1982 op. cit. contains an extensive discussion of this play, with regard to the theme of individuation. See pp. 126–44.

84. Strindberg, A. *Six Plays of Strindberg* (trans. Elizabeth Sprigge), Doubleday/Anchor, New York 1955 p. 193.

85. Sprinchorn 1982 op. cit. discusses the impact of Swedenborg's ideas (such as that of vastation, or what Swedenborg called 'being let into one's own internals, that is, into what is the spirit's own') on Strindberg.

86. Ibid., passim contains penetrating discussions of Strindberg's pictorial and musical sense. See also Smith, J.B. 'Strindberg's visual imagination' *Apollo* October 1970.

87. Vogelweith, G. *Psychothéâtre de Strindberg (Un Auteur en quête de metamorphose)* Editions Klincksieck, Paris 1972.

88. See Digby, G.W. *Meaning and Symbol* Faber and Faber, London 1955 pp. 25–58 for a detailed Jungian interpretation of Munch; Neumann 1966 op. cit. Chapter 4 'Creative Man and Transformation' is also of relevance here.

89. Jaffé 1989 op. cit. p. 39.

90. '. . . I don't believe that my art is morbid or sick — as . . . many . . . believe. They are people who do not understand the essence of art, nor do they know the history of art.' Edvard Munch, quoted in *The Major Graphics* Munch Museum, Oslo 1976 p. 79. A knowledge of shamanic symbolism deepens one's sympathy for Munch's views. For example, the extraordinary *Harpy* of 1900, where a naked-breasted, winged female hovers above Munch, claws ready to pluck up his skeletal body, has traditionally been seen as evidence of the painter's misogyny. But one should remember that Munch painted and sketched himself with female breasts in the mid-1920s (see Langaard, J.H. and Revold, R. *The Drawings of Edvard Munch* Kunsten Idag, Oslo 1968 p. 120). If *Harpy* is compared with the Inuit (Eskimo) and other Native American shamanic images in

Halifax 1982 op. cit. pp. 44–5, where Sun Birds/Eagles carry off their 'victim' — symbolising what Halifax calls 'the sacrifice of lower forces and the emergence of a higher order of existence' — then Munch's shaman-like concern for psychic growth and androgynous totality becomes evident. (This comparison was first suggested by Helen Smith, in an unpublished, final year BA (Hons) paper on shamanic themes in Munch and Strindberg, Brighton Polytechnic 1988.)

91. Quoted in *Edvard Munch 1863–1944* Arts Council of Great Britain, London 1974 p. 12.

92. Argüelles 1975 op. cit. p. 178.

93. Johnson 1989 op. cit. p. 12.

94. Quoted in Boe, A. *Edvard Munch* Editiones Poligrafa, Barcelona 1989 p. 28.

95. Ibid. p. 30.

96. See Varnedoe 1988 op. cit. passim and Kent, N. *Light and Nature in Late 19th Century Art and Literature* Uppsala 1990.

97. Bachelard, G. *The Poetics of Space* (trans. Maria Jolas), Beacon Press, Boston 1971 p. 208. For Bachelard, in images of compelling poetic reverie 'The *being-here* is maintained by a being from elsewhere.' For Lippincott's discussion of *Starry Night* see Lippincott, L. *Edvard Munch: Starry Night* Getty Museum Studies in Art, Malibu 1988.

98. The 'studies' and 'compositions' of trees from 1911–13 by Dutch painter Piet Mondrian (1872–1944) are the most remarkable example of this theme being taken into abstraction. See *Mondrian: from figuration to abstraction* Thames and Hudson, London 1988.

99. Ingolfsson, A. and Johannessen, K. *Kjarval: A Painter of Iceland* Iceland Review, Reykjavik 1981 p. 20.

100. Asger Jorn *Gedanken eines Künstlers* Verlag Galerie van de Loo, Munich 1966. Quoted in *La Grande Parade: Highlights in Painting After 1940* Stedelijk Museum, Amsterdam 1984 p. 162.

101. Widerberg, F. and Moller, A. *Frans Widerberg: One Hundred Pictures* J.M. Stenersens Forlag, Oslo 1982 pp. 12 and 18.

102. Eliade 1974 op. cit. pp. 504–11.

103. Hansen 1988 op. cit. p. 42.

104. Atkins, G. *Asger Jorn The Crucial Years: 1954–1964* Lund Humphries, London 1977 p. 127.

105. Ibid. p. 97.

106. Atkins, G. *Asger Jorn Supplement: Paintings*

1930–1973 Lund Humphries, London 1986 p. 16.

107. See e.g. Lambert, J.-C. *Cobra* (trans. Roberta Bailey) Sotheby Publications, London 1983; Gray, C. (ed.) *Leaving the 20th century: The Incomplete Work of the Situationist International* Free Fall Publications, London 1974; ICA *An Endless Adventure . . . A Situationist Scrapbook* Verso/ICA, London 1989; Marcus, G. *Lipstick Traces: A Secret History Of The Twentieth Century* Secker and Warburg, London 1989; Andersen, T. 'Asger Jorn and the Situationist International' in Sussman, E. (ed.) *On the passage of a few people through a rather brief moment in time: THE SITUATIONIST INTERNATIONAL 1957–1972* The MIT Press, Cambridge, Mass. and London, 1989. Shield, P. 'The Danish Ostriches', *Jong Holland No 5 COBRA edition* 1988 pp. 21–31, furnishes an extensive, detailed look at the COBRA phenomenon, discussing various different estimates of the group's importance. For an overview of the development of Appel — an artist of much shamanic consequence — see Hagenberg, R. (ed.) *Karel Appel: Dupe of Being* Editions Lafayette, New York 1989.

108. As did the work of the Icelandic artist Svavar Gudnason (1909–88). Many of Gudnason's vibrant, free-flowing paintings are as redolent of the Icelandic *genius loci* as are those of Kjarval. Marginally associated with COBRA, from which he was to distance himself, Gudnason produced much work in the 1940s — such as the 1941 *St John's Dream*, the magnificent *Song of Iceland* of 1944, and *Death Anguish* of 1945–7 — which contained an inspiring, shamanic quality of metamorphosis, realised through both spontaneous, semi-abstract expression and a lyrical organisation of what Peter Shield calls 'meltwater colours'. See Shield, P. 'The Connections With Denmark' in *Svavar Gudnason 1909–1988* Listafasan Islands (National Gallery of Iceland), Reykjavik 1990.

109. *Fin De Copenhague* was reprinted by Editions Allia, Paris 1985.

110. Some of this music can be heard on the soundtrack of Per Kirkeby's 1977 film *Asger Jorn*: produced for Denmark's Statens Filmcentral by Kraka Film.

111. See Atkins 1977 op. cit. pp. 47–8 for Jorn's comparison of *Stalingrad* with *Guernica*. On the non-idyllic nature of Danish primitivism, see Alloway, L. 'Danish art and primitivsm' *Living Arts*, London No 1 1963 pp. 44–52.

112. Ekelöf 1967 op. cit. p. 47.

113. Atkins, G. *Asger Jorn* Methuen, London 1964 (unpaginated).

114. See Tucker, M. 'Dreamer In A Landscape' in *Frans Widerberg* Newcastle Polytechnic Gallery, Newcastle upon Tyne 1986 pp. 33–5.

115. Bachelard 1987 op. cit. p. 15.

116. See Gelling, P. and Davidson, H.R.E. *The Chariot of the Sun and other rites and symbols of the Northern Bronze Age* J.M. Dent and Sons Ltd, London 1969.

117. Tucker 1986 op. cit. p. 36. For an overview of differing approaches to colour symbolism, see Wood, B. *The Healing Power of Colour* The Aquarian Press, Wellingborough 1985 pp. 11–45.

118. Ouspensky, P.D. *The Symbolism Of The Tarot* (trans. A.L. Pogossky) Dover Publications, New York 1976 interprets the Tarot through occult wisdom going back to alchemy, the Kabala, and ultimately, Hermes Trismegistus. Much of Ouspensky's commentary helps to throw light on not just Widerberg's *Tarot* series, but such other images of metamorphosis by the painter as the 1983 oil *Magician*. There are also echoes (or rather, anticipations) of both Ekelöf and Don Juan, as in the observation in the section 'The Hierophant' that 'The Path is in yourself, and Truth is in yourself and Mystery is in yourself.' Ibid. p. 47. For another, very different approach to the pictorial possibilities of the Tarot by a twentieth-century artist, see Pollack, R. *Salvador Dali's Tarot* Salem House, Salem 1985.

119. Tucker 1986 op. cit. pp. 11–12. Kierkegaard's concept of the 'indirect communication' needed to communicate 'capability' (as opposed to knowledge) is relevant here.

120. Quoted in Wiedmann 1979 op. cit. pp. 13 and 67.

121. Swedenborg, E. *Journal of Dreams 1743–1744* (trans. J.J.G. Wilkinson; ed. William Ross Woofenden) Swedenborg Foundation, New York 1977 p. 90. Gunnar Ekelöf quotes these lines at the end of his great study of the metamorphoses of 'a moment in time', the 1960 *A Mölna Elegy*. See Ekelöf, G. *A Mölna Elegy* (bi-lingual edition; trans. Muriel Rukeyser and Leif Sjöberg) Unicorn Press, Greensboro 1984 pp. 52–53.

122. Södergran, E. *Samlade Dikter* (Collected Poems) Wahlström and Widstrand, Stockholm 1987 p. 96 (this trans. M. Tucker).

123. The 1918 collection *September Lyre* was her great, contentious breakthrough. See Schoolfield, G.C. *Edith Södergran: Modernist Poet In Finland* Greenwood Press, Connecticut/London 1984 pp. 62–82; and for an overview of her status today, Ibid. pp. 133–5.

124. Quoted in Södergran, E. *Complete Poems* (trans. David McDuff) Bloodaxe Books, Newcastle upon Tyne 1984 p. 50.

125. Schoolfield 1987 op. cit. p. 134.

126. Södergran 1984 op. cit. p. 17.

127. Ibid. p. 103 ('The Whirlpool of Madness'); p. 78 ('Beauty'); p. 109 ('The Most Beautiful God'); p. 141 ('Roses').

128. Ibid. p. 154.

129. Ibid. p. 33. There are clear parallels with Ekelöf here, as there also are in her Igjugarjuk-like belief that 'Life's three greatest gifts: poverty, loneliness, suffering are treasured only by the wise man at their true value.' Ibid. p. 153.

130. Södergran, E. *Love and Solitude: Selected Poems 1916–1923* (bi-lingual edition; trans. Stina Katchadourian) Fjord Press, Seattle 1985 p. 137. The solar theme supplies a clear bridge between Nietzsche, Södergran and Widerberg, as does the colour sense of all three. Zarathustra was drawn to 'deep yellow and hot red', and Södergran loved red, blue and yellow – 'For my own paleness' sake', as she wrote in 'The Colours' Longing', in the 1916 *Poems*. See Södergran 1984 op. cit. p. 60.

131. Ibid. (Södergran) p. 183.

132. Ibid. p. 184. Radin 1957 op. cit. documents the simultaneous presence in 'primitive' cultures of polytheistic and monotheistic beliefs, and criticises the conventional wisdom that the history of religious belief reveals a linear progression from polytheistic animism to the monotheism of the so-called 'higher religions'. See pp. 342–74.

133. In what follows, I have emphasised the Nordic element in Garbarek's work. It should be pointed out that he has made many records of a more obviously 'international' orientation e.g. his contributions to George Russell's 1970 *Trip to Prillarguri* (Soul Note SN 1029), Keith Jarrett's 1977 *My Song* (ECM 1115) and Indian violinist and composer Shankar's 1984 *Song For Everyone* (ECM 1286). It is also the case that some of Garbarek's most Nordic-sounding work has been created from widely derived international sources. 'Dansere' (Dancers), for example, from the 1975 *Dansere* (ECM 1075), sounds like a perfect complement to the imagery and ideas of Munch's *Frieze of Life* – but its haunting theme is based upon a pentatonic scale from Bali. See Chapter 12.

134. Recorded with Jan Erik Vold, Bobo Stenson, Jon Christensen and Swedish bassist Palle Danielsson, *Ingentings Bjeller* (Norwegian Polydor 2664 388) is one of the finest of all poetry and jazz collaborations.

135. See e.g. Tucker, M. 'Jan Garbarek: Beyond the Nordic Ethos', *Jazz Journal International* October 1977 pp. 6–8 and 19; (Tucker) 'Jan Garbarek: The Poetics of Space', *The Wire* No 7 Summer 1984 pp. 17–21; Brodowski, P. and Szprot, J. 'Jan Garbarek: Mysterious Wayfarer', *Jazz Forum* No 86 1984 pp. 38–44. In 1974 Keith Jarrett wrote three pieces of music expressly for Garbarek's saxophone improvisations and string orchestra; the pieces were titled 'Numinor', 'Wind Song' and 'Luminessence'. All three have a spacious, Nordic quality of intense, questing reflection to them: in the light of Lopez's comments in *Arctic Dreams* about the Northern shaman's 'inexplicable searchlight' (see note 15 above), the title of the last piece acquires particular resonance. The recording *Luminessence* (ECM 1049) is discussed in Carr, I. *Keith Jarrett: The Man and His Music* Grafton Books/HarperCollins, London 1991 pp. 85–6, together with Jarrett's 1975 *Arbour Zena* (ECM 1070). The latter also featured Garbarek with strings; one particularly atmospheric piece was titled *Runes (Dedicated to the Unknown)*.

136. Personal communication January 1980. Some of this music evolved from improvisations which Garbarek had recently supplied for Edith Roger's production of Ibsen's *Brand* at the National Theatre in Oslo.

137. 'To Music' in Rilke, R.M. *An Unofficial Rilke* (trans. Michael Hamburger) Anvil Press, London 1981 p. 69.

138. 'Schubertiana' in Tranströmer, T. *Truth Barriers* (trans. Robert Bly) Sierra Club Books, San Francisco 1980 p. 23. Further to note 1 above, the survival of shamanic consciousness – of the path 'upward into/the depths' – in the Nordic countries this century is all the more worth noting in that these countries have done so much to establish principles of democratic modernity. To speak of the shamanic spirit in twentieth-century art is *not* to speak in any crude terms of 'either/or' (e.g. either 'Progress' or 'Barbarism') but rather in terms of the

possibilities of the richness of a 'both/and' approach (e.g. both social democracy *and* shamanism to life.

CHAPTER SEVEN

1. *The Two Towers* George Allen and Unwin Ltd, London 1965 pp. 98, 201 and 187–9.
2. *The Return of the King* George Allen and Unwin Ltd, London 1965, pp. 223–5.
3. Ibid. pp. 200–1.
4. Ibid.
5. Lewis quoted on jacket, ibid. Wilson quoted in Seymour-Smith, M. *Who's Who in Twentieth Century Literature* Weidenfeld and Nicholson, London 1976 p. 364. For a balanced assessment of Tolkien (focussing on his approach to the theme of the Tree of Life) from a feminist/ecological perspective, see Taplin, K. *Tongues in Trees: Studies in Literature and Ecology* Green Books, Bideford 1989, pp. 191–7. One should draw attention here to the importance of the presence of shamanic ideas in children's literature e.g. Alan Garner *The Owl Service* Peacock/Puffin, Harmondsworth 1969 and Ursula Le Guin *A Wizard of Earthsea* Puffin/Penguin, Harmondsworth 1971 (republished as part of the *Earthsea Trilogy* by Penguin in 1979).
6. Written at the foot of one of his sketches. See Lorca, F.G. *Deep Song and Other Prose* (ed. and trans. Christopher Maurer) Marion Boyars, London 1980 p. ix. For Lorca's art work, see Oppenheimer, H. *Lorca: The Drawings* Franklin Watts, New York and Toronto 1987. This includes the text of the lecture 'Thoughts on Modern Art' which Lorca gave in Granada in 1928, when he spoke of painting's post-Cézanne 'salvation'.
7. Ibid. (Oppenheimer) pp. 87–92.
8. *Ode to Walt Whitman and Other Poems* (trans. Carlos Bauer) City Lights Books, San Francisco 1988, p. iv.
9. See Whitman, W. *Leaves of Grass* Signet/New American Library, New York 1958 pp. 144–9 ('Brooklyn Bridge') and Lorca *Poet in New York* (ed. Christopher Maurer, trans. Greg Simson and Steven F. White) Viking/Penguin, Harmondsworth 1989. See pp. xvi–xvii for Lorca's 1928 lecture 'Imagination, Inspiration, Evasion', with its stress on the inspiration which enables the poet and reader to acknowledge mystery in the self-contained entity of the poem. Although *Poet in New York* has been called a surrealist work, it contains nothing of the automatic writing which Breton advocated in his *Surrealist Manifesto* of 1924.
10. 'Deep Song' in Lorca 1980 op. cit. p. 30.
11. Quoted in Faas, E. *Ted Hughes: The Unaccommodated Universe* Black Sparrow Press, Santa Barbara 1980, p. 15.
12. Tzara, T. 'Note on Art' (1917) in *Seven Dada Manifestos and Lampisteries* (trans. Barbara Wright) John Calder, London/Riverrun Press, New York 1977/81 p. 59.
13. On the Orpheus myth see Warden, J. 'Introduction' and Robbins, E. 'Famous Orpheus' in Warden, J. (ed.) *Orpheus: the Metamorphoses of a Myth* University of Toronto Press, Toronto 1982. Sewell, E. *The Orphic Voice: Poetry and Natural History* Routledge and Kegan Paul, London 1961 is an excellent study of the impact of Orphic ideas on attitudes to language and poetic knowledge from antiquity to Rilke, with particular emphasis on Romanticism. See also Kosinski, D.M. *Orpheus in Nineteenth-Century Symbolism* UMI Research Press, Ann Arbor 1989.
14. Ibid. (Sewell) p. 202.
15. Ibid. (*Prometheus* quote) p. 281 and 'A Defence of Poetry', *Complete Works* Vol VII p. 135. Quoted in Furst, L.R. *European Romanticism: Self-Definition* Methuen and Co, London 1980 p. 91.
16. Letter to Paul Demeny, 15 May 1871. *Rimbaud: Complete Works* (trans. Paul Schmidt) Picador/Pan Books, London 1988 p. 103. 'A Season in Hell' is the title of Rimbaud's great sequence of disturbed, multi-voiced and visionary poems from the early 1870s.
17. Ibid. p. 102.
18. Quoted in Bachelard 1971 op. cit. p. 170.
19. Sewell 1961 op. cit. p. 280.
20. Williams, R. 'Language and the Avant-Garde' in his *The Politics of Modernism* (ed. Tony Pinkney) Verso, London 1989 p. 71.
21. Quoted in *Mallarmé* (ed. and trans. Anthony Hartley) Penguin, Harmondsworth 1965 p. xxiii.
22. Apollinaire: *Selected Poems* (trans. Oliver Bernard) Penguin, Harmondsworth 1965 p. 19. Trismegistus, i.e. Hermes Trismegistus, Egyptian priest, philosopher, occultist and author of the famous reflection of the Smaragdine Tablet: 'That which is above is like that which is beneath, and that which is beneath is like that which is above, to work the miracles of one thing.'

23. 'Ein für alle Male/ist's Orpheus, wenn es singt.' *Sonnets To Orpheus* Part 1 Number 5 (this trans. M. Tucker). See MacIntyre, C.F. *Rilke: Sonnets To Orpheus* University of California Press, Berkeley and Los Angeles 1960 p. 11 and Bly, R. *Selected Poems of Rainer Maria Rilke* Harper and Row, New York 1981 p. 203 for slightly different translations.

24. Ibid. (Bly) p. 101.

25. Ekelöf 1967 op. cit. p. 16. (Originally in an essay of 1951.)

26. Pound, E. *Guide to Kulchur* New Directions, New York 1968 p. 55.

27. See Skelton, R. *Poetic Truth* Heinemann Educational Books, London 1978 for formal and philosophical justification of the idea that 'Poetry . . . does present itself as a kind of judgement of all other and more approximate modes of communication and decision . . .' (p. 116). See also the defence of poetry's 'otherness' in Bachelard 1969 and 1971 passim; Heidegger, M. *Poetry, Language, Thought* (trans. Albert Hofstader) Harper and Row, New York 1975 and Ward, J.P. *Poetry and The Sociological Idea* The Harvester Press, Brighton 1981. For the 'problematics' of such 'otherness' in modernism see Bradbury, M. and McFarlane, J. (eds.) *Modernism 1890–1930* Part Two section 5 'The Lyric Poetry of Modernism' and Hamburger, M. *The Truth of Poetry: Tensions in Modern Poetry from Baudelaire to the 1960s* Methuen, London and New York 1982 passim. See also the comments at the end of this chapter, concerning the work of Kenneth White.

28. Bachelard/Gaudin 1987 op. cit. p. lvi. See Bachelard 1971 op. cit. pp. 178–82 for the awakened, expansive health of the 'cosmic breathing' which poetic reverie can induce. For Bachelard, 'It is a poor reverie which invites a nap'. Ibid. p. 10.

29. Ibid. (Bachelard 1971) pp. 189 and 36.

30. Ibid. p. 190.

31. Ibid. p. 193.

32. Letter to his Polish translator, quoted in David Young's 'Introduction' to *Duino Elegies* (trans. David Young) W.W. Norton and Company, New York 1980 p. 10. The shamanic nature of much of Rilke's work is underlined when one considers e.g. 'the voice' which Rilke heard – the ecstatic inspiration – which precipitated the writing of the *Elegies* in the winter of 1912, and the euphoria which came over the poet after the completion of the work ten years later. See Wydenbruck, N. *Rilke: Man and Poet* John Lehmann, London 1949 pp. 205 and 325–31.

33. 'Reference Back' in *The Whitsun Weddings* Faber and Faber, London 1979 p. 40.

34. 'Passage West' in *Handbook For The Diamond Country: Collected Shorter Poems 1960–1990* Mainstream Publishing, Edinburgh 1990 p. 132 and 'The Wind At Seven Islands' in *The Blue Road* Mainstream Publishing, Edinburgh 1990 p. 69.

35. In the present context, it is interesting to note that chapter 8 of Jessie L. Weston's 1920 *From Ritual To Romance*, a book which Eliot drew heavily upon in *The Waste Land*, deals with the theme of the magician and healer in fertility ritual.

36. *Entretiens* p. 278, quoted in Wilson, J. *Octavio Paz: A study of his poetics* Cambridge University Press, Cambridge 1979 p. 33.

37. 'Improvised Poetics' (1968 discussion) in Ginsberg, A. *Composed on The Tongue* (ed. Donald Allen) Grey Fox Press, Bolinas 1980 p. 47.

38. See the discussion of the nightmare quality in Ginsberg's Orphic odyssey in Faas, E. (ed.) *Towards a New American Poetics: Essays and Interviews* Black Sparrow Press, Santa Barbara 1978 pp. 249–64. The work of Hughes is discussed in detail later in the present chapter.

39. Recent eco-feminist approaches to poetry (and such recent Goddess poetics as the work of Starhawk) are discussed towards the end of the present chapter.

40. See e.g. Bly, R. *The Kabir Book: Forty-Four of the Ecstatic Poems of Kabir* Seventies Press/Beacon Press, Boston 1977. See Sjöö and Mor 1987 op. cit. pp. 119–21 for the parallels between Sufism and shamanism.

41. See e.g. the discussion of breath by Ginsberg in Faas 1978 op. cit. and Ginsberg 1980 op. cit. passim. The New Zealand experimental writer, Richard von Sturmer (*b.* 1956) has developed his interest in Jung's notion of the collective unconscious in both free-flowing writing and the overtone chanting which he does with his long-term collaborator Charlotte Wrightson in 'The Humanimals' group. See O'Brien, G. and Cross, R. *Moments of Invention: Portraits of 21 New Zealand Writers* Heinemann Reed, Auckland, 1988, pp. 119–24.

42. Obviously, I have only indicated some of the more potent examples of the theme. (Two further examples which deserve at least a

mention here are W.B. Yeats's variously-inflected pursuit of esoteric vision and the high-pitched lyricism of much of Dylan Thomas's work.) An enormous expansion of the twentieth-century poet's sense of tradition occurs between Eliot's famous 1917 essay 'Tradition and the Individual Talent', which stressed an historical sense stretching through 'the whole of the literature of Europe from Homer [to the present day]', and the several anthologies of world-wide 'ethnopoetics' which Jerome Rothenberg has edited from the 1960s onwards. Eliot, T.S. *Selected Essays* Faber and Faber, London 1961 pp. 13–22; for detail on Rothenberg, see below.

43. E.g. the delightful *Dharma Poems*, recorded in London in the 1980s (no label information on the cassette).

44. Quoted in Faas 1978 op. cit. p. 89.

45. 'The Politics of Ethnopoetics' in Snyder, G. *The Old Ways: Six Essays* City Lights Books, San Francisco 1977 p. 42.

46. Quoted in Faas 1978 op. cit. p. 89.

47. 'The Yogin And The Philosopher' in Snyder 1977 op. cit. p. 12.

48. 'Walking' from *Excursions*. Quoted in Rothenberg, J. and Rothenberg, D. (eds.) *Symposium of The Whole: A Range of Discourse Toward an Ethnopoetics* University of California Press, Berkeley, Los Angeles and London 1983 p. 10.

49. *Walden, or, Life in the Woods* Signet/New American Library, New York 1960 p. 128.

50. Quoted in Read, H. *Arp* Thames and Hudson, London 1968 p. 142. For a thorough study of Arp's poetics (and a bi-lingual presentation of his poetry) see Last, R.W. *Hans Arp: The Poet of Dadaism* Oswald Wolff, London 1969.

51. Ibid. (Read)

52. Eliade 1974 op. cit. p. 510.

53. Ibid.

54. Material reworked from Rasmussen, K. *The Netsilik Eskimos* (1931) in Field, E. *Eskimo Songs and Stories* (1967). Quoted in Rothenberg and Rothenberg 1983 op. cit. p. 3.

55. Eliade 1974 op. cit. p. 510.

56. Rotherberg (ed.) 1985 op. cit. p. xxv (first ed. 1968).

57. See note 48. Also worth noting here is Rothenberg, J. (ed.) *Shaking The Pumpkin: Traditional Poetry of The Indian North Americas* Alfred Van Der Marck Editions, New York 1986.

58. Rothenberg, J. *Pre-faces and Other Writings* New Directions, New York 1981 p. 9.

59. Heidegger 1975 op. cit. p. 192.

60. Fischer 1963 op. cit. p. 27.

61. 'Poetry and History' (1959) in *Octavio Paz: Selected Poems* (ed. Charles Tomlinson) Penguin, Harmondsworth 1979 p. 15.

62. Wilson 1979 op. cit. p. 26.

63. Ibid. p. 62.

64. Ibid. p. 137. Reading Paz through the ideas of, for example, Eliade and Bachelard, Wilson's excellent text offers many insights into (the essentially shamanic nature of) Paz's quest to transform 'the wasteland' of twentieth-century consciousness.

65. Tzara 1981 op. cit. p. 75.

66. Ibid. p. 58.

67. *Flight out of Time: A Dada Diary* (ed. John Elderfield) Viking Press, New York 1974 p. 71. (Originally published 1927.) Quoted in Guss, D.M. (ed.) *The Language of the Birds: Tales, Texts, and Poems of Interspecies Communication* North Point Press, San Francisco 1985 p. 336. Guss's anthology belongs next to those by Rothenberg.

68. Ibid. (Ball). Quoted in Melzer, A. *Latest Rage the Big Drum: Dada and Surrealist Performance* UMI Research Press, Ann Arbor 1980 pp. 62–3. Other sources suggest that Ball's costume had been designed and made by the brothers Jules and Marcel Janco. See Marcus 1989 op. cit. p. 226.

69. Ibid. (Marcus) p. 227.

70. Melzer 1980 op. cit. p. 63. Melzer documents the strong influence which Kandinsky had upon Ball from c.1912 to 1914: see pp. 16–25.

71. Available in bi-lingual form as 'Incantation By Laughter' in Markov, V. and Sparks, M. (eds.) *Modern Russian Poetry* Macgibbon and Kee/Robert Cunningham and Sons Ltd, Alva 1966 p. 327.

72. Guss 1985 op. cit. p. 311. Translated by Barbara Einzig from the Russian edition: Valemir Khlebnikov, *Collected Works*, (ed. Y. Tynyanov and N. Stepanov) Wilhelm Fink Verlag, Munich 1968, Vol. 1, book 2: *Creations 1906–1916* p. 98.

73. Ibid. (Guss) p. 88.

74. Ibid. p. 89.

75. Ibid.

76. Ibid. pp. 92–4. From *The Selected Poetry of Vicentre Huidobro* (ed. and with an Introduction by David M. Guss) New Directions, New York 1981 pp. 158–9.

77. Esslin, M. *Artaud* Fontana, London 1976 p. 116.

78. *Modern Theatre: Seven Plays And An Essay* (trans. Thomas R. Buckmann) University of Nebraska Press, Lincoln 1966 p. 12.
79. Quoted in Hayman, 1977 op. cit. p. 77.
80. 'On the Balinese Theatre' (1931) in *Artaud on Theatre* (ed. Claude Schumacher) Methuen, London 1989 p. 92.
81. Ibid. pp. 93 and 96—7 ("Mise en scène' and Metaphysics' 1932).
82. Hayman 1977 op. cit. p. 81.
83. Ibid. pp. 104—14.
84. Ibid. p. 133.
85. Ibid. pp. 141 and 17—19.
86. Ibid. p. 18.
87. Artaud/Schumacher 1989 op. cit. p. 128.
88. Ibid. pp. 105 and 108.
89. For Artaud, the 'only value' of theatre lay in 'its agonising, magic relationship to reality and danger'. Ibid p. 100. The theatre and 'its double' — of 'metaphysics, plague, cruelty' — was 'the pool of energies which constitute Myths, which man no longer embodies', but which was embodied by the theatre: 'By this double I mean the great magical agent of which the theatre, through its forms, is only the figuration on its way to becoming the transfiguration.' Ibid p. 87. What Artaud called 'cruelty' — 'in the sense of hungering after life, cosmic strictness, relentless necessity, in the Gnostic sense of a living vortex engulfing darkness, in the sense of the inescapably necessary pain without which life could not continue' — was deemed an essential aspect of this transformational process. Ibid p. 107. Hayman 1977 op. cit. investigates the impact of such ideas on Peter Brook, Charles Marowitz and Peter Weiss; Jerzy Grotowski; Jean Genet and Eugene Ionesco; Julian Beck and Judith Malina; Joseph Chaikin; R.D. Laing and Michel Foucault. Hayman also suggests that Artaud 'catalysed' the multi-media idea of the 'Happening' which originated at Black Mountain College in 1952 when John Cage read Artaud's work. One also senses the spirit of Artaud — his shamanistic determination to wake up 'the living dead'- in the *Orgies, Mysteries, Theatre* projects of the Austrian Hermann Nitsch in the 1970s, as well as in much of the post-1970 performance art which has stressed what Roselee Goldberg calls 'the ritualized pain of self-abuse'. (Goldberg, R. *Performance Art: From Futurism to The Present* Thames and Hudson, London 1988 p. 165.)

From a shamanic point of view, one must hope that such pain has led its suffering practitioners toward a healing, holistic sense of 'transfiguration'. Chapter 3 of Kenneth White's *Le Monde d'Antonin Artaud* (Paris, Editions Camplexe, 1989), devoted to Artaud's theatre, is entitled 'La scène chamanique'. White argues that 'shamanic' theatre is a better term than those Artaud used: 'metaphysical', 'alchemical', 'theatre of cruelty', all of which hardly satisfied Artaud himself.
90. Innes, C. *Holy Theatre: Ritual and The Avant-Garde* Cambridge University Press, Cambridge, London and New York 1981 p. 139.
91. See Jacobs, F.R. 'Hughes and drama' in Sagar, K. (ed.) *The Achievement of Ted Hughes* Manchester University Press, Manchester 1983, esp. pp. 168—70.
92. Innes 1981 op. cit. p. 139.
93. Faas 1980 op. cit. p. 50.
94. Ibid. p. 186.
95. Ibid. p. 207.
96. Ibid. pp. 67—8.
97. Sagar 1983 op. cit. pp. 285—312.
98. Ibid. See e.g. Sweeting, M. 'Hughes and Shamanism' and Bradshaw, G. 'Creative Mythology in Cave Birds'. Hughes has long appreciated the emphasis upon the multidimensional Goddess spirit in nature in Robert Graves's 'historical grammar of poetic myth', *The White Goddess*. First published in 1948; reprinted several times, including an amended and enlarged edition, by Faber and Faber, London.
99. Ibid. (Sagar) p. 311.
100. 'In the Dark Violin of the Valley' in *River* (Poems by Ted Hughes. Photographs by Peter Keen) Faber and Faber, London 1983 p. 86.
101. 'Crow and the Birds' in *Crow: From the Life and Songs of the Crow* Faber and Faber, London 1974 p. 37.
102. 'That Morning' in Hughes and Keen 1983 op. cit. p. 72. See also Sagar 1983 op. cit. pp. 311—12.
103. Ibid. (Sagar) p. 93 (Gifford, T. and Roberts, N. 'Hughes and two contemporaries: Peter Redgrove and Seamus Heaney').
104. Ibid. pp. 102—4. Heaney is another, very different poet of clear, potentially healing shamanic power: see e.g. the sensitivity and economy with which the mythic 'word-hoard' of the past is used to develop a compassionate perspective upon recent Irish history in *North*

Faber and Faber, London 1975.

105. *The Moon Disposes: Poems 1954–1987* Secker and Warburg, London 1987 pp. 66–7.

106. Ibid. pp. 175–6.

107. *Dressed as For a Tarot Pack* Taxus, Exeter 1990 p. 6.

108. Sagar 1983 op. cit. p. 99.

109. Blurb to Shuttle, P. and Redgrove, P. *The Wise Wound: Menstruation And Everywoman* Victor Gollancz Ltd, London 1978.

110. Faas 1980 op. cit. p. 56.

111. 'Witches' in *Lupercal* Faber and Faber, London 1960 p. 48.

112. Shuttle and Redgrove 1978 op. cit. p. 196.

113. *The Spiral Dance* Harper and Row, San Francisco 1989 pp. 2 and 11 (thealogy is a word coined by religious scholar Naomi Goldberg from *thea*, the Greek word for Goddess).

114. Ibid. pp. 209–10.

115. Ibid. p. 124.

116. Ibid. p. 10.

117. Ibid. p. 143.

118. Plant, J. (ed.) *Healing the Wounds* Green Print/ The Merlin Press, London 1989 p. 117.

119. Ibid. p. 201.

120. Taplin 1989 op. cit. p. 20.

121. Details taken from White's lecture 'A Shaman dancing on the Glacier', published in *Artwork* No 50 June-July 1991 special supplement 'Burns, Beuys and Beyond' pp. 2–3. Kenneth White's *Incandescent Limbo*, published (though written originally in English) so far only in French, as *Les Limbos incandescents* (Denoël, 1976; new edition 1990) constitutes a modern shamanist initiation, particularly in the section 'A Short Introduction to Eskimo Studies'. For an outline biography and excellent bibliography of White, see *L'Itinéraire De Kenneth White* Bibliothèque municipale de Rennes 1990.

122. Ibid. (*Artwork* supplement).

123. *The Tribal Dharma: An Essay on the Work of Gary Snyder* Unicorn Bookshop, Carmarthen 1976.

124. 'Coastline' White 1990 (*Handbook for the Diamond Country*) op. cit. p. 55.

125. 'Ovid's Report' in *The Bird Path: Collected Longer Poems 1964–1988* Mainstream Publishing, Edinburgh 1990 p. 40.

126. White 1990 op. cit. (*Handbook*) p. 187. The concluding thoughts of Ernst Cassirer's *Language and Myth* Dover, New York 1953, which address the continued presence of myth in modern lyric poetry, are particularly applicable to White's work: 'Word and mythic image, which once confronted the human mind as hard realistic powers, have now . . . become a light, bright ether in which the spirit can move without let or hindrance. This liberation is achieved not because the mind throws aside the sensuous forms of word and image, but in that it uses them both as *organs* of its own, and thereby recognizes them for what they really are: forms of its own self-revelation.' p. 99.

127. White 1990 op. cit. (*Blue Road*) p. 143.

128. There is a fine blend of the spirit of the shaman and the trickster in some of these poems. For an example of direct contact, White follows a similar path, but in the Far East this time, in his Japan-Hokkaido book *The Wild Swans* (*Les Cygnes sauvages*), Paris, Grasset 1990.

129. *Le Chemin du Chaman* Pierre-Alain Pingoud (PAP), Lausanne 1990 p. 32 (trans. Kenneth White). The book is illustrated with a range of shamanic drawings from Altaic, Eskimo, European and African hunting cultures. When White wrote the book, he thought of it 'as a kind of ballet'. The Parisian-domiciled jazz saxophonist Steve Lacy (who in 1979 recorded parts of the *Tao Te Ching* to music, on *The Way* Hat Hut/hat ART 2029) has subsequently set *Le Chemin du Chaman* to music. With regard to contemporary 'native' shamanism in White's itinerary, see his translation (via the French ethnologist Jacques Lemoine) of the Hmong death-initiation poem 'Ki'ua ke', 'showing the way' Pandora, Bangkok 1983.

130. *Letters From Gourgounel* Jonathan Cape, London 1966 p. 9. The conclusion to this book is reminiscent of both the remarks of Jan Garbarek about the forest we have within us, wherever we go (see Chapter 6 above), and Jungian ideas of individuation: '. . . I think the forest is everywhere. It is in every man, just as every man is his own prison. Once you have escaped from your prison, and gone through the forest and the ocean of your self, you do not need a real retreat [such as White had experienced at Gourgounel]. You do not need the forest — or a church, or a monastery. The world is open before you. All you need to do — and want to do — is to walk through it.' (p. 144) Living at Gourgounel had taken White 'as far back as needful'. The point was then to walk 'through Gourgounel, to anywhere . . . Now I just want to keep going'. Ibid. Needless to say, White is as aware as the next thinking

person today that we *do* need real forests . . . and mountains . . . and oceans . . . and birds.

131. White 1990 op. cit. (*Blue Road*) p. 132.

132. Inaugural Text, April 1989. Anyone interested in the development of geopoetics can contact the Secretariat of the Institute International de Géopoétique, Chemin du Goaquer, 22560 TREBEURDEN, France.

133. Ibid.

134. Ibid.

135. Kenneth White's essays, amounting to a whole philosophy of culture, under the general title of *The Nomad Mind*, exist for the moment, in their entirety, only in French. It is very much hoped that they will soon be available in English.

CHAPTER EIGHT

1. Rudhyar, D. *The Magic of Tone and The Art of Music* Shambhala, Boulder and London 1982 pp. 6, 17 and 34.

2. Ibid. p. 34.

3. Lowenstein 1973 op. cit. p. xxiii.

4. Rudhyar 1982 op. cit. p. 25. Rudhyar discusses various numerological and philosophical bases of the idea of 'the sacred Tone'.

5. Roth, G. (with Loudon, J.) *Maps To Ecstasy: Teachings of an Urban Shaman* Mandala/ HarperCollins, London 1990 p. 26.

6. Ibid. One thinks of the recent political-ecological concerns of Sting, for example.

7. Ibid. p. 34.

8. Ibid. p. 62.

9. Innes 1981 op cit. p. 51. See also Wigman, M. *The Language of Dance* (trans. Walter Sorell) Wesleyan University Press, Middletown, Connecticut 1986.

10. Ibid. (Innes) p. 53.

11. Ibid. pp. 53–4 (from reviews of 1923–31).

12. Ibid. p. 54.

13. Bechet, S. *Treat It Gentle: An Autobiography* Da Capo Press, New York 1979 p. 127.

14. Whitcomb, I. *After The Ball: Pop Music from Rag to Rock* Penguin, Harmondsworth 1972 p. 89.

15. Bell, C. *Since Cézanne* Chatto and Windus, London 1929 p. 216 (first pub. 1922).

16. Larkin, P. *Required Writing: Miscellaneous Pieces 1955-1982* Faber and Faber, London and Boston 1983 pp. 291–3. Ironically enough, Coltrane recorded a moving tribute to Bechet on his 1960 album *Coltrane Plays The Blues* (London Atlantic HA-K 8017).

17. Rutherford 1986 op. cit. p. 13.

18. Sylvian, D. *Alchemy – An Index of Possibilities* (Virgin SYL 1). See Dilberto, J. 'David Sylvian: Maker of Earth-Bound Atmospheres' *Downbeat* March 1988 pp. 26–28 for Sylvian's encounter with jazz.

19. Quoted in Berendt, J-E. *Jazz: A Photo History* (trans. William Odom) Andre Deutsch Limited, London 1979 p. 221.

20. See Hodge, J.L., Struckmann, D.K. and Dorland Trost, L. *Cultural Bases of Western Racism and Group Oppression* Two Riders Press, Berkeley 1975 passim.

21. Thoreau 1960 op. cit. p. 15.

22. Ibid. pp. 10 and 150.

23. Weather Report *I Sing The Body Electric* (CBS S 64943).

24. Sleevenotes to *Weather Report* (CBS S 64521).

25. See Hamel, P.M. *Through Music to The Self* Compton Press, Tisbury 1978 and Berendt, J-E. *Nada Brahma: The World is Sound* East West Publications, London and The Hague 1987.

26. Machlis, J. *Introduction to Contemporary Music* J.M. Dent and Son Ltd, London 1963 p. 99.

27. See Bowers, F. *The New Scriabin* David and Charles, Newton Abbott 1974 pp. 43–100 and 124–6.

28. Small, C. *Music, Society, Education* John Calder, London 1977 p. 109.

29. Stravinsky: Introductory remarks to his own recording of *Le Sacre du Printemps* (CBS 72533).

30. See the discussion of Sibelius in Chapter 6; Holbrook, D. *Gustav Mahler and The Courage To Be* Vision Press, London 1975 (for a phenomenological approach to 'The creative work which Mahler does on time and structure, by way of escaping from the limitations of Western modes' pp. 29–30); Machlis 1963 op. cit. pp. 318–24 (for an introduction to Orff's integration of melody and speech and the *ostinato* primitivism of his deliberate archaism); Partsch, H. *Genesis of a Music* Da Capo, New York 1974 (Partsch developed a forty-three-note-to-the-octave scale, designed and built his own instruments, and produced music in the ancient, ritualistic spirit of a composite culture: see Mellers, W. *Music in a New Found Land: Themes and Developments in the History of American Music* Barrie and Rockcliff, London 1964 pp. 169–77 for a comparison of the ritualistic 'corporeality' of Partsch's music with that of Orff); Machlis 1963 op. cit. pp. 328–30 (for an introduction to Messiaen's synthesis of Eastern and Western elements and his use of

birdsong); Stockhausen, K. *Towards a Cosmic Music* (ed. and trans. Tim Nevill) Element Books, Shaftesbury 1989 (see below); and such compositions as *Sacrifice* (1962) and *November Steps* (1967) (Takemitsu) and *Drumming* (1971) and *Music for a Large Ensemble* (1978) (Reich).

31. From 'The Seven Days': quoted on back cover of Stockhausen 1989 op cit.

32. Ibid. p. 14.

33. Ibid. p. 120.

34. Available on Deutsche Grammophon 423 378—2, together with Stockhausen's instructions on the sort of 'nocturnal-erotic' costume which would be ideal for the performance.

35. Stockhausen 1989 op. cit. p. 98.

36. Ibid. p. 120.

37. Ibid. p. 13.

38. See Harner 1982 op. cit. pp. 64—9 for a discussion of the changes in the central nervous system produced by the 'repetitive sound . . . the steady, monotonous beat' of the Tungus shaman's drum, enhanced by 'the higher frequencies' of the bells and iron trinkets on his costume. See also Nicholson, S. (ed.) *Shamanism: An Expanded View of Reality* Quest/The Theosophical Publishing House, Wheaton 1987 passim. See Chapter 4 above for the comments of Ken Hyder on shamanic drumming. It is the strictly metronomic and manufactured quality of the electro-rhythms of the British House group The Shamen's 1990 *En-Tact* (TPLP 22 CD) which severely reduces the value of the energy (or NRG, as they prefer to spell it) of their would-be modern-tribalistic dance music.

39. Shapiro, N. and Hentoff, N. *The Jazz Makers* Peter Davies, London 1957 p. 43. For Dodds, anyone who wants to be a jazz drummer 'must be a musician. You can't be just anybody. Anybody can't drum. Anybody can beat a drum, but anybody can't drum.' Ibid. p. 19. Years later, Rashied Ali, the drummer who eventually replaced Elvin Jones in the John Coltrane group, made a similar (forceful) point about percussion instruments. See Simpkins 1975 op. cit. p. 207.

40. Quoted in Abrahams, R.D. *Positively Black* Prentice-Hall Inc, New Jersey 1970 pp. 157—8.

41. Lao Tsu *Tao Te Ching* (trans. Gia-Fu Feng and Jane English) Vintage Books, New York 1972 ('verse' 64).

42. Printed in *International Times* January 1967. Quoted in White, K. 1975 op. cit. p. 31.

43. Davies, E. 'Psychological Characteristics of Beatle Mania' in Denisoff, R.S. (ed.) *Sociology: Theories In Conflict* Wadsworth, Belmont 1972 p. 224.

44. Ibid. p. 229.

45. *An American Prayer* (Elektra ELK 52 111).

46. 'Shaman's Blues' is on *The Soft Parade* (Elektra EKS 75 005).

47. Hopkins, J. and Sugerman, D. *No One Here Gets Out Alive* Plexus, London 1980 p. 160. In Oliver Stone's 1991 film *The Doors*, the shamanic implications of Morrison's performances were underlined through the introduction of an explicit shamanic motif at certain key moments in the film.

48. Morrison, J. *The Lords. The New Creatures* Omnibus, London 1985 pp. 5 and 23—4.

49. Morrison, J. *Wilderness: The Lost Writings of Jim Morrison* Viking/Penguin, Harmondsworth 1988 p. 71. In 1989 I discussed the shamanic aspects of Morrison's persona with Genesis P-Orridge of Throbbing Gristle and Psychic TV. He made the point that Morrison's drink and drug problems epitomised the problem of encountering the extraordinary energy created by shamanic consciousness without having either the full understanding or traditional means necessary to control and develop it. Personal communication August 1989. (Extending the theme of shamanism in rock music, much of Psychic TV's *Live In Rekyjavik* (Temple Records 026/History 12), which partly documents the pagan wedding of Paula and Genesis P-Orridge in Iceland, contains passages of compelling, primal 'sound-power' e.g. the opening 'Those Who Do Not'. For P-Orridge's views on a series of related issues see *RE/SEARCH* Nos 4/5 San Francisco 1982 which also contains material on William S. Burroughs and Brion Gysin. The Byrds and Captain Beefheart and his Magic Band are but two further, very different rock groups who merit consideration from a shamanic perspective. See also Reynolds, S. 'Jah Wobble: Invading his heart' *The Wire* issue 93 November 1991 pp. 38—41 for Wobble's shaman-like growth from punk militancy to an individuated perception of the healing potentialities of music.) *Hekura: Yanomano Shamanism from Southern Venezuela* (QUARTZ 004) is an extraordinary document of the use of hallucinogenic drugs in shamanic healing. Periodically ingesting ebene powder (collected from tree bark) through their nostrils, the

shamans circle around a sick man, chanting, growling and screaming in freely phrased, but strongly rhythmical fashion. See the discussion by David Toop (who recorded the session) in '(Ghost) Riders in the Sky: Three Aspects of Shamanism' *PS* No 7 January-February 1981. On the question of hallucinogens and shamanism see Harner, M.J. (ed.) *Hallucinogens and Shamanism* Oxford University Press, New York 1978 and De Rios, M. D. (ed.) *Hallucinogens: Cross-Cultural Perspectives* Prism Press, Bridport 1990.

50. *Led Zeppelin* (Atlantic 250 008).

51. Sarlin, B. *Turn It Up! (I Can't Hear The Words)* Coronet/Hodder, London 1975 p. 17 and passim.

52. Goldberg, S. 'Bob Dylan and the Poetry of Salvation' in McGregor, C. (ed.) *Bob Dylan: A Retrospective* William Morrow and Co, New York 1972 p. 368. This is an unusually perceptive, wide-ranging article on Dylan, relating his work to both Romanticism and the East.

53. Mellers, W. *A darker shade of pale: A backdrop to Bob Dylan* Faber and Faber, London 1984 p. 137.

54. Ibid. pp. 137—8.

55. Yorke, R. *Van Morrison: into the music* Charisma/Futura, London 1975 p. 54.

56. 'Dweller on the Threshold' from *Beautiful Vision* (Mercury 6302 122). The lyric addresses the problem of 'penetrating the realm of glamour' in order to see oneself in true light, and was inspired by *Glamour – A World Problem* by Alice Bailey.

57. Anthony Wall (director) *One Irish Rover* BCC Arena March 1991.

58. Bly, R. *Iron John: A Book About Men* Addison-Wesley, New York 1990 passim.

59. 'Listen To The Lion' from *Saint Dominic's Preview* (Warner Bros. Records K 46172).

60. Wall 1991 op. cit.

61. John Lee Hooker *The Healer* (Silvertone Records ORE LP 508). Singer Gil Scott-Heron and The Last Poets have both addressed this theme from a jazz perspective: e.g. 'Lady Day and John Coltrane' from Heron's *Pieces of a Man* (Flying Dutchman/Philips 6369 415) and The Last Poets' 'Jazzoetry' and 'Bird's Word' from *Chastisement* (Blue Thumb BTS 39). For background to the theme of the 'wounded healer' in the Afro-American tradition, see Jones, L. *Blues People* William Morrow and Co,

New York 1973, Sidran, B. *Black Talk* Holt, Rhinehart and Winston, New York 1971 and Finn, J. *The Bluesman: The Musical Heritage of Black Men and Women in The Americas* Quartet Books, London 1986. See the comment by photographer and writer Val Wilmer, in her *Mama Said There'd Be Days Like This* The Women's Press, London 1991 p. 316. 'Church (gospel) singers and blues people are shamans who work *with* their listeners to establish and confirm eternal verities. And even those outside the common cultural bank can participate if they know the language.

62. McFerrin, B. *Medicine Music* (EMI CDP 792048 2).

63. Palmer, R. 'The Nelson Touch' *Jazz Journal International* September 1990 p. 11 (quoted from *Downbeat* April 24 1975). Needless to say, Nelson's comment should not be interpreted in the light of any insane rationalisation of the obscenity of slavery.

64. See Starr, F. S. *Jazz Red and Hot: The Fate of Jazz in the Soviet Union* Oxford University Press, New York and London 1983 and Zwerin, M. *La Tristesse de Saint Louis: Swing Under The Nazis* Quartet Books, London 1985.

65. Joans, T. *A Black Manifesto in Jazz Poetry and Prose* Signature/Calder and Boyars, London 1971 p. 73.

66. Hadler, M. 'Jazz And The Visual Arts' *Arts Magazine* June 1983 p. 100.

67. See Richter 1966 op. cit. p. 20; Melzer, A. 1980 op. cit. pp. 30—2, and Rothenberg, J. 1981 op. cit. p. 166.

68. Hadler 1983 op. cit. p. 96.

69. Johnson 1989 op. cit. p. 12.

70. Occhiogrosso, P. 'Anthony Braxton Explains Himself' *Downbeat* August 12 1976 p. 49.

71. Lock, G. *Forces In Motion: Anthony Braxton and the Meta-Reality of Creative Music* Quartet Books, London 1988 p. 63.

72. Ibid. p. 155.

73. Ibid. p. 182. See pp. 384—5 for some of the recordings which Crispell has made under her own name e.g. the 1987 *Gaia* (Leo Records).

74. 'Unit Structures: Cecil Taylor in conversation with Bill Smith' *Coda* March 1975 p. 2. In the same interview Taylor describes himself as 'a vehicle for certain ancestral forces that this body has been fortunate enough to hear and pass on to people, and together in a community situation we exercise certain conversations.' p. 6.

75. In Santano, G. 'Cecil Taylor: An American

Romantic' *Downbeat* June 1990 pp. 16—18 Taylor first casts some doubt on this quotation, but then reiterates the point of it by stressing how important dance is to him. See Stearns, M. and Stearns, J. *Jazz Dance: The Story of American Vernacular Dance* Collier-Macmillan Ltd, London 1968 and Thorpe, E. *Black Dance* Chatto and Windus Ltd, London 1989 for historical overviews of the relation of dance and jazz within the black tradition.

76. Lock 1988 op. cit. p. 316 (quoted from sleevenotes to *Live In The Black Forest*).

77. Taylor, C. 'Sound Structure of Subculture Becoming Major Breath/Naked Fire Gesture': poetry on the sleeve of mid-1960s *Unit Structures* recording (Blue Note BLP 4237).

78. *Communications* (JCOA 1001/2); *Silent Tongues* (Freedom FLP 40146); *Winged Serpent (Sliding Quadrants)* (Soul Note SN 1089); *For Olim* (Soul Note SN 1150); *In Florescence* (A&M 395286 — 2). For more of Taylor's poetry in performance, the 1987 *Tzotzil/Mummers/Tzotzil* (Leo LR 162) and *Live In Vienna* (Leo 408/409) are recommended. The latter contains an interesting interview with Taylor by Spencer A. Richards, revealing Taylor's strong affinity with the poetry of Robert Hayden; both records feature the quicksilver Thurman Barker on drums.

79. Jamal, M. (ed.) *ShapeShifters: Shaman Women in Contemporary Society* Arkana/Penguin, Harmondsworth 1987 p. 165.

80. Lock 1988 op. cit. p. 182.

81. Lynch, K. 'Cecil Taylor And The Poetics Of Living' *Downbeat* November 1986 p. 67. Taylor is unequivocal: 'Having spent quite some time in Japan, it became evident that the separation of mind and body is a Western sickness. Because it seems to me that the great poets do not separate the passion that they use. If anything, the passion instructs the nature of the intellect.' p. 24.

82. Johnson, H. and Pines, J. *Reggae: Deep Roots Music* Channel Four/Proteus Books, London 1982 p. 80.

83. See Williams, M. *The Jazz Tradition* Oxford University Press, New York 1970 pp. 3—15 for an incisive introduction to socio/psychological questions of jazz's 'meaning'. Williams's fundamental and well-argued point, that jazz involves 'discovery of one's worthiness from within', leads him to the Jungian-like conclusion that 'Perhaps in jazz, then, the gods, in some small way, prepare for their metamorphosis'

(p. 15). See also Berendt, J-E. 'Glosses on a Philosophy of Jazz' in Berendt, J-E (ed.) *The Story of Jazz* Barrie and Jenkins, London 1978.

84. Thoreau 1960 op. cit. p. 216.

85. Ibid. p. 216.

86. See Hamel 1978 op. cit. pp. 89—91 for a consideration of mathematical, magical and mythical approaches to musical time.

87. In 1984 Soul Note records released *Pieces of Time* (Soul Note SN 1078), a collaboration between drummers Kenny Clarke, Milford Graves, Andrew Cyrille and Famoudou Don Moye with sleevenotes by Max Roach. The music, especially the eight-minute 'Energy Cycles', is a rich, variegated mixture of layered, polyphonic structures and free flights of melodic and percussive imagination. In Spring 1990 Andrew Cyrille, the catalyst of the project, long-time collaborator with Cecil Taylor and one of the major drummers and band leaders of the past twenty-five years, spoke to me of his belief in the healing potentialities of such music. Cyrille has a very strong sense of learning from, inheriting and extending the drum tradition in jazz — keeping the music 'on the creative edge', while also preserving the archetypal power of the tradition *which has always been one of imagination and verve.* Personal communication, Spring 1990. See Wilmer, V. *As Serious as Your Life: The Story of The New Jazz* Quartet Books, London 1977 pp. 153—88 for the considerable degree to which such drummers as Cyrille, Graves, Sunny Murray and Rashied Ali have reflected on the healing import of their music. For Max Roach's views on the potentialities of percussion see Fox, C. 'Sit Down and Listen: The story of Max Roach' in Haydon, G. and Marks, D. (eds.) *Repercussions: A Celebration of African-American Music* Century Publishing, London 1985.

88. Count Ossie and The Rasta Family *Man From Higher Heights* (Vista Sounds VSLP 4060); Bob Marley and The Wailers *Legend* (Island BMW 1).

89. Ismael Ivo Notes to *Phoenix* (world premier October 1985, Berlin), Pegasos, Berlin (unpaginated). Ivo comes from Sao Paolo, which he describes as the largest industrial centre in South America and one of the most densely populated and violent cities in the world: the primitivism of his Pan-African art is anything but escapist or neglectful of history.

90. Finn 1986 op. cit. passim e.g. 'a good blues

performer must needs be something of a
sorcerer.' (p. 209). One of the great West
African *griots* (praise singers) of recent years is
the Mali singer Salif Keita. Keita's music — such
as the 1987 *Soro* (Stern's Africa Sterns 1020) —
combines the traditional wailing power of
Islamic singing with Western technology and
arrangements which are at times reminiscent of
James Brown. Born an albino, Keita — who has
lived in Paris since the early 1980s — has long
been conscious of himself as both an outsider
and a prophet: 'I think that all musicians, all
artists, are in some measure prophets. Art
comes from the heart and the heart is nearer to
God.' Hanly, F. and May, T. (eds.) *Rhythms of
The World* BBC Books, London 1989 p. 76.

91. Murray, C.S. *Crosstown Traffic: Jimi Hendrix and
post-war pop* Faber and Faber, London 1989
p. 145.

92. Ibid. p. 204.

93. 'Voodoo Chile' from *Electric Ladyland* (Polydor
823 359 – 2).

94. This is, of course, a contentious point. Some
musicians — such as Cecil Taylor and Vernon
Reid, guitarist with Living Colour — are more
than happy to celebrate the links between e.g.
James Brown or Sly Stone and jazz; others,
such as bebop guitarist Nathen Page, believe
that lines must be drawn and jazz's *particular*
history and achievement stressed. See e.g.
Smith/Taylor 1975 op. cit. p. 7; Shaar 1989 op.
cit. p. 130 and *Jazz Journal International* April
1991 p. 13. On the totality of the black music
tradition, see Wilmer, V. *The Face of Black Music*
(photographs by Valerie Wilmer. Introduction
by Archie Shepp) Da Capo Press, New York
1976. A reflection by Jimi Hendrix sets the tone
of this superb documentation of the African-
American experience, as expressed in music:
'Music is going to break the way. It's like the
waves of the ocean. You can't just cut out the
perfect wave and take it home with you. It's
constantly moving all the time.' Ibid.
(unpaginated).

95. A reference to French critic and record
producer Hughes Panassie's (in)famous
celebration of pre-bebop jazz and critique of
'progressive' or 'would-be artistic' jazz in his
The Real Jazz A.S. Barnes/The Jazz Book Club,
London 1967. See e.g. pp. 253–62, written in
1960 and sceptical of the lasting importance of
Ornette Coleman's innovations. (In fact, such
innovations helped to bring back to jazz much

of the soulfulness which Panassie loved, and
have been of great importance for the world-
wide development of jazz in the last thirty
years.)

96. See Rozelle, R.V., Wardlaw, A., and McKenna,
M.A. (eds.) *Black Art: Ancestral Legacy The
African Impulse In African-Amerian Art* Dallas
Museum of Art/Harry N. Abrams, New York
1990 pp. 254–55.

97. Lock 1988 op. cit. p. 12.

98. Jost, E. *Free Jazz* Universal Edition, Vienna
1975 p. 191. This book contains good
discussions of such other key developments
from Chicago as the various groups which
emerged from The Association For The
Advancement Of Creative Musicians which
pianist and composer Muhal Richard Abrams
established in the 1960s. Compositions such as
'The Bird Song' and the title track from
Abrams's 1968 recording *Levels and Degrees of
Light* (Delmark 413) typified the strong
mythopoeic concerns of such Chicagoans'
music, realised with a breadth of approach
which embraced the spaciousness of
impressionism as well as the fire of 1960s free
improvising. The Art Ensemble of Chicago, the
best-known of the groups to have emerged
from AACM, strike an unmistakably shamanic
note in their music. Hear, for example, the
myth-poem 'Illustrum' from *Fanfare for the
Warriors* (1973) on Atlantic ATL 50 304, where
the 'sun people' of the African diaspora battle
against the 'silver queen of the ghost world', or
the concern for ritualistic dynamics throughout
Urban Bushmen (1980) on ECM 1211/12. In
1990 the AEC made an excellent record with
Cecil Taylor, *Dreaming of the Masters* Vol 2
(DIW-846-E).

99. 'The Seeker' from *The Art Of Rahsaan Roland
Kirk* (Atlantic ATL 60042).

100. Daniels, D.H. 'Goodbye Pork Pie Hat: Lester
Young as Spiritual Figure' *Annual Review of Jazz
Studies* No 4 Transaction Books, New York
1988 p. 169. This important article (pp. 161–77)
provides essential material on the spiritual
context of innovative jazz activity. Although
Daniels does not mention shamanism, there are
shamanic implications in much of what he says.

101. DeMichael, D. 'John Coltrane And Eric Dolphy
Answer The Critics' *Downbeat* July 12 1979
p. 52. The article/interview first appeared in
Downbeat in 1962, and to be fair to DeMichael,
he was speaking for other critics (such as John

Tynan) much of the time. For a detailed study of Dolphy (who was inspired by aspects of the Western musical avant-garde as well as by the jazz tradition and birdsong) see Simosko, V. and Tepperman, B. *Eric Dolphy: A Musical Biography and Discography* Da Capo, New York 1979. A later alto saxophonist of note, Steve Coleman, has been inspired by the flight patterns of bees. See Alleyne, S. 'Steve Coleman: 21st Century Sax' *Straight No Chaser* Winter 1990 pp. 16–19.

102. David M. Guss 1985 op cit.
103. 'Theme For The Eulipions' from *The Return Of The 5000lb Man* (Warner Bros. WB 56 202).
104. Ullmann, M. *Jazz Lives: Portraits In Words and Pictures* Perigee/J.P. Putnam's Sons, New York 1980 p. 129.
105. Nicholson 1987 op. cit. p. 202.
106. The 1956 *Ezz-Thetic* (RCA PL 42187), 1960 *Jazz in The Space Age* (MCA MAPD 7031) and 1983 *So What* (Blue Note BT 85132) are representative examples of Russell's work. See Harrison, M. 'Rational Anthems' *The Wire* Nos 3/4/5, Spring/Summer/Autumn 1983.
107. The 1983 *Hemispheres* (Gramavision GR 8303) is a good example of Davis's unstereotypical music. Commissioned by choreographer Molissa Fenley for the evening-length dance *Hemispheres*, the shifts in the music's rhythmic density provided an appropriate structural counterpart to the unfolding myth-narrative of Èṣù-Ẹlẹgbára, the Pan-African Trickster figure who embodies the creative union of opposites (and who was identified with Satan by Western missionaries). Known as the divine linguist and guardian of the crossroads, this mediator of worlds clearly takes his/her place within the tradition of shamanism: in sculpture he/she is represented with well-defined female breasts.
108. See Hunt, D.C. 'Today's Jazz Artist: His Communication and Our Technological Age' in Rivelli, P. and Levin, R. (eds.) *Giants of Black Music* Da Capo, New York 1979. Written in 1969, Hunt's thoughts are addressed to the so-called 'New Thing' jazz of the 1960s. However, his words apply to all creative jazz, from Louis Armstrong onwards: 'The contemporary jazz artist is a valuable spokesman. Philosophically, he has the beautiful capacity, through a musical instrument, to dramatize the human condition. His artistic talking, shouting, singing, moaning, and crying serve to awaken us to the artificial living patterns of our society — the slightness of understanding, the easy acceptance — all that

reeks of sterility . . . The alternative to man as a slave in a world of central control is a rebirth of man as a spiritual animal. Recognition of today's jazz artist and his continual focus on the human approach to universal truth will aid in that rebirth.' p. 66. See also Levin, R. 'The New Jazz and the Nature of its Enemy' in Sinclair, J. and Levin, R. (eds.) *Music and Politics* The World Publishing Company, New York 1971 pp. 78–86.

109. Cole 1976 op. cit. p. 11 (the comment was made in an interview of 1962).
110. DeMichael 1967 op. cit. p. 52.
111. Cole 1976 op. cit. p. 33 From the point of view of a shamanic understanding of Coltrane's music, this book is indispensable for its cross-cultural connections and synthesis of technical analysis and emotional perception. In what follows, I have largely concentrated on Coltrane himself: for a closely reasoned analysis of the essential role of other musicians — particularly Elvin Jones — in the development of the saxophonist's music, Cole's book is highly recommended.
112. Ibid. p. 32.
113. See the posthumously released *Cosmic Music* (Impulse/Coltrane Records AS 9148) and the interview with Frank Kosky in the latter's *Black Nationalism and the Revolution in Music* Pathfinder Press, New York 1972 e.g. Coltrane's idea that true power 'is to be part of all, and the only way you can be part of all is to understand it. And when there's something you don't understand, you have to go humbly to it' p. 242. On Sufism see Shah, I. *The Sufis* Star/W.H. Allen, London 1977. Many jazz musicians of the post-bebop era became involved with Islam, Sufism or the Baha'i Faith. See e.g. Gillespie, D. (with Fraser, A.) *To Be Or Not To Bop: The Autobiography of Dizzy Gillespie* W.H. Allen and Co, London 1980 pp. 473–76. Gillespie's thoughts on the origin of the word 'jazz' and the music's relation to both painting and social change are extremely interesting: 'Jazz is an African word [from Malenke *jasi* meaning to act out of the ordinary, thus to speed up, to excite, to act uninhibited]. It doesn't detract from the importance, the seriousness, or the dignity of our music [as some musicians and critics have suggested] . . . In improvisation, the first thing you must have is the sight of a gifted painter. You've got to . . . see colours and lines in music . . . The role

of music goes hand in hand with social reformation – the changing of society to make things right because music is a form of worship.' Ibid. pp. 492–3.

114. One of the strangest comments ever made about Coltrane is that by Richard Cook in his article 'John Coltrane: Every Time I Hear The Sound': 'Coltrane is almost never tender . . . Emotional touchstones are subsumed by the torrent of [his] playing. We can search for nobility, anger or sadness and fail to locate any of them . . . nothing rests long enough to take the clear shape of a communicated feeling.' *The Wire* No 22 December 1985 p. 32.

115. See Cole 1976 op. cit. pp. 178–83 for the development of this 'speaking in tongues' by Coltrane and such collaborators as Dolphy and Pharoah Sanders from *c.*1961 to 1965/66. Describing the playing of two notes at a time by both Coltrane and Sanders at the beginning of the 1965 *Meditations*, Cole says 'it sounds like birds, or gives the image of birds gathering'. p. 183.

116. Simpkins 1975 op. cit. p. 209.

117. Kofsky 1972 op. cit. pp. 221–43.

118. See Thomas, J. C. *Chasin' The Trane: The music and mystique of John Coltrane* Elm Tree Books, London 1976 p. 103 for a comparison of the nature of the 'lingering melancholy, a visceral sadness' in the sound of Stan Getz with the (more universal) sense of melancholy and longing in Coltrane. Later, Thomas quotes John Taggart's comparison of Coltrane's approach to music with 'some of the procedures Castaneda talks about in the Don Juan books', but does not go into specific detail. p. 133.

119. Wilmer 1977 op. cit. p. 43 offers an incisive summary of Coltrane's personal impact on many, pointing out e.g. how his respect for his wife's contribution to music started many players thinking about including women in their music. Alice Coltrane has made a particularly revealing comment about her husband's music: 'A higher principle is involved here. Some of his latest works aren't musical compositions. I mean they weren't based entirely on music. A lot of it has to do with mathematics, some on rhythmic structure and the power of repetition, some of elementals. *He always felt that sound was the first manifestation in creation before music.*' Cole 1976 op. cit. p. 173.

120. See Hamel 1976 op. cit. pp. 112 and 119–20 for a summary of Lama Govinda's discussion of

the meaning of Om in his *Foundations of Tibetan Mysticism*. The extent and depth of Coltrane's reading in Eastern philosophy is hard to assess. He was familiar with the work of Kahlil Gibran; fellow saxophonist Sonny Rollins had once suggested *Autobiography of a Yogi* to him, and pianist Bill Evans recommended Krishnamurti's *Commentaries on Living.* See Thomas 1976 op. cit. p. 91. As already remarked, the humility which Coltrane reveals in the interview in Kofsky 1972 op. cit. is redolent of Sufi beliefs.

121. Cole 1976 op. cit. p. 94. This simple phrase bears much reflection.

122. Archie Shepp sleevenote to *Mama Too Tight* (Impulse SIPL 508).

123. *Music Is The Healing Force of The Universe* (Impulse AS 9191).

124. Ken Hyder believes that, in its constantly shifting patterns of sound and freedom from metronomic regularity, the drumming of Sunny Murray on the *Spiritual Unity* recording is very similar to shamanic archetypes. (See note 38 above.) He also believes that Murray's half Native American heritage is important to consider here. Personal communication, April 1991.

125. Leon Thomas quoted in Nat Hentoff's sleevenotes to *Spirits Known and Unknown* (Flying Dutchman/Philips 6373 001). Also available in Rivelli and Levin 1979 op. cit. pp. 113–117.

126. Ibid. Joe Lee Wilson (*b.*1935) is another outstanding Afro-American singer who has developed the scat tradition of jazz singing into shaman-like areas of primal power. He has also done much to emphasise the crucial role of the blues in jazz. Hear e.g. 'Mode For Trane', his splendid tribute to Coltrane on *Secrets From The Sun* (Inner City 1042).

127. Don Cherry quoted in Joachim-Ernst Berendt's sleevenotes to *Actions* (Philips 6305 153).

128. Taylor, A. *Notes And Tones: Musician To Musician Interviews* Quartet Books, London 1983 p. 176.

129. Jost 1975 op. cit. p. 162.

130. Sun Ra *Purple Night* (A&M 395 324 – 2). CODONA made three records: ECM 1132, 1177 and 1243. Other works featuring Cherry which are of especial interest in the present context are the 1973 *Eternal Now* (Sonet SNTF 653), with its strong atmosphere of Asian meditation; Collin Walcott's *Grazing Dreams* (ECM 1096) from 1977; the 1981 *Bitter Funeral*

Beer (ECM 1179), released under drummer/percussionist Bengt Berger's name and based on funeral music from Ghana; the two duo collaborations with drummer Ed Blackwell – the 1969 *Mu* (Affinity AFF 17) and 1982 *El Corazon* (ECM 1230) – and the 1979 *Old and New Dreams* (ECM 1154), with fellow Ornette Coleman collaborators Blackwell, Dewey Redman and Charlie Haden. Bassist Haden's 'Song For The Whales' on this last recording is a statement of shaman-like empathy for the natural world: some extraordinary arco work near the bridge of the bass conjures something of the mystery of this threatened species's existence.

131. Lange, A. 'The Keith Jarrett Interview' *Downbeat* June 1984 p. 18.
132. Carr 1991 op. cit. p. 154.
133. Ibid. p. 41.
134. Jarrett, K. sleevenotes to *Concerts* (ECM 1227/28/29).
135. *Death and The Flower* (Impulse AS 9301) and *The Survivors' Suite* (ECM 1085) are good examples of the former; *Belonging* (ECM 1050) and *Personal Mountains* (ECM 1382) of the latter.
136. *Invocations/The Moth and The Flame* (ECM 1201/02).
137. Carr 1991 op. cit. pp. 160–1.
138. Keith Jarrett sleevenotes to *Spirits* (ECM 1333/4).
139. Carr 1991 op. cit. p. 28.
140. Title of 1976 American quartet recording *Eyes of The Heart* (ECM 1150); sleevenotes to *Changeless* (ECM 1392); Lange 1984 op. cit. p. 19. The title of the beautifully sprung, funky blues which 'headlined' Jarrett's 1990 Town Hall, New York live recording with Peacock and De Johnette could not have been more appropriate: *The Cure* (ECM 1440).
141. In what follows I only have room to suggest a small fraction of the relevant material. See Burwell, P. 'Radical Structure' *Studio International* November/ December 1976 for a wide-ranging discussion of free improvisation within a largely British context, including such diverse musicians as saxophonist Evan Parker and drummer/percussionist Frank Perry – both of whose work can be related to shamanic ideas e.g. Parker's playing on The Alexander von Schlippenbach Quartet's *The Hidden Peak* (FMP 0410) and Frank Perry's solo recording *Deep Peace* (QUARTZ 007). Drummer and percussionist Burwell's various points concerning the freeing of musical performance from the alienating grasp of commodity culture have clear shamanic implications: Burwell's argument is advanced with references to Carlos Castaneda and Claude Lévi-Strauss. David Toop, with whom Burwell often worked at the time, was one of the first commentators on jazz to emphasise the shamanic nature of the work of certain jazz/free drummers: see his 'An Open Letter to Richard Williams' *Musics* No 16 February 1978 p. 19. A key question with regard to the relation of free improvisation to shamanism is the extent to which practitioners of the former are interested in archetypes of expression, be they those of structure or feeling. For some free improvisers, the very idea of playing song-like melody is heresy.
142. *Nan Madol* (Japo 60007; re-released on ECM). Alice Coltrane has done much to advance the use of the harp in jazz.
143. *Satu* (ECM 1088). See Vahasilta, T. 'Edvard Vesala: a drummer from the north' *Jazz Forum* No 92 1/1985.
144. *Springbird* (Leo Records 005) See Sermila, J. 'Juhani Aaltonen' *Jazz Forum* No 42 4/76.
145. Feigin, L. (ed.) *Russian Jazz: New Identity* Quartet Books, London 1985 p. 113 contains extracts from the enthusiastic Western reviews. (NB: The London-based Leo Records, which is run by Leo Feigin, should not be confused with Edvard Vesala's Finnish-based company of the same name.) The *Live In Leningrad* release by Arkhangelsk (Leo LR 135) should also be mentioned here, for there are strong echoes of shamanism in this sextet's blend of electronics, hypnotic drum patterns, crying vocalese and more traditional elements of jazz.
146. Ibid. p. 120 It is refreshing to see Yukechev mentioning Oscar Peterson in this context. The spiritual worth of Peterson's work has sometimes been maligned by lazy-eared critics (and musicians) who profess to hear nothing but exceptional technique in his playing. For a thoroughly researched appreciation of Peterson's essentially Romantic art see Palmer, R. *Oscar Peterson* Spellmount Books, Tunbridge Wells 1984.
147. Feigin 1985 op. cit. p. 117.
148. Ibid. p. 117.
149. Ibid. p. 115.
150. Ibid. p. 42.
151. Ibid. p. 42.

CHAPTER NINE

1. Hitchcock, J.T. 'A Nepali shaman's performance as theater' in Brodsky, T. et al (eds.) 1977 op. cit. p. 42.

2. Bergman, I. 'On Dreams, the Subconscious and Filmmaking' in Petrić, V. (ed.) *Film and Dreams: An Approach to Bergman* Redgrave Publishing Company, P.O. Box 67, South Salem, New York 1981 p. 53.

3. Petrić, V. 'Film and Dreams: A Theoretical-Historical Survey' in ibid. p. 23. This essay offers exactly what its title suggests: among its many felicities, one should single out here the distinction between the hypnagogic state — the period of time before going to sleep at night when it is difficult to say whether we are in fact awake or asleep — and the hypnopompic period which occurs when we awake from sleep. (These distinctions are derived from Charles Tart 'Between Waking and Sleeping: The Hypnagogic State' in *Altered States of Consciousness* Anchor Books, New York 1972 p. 75.) Also important is the similarity which Petrić establishes between 'lucid dream' and film viewing. In either case, the self-consciousness, or knowledge, of being in a either a dream or cinema does not cancel the 'suspension of disbelief' which occurs in the face of the power of the (dream or film) imagery. Ibid. p. 7.

4. Quoted in Stephenson, R. and Phelps, G. *The Cinema as Art* Penguin Books, Harmondsworth 1989 (revised edition) p. 236. It is worth noting that film has supplied a fine, albeit flawed parody of many of the primitivistic themes of the present book, in British director Robert Day's 1960 *The Rebel*. Set mostly in a mythical Paris of bohemian artists and sharp dealers and critics, *The Rebel* stars the late comedian Tony Hancock, who plays a frustrated clerk and would-be artistic iconoclast. The film strings together a series of faintly absurd clichés about the regenerative powers of modern art: few aspects of primitivistic modernism (whether aesthetic or sociological) escape unscathed, as Hancock increasingly warms to his Trickster-like role. However, in retrospect, the final impression the film gives is one of sadness: sadness that Hancock here came so close to the sort of Jungian and shamanic ideas that — had he take them more seriously — might have prevented his decline into alcoholism and eventual suicide in 1967.

5. Tarkovsky, A. *Sculpting In Time: Reflections on The Cinema* (trans. Kitty Hunter-Blair) The Bodley Head, London 1986 p. 66.

6. Richter, H. *The Struggle for the Film* (trans. Ben Brewster) Wildwood House Ltd, Gower Publishing Co., Aldershot 1986 pp. 41–2.

7. Ibid. p. 42.

8. Ibid. p. 163.

9. Eliade 1975 op. cit. p. 126.

10. Berger, J. *Ways Of Seeing* BBC/Pelican/Penguin Books, Harmondsworth 1972 p. 34.

11. This is perhaps an appropriate moment to emphasise that I am of course aware that there have been many good things about the twentieth century: this book was written in the spirit of neither sentimental escapism nor Luddite protest (or at least, not consciously so).

12. Benjamin, W. 'The Work of Art in The Age of Mechanical Reproduction' in *Illuminations* (trans. Harry Zohn) Fontana/Collins, London and Glasgow 1973 p. 224.

13. Ibid. p. 226.

14. Quoted ibid. p. 229.

15. Quoted ibid. p. 229.

16. Ibid. p. 235.

17. Ibid. p. 240.

18. Ibid. pp. 240 and 242–3.

19. Sociologists may answer that such facetious objections are met by the precision with which they have refined their various analytical and descriptive tools. But it is the melancholy fate of sociology to be stranded somewhere between the creativity of the history of ideas (in the sense that Benjamin's essay is an essay in the history of ideas) — a creativity that is not always answerable to empiricists's ideas of 'truth' — and the ultimate inertia of empiricism.

20. Benjamin 1973 op. cit. p. 235.

21. Tarkovsky revealed that he had great difficulty editing the film, 'every scene of which was rooted in personal biography'. *Mirror* was 'not edited in anything like the usual manner': Tarkovsky spoke of 'pushing the various parts of the film around' at the end of shooting, in order find out exactly what sort of film he had made. *Andrei Tarkovsky* (producer Charlie Pattinson) BBC Arena 1987. The positive reactions which *Mirror* elicited from a socially-diverse range of viewers can be read in Tarkovsky 1986 op. cit. pp. 8–12.

22. Biró, Y. *Profane Mythology: The Savage Mind of Cinema* (trans. Imre Goldstein) Indiana University Press, Bloomington 1982 p. 19.

23. Ibid. pp. 19 and 24.

24. Ibid. p. 39.
25. Richter 1986 op. cit. p. 164.
26. Cousineau (ed.) 1990 op. cit. p. 182.
27. Ibid. pp. 180–4.
28. Ibid. p. 181.
29. Biró 1982 op. cit. p. 83.
30. Ibid. p. 84. Biró offers some interesting insights, nevertheless, into the beauty of what she sees as the 'cheerless and ominous world' of nature in Bergman's films. See pp.111–12.
31. Richter 1986 op. cit. p. 163. Richter derived this thought from the Russian director Sergei Eisenstein (1898–1948).
32. Prince, S. *The Warrior's Camera: The Cinema of Akira Kurosawa* Princeton University Press, Princeton, New Jersey 1991 p. 291.
33. Søren Kierkegaard (1813–55). Quoted from his *Journals and Papers* in Oden, T.C. (ed.) *Parables of Kierkegaard* Princeton University Press, Princeton, New Jersey 1978 p. xv.
34. Prince 1991 op. cit. p. 112. *Ikiru*, the Japanese title of the film, is the intransitive verb meaning 'to be'. *How* to be has always been the question for Kurosawa: while the bulk of his work is distinguished by its humanist concerns, the shamanic pursuit of the rebirth of a cosmic dimension is no less remarkable, especially in the later work.
35. Ibid. pp. 235–47.
36. Ibid. p. 149.
37. Quoted in ibid. p. 257.
38. At the time of its release, at least one English critic suggested that in *Dreams* Kurosawa had finally succumbed to sentimentality. While parts of the last sequence of the film — 'Watermill Village' — might fairly be accused of a sentimentalisation of Taoist beliefs, the power of the remainder of the film seems to me to be entirely in keeping with the animistic force of Kurosawa's life-long search for a language of healing, mythopoeic power. Kurosawa's late films have caused critics problems: for example, Audie Block's comment in *Japanese Film Directors* Kodansha International, New York 1978 p. 180 that 'The shantytown atmosphere of *Dodeskaden* is hard to find in contemporary wealthy Japan, and the man in unspoiled nature represented by Dersu is hard to find anywhere in the world' illustrates this critic's belief that the late films embody a 'didactic remoteness'. But at the same time, such a comment diminishes the extraordinary resonance of that mythic *tension* between the forces of history and cosmos

which has long been a crucial part of Kurosawa's essentially shamanic art.
39. Press conference at Hotel du Cap, Antibes. Material issued as part of the publicity for the London showing of *Dreams* summer 1990.
40. The influence of the lighting of a forest landscape in Kurosawa's *Rashomon* (which won the Grand Prize in Venice in 1951) on Bergman might be inferred from several of his films of the mid-1950s; with regard to *The Virgin Spring* (1959) it would seem as though Bergman wished to pay homage to the ritual elements of Kurosawa's mid-1950s work. Bergman himself has suggested that the references to Kurosawa became too overt in this film. For Kurosawa's influence on Tarkovsky, and especially in *Andrei Roublov*, see Le Fanu, M. *The Cinema Of Andrei Tarkovsky* British Film Institute, London 1987 p. 48.
41. See Leszczylowski, M. 'A Year with Andrei' *Sight and Sound* Vol 56 No 4 Autumn 1987 p. 284: 'The two men could see each other at a distance of about fifteen metres. What followed staggered me: each made an about turn, as sharply as though following some elaborate drill, and each made off in his separate direction. Thus the two great ones of this world [who in the past had expressed a desire to meet] passed by without touching.'
42. Bergman, I. *The Magic Lantern: An Autobiography* (trans. Joan Tate) Hamish Hamilton Ltd, London 1988 p. 73.
43. Ibid.
44. Of course, Bergman's art must in turn be seen within the Nordic tradition which stretches back through Carl Dreyer (1889–1968) to Victor Sjöström (1879–1960), who played the lead role of Victor Borg for Bergman in *Wild Strawberries*. See Hardy, F. *Scandinavian Film* The Falcon Press, London 1952 and Harcourt, P. *Six European Directors* Penguin, Harmondsworth 1974 Chapter 5 'The Troubled Pilgrimage of Ingmar Bergman'. To give only one specific example of the correspondences between the film language of Bergman and Tarkovsky, think of the opening shot of *Through a Glass Darkly*, where — to the grave tones of Bach's *Suite no 2 for cello* — Bergman fills the screen with a reverie of cloud and sky, reflected in limpid, still water. There is something absolutely 'right' about the fact that during his last film, *The Sacrifice*, Tarkovsky worked with cameraman Sven Nykvist, who filmed this shot — and so

many others, of course — for Bergman.

45. For a selection of critical perspectives, see e.g. Kaminsky, S.M. and Hill, J.F. (eds.) *Ingmar Bergman: Essays in Criticism* Oxford University Press, Oxford, London, New York 1975. Bergom-Larsson, M. *Ingmar Bergman and Society* The Tantivy Press, London 1978 is a good example of a critic approaching Bergman from a (relatively sensitive) left-wing perspective. Bergom-Larsson locates Bergman's work — particularly his seeming obsession with the problematics of the role of the modern artist — within both the general ideological contradictions of bourgeois society and the increase in State intervention in all aspects of post-World War Two Swedish life. A common (and in my view, particularly inapposite) left-wing criticism of Bergman in the 1960s was that his films 'abstracted' humanity from the socio-historical realm, and were therefore 'ideologically regressive'. For Bergman's response to such criticisms, see e.g. Livingston, P. *Ingmar Bergman and the Rituals of Art* Cornell University Press, Ithaca and London 1982 p. 170 and passim.

46. *Persona* is one of the most important films of the 1960s, and like a good deal of Bergman's work, has not lost any of its power today. See Blackwell, M.J. *Persona: The Transcendent Image* University of Illinois Press, Urbana and Chicago 1986, which includes a bibliography of essays and books about the film. For an application of both Freudian and Jungian perspectives to this film, see Houston, B. and Kinder, M. *Self and Cinema: A Transformalist Perspective* Redgrave Publishing Company, Pleasantville, NY 1980. (See p. 29 for the development of the anima in Bergman's work.)

47. Progoff, I. 'Waking Dream and Living Myth' in Campbell, J. (ed.) *Myths Dreams and Religion* Spring Publications, Inc. Dallas 1988 pp. 193–4. Bergman's comments are taken from a transcript of the interview supplied by Radio TV Reports, Inc, Public Broadcast Laboratory, WNDT-TV, New York. See also *Bergman on Bergman* (interviews with Ingmar Bergman by Stig Björkman, Torsten Manns, Jonas Sima) (trans. Paul Britten Austin) Secker and Warburg, London 1973 p. 164. Bergman speaks of 'the total dissolution of all notions of an other-worldly salvation' that he experienced in the early 1960s, and the growth instead of 'a sense of the holiness — to put it clumsily — to be

found in man himself. The only holiness which really exists. A holiness wholly of this world.' One can imagine that theologians and psychologists might care to debate the import of Bergman's words for some considerable time: for theologically-inflected interpretations of Bergman, see Gill, J.H. *Ingmar Bergman and The Search for Meaning* William B. Erdmans Publishing Company, Grand Rapids, Michigan 1969 and Gibson, A. *The Silence of God: Creative Response to The Films of Ingmar Bergman* Harper and Row Publishers, New York, Evanston and London 1970.

48. Ibid. (Progoff) p. 195.

49. See Livingston 1982 pp. 92–3 and passim. Apart from being one of the essential volumes of Bergman criticism, Livingston's book is one of the most important of all post-Eliade considerations of the role of the 'sacred' in twentieth-century art, exploring the question of violence and 'liminality', for example, in illuminating detail.

50. It may seem strange to see humour mentioned in a discussion of Bergman, but one should remember that he has made at least one internationally successful comedy, the 1955 *Smiles of a Summer Night* (the success of which facilitated the financing of *The Seventh Seal* — itself a film of no little humour, despite its prevalent mood of anguished quest). The range of humour in Bergman is in fact large, and merits an in-depth study.

51. Livingston 1982 op. cit. pp. 107–9.

52. For Bergman's Erasmus speech see Bergman, I. *Persona and Shame: The Screenplays of Ingmar Bergman* Calder and Boyars, London 1972 pp. 1–5.

53. It is precisely the *acknowledgement* and *working through* of the darker sides of life which gives Bergman's work much of its shamanic power.

54. Vesaas 1971 op. cit. 'Beyond One's Grasp' p. 153.

55. In terms of Bergman's intellectual and artistic development, one wonders how much attention he has paid to the work of Pär Lagerkvist and Gunnar Ekelöf, two authors whose various concerns would seem to be close to his own. (His interest in Strindberg is legendary.) Surprisingly, neither is mentioned in *The Magic Lantern*.

56. Sontag, S. *Styles of Radical Will* Secker and Warburg, London 1969 p. 143. The remark is taken from Sontag's essay on *Persona*, pp. 123–45.

57. Le Fanu 1987 op. cit. p. 121.

58. Tarkovsky 1986 op. cit. p. 63.

59. Gaston Bachelard believed that it was difficult, if not impossible, for a poet to empathise with all four of the elements to truly productive effect. From a Bachelardian perspective, therefore, Tarkovsky would seem to present a very special case of synthetic consciousness. Bachelard's work on the poetics of reverie could seem to have been 'made' for Tarkovsky.

60. Tarkovsky 1986 op. cit. p. 63.

61. Ibid. pp. 63–4.

62. Stephenson and Phelps 1989 op. cit. p. 122.

63. They are also, at times, noticeable for their seeming espousal of reactionary views e.g. the sacristan's advice to Evgenia, in *Nostalgia*, that a woman's role in the world is to have, and care for, children. While the *auteur* theory of cinema should certainly be applied to Tarkovsky, one should beware of reading every such 'statement' in his films as evidence of *his* ideology, pure and simple. Just as the Christian elements in Tarkovsky's films have to be seen within the wider, pan-religious nature of his work, so should any critique of the alleged reactionary nature of that work acknowledge the complexity of Tarkovsky's 'world view' e.g. the 'deconstruction' of stereotypes about 'masculinity', the Taoist emphasis on tenderness and humility – and above all, the strengthening of the values of anima by which his work is distinguished.

64. Apart from Bach, the film also uses Zen-inflected Japanese flute music and Saami *joiks*. The story which Alexander tells his son at the beginning of the film is of an Orthodox monk, Pamve, and his instructions to his disciple Kolov to water a dead tree with ritual regularity, so that it may come back to life: Kolov does. But as Alexander contemplates the tree which he and 'Little Man' have erected by the seashore, he is reminded of the Ikebana floral arrangements of Japanese culture. Tarkovsky's work is full of such cross-cultural resonances.

65. De Baecque, A. *Andrei Tarkovski* Cahiers Du Cinema/Collection 'Auteurs', Paris 1989 pp. 23–7. De Baecque makes many incisive points about Tarkovsky, not least concerning the director's ability to imply the infinite through the intimate. Tarkovsky himself spoke of his desire to avoid all traces of oratory, or 'propagandist speech', and to offer instead films

which might be 'the occasion for a deeply intimate experience'. Tarkovsky 1986 op. cit. p. 183.

66. Tarkovsky, A. *Time within Time: The Diaries 1970–1986* (trans.Kitty Hunter-Blair) Seagull, Calcutta 1991 p. 169.

67. Ibid. p. 181. See Tarkovsky 1986 op. cit. p. 193 for the shaman-like view that '. . . it is only through spiritual crisis that healing occurs. A spiritual crisis is an attempt to find oneself, to acquire new faith.' See also p.188, where Tarkovsky suggests that 'True artistic inspiration is always a torment for the artist, almost to the point of endangering his life. Its realisation is tantamount to a physical feat.' Sadly, the last words were to prove all-too-prophetic for Tarkovsky.

68. The term 'signature of things' comes from the Protestant mystic Jacob Boehme (1575–1624), whose ideas have had a considerable impact on twentieth-century art. See Tuchmann (ed.) 1986 op. cit. passim. Has any other film maker done as much as Tarkovsky to intimate the animistic path which links psychic individuation with 'the signature of things'? Here lies a great part of his genius. In speaking of Tarkovsky as a genius (as I would also do of Bergman) I am of course aware, as both directors certainly were, of the essentially co-operative nature of filmmaking. I use the term genius in the sense of Coleridge's words (see Chapter 2) i.e. indicating exceptional qualities of an individuated relation to the world.

69. Alexander, L. 'Andrey Tarkovsky – Enigma And Mystery' *Soviet Film* July 1989 p. 36. See also Tarkovskaya. M. (ed.) *About Andrei Tarkovsky* Progress Publishers, Moscow 1990 pp. 298–315.

70. Ibid. (*Soviet Film*).

71. Schrader, P. *Transcendental Style in Film: Ozu, Bresson, Dreyer* Da Capo, New York 1988 pp. 162–6.

CHAPTER TEN

1. Klepac, L. (ed.) *Marino Marini Etchings and Lithographs* The Art Gallery of Western Australia, Perth 1980 p. 9. For qualification of the somewhat simplistic picture of Renaissance psychology which Marini's words may suggest, see Hillman 1977 op. cit. pp. 193–228.

2. Eliade, M. *The Sacred and The Profane: The Nature of Religion* (trans. Willard R. Trask)

Harvest/Harcourt, Brace and World, Inc. New York 1959 p. 64.

3. Moffitt, J.F. 'Marcel Duchamp: Alchemist of the Avant-Garde' in Tuchmann (ed.) 1986 op. cit. p. 261. See also Burnham, J. *Great Western Salt Works: essays on the meaning of Post-Formalist art* George Braziller, New York 1974 pp. 71—88 'The purposes of the ready mades'.

4. Ibid. (Moffitt) p. 261.

5. Bachelard 1971 op. cit. p. 157.

6. For an introduction to Fluxus see Phillpot, C. and Hendricks, J. *Fluxus: Selections from the Gilbert and Lila Silverman Collection* The Museum of Modern Art, New York 1988.

7. O'Doherty, B. *The Voice and the Myth: American Masters* Universe Books, New York 1988 p. 281. See especially Cornell's *Sun Box* of c.1956, reproduced on p. 269.

8. Vastokas, J. 'The Interdimensional Landscape: archetypal imagery in the work of Tony Urquart' *Artscanada* May 1973 p. 33.

9. Lipsey 1988 op. cit. p. 243.

10. Ibid. p. 242.

11. Shanes, E. *Constantin Brancusi* Abbeville Press, New York 1989 pp. 18—19.

12. Ibid. p. 101.

13. Eliade, M. *The Myth of the Eternal Return, or, Cosmos and History* (trans. Willard R. Trask) Bollingen Series/Princeton University Press 1974 p. 34.

14. Eliade, M. 'Brancusi and Mythology' in *Ordeal by Labyrinth: Conversations with Claude-Henri Rocquet* (trans. Derek Coltman) University of Chicago Press, Chicago and London 1982 p. 196.

15. For the African emphasis, see Geist, S. 'Brancusi' in Rubin, W. (ed.) *Primitivism In 20th Century Art* Vol 11 Museum of Modern Art, New York 1984 pp. 345—67; for the Romanian perspective see Comarnesco, P., Eliade, M., Jianou, I. and Noica, C. *Brancusi* Arted Editions D'Art, Paris 1982. (Eliade 1982 op. cit. is a translation from the latter volume).

16. Lipsey 1988 op. cit. pp. 244 and 242.

17. Eliade 1974 op. cit. (. . . *Cosmos and History*) pp. xiii—xiv.

18. Eliade 1959 op. cit. p. 13.

19. For Eliade, 'archaic man certainly has the right to consider himself more creative than modern man, who sees himself as creative only in respect to history. Every year, that is, archaic man takes part in the repetition of the cosmogony, the creative act *par excellence*.' Eliade

1974 op. cit. (. . . *Cosmos and History*) p. 158.

20. Eliade 1959 op. cit. p. 44.

21. Ibid. pp. 32—4.

22. Ibid. p. 64.

23. Ibid. p. 57.

24. Eliade 1974 op. cit. (*Shamanism*) pp. 259—87 'Shamanism and Cosmology'.

25. Eliade 1972 op. cit. p. 246 and Cousineau (ed.) 1990 op. cit. p. 167.

26. A fascinating book remains to be written on the relation between the ideas of Jung and Eliade. Eliade, M. *Autobiography Volume 11 1937–1960 Exile's Odyssey* University of Chicago Press, Chicago and London 1988 pp. 162 reveals how after reading *Le chamanisme* in the early 1950s, Jung wrote enthusiastically to Eliade, to say that he had found confirmation for some of his hypotheses in 'the oneiric and psychopathological experience of shamanic initiation rites'. Eliade and Jung met at Ascona, where they talked for several hours. While Eliade was interested in the idea of the collective unconscious, he makes it clear that his use of the term 'archetype' in *The Myth of the Eternal Return* came from 'its original, Neoplatonic model of "paradigm, exemplary model"', and suggests that he made a mistake in using a term which could be confused with Jung's psychological idea: 'I should have used the expression "exemplary model" as I have, in fact, since then.'

27. See Geist, S. *Brancusi/The Kiss* Icon Editions/ Harper and Row, New York and London 1978 for a thorough study of the various versions of this key work.

28. Geist, S. *Brancusi: A Study of the Sculpture* Hacker Art Books, New York 1983 pp. 57—8 and Lipsey 1988 op. cit. p. 236.

29. Ibid. (Lipsey) p. 234.

30. Ibid. p. 242.

31. See Shanes 1989 op. cit. pp. 83—97 for a well-considered and beautifully illustrated discussion of this ensemble, which besides *Endless Column* comprises *Gate of the Kiss* and *Table of Silence*.

32. Eliade 1982 op. cit. p. 199.

33. Lipsey 1988 op. cit. p. 239. Brancusi also called *Endless Column* 'the negation of the Labyrinth'. Ibid.

34. Ibid. p. 244.

35. Hulten, P., Dumitresco, N. and Istrati, A. *Brancusi* Faber and Faber, London and Boston 1988 p. 25.

36. I have not been to Tîrgu-Jiu. A photograph in

Shanes 1989 op. cit. p. 86 reveals how *Endless Column* appears to grow upwards from out of the depths of the ground, an impression confirmed by Eric Shanes when I spoke to him about the sculpture in summer 1991.

37. Eliade 1982 op. cit. p. 201.
38. Shanes 1989 op. cit. pp. 93—4.
39. Bachelard 1969 op. cit. p. 32.
40. Read, H. 1968 op. cit. p. 93.
41. Hammacher, A.M. *Barbara Hepworth* Thames and Hudson, London 1987 p. 117.
42. See Moore, H. *Henry Moore at The British Museum* British Museum Publications Ltd. London 1981 for Moore's recollections of the effect the collection had upon him in the 1920s and 1930s. See also Wilkinson, A.G. *The Drawings of Henry Moore* Art Gallery of Ontario/Tate Gallery Publications, London 1977. For critiques of Moore's 'essentialist' view of tribal sculpture see e.g. Hiller (ed.) op. cit. passim.
43. Neumann, E. *The Archetypal World of Henry Moore* (trans. R.F.C. Hull) Bollingen Series/Pantheon Books, New York 1959 p. 27.
44. Berthoud, R. *The Life of Henry Moore* Faber and Faber, London and Boston 1987 p. 125. Lipsey 1988 op. cit. pp. 286—96 discusses Moore's eventual acknowledgement of the power of classicism at its best.
45. Compton, S., Cork, R., and Fuller, P. *Henry Moore* Royal Academy of Arts/Weidenfeld and Nicolson, London 1988 p. 35.
46. Berthoud 1987 op. cit. p. 176.
47. Neumann 1959 op. cit. p. 44.
48. Ibid. p. 46.
49. Neumann calls Moore a 'spirit seer' (ibid. p. 74), admiring him for his ability to counter patriarchy's one-sided, mechanistic view of life through his engagement with aspects of the Great Mother and 'the Feminine in and for itself' archetypes (pp. 128—30). He suggests that from the point of view of depth psychology, the quality of *participation mystique* in Moore's work means that his sculptures 'actually are the earth for an ego bound to the unitary world by haptic experience, and are not just models or symbols for it'. Ibid. p. 57. Presented with a copy of Neumann's book, Moore read only the first chapter, on the grounds that 'it explained too much about what my motives were and what things were about'. (Compton, Cork and Fuller 1988 op. cit. p. 34.) It would seem that from his intuitive faith in the unconscious,

Moore was able to anticipate the return to the Goddess which has been such a feature of feminist/women's art in the last twenty or so years. On the Great Mother, see Neumann, E. *The Great Mother: An Analysis of the Archetype* Bollingen Series/Princeton University Press 1974. On the impact of James Lovelock's late-1970s 'Gaia Hypothesis' upon feminist/Goddess-oriented art, see Gadon 1990 op. cit. passim.

50. Shanes 1989 op. cit. p. 78.
51. Hammacher 1987 op. cit. pp. 42—3. Hammacher draws this distinction with regard to what he sees as the different approach of Hepworth and Moore to the motif of the hole in sculpture.
52. See Bord, J. and C. *The Secret Country: More Mysterious Britain* Paladin/Granada Publishing Ltd, London 1980 pp. 35 and 46 for the traditional belief in healing stones: passing a sick child through the hole of a standing stone could symbolize rebirth. I am not suggesting that the motif of the hole in Hepworth's sculpture arose out of any directly parallel feeling or belief. However, as with Moore, the 'feeling-tone' of Hepworth's work may well have more in common with the mythopoeic roots of such beliefs than with purely 'abstract' or formal concerns. See her discussion of this point in Bowness, A. (ed.) *The Complete Sculpture of Barbara Hepworth 1960—9* Lund Humphries, London 1971 p. 13.
53. Written for *Unit One*. Quoted in Osborne, H. (ed.) *The Oxford Companion to Twentieth Century Art* Oxford University Press, Oxford and New York 1988 p. 255.
54. Hepworth, B. *Drawings From a Sculptor's Landscape* Cory Adams and Mackay, London 1966 p. 11.
55. Bowness (ed.) 1971 op. cit. p. 14.
56. Hepworth believed that no matter how developed our experience of the world had become in the twentieth century, 'we always come back to the fact that we are human beings of such and such a size, biologically the same as primitive man, and that it is through drawing and observing, or observing and drawing, that we equate our bodies with our landscape. A sculptor's landscape . . . is a primitive world; but a world of infinite subtle meaning.' Hepworth 1966 op. cit. p. 13. I would argue that rather than any biological parallel, it was Hepworth's feeling for the archetypal

'cosmicity' of life which linked her with the 'cosmicity' with which so-called primitive culture endowed nature.

57. Lipsey 1988 op. cit. p. 355.
58. Friedman, M. *Noguchi's Imaginary Landscapes* Walker Art Center, USA 1978 p. 7.
59. Lipsey 1988 op. cit. p. 342.
60. Ibid. p. 351.
61. Ibid. p. 338.
62. Ibid. p. 351.
63. Harry Chapin, quoted from *The Arts* Vol 8 No.7 (July 1979) p. 3 in Lippard, L.R. *Overlay: Contemporary Art and The Art of Prehistory* Pantheon Books, New York 1983 pp. 51–2.
64. Anne Seymour 'Walking in Circles' in Richard Long *Walking in Circles* Thames and Hudson, London 1991 p. 7.
65. See Long, R. and Seymour A. 'Fragments Of A Conversation' and Richard Cork 'An Interview With Richard Long' ibid. passim.
66. Long, R. and Giezen, M. *Richard Long in Conversation Part Two* MW Press, Noordwijk, Holland 1986 p. 7.
67. Long and Seymour 1991 op. cit. p. 45.
68. Long and Giezen 1986 op. cit. p. 17.
69. Ibid. p. 9.
70. Ibid. pp. 26 and 23.
71. Gimbutas, M. *The Language of The Goddess* Thames and Hudson, London 1989 p. 321.
72. Ibid. p. 311.
73. Ibid.
74. Lippard 1983 op. cit. p. 62. Ernst's work is discussed in Chapter 11.
75. Gadon 1990 op. cit. p. 359.
76. Ibid. p. 346.
77. Ibid.
78. See e.g. ibid. and Lippard 1983 op. cit. passim. Unfortunately, space precludes consideration of all of these artists: I consider Edelson's work most relevant to the present context. The other artists' work is well-discussed and illustrated in the aforementioned sources.
79. Lippard 1983 op. cit. p. 69.
80. Gadon 1990 op. cit. p. 273.
81. Ibid.
82. Levy 1988 op. cit. pp. 59–60. Quoting from Edelson, M.B. *Seven Cycles: Public Rituals* (with an Introduction by Lucy R. Lippard) Mary Beth Edelson, 110 Mercer Street, New York, New York 10012 1980 pp. 33–4.
83. Beuys, J. and Kuoni, C. (ed.) *Energy Plan For The Western Man: Joseph Beuys in America* Four Walls Eight Windows, New York 1990 p. 203

(from a 1982 conversation with Lama Sogyal Rinpoche).
84. Tisdall, C. *Joseph Beuys* The Solomon R. Guggenheim Foundation, New York/Thames and Hudson, London 1979 p. 6.
85. Beuys/Kuoni 1990 op. cit. p. 32.
86. Ibid. p. 85 'To be a teacher is my greatest work of art. The rest is the waste product, a demonstration.' (1969 interview.) For Beuys's views on art and politics, see e.g. Schellmann, J. (ed.) *Joseph Beuys Multiples* Edition Schellmann, Munich and New York 1985 unpaginated (June 1977 interview).
87. Wiedmann 1979 op. cit. p. 11. Beuys was fond of quoting Nietzsche – 'Man is a sick animal'. For a thorough discussion of his work in relation to Romanticism and subsequent socio-cultural questions regarding healing see Murken, A.H. *Joseph Beuys und die Medizin* F. Coppenrath Verlag, Munster 1979 (text in English).
88. Schellmann 1985 op. cit. (December 1970 interview).
89. *Joseph Beuys Drawings* Victoria and Albert Museum, London 1973 contains an excellent selection of Beuys's drawings; Anne Seymour's essay 'The Drawings of Joseph Beuys' discusses the shamanic theme in Beuys's work in close detail. See also her essay in *Beuys. Klein. Rothko. Transformation and Prophecy* Anthony d'Offay Gallery, London 1987.
90. See Levin, K. 'Joseph Beuys: The New Order' in her *Beyond Modernism: Essays on Art from the 70s and 80s* Icon/Harper and Row, New York 1988 pp. 172–85 for an investigation of what she sees as the transmuted echoes of Nazism in Beuys's work.
91. Tisdall 1979 op. cit. p. 25 and Eliade 1974 op. cit. (*Shamanism*) p. 154.
92. Beuys/Kuoni 1990 op. cit. p. 256 and Moffitt, J.H. *Occultism in Avant-Garde Art: The Case of Joseph Beuys* UMI Research Press, Ann Arbor and London 1988 p. 10. (*Vis à vis* note 90 above, it is worth remarking Moffitt's observation that Hitler declared Steiner 'the greatest enemy of the Nazi Party' and tried to have him assassinated in 1922. Ibid. p. 116.)
93. Wilson, C. *Rudolf Steiner: The Man and His Vision* The Aquarian Press, Wellingborough 1986 p. 37.
94. Moffitt 1988 op. cit. p. 165.
95. Ibid. p. 167.
96. Tisdall 1979 op. cit. p. 23.

97. Moffitt 1988 op. cit. p. 109.
98. Tisdall 1979 op. cit. pp. 101–05.
99. My comments are based on the video of the action which was shown, together with other videos of Beuys's work, at the Anthony d'Offay Gallery, London, June-August 1990, as a complement to the Beuys show 'The End Of The Twentieth Century'. See Tisdall, C. *Joseph Beuys: Coyote* Schirmer/Mosel, Munich 1988.
100. Tisdall 1979 op. cit. p. 101.
101. Ibid. p. 228.
102. Snyder 1977 op. cit. p. 88.
103. Bastian, C. and H., and Simmen, J. *Joseph Beuys Drawings* National Galerie, Berlin/Prestel-Verlag, Munich 1979 p. 97.
104. Tisdall 1979 op. cit. p. 232.
105. Ibid. p. 105.
106. Another potent example of the wider impact of Beuys's ideas is the effect they had on Jimmy Boyle, a one-time Scottish prisoner and ex-gangster who, as Tisdall recounts, 'while serving a life sentence for murder in HM Prison Barlinnie in Glasgow saw photographs of *Coyote*, through Richard Demarco, identified with the coyote, and initiated a friendship with Beuys.' (Ibid. p. 235.) Boyle had been sculpting since 1972; his increasing engagement with art played a key role in his passage from peer-group monster to compassionate political thinker. In a lecture which he gave at Brighton Polytechnic in autumn 1989, Boyle placed particular emphasis upon the positive psychological and social import of Beuys's ideas about creativity. See Carrell, C. and Laing, J. (eds.) *The Special Unit, Barlinnie Prison: Its Evolution through its Art* Third Eye Centre, Glasgow 1982.
107. 'Interview with Richard Demarco' in Beuys/Kuoni 1990 op. cit. pp. 109–16. See also *Joseph Beuys 7000 Oaks* Free International University/DIA Art Foundation, Cologne 1982.
108. Beuys/Kuoni 1990 op. cit. p. 179. In this chapter, I have tried to indicate some of the chief aspects of the shamanic spirit in twentieth-century sculpture. The potential field of inquiry is vast; the Russian Ilya Kabakov, the American Nancy Graves, the Polish Jerzy Bereś and the British David Kemp, Jan Marshall and Nigel Rolfe are six further artists, for example, whose work repays attention from a shamanic perspective. See e.g. Davies, P. and Knipe, T. (eds.) *A Sense of Place: Sculpture in Landscape* Sunderland Arts Centre Ltd. Ceolfrith Press

No. 73 1984 pp. 120–1 for the 'post-technological shamanism' of Kemp's *Birdman's Hut*, the 'future relic' which he made in Grizedale Forest, England and Museum of Modern Art, Oxford *Art At The Edge: Contemporary Art from Poland* MOMA, Oxford 1988 for the totem-like constructions and assemblages of Bereś. See Chapter 12 below for a further consideration of the shamanic spirit in contemporary sculpture.

CHAPTER ELEVEN

1. Eliade 1974 op. cit. (*Shamanism*) p. 98.
2. See Eliade/Murray 1968 op. cit. and Heinberg 1990 op. cit.
3. Tranströmer/Fulton 1987 op. cit. p. 150.
4. Jung (ed.) 1974 op. cit. pp. 84–5.
5. 'The Half-made Heaven', from Tranströmer T. *Dikter* (Collected Poems) Manpocket/Albert Bonniers, Stocholm 1984 p. 64 (this trans. M. Tucker). See also Tranströmer/Fulton 1987 op. cit. pp. 64–5; Fulton translates the title as 'The Half-Finished Heaven'. My translation is largely based upon that of Fulton; in discussion he has approved these few changes. (Personal communication November 1991.) Fulton made the good point to me that 'half-made' should not be taken to imply something incomplete, as in the sense of unfinished or badly made, but rather something on the way to *being* made.
6. In exhibitions held at Zurich's Galeria Dada in 1917, African sculpture and drawings by children were displayed next to Dadaist collages and reliefs; in the Dada room which they arranged in a Cologne exhibition of November 1919, Ernst and Baargeld showed paintings by naifs and the inmates of a local mental asylum next to their own work. (Well meant as they were, such juxtapositions would help feed the development of the grossly misleading primitivistic myth of Noble (tribal) Savage = child = madman.) Cowling, E. 'An other culture' in Ades, D. (ed.) *Dada and Surrealism Reviewed* Arts Council of Great Britain, London 1978 p. 453.
7. Herrera, H. *Frida Kahlo* Bloomsbury, London 1989 p. 228.
8. See Cowling 1978 op. cit. and Cowling, E. 'The Eskimos, The American Indians And The Surrealists' *Art History* Vol. 1 No. 4 December 1978. One translation of 'Surréalisme' might be 'a greater reality'. As Cowling documents, the

mythologically rich art of the Inuit (Eskimo) and North West Coast Native American tribes encouraged the Surrealists in their animistic pursuit of what Breton called 'the elaboration of a *collective myth* appropriate to our time'. Cowling (*Art History*) p. 497.

9. See Waldberg, P. *Surrealism*, Thames and Hudson, London 1966 pp. 66—72 and Breton, A. *What Is Surrealism? Selected Writings* (ed. Franklin Rosemont) Pluto Press, London 1989 passim. Surrealism assumed its name from the poet Apollinaire, who designated as *surréaliste* a drama which he wrote in 1916 called *Les Mamelles de Tiresias* (The Breasts of Tiresias). It was from Apollinaire, said Breton, that he first heard the quintessential Surrealist words 'I marvel'.

10. Ibid. (Breton) pp. 160—8. Breton's novel *Nadia* ends with the words 'Beauty will be convulsive or it will not be at all'.

11. The 1986 *L'Amour Fou* exhibition at the Hayward Gallery, London, addressed these themes. See e.g. Ades, D. *An Introduction to Photography and Surrealism* Arts Council of Great Britain, London 1986.

12. Breton 1989 op. cit. p. 369.

13. *Time*, 21 April 1947. Quoted in Schneede, U.M. 'Sightless Vision: Notes on the Iconography of Surrealism' in Spies, W. (ed.) *Max Ernst: A Retrospective* Prestel-Verlag, Munich/Tate Gallery, London 1991 p. 354.

14. Ibid. p. 354.

15. Chadwick, W. *Women Artists and the Surrealist Movement* Thames and Hudson, London 1991, offers a carefully reasoned interpretation of Kahlo's work in the light of the theme of female/earth analogies (transcending the patriarchal cliché of 'woman is to nature as man is to culture'). See Chapter 4 'The Female Earth', where Chadwick suggests that in *Roots* 'woman nourishes the earth with her own body, rather than the more conventional reverse'. She also offers the idea (through reference to an article by Terry Smith) that the painting may be 'a biting commentary on fertility and nature' pp. 160—1.

16. Herrera 1989 op. cit. p. 263.

17. Breton 1989 op. cit. p. 45.

18. Secrest, M. *Salvador Dali: The Surrealist Jester* Weidenfeld and Nicholson, London 1986 p. 196.

19. A typical example was furnished by the Benson and Hedges campaign of the late 1970s, which offered a 'surreal' displacement of the unhealthy consequences of smoking through the visual equation of a cigarette packet with the golden aura of sunshine flooding through an open door.

20. Argüelles 1975 op. cit. p. 221.

21. Ibid. p. 195. For Dubuffet on Outsider Art see e.g. 'Art Brut In Preference To The Cultural Arts' in Weiss, Allen S. (ed.) *Art Brut: Madness and Marginalia, Art and Text* No 27 December-February 1988 Paddington, New South Wales pp. 30—3.

22. Ibid. (Argüelles) p. 198.

23. Ibid. p. 197.

24. Cardinal, R. *Outsider Art* Studio Vista, London 1972 pp. 57—8.

25. Argüelles 1975 op. cit. p. 199.

26. Thévoz, M. *Art Brut* Skira, Geneva/Academy Editions, London 1976 pp. 115—16.

27. These comments are based on both the relatively extensive show of Wölfli's work which took place at the Kunstmuseum Bern in Summer 1985 and reproductions of Wölfli's work in a number of sources.

28. Which is not to say that 'Saint Adolf 11' does not deserve his place somewhere on the shamanic Tree of Life. I have taken the case of Wölfli as a particularly good example of the claims often made for Art Brut: see the magazine *Raw Vision* (ed. John Maizels), London 1989, for a fascinating range of material on a variety of other 'outsider artists', some of whom, such as the French sculptor, poet and seer Chomo (*b*.1907), clearly exhibit shamanic concerns in their work. See, e.g. Cardinal, R. 'Within Us These Traces' *Art and Text* No 27 op. cit. 1988, pp. 46—51 for consideration of shamanic/Orphic themes in the work of French outsider artist Michel Nedjar, and pp. 53—9 for Nedjar's own comments on his work.

29. See Chadwick 1991 op. cit. for a thorough treatment of women artists and Surrealism. For the majority of these artists, Freud played a much less important role (if he played one at all) than Jung.

30. Orenstein 1990 op. cit. p. 18.

31. Ibid. p. 19.

32. Ibid. passim. See also Chadwick 1991 op. cit. passim.

33. Ibid. (Orenstein) pp. 10—11, 20 and 111.

34. Chadwick 1991 op. cit. pp. 191—7.

35. Orenstein 1990 op. cit. p. xxi. Carrington's *The Hearing Trumpet*, a splendid novel of Tricksterish

humour, was published by Virago Press in London, 1991, with an introduction by Helen Byatt.

36. Ibid. pp. 10 and 44–5.
37. See Chadwick 1991 op. cit. p. 176 for colour reproduction. Like a lot of Surrealist painting which presents what amounts to a static illustration of a dream-vision, rather than a painterly, improvised stimulus to dream, the image is uncannily close to kitsch.
38. Orenstein 1990 op. cit. p. 10.
39. Ibid. pp. 61–3.
40. Ibid. p. 61.
41. Ibid. p. 61. See also Schlieker, A. (ed.) *Leonora Carrington: Paintings, drawings and sculptures 1940–1990* Serpentine Gallery, London 1991, for essays by Marina Warner and Whitney Chadwick.
42. Those who subscribe to Clive Bell's idea of 'significant form' from a strictly formalist viewpoint have a hard time understanding (or even acknowledging) the significance of both Expressionism and Surrealism, with their clear emphasis on psychic/social content. Ernst's exploration of the technique of *frottage* (rubbing) is a good example of the blend of (improvised) formal and psychic strength that can inform the shamanic spirit in twentieth-century art. It is, of course, a major argument of this book that 'significant form' can signify far more than purely formalist values, an idea that is implicit (but relatively undeveloped) in Bell 1981 op. cit. As documented in Chapter 3 above, Bell spoke of 'significant form' in art as embodying metaphysical ideas: the 'ecstasy' that can free us from 'the arrogance of humanity' (pp. 54–5).
43. See Spies (ed.) 1991 op. cit. p. 267 for colour reproduction.
44. Cowling 1978 (*Art History*) op. cit. p. 495. See Spies, W. *Max Ernst: Loplop The Artist's Other Self* Thames and Hudson, London 1983 for a thorough treatment of the Loplop motif. In one of his poems, Paul Eluard characterised Ernst thus: 'Swallowed up by feathers and left to the seas, he has translated his shadow into flight, into the flight of the birds of freedom.' Quoted in Bischoff, U. *Max Ernst*, Taschen, Cologne 1988 pp. 50–1.
45. Spies (ed.) 1991 op. cit. p. 33.
46. The last two paintings are much 'looser' and rhythmical in their handling of subject matter, colour and line than is normal with Ernst, suggesting something of a major psychic breakthrough. See Spies ibid. pp. 270 and 273 for colour reproductions.
47. Ibid. p. 33.
48. Spies 1983 op. cit. p. 73.
49. See note 42 above.
50. Spies (ed.) 1991 op. cit. p. 309.
51. Max Ernst 'Inspiration to Order' in Ghiselin, B. (ed.) *The Creative Process* Mentor/New American Library, New York 1952 p. 64. Ernst drew attention to the earlier and famous advice of Leonardo da Vinci, concerning e.g. the inspiration to be drawn from looking at the textures of an old wall.
52. Ernst/Ghiselin 1952 op. cit. p. 65.
53. Ibid.
54. See Spies (ed.) 1991 op. cit. pp. 232–3 for two versions of the picture.
55. Quoted in Wilson, S. 'Max Ernst and England' ibid. p. 371. Novalis suggested that 'There exist great resemblances between madness and enchantment. The enchanter is an artist of madness.' Quoted in Waldberg 1966 op. cit. p. 27. From a shamanic point of view, it is the *control* of the process of both 'madness' and enchantment that is crucial.
56. A production which some Surrealists deplored as toadying to bourgeois tastes. See e.g. Spies (ed.) 1991 p. 301.
57. See Bachelard 1969 op. cit. p. 208.
58. Quoted in Jouffroy, A. *Miró* (trans. Charles Lynn Clark) Art Data, England 1987 p. 101. Waldberg 1966 op. cit. has 'scale' instead of 'ladder' here: see p. 81.
59. Ibid. (Jouffroy) p. 101.
60. According to Jacques Dupin in his study *Joan Miró: Life and Work* Harry N. Abrams, New York 1961 p. 99.
61. It may not be without interest to recall that Miró's father was a successful goldsmith, and his paternal grandfather a noted blacksmith. See Eliade 1974 op. cit. (*Shamanism*) pp. 470–7 for the mythology of 'power over fire' shared by shamans and smiths. According to Eliade 'The craft of the smith ranks immediately after the shaman's vocation in importance.' (p. 470) Late in his career, Miró would create several 'burned pictures' as a protest against what he saw as the increasing commodification of art in capitalist society.
62. Rowell 1987 op. cit. p. 153.
63. Dupin 1961 op. cit. p. 474. Sweeney, M. 'Miró And The Rural Environment' in Sekules, V. (ed.) *The Touch of Dreams: Joan Miró Ceramics and*

Bronzes 1949–1980 Sainsbury Centre for Visual Arts, Norwich 1985 contains a good discussion of Miró's primitivism in the context of the complexity of the relationships between country and city in Catalonia.

64. Erben, W. *Joan Miró 1893–1983: The Man and His Work* Taschen, Cologne 1988 p. 139. The impeccably attired Miró spoke of himself as being like a 'Madman' or 'Savage' in the studio: see Raillard 1989 op. cit. p. 7.

65. Letter of August 11, 1918 to J.F. Rafols. Rowell 1987 op. cit. p. 57.

66. '. . . the horizon . . .' is part of a line from Paul Eluard *Repetitions* Paris 1922. Quoted in Krauss, R. and Rowell, M. *Joan Miró: Magnetic Fields* The Solomon R. Guggenheim Foundation, New York 1972 p. 69 (I have substituted 'unbuckled' for 'unknotted').

67. Corredor-Mattheos, J. *Miró's Posters* Ediciones Poligrafa, S.A., Barcelona 1987 p. 15.

68. Dupin 1961 op. cit. p. 477.

69. Miró had an uncanny ability to be possessed. According to Erich Neumann, 'Every transformative or creative process comprises stages of possession. To be moved, captivated, spellbound, signify to be possessed by something; and without such a fascination and the emotional tension connected with it, no concentration, no lasting interest, no creative process, are possible.' As Neumann says, such possession can lead to 'either a one-sided narrowing or an intensification and deepening' of the psyche. It is a large part of Miró's greatness that he consistently sought to intensify, deepen, and broaden both his feelings for the world and his artistic language. See Neumann 1966 op. cit. pp. 177–8.

70. See Miró, J. *Ceci est la couleur de mes rêves: entretiens avec Georges Raillard* Seuil, Paris 1977 pp. 26 and 65 and passim.

71. Ibid. pp. 187–94.

72. See Malet, R.M. 'From the murder of painting to the Constellations' and Jeffett, W. 'A "Constellation" of Images. Poetry and Painting, Joan Miró 1929–1941' in *Joan Miró: Paintings and Drawings 1929–41* Whitechapel Gallery, London 1989. Miró spoke of wanting 'to hit the spectator with a straight right between the eyes before he has time for a second thought'.

73. Penrose, R. *Miró* Thames and Hudson, London 1988 pp. 181–201. A selection of Miró's graphics can be found in Taillandier, Y. *Indelible Miró* Tudor, New York 1972.

74. See Malet and Jeffett 1989 op. cit. Miró created at least two major public protests against fascism, in the large mural *The Reaper* (also known as *Catalan Peasant in Revolt*), which he painted in the Spanish Pavilion of the 1937 Exposition Internationale, and the 1937 *Aidez L'Espagne* (Help Spain) poster of the same year.

75. See Price 1989 op. cit. p. 19. Also quoted in Brighton Museum Exhibition 'Exotics: North American Indian Culture and the European', Brighton Museum and Art Gallery May-June 1991.

76. Eliade 1975 op. cit. Preface (unpaginated).

77. Ibid.

78. Dupin 1961 op. cit. p. 360.

79. Al-'Arabi/Nicholson 1978 op. cit. p. 67.

80. Dupin 1961 op. cit. p. 360 and Penrose 1988 op. cit. p. 105. See also Paz 1987 op. cit. Chapter 14 'Constellations: Breton and Miró'.

81. From the 'large Palma notebook' of 1940–41. See Picon, G. *Joan Miró: Catalan Notebooks* Skira, Geneva/Academy Editions, London 1977 p. 116.

82. Quoted in Frank, E. *Pollock* Abbeville Press, New York 1983 p. 39.

83. Picasso and Miró meant a great deal to Pollock at this time. Pollock's mature achievement would later have a strong effect on Miró, who described Pollock's first individual show in Paris, which he saw in 1952, as 'a revelation'. See Jouffroy 1987 op. cit. p. 98.

84. Reproduced in Frank 1983 op. cit. pp. 22 (*Bird*) and 35 (*Naked Man*). In what follows concerning Pollock's upbringing, I have drawn in particular upon Rushing, W.J. 'Ritual and Myth: Native American Culture and Abstract Expressionism' in Tuchmann (ed.) 1986 op cit. I have followed Rushing's various uses of the terms 'Native American' and 'Indian'.

85. See the discussion in Segaller, S. and Berger, M. *Jung: The Wisdom of The Dream* Channel 4/Weidenfeld and Nicholson, London 1989 pp. 141–4, which draws parallels between the process of Navaho healing and Jungian ideas.

86. Rushing 1986 op. cit. pp. 282–3.

87. See Ashton, D. *The Life and Times of the New York School* Adams and Dart, Bath 1972 pp. 102–3.

88. Ibid., passim and Rushing 1986 op. cit. passim.

89. Ibid. (Rushing) p. 274.

90. Waldman 1978 op. cit. p. 39.

91. Newman spoke of 'the naked, exalted moment' in the 1940s when a sense of absolute

hopelessness was transmuted into (mythopoeic) potentiality.

92. Ashton 1972 op. cit. p. 154.

93. Kirk Varnedoe (who coined the 'caricatured cowboy existentialist' epithet) discusses this myth in his 'Abstract Expressionism', in Rubin, W. (ed.) 1984 op. cit. pp. 643–4. The critic Harold Rosenberg's famous 'existentialist' description of Abstract Expressionism as action painting annoyed Pollock, who described his own work in the following animistic terms: 'When I am *in* my painting, I'm not aware of what I'm doing. It is only after a sort of "get acquainted" period that I see what I have been about. I have no fears about making changes, destroying the image, etc., because the painting has a life of its own. I try to let it come through. It is only when I lose contact with the painting that the result is a mess. Otherwise there is pure harmony, an easy give and take, and the painting comes out well.' From *Possibilities 1* 1947–8, quoted in O'Hara, F. *Art Chronicles 1954–1966* George Braziller Inc, New York 1975 p. 39.

94. Rushing 1986 op. cit. p. 292.

95. For a detailed investigation of Davie's music and its relation to Romanticism see Tucker, M. 'Music Man's Dream' in *Alan Davie* Lund Humphries, London 1992.

96. In the early 1950s, Davie was employed by the Scottish painter William Johnstone (1897–1981) at London's Central School. Johnstone was very interested in both the unconscious and Surrealism.

97. Quoted in Tucker 1992 op. cit. p. 82. On the Orphic/shamanic qualities in Davie's work see also Macmillan, 1992 op. cit. and (in the same volume) Patrizio, A. and Hare, B. 'An Interview with Alan Davie'.

98. Davie, A. 'Personal Thoughts' *The Times Educational Supplement* 24 June 1960. Few exhibitions can have done so much to stimulate interest in this 'mystical key' as the retrospective which Alan Davie had at the McLellan Galleries, Glasgow, January–March 1992. Featuring work from all stages of Davie's career, the exhibition was a virtual 'Chartres cathedral' of the twentieth-century shamanic imagination in painting. See *Solo: the Alan Davie exhibition*, McLellan Galleries, Glasgow 1992 with the essay 'A Handful of Sounds: the art of Alan Davie' by Andrew Patrizio and James Coxson.

99. Hillman 1987 op. cit. pp. 3 and 50.

100. See Tucker 1992 op. cit. passim.

101. See Patrick, K. 'An Interview with Alan Davie' *The Green Book* Vol 111 No 3 1989 for aspects of Davie's relation with the British art establishment.

102. Bowness, A. (ed.) *Alan Davie* Lund Humphries, London 1967 p. 19.

103. The yin/yang theme is also present in the contrast between the rounded nature of many of de Saint Phalle's sculptures and the spiky forms of the surreal machine-sculptures which her late husband Jean Tinguely (1925–91) made for the garden. For detail on the complementary yin/yang relation, see Watts 1981 op. cit. pp. 21–36. The shamanic balance that can be discerned in the Jungian idea of individuation has much in common with this ancient Chinese perception of the mutual interdependence of elements of male/female, light/dark, heaven/earth within each personality – no matter what its gender.

104. Transcript of interview with Niki de Saint Phalle, Gimpels Fils Gallery, London (unpublished). My research into the Tarot garden of de Saint Phalle was greatly aided by both the kindness of Alan Davie in giving me access to visual material and a final year BA (Hons) unpublished paper on the garden by Hilary Prosser (Brighton Polytechnic 1991). See *Tarot Cards in Sculpture by Niki de Saint Phalle* Guiseppe Ponsio, Milan 1985.

CHAPTER TWELVE

1. Worrall, S. 'Anyone for virtual tennis?' *The Sunday Times Magazine* May 26 1991 p. 20.

2. Ibid. p. 26.

3. Ibid. p. 21.

4. Ibid. p. 22. *A Separate Reality: Further Conversations with Don Juan* was first published in 1971.

5. Quoted by Worrall 1991 op. cit. See McLuhan, M. and Fiore, Q. *The Medium Is The Massage* Penguin, Harmondsworth 1967 passim for McLuhan's idea of the 'global village' implicit in the extension of electronic technology. While I have discussed certain key aspects of the technology of twentieth-century shamanism in Chapter 9, from a sociological point of view, the question of 'electronic retribalisation' this century clearly merits a separate study. Personally, I must admit to being more inspired

by learning of such twentieth-century examples of inter-species communication as flautist Paul Horn's apparent curing of the depression of Haida, a so-called killer whale, or poet Heathcote Williams's being 'Smitten by the shamanistic glimmer' of a dolphin's eye, than I am by contemplating the possibility of the world-wide availability of VR. See Horn, P. and Underwood, L. *Inside Paul Horn* HarperCollins, San Francisco 1990 pp. 177–82 and Williams, H. *Falling For a Dolphin* Jonathan Cape, London 1990 p. 96.

6. Worrall op. cit. p. 26.

7. One might see the 'shamanic claims' made for Virtual Reality as a Computer Age equivalent to Aldous Huxley's (more refined) argument for a mescaline-induced 'shortcut' to spiritual wisdom in his *The Doors of Perception* (1954; many subsequent Penguin eds.). See the critique of Huxley in Zaehner, R.H. *Mysticism Sacred and Profane* Oxford University Press, London, Oxford and New York 1973 (first ed. 1957).

8. Starhawk 1989 op. cit. pp. 214 and in Plant (ed.) 1989 op. cit. p. 175. On trendiness and shamanism see *i-D Magazine* No 99, December 1991, pp. 61–3.

9. Ibid. (Plant and Starhawk).

10. Ibid. (Starhawk).

11. The point about our *all* being ethnic is made by Mary Beth Edelson in an interview with Mel Watkin of November 1988 and September 1989. See Edelson, M.B. *Shape Shifter: Seven Mediums* Mary Beth Edelson, 110 Mercer St. New York 1990 p. 9.

12. Halifax 1979 op. cit. pp. 86–7.

13. Jamal (ed.) 1987 op. cit. p. 159.

14. Ibid. pp. 159–60. For the 'rainbow symbolism' of traditional shamanism see Eliade 1974 op. cit. (*Shamanism*) p. 132–5.

15. Lawrence, D.H. *The Rainbow* Penguin, Harmondsworth 1965 pp. 495–6.

16. Mathey, J.F. *Hundertwasser* Bonfini Press, Naefels 1985 p. 23.

17. Ibid. pp. 86–91.

18. Ibid. pp. 92–3.

19. Koschatzsky, W. *Hundertwasser: The Complete Graphic Work 1951–1986* (trans. Charles Kessler) Rizzoli, New York 1986 p. 21. Hundertwasser has often produced enormous editions of his graphic work, deliberately lessening the market value of the work in an attempt to reach as many people as possible. 'I want to show how simple it is, basically,' he once said, 'to find

paradise on earth.' Mathey 1985 op. cit. p. 14. Compare the belief of Henry Miller that 'The earth is a paradise . . . We only have to make ourselves fit to inhabit it.' Quoted in Cowan, J. *Letters From a Wild State: An Aboriginal Perspective* Element Books Ltd, Longmead, Shaftesbury 1991 p. 1.

20. Quoted from Dudley, D. 'Brancusi', *Dial 82* (February 1927) in Shanes 1989 op. cit. p. 107.

21. Ibid. (Shanes) p. 100.

22. Eliade 1972 op. cit. p. 14.

23. Ibid. p. 38.

24. Eliade 1965 op. cit. p. 24.

25. Eliade 1972 op. cit. p. 83.

26. Sutton, P. (ed.) *Dreamings: The Art of Aboriginal Australia* Viking/Penguin Books, Harmondsworth 1989 p. 3.

27. See *Andrej Jackowski: The Brides and Other Paintings* Marlborough Fine Art (London) Ltd. 1989 p. 5 and Jackowski, A. and Hyman, T. 'Holding The Tree' *Resurgence* issue 142 September/October 1990 p. 32. See also Hicks, A. *The School of London: the resurgence of contemporary painting* Phaidon, Oxford 1989 pp. 74–80. Apart from Jackowski, several of the painters whom Hicks discusses — particularly Ken Kiff (*b.*1935) and John Bellany (*b.*1942) — have produced work which is strongly redolent of animistic, shamanic ideas. It is worth noting here that *The Beekeeper's Son*, the painting with which Jackowski won the prestigious John Moores Prize in 1991, featured the shamanic motif of a flying figure.

28. Cousineau (ed.) 1990 op. cit. p. 66.

29. Ibid. p. 139.

30. Quoted from Brancusi exhibition catalogue, Brummer Gallery, New York 1926 in Shanes 1989 op. cit. p. 105.

31. Cousineau (ed.) 1990 op. cit. p. 64.

32. Ibid. p. 166.

33. Ibid. p. 155.

34. It is for this reason, above all, that the many contributions of Mircea Eliade to twentieth-century thought are of such value. Any overall critique of primitivism which does not address the issues of 'cosmos and history' highlighted by Eliade is, to my mind, seriously flawed.

35. 'Digging' in Heaney, S. *Selected Poems 1965–1975* Faber and Faber, London and Boston 1981 pp. 10–11.

36. Quoted in Nairne, S. (ed.) *State of The Art: Ideas and Images in the 1980s* Channel 4 Television

Company Ltd/Chatto and Windus, London 1987 p. 42.

37. See Cirlot, J.E. *A Dictionary of Symbols* (trans. Jack Sage) Routledge, London and New York 1988 pp. 253–4. As with his imagery of scorched fields, Kiefer's eagle imagery is ambiguous, an ambiguity heightened by his use of materials: the wings of his giant eagles are often made of lead.

38. Rosenthal, M. *Anselm Kiefer* Philadelphia Museum of Art/Prestel-Verlag, Munich 1987 p. 12.

39. The image is reproduced in colour, ibid. p. 16.

40. See ibid. passim for an extensive consideration of alchemical themes in Kiefer's work.

41. *Sigmar Polke* San Francisco Museum of Modern Art 1990 p. 15.

42. See the discussion of 'aura' and mechanical reproduction in Chapter 9 above.

43. 'The Daemon And Sigmar Polke' in *Polke* op. cit. p. 19. See *Parkett* No 30 Zurich 1991 'Collaboration. Sigmar Polke' for a variety of perspectives on Polke's approach to the dialectic of culture and nature.

44. Halifax 1979 op. cit. p. 91.

45. See references to Chapters 6 and 8 plus e.g. Jarrett, K. *Belonging* (ECM 1050); Towner, R. *Solstice* (ECM 1060); Connors, B. *Of Mist and Melting* (ECM 1120); Haden, H., Garbarek, J. and Gismonti, E. *Magico* (ECM 1151); Darling, D. *Cycles* (ECM 1219); Weber, E. *Chorus* (ECM 1288); Karaindrou, E. *Music For Films* (ECM 1429); Giger, P. *Alpstein* (ECM 1426) and Gurtu, T. *Living* Magic (CMP CD 50). See also the 1991 *Star* (ECM 1944) by Garbarek, Miroslav Vitous and Peter Erskine. On the breadth of Garbarek's music, see Tucker, M. *Programme Notes* to Jan Garbarek Quartet Contemporary Music Tour Spring 1987, Arts Council of Great Britain, London 1987.

46. Bourne, M. 'Jan Garbarek's Scandinavian Design' *Downbeat* Vol 53 No 7 July 1986.

47. *Witchi Tai To* (ECM 1041) with bassist Palle Danielsson and drummer Jon Christensen.

48. *Comin' and Goin'* (Antilles New Directions ANCD 8706) This excellent recording from 1983 is a prime example of the 'path we've never ever had before', combining as it does vocal and rhythmic aspects of Pepper's rich Native American heritage with aspects of post-Ornette Coleman jazz. Among the contributing musicians are electric guitarists John Scofield and Bill Frisell, Don Cherry, Collin Walcott

and Nana Vasconcelos. On the use of peyote today, see Mount, G. (ed.) *The Peyote Book: A Study of Native Medicine* (2nd ed.) Sweetlight Books, Arcata, California, 1987.

49. *Gula Gula* (Real World RWMC 13).

50. Missionary work increased particularly in the seventeeth and eighteenth centuries. See Bäckman and Hultkrantz 1978 op. cit. passim and Nordic Arts Centre, Helsinki *Sámi Art* NAC 1984 p. 8, where it is suggested that the shamans themselves were persecuted. See also Ahlbäck, T. and Bergman, J. (eds.) *The Saami Shaman Drum (based on papers read at the Symposium on the Saami Shaman Drum held at Åbo, Finland on 19–20 August 1988)* Almqvist and Wiksell International, Stockholm 1991 pp. 28–51.

51. Gaup, A. *Trommereisen* Gyldendal Norsk Forlag, Norway 1988.

52. Allwood, M. (ed.) *Modern Scandinavian Poetry* Anglo-American Center/Dreyers Forlag Oslo 1982 p. 154. For an introduction to Saami culture, with bibliography, see Manker, E. *People of Eight Seasons: The Story of The Lapps* Nordbok, Gothenburg 1975 (English text).

53. Ibid. (Allwood) p. 154.

54. Valkeapää, N-A. *Solen, Min Far* DAT, Norway 1990.

55. Valkeapää, N-A. *Vindens veier* Tiden Norsk Forlag, Norway 1990.

56. Valkeapää, N-A. and Kotilainen, E. *Beavi, Áhčážan* (DAT CD 4).

57. Valkeapää 1990 op. cit. (*Vindens veier*) (unpaginated). In 1991 Valkeapää won the Nordisk Råds Pris for Literature.

58. Erdoes, R. *Crying For a Dream* Bear and Co Publishing, Santa Fe 1990 p. 95.

59. Ibid. p. 34.

60. Ibid. p. 56. Swann, B. and Krupat, A. (eds.) *I Tell You Now: Autobiographical Essays by Native American Writers* University of Nebraska Press, Lincoln and London 1987 is an excellent compilation of reflections upon questions of Native American identity today. In the present context, the essay by Duane Niatum, poet and editor of *Harper's Book of Twentieth-Century Native American Poetry* is particularly interesting: Niatum talks of the inspiration which he has drawn from his family background — the fundamental intuition of the wholeness of the universe — as well as from such artists as Matisse, Klee and Brancusi. He speaks of his love of jazz, and of his deep regard for 'the

magic we find in the dream' — a dream which Niatum experiences through both the depths of his own Klallam tribe culture and the work of a poet such as Pablo Neruda, who for Niatum has come as near to defining the impossible — the nature of the poet's calling — as possible: 'He said we must give back to the people their own impulse to break into song, unite the community in the oldest bond of Nature: the impulse to sing.' pp. 133 and 135. See Zolla, E. *The Writer and the Shaman: A Morphology of the American Indian* (trans. Raymond Rosenthal) Harcourt Brace Jovanovich Inc, New York 1973 for a survey of attitudes towards Native Americans, as expressed in literature from Puritanism to the rise of a Native American literature.

61. See Clarke, R. and Hindley, G. *The Challenge of the Primitives* Jonathan Cape, London 1975 and Diamond, S. *In Search of The Primitive: A Critique of Civilization* Transaction Books, New Brunswick and London 1981 for pointed discussion of how much so-called advanced industrial society might learn from the cultures which it has sought to either exploit or destroy.

62. See also, e.g., Pepper's work on Charlie Haden's 1982 big band album (with arrangements by Carla Bley) *The Ballad of The Fallen* (ECM 1248) and on Tony Hyman's 1989—90 *Oyaté* (nato VG662 669 003), a tribute to the spirit(s) of Native America.

63. The work is reproduced in Ray, D.J. *Eskimo Art: Tradition and Innovation in North Alaska* Index Of Art In The Pacific Northwest, No 11/Henry Art Gallery/University of Washington Press, Seattle and London 1977 p. 260. *Eskimo Art* was published in tandem with the exhibition of that name at the Henry Art Gallery, Washington 1977.

64. Roszak 1973 op. cit. p. 350. See Brett, G. 'Unofficial Versions' in Hiller, S. (ed.) 1991 op. cit. pp. 125—6 for an incisive discussion of the instructive case of Tatlin's invention of an 'air bicycle', or glider, in 1929—31. Tatlin wanted to give 'the feeling of flight' back to people: but the conception and development of *Letatlin* (a combination of the Russian verb 'to fly' and Tatlin's name) found its inventor caught between poetry and technology, ancient symbolism and contemporary mechanics. According to Camilla Gray, Tatlin (1885—1953) 'devoted the last thirty years of his life to a glider which never left the ground'. Gray, C.

The Russian Experiment in Art 1863–1922 Thames and Hudson, London 1976 p. 180.

65. Carpenter, E. *Eskimo Realities* Holt, Rhinehart And Winston, New York, Chicago, San Francisco 1974 documents the shift from traditional to Western-inflected values in twentieth-century Inuit culture; from, for example, the lack of 'a single, favored point of view, hence, a base' in traditional ivory carvings to the 'massive, heavy and fragile [stone] carvings designed to be set in place and viewed by strangers.' Stone carving, suggests Carpenter, was developed in Canadian Eskimo culture only after 1949 and 'the teachings and promotions of James Houston, an artist representing, first, the Canadian Handcraft Guild and, later, the Canadian government.' For Carpenter, the result was that 'The traditional role of art is gone: object has replaced art'. pp. 132 and 192. Carpenter offers a thorough investigation of both the 'world view' of this traditional culture (with considerably different approaches to space, time, sound and smell from our own) and the impact of Westernisation upon it. See also Carpenter, E. 'The Eskimo Artist' in Otten, C.M. (ed.) *Anthropology and Art: Readings in Cross-Cultural Aesthetics* The Natural History Press, New York 1971 pp. 163—71.

66. See Blodgett, J. 1979 op. cit. passim and the discussion of the destructive impact of the 1896—1900 Alaskan goldrush upon traditional Inuit values in Ray, D.J. *Eskimo Masks: Art and Ceremony* University Of Washington Press, Seattle And London 1967 pp. 1—3. See pp. 4—24 for the fundamental importance of the mask to the traditional shaman. In 'Dances Inspired By Shamanism', *Artweek* Vol 16 No 43 December 21 1985, Elizabeth Richardson draws attention to the continued importance of the use of masks in the work of the contemporary dancer, choreographer and ethnographer Patricia Bulitt, who draws strongly upon Alaskan Inuit shamanic tradition.

67. See e.g. Clark, J. and McCaughey, P. *Sidney Nolan: Landscapes and Legends a retrospective exhibition 1937–1987* National Gallery of Victoria/ International Cultural Corporation of Australia Limited, Sydney 1987 and Gunn, G. *Arthur Boyd: Seven Persistent Images* Australian National Gallery, Canberra 1985.

68. See O'Ferrall, M. 'Australian Aboriginal Art: Convergence and Divergence' in 1990 Venice Biennale *Australia: Rover Thomas – Trevor Nickolls*

The Art Gallery of Western Australia, Perth 1990 on behalf of the Visual Arts/Crafts Board and Aboriginal Arts Unit, Australia Council. For the diversity of Aboriginal art this century, and the complexities of such issues as the rights to both 'Dreamtime' and land which it can raise, see e.g. Sutton (ed.) 1988 op. cit. passim. See also Chatwin, B. *The Songlines* Picador/Pan Books Ltd London 1988.

69. Isaacs, J. *Aboriginality: Contemporary Aboriginal Paintings and Prints* University of Queensland Press, Queensland 1989. The selection of artists whom I have chosen to list below does not imply any qualitative judgement with regard to the other artists — such as Jimmy Pike and Euphemia Bostock — whom Isaacs discusses, and whose work should be of equal interest to anyone interested in the questions addressed by the present chapter.

70. See ibid. and Caruna, W. and Isaacs, J. (eds.) special *Art Monthly Australia* supplement 'The land, the city — The emergence of urban Aboriginal art', published by Art Monthly Australia, c/o Arts Centre, Australian National University, GPO Box 4, Canberra, ACT2601 at the time of the 1990 Venice Biennale. This includes both an extensive interview with Foley and an interesting overview of some of the problematics of contemporary American reaction to modern Aboriginal art.

71. Carpenter 1971 op. cit. underlines parallels between traditional Inuit conceptions of space and time and the work of such twentieth-century Western artists as Joyce, Pound and Klee e.g. 'I do not think it accidental that it is in Paul Klee's work that we see the closest parallels with Eskimo art, for in both there is a structuring of space by sound' (p. 167). Why, therefore, should modern Inuits not express themselves in the two-dimensional forms used by Klee? I am aware that such a question raises a wide and complex range of issues: see Otten (ed.) 1971 op. cit. passim; Sutton (ed.) 1989 op. cit. passim and Hiller (ed.) 1991 op. cit. passim for a variety of perspectives on questions of tradition, modernity and creativity in 'tribal' cultures today.

72. Ross, J. 'Healing the World's Ills: California Indian Shamanism at the C.E. Smith Museum, Hayward' *Artweek* Vol 21 10 May 1990 pp. 12—13.

73. Ibid.

74. Sinclair, L. and Pollock, J. *The Art of Norval*

Morrisseau Methuen Publications, Toronto, New York, London, Sydney 1979 p. 7.

75. Ibid. It is understandable that Morrisseau has experienced considerable personal tensions regarding his position 'between worlds', as it were. See ibid. passim. As Morrisseau's development reveals, the building of the 'rainbow bridge' of the new shamanic consciousness can involve complex, demanding, and often painful issues of identity. In emphasising the positive aspects of Brook Medicine Eagle's image of the future, it is in no way my intention to minimise the necessity of facing such issues.

76. This 1975 acrylic painting is illustrated ibid. p. 115 and also in Martin, J-H. et al *Magiciens de la terre* Centre Georges Pompidou, Paris 1989 p. 205. This exhibition precipitated criticism comparable to that given to the MOMA 1984 'Primitivism' show. See Araeen, R. (ed.) 'Magiciens de la terre' *Third Text* No 6 special issue, London Spring 1989.

77. Ibid. (Sinclair and Pollock) p. 45.

78. Gablik, S. 'Art In The Age of Ecology' *Resurgence* issue 147 July/August 1991 p. 43.

79. Ibid. See also Gablik, S. *The Reenchantment of Art* Thames and Hudson, London 1991.

80. *The Journey: A Search For The Role of Contemporary Art in Religious and Spiritual Life* Usher Gallery/Redcliffe Press, Lincolnshire 1990 p. 30. This catalogue contains an interesting essay by Don Cupitt, entitled 'The Abstract Sacred', where Cupitt argues that from Van Gogh to Richard Long and beyond, modern art does contain a strong religious element — an element rooted in feelings for the earth. It 'must not be reified, nor must it be thought of as an Eternal One. It is something for which we have no developed vocabulary, but of which art has made us aware. It may be a starting point for the religion of the future.' Ibid. pp. 102—3. It has been the purpose of the present book to argue that, on the contrary, we have an extremely well-developed vocabulary for the religious implications of much modern art. It is instructive to read Cupitt in the light of Eliade 1965 and 1975 op. cit., for example. On the work of Jennifer Durrant, see *Jennifer Durrant Paintings* Serpentine Gallery/Arts Council of Great Britain 1987, where much in David Miller's essay 'Jennifer Durrant and the Poetics of Painting' addresses issues similar to those raised in Chapter 2 above.

81. Quoted from a 16 May 1964 interview in *Vrij Nederland* in *King Of Arts: Anton Heyboer* Contempo Modern Art Gallery, Eindhoven 1988 p. 21 (English text).

82. Ibid. p. 147.

83. See Sizoo, H. 'Anton Heyboer, expressionist philosopher and philosopher among expressionists' in *DA + AT: Dutch Art + Architecture Today* Eindhoven/Amsterdam December 1982 pp. 7–13.

84. Spence, J. *Putting Myself in The Picture: A Political, Personal and Photographic Autobiography* Camden Press Ltd, London 1986 p. 212.

85. Ibid. p. 215. On phototherapy, see Krauss, D.A. and Fryrear, J.L. (eds.) *Phototherapy in Mental Health* Charles C. Thomas, Publisher, Springfield, Illinois 1983, which includes an excellent bibliography.

86. Lawlis, F. 'Shamanic Approaches in a Hospital Pain Clinic' in Doore, G. (ed.) 1988 op. cit. p. 149. See also Achterberg, J. *Imagery in Healing: Shamanism and Modern Medicine* New Science Library/Shambhala, Boston 1985.

87. Edelson 1990 op. cit. pp. 49 and 51.

88. Lippard, L.R. 'American Landscapes' in Bridges, M. *Markings: Aerial Views of Sacred Landscapes* Phaidon, Oxford 1986 p. 56. (Also contains essays by Maria Reiche, Charles Gallenkamp and Keith Critchlow.)

89. Ibid.

90. Goldberg, V. 'A Terrible Beauty' in *ARTnews* Vol 90, No 6 Summer 1991 p. 107.

91. Neizvestny, E. (with Leong, A.) *Space, Time, and Synthesis in Art: Essays on Art, Literature, and Philosophy* Mosaic Press, Oakville, New York, London 1990 passim. The theme of Neizvestny's book is supplied by the *credo* of Dostoevsky: 'Beauty will save the world'. Neizvestny's post-Cubist vision of art is able to synthesise the symbolism of the Moebius strip with reflections upon the tradition of the 'holy fool' in Russian culture: much of his thought has a strong shamanic dimension to it, as Neizvestny himself makes apparent. His views on the ironies of Soviet censorship are worth pondering here: 'The poet Osip Mandelstam once said to his wife: "The Soviet Union is the only country in the world that takes poetry seriously. It will kill you for it." The USSR is the only society in modern times that attributes magical powers and meaning to art. And rightly so. Its only mistake is praying to the wrong god. Soviet authorities believe that if a sculptor models a handsome, patriotic and heroic person, everyone will be transformed immediately into a hero . . . In short, the Soviet state believes in magical incantations and regards the artist as a shaman.' (p. 50)

92. Cembelast, R. 'The Ecological Art Explosion' in *ARTnews* 1991 op. cit. p. 99. This valuable article traces the growth of ecological consciousness among artists and arts administrators from the early 1960s — following the impact of Rachel Carson's *Silent Spring* (1962) — to the present. The article covers developments world-wide: among the artists whose work is discussed are Newton and Helen Mayer Harrison, Rebecca Howland, Agnes Denes, Joseph Beuys, Karen Stahlecker, Nancy Holt, Alan Sonfist, Buster Simpson and Ian Hunter.

93. Chadwick, H. *Enfleshings* Secker and Warburg, London 1989 p. 58.In making 'autobiographies of sensation', Chadwick hopes 'to find a resolution between transcience and transcendence'. Ibid. p. 41. Marina Warner's essay 'In the Garden of Delights' explores the complex play of 'nature' and 'culture' in Chadwick's multi-layered, metamorphosing reclamation of Paradisal consciousness.

94. Ibid. p. 54.

95. Pettersson, J.A. 'Kjartan Slettemark And The Sixties' in *Siksi*, Helsinki 1989 No 4 pp. 10–15. See also Bløndal, T. (ed.) 1986 op. cit. pp. 125–6 for discussion of the violent Scandinavian debate precipitated by Slettemark's anti-war *Report from Vietnam* picture (1965). Monica Sjöö has described Slettemark as 'a shaman of modern art, if ever there was one'. Personal communication, January 1990.

96. Ohsuka was speaking in director Michael Blackwood's television programme *Butoh: Body on The Edge of Crisis*, broadcast on BBC TV September 1991. The programme traced the legacy of the ideas of the late Tatsumi Hijikata (*d.*1986) concerning the Butoh — 'dance of darkness' — which he developed from the late 1950s onwards. See Holborn, M. *Beyond Japan: a Photo Theatre* Barbican Art Gallery/Jonathan Cape, London 1991 p. 94–6 for the view that in such (in)famous dances as the 1968 *Revolt of the Flesh* Hijikata 'writhed like a possessed shaman', performing a dance that was of neither East nor West. As Holborn documents, Butoh grew partly out of the Japanese reaction to the Americanisation of post-World War Two Japan;

nevertheless, it is often set to Western music. As contemplative as it is highly theatrical, Butoh's free-ranging yet highly disciplined exploration of the body's being-in-the-world mixes animism and androgyny, sexuality and spirituality in a manner which is at times highly reminiscent of shamanism. For another, more overt 'revival' and development of shamanism in recent years in the East, see Durland, S. 'On The Side of The Deepest Soul on Earth: An Interview with Ja Kyung Rhee and Hye Sook of Theatre 1981' in *High Performance* No 45, Vol 12 No 1 Spring 1989 pp. 28–31. A collaborative group of Korean-American artists, Theatre 1981 have combined traditional Korean theatrical and ritual forms with experimental performance techniques. Drawing upon both feminist ideas and the symbolism of shamanism, their involvement with political and spiritual issues eschews didacticism in pursuit of a deeper level of catharsis. The interview reveals the strong resistance with which shamanic ideas are now met in Christianised Korea. On traditional Korean shamanism, see Guisso, R. and Yu, C-S. *Shamanism: The Spirit World of Korea* Asian Humanities Press, Berkeley, California 1988.

97. Catling, B. *The Stumbling Block its Index* Book Works, London 1990 (unpaginated). Sinclair describes Catling as a genuine *Hexenmeister*, a master of signatures and correspondences. There is a strong mediumistic quality to Catling's work, a quality which emerges with particular force in the title of one of his pieces from the mid-1980s: *On Touching, Haunting and Marking a Silent Room* (1986). See *Brian Catling: An Installation And Five Performances* The Museum of Modern Art, Oxford 1989.

98. Sinclair, I. 'A New Vortex: The Shamanism of Intent' in *Modern Painters* Vol 4 No 2 Summer 1991 p. 51.

99. The exhibition included, for example, a poetry reading by Tom Lowenstein (*b*.1941), whose various translations of Inuit poems and ethnogaphic work in Alaska are but part of the work he has done over the years to help preserve and develop shamanic consciousness. See e.g. Lowenstein, T. 1973 op. cit. and Lowenstein, T. *Filibustering In Samsara* The Many Press, London 1987 — the latter a collection of Lowenstein's own poems, which include some complex meditations on the interplay and clash of contexts in contemporary experience. See

pp. 37–41 for an extended meditation on the idea that the ascensional, abstracted 'rectangular' aspect of the stick-like Lascaux shaman figure intimates the eventual dominance of 'technocratic' consciousness. (For a different interpretation of this supremely enigmatic image, see Thompson, W.I. *The Time Falling Bodies Take To Light: Mythology, Sexuality and the Origins of Culture* St Martin's Press, New York 1981 pp. 110–117. Using ideas from Jungian and Tantric thought, and drawing upon Marija Gimbutas's documentation of the bird-snake complex in prehistoric Central Europe, Thompson stresses the integrative nature of the whole image: 'If the man is a shaman, and the bison is an image of the Great Goddess, then the bison could be an epiphany of the Goddess coming to the shaman in the power vision that sets him apart from ordinary men. In the center of the picture is a staff with a bird on the top, and this seems related to the fact that the man is shown with a bird's head. The staff with a bird on top, whether as totem pole or caduceus, is an ancient and universal symbol . . . If the bird on top of the staff is a sign of . . . Tantric transformation, then the bird head on the man indicates that he is one whose consciousness can fly into the sky; he is no ordinary man, he is a shaman, an initiate who has won the favour of the divine feminine, the Shakti, the Great Goddess . . .')

100. Sinclair, I. *The Shamanism of Intent: Some Flights of Redemption* Goldmark Gallery, Uppingham 1991 p. 5.

101. Ibid. p. 10.

102. Edelson 1990 op. cit. p. 10.

103. Ibid. p. 7.

104. Ibid. p. 11.

105. Niki de Saint Phalle *The Wounded Animals* Gimpel Fils London/Gimpel Weitzenhoffer New York 1988 (unpaginated). See also Niki de Saint Phalle *Oeuvres des années 80* Galerie de France/J.G.M. Galerie 1989.

106. Bowness 1967 op. cit. p. 16.

107. Hyder 1991 op. cit. p. 32. Throughout the Siberian part of this tour, says Hyder, 'references to shamanism and its spiritual role kept coming up.' . . . 'In Abakan, we were interviewed by a radio journalist, Sanka Kostiakov, who turned out to be a recent candidate for the supreme soviet. This 26-year old just failed to be elected. He is a leading member of the Khakassian People's Movement

whose platform includes the demand for the return of shamanism. He said that the Russian culture had robbed his people of their spirituality, and that shamans had been shot in the 1930s.' Ibid.

108. Attributed to Bernard of Chartres by John of Salisbury *Metalogicon* (12th century). See Collard and Contrucci 1988 op. cit. p. 10 for the information (via Jane Harrison) that ' "giant" means "earthling", and so does "titan", that is, creatures born of Ge (Gaia) and Titaia, ancient names of Mother Earth'.

Selected Bibliography

Achterberg, J. *Imagery in Healing: Shamanism and Modern Medicine* New Science Library/Shambhala, Boston 1985.

Ades, D. (ed.) *Dada and Surrealism Reviewed* Arts Council of Great Britain, London 1978.

Ahlbäck, T. and Bergman, J. (eds.) *The Saami Shaman Drum (based on papers read at the Symposium on the Saami Shaman Drum held at Åbo, Finland on 19–20 August 1988)* Almqvist and Wiksell International, Stockholm 1991.

Araeen, R. (ed.) 'Magiciens de la terre' *Third Text* No 6 special issue, London Spring 1989.

Argüelles, J.A. *The Transformative Vision* Shambhala, Berkeley 1975.

Asatchaq, Tukummiq and Lowenstein, T. *The Things That Were Said of Them: Shaman Stories from Tikigaq* University of California Press, Berkeley, Los Angeles and London 1992.

Bachelard, G. *The Poetics of Space* (trans. Maria Joles) Beacon Press, Boston, Massachusetts 1971.

Bachelard, G. *The Poetics of Reverie: Childhood, Language and the Cosmos* (trans. Daniel Russell) Beacon Press, Boston, Massachusetts 1971.

Bachelard, G. *On Poetic Imagination and Reverie* (ed. and trans. Colette Gaudin) Spring Publications, Inc, Dallas, Texas 1987.

Bäckman, L. and Hultkrantz, Å. *Studies in Lapp Shamanism* Stockholm Studies In Comparative Religion 16/Almqvist and Wiksell International, Stockholm 1978.

Bancroft, A. *Origins of The Sacred: The Spiritual Journey in Western Tradition* Arkana/Routledge and Kegan Paul, London 1987.

Bataille, G. *Lascaux or The Birth of Art* Macmillan London Ltd 1980.

Bates, B. *The Way of Wyrd: Tales of an Anglo-Saxon Sorcerer* Harper and Row Publishers, New York 1983.

Bates, B. *The Way of The Actor: A new path to personal knowledge and power* Century Hutchinson Ltd, London 1986.

Beane, W. C. and Doty, W.G. (eds.) *Myths, Rites, Symbols: A Mircea Eliade Reader* (two volumes) Harper and Row Publishers, New York 1975.

Bell, M. *Primitivism* Methuen and Co Ltd, London 1972.

Benjamin, W. *Illuminations* (trans. Harry Zohn). Edited and with an Introduction by Hannah Arendt. Fontana, London 1973.

Berendt, J-E. *Nada Brahma: The World is Sound* East West Publications, London and The Hague 1987.

Biró, Y. *Profane Mythology: The Savage Mind of the Cinema* (trans. Imre Goldstein) Midland/Indiana University Press, Bloomington 1982.

Blacker, C. *The Catalpa Bow: A Study of Shamanistic Practices in Japan* George Allen and Unwin Ltd, London 1986.

Blodgett, J. *The Coming and Going of The Shaman: Eskimo Shamanism and Art* The Winnipeg Art Gallery, Manitoba 1979.

Brodzsky, A.T., Danesewich, R., Johnson, N. (eds.) *Stones, Bones and Skin: Ritual and Shamanic Art* Artscanada/The Society for Art Publications, Toronto 1977.

Campbell, J. *The Hero with a Thousand Faces* Abacus/Sphere Books Ltd, London 1975.

Campbell, J. *The Masks of God Vol 1: Primitive Mythology* Penguin Books Ltd, Harmondsworth 1982.

Campbell, J. *The Masks of God Vol 4: Creative Mythology* Penguin Books Ltd, Harmondsworth 1976.

Campbell, J. *Myths To Live By* Condor/Souvenir Press (Educational and Academic) Ltd, London 1973.

Campbell, J. *The Way of The Animal Powers. Historical Atlas of World Mythology Vol. 1* Times Books Ltd, London 1984.

Campbell, J. and Moyers, B. *The Power of Myth* Doubleday, New York and London 1988.

Campbell, J. (ed.) *Myths Dreams and Religion* Spring Publications, Inc, Dallas Texas 1988.

Cardinal, R. *Outsider Art* Studio Vista, London 1972.

Cassirer, E. *Language and Myth* Dover Publications Inc, New York 1953.

Castenada, C. *The Teachings of Don Juan: a Yaqui way of knowledge* Ballantine Books, New York 1973.

Castaneda, C. *A Separate Reality* Penguin Books Ltd, Harmondsworth 1986.

Castaneda, C. *Tales of Power* Simon and Schuster, New York 1974.

Castaneda, C. *Journey To Ixtlan: The Lessons of Don Juan* Penguin Books Ltd, Harmondsworth 1987.

Cazeneuve, J. *Lucien Lévy-Bruhl* (trans. Peter Riviere) Basil Blackwell, Oxford.

Cembalest, R. 'The Ecological Explosion'. *ARTnews* Vol. 90, No 6, summer 1991.

Charbonnier, G. (ed.) *Conversations with Claude Lévi-Strauss* (trans. John and Doreen Weightman) Jonathan Cape, London 1970.

Clarke, R. and Hindley, G. *The Challenge of the Primitives* Jonathan Cape, London 1975.

Cook, R. *The Tree of Life: Image For The Cosmos* Thames and Hudson Ltd, London 1988.

Cousineau, P. (ed.) *The Hero's Journey: Joseph Campbell on his Life and Work* Harper and Row Publishers, San Francisco 1990.

Cowan, J. *Letters From a Wild State: An Aboriginal Perspective* Element Books Ltd, Longmead, Shaftesbury 1991.

Cowling, E. 'The Eskimos, The American Indians and The Surrealists' *Art History* Vol 1 No 4 December 1978.

Cutts, S. et al *The Unpainted Landscape* Coracle Press, London/The Scottish Arts Council/Graeme Murray Gallery, Edinburgh 1987.

Davenport, D. and Jochim, M.A. 'The Scene in the shaft at Lascaux' *Antiquity* 62 1988.

Davies, P. and Knipe, T. (eds.) *A Sense of Place: Sculpture in Landscape* Sunderland Arts Centre Ltd/Ceolfrith Press no 73 1984.

Diamond, S. *In Search of The Primitive: A Critique of Civilization* Transaction Books, New Brunswick and London 1981.

Donoghue, D. *The Arts Without Mystery* The British Broadcasting Corporation, London 1983.

Doore, G. (ed.) *Shaman's Path: Healing, Personal Growth and Empowerment* Shambhala, Boston and London 1988.

Drury, N. *The Shaman and The Magician: Journeys Between the Worlds* Routledge and Kegan Paul, London 1982.

Drury, N. *Vision Quest: A Personal Journey Through Magic and Shamanism* Prism Press, Bridport 1989.

Drury, N. *The Elements of Shamanism* Element Books Ltd, Longmead, Shaftesbury 1989.

Duerr, H. P. *Dreamtime: Concerning the Boundary between Wilderness and Civilization* (trans. Felicitas Goodman) Basil Blackwell, Oxford 1987.

Ehrenzweig, A. *The Hidden Order of Art* Paladin/Granada Publishing Ltd, London 1970.

Eliade, M. *The Myth of The Eternal Return, or, Cosmos and History* (trans. Willard R. Trask) Bollingen Series 46/Princeton University Press 1974.

Eliade, M. *The Sacred and The Profane: The Nature of Religion* (trans. Willard R. Trask) Harvest/Harcourt, Brace and World, Inc, New York 1959.

Eliade, M. *The Quest: History and Meaning in Religion* The University of Chicago Press, Chicago and London 1975.

Eliade, M. *Myth and Reality* George Allen and Unwin Ltd, London 1964.

Eliade, M. *Myths, Dreams and Mysteries: The Encounter Between Contemporary Faiths and Archaic Reality* (trans. Philip Mairet) The Fontana Library of Theology and Philosophy/Collins, London and Glasgow 1972.

Eliade, M. *Shamanism: Archaic Techniques of Ecstasy* (trans. Willard R. Trask) Bollingen Series 76/Princeton University Press 1974.

Eliade, M. *Ordeal by Labyrinth: Conversations with Claude-Henri Rocquet* (trans. Derek Coltman) University of Chicago Press, Chicago and London 1982.

Eliade, M. 'The Sacred and The Modern Artist' *Criterion*, Divinity School, University of Chicago 1965 Vol 4 Pt 2.

Eliade, M. 'The Yearning for Paradise in Primitive Tradition' in Murray, H.A. (ed.) *Myth and Mythmaking* Beacon Press, Boston 1968.

Eliade, M. 'A conversation with Mircea Eliade' *Encounter* Vol LIV No 3 pp. 21–7.

Faas, E. *Towards a New American Poetics: Essays and Interviews* Black Sparrow Press, Santa Barbara 1978.

Faas, E. *Ted Hughes: The Unaccommodated Universe* Black Sparrow Press, Santa Barbara 1980.

Fairchild, H.N. *The Noble Savage: A Study in Romantic Naturalism* Russell and Russell, New York 1961.

Fitzhugh, W.W. and Crowell, A. *Crossroads of Continents: Cultures of Siberia and Alaska* Smithsonian Institution Press, Washington 1988.

Frey-Rohn, L. *Nietzsche: A Psychological Approach to his Work* Daimon Verlag, Einsiedeln 1988.

Gablik, S. *Has Modernism Failed?* Thames and Hudson Ltd, London 1985.

Gablik, S. *The Reenchantment of Art* Thames and Hudson Ltd, London 1991.

Gadon, E.W. *The Once and Future Goddess* The Aquarian Press, Wellingborough 1990.

Giedion, S. *The Eternal Present: A Contribution on Constancy and Change* Oxford University Press, London 1962.

Gimbutas, M. *The Language Of The Goddess* (with a foreword by Joseph Campbell) Thames and Hudson Ltd, London 1989.

Goldwater, R. *Primitivism in Modern Art* The Belknap Press of Harvard University Press, Cambridge, Massachusetts and London 1986 (revised edition).

Grim, J.A. *The Shaman: Patterns of Religious Healing Among the Ojibway Indians* University of Oklahoma Press, Norman and London 1987.

Guisso, R. and Yu, C-S. *Shamanism: The Spirit World of Korea* Asian Humanities Press, Berkeley, California 1988.

Guss, D.M. (ed.) *The Language of the Birds: Tales, Texts, and Poems of Interspecies Communication* North Point Press, San Francisco 1985.

Halifax, J. *Shamanic Voices: The Shaman as Seer, Poet and Healer* Pelican/Penguin Books Ltd, Harmondsworth 1980.

Halifax, J. *Shaman: The Wounded Healer* Thames and Hudson Ltd, London 1982.

Hamel, P.M. *Through Music to The Self* The Compton Press, Tisbury 1978.

Harner, M.J. (ed.) *Hallucinogens and Shamanism* Oxford University Press, New York 1978.

Harner, M.J. *The Way of The Shaman: A Guide to Power and Healing* Bantam Books, Toronto, New York, London and Sydney 1982.

Hatto, A.T. *Shamanism and Epic Poetry in Northern Asia* School of Oriental and African Studies, University of London 1970.

Heidegger, M. *Poetry, Language, Thought* (trans. Albert Hofstader) Harper and Row Publishers, New York 1975.

Heinberg, R. *Memories and Visions of Paradise: Exploring the Universal Myth of a Lost Golden Age* The Aquarian Press, Wellingborough 1990.

Hiller, S. (ed.) *The Myth of Primitivism: Perspectives on art* Routledge, London 1991.

Hillman, J. *Anima: An Anatomy of a Personified Notion* Spring Publications, Inc, Dallas, Texas 1985.

Hillman, J. *The Thought of the Heart* (Eranos Lectures 2) Spring Publications, Inc, Dallas, Texas 1987.

Hodin, J. P. *Modern Art and The Modern Mind* The Press of Case Western Reserve University, Cleveland and London 1972.

Innes, C. *Holy Theatre: Ritual and The Avant-Garde* Cambridge University Press, Cambridge, London and New York 1981.

Institute of Contemporary Art, University of Pennsylvania *Masks Tents Vessels Talismans* Exhibition catalogue 1979.

Jaffé, A. *Was Jung a Mystic? and Other Essays* Daimon Verlag, Einsiedeln 1989.

Jamal, M. (ed.) *Shape Shifters: Shaman Women in Contemporary Society* Arkana/Penguin Books Ltd, Harmondsworth 1987.

Jaspers, K. *Strindberg and Van Gogh* The University of Arizona Press, Tuscon 1977.

Johnson, R.A. *Ecstasy: Understanding The Psychology of Joy* Harper and Row Publishers, San Francisco 1989.

Jung, C.G. (ed.) *Man and his Symbols* Aldus Books/Jupiter Books, London 1974.

Jung, C.G. *Psychology and Alchemy* Routledge, London 1989.

Jung, C.G. *Memories, Dreams, Reflections* Flamingo/Fontana Paperbacks, London 1988.

Jung, C.G. *The Spirit in Man, Art and Literature* (trans. R.F.C. Hull) Ark Paperbacks/Routledge, London 1989.

Jung, C.G. *Four Archetypes: Mother. Rebirth. Spirit. Trickster* Ark Paperbacks/Routledge, London 1988.

Jung, C.G. *Essays on Contemporary Events: Reflections on Nazi Germany* Ark Paperbacks/Routledge, London 1988.

Kalweit, H. *Dreamtime and Inner Space: The World of The Shaman* Shambhala, Boston and London 1988.

Kaye, N. 'Ritual and Renewal: Reconsidering the Image of the Shaman' *Performance* No 59, Winter 1989/90.

Knapp, B.L. *Music, Archetype, and The Writer: A Jungian View* The Pennsylvania State University Press, University Park and London 1988.

Kosinski, D.M. *Orpheus in Nineteenth-Century Symbolism* UMI Research Press, Ann Arbor 1989.

Lane, J. *The Living Tree: Art and The Sacred* Green Books, Hartland, Bideford 1988.

Larsen, S. *The Shaman's Doorway: Opening Imagination to Power and Myth* Station Hill Press, Barrytown, New York 1988 (revised edition).

Lévi-Strauss, C. *Structural Anthropology* (trans. Claire Jacobsen and Brooke Grundfest Schoepf) Allen Lane/The Penguin Press, London 1969.

Lévi-Strauss, C. *The Savage Mind* Weidenfeld And Nicolson, London 1972.

Levin, D.M. *The Body's Recollection of Being: Phenomenological Psychology and The Deconstruction of Nihilism* Routledge and Kegan Paul, London 1985.

Levy, M. 'The Shaman Is a Gifted Artist: Shamanism in the work of Yves Klein, Joseph Beuys, Mary Beth Edelson and Karen Finlay' *High Performance* Vol 11, No 61, Los Angeles 1988.

Lewin, R. 'Stone Age Psychedelia' *New Scientist* Vol 130 No 1772 June 8 1991.

Lewis, I.M. *Ecstatic Religion: An Anthropological Study of Spirit Possession and Shamanism* Pelican/Penguin Books Ltd, Harmondsworth 1975.

Lippard, L.R. *Overlay: Contemporary Art and The Art of Prehistory* Pantheon Books, New York 1983.

Lipsey, R. *An Art of Our Own: The Spiritual in Twentieth-Century Art* Shambhala, Boston and Shaftesbury 1988.

Livingston, P. *Ingmar Bergman and the Rituals of Art* Cornell University Press, Ithaca and London 1982.

Lommel, A. *Shamanism: The beginnings of art* McGraw-Hill Book Company, New York and Toronto/Evelyn, Adams and Mackay Ltd 1967.

Lowenstein, T. *Eskimo Poems From Canada and Greenland* (translated by Tom Lowenstein from material originally collected by Knud Rasmussen) Allison and Busby, London 1973.

Lowenstein, T. *Ancient Land: Sacred Whale* Bloomsbury, London 1992.

Lunt, A. *Apollo Versus the Echomaker: A Laingian Approach to Psychotherapy, Dreams and Shamanism* Element Books Ltd, Longmead, Shaftesbury 1990.

Macmillan, D. 'Magic Pictures' in *Alan Davie: works on paper* Talbot Rice Gallery, University of Edinburgh/British Council, London 1992.

Martin, J-H et al *Magiciens de la terre* Centre Georges Pompidou, Paris 1989.

Milner, M. *On Not Being Able To Paint* Heinemann Educational Books, London 1987.

Neihardt, J.G. *Black Elk Speaks* University of Nebraska Press, Lincoln and London 1989.

Neumann, E. *Art and The Creative Unconscious* (trans. Ralph Mannheim) Harper Torchbooks/The Bollingen Library, Harper and Row Publishers, New York 1966.

Nicholson, S. (ed.) *Shamanism: An Expanded View of Reality* Quest/The Theosophical Publishing House, Wheaton 1987.

Orenstein, G.F. *The Reflowering of the Goddess* Pergamon Press, New York 1990.

Plant, J. (ed.) *Healing the Wounds: The Promise of Ecofeminism* Green Print/The Merlin Press, London 1989.

Paolozzi, E. *Lost Magic Kingdoms* British Museum Publications, London 1985.

Price, S. *Primitive Art in Civilized Places* The University of Chicago Press, Chicago and London 1989.

Radin, P. *Primitive Man as a Philosopher* Dover Publications Inc, New York 1957.

Ray, D.J. *Eskimo Masks: Art and Ceremony* University of Washington Press, Seattle and London 1967.

Ray, D.J. *Eskimo Art: Tradition and Innovation in North Alaska* University of Washington Press, Seattle and London 1977.

Reichel-Dolmatoff, G. *Shamanism and Art of The Eastern Tukanoan Indians* Institute of Religious Iconography, State University of Groningen/E.J. Brill, Leiden, New York, Copenhagen and Cologne 1987.

Richter, H. *The Struggle for the Film* (trans. Ben Brewster) Wildwood House, Aldershot 1986.

Roszak, T. *The Making of a Counter Culture: Reflections on the Technocratic Society and Its Youthful Opposition* Faber and Faber, London 1970.

Roszak, T. *Where The Wasteland Ends: Politics and Transcendence in Post Industrial Society* Faber and Faber, London 1973.

Roth, G. (with Loudon, J.) *Maps To Ecstasy: Teachings of an Urban Shaman* Mandala/HarperCollins, London 1990.

Rothenberg, J. (ed.) *Technicians Of The Sacred: A Range of Poetries from Africa, America, Asia, Europe and Oceania* University of California Press, Berkeley, Los Angeles and London 1985 (2nd edition).

Rothenberg, J. and Rothenberg, D. (eds.) *Symposium of The Whole: A Range of Discourse Towards an Ethnopoetics* University of California Press, Berkeley, Los Angeles and London 1983.

Rothenberg, J. *Pre-faces and Other Writings* New Directions, New York 1981.

Rubin, W. (ed.) *'Primitivism' in 20th Century Art* (two volumes) The Museum of Modern Art, New York 1984.

Rudhyar, D. *The Magic of Tone and The Art of Music* Shambhala, Boulder and London 1982.

Rutherford, W. *Shamanism: The Foundations of Magic* The Aquarian Press, Wellingborough 1986.

Schrader, P. *Transcendental Style In Film: Ozu, Bresson, Dreyer* Da Capo Press, New York 1988.

Segaller, S. and Berger, M. *Jung: The Wisdom of The Dream* Channel 4/Weidenfeld and Nicholson, London 1989.

Sewell, E. *The Orphic Voice: Poetry and Natural History* Routledge and Kegan Paul, London 1961.

Sinclair, I. *The Shamanism of Intent: Some Flights of Redemption* Goldmark Gallery, Uppingham 1991.

Sjöö M. and Mor, B. *The Great Cosmic Mother: Rediscovering the Religion of The Earth* Harper and Row, San Francisco 1987. (Revised edition 1991.)

Starhawk *The Spiral Dance: A Rebirth of The Ancient Religion of The Great Goddess* Harper and Row Publishers, San Francisco 1989 (revised edition).

Steiner, G. *Real Presences: is there anything* in *what we say?* Faber and Faber, London 1989.

Tarkovsky, A. *Sculpting in Time: Reflections on The Cinema* (trans. Kitty Hunter-Blair) Faber and Faber, London and Boston 1989 (revised edition).

Thévoz, M. *Art Brut* Academy Editions, London 1976.

Thompson, W.I. *The Time Falling Bodies Take to Light: Mythology, Sexuality and the Origins of Culture* St Martin's Press, New York 1981.

Tisdall, C. *Joseph Beuys* The Solomon R. Guggenheim Foundation, New York/Thames and Hudson Ltd, London 1979.

Toop, D. '(Ghost) Riders in the Sky: Three Aspects of Shamanism', *P.S.* No 7, London 1981.

Torgovnick, M. *Gone Primitive: Savage Intellects, Modern Lives* The University of Chicago Press, Chicago and London 1990.

Tuchmann, M.(ed.) *The Spiritual in Art: Abstract Painting 1890–1985* Los Angeles County Museum of Art/Abbeville Press, New York 1986.

Tucker, M. 'Dreamer In A Landscape' in *Frans Widerberg: A Retrospective Exhibition* Brighton Polytechnic Gallery/Newcastle Polytechnic Gallery, Newcastle upon Tyne 1986.

Tucker, M. 'Not the Land, but an Idea of a Land' in Freeman, J. (ed.) *Landscapes from a High Latitude: Icelandic Art 1909–1989* Lund Humphries, London 1989.

Tucker, M. 'Music Man's Dream' in *Alan Davie: with essays by Douglas Hall and Michael Tucker* Lund Humphries, London 1992.

Usher Gallery *The Journey. A Search For The Role of Contemporary Art in Religious and Spiritual Life* The Usher Gallery/Redcliffe Press Ltd, Lincolnshire 1990.

Vassar College Art Gallery *Primitive Presence in the '70s* Exhibition catalogue 1975.

Ward, J.P. *Poetry and The Sociological Idea* The Harvester Press, Brighton 1981.

Warden, J. (ed.) *Orpheus: The Metamorphoses of a Myth* University of Toronto Press, Toronto 1982.

White, K. *Pilgrim of the Void: travels in South-East Asia and the North Pacific* Mainstream Publishing Ltd, Edinburgh and London 1992.

Wiedmann, A. *Romantic Roots In Modern Art. Romanticism and Expressionism: A Study in Comparative Aesthetics* Gresham Books, Unwin Brothers Ltd, The Gresham Press, Old Woking 1979.

Wilkinson, A.G. *Gauguin To Moore: Primitivism In Modern Sculpture* Art Gallery of Ontario 1981.

Wilmer, V. *The Face Of Black Music* (photographs by Valerie Wilmer. Introduction by Archie Shepp) Da Capo Press, New York 1976.

Zolla, E. (trans. Raymond Rosenthal) *The Writer and the Shaman. A Morphology of the American Indian* Harcourt Brace Jovanovich Inc, New York 1973.

Index